Canadian Business Law

Custom Edition for the Certified General Accountants
Association of Canada

Taken from:
Business Law in Canada, Ninth Edition
by Richard A. Yates, Teresa Bereznicki-Korol, and Trevor Clarke

The Law and Business Administration in Canada, Twelfth Edition
by J. E. Smyth, D. A. Soberman, A. J. Easson, and S. A. McGill

Managing the Law: The Legal Aspects of Doing Business, Third Edition
by Mitchell McInnes, Ian R. Kerr, and J. Anthony VanDuzer

Cover Art: Courtesy of Corbis

Taken from:

Business Law in Canada, Ninth Edition
by Richard A. Yates, Teresa Bereznicki-Korol, and Trevor Clarke
Copyright © 2011, 2008, 2005, 2002, 1999, 1995, 1992, 1989, 1986 by Pearson Canada Inc.
Published by Prentice Hall
Toronto, Ontario

The Law and Business Administration in Canada, Twelfth Edition
by J. E. Smyth, D. A. Soberman, A. J. Easson, and S. A. McGill
Copyright © 2010, 2007, 2004, 2001, 1998, 1995, 1991, 1987, 1983, 1976, 1968, 1964 by
Pearson Canada Inc.
Published by Prentice Hall

Managing the Law: The Legal Aspects of Doing Business, Third Edition
by Mitchell McInnes, Ian R. Kerr, and J. Anthony VanDuzer
Copyright © 2011, 2007, 2003 by Pearson Canada Inc.
Published by Prentice Hall

This special edition published in cooperation with Pearson Learning Solutions.

Pearson Learning Solutions, 501 Boylston Street, Suite 900, Boston, MA 02116
A Pearson Education Company
www.pearsoned.com

Printed in Canada

1 2 3 4 5 6 7 8 9 10 V0YA 16 15 14 13 12 11

000200010271281954

BK

ISBN 10: 1-256-49211-6
ISBN 13: 978-1-256-49211-5

Contents

Chapter 1

Introduction to the Legal System   1

WHAT IS LAW?   1

CATEGORIES OF LAW   2

ORIGINS OF LAW   3
Civil Law Legal System   3
Common Law Legal System   5

SOURCES OF LAW   8
Common Law   8
Equity   9
Statutes   10

LAW IN CANADA   11
Confederation   11
Constitution and Division of Powers   12
Conflicting Powers   15
Delegation of Powers   17
Agreements to Share Powers   17
Legislation   18

PROTECTION OF RIGHTS AND FREEDOMS   20
Canadian Bill of Rights   20
Charter of Rights and Freedoms   21
Charter Provisions   24
The Importance of the Changes   36
Human Rights Legislation   36

APPENDIX READING   41
How Is Law Linked to Morals and Ethics?   41
Is It Ever Right to Break the Law?   42
How Does Law Influence Behaviour?   43

Chapter 2

The Resolution of Disputes—The Courts and Alternatives to Litigation   47

THE COURTS   48
Trial Courts of the Provinces   50
Courts of Appeal of the Provinces   53
Courts at the Federal Level   54

THE PROCESS OF CIVIL LITIGATION   55
Limitation Periods   55
Jurisdiction   56
Pre-Trial Procedures   59

The Trial   61
Judgment   62
Enforcement   63
Judicial Remedies Before Judgment   66

HOW LAWYERS BILL THEIR CLIENTS   67

ALTERNATIVES TO COURT ACTION   68

WHAT IS ALTERNATIVE DISPUTE RESOLUTION?   68
ADR Mechanisms   70

Chapter 3

The Law of Torts   78

THE SCOPE OF TORT LAW   78

DEVELOPMENT OF THE TORT CONCEPT   79

THE BASIS FOR LIABILITY   79
Fault   79
Strict Liability   80
Social Policy   81
Vicarious Liability   81

INTENTIONAL TORTS   82
Trespass to Person: Assault and Battery   83
Trespass to Land   85
Trespass to Chattels, Conversion, and Detinue   87
False Imprisonment   89
Malicious Prosecution   90
Private Nuisance   92
Defamation   94
Libel and Slander   98
Product Defamation (Injurious Falsehood)   103
Successfully Establishing a Tort Claim   104

OTHER TORTS IMPACTING BUSINESS   105
Inducing Breach of Contract   106
Interference with Economic Relations   108
Intimidation   108
Deceit (Fraudulent Misrepresentation)   109
Conspiracy   109
Passing Off   110
Misuse of Confidential Information   110

PRIVACY   111

TORTS ONLINE   115

REMEDIES   116

Chapter 4
Negligence   120

NEGLIGENCE   120
　Duty of Care   121
　Standard of Care   123
　Causation   124
　Remoteness of Damage   125
　Economic Loss   127
　Burden of Proof   128
　The Plaintiff's Own Conduct   129
PRODUCT LIABILITY   130

Chapter 5
Professional Liability   136

PROFESSIONAL LIABILITY: THE LEGAL
DILEMMA   136
　Liability of Professionals   137
　Contractual Duty   137
　Fiduciary Duty   137
　Duty in Tort   140
　The Choice of Action   141
LIABILITY FOR INACCURATE STATEMENTS   142
　Misrepresentation   142
　The *Hedley Byrne* Principle   143
　Limits to the *Hedley Byrne* Principle   144
　Omissions   147
THE STANDARD OF CARE FOR
PROFESSIONALS   148
CAUSATION   150
THE ROLE OF PROFESSIONAL
ORGANIZATIONS   150
　Responsibilities and Powers   150
　Codes of Conduct   152
　Discipline   154
　Conflict of Duty Towards Clients and
　the Courts   154
MULTI-DISCIPLINARY PARTNERSHIPS   155
APPENDIX READING   156
　Law and Business Ethics   156
　　Business Ethics   156
　　Codes of Conduct   157

Chapter 6
Formation of Contracts: Offer, Acceptance, and Consideration   160

THE CONTRACTUAL RELATIONSHIP   160
　Definition of Contract   160
　Elements of a Contract   161
　Important Terms and Definitions   162
　Consensus   163
　Offer   164
　Acceptance   172
CONSIDERATION   178
　The Price One Is Willing to Pay   178
　Adequacy of Consideration   180
　Gratuitous Promises Are Not Consideration   182
　Examples of Valid Consideration   184
　Exceptions to the General Rule   185
APPENDIX READING   188
　Formation of Internet Contracts   188

Chapter 7
Formation of Contracts: Capacity, Legality, and Intention   193

CAPACITY   193
　Minors/Infants   193
　Insanity and Drunkenness   199
LEGALITY   200
　Contracts Performed Illegally   200
　Contracts Formed Illegally   202
INTENTION   209
FORM OF THE CONTRACT   212
　The Requirement of Writing   212

Chapter 8
Factors Affecting the Contractual Relationship   221

MISTAKE   221
　Shared Mistake   223
　Misunderstanding   225
　One-Sided Mistake   226
　Rules of Interpretation   230

MISREPRESENTATION   233
  Allegation of Fact   235
  Silence or Non-Disclosure   236
  False Statement   237
  Statement Must Be Inducement   237
  As a Term of the Contract   238
  Innocent Misrepresentation   238
  Fraudulent Misrepresentation   239
  Negligent Misrepresentation   241

DURESS AND UNDUE INFLUENCE   242
  Duress   242
  Undue Influence   244
  Unconscionable Transactions   246

PRIVITY OF CONTRACT AND ASSIGNMENT   248
  Privity   248
  Assignment   252
  Negotiable Instruments   256

APPENDIX READING   257
  Vicarious Performance   257
    How It Occurs   257
    When Is Vicarious Performance Allowed?   257
    Tort Liability   258

Chapter 9
The End of the Contractual Relationship   261

PERFORMANCE   261
  Tender   263

BREACH   264
  Conditions and Warranties   265
  Exemption Clauses   266
  Fundamental Breach   268
  Repudiation   270

DISCHARGE BY AGREEMENT   272
  Contractual Terms   275

FRUSTRATION   275
  Circumstances Not Constituting Frustration   277
  Effect of Frustration   279

REMEDIES FOR BREACH OF CONTRACT   281
  Damages   281
  Limitations on Recoverable Damages   282
  Equitable Remedies   285

Chapter 10
Special Contracts: Sales and Consumer Protection   293

THE SALE OF GOODS   294
  Scope of the *Sale of Goods Act*   294
  Title and Risk   296
  Rights and Obligations of the Parties   299
  Remedies on Default   308

CONSUMER PROTECTION   310
  Federal Legislation   311
  Provincial Legislation   316

Chapter 11
Special Contracts: Employment   330

WHAT IS EMPLOYMENT?   330
  The Control Test   330
  The Organization Test   332

THE LAW OF MASTER AND SERVANT   333
  The Employment Contract   333
  Termination   336
  Liability of Employer   345
  Legislation   346

COLLECTIVE BARGAINING   357
  Legislation   358
  Organization of Employees   360
  Bargaining   362
  Terms of Collective Agreements   365
  Strikes and Lockouts   367
  Picketing   369
  Public Sector and Essential Services   370
  Union Organization   371

Chapter 12
Special Contracts: Insurance   375

INSURANCE   375
  The Insurance Industry   375
  Types of Insurance   376
  Insurable Interest   380

LIMITATION CLAUSES   381
  Ambiguities Resolved in Favour of the Insured   381
  Contract of Utmost Good Faith   382
  Subrogation   385
  Bonding   385

Chapter 13
Special Contracts: Leases 387

INTRODUCTION 387

LEASING 387

TYPES OF CHATTEL LEASE 388
Operating Leases 388
Purchase Leases 388
Security and Finance Leases 389
Sale-and-Leaseback 390

REASONS FOR CHATTEL LEASING 390

COMMON TERMS IN CHATTEL LEASES 391
Duration 391
Rent 391
Insurance and Other Costs Payable
by the Lessee 391
Purchase Option 391
Early Termination—Minimum Payment 391
Implied Terms 392

RIGHTS OF THE PARTIES 393
The Lessor 393
The Lessee 394

Chapter 14
Secured Transactions and Priority Interests 396

METHODS OF SECURING DEBT 396
Personal Property 397
Guarantees 406
Other Forms of Security 410

BANKRUPTCY 410
Introduction 410
The Process 412
Alternatives to Bankruptcy 414
Priority Among Creditors 417
Offences 419
After Discharge 423

NEGOTIABLE INSTRUMENTS 424

Chapter 15
Agency and Partnership 433

INTRODUCTION 433

THE AGENCY RELATIONSHIP 434
Formation by Contract 434

AUTHORITY OF AGENTS 435
Actual Authority 436

Apparent Authority—Authority Created by
Estoppel 436
Ratification 439
Agency by Necessity 441

THE RIGHTS AND RESPONSIBILITIES OF THE
PARTIES 442
The Agent's Duties 442
The Principal's Duties 447
Undisclosed Principals 447
The Third Party 449
Liability for Agent's Tortious Conduct 450
Termination of Agency 453
Specialized Agency Relationships 454

TYPES OF BUSINESS ORGANIZATION 455

THE SOLE PROPRIETORSHIP 456
Government Regulations 456
Liability 457

PARTNERSHIP 457
Legislation 458
Creation of the Partnership 458
The Partner as an Agent 464
Vicarious Liability 465
Unlimited Liability 465
Registration 467
Rights and Obligations of the Parties 468
Advantages of Partnership 470
Dissolution of a Partnership 471
Distribution of Assets and Liabilities 473
Limited Partnerships 473
Limited Liability Partnerships 474

Chapter 16
The Nature of a Corporation 480

INTRODUCTION 480

THE NATURE OF A CORPORATION 480
The Corporation as a Legal Person 480
Characteristics of Corporations and
Partnerships 481
Consequences of Separate Corporate
Personality 483
Limitations on the Principle of Separate Corporate
Existence 486

METHODS OF INCORPORATION 488
Early Methods of Incorporation 488
Incorporation Statutes 488
The Choice of Jurisdiction 490

THE CONSTITUTION OF A CORPORATION 491
Articles of Incorporation 491

The Corporate Name   491
By-laws   492

TYPES OF BUSINESS CORPORATIONS   494
Public and Private Corporations   494
Corporate Groups   495
Professional Corporations   495

CORPORATE CAPITAL   497
Equity and Debt   497
Share Capital   497
Par Values   497

CORPORATE SECURITIES   498
The Distinction Between Shares and Bonds   498
Rights of Security Holders   499
The Transfer of Corporate Securities   500

Chapter 17

Corporate Governance: The Internal Affairs of Corporations   504

INTRODUCTION   504

WHAT IS CORPORATE GOVERNANCE   504

CORPORATE GOVERNANCE OF PUBLICLY TRADED CORPORATIONS   505

THE STRUCTURE OF THE MODERN BUSINESS CORPORATION   506

DIRECTORS   508
The Role of the Directors   508
Appointment and Removal of Directors   510

OFFICERS   511

DUTIES OF DIRECTORS AND OFFICERS   512
What Duties Are Owed?   513
To Whom Are Directors' and Officers' Duties

Owed?   513
Defences to Breach of Duty   515
Strict Liability   516
Specific Conduct Involving Conflicts of Interest   517
Insider Trading   520

SHAREHOLDERS   522
The Role of Shareholders   522
Private Corporations   522
Rights Attached to Shares   523
Meetings and Voting   523
Financial Rights   526
The Right to Information   528
Duties of Shareholders   530

THE ROTECTION OF MINORITY SHAREHOLDERS   532
Majority Rule   532
The Appraisal Remedy   532
The Derivative Action   532
Winding Up   533
Oppression Remedy   534

SHAREHOLDER AGREEMENTS   536
Advantages   536
Unanimous Shareholder Agreements   537

APPENDIX READING   538
Contractual Liability   538

Glossary   541

Index   552

Chapter 1

Introduction to the Legal System

1. Determine a functional definition of "law"
2. Identify the types of law that exist in Canada
3. Distinguish between common law and civil law
4. Identify the sources of Canadian law
5. Identify the three elements of Canada's Constitution
6. Explain how legislative power is divided in the Constitution
7. Detail how legislation is created in the parliamentary system
8. Describe the rights and freedoms protected by the *Charter of Rights and Freedoms*

WHAT IS LAW?

Most of us recognize the rules and regulations that are considered law and understand that law plays an important role in ordering society, but knowing that does not make it easy to come up with a satisfactory, all-inclusive definition. Philosophers have been trying for centuries to determine just what "law" means, and their theories have profoundly affected the development of our legal system. Law has been defined in moral terms, where only good rules are considered law (natural law theorists). Others have defined law by looking at its source, stipulating that only the rules enacted by those with authority to do so qualify as law (*legal positivists*). And some have defined law in practical terms, suggesting that only those rules that the courts are willing to enforce qualify as law (*legal realists*). Legal positivism helped shape the concept of law in Canada, where parliamentary supremacy requires that we look to the enactments of the federal parliament or provincial legislatures as the primary source of law. In the United States, however, a more pragmatic approach to law based on legal realism has been adopted. It allows judges to factor in current social and economic realities when they make their decisions.

No wholly satisfactory definition of law

For our purposes, the following simplified definition is helpful, if we remember that it is not universally applicable. **Law is the body of rules made by government that can be enforced by the courts or by other government agencies**. In our

Definition

daily activities, we are exposed to many rules that do not qualify as law. Courtesy demands that we do not interrupt when someone is speaking. Social convention determines that it is inappropriate to enter a restaurant shirtless or shoeless. Universities and colleges often establish rules of conduct for their students and faculty. These rules do not fall into our definition of law because the courts do not enforce them. But when there is a disagreement over who is responsible for an accident, a question as to whether a crime has been committed, or a difference of opinion about the terms of a contract or a will, the participants may find themselves before a judge. Rules that can be enforced by the courts govern these situations; thus, they are laws within the definition presented here.

Government agencies also enforce the law

A person dealing with government agencies, such as labour relations boards, workers' compensation boards, or city and municipal councils, must recognize that these bodies are also able to render decisions in matters that come before them. The rules enforced by these bodies are also laws within this definition.

Do not confuse law and morality

While the definition of law as enforceable rules has practical value, it does not suggest what is just or moral. We must not assume that so long as we obey the law we are acting morally. Legal compliance and ethical behaviour are two different things, and people must decide for themselves what standard they will adhere to. Many choose to live by a personal code of conduct demanding adherence to more stringent rules than those set out in the law, while others disregard even these basic requirements. Some think that moral values have no place in the business world, but in fact the opposite is true. There is now an expectation of high ethical standards in business activities, and it is hoped that those who study the law as it relates to business will appreciate and adhere to those higher standards. We must at least understand that whether we are motivated by divine law, conscience, moral indifference, or avarice, serious consequences may follow from non-compliance with the body of rules we call law.

CATEGORIES OF LAW

Substantive law includes public and private law

Law consists of rules with different but intersecting functions. The primary categories are substantive and procedural laws. **Substantive law** establishes not only the rights an individual has in society but also the limits on his or her conduct. The rights to travel, to vote, and to own property are guaranteed by substantive law. Prohibitions against theft and murder as well as other actions that harm our neighbours are also examples of substantive law. **Procedural law** determines how the substantive laws will be enforced. The rules governing arrest, investigation, and pre-trial and court processes in both criminal and civil cases are examples. Law can also be distinguished by its public or private function. **Public law** includes constitutional law that determines how the country is governed and the laws that affect an individual's relationship with government, including criminal law and the regulations created by government agencies. **Private law** involves the rules that govern our personal, social, and business relations, which are enforced by one person suing another in a private or civil action. Knowing the law and how it functions allows us to structure our lives as productive and accepted members of the community and to predict the consequences of our conduct. Business students study law because it defines the environment of rules within which business functions. In order to play the game, we must know the rules.

Figure 1.1 A Map of the Law

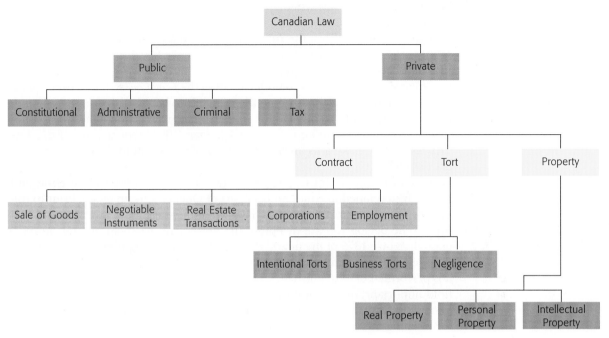

ORIGINS OF LAW

Nine of the ten Canadian provinces and the three territories have adopted the common law legal system developed over the last millennium in England. For private matters, Quebec has adopted a system based on the *French Civil Code.* Although this text focuses on common law, understanding it may be assisted by briefly examining the basic differences between the common law and civil law legal systems. It is important to note that the term *civil law* has two distinct meanings. The following discussion is about the **civil law legal system** developed in Europe and now used in many jurisdictions, including Quebec. The terms *civil court, civil action,* and *civil law* are also used within our common law legal system to describe private law matters and should not be confused with the *Civil Code* or civil law as used in Quebec.

Quebec civil law; all other provinces common law

Civil Law Legal System

Modern civil law traces its origins to the Emperor Justinian, who had Roman law codified for use throughout the Roman Empire. This codification became the foundation of the legal system in continental Europe. Its most significant modification occurred early in the 19th century, when Napoleon revised it. The *Napoleonic Code* was adopted throughout Europe and most of the European colonies. Today, variations of the *Civil Code* are used in all of continental Europe, South America, most of Africa, and many other parts of the world, including Quebec. The most important feature of French civil law is its central *Code*—a list

***Civil Code* used throughout much of the world**

of rules stated as broad principles of law that judges apply to the cases that come before them. Under this system, people wanting to know their legal rights or obligations refer to the *Civil Code*.

Quebec courts rely on the rules set out in the *Code* to resolve private disputes in that province. While civil law judges are influenced by decisions made in other cases, and lawyers will take great pains to point out what other judges have done in similar situations, the key to understanding the *Civil Code* system is to recognize that ultimately the *Code* determines the principle to be applied. Prior decisions do not constitute binding precedents in a civil law jurisdiction. The most recent Quebec *Civil Code* came into effect on 1 January 1994.[1] One-quarter of the 1994 *Code* is new law, making its introduction a significant event in the evolution of the law of Quebec.

One of the effects of the new *Code* was to make the doctrine of good faith (recently developed in common law) part of Quebec's contract law. Prior to this, the law was similar to the common law, where the obligation to act in good faith toward the person you are dealing with applied only when special relationships existed. Article 1375 of the new *Code* states that contracting parties "shall conduct themselves in good faith both at the time the obligation is created and at the time it is performed or extinguished."[2] This means that the parties can no longer withhold important information or fail to correct erroneous assumptions that they know have been made by the other side without exposing themselves to an action for violating this obligation of good faith.

To illustrate how the law is applied in a civil law legal system as opposed to a common law legal system, consider the situation involving a person suffering injury because of the careless act of another. If a person was seriously burned in Quebec, as a result of being served overly hot coffee in a pliable paper cup at a fast-food restaurant drive-through, the victim would turn to the Quebec *Civil Code* to determine his or her rights. Articles 1457 and 1463 of the most recent *Code* state the following:

> 1457. Every person has a duty to abide by the rules of conduct which lie upon him, according to the circumstances, usage or law, so as not to cause injury to another. Where he is endowed with reason and fails in this duty, he is responsible for any injury he causes to another person and is liable to reparation for the injury, whether it be bodily, moral, or material in nature.
>
> He is also liable, in certain cases, to reparation for injury caused to another by the act or fault of another person or by the act of things in his custody.
>
> 1463. The principal is liable to reparation for injury caused by the fault of his agents and servants in the performance of their duties; nevertheless, he retains his recourses against them.

Thus, applying article 1457, the server may be held liable to the customer. But if in a subsequent identical case, the Court applied both articles 1457 and 1463, the employer could be held liable in addition to the employee, increasing the likelihood that the customer would actually recover any damages awarded by the court. Since the courts in a civil law jurisdiction are not required to follow

Civil Code provides predictability

Quebec uses *Civil Code* to resolve private disputes

Civil Code recognizes doctrine of good faith

Civil Code also applied to tort cases

[1.] *Civil Code of Quebec*, S.Q. 1991, c. 64.*Civil Code of Quebec*, S.Q. 1991, c. 64.

[2.] *Ibid.*, Art. 1375.

each other's decisions, two very similar cases may be decided differently. The end result is shaped by the specific "law" or article of the *Code* that is applied to the facts of a case.

In a common law jurisdiction, liability may also be imposed on both the employer and the employee who caused injury due to the application of the principles of negligence and vicarious liability. But in a common law jurisdiction, the doctrine of following precedent would demand that the courts look to similar cases for the principles to be applied. Thus, if a litigant can point to a case similar to her own, where a superior court imposed liability on both the employee (server) and the employer (restaurant), it is likely that a similar decision will be delivered in her case.

There are many important differences between civil law and the principles of common law. In this text, we have limited the discussion to common law—while there are many similarities, care should be taken not to assume that the same principles apply to Quebec or other civil law jurisdictions.

Consistency is reduced where preceding court decisions can be ignored

Following precedent increases consistency and predictability

Common Law Legal System

As Roman civil law was taking hold in Europe, relations between the existing English and French kingdoms were frequently strained. It has been suggested that this strain is the reason England maintained its unique common law system of justice rather than adopting the more widely accepted Roman civil law. The early Norman kings established a strong feudal system in England that centralized power in their hands. As long as they remained strong, they maintained their power; but when weak kings were on the throne, power was surrendered to the nobles. The growth of the common law legal system was much affected by this ongoing struggle for power between kings and nobles and later between kings and parliament.

Common law grew from struggle for power

During times when power was decentralized, the administration of justice fell to the local lords, barons, or sheriffs, who would hold court as part of their feudal responsibility. Their courts commonly resorted to such practices as trial by battle or ordeal. Trial by battle involved armed combat between the litigants or their champions, and trial by ordeal involved some physical test. The assumption was made that God would intervene on behalf of the righteous party. Strong kings, especially Henry II, enhanced their power by establishing travelling courts, which provided a more attractive method of resolving disputes. As more people used the king's courts, their power base broadened, and their strength increased. The fairer the royal judges, the more litigants they attracted. Eventually, the courts of the nobles fell into disuse. The function of the royal courts was not to impose any particular set of laws but to be as fair and impartial as possible. To this end, they did not make new rules but enforced the customs and traditions they found already in place in the towns and villages they visited. The judges also began to look to each other for rules to apply when faced with new situations.

Henry II established travelling courts

Common law principles came from the common people—their traditions and customs

STARE DECISIS

Gradually, a system of justice developed in which the judges were required to follow each other's decisions. This process is called ***stare decisis***, or "following precedent." Another factor that affected the development of *stare decisis* was the creation of appeal courts. Although the process of appeal at this time was rudimentary, trial judges would try to avoid the embarrassment of having their decisions overturned and declared in error. Eventually, the practice of following

Judges follow decisions—if made within that court's hierarchy

precedent became institutionalized. The most significant feature of our legal system today is that the decision of a judge at one level is binding on all judges in the court hierarchy who function in a court of lower rank, provided the facts in the two cases are similar.[3] Thus, a judge today hearing a case in the Court of Queen's Bench for Alberta would be required to follow a similar decision laid down in the Court of Appeal for Alberta or the Supreme Court of Canada, but would not have to follow a decision involving an identical case from the Court of Appeal for Manitoba.[4] Such a decision would be merely persuasive, since it came from a different jurisdiction. Because the Supreme Court of Canada is the highest court in the land, its decisions are binding on all Canadian courts.

CASE SUMMARY 1.1

Inconsistent Interpretations—Significance of Having a Supreme Court: *R. v. Keegstra*[5] and *R. v. Andrews*[6]

Each province in Canada has its own hierarchy of courts, thus a ruling from the highest court in one province may conflict with decisions from other courts. Consider the dilemma faced by the police in enforcing Canada's *Criminal Code* following the decisions in the *Keegstra* and *Andrews* cases. Both cases involved charges laid under section 319(2) of the *Code*, prohibiting wilful promotion of hatred against identifiable groups.

Keegstra had been teaching students in Eckville, Alberta, that the holocaust was a hoax. Andrews was also spreading anti-semitic, white supremacist hate literature. In the *Keegstra* case, the charges were set aside when the Alberta Court of Appeal declared the legislation to be unconstitutional. Keegstra successfully argued that the *Criminal Code* prohibition violated his freedom of expression as guaranteed by the *Charter of Rights and Freedoms*. But in the *Andrews* case, the Ontario Court of Appeal upheld the constitutionality of the same charges even though it had the benefit of the Alberta decision. It simply chose not to follow it.

Courts from different provinces are not bound to follow each other's decisions. Consequently, Canadians may face situations where charges cannot be laid in one province, whereas similar conduct will result in criminal prosecution in others. The police could not pursue hate crimes in Alberta because the Alberta Court of Appeal had ruled the law unconstitutional. Yet in Ontario, similar conduct drew charges.

The Supreme Court of Canada ruled on the *Keegstra* and *Andrews* appeals simultaneously. It declared section 319 constitutional, finding that although freedom of expression is violated by the *Code*, these infringements are justifiable under section 1 of the

---

[3.] See *Toronto Star Newspapers Ltd. v. The Queen,*[2007]84 O.R. (3d) 766 (Ont. H.C.J.), where the applicants argued that the court could depart from an earlier 1984 decision of the Ontario Court of Appeal, which upheld mandatory publication bans. The judge declared that "the question put to the Court of Appeal in Global is indistinguishable from the one I am asked to consider. I find I have no authority to reconsider Global. Until such time as the Court of Appeal or the Supreme Court of Canada finds that Global was wrongly decided, it remains the law in Ontario."

[4.] Strictly speaking, a judge is not bound to follow decisions made by other judges in a court at the same level in that province. However, the practical effect is the same, since these judges must follow their colleagues' decisions "in the absence of strong reason to the contrary." *R. v. Morris*, [1942] O.W.N. 447 (Ont. H.C.J.).

[5.] [1988] A.J. No. 501 (C.A.), rev'd [1990] 3 S.C.R. 870.

[6.] [1988] O.J. No. 1222 (C.A.); [1990] 3 S.C.R. 870.

Charter. Prohibiting communications that are hateful and harmful was found to be justifiable, even if freedom of expression is thus curtailed, for the good of society as a whole. Charges for inciting hatred were thus tried against Keegstra and he was eventually convicted.

SMALL BUSINESS PERSPECTIVE

These cases demonstrate that one law may be interpreted and enforced differently from province to province. A sophisticated businessperson cannot assume that laws will receive similar interpretation across the country.

The role *stare decisis* plays in the English common law legal system is similar to the role the *Civil Code* plays in the French system. It allows the parties to predict the outcome of the litigation and thus avoid going to court. However, a significant disadvantage of following precedent is that a judge must follow another judge's decision even though social attitudes may have changed. The system is anchored to the past, with only limited capacity to make corrections or to adapt and change to meet modern needs. Opposing legal representatives present a judge with several precedents that support their side of the argument. The judge's job is to analyze the facts of the precedent cases and compare them with the case at hand. Since no two cases are ever exactly alike, the judge has some flexibility in deciding whether or not to apply a particular precedent. Judges try to avoid applying precedent decisions by finding essential differences between the facts of the two cases if they feel that the prior decision will create an injustice in the present case. This process is referred to as **distinguishing the facts** of opposing precedents. Still, judges cannot stray very far from the established line of precedents.

Stare decisis provides predictability

Results in an inflexible system

A judge must choose among precedents

CASE SUMMARY 1.2

Lower Court Judge Must Follow Decision of Higher Court: *R. v. Clough*[7]

Ms. Clough was convicted in a B.C. Provincial Court of possession of cocaine for the purposes of trafficking and also for possession of a small amount of marijuana. At the time of sentencing, the provincial court judge had to decide whether this was an appropriate case to impose a conditional sentence on Ms. Clough or a harsher sentence involving a jail term. He was asked to take into consideration the Supreme Court of Canada decision in *R. v. Proulx*,[8] setting out certain guidelines for sentencing in these circumstances, and the British Columbia Court of Appeal decision in *R. v. Kozma*,[9] which upheld the imposition of a conditional sentence in a similar matter.

[7.] [2001] B.C.J. No. 2336 (C.A.).

[8.] *R. v. Proulx*, [2000] 1 S.C.R. 61.

[9.] [2000] B.C.J. No. 1595 (C.A.).

The B.C.C.A. had considered the *Proulx* judgment before reaching its decision in the *Kozma* matter. But the Provincial Court Judge in this case stated that the B.C.C.A. had wrongly decided the *R. v. Kozma* case and refused to follow it. He imposed a sentence of eight months on Ms. Clough, and that decision was appealed to the B.C.C.A.

The Court of Appeal stated that the Provincial Court Judge had the authority to find that the facts in this case were different and not apply the *Kozma* decision for that reason, but it was not within his power to refuse to follow the decision of a senior court on the basis that the case had been wrongly decided. "That was not for him to say." The Court of Appeal stated in its judgment that the Provincial Court Judge "was bound by the rule of *stare decisis* to accept the decisions of this court to the extent that they may apply to the case before him." Thus, the Court of Appeal overturned his decision, removed the eight-month jail term, and substituted a conditional sentence on Ms. Clough.

This case nicely illustrates how *stare decisis* works today. The Supreme Court of Canada made a decision in the *R. v. Proulx* case, and the British Columbia Court of Appeal interpreted and applied that decision in *R. v. Kozma*. Whereas the Supreme Court of Canada could declare the *Kozma* decision erroneous and refuse to apply it (or even overturn it on appeal), the Provincial Court of British Columbia was required to follow the *Kozma* decision, it being from a superior court.

DISCUSSION QUESTIONS

Should a lower court be required to follow the decision of a higher court that it believes has been wrongly decided? What about the requirement of following a precedent when the reason for it has long since disappeared? Consider the arguments for and against the application of *stare decisis*.

SOURCES OF LAW

Common Law

Customs and traditions major source of common law

Common law borrows from:
- **Roman civil law**
- **Canon law**
- **Law merchant**

At an early stage in the development of common law, three great courts were created: the court of common pleas, the court of king's bench, and the exchequer court, referred to collectively as the **common law courts**. The rules developed in the courts were called "common law" because the judges, at least in theory, did not create law but merely discovered it in the customs and traditions of the people to whom it was to be applied. However, the foundation for a complete legal system could not be supplied by local custom and tradition alone, so common law judges borrowed legal principles from many different sources. Common law borrows from **Roman civil law**, which gave us our concepts of property and possessions. **Canon** or **church law** contributed law in relation to families and estates. Another important European system that had an impact on common law was called the **law merchant**. Trading between nations was performed by merchants who were members of guilds (similar to modern trade unions or professional organizations), which developed their own rules to deal with disputes between members. As the strength of the guilds declined, common law judges found themselves dealing increasingly with disputes between merchants. The law merchant was then adopted as part of the English common law, and it included laws relating to negotiable instruments, such as cheques and promissory notes.

Equity

Common law courts had some serious limitations. Parties seeking justice before them found it difficult to obtain fair and proper redress for the grievances they had suffered. Because of the rigidity of the process, the inflexibility of the rules applied, and the limited scope of the remedies available, people often went directly to the king for satisfaction and relief. The burden of this process made it necessary for the king to delegate the responsibility to the chancellor, who, in turn, appointed several vice-chancellors. This body eventually became known as the **Court of Chancery**, sometimes referred to as the **Court of Equity**. It dealt with matters that, for various reasons, could not be handled adequately or fairly by the common law courts. The Court of Chancery did not hear appeals from the common law courts; rather, it provided an alternative forum. If people seeking relief knew that the common law courts could provide no remedy or that the remedy was inadequate, they would go to the Court of Chancery instead. Initially, the Court of Chancery was unhampered by the rules of precedence and the rigidity that permeated the common law courts, and could decide a case on its merits. The system of law developed by the Court of Chancery became known as the **law of equity**. This flexibility, which was the most significant asset of equity, was also its greatest drawback. Each decision of the Court of Chancery appeared arbitrary; there was no uniformity within the system; and it was difficult to predict the outcome of a given case. This caused friction between the chancery and the common law judges, which was solved, to some extent, by the chancery's adopting *stare decisis*. This caused the same problems found in the common law courts. The chancery courts eventually became as formal and rigid as the common law courts. Finally, the two separate court systems were amalgamated by the *Judicature Acts of 1873–1875*.[10] This merger happened in Canada as well, and today there is only one court system in each of the provinces.

Although the two court systems merged, the bodies of law they had created did not, and it is best still to think of common law and equity as two distinct bodies of rules. Originally, the rules of equity may have been based on fairness and justice, but when a person today asks a judge to apply equity, they are not asking for fairness: they are asking that the rules developed by the courts of chancery be applied to the case. Equity should be viewed as a supplement to, rather than a replacement of, common law. Common law is complete—albeit somewhat unsatisfactory—without equity, but equity would be nothing without common law. The courts of chancery were instrumental in developing such principles in law as the trust (in which one party holds property for another), and also provided several alternative remedies, such as injunction and specific performance, that will be examined later in the text.

The common law provinces in Canada administer both common law and equity, and judges treat matters differently when proceeding under equity as opposed to common law rules. Of course, judges must always be alert to the fact that any applicable parliamentary statute will override both.

---

10. *Judicature Acts*(1873–1875) 31 Geo. III.

Common law rigid

Courts of Chancery provided relief

Resulting in the law of equity

Conflict resulted in rigidity in chancery as well

Equity today does not simply mean fairness

Equity supplements the common law

Statutes

In many situations, justice was not available in either the common law or chancery courts, and another method was needed to correct these inadequacies. The English Civil War of the 17th century firmly established the principle that Parliament, rather than the king, was supreme, and from that time, Parliament handled any major modification to the law. Parliamentary enactments are referred to as statutes or legislation and take precedence over judge-made law based on either common law or equity.

It is important to remember that government has several distinct functions: legislative, judicial, and administrative. Parliament legislates or creates the law, as do each of the provincial legislatures; the judicial branch is the court system, and the judiciary interprets legislation and makes case law; the executive branch and its agencies administer and implement that law. Organizations such as the RCMP, the Employment Insurance Commission, and the military are part of the executive branch of government. Often, legislation creating such bodies (the enabling statute) delegates power to them to create regulations (the subordinate legislation). Through those regulations, government agencies implement and accomplish the goals of the enabling statute and enforce its terms. Similarly, municipal

Table 1.1 Sources of Law in Canada

Branch of Government	Legislative	Executive	Judicial
Who fills these positions?	Federally: Parliament	Prime Minister and Cabinet Ministers together with each department's civil servants/ bureaucrats	Judges appointed by the various provinces and federally appointed justices
	Provincially: Legislative Assemblies	Premier and the Cabinet together with each department's civil servants/bureaucrats	
Type of law made	Statute law (legislation)	Subordinate legislation • regulations made by order-in-council or as authorized by legislation • bylaws made by municipal governments	Case law
Examples	(Federal) • *Immigration and Refugee Protection Act* • *Criminal Code*	(Federal) Immigration and Refugee Protection Regulations	(Federal) The decision of the Supreme Court of Canada in *R. v. Keegstra*
	(Provincial) • *Workers' Compensation Act* • *Traffic Safety Act* • *Business Corporations Act*	(Provincial) Workers' Compensation Regulations	(Provincial) The decision of the Ontario Court of Appeal in *Haig v. Canada*

bylaws operate as subordinate legislation. A provincial statute, such as *Ontario's Municipal Act, 2001*,[11] may enable municipalities to pass bylaws, but only with regard to matters stipulated in the *Act.*

For the businessperson, these statutes and regulations have become all-important, setting out the specific rules governing business activities in all jurisdictions. Although judge-made law still forms the foundation of our legal system, it is statutes and regulations that control and restrict what we can do and determine what we must do to carry on business in Canada today. See Table 1.1 for a summary of the sources of law in Canada.

LAW IN CANADA

Confederation

Canada came into existence in 1867, with the federation of Upper and Lower Canada, Nova Scotia, and New Brunswick. Other provinces followed, with Newfoundland being the most recent to join Confederation. Every jurisdiction except Quebec adopted the English common law legal system. Quebec elected to retain the use of the French civil law legal system for private matters falling within provincial jurisdiction.

Confederation was accomplished when the British Parliament passed the *British North America Act* (*BNA Act*), now renamed the *Constitution Act, 1867.*[12] The *BNA Act*'s primary significance is that it created the Dominion of Canada, divided power between the legislative, executive, and judicial branches of government, and determined the functions and powers of the provincial and federal levels of government. The preamble to the *BNA Act* says that Canada has a constitution "similar in principle to that of the United Kingdom"; that is, we claim as part of our constitution all the great constitutional institutions of the United Kingdom, such as the *Magna Carta* and the *English Bill of Rights*. Also included are such unwritten conventions as the **rule of law**, which recognizes that although Parliament is supreme and can create any law considered appropriate, citizens are protected from the arbitrary actions of the government. All actions of government and government agencies must be authorized by valid legislation. In addition, our constitution includes those acts passed by both the British and Canadian Parliaments subsequent to the *Constitution Act, 1867* that have status beyond mere statutes, such as the *Statute of Westminster* (1931) and the *Constitution Act, 1982*,[13] which includes the *Charter of Rights and Freedoms*. The most recent addition to the constitutional statutes is the *Constitution Act, 1999* (Nunavut).[14]

BNA Act **created Canada and divided powers**

More to Canadian Constitution than *BNA Act* **and** *Charter*

Canada's Constitution is, in essence, the "rulebook" that government must follow. It is comprised of three elements: (1) statutes, such as the *Constitution Act, 1982* and the statutes creating various provinces; (2) conventions, which are unwritten rules dictating how the government is to operate and include the rule of law; and (3) case law on Constitution issues, such as whether the federal or provincial government has jurisdiction to create certain statutes.

---

11. S.O. 2001, c. 25.

12. *Constitution Act, 1867*(U.K.), 30 & 31 Vict., c. 3, reprinted in R.S.C. 1985, App. II, No. 5 (formerly the *British North America Act,1867*).

13. *Constitution Act, 1982*, being Schedule B to the *Canada Act 1982* (U.K.), 1982, c. 11.

14. S.C. 1998, c. 15, Part II; (in force 1 April 1999).

CASE SUMMARY 1.3

The Power to Prorogue Parliament[15]

Within two months of the October 2008 federal election, Canadians were facing the prospect of going to the polls again. The decision of whether to prorogue (adjourn) Parliament or not rested with the Governor General, Michaelle Jean. Canadians learned that reserve powers, vested in the head of state (the Queen, as represented by the Governor General and Lieutenant-Governors), are protected by unwritten constitutional conventions. These reserve powers include the power to dismiss a Prime Minister, to dissolve Parliament (or not), and to delay or refuse royal assent to legislation.

Since the King-Byng affair in 1926, the convention (unwritten rule) has been that the Governor General is expected to take the advice of the sitting Prime Minister. This convention arose on the heels of the then Governor General's (Lord Byng's) decision to ignore the wishes of the Prime Minister (McKenzie King) to dissolve Parliament. Instead the Governor General called upon the Leader of the Opposition to lead Parliament, which proved to be futile since the opposition did not have the support of the House of Commons. The minority government was soon defeated and an election had to be called anyway.

In December 2008, the leaders of the Liberal and New Democratic parties formed a coalition and, with the support of the Bloc Québécois, planned to defeat Harper's Conservatives during the first sitting of Parliament. Harper thus asked the Governor General to prorogue Parliament until a new budget could be presented. In deciding to prorogue Parliament, the Governor General essentially dealt a death-blow to the coalition and allowed the Conservatives a chance to win back the confidence of the House.[16]

DISCUSSION QUESTIONS

Did the Governor General essentially follow the convention that arose as a consequence of the King-Byng affair? Under what circumstances might it be acceptable for the Governor General not to follow the advice of a Prime Minister?

For the person in business, it must be remembered that the effect of Confederation was not simply to create one country, with one set of rules. Each province was given the power to establish rules in those areas over which it had jurisdiction. As a consequence, businesses operating within and between provinces must comply with federal, provincial, and municipal regulations. In spite of the opportunity for great divergence among the provinces, it is encouraging to see how similar the controls and restrictions are in the different jurisdictions.

Constitution and Division of Powers

In Canada, as in Britain, Parliament is supreme and traditionally has had the power to make laws that cannot be overruled by any other body and are subject only to the realities of the political system in which they function. In addition, the *Constitution Act, 1867* and the *Charter of Rights and Freedoms* place some limitations

---

[15] For more information on this Constitutional spectacle, see online: http://www.cbc.ca/canada/story/2008/12/02/f-governor-general.html (accessed May, 2009).

[16.] See "The Delicate Role of the Governor General," http://www.cbc.ca/canada/story/2008/12/02/f-governor-general.html. To view a video clip summarizing the King-Byng affair, see http://archives.cbc.ca/politics/federal_politics/clips/11688/, May 13, 2009).

on this supremacy. Unlike the United Kingdom, Canada has a federal form of government with 11 different legislative bodies, each claiming the supreme powers of Parliament.

The *Constitution Act, 1867* assigned different legislative powers to the federal and provincial governments. The powers of the federal government are set out primarily in section 91 of the *Constitution Act, 1867*, and those of the provincial governments in section 92. The federal government has power over such matters as banking, currency, the postal service, criminal law (although not its enforcement), and the appointment of judges in the federal and higher-level provincial courts. The federal government passes considerable legislation affecting such matters as the regulation of all import and export activities, taxation, environmental concerns, money and banking, interprovincial and international transportation, as well as important areas of intellectual property, such as copyrights, patents, and trademarks. The provinces have jurisdiction over such matters as hospitals, education, the administration of the courts, and commercial activities carried on at the provincial level.

Constitution Act and *Charter* limit power of federal and provincial governments

Constitution Act (1867) divides powers between federal and provincial governments

Federal powers set out in sec. 91

Provincial powers set out in sec. 92

Thus, most business activities that are carried on within the province are governed by provincial legislation or municipal bylaws, including statutes dealing with the sale of goods, consumer protection, employment, workers' compensation, collective bargaining, secured transactions, incorporation, real estate, and licensing. For industries that fall within federal jurisdiction, such as banking and the railways, there are corresponding federal statutes, such as collective bargaining and incorporation legislation. Under the "Peace, Order, and Good Government" (P.O.G.G.) clause (found in the introduction to section 91), the federal government has residual power to make law with respect to things not listed in the *Constitution Act, 1867,* such as broadcasting and air transportation. Under section 92(16), the provinces are given broad powers to make law with respect to all matters of a local or private nature. It is important to note that these assigned areas of jurisdiction are concerned with the nature of the legislation being passed, rather than the individuals or things affected. Thus, the federal government's power to pass banking legislation allows it to control anything to do with banking, including interest rates, deposits, and how those deposits are invested. The division of powers accomplished by sections 91 and 92 of the *Constitution Act, 1867* has been very important in the development of Canada as a nation and, until the recent entrenchment of the *Charter*, was the main consideration of courts when faced with constitutional questions. In these jurisdictional disputes between governments, where competing governments claim to control a particular activity, the courts are called upon to act as a referee. See Table 1.2 for a summary of the division of powers.

Sections 91 and 92 deal with types of legislation, not things

Table 1.2   Division of Powers

Federal—Section 91	Provincial—Section 92
Trade and commerce	Municipal institutions
Employment insurance	Hospitals (and health care)
Raising monies by any mode of taxation	Direct taxation within the province
Criminal law (although not its enforcement)	Administration of justice within the province
Banking, currency, postal service	Property and civil rights
Residual power under the "P.O.G.G." clause	Generally, matters of a local or private nature

Challenging Provincial Forfeiture Laws: *Chatterjee v. Ontario (Attorney General)*[17]

Chatterjee, a university student, was being arrested for breach of probation when the police coincidentally found $29 000 in cash and items associated with drug trafficking in his car, but no drugs. No charges were laid relating to the money, nor was Chatterjee charged with any drug-related activity. Nonetheless, the Attorney General applied for and obtained an order allowing the Crown to keep the money and equipment, as proceeds of unlawful activity under Ontario's *Remedies for Organized Crime and Other Unlawful Activities Act*, also known as the *Civil Remedies Act (CRA)*. Chatterjee challenged the constitutional validity of the *CRA*, arguing that the province did not have the right to seize proceeds of crime since criminal law is a matter of federal, not provincial, jurisdiction.

The Supreme Court of Canada unanimously upheld the provincial law, since the dominant feature related to "property and civil rights," is a provincial matter. While its provisions may incidentally overlap with criminal law, "the fact that the CRA aims to deter federal offences as well as provincial offences, and indeed, offences outside of Canada, is not fatal to its validity."

As stated by Binnie, J. for the Court: "The CRA was enacted to deter crime and to compensate its victims. The former purpose is broad enough that both the federal government (in relation to criminal law) and the provincial governments (in relation to property and civil rights) can validly pursue it. The latter purpose falls squarely within provincial competence. Crime imposes substantial costs on provincial treasuries. Those costs impact many provincial interests, including health, policing resources, community stability and family welfare. It would be out of step with modern realities to conclude that a province must shoulder the costs to the community of criminal behaviour but cannot use deterrence to suppress it."

SMALL BUSINESS PERSPECTIVE

This case is interesting because the party raising the constitutional challenge was not a government, but rather, an individual. Thus if one finds oneself objecting to a particular law, one might solve the issue by challenging the constitutional validity of the enactment!

Courts examine the essence of laws in constitutional challenges

When determining the constitutional validity of legislation, the courts often resolve the issue by looking at the "pith and substance" of the challenged law. In other words, what is the main purpose of the law and does the government which enacted the law have the constitutional jurisdiction to regulate that concern. Such was the approach taken in the *Reference re Firearms Act* (Can.) case.[18] In 1995, Parliament amended the *Criminal Code* by enacting the *Firearms Act*.[19] The amendments require all holders of firearms to obtain licences and register their guns. Alberta, backed by Ontario, Saskatchewan, Manitoba, and the territories, chal-

---

[17] 2009 SCC 19.

[18] [2000] 1 S.C.R. 783.

[19] S.C. 1995, c. 39.

lenged the law, arguing it was a brazen intrusion on private property and civil rights, a provincial power according to section 92(13) of the *Constitution Act, 1867*. The opponents argued that the new law would do no more to control gun crimes than registering vehicles does to stop traffic offences.

The Supreme Court of Canada upheld the *Firearms Act* as **intra vires** Parliament, meaning that it was within its power. It found that the *Act* constitutes a valid exercise of Parliament's jurisdiction over criminal law because its "pith and substance" is directed to enhancing public safety by controlling access to firearms. Because guns are dangerous and pose a risk to public safety, their control and their regulation as dangerous products were regarded as valid purposes for criminal law. In essence, the law was determined to be criminal in focus. The *Act* impacted provincial jurisdiction over property and civil rights only incidentally. Accordingly, the *Firearms Act* was upheld as a valid exercise of federal power under section 91(27) of the *Constitution Act, 1867*.

> Laws upheld if interference with another jurisdiction's power is incidental

Conflicting Powers

On occasion, one level of government passes legislation that may infringe on the powers of another. For example, municipal governments have tried to control prostitution or pornography, using their zoning or licensing power, when in fact these matters are controlled by criminal law, a federal area.[20] Such bylaws have been struck down as **ultra vires** (beyond one's jurisdiction or power) by the courts, as veiled attempts to control moral conduct, matters to be dealt with under criminal jurisdiction. Municipalities sometimes try to dramatically increase the licensing fee charged to a business to accomplish the same purpose, often with the same result.

> Validity of statute determined by its true nature

One level of government cannot invade the area given to another by trying to make it look like the legislation is of a different kind. This is called colourable legislation and the court simply looks at the substance of what the governing body is trying to do, as opposed to what it claims to be doing, and asks whether or not it has that power.

CASE SUMMARY 1.5

Municipal Bylaw to Ensure Covering of Breasts: *Maple Ridge (District) v. Meyer*[21]

A quiet B.C. community was shocked to see Ms. Meyer bare her breasts at a public swimming pool—after all, she was no longer a child! The response was an amendment to the Maple Ridge Park bylaw, making it an offence punishable by a fine of $2000 and six months' imprisonment to appear in a park unclothed. "Clothed" was defined to require females over the age of eight years to fully cover their nipples and areolae with opaque apparel. The Court determined that the amendment to the bylaw was motivated by complaints regarding morality, modesty, and embarrassment. The bylaw created a stricter

---

20. *R. v. Westendorp*, [1983] 1 S.C.R. 43.

21. [2000] B.C.J. No. 1154 (B.C.S.C.).

standard regarding nudity than that found in the *Criminal Code*. It imposed strict liability whereas under the *Code* defences were available; further, it criminalized the conduct of girls as young as nine years old. The Court struck the bylaw down as *ultra vires* the legislative competence of Maple Ridge, finding it a "colourable attempt to regulate morality and thus displace the federal jurisdiction in respect of criminal law."

DISCUSSION QUESTIONS

In light of the division of powers, can you think of other laws that may be characterized as colourable legislation? Who can challenge such legislation and how is this done?

When provincial and federal laws conflict, follow federal

The powers of the federal and provincial governments can overlap considerably. When overlap does take place, the principle of **paramountcy** may require that the federal legislation be operative and that the provincial legislation go into abeyance and no longer apply. If the overlap between provincial and federal legislations is merely incidental, both are valid, and both are operative. An individual must obey both by adhering to the higher standard, whether provincial or federal. It is only when the laws are such that only one can be obeyed that a true conflict exists, and then the federal provision will prevail.

CASE SUMMARY 1.6

Another Challenge Goes Up in Smoke: *Rothmans, Benson & Hedges Inc. v. Saskatchewan*[22]

The Federal *Tobacco Act* permitted manufacturers and retailers to display tobacco products and to post signs setting out availability and prices. Saskatchewan passed the *Tobacco Control Act* prohibiting all advertising, display, and promotion of tobacco products in any location where they might be seen by someone under 18. The provincial statute was challenged by Rothmans, Benson & Hedges Inc. on the basis that it was in conflict with the federal *Act*, and because of the principle of paramountcy it could not stand. It was clearly established that the federal legislation was valid and within the competency of the federal government under its criminal law power described in section 91(27) of the *Constitution Act, 1867*. The provincial legislation was presumably valid under the provincial powers set out in section 92 of the *Constitution Act, 1867*. The problem was to determine whether the provincial *Act* could stand given the federal intrusion into the area.

The Supreme Court of Canada concluded that the federal *Tobacco Act* didn't actually permit advertising in those areas prohibited by the provincial legislation; its restrictions were simply not as broad as those covered by the provincial *Act*. The Court found that the two statutes were not in conflict; one simply went further than the other. It was possible for the retailers and manufactures to obey them both by following the higher standard set out in the provincial *Act*. Thus if young people were prohibited from coming

22. [2005] 1 S.C.R. 188.

into a place where there was such advertising, such as a bar or pub, the merchant would be in compliance with both the federal and the provincial *Acts*. Further the court determined that since the purpose of the federal *Act* was to promote public health and restrict the use of tobacco products, the provincial legislation did not frustrate the purpose. Thus, finding no conflict, the court found the provincial *Act* valid and binding.

The case not only illustrates that when there is a true conflict between valid federal and valid provincial legislation, the federal act will prevail, but also shows that often what appears to be a conflict is not. Generally, when it is possible to obey both statutes, there is no conflict and both are valid.

SMALL BUSINESS PERSPECTIVE

The above case demonstrates an interesting tactic—if a particular law restricts the profitability of one's business, one may be able to challenge its constitutionality. If the challenge is successful, the courts can strike the law down, resolving the problem for you

Delegation of Powers

Since neither the federal nor the provincial levels of government are considered inferior legislative bodies, both are supreme parliaments in their assigned areas. Over the years, for various reasons, these bodies have sometimes found it necessary to transfer the powers given to them to other levels of government. However, direct delegation between the federal and provincial governments is prohibited. For example, during the Depression of the 1930s, it became clear that a national system of unemployment insurance was needed. The provinces, having jurisdiction in this area, attempted to delegate their power to the federal government. The Supreme Court held that they could not do so, as it was an "abdication" of the "exclusive powers" given to the provinces under the *Constitution Act, 1867*. To make unemployment insurance an area of federal responsibility, the British Parliament needed to amend the constitution. This amendment is now incorporated in section 91, subsection (2A) of the *Constitution Act, 1867*.

Although direct delegation is prohibited, it is possible for the federal and provincial governments to delegate their powers to inferior bodies, such as boards and individual civil servants; in fact, this is usually the only way that governmental bodies can conduct their business. It is thus possible for the federal government to delegate its power in a particular area to a provincial board or a provincial civil servant. Similarly, a province can give powers to federal boards, since these are also inferior bodies. In this way, governments overcome the prohibition against delegation.

Direct delegation prohibited

Indirect delegation permitted

Agreements to Share Powers

Another means used to circumvent the constitutional rigidity created by the 1867 division of powers is by federal and provincial government agreements to share powers. These agreements may consist of *transfer-payment schemes*, or conditional grants under which the transfer of funds from the federal government is tied to conditions on how the money is to be spent. Through such schemes, the federal government can exercise some say as to how a provincial government operates programs that fall under the province's constitutional area of control. The federal government may set certain national standards to which the funding is tied and in this fashion ensure that all Canadians have access to similar levels of service.

Transfer-payment schemes in the areas of health, social programs, and education are examples of provincial areas where the federal government provides considerable funding along with the imposition of national standards or other conditions on the provinces. At the time of Confederation, government spending on these services was minuscule. Now these areas may account for two-thirds of all government spending. The provinces, with their restricted taxing powers, would have difficulty providing these services without federal funding. In the fairly recent past the federal government dramatically cut payments to support health and social programs in the provinces, but more recently these transfer payments have been at least partially restored.

Legislation

Legislation is introduced to the parliamentary process in the form of a **bill**, which goes through a sequence of introduction, debate, modification, and approval that is referred to as first, second, and third readings. When a bill is finally enacted, it has the status of a statute (although it may still be referred to as a bill or an act). Such a statute does not have the status of law until it receives the approval (signature) of the Governor General at the federal level or the Lieutenant-Governor in a province, a process referred to as receiving **royal assent**. The Governor General and the Lieutenant-Governors are the Queen's representatives in Canada and can sign on behalf of the Crown. Current convention (practice) in Canada directs the Queen's representatives to sign as the government in power directs them, and such approval is therefore usually a formality. The government may use this requirement to delay the coming into effect of legislation, and care should therefore be taken when examining an act to make sure that it has received royal assent. The statute itself may have provisions for different parts of it to come into force at different times. There are many examples where whole acts, or portions of them, have no legal effect for these reasons. See Figure 1.2 for a summary of the traditional process for passing bills.

Statutes must receive royal assent

The Government of Canada publishes a compilation of these statutes annually; the collection can be found in most libraries, under *Statutes of Canada*. The federal government has summarized and published all current statutes in the *Revised Statutes of Canada* in 1985, cited as R.S.C. (1985). It is not necessary to go back any earlier than this compilation to find current legislation. Indexes and guides are provided to assist in the process of finding the federal statutes and subsequent amendments.

Federal and provincial statutes compiled and published

Similarly, each province annually publishes the statutes passed by its legislative assembly and provides a compilation in the form of revised statutes. Unfortunately, there is no uniformity in the timing of the revisions, and each province has revised and compiled its statutes in a different year. Most jurisdictions provide official or unofficial consolidated updates of their statutes online as an ongoing service. These statutes, along with useful commentary about new legislation, are currently available on the internet at their respective government's website. The Access to Justice Network provides easy access to the laws across the country (see its website at **www.acjnet.org**) as does the Canadian Legal Information Institute (**www.canlii.org**).

Regulations also published

Statutes often empower government agencies to create further rules to carry out their functions. As long as these regulations meet the terms of the statute,

Figure 1.2 Traditional Passage of Bills

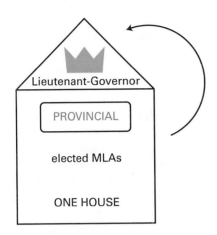

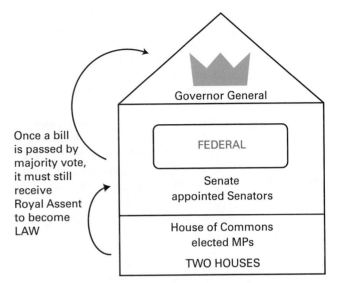

First Reading—Bill is introduced in the Legislative Assembly. Customarily passes first reading without debate.

Second Reading—Bill is read again. Now debated. After approval, it may go to Committee of the Whole for review and amendment. Committee of the Whole must approve all bills before they can receive a third reading.

Third Reading—Bill is read again. Final debate. **VOTE** held.

Once a bill is passed by majority vote, it must still receive Royal Assent to become LAW

First Reading—Introduction (by government, by private member, or possibly by all-party committee*¹). Bill is printed. May go to all-party committee after approval.*²

Second Reading—Bill is debated. After approval in principle, the Bill goes to all-party committee, which may recommend amendments.

Third Reading—Final debate and **VOTE**.

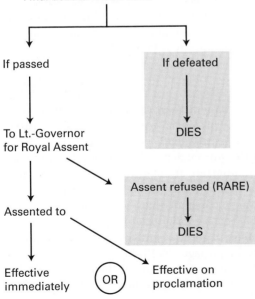

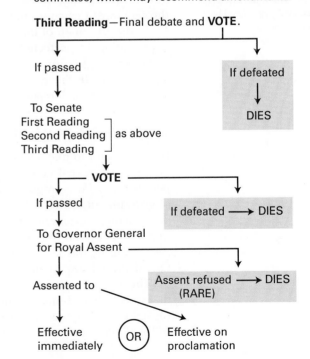

The Federal Government now allows for two variations from the "traditional" passage of bills.*¹ A motion may be tabled for a Committee to prepare and introduce a bill.*² Bills may now be referred to Committee *before* second reading. In any event, a bill goes to Committee only *once*.

they have the effect of law. They are also published and are available to the public as *Regulations of Canada* or of the respective provinces. Cities and municipalities pass bylaws under their statutory authority in the same way, and these too are published and made available by those jurisdictions. Statutes passed within the power of the respective governments as set out in the *Constitution Act, 1867* and other constitutional provisions override any previous law in place, whether judge-made law (common law or equity) or prior legislation.

Judges interpret and apply statutes

A trial judge required to deal with a statute must first determine what it means. This task is not always easy, since it is difficult for those drafting the law to anticipate all of the situations in which it will be applied. The judge must then determine whether, under the *Constitution Act, 1867* and other constitutional provisions, the legislative body that passed the statute in question had the power to do so. When a judge interprets and applies a statute, that decision becomes a precedent, and henceforth the statute must be interpreted in the same way by courts lower in the court hierarchy.

Decisions create precedents

PROTECTION OF RIGHTS AND FREEDOMS

As noted earlier in this chapter, the preamble of the *Constitution Act, 1867* states that Canada will have "a Constitution similar in principle to that of the United Kingdom." The courts have interpreted that phrase as importing into Canada the unwritten conventions and traditions of government developed in the United Kingdom over the centuries. Among those unwritten conventions are the practices of protecting and preserving fundamental rights and freedoms. Canada has, thus, inherited the British tradition of protecting human rights and individual freedoms through unwritten conventions (practices) as supported by common law.

Rights and freedoms were historically protected by convention

In the aftermath of the Second World War, concern arose over the adequacy of entrusting the protection of personal rights and freedoms to common law. Two streams of legislation developed, one dealing with protecting human rights against abuses by the government and the second aimed at protecting individuals against discrimination and intolerance by society at large.

Canadian Bill of Rights

It is important to understand that the basic human rights protections set out in ordinary statutes passed by the federal or provincial governments may not protect people from abuses by government. Because Canada adopted the British method of government, which is based on the supremacy of Parliament, the provincial and federal governments were free to interfere at will with civil rights through legislation. One need look no further than the way the Japanese Canadians were treated during the Second World War to conclude that it could be dangerous for Canadians to leave the protection of their basic rights to the political process.

The first attempt at limiting the federal government's power to pass legislation that violates basic human rights was the passage (in 1960) of the *Canadian Bill of Rights*.[23] Because it was not entrenched in the Constitution, the courts viewed the *Bill of Rights* as just another statute that could be repealed, amended, or simply

---

[23.] S.C. 1960, c. 44.

overridden by any subsequent federal statute. Furthermore, when asked to apply the *Bill of Rights*, the courts approached its provisions in the same narrow, restrictive way that they did any other legislation, thus significantly limiting its scope and effect. For example, when federal legislation passed subsequently was found to be in conflict with the provisions of the *Bill of Rights*, instead of applying the *Bill of Rights* and limiting the operation of the new statute, the courts would treat the new legislation as overriding the old and would disregard the provisions that conflicted with the new legislation. This, of course, effectively defeated the purpose of the *Bill of Rights*, and while it is still considered law in Canada, its effectiveness is extremely limited. Something more was needed.

Bill of Rights just another statute

Charter of Rights and Freedoms

A constitutional guarantee of basic rights and freedoms arose in 1982 following a series of constitutional conferences. *The Constitution Act, 1982*[24] was simultaneously enacted in Canada and the United Kingdom. In the latter, it was contained in a statute called the *Canada Act 1982*.[25] One effect of these enactments was to make a very significant addition to the Canadian Constitution in the form of the Canadian *Charter of Rights and Freedoms*.

The effect of including the *Charter* in our Constitution is twofold. First, neither the federal government nor the provinces have the power to modify or otherwise interfere with the basic rights set out in the *Charter* except through constitutional amendment. Ordinary legislation will not override the *Charter* simply because it is passed after the *Charter*. The provisions are said to be entrenched in the Constitution and are, as declared in section 52 of the *Constitution Act, 1982*, "the supreme law of Canada." The section goes on to state: "Any law that is inconsistent with the provisions of the Constitution is, to the extent of that inconsistency, of no force or effect." In other words, the *Charter* and the rights protected by it come first.

The Constitution includes the *Charter*

Constitution including the *Charter* is the supreme law of Canada

Second, the burden of protecting those rights has shifted from the politicians to the judges. Now, an individual who feels that his or her rights have been interfered with by legislation or other forms of government action can seek redress from the courts, relying on the provisions of the *Charter*. The courts can remedy a violation of rights by excluding evidence improperly secured and can grant any remedy deemed just in the circumstances.[26] The courts can even strike down statutes that infringe on those rights. Hence, the doctrine of parliamentary supremacy has been to some extent limited, the courts now being able to check the power of Parliament and the legislatures in those areas covered by the *Charter*.

Courts are empowered to strike down offending statutes

LIMITATIONS

There are three important limitations on the entrenchment of these basic rights. Section 1 of the *Charter of Rights and Freedoms* allows "reasonable limits" on those rights and freedoms when limiting them can be "demonstrably justified in a free and democratic society." This gives the courts the power to interpret the provisions of the *Charter* to avoid an unreasonable result. The rights and freedoms set

---

24. Schedule B to the *Canada Act 1982* (U.K.) 1982, c. 11.

25. *Canada Act 1982*, (U.K.) 1982, c. 11.

26. *Canadian Charter of Rights and Freedoms*, s. 24, Part I of the *Constitution Act 1982*, being Schedule B to the *Canada Act 1982* (U.K.), 1982, c.11.

out in the *Charter* are, therefore, not absolute. For example, the *Charter* guarantees freedom of expression, but there would be little dispute that libel, slander, or hardcore pornography must be controlled.

The Supreme Court was asked in *Hill v. Church of Scientology of Toronto* (1995)[27] to give effect to the freedom of expression provision of the *Charter* by dismissing a defamation action against the Church and its representative, especially where the remarks were directed at a government official or Crown prosecutor. The Court found that the laws of defamation were, under section 1, a reasonable limitation on the operation of the freedom of expression clause of the *Charter,* thus confirming the lower court's finding of defamation and the highest defamation award up to that time in Canada.

> **Government cannot interfere with basic rights and freedoms except if reasonable to do so**

The interests of the public are considered when applying section 1. Nonetheless, a law that restricts *Charter* rights, though apparently justified, will be rejected if it goes too far. For example, section 1 of the *Charter* was used to justify the imposition of reasonable limits on the rights of prisoners; prisoners serving two years or more in jail could not vote in federal elections. The Federal Court of Appeal found that the voting bans violated section 3 of the *Charter* but were justifiable in light of the objectives of the amended *Canada Elections Act,* specifically the fostering of civic responsibility and respect for the rule of law.[28] These objectives were important enough to warrant (in some cases) a compromise of *Charter* rights. But on further appeal, the Supreme Court of Canada overturned this decision, reasserting prisoners' right to vote. (See Case Summary 1.10 later in this chapter.)

CASE SUMMARY 1.7

Government Reneges on Agreement: *Newfoundland (Treasury Board) v. Newfoundland and Labrador Association of Public and Private Employees*[29]

In this case a significant pay inequity had been identified between female health-care workers and their male counterparts in Newfoundland. The government of Newfoundland and Labrador had entered into an agreement to correct the problem in 1988, including the making of substantial payments to address this pay inequity. The agreement was not implemented, and in 1991 the government brought in legislation, the *Public Sector Restraint Act (Nfld.),* which contained provisions to delay the imposition of the increases meant to correct the imbalance and to eliminate the accumulated arrears altogether. Essentially, the government wiped out $24 million it owed to its employees to correct the imbalance under the agreement. The union took this to arbitration, and the arbitration board decided in the union's favour, finding that the employees' section 15 equality rights under the *Charter* had been infringed. The government appealed and the matter eventually came before the Supreme Court of Canada. The Supreme Court agreed that the section 15 equality rights of the female employees had

---

27. [1995] 2 S.C.R. 1130.

28. *Sauvé v. Canada (Chief Electoral Officer),* [2002] 2 F.C. 119 (C.A.), rev'd [2002] S.C.J. No. 66.

29. [2004] 3 S.C.R. 381.

been infringed. There was a clear case of gender discrimination here. The agreement was designed to correct a historical discrimination, which the government itself acknowledged existed. But the Court also held that because of the serious financial crisis then being experienced by the government of Newfoundland and Labrador, their actions in refusing to pay and delaying the increases was a reasonable limitation "prescribed by law as can be demonstrably justified in a free and democratic society" under section 1 of the *Charter*. This case illustrates how section 1 of the *Charter* can be used to justify some pretty serious deviations from the basic rights and freedoms set out in the *Charter*.

DISCUSSION QUESTIONS

Should the rights and freedoms listed in the *Charter* be absolute or are the exceptions listed under sections 1 and 33 acceptable given the requirements of efficient government and justice?

The second limitation is contained in section 33, and is referred to as the "notwithstanding clause." It allows each of the provinces and the federal government to override the basic rights contained in section 2 and sections 7 through 15 of the *Charter* simply by stating that the new legislation operates "notwithstanding" (regardless of) the *Charter*. The sections that can be overridden in this way include **fundamental freedoms** (such provisions as freedom of conscience and religion, of thought and belief, of opinion and expression, and of assembly and association); **legal rights** (the right of life, liberty, and security of person; security against unreasonable search and seizure, arbitrary imprisonment and detention); and **equality rights** (the right not to be discriminated against on the basis of gender, age, religion, race, or colour; and the guarantee of equality before the law).

It would appear that section 33 weakens the *Charter of Rights and Freedoms* considerably. The supremacy of Parliament appears to have been restored, at least in relation to the designated sections. It was originally hoped that most provinces would find the political cost too great to override the *Charter* in this way and, as a result, would refrain from doing so; for the most part, this has been the case. Quebec, however, used the notwithstanding clause to support language legislation restricting the use of English on business signs in that province. This legislation clearly violates the *Charter's* guarantee of freedom of expression, but the Quebec government gambled that the majority of the electorate would favour such protection of the French language. There are very few other examples of the clause's being used, and Alberta's experiments with invoking the clause have been controversial.[30] The notwithstanding clause does not apply to the sections guaranteeing democratic rights (the right to vote, to elect members to Parliament and the legislative assemblies), mobility rights (the right to enter and leave Canada), or language rights (the right to use both official languages). In addition, the rights of aboriginal people and the rights guaranteed to both genders cannot be overridden by the federal or provincial governments.

Use of notwithstanding clause may be a political gamble

---

30. Alberta had used the notwithstanding clause to override equality rights when it passed the *Marriage Act* provisions restricting marriage to a man and a woman. The clause was used to deny same sex couples the ability to marry. The sunset clause caused that override to expire in 2005. See *Marriage Act*, R.S.A. 2000, c. M-5, s. 2.

Sunset clause

A "sunset clause" is applied to the operation of section 33. If the notwithstanding clause is invoked, the statute must be re-enacted by that legislative body every five years. This forces a re-examination of the decision to override the *Charter*, after the intervening event of an election where the use of the notwithstanding clause can be made an issue. New legislators may not be as willing to pay the political cost of using the notwithstanding clause.

The third limitation is the restriction of the operation of the *Charter* to government and government-related activities. Section 32(1)(a) declares that the *Charter* applies only to matters falling within the authority of "the Parliament and Government of Canada" and the territories, and section 32(1)(b) makes the *Charter* apply "to the legislature and government of each province." A serious problem facing the courts is determining just where government stops and government institutions acting in a private capacity start. Are government institutions—universities, schools, hospitals, and Crown corporations such as the CBC—affected?

Charter applies only to the government—but where does government stop?

While there are still many questions, it does seem clear that when such institutions are acting as an arm of government, the *Charter* applies. Certainly the *Charter* applies to the legislation creating these institutions and to the services provided directly by government departments, including the police and military. When government agencies act in their private capacity (for example, in employee relations), the appropriate federal or provincial human rights legislation applies; such legislation must, in turn, comply with the provisions of the *Charter*. If a section of a statute is in conflict with the provisions of the *Charter*, the offending section will be void, or an appropriate section will be added. In the *Vriend* case[31] (discussed in Case Summary 1.16), the Supreme Court of Canada showed its willingness to interpret into the Alberta statute a provision prohibiting discrimination on the basis of sexual orientation, rather than overturning the statute. Occasionally, the courts have declared legislation invalid but have stayed (held in abeyance) their decision to give the legislators an opportunity to amend the statutes themselves.[32]

Charter probably applies to private institutions acting as arms of government

While the *Charter* directly affects an individual's relationship with government, it only indirectly affects the relationships between individuals and between individuals and private institutions. Human rights legislation impacts these latter relationships, but these federal and provincial human rights codes must comply with the *Charter*. It is also important to remember that the provisions of the *Charter* apply not only to the regulations and enactments of these government bodies and institutions but also to the conduct of government officials employed by them. These officials derive their authority from provincial or federal enactments. If they are acting in a way that violates the provisions of the *Charter*, either they are not acting within their authority, or the statute authorizing their conduct is itself in violation of the *Charter*. In either case, such offending conduct can be challenged under the *Charter*.

Charter Provisions

A brief summary of the types of rights and freedoms Canadians now enjoy because of the *Charter of Rights and Freedoms* follows. The *Charter* sets out several rights that are available in some cases only to citizens of Canada and in other cases

---

[31.] *Vriend v. Alberta*, [1998] 1 S.C.R. 493.

[32.] See *Haig v. Canada* (1992), 9 O.R. (3d) 495 (Ont. C.A.).

to everyone in the nation. The extent of these rights and freedoms, their mean-ing, and the limitations on those rights are still being defined by court decisions. Recourse is available through the courts if the declared rights are interfered with by laws or by the acts of government agents. The courts have been empowered under section 24 of the *Charter* to "provide such remedies as the court considers appropriate and just in the circumstances." These powers are in addition to the inherent power of the court to declare that the offending legislation or conduct is of no effect. This provision allows the courts to award damages, injunctions, and other remedies, when otherwise they would have had no power to do so. Section 24 also gives a judge the power in a criminal matter to exclude evidence that has been obtained in a way that violates the *Charter* rights of the accused, if its admis-sion "would bring the administration of justice into disrepute."

FUNDAMENTAL FREEDOMS

Section 2 of the *Charter* declares certain underlying fundamental freedoms avail-able to everyone in Canada. These are freedom of conscience and religion,[33] free-dom of belief, opinion, and expression; and freedom of assembly and association. The *Charter* protects the right to believe in whatever we wish, to express that belief, and to carry on activities associated with it free from interference. When the expression of those freedoms or the activities associated with them interferes with the freedoms of others, the courts may restrict those freedoms by applying section 1 of the *Charter*.

Freedom of expression, which includes freedom of the press, is an extremely important provision for preserving the democratic nature of Canada, and our courts are very careful to uphold these freedoms. Still, there are many limitations on them, such as the laws of defamation and obscenity.

> Everyone in Canada has right to freedom of conscience and religion; of thought, belief and opinion; of the press; of peaceful assembly; of association

---

CASE SUMMARY 1.8

Sunday Shopping: Does It Prevent Corporations from Going to Church? *R. v. Big M Drug Mart Ltd.*[34]

Big M Drug Mart Ltd. was charged with violation of the *Lord's Day Act*, which required that all such businesses be closed on Sunday. This statute was enacted by the federal government under its criminal law power long before the enactment of the *Charter*. It compelled the observance of a religious duty by means of prohibitions and penalties. This matter went to the Supreme Court of Canada, which held that the *Lord's Day Act* was invalid and of no effect because it interfered with the right of freedom of conscience and religion. It did not matter that the applicant was a corporation incapable of having a conscience or beliefs. Any accused, whether corporate or individual, may defend a crim-inal charge by arguing that the law under which the charge is brought is constitutionally invalid.

[33.] See *R. v. Hutterian Brethren of Wilson Colony*, [2007] A.J. No. 518 C.A., wherea regulatory amend-ment, which required that all drivers' licences include a photo of the licence, violated the respondents' rights of freedom of religion and equality under the *Charter* and was not justified under s. 1. The appeal to the Supreme Court of Canada was heard and reserved October 7, 2008. [2007] S.C.C.A. No. 397.

[34.] [1985] 1 S.C.R. 295.

Compare this to the decision in *London Drugs Ltd. v. Red Deer (City)*,[35] which involved a similar requirement that businesses close one day a week. In that case, however, the bylaw was upheld. It simply required the business to be closed one day a week. The bylaw specified Sunday as a default, but allowed the business to specify another day if it wished. That made it secular rather than religious with the object of simply giving the employees one day in the week free of work. This treated all businesses equally since they had a choice as to when to close.

SMALL BUSINESS PERSPECTIVE

Apparently, it is open to governments to impose restrictions upon business hours by just avoiding any reference to religion. Just as the *Charter* can be used to challenge legislation, legislators are free to achieve desired ends, so long as rights and freedoms are not violated in the process.

CASE SUMMARY 1.9

The Signs of the Times: *Vann Niagara Ltd. v. The Corporation of the Town of Oakville*[36]

The corporation of the town of Oakville, Ontario, had passed a bylaw in 1994 that prohibited the erecting of billboards in the municipality, except those that advertised an activity taking place on the premises where the sign was located. Vann Niagara Ltd. applied for permission to erect 86 billboards in the industrial part of the town, but this was turned down because of the bylaw. Vann Niagara challenged that decision, claiming that it violated the company's rights under the freedom of expression provision (section 2b) of the *Charter of Rights and Freedoms*.

The Ontario Court of Appeal held in this case that indeed the company's rights to freedom of expression had been infringed. The *Charter* protects freedom of expression whether it relates to political, social, or commercial expression. Although Vann Niagara was a commercial entity and the expression was for a commercial purpose, its right to do so was still protected under section 2b of the *Charter*. The Court also found that this infringement was not justifiable under section 1 of the *Charter*. The stated objective of the bylaw, to preserve the small-town character of the municipality, did not justify the total ban on billboards. The Court could not agree that such signs erected in an industrial area as requested would have a negative effect on the character of the town and so the bylaw went too far. Note that the implementation of the decision was suspended for six months for the municipality to bring the bylaw into compliance with the *Charter*.

Compare this to the *R. v. Bryan* case,[37] where the Canada Elections Act prohibited the publication of election results from other parts of the country in British Columbia before the polls closed on election night. The objective here was to make sure that the B.C. electors had the opportunity to make their own decisions unaffected by what was hap-

---

[35] [1987] A.J. No. 815 (Q.B.); appeal dismissed [1988] A.J. No. 701 (C.A.); leave to appeal to S.C.C. refused [1988] S.C.C.A. No. 246.

[36] [2002] O.J. No. 2323 (C.A.).

[37] [2007] S.C.J. No. 12.

pening in the rest of the country. This was also clearly an infringement of the right of freedom of expression as guaranteed in the Charter, but in this case the Court held that the Act was a reasonable limitation under section 1 considering the importance of ensuring voting unaffected by outside interference, and that the Act went no further than was necessary to accomplish that objective. The conviction stood.

These two cases illustrate not only the protection of freedom of expression under the *Charter* but also the limitation provisions under section 1. The issue for the Courts is deciding when the limitation provisions will come into operation and when they won't.

The Supreme Court of Canada has stated that collective bargaining is the "most significant collective activity through which freedom of association is expressed in the labour context."[38] Laws that restrict collective bargaining rights are thus subject to *Charter* scrutiny. Accordingly, in *Fraser v. Ontario (Attorney General)*[39] the Court of Appeal unanimously supported the agricultural workers whose collective bargaining rights were inadequately protected by the *Agricultural Employees Protection Act*. Whereas this legislation enabled agricultural workers to form associations that could make representations to employers about working conditions, it did not allow them to bargain collectively. Further, employers were under no obligation to listen in good faith and the law contained no dispute resolution mechanism. The Court declared the law unconstitutional, but gave the Ontario government 12 months to draft a new *Act*.

Similarly, members of the RCMP successfully challenged the regulations to the *Public Service Labour Relations Act*, which excluded the RCMP from collective bargaining. In *Mounted Police Assn. of Ontario v. Canada (Attorney General)*,[40] Justice MacDonnell found that the RCMP Staff Relations Representation Program (SRRP) was not an independent association formed by or chosen by the police officers. It merely was a mechanism for consultation. Essentially, the Program was an entity created by management to avoid unionization. Since the regulations blocked collective bargaining rights of RCMP members, they were unconstitutional. This declaration was suspended for 18 months to give Parliament a chance to provide a statutory framework for collective bargaining.

When employer rights are interfered with by inappropriate trade union activity, limits may be imposed on the right to peaceful assembly. The rights to peaceful assembly and freedom of association have likewise been limited when riots may occur.

Note that section 2 is one of the areas of the *Charter* that can be overridden by the use of the notwithstanding clause (section 33).

DEMOCRATIC RIGHTS

Sections 3, 4, and 5 protect our rights to vote and to qualify to be elected to the House of Commons or the provincial legislative assemblies. Reasonable limitations can be put on the right to vote, restricting those who are underage and,

---

[38] *Health Services and Support—Facilities Subsector Bargaining Assn. v. British Columbia*, [2007] S.C.J. No. 27, at p. 66.

[39] [2008] O.J. No. 4543; Notice of Appeal to S.C.C. filed May 2009, [2009] S.C.C.A. No. 9.

[40] [2009] O.J. No. 1352 (Sup.Ct.J.).

Maximum duration is five
years unless crises loom

Right to vote, to be elected,
duty to have government sit
annually

most likely, the mentally incompetent. But the abuses of the past, where racial groups were denied the vote, are now prohibited. These rights were protected in the past by constitutional convention, but now they are enshrined in the *Charter*. Section 4 ensures that there will be an election at least every five years, except in times of war, and section 5 requires that the elected body be called into session at least once every 12 months. The government in power still has the right to decide when to call an election within that five-year period and also whether to call the session into sitting more often than the "once every 12 months" minimum. The government also has the power to determine what that session will consist of, which also gives some potential for abuse. These sections cannot be overridden by the notwithstanding clause (section 33), a distinction of which the courts have taken notice (see Case Summary 1.10).

CASE SUMMARY 1.10

Ballot Boxes in Jails: *Sauvé v. Canada (Chief Electoral Officer)*[41]

All prison inmates were prohibited from voting in federal elections by the former provisions of the Canada Elections Act. That Act was held unconstitutional as an unjustified denial of the right to vote, guaranteed by section 3 of the *Charter in Sauvé v. Canada (Attorney General)*.[42] Parliament responded to this litigation by changing the Act, denying the right to vote to a smaller group—those inmates serving sentences of two years or more. The issue in this case was whether the new provisions were likewise unconstitutional. It was argued that they violated the right to vote (section 3) and equality rights as protected by section 15. The Crown conceded that the Act contravened section 3 of the Charter. The key issue was thus whether this restriction could be demonstrably justified under section 1.

The Court decided that the violation was not justified. As stated by Chief Justice McLachlin: "The right to vote, which lies at the heart of Canadian democracy, can only be trammeled for good reason. Here the reasons do not suffice... Charter rights are not a matter of privilege or merit, but a function of membership in the Canadian polity that cannot be lightly set aside. This is manifestly true of the right to vote, the cornerstone of democracy, exempt from the incursion permitted on other rights through s. 33 override."

DISCUSSION QUESTIONS

The fact that the notwithstanding clause cannot be used to override democratic rights was emphasized in the above decision. What does this suggest about the inviolability of mobility rights and language rights?

---

41. [2002] 2 F.C. 119 (C.A.), rev'd [2002] S.C.J. No. 66.

42. [1993] 2 S.C.R. 438.

MOBILITY RIGHTS

Section 6 of the *Charter* ensures that Canadians can travel and live anywhere within the geographic limitations of Canada as well as enter and leave the country at will. It also ensures that all Canadians have the right to earn a livelihood in any part of Canada. But again these assurances are qualified. Programs that are of general application in a province or region can be valid even though they appear to interfere with these rights. In the field of employment, for instance, provincial licensing and educational requirements may prevent people trained and licensed in other parts of the country from carrying on their chosen profession without requalifying in that province. Section 6(4) specifically allows for programs that are designed to better the condition of those "who are socially or economically disadvantaged," even when those programs interfere with the mobility rights of other Canadians who might want to take advantage of the programs but are prohibited from doing so.

> Citizens enjoy right to enter and leave Canada

CASE SUMMARY 1.11

Resident Non-Resident Asserts the Right to Earn a Living: *Basile v. Attorney General of Nova Scotia*[43]

Under the Direct Sellers' Licensing and Regulation Act,[44] anyone involved in the activity of direct selling (door-to-door sales) in Nova Scotia had to be a resident of that province. Mr. Basile was a bookseller and a resident of Quebec. He applied for a licence to sell in Nova Scotia and was refused because he was not a permanent resident, as required by the statute. He challenged this decision as a violation of his mobility rights under the *Charter of Rights and Freedoms*. This was clearly an infringement of the mobility rights under the Charter, which gave any Canadian the right to travel to and earn a living in any part of the country. The main difficulty was to decide whether this fell into one of the exceptions set out in either section 6(3)(a) (laws of general application) or the reasonable limitation clause in section 1 of the Charter. The Court held that this did not qualify as a law of general application, since it was directed at one specific group—non-residents. Further, since no evidence had been presented that would support the argument that this was a reasonable limitation as required under section 1 of the Charter, Mr. Basile was successful, and the offending section was declared by the Court to be "of no force and effect."

SMALL BUSINESS PERSPECTIVE

Mr. Basile was successful in asserting his mobility rights and in having the restricting legislation struck down. But would a business or corporation be able to raise a similar argument? Consider to whom mobility rights are extended.

---

43. [1984] N.S.J. No. 337 N.S.S.C. (App.Div.).

44. S.N.S. 1975, c. 9.

LEGAL RIGHTS

The rights listed under this heading are intended to protect individuals from unreasonable interference from the government or its agents and to ensure that when there is interference, it is done in a way that is both procedurally fair and consistent with basic principles of fundamental justice. It is important to note that the protection provided in this section does not extend to interference with property rights. There is no specific reference to property rights in the *Charter*.

Section 7 states that we have the right to life, liberty, and the security of person and the right not to have these rights taken away, except in accordance with the "principles of fundamental justice." In the *Baker* case, where the Supreme Court examined the procedure followed at deportation hearings, Justice L'Heureux-Dubé summarized what is required by the principles of procedural fairness. "The values underlying the duty of procedural fairness relate to the principle that the individual or individuals affected should have the opportunity to present their case fully and fairly, and have decisions affecting their rights, interests, or privileges made using a fair, impartial, and open process, appropriate to the statutory, institutional, and social context of the decision."[45] The requirements of fundamental justice include procedural fairness but go further. Certain underlying principles considered basic to our legal system would also be included. An example would be the rule of law discussed above.

Everyone has a right to life, liberty, and security of person

Everyone is entitled to procedural fairness

CASE SUMMARY 1.12

Duty to Assist Citizens: *Khadr v. Canada (Prime Minister)*[46]

In April 2009, almost seven years after Omar Khadr was arrested (at age 15) in Afghanistan for allegedly throwing a grenade that caused the death of a U.S. soldier, the Federal Court required the Canadian government to request that Khadr be repatriated. Khadr had been detained at Guantanamo Bay in Cuba, and the Canadian government had refused to intervene in his behalf. At issue was whether Khadr's *Charter* rights under section 7 were violated by his continued detention, as the legal regime at Guantanamo violated Geneva Conventions.

Justice O'Reilly noted that when a person's life, liberty, and security are at stake, the *Charter* requires Canadian officials to respect principles of fundamental justice. In doing so, officials should consider factors specific to the claimant, such as his age, his need for medical attention, his presence in an unfamiliar, remote, and isolated prison with no family contact, as well as his lack of education. Justice O'Reilly ruled: "I find that the Government of Canada is required by s. 7 of the *Charter* to request Mr. Khadr's repatriation to Canada in order to comply with a principle of fundamental justice, namely, the duty to protect persons in Mr. Khadr's circumstances by taking steps to ensure that their fundamental rights, recognized in widely-accepted international instruments such as the Convention on the Rights of the Child, are respected. The respondents did not offer any basis for concluding that the violation of Mr. Khadr's rights was justified under s. 1 of the *Charter*.

---

45. *Baker v. Canada (Minister of Citizenship and Immigration)*, [1999] 2 S.C.R. 817, at 841.

46. 2009 FC 405; note: Leave to appeal to the S.C.C. granted on 4 September 2009.

"The ongoing refusal of Canada to request Mr. Khadr's repatriation to Canada offends a principle of fundamental justice and violates Mr. Khadr's rights under s. 7 of the *Charter*. To mitigate the effect of that violation, Canada must present a request to the United States for Mr. Khadr's repatriation to Canada as soon as practicable."

DISCUSSION QUESTIONS

The Court has recognized that the Crown has a duty to protect its citizens. Do you find the above ruling reassuring? Note that the federal government's subsequent appeal to the Federal Court of Appeal was unsuccessful. It remains to be seen whether a further appeal will be brought.

Sections 8 and 9 prohibit such activities as unreasonable search and seizure and arbitrary imprisonment. Subsequent sections provide for the right to be informed of the reason for an arrest, the right to retain counsel, the right to be tried within a reasonable time, the presumption of innocence, the right not to be tried twice for the same offence, and the right not to be subjected to any cruel or unusual punishment. The common theme here is to protect people from abusive, arbitrary, or unequal application of police and prosecutorial power. Not only is the individual protected in the event of such an abuse, but the provisions also serve to discourage the police and prosecutors from acting outside the law. The powers given to the courts further help to persuade the law-enforcement community to act properly by allowing the court to exclude evidence obtained in violation of these provisions, where not to do so "would bring the administration of justice into disrepute" (see section 24(2)). These basic legal rights can be overridden by the invocation of the notwithstanding clause.

Everyone to be secure from unreasonable search, seizure, detention, or imprisonment

CASE SUMMARY 1.13

A Right to Die? *Rodriguez v. British Columbia (Attorney General)*[47]

Does the right to life as guaranteed by section 7 of the *Charter* also protect the right to die? Sue Rodriguez, a terminally ill patient, sought the assistance of a physician to commit suicide. The *Criminal Code of Canada*, however, prohibits aiding a person to commit suicide, so Rodriguez argued that this violated her rights under sections 7, 12, and 15(1) of the *Charter*. Rodriguez also argued that the guarantee of security of person found in section 7 protected her right to decide what would happen to her body. Control over one's body would be violated if she could not choose to die. She claimed that as her health deteriorated, she would no longer be able to end her own life. The *Code*, to the extent that it bars a terminally ill person from a "physician assisted suicide," in effect creates inequality. It prevents persons physically unable to end their lives unassisted from

---

47. [1993] 3 S.C.R. 519.

choosing suicide, when that option is, in principle, available to other members of the public without contravening the law (since commission of suicide is not a punishable offence or crime). Finally, Rodriguez claimed that forcing her to live in a degenerated body would be cruel and unusual treatment.

In a split decision, the Supreme Court of Canada determined that the right to security of person also had to be viewed in light of the sanctity of life, the right to life also being specifically guaranteed under section 7. Section 12 was not violated by the *Code*, as a prohibition of assisted suicide is not a form of "treatment" by the state. Finally, the majority determined that if equality rights were violated by the *Code*, this violation would be justifiable under section 1. Criminalizing assisted suicide was to protect the sanctity of life and prevent abuses. Out of concern that decriminalization of euthanasia might lead to abuses, the Court was not prepared to go down the path toward it. "Active euthanasia," or doctor-assisted suicide, remains illegal in Canada.

DISCUSSION QUESTIONS

The basic question here goes beyond the *Charter*, requiring us to think about the sanctity of human life in our society. Should someone be allowed to assist another to end life? Will the plea of terminally ill patients pressure politicians to legislate guidelines for doctor-assisted suicide? What do you think?

EQUALITY RIGHTS

Every person is to be equal before and under the law

The equality rights set out in section 15 of the *Charter* prohibit discrimination in the application of the law on the basis of gender, religion, race, age, or national origin and ensure that all people in Canada have the same claim to the protection and benefits of the law. This means that the various provisions of the federal and provincial laws must be applied equally to all. Any time a distinction is made in any provincial or federal law or by a government official on the basis of one of these categories, it can be challenged as unconstitutional. Even where the discrimination relates to a category not listed, there is a general prohibition against such discrimination, and so victims will be protected.[48] The courts tend to interpret the Constitution and its provisions broadly. Thus, even though section 15 makes no reference to sexual preference, the courts have had no difficulty in concluding that a denial of benefits to same-sex couples is prohibited because it discriminates against applicants on the basis of their sexual orientation.

It is important to note that section 15(2) provides for affirmative-action programs. When a provision is intentionally introduced that has the effect of discriminating against one group of people, it may still be allowed if its purpose is to correct an imbalance that has occurred through discrimination in the past. Thus,

---

[48.] See *Morrow v. Zhang*, [2008] A.J. No. 125, where two motorists who had suffered soft tissue injuries as a result of motor vehicle collisions succeeded in challenging the validity of Alberta's Minor Injury Regulations. The regulations, which restricted the right to sue a tortfeasor to $4000 (for damages for pain and suffering) was struck down as a violation of their rights under ss. 7 and 15(1). In stark contrast, the Nova Scotia Supreme Court essentially ruled the opposite in *Hartling v. Nova Scotia (Attorney General)* 2009 NSSC 38. The appeal on the *Morrow* case resulted in the Alberta Court of Appeal concluding that *Charter* rights had not been infringed. [2009] A.J. No. 621 (C.A.). Further appeals are anticipated.

CASE SUMMARY 1.14

Courts Prompt Significant Legislative Changes: *M. v. H.*[49]; *Halpern v. Canada (Attorney General)*[50]

Two women cohabited in a same-sex relationship for 10 years. When their relationship broke down, M. applied for spousal support under Ontario's *Family Law Act*. She argued that the opposite-sex definition of spouse was discriminatory and unconstitutional, as it included married persons and heterosexual couples who had cohabited without marrying, but failed to include same-sex couples. The Courts found the definition violated section 15(1) of the *Charter* as it formally distinguished between M. and others on the basis of sexual orientation. The lower courts favoured "reading in" a non-discriminatory definition of spouse to the legislation, to enable same-sex couples to claim spousal support. The Supreme Court of Canada, however, dismissed the appeal, and chose to sever the offending section from the legislation. It suspended its declaration for six months to allow the government time to amend the legislation. This would mean that if the government didn't create new legislation, the Supreme Court's decision would result in no spousal benefits being available to either heterosexual or homosexual unmarried couples. In response to this case, the Ontario government amended 67 statutes to extend similar benefits to non-married couples, regardless of their sexual orientation.

In the *Halpern* case, the Ontario Court of Appeal took a different approach when asked to review the common law definition of marriage. It declared the definition of marriage as "one man and one woman" to be invalid as it offends equality rights. It reformulated the definition to the "voluntary union for life of two people to the exclusion of all others" and declared this definition to have immediate effect. Consequently, numerous same-sex couples rushed to secure marriage licences. The federal government responded by referring a proposed bill on same-sex marriages to the Supreme Court of Canada for review.[51] After the Supreme Court affirmed the validity of the proposed legislation and the authority of the federal parliament to define marriage, Parliament proceeded to redefine marriage to include same-sex couples.[52]

DISCUSSION QUESTIONS

Parliament remains supreme in Canada, so long as it does not violate the Constitution. Knowing what you do about the *Charter*, what steps could Parliament have taken if it wished to preserve the traditional definition of marriage?

---

the government may intentionally set out to hire women or specific ethnic minorities to get a better balance in the civil service. This is permissible even though it will have the effect of preventing people of other groups, such as Caucasian men, from having an equal opportunity to obtain those same jobs. Universities often have similar programs to encourage minorities to enter faculties or professions to correct historical imbalances.

---

49. [1999] 2 S.C.R. 3.

50. [2003] O.J. No. 2268 (C.A.).

51. *Reference re: Same-Sex Marriage*, [2004] 3 S.C.R. 698.

52. *Civil Marriage Act*, S.C. 2005, c. 33.

In addition to the provisions set out in section 15, there are other provisions in the *Charter* setting out equality rights. Section 28 guarantees that the provisions of the *Charter* apply equally to males and females. Equality rights (protected by section 15) can be overridden by the operation of the notwithstanding clause, but section 28 cannot be overridden.

Section 35 states that the *Charter* in no way affects the aboriginal and treaty rights of the native people of Canada. Although this last provision may have the effect of preserving inequality rather than eliminating it, the object of this section was to ensure that during the process of treaty negotiations and land claim disputes between the provincial governments and the native groups of Canada nothing in the *Charter* would interfere with the special-status rights associated with that group. Section 33 cannot be used to override the protection given to the position of the aboriginal people of Canada.

Although these *Charter* provisions apply only in our dealings with government, it is important for businesspeople to remember that these equality provisions are the essence of most provincial and federal human rights legislation. Since those statutes must comply with the *Charter* provisions, the *Charter* indirectly controls business practices (see Case Summary 1.16, which discusses *Vriend v. Alberta*). In addition, there are many examples of provincial and federal legislation that require all those working on government-funded projects to comply with special federal and provincial programs aimed at correcting past injustices. These special requirements may range from fair-wage policies (where non-union businesses must pay wages comparable with union-negotiated wages) to programs requiring the hiring or promotion of disadvantaged minorities or the correction of gender imbalances in the workforce.[53]

LANGUAGE RIGHTS

French and English have equal status—Canada and New Brunswick

The part of the *Charter* headed "Official Languages of Canada" outlined in sections 16 to 22 ensures that French and English have equal status and that the rights of minorities to use those languages are protected.[54] Of the Canadian provinces, only New Brunswick is officially bilingual, and so section 16 of the *Charter* declares that English and French are the official languages of Canada (federally) and of New Brunswick. All federal government activities, including court proceedings, publications, and other services where numbers warrant, must be available in both official languages. Similar rules are established for New Brunswick. Note that some language rights are set out in the *Constitution Act, 1867*. For example, section 3 requires that Quebec provide court services in English as well as French. *The Constitution Act (1867)* also requires that Manitoba provide many government services in both English and French.

[53.] See, for example, the federal *Employment Equity Act*, S.C. 1995, c. 44.

[54.] For an example, see *R. v. Beaulac,* [1999] 1 S.C.R. 768, where the accused succeeded in appealing his conviction on murder charges and a new trial was ordered because the trial judge refused his request for a trial before a bilingual judge and jury. The trial arose in the province of British Columbia, and although the accused could express himself in English, his own official language was French.

CASE SUMMARY 1.15

Traffic Ticket Challenge May Require Translation of Alberta's Laws: *R. v. Caron*[55]

It is amazing what fighting a traffic ticket might lead to. Gilles Caron, a francophone truck driver, challenged the $54 traffic ticket, arguing that his constitutional right to a hearing in French was violated. Alberta's 1988 *Languages Act* revoked French language rights, but Caron argued this law was unconstitutional.

Expert testimony was introduced, revealing that a key piece of historical evidence was missing when the *Languages Act* was passed. Records established that Rupert's Land (from which Alberta was carved) agreed to join Canada only if French language rights were protected. Judge Wenden ruled the *Languages Act* unconstitutional and Caron was found not guilty of the traffic violation.

The ruling could mean that Alberta's laws must be translated to French.

DISCUSSION QUESTIONS

Who should bear the cost of *Charter* challenges? Note that Caron obtained an order directing the Crown to provide approximately $94 000 to him for legal costs incurred during the trial. While the traffic ticket charges were minor, the trial occupied more than 80 days because the respondent raised the issue of French language rights. The government appealed the funding order, but lost.[56] Leave to appeal to the Supreme Court of Canada on this issue was granted in 2009.[57]

Minority-language educational rights, outlined in section 23, are guaranteed for the citizens of Canada, ensuring that those whose first language is English or French and who received their primary education in English or French, or have had one of their children educated in English or French, have the right to have their other children educated in that language. People who are immigrants to Canada have no such rights, no matter what their native language may be. Note that the right to be educated in English or French applies only where community numbers warrant the expense of setting up such a program. Language rights and minority-language educational rights cannot be overridden by section 33 of the *Charter.*

SECTION 52

The Constitution Act, 1982 makes other important changes to Canada's Constitution. In addition to declaring that the Constitution is the "supreme law of Canada," section 52 also sets out all the statutes that have constitutional status in an attached schedule. Important amendments are also made to the *Constitution Act, 1867,* creating section 92A, which expands the power of the provinces to make law with respect to non-renewable natural resources, including the generation of electric power and forestry resources.

---

55. 2008 A.B.P.C. 232.

56. [2008] A.J. No. 268 (C.A.); see also [2009] A.J. No. 70 (C.A.).

57. [2009] S.C.C.A. No. 128.

The Importance of the Changes

The significance of the 1982 additions to the Constitution cannot be overemphasized. The *Charter of Rights and Freedoms* will continue to affect the development of Canadian law over the next century. Traditionally, Canadian courts had adopted the position that their function was to apply the law as it existed. If the law needed to be changed, the judiciary left the job to Parliament and the legislative assemblies. It is clear that the courts have been forced to play a more active role and create new law through their interpretation and application of the provisions of the *Charter*. The broad, generalized nature of the *Charter* provisions contributes to this more expansive role of the courts. Statutes have traditionally been interpreted in a very narrow way, and because of this they are always very carefully and precisely worded. But the *Charter* provisions are generalizations, and the courts must therefore interpret these broad statements, filling in the gaps and thus making new law.

The *Constitution Act, 1982* also eliminated the requirement that any major change involving Canada's Constitution had to be made by an act of the Parliament of Great Britain. Because the original *BNA Act* was an act of the British Parliament, any changes to it had to be made by that body. When the provinces and the federal government agreed on a formula for amending the Constitution, the British Parliament passed the *Canada Act*,[58] making Canada completely independent of Britain. It should be emphasized that although Canada's ties to the British Parliament have been severed, our relationship with the monarch remains. The Queen remains the Queen of Canada, just as she is the Queen of the United Kingdom, Australia, New Zealand, and other independent nations.

Quebec did not agree with patriating the Constitution

Quebec, however, did not assent to this document. Subsequently, another important agreement that attempted to change this amending formula was drawn up; this agreement was known as the Meech Lake Accord. However, the Accord did not receive the required unanimous approval by the provinces within the specified time limit. Its failure and the failure of the subsequent Charlottetown Accord (which went to a national referendum) have created a constitutional crisis in Canada, with Quebec seeking independence. The pro-separatist government in Quebec took the question of sovereignty to a provincial referendum in 1996, which failed by a margin of only 1 percent. Thereafter, the federal government submitted a Reference to the Supreme Court of Canada[59] to determine whether Quebec could unilaterally secede from Canada. Discussions regarding granting Quebec distinct status in Canada have occasioned much debate and dissension within the federation. The question of whether Quebec will remain in Canada continues to be an important and troubling issue for Canada.

Human Rights Legislation

Whereas the *Canadian Bill of Rights* and the *Charter* address protecting individuals' rights from abuses by government, various federal and provincial statutes have been enacted with the aim of protecting an individual's rights from abuse by other members of the public. Initially, human rights legislation was designed to stop discrimination against identifiable minority groups in specific areas, such as hotels

---

58. *Canada Act 1982* (U.K.) 1982, c. 11.

59. *Reference Re Secession of Quebec*, [1998] 2 S.C.R. 217.

and restaurants. (See *Racial Discrimination Act, 1944* of Ontario.[60]) Today's statutes are broader in scope, protecting individuals against human rights violations by the public at large, in a variety of settings. The *CanadianHuman Rights Act*[61] is one example.

The *Canadian Human Rights Act (CHRA)* applies to abuses in sectors regulated by federal legislation, such as the broadcast and telecommunication industries; similar provincial statutes apply only in areas controlled by provincial legislation.[62] For example, if one is employed by a bank, any human rights complaints concerning activities at work would be brought before the Canadian Human Rights Commission (CHRC), as banks are federally regulated; whereas if one was employed by a provincially regulated retailer, those human rights complaints would be addressed by the provincial human rights commission. These statutes aim at ensuring that individuals will have access to employment (including membership in professional organizations and unions) without facing barriers created through discrimination. Access to facilities and services customarily available to the public, as well as to accommodation (tenancies), is likewise addressed.

These acts prohibit discrimination relating to gender, religion, ethnic origin, race, age, disabilities, and various other prohibited grounds. The *CHRA* now specifically protects against discrimination on the grounds of sexual orientation and pardoned criminal conviction; not all provincial legislation goes so far. Where protection against discrimination on the basis of sexual orientation has been left out of human rights legislation, the courts have shown a willingness to imply the existence of this protection. The principle applied is that under the *Charter of Rights and Freedoms*, every individual is entitled to the "equal protection and equal benefit of the law"; therefore, such rights ought to have been included. In the process, the courts are effectively rewriting statutes.

> **Human rights legislation prohibits discrimination on certain grounds**

CASE SUMMARY 1.16

Equality Issues Resolved by the Courts: *Vriend v. Alberta*[63]

In 1987, Delwin Vriend was employed by a private religious school in Alberta. His job performance was not in question, but he was dismissed after he "disclosed his homosexuality." He complained under the Alberta *Individual's Rights Protection Act (IRPA)* to the Alberta Human Rights Commission, claiming that he had been discriminated against because of his sexual orientation. He was told that he could not make such a complaint because the *Act* did not provide protection against discrimination due to sexual orientation.

[60.] S.O. 1944, c. 51.

[61.] R.S.C. 1985, c. H-6.

[62.] See: *Human Rights Code*, R.S.O. 1990, c. H-19; *Charter of Human Rights and Freedoms*, R.S.Q. c. C-12; *Alberta Human Rights Act, R.S.A. 2000, c. 25-5*; *Human Rights Code*, R.S.B.C. 1996, c. 210; *Saskatchewan Human Rights Code*, S.S. 1979, c. S-24.1; *The Human Rights Code*, S.M. 1987–88, c. 45, C.C.S.M. c. H175; *Human Rights Act*, R.S.N.B. 1973, c. H-11; *Human Rights Code*, R.S.N.L. 1990, c. H-14; *Human Rights Act*, R.S.N.S. 1989, c. 214; *Human Rights Act*, R.S.P.E.I. 1988, c. H-12; *Consolidation of Fair Practices Act*, R.S.N.W.T. 1988, c. F-2 (as duplicated for Nunavut by s. 29 of the *Nunavut Act*, S.C. 1993, c. 28); *Human* Rights Act, R.S.Y. 1986, c.11.

[63.] [1998] 1 S.C.R. 493 (S.C.C.).

This case went to the Supreme Court of Canada, which agreed with the trial court that the protections given by the *Act* were under-inclusive, protecting some but not all from discrimination. The Supreme Court rewrote the provincial statute so that it complied with section 15 of the *Charter of Rights and Freedoms*. It read sexual orientation into the impugned provisions of the *IRPA*, reasoning that this was the most appropriate way of remedying the under-inclusiveness. In light of the *Act's* preamble and stated purpose, if the legislature had the choice of having no human rights statute or having one that extended protection to those historically facing discrimination—such as homosexuals—the latter option would be chosen.

This case is interesting because it raises the issue of how far the courts can go in shaping the law. Here the Supreme Court has effectively rewritten provincial legislation it found to have violated *Charter* rights.

DISCUSSION QUESTIONS

What do you think? Is "judicial legislating" proper under Canada's Constitution? Or should the courts merely declare whether legislation is constitutional or not, and then allow the legislators time to amend any contravening legislation?

It is interesting to reflect upon the evolution of human rights protection. Three decades ago, discrimination based on sexual orientation was not specifically prohibited. Passage of the *Charter* enabled individuals to challenge laws that denied equal treatment. Cases like the *Vriend* decision brought the issue of discrimination based on sexual orientation to the attention of the public. As public sensitivity increased, the protection given to same-sex relationships expanded. The denial of marriage licences was held to be unconstitutional; eventually, the federal government was pressured to redefine marriage and sought the Supreme Court's input in the *Reference re: Same-Sex Marriage* case.[64] Now the protections extended to same-sex marriages equal those extended to traditional marriages.

Human rights commissions hear complaints

Both the federal and the provincial governments have set up special human rights tribunals authorized to hear complaints of human rights violations, to investigate, and, where appropriate, to impose significant sanctions and remedies. There are time limits to consider: a complaint before the CHRC, for example, must be filed within 12 months of the alleged incident. The Commission then proceeds to attempt settlement of the complaint through conciliation and investigation. If all else fails, a panel hearing is convened.

An issue that has arisen since the adoption of the *Charter of Rights and Freedoms* is whether these human rights acts go far enough. The protections extend only to certain areas as identified by the specific federal or provincial legislation—typically, employment, tenancies, public facilities and services, and public signs and notices. Private clubs can still discriminate as to who they will admit as members because discrimination by private facilities is not prohibited by the legislation. This explains why some golf clubs, for example, do not have female members.

Another area addressed by human rights legislation is harassment. The offending conduct in question usually involves the misuse of a position of power

---

64. [2004] 3 S.C.R. 698.

or authority to obtain a sexual or some other advantage. Protection against sexual harassment exists because sexual harassment is regarded as a form of discrimination on the basis of gender. Protection against other forms of harassment, although not specifically addressed by legislation, is now being addressed by employers in their policy manuals and in collective agreements. Commission decisions recognize that when there is discrimination in the workplace or where public services are provided, there is a duty not to discriminate and also a duty to take reasonable steps to accommodate any person who may be discriminated against. This may require anything from creating wider spaces between workstations to accommodate a wheelchair to providing a digital reader for a blind person. Failure to accommodate religious beliefs may result in the employer's being required to take reasonable steps to rearrange work schedules so that employees are not obligated to work on their day of worship. The field of employment is impacted significantly by human rights legislation.

CASE SUMMARY 1.17

Duty to Accommodate Those Facing Discrimination: *Ontario Human Rights Commission et al. v. Simpsons-Sears Ltd.*[65]

The clerks employed at a particular branch of Simpsons-Sears Ltd. were required to work some Friday nights and two out of every three Saturdays. Mrs. O'Malley, who was a clerk at Sears for three years before joining the Seventh-day Adventist Church, informed her manager that she could no longer work on their Sabbath day (Friday night to Saturday night). Her employment was terminated, and she was hired back part-time to accommodate these restrictions. She wanted to continue working full-time and laid a complaint with the Ontario Human Rights Commission on the basis of discrimination against her because of her creed. The matter went all the way to the Supreme Court of Canada, which held that discrimination had, in fact, taken place. It was not necessary to show that there was an intention to discriminate, only that there was discrimination in fact. Even where the rule or practice was initiated for sound economic and business reasons, it could still amount to discrimination. The employer was required to take reasonable steps to try to accommodate the religious practices of this employee, short of creating undue hardship on the business. The business had failed to show any evidence of accommodation or that to accommodate would have created undue hardship, and so the complaint was upheld. Simpsons-Sears was required to pay Mrs. O'Malley the difference in wages between what she had made as a part-time employee and what she would have made as a full-time employee.

SMALL BUSINESS PERSPECTIVE

Human rights legislation forces employers to be sensitive to the diverse needs of employees and accommodate their differences. Employers may complain about this added inconvenience or added obligation, but if employees are treated respectfully,

---

[65.] *[1985] S.C.J. No. 74.*

they may respond in kind. Greater loyalty from the workforce may well offset any additional costs borne by the employer. This case highlights the necessity of being familiar with human rights legislation as an employer or provider of services or accommodation. Failure to take reasonable steps to accommodate the different needs of different people may lead to a finding of unlawful discrimination. The consequences may be costly.

Part of the mandate of human rights commissions is to promote knowledge of human rights and to encourage people to follow principles of equality. The prohibition of discriminatory signs and notices assists in that end. The federal *CHRA* goes even further and deems it a discriminatory practice to communicate hate messages "telephonically or by means of a telecommunication undertaking within the legislative authority of Parliament."[66] In 2002, Ernst Zundel's internet site was found to have contravened section 13 of the *Act*. This was Canada's first-ever human rights complaint involving an internet hate site. The Canadian Human Rights Tribunal concluded that the site created conditions that allow hatred to flourish.

Amendments to the *Canadian Human Rights Act (CHRA)* impacting the First Nations governments came into force in June 2008. Since 1977, the *CHRA* did not apply to the federal government and First Nations governments for decisions authorized by the *Indian Act*. Complaints arose largely from First Nations women who married non-status Indians and were thus exposed to discriminatory treatment; these women were not able to seek remedies under the *CHRA*.

This exemption from the *CHRA* was removed and gender equality stipulations were expressly protected.[67]

CASE SUMMARY 1.18

Family Needs Require Support: *Health Sciences Association of British Columbia v. Campbell River and North Island Transition Society*[68]

Mrs. Howard worked as a child and youth support worker, working part-time regular hours between 8:30 a.m. and 3:00 p.m., Monday through Thursday. She also had a 13-year-old son who had severe behavioral problems requiring psychiatric supervision and treatment. After school Mrs. Howard looked after her son, but when her employer unilaterally changed her employment hours from 11:30 a.m. to 6:00 p.m., Monday through Thursday, she could no longer do this. Her union filed a grievance on her behalf, claiming that her rights under the *B.C. Human Rights Code* not to be discriminated against on the basis of family status had been violated. The Court had to decide whether the action of the employer in changing her work hours amounted to discrimination on the basis of family status in contravention of the *Code*. The Court decided that since there

---

[66] Canadian Human Rights Act, R.S. 1985, c. H-6, s. 13.

[67] Section 67 of the Canadian Human Rights Act restricted the ability of First Nations people living on reserve to file a complaint against band councils or the federal government. It was repealed by Bill C-21 effective June 18, 2008.

[68] 2004 BCCA 260.

was a significant parental obligation to take care of her son in these circumstances, the action of the employer in changing her work hours was a significant interference with that obligation, and therefore constituted discrimination on the basis of family status and a violation of the *Code*.

SMALL BUSINESS PERSPECTIVE

Human rights legislation may actually go further in protecting basic rights than does the *Charter*. Even when the employer is the government, it may be more appropriate to turn to human rights mechanisms, rather than to the *Charter*, to redress discrimination in the workplace.

Although the *Charter of Rights and Freedoms* has justifiably been given a great deal of attention in recent times, for businesspeople, the human rights codes in force in the various provinces are of greater concern. These codes not only govern how employees are to be treated but also apply to the treatment of customers and those with whom business is conducted. In fact, a significant number of cases before human rights commissions deal with complaints arising from business interactions, usually because of questionable customer-relations practices. A nightclub, for example, that typically demands identification only from customers of certain racial backgrounds may be investigated on allegations of discriminating when granting access to a public facility.

 REDUCING RISK 1.1

Businesspeople are well advised to become familiar with the human rights legislation in place where they do business and to make sure that their activities comply with these laws. In addition to requiring offenders to pay compensation and damages to those aggrieved, human rights commissions often require public apologies when discriminatory practices have been condoned. The resulting damage to the goodwill and reputation of the business simply is too great to ignore.

APPENDIX READING

How Is Law Linked to Morals and Ethics?

Law, morals, and ethics are interrelated. Individuals "must" comply with the law—it is not optional. Therefore, laws must be *just* so that the majority of society views them as achieving a fair result and voluntarily complies. Most laws naturally evolve from basic moral principles that all people accept.[69] Still, law often reflects

---

69. Natural law theory has two streams. One stream involves a foundation of religious principles linked to ancient societies where religious leaders held law-making powers. The 17th-century Dutch philosopher Grotius revived the second theory of natural law based on fundamentally rational moral principles independent of religion. One of the most eloquent expressions that combines these two views of natural law, based on the teachings of the 17th-century English philosopher John Locke, is found in the Declaration of Independence of the United States: "We hold these truths to be self-evident: that all men are created equal, that they are endowed by their Creator with certain unalienable rights, that among these are life, liberty and the pursuit of happiness" (italics added).

only a minimum standard acceptable to most people. Morals, on the other hand, are *optional* standards of behaviour that people "ought" to observe even though they are not compulsory. Similarly, ethical behaviour is generally considered to be a higher standard than the law involving concepts of integrity, trust, and honour. Although legal philosophers try to create clear distinctions, the categories overlap.[70] For example, lying is always unethical and immoral and sometimes against the law. The law imposes ethical obligations of trust and integrity on some positions, such as directors of corporations, lawyers, and doctors. When unethical and immoral behaviour are recognized by the majority of society as unacceptable, it is likely that a law will be introduced to regulate the conduct. Therefore, the moral and ethical values of society as a whole shape the development and direction of the law.

Is It Ever Right to Break the Law?

Even an effective, democratic legal system still leaves us with a number of difficult issues: Is it ever right to break the law? Is "law" the same thing as "justice"? What if a law is unjust? Intelligent, moderate men and women generally agree that there are times when an individual is justified in breaking the law, although they would add that, generally speaking, the law should be obeyed. They would also agree that there are unjust laws, but even these ought to be obeyed because of the chaotic consequences for society if many people failed to obey them. Even while trying to get unjust laws changed by normal, lawful means, we should still comply with them.

ILLUSTRATION 1.1

Mary Brown was at home tending her sick 18-month-old baby. He had a high temperature caused by an undetermined virus. Suddenly she realized that the child had lapsed into a coma. Fearing that he was in a state of convulsion and might die, she rushed him to her car and drove to the nearest hospital. Within a few moments she was driving 110 km/h in a 50 km/h zone. On arrival at the hospital, the child was placed in emergency care, and the doctor commended her for having saved the life of her child. A police officer arrived on the scene and presented her with a summons for dangerous driving.

Mary Brown drove her car far in excess of the speed limit—a speed limit designed to promote safety. She endangered the lives of other users of the streets, but she did so in order to save the life of her own child. She would not argue that the 50 km/h speed limit was unreasonable or unjust, but only that in the circumstances she was justified in breaking the law or, possibly, that the law should not apply to that particular situation. Nonetheless, the law was apparently broken.

[70.] The 18th-century philosopher David Hume pioneered the theory of *positive law* which clearly distinguishes between those laws one must comply with and moral obligations that one "ought" to observe. Those that require clear distinctions between these two categories are known as legal positivists. John Austin, a 19th-century philosopher, advanced the theory of legal positivism by designating law as that proclaimed by the sovereign ("the King of Parliament"). Modern legal thinkers have abandoned the sovereign source of law in favour of a *basic law* (a constitution or founding document) that is recognized by citizens and empowers lawmakers.

Law and justice, then, may not always coincide. But, one may ask, "Is an unjust law really law?" In some rare circumstances, it has been argued that a law is so atrociously unjust that it need not be obeyed by anyone. Conversely, is there any point in having a law that no one will obey, such as prohibition or music downloading? These perplexing questions demonstrate the link between law and ethics. Law must be rooted in the ethical and moral values of the society in order to be effective.

How Does Law Influence Behaviour?

First, we hope that individuals voluntarily comply with the law simply because it is the law and the vast majority of us instinctively understand the need to "obey the rules."

However, to further encourage compliance most laws trigger penalties or consequences when they are broken. When a person breaks the law they are held responsible for the consequences; this is often described as **legal liability**. How offensive society finds the conduct determines what area of the law regulates it and therefore what type or types of legal liability it will attract. If lawmakers view the conduct as extremely offensive to society as a whole, such as murder, they will consider it a matter of public law, require the government to enforce the law, and impose the most serious consequences, that of **criminal liability**. If society views the conduct as less offensive but still necessary for an orderly society, such as proper driving habits, it may only expose the conduct to **regulatory or quasi-criminal liability** and the government will generally ticket offenders. Alternatively, if lawmakers designate the conduct as primarily a private matter affecting only the parties involved, such as a tenant failing to pay rent, it will be considered a matter of private law and persons harmed by the conduct will be responsible for enforcing the law through private or civil lawsuits. This type of liability is known as **civil liability**. These three forms of liability are the tools used by lawmakers to encourage people to abide by the law.

legal liability
responsibility for the consequences of breaking the law

criminal liability
responsibility arising from commission of an offence against the government or society as a whole

regulatory or quasi-criminal liability
responsibility arising from breaches of less serious rules of public law often enforced through specialized regulatory tribunals set up by the government for specific purposes

civil liability
responsibility arising from a breach of a private law enforced through a lawsuit initiated by the victim

CHECKLIST	**What Types of Legal Liability Do Lawmakers Use to Control Individual Behaviour?**

- Criminal liability
- Regulatory or quasi-criminal liability
- Civil liability

ILLUSTRATION 1.2

In 2004 the federal government announced plans to decriminalize possession of recreational use marijuana. This sparked a debate about whether society's attitude towards marijuana use had changed. Some people misunderstood the plan as one that would legalize marijuana use when, in fact, the conduct was to remain illegal as a regulatory offence.

It is possible for one event to attract all three types of liability.

ILLUSTRATION 1.3

A business releases chemicals into the groundwater contrary to the environmental emissions standards. Local residents drink the contaminated water and die. The company would face criminal liability if charged by the government with the offence of criminal negligence causing death. It could also be fined for breach of the particular environmental regulations and it would also likely be sued by the victims' families for the losses associated with the deaths of their loved ones.

SUMMARY

A workable definition

- Law is the body of rules made by government that can be enforced by courts or government agencies

Categories of law

- Substantive law governs behaviour
- Procedural law regulates enforcement processes
- Public law comprises constitutional, criminal, and administrative laws
- Private law involves one person's suing another

Origins of law

- Codes in civil law jurisdictions
- Judge-made laws and precedents in common law jurisdictions

Sources of Canadian law

- Common law
- Equity from chancery courts
- Statutes—legislation of federal and provincial governments

Constitution of Canada

- *Constitution Act, 1867 (BNA Act)*
- *Constitution Act, 1982* including the *Charter of Rights and Freedoms*
- Various other statutes
- Various statutes that have Constitutional status
- Conventions and traditions
- Case law on constitutional issues

Constitution Act, 1867

- Created the Dominion of Canada and established its structures
- Divides power between federal and provincial governments
- Legislative powers are set out in sections 91 and 92
- Courts interpret and rule on constitutional issues

Charter of Rights and Freedoms

- All legislation must be compliant with the *Charter*
- Applies to relationships with government
- Limited by sections 1, 32, and 33

Human rights legislation

- Federal—provides protection against discrimination by businesses that fall under federal jurisdiction
- Provincial—protects individuals in private relationships; addresses discriminatory practices by parties under provincial regulation

---

QUESTIONS

1. Why is it difficult to come up with a satisfactory definition of law?

2. Where do we look to predict the outcome of a legal dispute:
   a. in a common law system?
   b. in a civil law system?

3. Explain how the use of previous decisions differs in civil law and common law jurisdictions.

4. Describe what is meant by the following statement: "Common law judges did not make the law, they found it."

5. Describe the advantages and the disadvantages of the system of *stare decisis*.

6. Describe the problems with the common law system that led to the development of the law of equity.

7. Detail what was accomplished by the *Judicature Acts of 1873–1875*.

8. Explain what is meant by the phrase "the supremacy of Parliament."

9. What effect will a properly passed statute have on inconsistent judge-made law (case law)?

10. Outline how a parliamentary bill becomes law.

11. Using the principles of *stare decisis,* explain how judges determine whether they are bound by another judge's decision in a similar case.

12. What is included in Canada's Constitution?

13. What is the effect of sections 91 and 92 of the *Constitution Act, 1867,* formerly the *British North America Act*?

14. How did the *Constitution Act, 1867* limit the power of the federal and provincial governments? How is it possible, given the division of powers, to have identical provisions in both federal and provincial legislations and have both be valid?

15. Explain what is meant by the doctrine of paramouncy. When does the doctrine apply?

16. Describe the limitations on the federal and provincial governments' powers to delegate their authority to make laws.

17. Identify the limitations of human rights legislation.

18. Explain how the *Constitution Act, 1982*, including the *Charter of Rights and Freedoms*, affects the doctrine of supremacy of Parliament.

19. Explain any limitations that apply to the rights and freedoms listed in the *Charter*.

20. Give examples of democratic rights, mobility rights, legal rights, and equality rights as protected under the *Charter*. Give examples of three other types of rights protected under the *Charter*.

21. How do human rights codes differ in their application from the *Charter of Rights and Freedoms*?

Chapter 2

The Resolution of Disputes— The Courts and Alternatives to Litigation

CHAPTER OBJECTIVES

1. Describe the court system in Canada
2. Outline the process of civil litigation
3. Explain the nature and function of regulatory bodies
4. Identify the restrictions on the decision-making power of such bodies
5. Explain the power of the courts to review the decisions of these bodies
6. Describe the alternative dispute resolution (ADR) methods—negotiation, mediation, arbitration
7. Identify the advantages and disadvantages of ADR

In addition to hearing criminal matters, the courts have been charged with the duty of adjudicating civil or private disputes, including assessing liability for injuries and awarding compensation when someone has been harmed by the actions of another. But having the court settle those claims can be an expensive and time-consuming process. While it is always a good idea for the parties to try to resolve their own disputes, when this is not possible they can turn to the courts to adjudicate a resolution. In this chapter, we examine the structure of the courts in Canada and then look at the litigation process, from the initial claim to the enforcement of a judgment. Also discussed in this chapter is the important area referred to as administrative law, which concerns itself with decisions made by an expanding government bureaucracy that affect businesses and individuals. These decision-making bodies often look like courts, though they are not, and their decision-making powers are sometimes abused. Restrictions on the powers of such decision makers and how those decisions must be made as well as what we can do when those restrictions are violated will be discussed in the second part of this chapter. The final part of this chapter outlines a variety of alternatives to the litigation process, along with a review of the reasons why businesspeople might choose negotiation, mediation, or arbitration over courts in resolving their disputes.

THE COURTS

The process described below outlines the various procedures used at the trial level of the superior courts; students should note that the actual procedure may vary with the jurisdiction. Procedural laws ensure that the hearing will be fair, that all litigants have equal access to the courts, and that parties have notice of an action against them and an opportunity to reply.

Trials open to public

As a general rule, Canadian courts are open to the public. The principle is that justice not only must be done but also must be seen to be done; no matter how prominent the citizen and no matter how scandalous the action, the procedures are open and available to the public and the press. There are, however, important exceptions to this rule. When the information coming out at a trial may be prejudicial to the security of the nation,[1] the courts may hold in-camera hearings, which are closed to the public. When children are involved, or in cases involving sexual assaults, the more common practice is to hold an open hearing but prohibit the publication of the names of the parties.[2]

Both criminal and civil functions

The courts in Canada preside over criminal prosecutions or adjudicate in civil disputes. While civil matters are the major concern of this text and criminal law is discussed only incidentally, it should be noted that there are some important differences between civil and criminal actions. In civil actions, two private persons use the court as a referee to adjudicate a dispute, and the judge (or, in some cases, the judge with a jury) chooses between the two positions presented. The decision will be made in favour of the side advocating the more probable position. The judge, in such cir-

Civil test—balance of probabilities

cumstances, is said to be deciding the matter on the balance of probabilities, which requires the person making the claim to show the court sufficient proof so that there is greater than 50 percent likelihood that the events took place as claimed.

Criminal prosecutions are quite different. When a crime has been committed, the offence is against the state and the victims of the crime are witnesses at the trial. The government pursues the matter and prosecutes the accused through a Crown prosecutor. Since the action is taken by the government (the Crown) against the accused, such cases are cited as, for example, "*R. v. Jones.*" (The R. stands for either Rex or Regina, depending on whether a king or queen is enthroned at the time of the prosecution.) While a civil dispute is decided on the balance of probabilities, in a criminal prosecution the judge (or judge and jury) must be convinced beyond a reasonable doubt of the guilt of the accused. This is

Criminal test—beyond reasonable doubt

a much more stringent test in that even when it is likely or probable that the accused committed the crime, the accused must be found "not guilty" if there is any reasonable doubt about guilt.

As illustrated by Case Summary 2.1, a person might be faced with both a civil action and a criminal trial over the same conduct, and as occurred here, even though a person was acquitted at the criminal trial he may still be found liable in the civil action. While there may not be enough proof to establish beyond a reasonable doubt

May face both criminal and civil trial for same matter

that the accused committed the crime, there may be enough evidence to show that he probably committed the wrong. Another recent example involves a woman in British Columbia who won a $50 000 civil judgment against the man she accused of raping her even after a criminal prosecution had acquitted him of the sexual assault.[3]

[1.] See *Ruby v. Canada (Solicitor General)* for a recent discussion of the issue of open courts.

[2.] *John Doe v. Smith* provides a concise summary of the law on this issue.

[3.] *J.L.L. v. Ambrose.* The criminal prosecution is unreported in case reports, but was reported in *The Vancouver Sun* (25 February 2000).

CASE SUMMARY 2.1

What Is the Appropriate Burden of Proof? *Rizzo v. Hanover Insurance Co.*[4]

Rizzo owned a restaurant that was seriously damaged by fire. When he made a claim under his insurance policy, the insurer refused to pay on the basis of its belief that Rizzo had started the fire himself. It was clear that the fire was intentionally set and that it was done with careful preparation. Because the restaurant business had not been doing well and Rizzo was in financial difficulties, the finger of blame was pointed at him. Other evidence damaged his credibility. The Ontario High Court in this case had to decide what burden of proof the insurer should meet. Because the conduct that Rizzo was being accused of was a crime, he argued that it should be proved "beyond a reasonable doubt." The Court held that because this was a civil action, it was necessary only that the insurer establish that Rizzo was responsible for setting the fire "on the balance of probabilities" and that it had satisfied that burden. "I have found on balance that it is more likely than not that the plaintiff did take part in the setting of the fire." As a result, Rizzo's action against the insurer was dismissed. Note that the fact that Rizzo had been acquitted of arson in a criminal proceeding was inadmissible in a civil proceeding as proof that he had not committed the arson.

DISCUSSION QUESTIONS

Should there be two different standards of proof? Wouldn't it be better to require the higher standard of proof even in civil matters? What effect would that have on the amount of civil litigation taking place in our courts?

Criminal law is restricted to the matters found in the *Criminal Code,* as well as certain drug control legislation and a few other areas under federal control that have been characterized as criminal matters by the courts. There is a much broader area of law that subjects people to fines and imprisonment but does not qualify as criminal law. This involves regulatory offences, sometimes referred to as quasi-criminal matters, and includes such areas as environmental, fishing, and employment offences as well as offences created under provincial jurisdiction, including motor vehicle, securities, and hunting offences.

Regulatory offences

The provincial and federal governments have authority to create enforcement provisions including fines and imprisonment for laws that have been enacted under the powers they have been given under the *Constitution Act, 1867.* These regulatory offences are manifestations of the exercise of that power. Only the federal government has the power to make criminal law, and although people may be punished with fines, and sometimes even imprisonment, for violations of these regulatory offences, the violations do not qualify as criminal acts. People charged under these provisions usually go through a process similar to prosecution of a summary conviction offence under the *Criminal Code.*[5]

[4.] (1993), 14 O.R. (3d) 98 (C.A.), leave to appeal to S.C.C. refused, [1993] S.C.C.A. No. 488.

[5.] To view a flowchart depicting the criminal justice process followed when adults are prosecuted for commission of a crime, go to "Overview of the Justice System: The Criminal Justice Process—Adults," www.justice.gov.ab.ca/criminal_pros/process_adults.aspx.

Trial Courts of the Provinces

The nature and structure of the courts vary from province to province but there are essentially four levels, including the Supreme Court of Canada. (Figure 2.1 provides an outline of Canada's court system.) At the lowest level are the Provincial Courts (their titles may be different in some provinces or territories).

Lower and superior courts

These courts have a criminal jurisdiction over the less serious criminal matters that are assigned to magistrates and judges under the *Criminal Code*. As a separate body, but usually as a division of the provincial courts, most jurisdictions also have small claims courts and family courts. Small claims courts deal with civil matters that involve relatively small amounts of money, no more than $5000 to $25 000 depending on the province.[6] Family courts handle family matters, such as custody issues that arise once the parents have separated. Enforcement of maintenance and alimony can also be dealt with by these courts, but they have no jurisdiction to issue divorces, which must be obtained in the superior trial court.[7] Some provinces maintain separate youth justice courts while others designate the family court to fulfill this function. These deal with offences under the *Youth Criminal Justice Act*.[8] In Canada, youth offenders aged 12 to 18 years are subject to the same *Criminal Code* provisions as adults, but are subject to a different level of punishment, and so the role of youth courts is very important.

The judges in the provincial courts are appointed and paid by the relevant provincial government. The mandatory age of retirement varies from province to province. For example, in Ontario, judges must retire upon reaching the age of 65; in Alberta, upon reaching the age of 70; and in New Brunswick, upon reaching the age of 75.[9]

The highest trial level court, referred to generally as the superior court of a province (the specific name varies with the jurisdiction), has an unlimited monetary jurisdiction in civil matters and deals with serious criminal matters. Some provinces have also retained specialized courts, referred to as **surrogate** or **probate courts**, dealing with the administration of wills and estates. In most jurisdictions, however, this is now just a specialized function of the superior court. Similarly, bankruptcy courts operate within the superior court system. These courts deal with the legal aspects of bankruptcy and must comply with the procedural rules set out in the *Bankruptcy and Insolvency Act*.[10]

It is before the trial courts that the disputing parties in a civil case first appear and testify, the witnesses give evidence, the lawyers present arguments, and judges make decisions. When both a judge and a jury are present, the judge makes findings of law, and the jury makes findings of fact. When the judge is acting alone, which is much more common, especially in civil matters, the judge decides both

Questions of law and fact

matters of fact and matters of law. Matters of fact are those regarding the details of

---

[6.] In Alberta, British Columbia, Nova Scotia, and the Yukon, the monetary jurisdiction of the small claims courts is $25 000, while in Saskatchewan and Newfoundland and Labrador, the jurisdiction is $5000. The monetary jurisdiction in Ontario is to change from $10 000 to $25 000 on 1 January 2010.

[7.] *Divorce Act*, R.S.C. 1985 (2nd Supp.), c. 3, s. 2(1).

[8.] S.C. 2002, c. 1. This legislation replaced the *Young Offenders Act* on 1 April 2003.

[9.] See *Courts of Justice Act*, R.S.O. 1990, c. 43, s. 47, *Provincial Court Act*, R.S.A. 2000, c. P-31, s. 9.22, and *Provincial Court Act*, R.S.N.B. 1973, c. P-21, s. 4.2. In Ontario and Alberta, judges can be reappointed for a term of one year, to the age of 75.

[10.] R.S.C. 1985, c. B-3.

Figure 2.1 Outline of Canada's Court System[11]

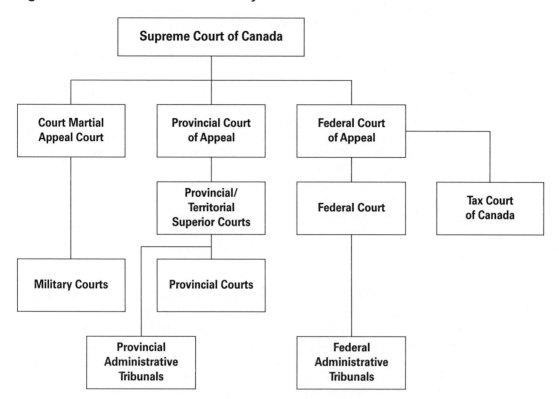

an event. For example, was Erasmus at the corner of Portage and Main in the city of Winnipeg at 7:00 a.m. on 5 March 2007? Did a portion of the building owned by Bereznicki fall on Erasmus? Was he paralyzed as a result of his injury? Was Bereznicki aware of the danger? Had she taken steps to correct it? Questions of law, on the other hand, concern the rules or laws that are to be applied in the situation. For example, was Bereznicki obliged to keep the outside of her building in good repair? Would this obligation be affected if Bereznicki were unaware of the danger? The trial itself is discussed in more detail under "The Process of Civil Litigation," below.

RECENT DEVELOPMENTS

Canada's system of courts is dynamic; it is constantly changing to reflect changes in Canadian society. For example, several innovations have recently been made by various governments. For a full understanding of the court system, it is necessary to review these innovations.

Court reforms dictate change

[11.] Department of Justice Canada, http://canada.justice.gc.ca/eng/dept-min/pub/ccs-ajc/page3.html. Note: The Federal Court Trial Division changed its name to Federal Court on 2 July 2003. See explanation on p. 54.

Drug treatment courts have been established in several large Canadian cities. The emphasis in these courts is on the treatment of addicts, not incarceration. Non-violent offenders involved in minor drug offences agree to be bound by the terms of a structured outpatient program designed to reduce their dependence on drugs. They are released on bail, subject to random drug tests, and must appear regularly in court. If they demonstrate control of their addiction, the criminal charges are stayed, or the offender receives a non-custodial sentence. If they cannot demonstrate such control, they are sentenced in the normal way. Research appears to indicate that drug treatment courts are more successful in preventing addicts from re-offending than the traditional court system involving incarceration, and that the yearly cost per participant is far below what it costs per year to maintain an offender in jail.[12]

Domestic violence courts have been established in several provinces in Canada. Ontario has a Domestic Violence Court Program in each of the province's 54 court jurisdictions.[13] These courts deal with spousal, elder, and child abuse. While the structure and jurisdiction of these courts vary from province to province, most of them offer specialized investigations by police, counselling for first-time offenders, prosecution of repeat offenders by specialized prosecutors, and support services for victims.

Unified family courts have jurisdiction over all legal issues related to the family and do not deal with any other types of cases. Such courts have been created in several provinces. This simplifies the court process, which can be extremely complicated due to the overlapping jurisdiction of the federal government and the provincial governments. In addition, the court procedures and rules for family cases have been simplified. As is the case with all specialized courts, judges in unified family courts develop expertise in family law.

As health-care services involving mentally ill persons have declined in recent years, the criminal justice system has seen an increase in the number of accused persons with mental illnesses. As criminal courts are not designed to identify and address the mental health concerns of accused persons, several of the provinces have implemented "mental health courts." These are specialized courts that focus on the treatment and rehabilitation (rather than the punishment) of those who have committed criminal acts due to mental disorders. Judicially monitored programs involving a multidisciplinary team (judges, lawyers, psychologists, nurses, community caregivers) encourage voluntary treatment over punishment. This allows accused persons with mental disorders the opportunity to access appropriate resources and services while ensuring public safety.

The Nunavut Court of Justice, established in 1999, is Canada's first single-level court. Judges in this court are given the powers of both the superior trial courts and the territorial courts. These judges can, therefore, hear all of the cases that arise in the territory. The court is a "circuit court," which travels throughout the territory hearing cases.

Sentencing circles are found in several provinces and are used primarily at the provincial court level for cases involving aboriginal offenders and victims. Sentencing circles are not courts. They involve all interested persons meeting in a circle to discuss the offence, including sentencing options. The circle may suggest

---

[12.] "Canada's First Drug Court Breaks the Cycle of Drugs and Crime," *LawNow* 26:4 (February/March 2002), "Drug Treatment Court: Not a Free Ride," *LawNow* 33:2 (November/December 2008).

[13.] Ontario Ministry of the Attorney General, Domestic Violence Court (DVC) Program, www.attorneygeneral.jus.gov.on.ca/english/about/vw/dvc.asp.

restorative community sentences, including restitution to the victim and treatment or counselling of the accused. The judge is not bound to accept a circle sentence. A judge in Saskatchewan created controversy when he granted a sentencing circle in a recent high-profile case involving two young children who froze to death.[14]

Aboriginal persons have been over-represented in Canadian prisons in recent years. An initiative to try to remedy this involves the establishment of specialized courts dedicated to serving Aboriginals. In these courts, charges against aboriginal accused are heard such that cultural sensitivity and respect are incorporated into the criminal justice process. Alberta, British Columbia, Ontario, and Saskatchewan have established aboriginal courts.

It is clear that the Canadian court system will continue to evolve in an effort to improve its success in helping Canadians resolve their disputes fairly. These reforms are taking place with respect to the structure of the courts themselves, as well as the processes involved at both the criminal and civil level. It must be clearly understood, however, that many of the suggested reforms are strenuously resisted on the grounds that they threaten to damage a very effective system that is the envy of much of the world. Retired Supreme Court Justice Frank Iacobucci has urged caution before we embark on such reforms. "We must not take what we have for granted, and we must be particularly vigilant so that in our quest for improvement, we don't desert the values and procedures that have brought us to this level of excellence."[15]

Not all are in favour of reforms

Courts of Appeal of the Provinces

Each province's appellate court hears appeals from the lower courts of that province. They must hear a matter before it can go to the Supreme Court of Canada. In most cases, this is the court of last resort. When one of the parties is dissatisfied with the decision of a provincial trial court and an error in law or procedure is identified, the decision may be successfully appealed. As a general rule, an appeal court will consider a case only when questions of law are in dispute, not questions of fact. But many appeals are based upon questions of mixed law and fact, where the rules that are applied are inseparably connected to the facts that are found. Whether a person lived up to the standards of a reasonable person in a given situation would be an example of such a question of mixed law and fact.

Appellate courts

The court exercising an appellate jurisdiction does not hold a new trial. The assumption is that the judge (or judge and jury) who saw and heard all of the evidence presented at trial is (are) best qualified to determine questions of fact. The appeal court judges (usually three) read the transcript of the trial, as well as the trial judge's reasons for decision. They then deal with the specific objections to the trial judge's decision submitted by the appellant's lawyers, hearing the arguments of both the appellant and the respondent.

The judges who serve on provincial superior and appeal courts are appointed by the federal government from a list of candidates supplied by the provinces.[16] Once appointed, the judges have tenure until they retire (by age 75) or are appointed to new positions. They can be removed from the bench only for serious

---

[14.] "Father of Girls Who Froze to Death Gets Sentencing Circle" (7 January 2009), CBC News Online, www.cbc.ca/canada/saskatchewan/story/2009/01/07/pauchay-sentencing.html.

[15.] *Lawyers Weekly* 24:9 (2 July 2004.)

[16.] Part VII of the *Constitution Act, 1867.*

misconduct,[17] but not as the result of making an unpopular decision or one that is unfavourable to the government.

Courts at the Federal Level

Federal Court and Federal Court of Appeal

The Federal Court and Federal Court of Appeal serve a function similar to that of the provincial superior courts. Until 2 July 2003, the Federal Court of Canada had a trial division and an appellate division. On that date, the *Courts Administration Service Act*[18] came into effect, making the two divisions of the Federal Court separate courts. The Trial Division became the Federal Court, a trial court. It hears disputes that fall within the federal sphere of power, such as those concerning copyrights and patents, federal boards and commissions, federal lands or money, and federal government contracts. The Federal Court of Appeal kept its previous name; it is an appellate court. It hears appeals from the Federal Court. Both of the federal courts can hear appeals from decisions of federal regulatory bodies and administrative tribunals. The role of these quasi-judicial bodies will be discussed below under the heading "Administrative Law." An appeal from the Federal Court of Appeal goes directly to the Supreme Court of Canada.

The Tax Court of Canada is another very specialized court, which was established in 1983 to hear disputes concerning federal tax matters. This body hears appeals from assessment decisions made by various federal agencies enforcing taxation statutes, such as the *Income Tax Act*, the *Employment Insurance Act*, and the *Old Age Security Act*. Pursuant to the *Courts Administration Service Act*, the Tax Court of Canada became a superior court on 2 July 2003; its powers and jurisdiction did not change. The courts that hear cases involving the military are also specialized courts; a discussion of these courts is beyond the scope of this text.

Supreme Court of Canada

The Supreme Court of Canada is the highest court in the land. It has a strictly appellate function as far as private citizens are concerned. There are nine judges appointed by the Government of Canada, according to a pattern of regional representation.[19] A quorum consists of five judges, but most appeals are heard by a panel of seven or nine judges. There is no longer an automatic right of appeal to the Supreme Court of Canada (except in criminal cases where a judge in the appellate court dissented on a point of law, or when an appellate court sets aside an acquittal and enters a verdict of guilty).[20] In all other cases, leave to appeal must be obtained from the Supreme Court, and such leave will be granted only if a case has some national significance. The Supreme Court hears both criminal and civil cases. In addition, it is sometimes asked to rule directly on constitutional disputes involving federal and provincial governments. For example, the federal government submitted a Reference to the Supreme Court of Canada in February 1998, asking whether Quebec could unilaterally secede from Canada.[21] Decisions of the Supreme Court set binding precedents for all other courts in Canada.

Supreme Court decisions set binding precedents

---

17. *Judges Act*, R.S.C. 1985, c.J-1, s. 65(2).

18. S.C. 2002, c. 8.

19. Three of the judges must be from the province of Quebec, pursuant to the *Supreme Court Act*, R.S.C. 1985, c. S-26, s. 6.

20. *Criminal Code*, R.S.C. 1985, c. C-46, s. 691.

21. *Reference Re Secession of Quebec*, [1998] 2 S.C.R. 217. Another reference to the Supreme Court was submitted to determine whether the federal government had the power to authorize same-sex marriages. That positive decision was rendered 9 December 2004. *Reference Re Same-Sex Marriage*, [2004] S.C.J. No. 75, 2004 S.C.C. 79.

THE PROCESS OF CIVIL LITIGATION

Most of this text deals with matters of substantive law (that is, law that summarizes rights and obligations of the "you can" or "you can't" variety) rather than procedural law (that is, law that deals with the process by which we enforce those rights and obligations). But it is important to be familiar with the procedures involved in bringing a dispute to trial, if only to understand the function of lawyers and the reasons for the expense and delay involved. Before a decision is made to sue someone, all avenues for settling the dispute outside of litigation ought to be exhausted. Alternative methods for resolving legal disputes have been developed, including negotiation, mediation, and arbitration. Often the court requires the disputing parties to have tried these dispute-resolution mechanisms before a trial procedure will be instigated. The litigation procedures may vary somewhat from province to province, but they are substantially the same in all common law jurisdictions. They apply to most superior courts. (One of the distinguishing characteristics of small claims courts is that this involved procedure has been streamlined significantly, eliminating many of the steps described.) The discussion below is based on the procedure followed in British Columbia. Figure 2.2 sets out the process of civil litigation.

Timely start to action necessary

Should try to settle dispute

Some variations from province to province

Limitation Periods

Whether to remove ongoing uncertainty or to ensure fairness when memories dim or witnesses become unavailable, court action must be brought within a relatively short time from the event giving rise to the complaint. This time is referred to as a **limitation period**. In most provinces, for example, a person who is owed money from a simple sale of goods transaction must bring an action against the debtor within six years of the failure to pay the debt.[22] The plaintiff must commence an action by filing the appropriate pleading (the writ of summons or the statement of claim) with the appropriate court. Failure to fulfill that step within the limitation period will result in the plaintiff being barred from pursuing the action. This time limitation will vary depending on the jurisdiction and the nature of the complaint involved, and may be embodied in several different statutes in a province.

With the expiry of the limitation period and the threat of court action removed, the potential defendant is not likely to settle out of court and the plaintiff is left with no recourse. For this reason, it is important for a person involved in a potential lawsuit to quickly get the advice of a lawyer regarding the relevant limitation period. Whether the limitation period had expired is the problem facing the court in the Canada's Wonderland case discussed in Case Summary 2.2. This case shows that a person not only has to sue for the right thing—in this case, negligence—but he also has to do so in a timely manner.

Expiration of limitation period prohibits suing

[22.] But in Alberta, the *Limitations Act* states that most lawsuits (including those for breach of contract and tort) must be commenced within two years of discovering the claim, or within 10 years from the date when the claim arose, whichever period expires first. Ontario has a similar system, except that the ultimate limitation period is 15, rather than 10, years, pursuant to the *Limitations Act, 2002*. Both the Alberta *Act* (ss. 8–9) and the Ontario legislation (s. 13) carry forward the rule that a written acknowledgment, or part payment, of a debt before a limitation period expires revives the limitation period, which begins again at the time of the acknowledgment or part payment. The Alberta legislation (s. 7) also allows the parties to extend a limitation period, by agreement. In British Columbia, no action may be brought after 30 years from the time the right to do so arose (*Limitation Act*, R.S.B.C. 1996, c. 266, s. 8(1)(c)).

Figure 2.2 Process of Civil Litigation

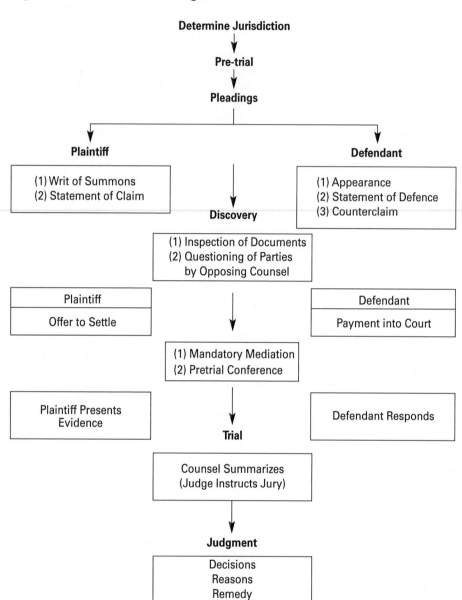

Jurisdiction

The first step when suing is to determine which court should hear the action. The proper geographic jurisdiction in which to bring an action can be a very difficult question, but generally the plaintiff or person bringing the action can choose a court in the area where the defendant resides or in the area where the matter complained about arose. If a traffic accident that happened in Alberta involved one driver from British Columbia and one from Ontario, the Ontario driver would have to sue in British Columbia or Alberta.

CASE SUMMARY 2.2

Does a Judge Have Discretion to Extend a Limitation Period? *Joseph v. Paramount Canada's Wonderland* [23]

Joseph suffered an injury at Paramount's amusement park. His lawyer prepared a statement of claim, but his assistant did not file it before the limitation period expired. She believed that the relevant limitation period was six years. However, in Ontario, the *Limitations Act, 2002* established a basic two-year limitation period and an ultimate limitation period of 15 years. (The basic limitation period runs from when the claim is discovered.) When the lawyer realized the error that had been made, he filed and served the statement of claim. The Defendant applied for a ruling that the action was barred, as the limitation period had expired. A Judge of the Superior Court of Justice held that the action was barred by the two-year limitation period provided by the new *Act*. The Judge also held, however, that he had discretion under the common law doctrine of special circumstances to extend the time to commence an action, as long as there was no prejudice to the defendant that could not be compensated for with either costs or an adjournment.

The Court of Appeal briefly discussed the aim of the new *Act* ("to balance the right of claimants to sue with the right of defendants to have some certainty and finality in managing their affairs"). It also discussed some of the reforms introduced by the new *Act*, such as the doctrine of discoverability. With respect to the special circumstances doctrine, the Court held that the Ontario legislature did not intend that the courts would continue to have discretion to extend the limitation periods under the new *Act*, which was intended to be comprehensive.

DISCUSSION QUESTIONS

If the special circumstances doctrine no longer applies, and a claim is not filed prior to the expiration of the limitation period because of a mistake by a lawyer's assistant, is the plaintiff out of luck? Is there anyone who could be held liable for the damages she may have recovered if her lawsuit had proceeded? If there is an ultimate limitation period, claims that have not been discovered prior to the expiration of the period can never be pursued. Is that fair?

The internet has complicated this to some extent since its messages are received in all jurisdictions. Where the internet is involved, a court is more likely to allow an action to proceed if there has been some sort of interaction or transaction over the internet with a resident of that province.[24] Still a court can refuse to hear a case if it believes that another jurisdiction would be more appropriate. There can also be serious jurisdictional problems when a successful litigant tries to enforce that judgment in another jurisdiction.

[23.] (2008), 90 Ont. R. (3d) 401 (C.A.).

[24.] *Easthaven Ltd. v. Nutrisystem.com Inc.* (2001), 202 D.L.R. (4th) 560 (Ont. Sup. Ct.).

Once the province has been chosen, the plaintiff must then choose the court in which to commence the litigation. In a civil action, this is either the province's small claims court or superior court. The monetary jurisdiction of the small claims court varies from province to province, as discussed above. Although it is simpler and less expensive to bring an action in the small claims court, a disadvantage is that that court is restricted in the costs it can award. The costs incurred for representation by a lawyer usually cannot be recovered. On the other hand, the procedure followed at the small claims court has been significantly streamlined. It is designed to enable ordinary people to present their legal problems without the need to hire a lawyer. Hiring a lawyer, asking a friend to assist in court, or handling the action on one's own are all options.

Small claims court is simple but only minimal costs are recoverable

---

CASE SUMMARY 2.3

When Does a Court Have Jurisdiction? *UniNet Technologies Inc. v. Communications Services Inc.*[25]

1. Entered licence agreement

UniNet ⟷ ALA ⟷ CSI

3. Entered licence agreement

2. Terminated licence agreement

"ALA," a corporation formed in St. Vincent and the Grenadines, granted UniNet, a B.C. corporation, a 99-year licence to use a domain name for the development and operation of an online gambling licence. UniNet sublicensed the name to Poker.com, a Florida corporation. Communication Services Inc. (CSI) was incorporated, by the principals of ALA, in Samoa, a country with strong asset protection laws that would protect the assets of the directors and officers of CSI and ALA from foreign claims and judgments. UniNet claimed that ALA wrongfully terminated the licence agreement and then transferred the domain name to CSI. The issue was whether B.C. courts had jurisdiction over the court proceeding. The lower court held that the B.C. courts had such jurisdiction.

The licence agreement between ALA and UniNet indicated that it was to be interpreted by the laws of British Columbia and that the B.C. courts were to have jurisdiction over any relevant litigation. It also required that any dispute arising out of the licence agreement was to be resolved by arbitration under B.C. legislation. UniNet had commenced such arbitration with respect to the termination of the agreement.

The Court of Appeal held that the test as to whether a court has jurisdiction is "whether the plaintiff has established that there is a 'real and substantial connection between the court and either the defendant or the subject-matter of the litigation.'" The Court considered that the licence agreement was governed by the law of British Columbia, that the parties had agreed to the jurisdiction of B.C. courts, that the right to use and own the domain name was being determined in arbitration in British Columbia, that the licence agreement was entered into in British Columbia, and that the agreement may have been performed, at least in part, in British Columbia. CSI argued that it was not

---

25. (2005), 251 D.L.R. (4th) 464, (2005), 38 B.C.L.R. (4th) 366 (C.A.).

a party to the licence agreement. The Court held that the litigation was about whether CSI received the domain name from ALA in breach of its obligations under the licence agreement with UniNet, and was therefore a natural continuation of the arbitration being held in British Columbia. The Court ruled that the cumulative effect of all of these factors gave the B.C. courts jurisdiction over the litigation.

REDUCING RISK 2.1

To avoid problems, those doing business over the internet should specify what law is to apply to transactions entered into with customers and which courts are to have jurisdiction over relevant litigation. When business is solicited, it would also be wise to include disclaimers setting limits on the parties who can enter into such transactions. Such disclaimers would be similar to those contained in product warranties, namely: "Void where prohibited by law" or "Available only to residents of Canada." If a business creates a website and uses it to do business in other jurisdictions, not only will it be subject to the law of those jurisdictions, but also any resulting litigation may be conducted in the courts of those jurisdictions.

Pre-Trial Procedures

The traditional way to commence an action in a superior court was for the plaintiff to issue a **writ of summons** (this has been abandoned in most provinces but is still used in British Columbia). Where the writ of summons is still in use, if the defendant chooses to dispute the claim, he must promptly file an **appearance** with the court clerk. The second step (the first in provinces where the writ of summons is not used) requires a **statement of claim** to be served on the defendant. The statement of claim sets out in detail the plaintiff's allegations. It must be filed with the court clerk and served on the defendant. The defendant must then prepare and file a **statement of defence**, in which he provides answers to the claims of the plaintiff stating areas of agreement, disputed claims, and contrary allegations.

Writ of summons
Appearance
Statement of claim

Statement of defence

If the defendant believes that he is the real victim, he can also file a **counterclaim**. This is similar to a statement of claim. A counterclaim requires the filing of a statement of defence from the plaintiff in response.

Counterclaim

The documents used to start and defend a lawsuit constitute the **pleadings**. The purpose of the pleadings is not to argue and justify positions; rather, the parties are merely stating the claims giving rise to the dispute and establishing the required elements of the legal action. If either party believes that the documents do not make the other party's position completely clear, she may ask for clarification or further information. Once the pleadings have closed, the parties have the right to apply to set a date for trial and begin the process of discovery. Throughout the pre-trial process, the parties have the right to—and often do—make applications to the court for direction regarding what details have to be disclosed, what questions have to be answered, and other matters that may arise.

The process of discovery has two distinct parts:

Documents may be used at trial

1. Discovery of documents. Each party has the right to inspect any document in the possession of the other party that may be used as evidence in the trial. This includes email and computer files on a disk or a hard drive.

Statements made under oath may be used at trial

2. Examination for discovery. The parties (with their lawyers) meet before a court reporter and, under oath, are asked detailed questions relevant to the problem to be tried. The parties are required to answer these questions fully and truthfully. Everything said is recorded, and may be used later at the trial. This examination process generally applies to only the parties to the action, not to witnesses. When corporations are involved, a representative who has personal knowledge of the matter may be examined. As part of a general reform of the litigation process in some provinces and in an attempt to reduce the costs of an action, the examination for discovery has been eliminated in actions involving smaller amounts.[26] Other provinces have limited the amount of time given to the examination process.[27]

In most jurisdictions, a pre-trial conference must be scheduled. This is a meeting of the parties, their lawyers, and the judge. It is held to determine which issues remain to be tried and whether the parties can themselves resolve the dispute. In fact, most disputes are resolved by the parties during these pre-trial processes.

Offer to settle

Another tool often available to parties before a trial is an **offer to settle.** Either party can make an official offer to settle; if it is accepted, that ends the matter. If it is refused and the judgment at the trial is different from the offer made, the costs awarded are adjusted to punish the parties for failing to act more reasonably.

If Jones was claiming $200 000 against Smith for an automobile accident, Smith could make an offer to settle (a "payment into court") of $150 000. The judge would know nothing about such a payment. If the eventual judgment was for more than $150 000, costs would be awarded as normal, since Jones acted reasonably in refusing to accept the offer. But if the judgment was for less than $150 000, obviously Jones would have been better off accepting the payment. Because he

---

! REDUCING RISK 2.2

The discovery stage is an extremely important part of the litigation process; cases are often won or lost at this point. When parties testify under oath at discovery, they often make admissions or incorrect statements that come back to haunt them at the trial. Admissions of fact that may not seem important at the time may become crucial at the actual trial, and a party is bound by those admissions. A false claim can be investigated before trial, and the party can be forced to recant at the trial, bringing her credibility into question. This means that what is said at the discovery stage often determines the outcome of the case, compelling the parties to come to a settlement. For businesses, it is extremely important that the person who testifies at discovery not only be familiar with the matter, but also be well prepared and appreciate the importance of her testimony and its potential impact on the legal action.

[26.] Under Ontario's Simplified Procedure, for example, examination for discovery is not permitted for actions involving less than $50 000 (Ontario *Rules of Civil Procedure*, r. 76).

[27.] In Alberta, the Streamlined Procedure for cases involving $75 000 or less sets a six-hour limit for examinations for discovery (Alberta, *Rules of Court*, r. 662). In British Columbia, there is a two-hour limit on examinations for discovery for Fast Track Litigation (British Columbia, *Supreme Court Civil Rules*, r. 66). Rule 68, the "Expedited Litigation Project Rule," has been in force province-wide since 1 January 2008. It also allows for a two-hour examination for discovery. New civil rules are scheduled to be implemented on 1 July 2010. They will probably include new fast track litigation rules.

acted unreasonably in not doing so, he would be denied compensation for the legal expenses incurred from the time of his refusal of the offer. The plaintiff can also make an offer to settle, showing a willingness to take less than originally claimed. If this is unreasonably refused by the defendant, he will be required to pay greater costs due to his failure to accept a fair settlement.

RECENT INITIATIVES

While it is obvious that the purpose of this long, involved, and expensive pre-trial process is to encourage the parties to reach a settlement and thereby avoid a trial, it is also clear that such a process results in frustrating delays for the parties. For this reason, the provinces have implemented reforms to speed up the litigation process, especially when smaller amounts are involved. British Columbia and Alberta, for example, allow for Summary Trials, where evidence is adduced by **affidavit** instead of by the testimony of witnesses.[28] British Columbia also provides for Fast Track Litigation for trials that can be completed within two days;[29] Alberta's Streamlined Procedure applies to trials involving claims of $75 000 or less.[30] Ontario and Saskatchewan have a Simplified Procedure for claims of $50 000 or less,[31] New Brunswick[32] and Prince Edward Island[33] have procedures for Quick Rulings, and Manitoba has implemented Expedited Trials and Expedited Actions.[34] Some provinces, including Ontario and Saskatchewan, have introduced Mandatory Mediation.[35] Several provinces, including Ontario, have started mandatory case management, which involves judicial supervision of the specific steps in the litigation process.[36] Ontario now regulates paralegals, which provides people involved in disputes with an alternative to hiring lawyers.[37] The objectives of reducing costs and delay—and of making the justice system more accessible—have motivated all jurisdictions to create small claims courts where the procedures have been dramatically simplified and costs reduced accordingly. It is important for businesspeople to understand that these changes, and all of the other changes to the justice system discussed above, have provided them with increased opportunity to utilize the system when necessary.

Recent initiatives

Payment into court

The Trial

Because the burden of proof at trial rests with the plaintiff, the plaintiff's case and witnesses are presented first. The plaintiff's lawyer assists witnesses in their testimony by asking specific questions, but the types of questions that may be asked are very restricted. For example, the plaintiff's lawyer is prohibited from asking

---

[28.] British Columbia, *Supreme Court Civil Rules, ibid.* r. 18A, and Alberta, *Rules of Court,ibid.* Part 11.

[29.] British Columbia, *Supreme Court Civil Rules, ibid.* r. 66.

[30.] Alberta, *Rules of Court, supra* note 28, Part 48.

[31.] Ontario, *Rules of Civil Procedure, supra* note 27, r. 76, and Saskatchewan, *Queen's Bench Rules*, Part 40.

[32.] New Brunswick, *Rules of Court*, Rule 77.

[33.] Prince Edward Island, *Rules of Civil Procedure*, Rule 75.

[34.] Manitoba, *Court of Queen's Bench Rules*, Rule 20 and Rule 20A.

[35.] Ontario, *Rules of Civil Procedure, supra* note 26, r. 24.1, and Saskatchewan, *Queen's Bench Act, 1998*, S.S. 1998, c. Q-1.01, s. 42.

[36.] *Ibid.* r. 77.

[37.] Paralegals are regulated by the Law Society of Upper Canada. See the Paralegal Society of Ontario website at www.paralegalsociety.on.ca/. See the section on Paralegal Regulation on the LSUC website at: www.lsuc.on.ca/paralegals/.

Plaintiff presents its case first—defendant cross-examines

leading questions, in which the answer is suggested (such as, "You were there on Saturday, weren't you?"). When the plaintiff's lawyer completes this direct examination of the witness, the defendant's lawyer is given the opportunity to cross-examine the witness. In cross-examination, the defence has more latitude in the type of questions asked and so is permitted to ask leading questions. When the opposing lawyer believes that the lawyer questioning the witness is abusing the process by asking prohibited questions, she can object to the question. The judge rules on the objection, deciding whether to permit the question or order the lawyer to withdraw it. The rules governing the type of testimony that can be obtained from witnesses—and, indeed, all other types of evidence to be submitted at a trial—are referred to as the **rules of evidence**. (These rules are very complex and beyond the scope of this text.) If something new arises from the cross-examination, the plaintiff's lawyer re-examines the witnesses on those matters. When the plaintiff has completed presenting evidence, the lawyer for the defence will then present its case calling witnesses and presenting evidence that supports its side, and the plaintiff cross-examines. After both sides have finished calling witnesses, the plaintiff's lawyer and then the defendant's lawyer are allowed to summarize the evidence and make arguments to the court. Again, if anything new comes up, the other party is given a chance to respond to it.

When the plaintiff is finished, the defence then presents its case

Judgment

If a jury is involved (which is not very common in civil cases), the judge will instruct it on matters of law. The jury then retires to consider the case and returns to announce its decision to the judge. The function of the jury is to decide questions of fact; the judge decides questions of law. Where the matter is heard by a judge alone, a decision may be delivered immediately; however, it is more common for the judge to hand down a judgment in writing some time later that includes reasons for the decision. These reasons can form the basis for an appeal.

Juries determine questions of fact

COSTS

The cost of retaining a lawyer to sue someone is often prohibitive; some creditors may decide to write off a debt rather than incur this outlay. In small claims courts, the presence of a lawyer is the exception rather than the rule, mainly because the winning party usually will not recover the costs of obtaining the services of a lawyer from the losing party. In higher-level courts, lawyers are generally essential, although parties do have the right to represent themselves. Although legal fees are usually the greater part, other expenses are often incurred, such as the costs of obtaining transcripts from the discovery process and the fees paid to secure specialized reports from experts.

REDUCING RISK 2.3

The delay and costs associated with litigation, as well as the lack of control over the process and outcome, have contributed to its decreasing popularity. For businesspeople, finding themselves in court should normally be viewed as a failure. Considerable care should be taken to avoid disputes, or to attempt to settle them before litigation becomes necessary. When a settlement cannot be reached by the parties, and both parties are willing, it is sometimes advantageous to explore some of the alternatives to litigation that are available. (These are discussed below.) However, in some situations—especially when it may be necessary to enforce the court's decision—litigation may be the best option available.

Even the winning party must pay her own legal expenses. She may, however, obtain as part of the judgment an order for "costs." This means that the defendant will be required to compensate the successful plaintiff for at least a portion of her legal expenses. While a judge always has discretion when awarding costs, **party and party costs** are usually awarded to the victorious party in a civil action. Party and party costs are determined using a predetermined scale and normally fall short of the actual fees charged.[38] Consequently, the plaintiff will usually have to pay some legal expenses even when she is successful. There is, of course, always the risk that a party may lose the action and have to pay all of her own legal expenses as well as the winning party's costs. If the judge finds the conduct of the losing party objectionable (for example, if an action is "frivolous and vexatious"), then he may award the winning party the higher **solicitor and client costs**.

Losing party usually pays costs

Legal expenses usually not completely recoverable

REMEDIES

One of the things that must be decided when a civil suit is begun is what the plaintiff will ask the court to do. The most common remedy requested in a court action is monetary payment in the form of **damages**, which are designed to compensate the victim for any loss suffered. **General damages** are based on estimates, such as when the court awards compensation to a litigant for pain and suffering or for future lost wages. **Special damages**, on the other hand, are calculated to reimburse the litigant for expenses or costs incurred before the trial. **Punitive** or **exemplary damages** are intended not to compensate the victim but rather to punish the wrongdoer for outrageous or extreme behaviour. This may result in a windfall for the victim. Punitive damages will be awarded only in very serious cases, such as a sadistic physical attack, or when an insurer pursued an unfounded allegation of arson against a vulnerable insured.[39]

Damages involve payment of money

In rare cases, remedies other than damages may be awarded. The court can order money incorrectly paid to the defendant to be restored to the rightful owner. In some circumstances, it is also possible to obtain an **accounting**, which results in any profits derived from the defendant's wrongful conduct to be paid over to the victim. The court also has the power to order an **injunction** stopping wrongful conduct or correcting some continuing wrong. The court may compel proper performance of a legal obligation by **specific performance**. In some situations, it may be appropriate for the courts to simply make a **declaration** as to the law and the legal rights of the parties.

Other remedies

Enforcement

Even when the litigation process is completed and judgment is obtained, there is no guarantee that the amount awarded will be paid. There may no longer be a dispute over liability, but if the **judgment debtor** refuses to pay, steps must be taken by the plaintiff, now the **judgment creditor**, to enforce the judgment. If the judgment debtor cannot pay and owns no assets (a "dry judgment"), it was likely unwise to have pursued the action in the first place. The successful plaintiff not only will get nothing from the defendant, but also will have to pay his own legal expenses. On the other

A judgment does not ensure payment

---

38. In Alberta, for example, party and party costs are usually awarded for actions in the Court of Queen's Bench pursuant to Schedule C of the *Rules of Court, supra* note 28.

39. *Whiten v. Pilot Insurance Co.*, [2002] 1 S.C.R. 595.

CASE SUMMARY 2.4

Is Specific Performance Always an Appropriate Remedy for Land Transactions? *Semelhago v. Paramadevan*[40]

Although damages or monetary compensation is the common remedy in a civil action, sometimes the court will order the equitable remedy of specific performance. In land transactions, it was thought that because all land is unique, specific performance would always be available—at least until this case was decided by the Supreme Court of Canada. Semelhago agreed to purchase from Paramadevan a house that was under construction, for $205 000. When it was time to perform the contract, Paramadevan refused, and this action was brought. Semelhago asked for the remedy of *specific performance*—or, as permitted by statute, damages in lieu of specific performance. At the trial he elected to receive damages, and the Court awarded him $125 000 damages in lieu of specific performance. The reason for this high award was that the market value of the house had risen from the $205 000 agreed upon at the time the contract was made to $325 000 at the time of trial. Paramadevan appealed the award, and the Appeal Court reduced it by the amount of the interest that Semelhago would have had to pay to finance the purchase of the house over the period from when the contract was entered into until the trial, saying that damages should reflect not only the increase in the value of the house from the time of the contract, but also the interest that would have been paid out had the deal closed as required by the contract. This reduced the damages to just less than $82 000.

The purpose of such damages is to put the victim in the position he would have been in had the contract been properly performed—and, so, the interest he would have had to pay should have been taken into consideration. The Supreme Court of Canada stated that specific performance should not always be considered the appropriate remedy in such land transaction disputes. It then refused to further reduce the award, and also refused to take into consideration the increased value of the house that Semelhago had intended to sell to acquire the one in question, but which he had instead retained. This case shows the factors that will be taken into consideration when assessing damages to be paid. An important statement that came out of the case was that it should no longer be thought that all land is unique, and that specific performance is therefore not always appropriate in a land transaction.

DISCUSSION QUESTIONS

Consider the remedies available to a court in a civil action. Here the Court refused to grant specific performance, but took into consideration the increasing values of the property and interest costs that would have been incurred when awarding damages. Were these appropriate considerations in the circumstances? Should remedies be limited to monetary compensation in most cases? Should damages always simply compensate or are there situations where punitive damages should be awarded?

hand, if the judgment debtor has prospects of owning future assets, the judgment does remain enforceable for several years and could be enforced in the future. The plaintiff must consider all of these factors—as well as the risk of losing the action—when deciding whether to proceed with an action against the defendant.

---

40. [1996] 2 S.C.R. 415.

ENFORCING JUDGMENT

The process to follow when enforcing a judgment is set out in Figure 2.3. Once judgment has been obtained, most provinces provide for a further hearing, sometimes called an **examination in aid of execution**[41] to determine the judgment debtor's assets and income that can be seized or garnished to satisfy the judgment. The plaintiff can question the judgment debtor (who is under oath) about her property, income, debts, recent property transfers, and present and future means of satisfying the judgment. At the conclusion of the process, the plaintiff can take appropriate steps to execute against particular property or income to recover the judgment.

Hearing to enforce judgment

SEIZURE OF PROPERTY

The execution process allows for the **seizure** and eventual sale of the debtor's property to satisfy the judgment. The property is seized by a government official (or in some provinces by a private business designated for that purpose[42]) who, after deducting a fee, sells it, usually through public auction. The proceeds are distributed first to **secured creditors**, then to preferred creditors and, finally, on a

Property may be seized and sold

Figure 2.3 Enforcement of Judgment

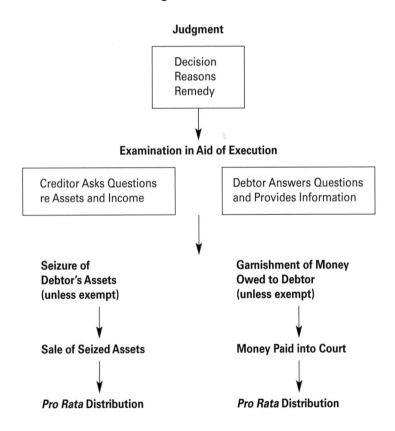

---

41. In Alberta, this hearing is called an examination in aid of enforcement—*Rules of Court, supra* note 28, r. 371–372. Instead of conducting an examination, the plaintiff may attempt to determine the information by requiring the judgment debtor to complete a financial report, verified by statutory declaration (in Alberta *Rules of Court*, r. 370).

42. In Alberta, a "civil enforcement agency" pursuant to the *Civil Enforcement Act*, R.S.A. 2000, c. C-15.

Proceeds of sale shared by all creditors

pro rata or proportionate basis, to the remaining unsecured creditors. **Secured creditors** used the property in question as security for a loan or other indebtedness, and so they have first claim to the proceeds from its sale, up to the amount secured. **Preferred creditors** are those who, by legislation, must be paid before other unsecured creditors. Landlords, owed unpaid rent, and employees, owed unpaid wages (both for a limited number of months), are examples of preferred creditors.

Some properties are exempt from seizure

Not all property is subject to seizure. The "necessities of life" are exempt from seizure. Exempt assets vary from province to province, but generally include—within specified limits—food, clothing, household furnishings, tools or other personal property needed to earn income, motor vehicles, and medical and dental aids. It should be noted that real property (land and buildings) can be seized to satisfy a judgment, but that the method employed varies with the jurisdiction. Often, registering the judgment against the real property is enough to pressure the debtor to pay. But when this is not enough, the property can be sold to satisfy the judgment.

Funds owed to debtor can be garnished

Garnishment involves the interception of funds owed to the judgment debtor and the payment of those funds into court. A creditor may garnish funds such as wages earned by the debtor but not yet paid to him, or the balance of the debtor's bank account. The legislation governing garnishment varies from province to province. Typically, when wages are garnished, the judgment debtor is entitled to an employment earnings exemption, which will vary depending on such factors as the amount earned and the debtor's number of dependants.[43] Once the required documentation is served on the garnishee (the person owing money to the judgment debtor), she must pay the amount owing (less the employment earnings exemption, if applicable) to the court, which then disburses the funds to the creditors.

Judicial Remedies Before Judgment

Pre-judgment remedies limited

Although most methods of execution require that a judgment first be obtained, some judicial remedies may be available to a creditor even before judgment. These are extraordinary remedies that are normally granted only when there is risk that the debtor's property will be removed from the jurisdiction or otherwise made unavailable to the creditor. While bank accounts and other debts can sometimes be attached before judgment, garnishing wages before judgment is usually not permitted.[44] New Brunswick and Nova Scotia do not permit any form of garnishment before judgment. When property other than money is involved, and there is risk of its being removed or sold, the creditor may be able to obtain a court order allowing seizure. This is not a judgment, but rather an interim order granted by the court before the actual trial to ensure that the goods will be available to satisfy a judgment if one is ultimately granted. Another remedy available in some situations is an injunction to a third party from paying out money owed to the debtor. This remedy does not direct those funds to the creditor, but it does prevent them from going to the debtor—who may dissipate or abscond with them.[45]

---

43. In Ontario, for example, 80 percent of a person's wages are usually exempt from garnishment—*Wages Act*, R.S.O. 1990, c. W. 1, s. 7.

44. See, for example, s. 3(4) of the *Court Order Enforcement Act*, R.S.B.C. 1996, c. 78.

45. In Alberta, the *Civil Enforcement Act*, *supra* note 43, Part 3, enables claimants to apply for attachment orders, which can allow both seizure and garnishment before judgment is obtained.

HOW LAWYERS BILL THEIR CLIENTS

One of the reasons people don't retain lawyers even when they clearly require legal advice is that they are afraid of the cost. While the provision of legal services is not cheap, an understanding of how lawyers bill their clients will help someone determine whether to retain a lawyer. In this regard, the issue of fees should be discussed during the initial consultation with the lawyer.

Every legal problem is unique. Also, there are many factors a lawyer will consider when calculating the fee to charge a client. It is therefore important that the client understand from the very beginning exactly how the lawyer will bill him for providing assistance with his particular problem. It is prudent to confirm this understanding in a fee agreement with the lawyer.

Each of the provincial law societies provides online information on lawyers' fees.[46] It appears that there are three main ways that lawyers calculate their fees. First, the lawyer may charge a fixed fee for the work required, regardless of the time involved. This method of billing is often used for specific tasks, such as preparing a will, purchasing a house, or incorporating a business.

Second, the lawyer may bill the client for all of the time she spends working on his file, using her hourly rate. Hourly rates usually vary with the number of years that the lawyer has been practising law. A senior lawyer may have a higher hourly rate than a junior lawyer, but the experience of the senior lawyer may enable her to complete the required legal work more efficiently, perhaps resulting in a fee lower than that charged by the relatively inefficient junior lawyer, who will be learning as she does the work.

Third, the lawyer may receive a percentage of the amount the client collects, either through a settlement or a court judgment. If the client does not collect anything, then the lawyer does not receive anything. This is a contingency fee agreement, which is often appropriate in personal injury claims, or product liability cases, when the client does not have any funds to pay the lawyer at the beginning of the case. The provincial law societies may restrict the use of contingency fee agreements, or set a maximum contingency fee for certain types of cases. The Law Society of British Columbia, for example, does not permit contingency fee agreements for family cases involving child custody or access. The maximum contingency fee allowed in claims for personal injury or wrongful death resulting from a motor vehicle accident is one-third of the amount received; for all other personal injury or wrongful death cases, the limit is 40 percent of the amount received.[47]

The client is also responsible for paying the out-of-pocket costs incurred by the lawyer on the client's behalf. These costs are called **disbursements**. Disbursements usually include costs such as the court fees for filing documents, long distance telephone charges, courier charges, the fee charged by an expert for testifying or preparing a report, and photocopying costs.

If a client decides to hire a lawyer, and the lawyer agrees to represent the client, the lawyer will usually request that a **retainer** be paid before she commences work on the matter. A retainer works as a deposit. The amount paid by the client is deposited into a trust account, to the credit of the client. When the lawyer bills the

Discuss fees with lawyer

Lawyer may bill on basis of fixed fee

or on basis of time spent and hourly rate

or as a contingency fee

Client responsible for disbursements

Retainer is a deposit

[46.] See the Law Society of Alberta, *supra* note 7 at www.lawsocietyalberta.com/LSA_Archives/index.cfm?page=arclawyerfees_iRQG4U.cfm; the Law Society of British Columbia, *supra* note 7 at www.lawsociety.bc.ca/public/lawyers_fees/types_fees.html; and the Law Society of Upper Canada, *supra* note 7 at www.lsuc.on.ca/public/a/faqs-finding-a-lawyer/index.cfm#8.

[47.] *Ibid.*

client, the amount owed will be paid from the retainer. The lawyer may require the client to "top up" the retainer as funds are withdrawn from the trust account.

ALTERNATIVES TO COURT ACTION

Businesspeople involved in private disputes are well advised to avoid litigation whenever possible because of the high costs, long delays, and likelihood of dissatisfaction with the results. In this section, we will discuss the various alternatives that can be used instead of—or in conjunction with—the litigation process. Many jurisdictions are now questioning the efficiency of the present civil justice system and are looking for better alternatives. Compulsory mediation, for example, has been incorporated as part of the litigation system in several jurisdictions. (In Ontario, the mandatory mediation component of the case management system appears to have been successful in increasing the resolution rate of disputes before trial and in reducing costs to the parties.[48])

Alternative dispute resolution (ADR) and litigation can work hand in hand, with the threat of one encouraging the parties to take advantage of the other. (The "Collaborative Family Law Process" involves an ADR approach in which litigation cannot even be threatened.[49]) Even if the matter does go to court, negotiation and mediation can be used at any stage in the litigation process, including post-judgment, when the parties wish to avoid an appeal. Note that the comments below with respect to the value of ADR apply equally to processes before administrative tribunals and other government decision-making bodies.

WHAT IS ALTERNATIVE DISPUTE RESOLUTION?

Any strategy that is used as a substitute for court action qualifies as a method of ADR, but there are three main approaches: (1) **Negotiation**—when the decision making is left in the hands of the disputing parties to work out for themselves; (2) **Mediation**—when a neutral third party assists the parties in coming to a resolution on their own; and (3) **Arbitration**—when a third party makes a binding decision in the matter under dispute.

Negotiation
Mediation
Arbitration

Table 2.1 compares these methods with litigation. They are discussed in more detail later in this section.

ADVANTAGES OF ADR VERSUS LITIGATION

There are some significant advantages in choosing an alternative to litigation. One is the retention of control of the matter by the people most affected by it. Rarely does a court judgment compensate the parties for all their time, money, and personal and business resources expended. It is, therefore, vitally important that businesspeople maintain control over the problem-solving process and appreciate the disadvantages of placing the matter in the hands of lawyers and the court when doing so can be avoided.

ADR leaves control in the hands of the parties

Most of the delays in litigation occur because of the lengthy pre-trial process and the problems of scheduling court personnel and facilities. When other reso-

Less delay with ADR

[48.] See Helen Burnett, "Pilot Project Meets Many of its Goals" *Law Times*, (21 April 2008), www.lawtimesnews.com/200804213999/Headline-News/Pilot-project-meets-many-of-its-goals.

[49.] See the discussion at www.collaborativelaw.ca/right_choice.php.

Table 2.1 Summary and Comparison of Litigation and ADR Methods

	Litigation	Arbitration	Mediation	Negotiation
Control	Low	Low	High	Highest
Delay	Lengthy	Moderate	Brief	Briefest
Cost	High	Moderate	Low	Low
Privacy	Low	Moderate	High	Complete
Flexibility	Low	Moderate	High	Highest
Good Will	Unlikely	Possible	Likely	Ensured
Predictability	High	Reasonable	Low	Low
Appealability	Usually	Moderate	None	None
Visibility	High	Moderate	None	None

lution processes are used, there are fewer procedural and scheduling delays because these matters are controlled by the parties themselves.

An ongoing court battle can be very distracting to a corporation's directors, managers, and employees. Key people may find themselves involved over a considerable period of time in overseeing the process, providing information, or preparing to testify. Much of this can be avoided by looking to an alternative method of resolving these disputes.

Less distraction with ADR

The fact that there is faster resolution of the matter with a simplified process involving fewer parties and fewer lawyers but with continued access to expert witnesses if needed contributes to a significant cost saving. Also, indirect considerations, such as the fact that the matter can be kept private, avoiding negative publicity and the disclosure of sensitive information, and the reduced risk of an adverse judgment, make an ADR approach more attractive.

Less expense with ADR

Risk of adverse judgment reduced

An American case against fast-food chain McDonald's illustrates the risk of insisting on litigation. In that case, a woman was injured when a cup of extremely hot coffee spilled on her as she removed the lid to add sugar. She suffered serious burns and spent some time in hospital. She had asked for some small compensation from McDonald's and was rebuffed. When the matter went to trial, the jury awarded more than $2.7 million in punitive damages. (Note that the trial judge later reduced the punitive damages to $480 000; the $160 000 compensatory damages award remained intact.) This could have been avoided had the representatives of McDonald's simply negotiated reasonably with her in the first place.[50]

One of the costs of a protracted conflict is the breakdown in the relationship between the parties. Litigation—in which questioning the opposition's credibility and honesty is routine—is adversarial in nature, often resulting in bitterness and animosity between the parties, thereby poisoning any future business relationship. In contrast, a quick settlement using ADR techniques may actually strengthen the relationship.

Good relationship can be retained with ADR

Another attractive feature of ADR is its flexibility. The parties remain in control, allowing them to accommodate the needs of multiple parties and competing interests. Even cultural differences can be taken into consideration. ADR can even be used to resolve internal disputes within an organization, often in an informal atmosphere with a quick resolution that is satisfactory to all.

ADR provides more flexibility

---

50. *Liebeck v. McDonald's Restaurants, P.T.S. Inc.*, 1995 WL 360309 (N.M. Dist. Ct. 1994).

ADR can resolve conflicts between businesses operating internationally

It should also be noted that when international trade is involved, ADR methods are much more common, especially when dealing with businesses that are in a civil law jurisdiction. Organizations have been established throughout Canada to assist in the conduct of such processes.[51] Legislation enabling the enforcement of arbitrated awards strengthens their usefulness.[52]

DISADVANTAGES OF ADR VERSUS LITIGATION

It must also be emphasized that there are many situations in which ADR should be avoided. The qualities of judicial fairness and impartiality associated with the litigation process are not always present in ADR. The court has no prior interest in the parties or their problems, but it does have extraordinary powers to extract information from the parties that do not exist outside the litigation process. A

ADR cannot ensure full disclosure

mediator cannot ensure that all relevant information has been brought forward. In the court system, there are safeguards and rules in place to ensure that each side gets a fair hearing. Because there are few rules or required procedures, ADR may not be able to provide this assurance. The court strives to balance the process so that neither side can take unfair advantage of the other, although this balance

ADR does little to overcome a power imbalance

may be compromised when only one side can afford extensive legal help. If parties are using ADR, and there is a power imbalance, there is the danger that the stronger party will take advantage of the weaker. In contrast, the discovery process does much to level the playing field where such inequality exists.

ADR cannot ensure consistent outcomes

Other advantages of litigation are that the decision will be based on, or set a precedent, and that the decisions will normally be made public and thus be an effective deterrent to similar behaviour. (In fact, concern has been expressed by judges and academics that the case law will not develop because mediation and arbitration are becoming much more popular than litigation, and they are private.[53]) There are also effective tools available for enforcing the judgment as well as a right to appeal the decision.

ADR agreements not enforceable or appealable

It must always be remembered that what is a disadvantage to one party may be the most attractive feature of the chosen process to another. As in all business decisions, sound, properly informed judgment is needed in deciding between ADR and litigation in any given situation.

ADR Mechanisms

Upon concluding that ADR is a viable option, the businessperson must then decide which of the various strategies would be most effective in resolving the dispute.

NEGOTIATION

Negotiation should be tried first

Negotiation should be the first recourse for people who find themselves in a disagreement—too often, it is the last. Negotiation involves the parties or their representatives meeting to discuss the problem to come to an agreement as to how it should be resolved. Both sides must be willing to enter into negotiations, and the goal must be to find a solution even if that means making concessions. Negotiation can be as simple as a phone conversation, an exchange of correspon-

---

[51.] For example, the British Columbia International Commercial Arbitration Centre at www.bcicac.com.

[52.] See, for example, *International Commercial Arbitration Act*, R.S.B.C. 1996, c. 233.

[53.] See Daryl-Lynn Carlson, "Family Lawyers Flocking to ADR" *Law Times* (11 June 2007), online: http://www.lawtimesnews.com/200706182260/Headline-News/Family-lawyers-flocking-to-ADR.

dence, or sitting down together in a private meeting; any meeting with the goal of resolving a dispute qualifies as a negotiation.

Because the process is cooperative and non-binding, either side can withdraw from the negotiations if the other is being unreasonable or intransigent; the parties may then elect to move on to some other means of dealing with the matter. An understanding of the law surrounding the dispute will help the parties recognize the consequences of a failure to settle as well as the relative strength or weakness of the position they are taking.

Successful negotiation requires an understanding of the issues and a willingness to cooperate and compromise. A competitive approach that tries to best the other party will likely not resolve underlying issues. Similarly, there is danger in being too willing to accommodate demands from the other side. It may not always be possible to reach a win–win solution, but satisfactory results often involve both sides cooperating to minimize their losses. Of course, there is always the danger of being subjected to unethical behaviour or coercion, and since not everyone can be a skilled negotiator, any decision to take this course of action must be made weighing all of the advantages and disadvantages. **Negotiation requires cooperation and compromise**

When there is a lack of skill or experience, or when one party is in a more powerful position, it is often wise to negotiate through a representative. While this involves extra costs and a certain amount of loss of control, it has the advantage of overcoming the lack of skill problem and creates a buffer between the parties so that a more powerful personality can be resisted. When lawyers are used, care must be exercised to choose one that is skilled in negotiation and not simply predisposed to litigation. There is a further advantage of the lawyer's better understanding the legal issues involved, and if the matter does proceed to litigation, the lawyer is already involved in the process. It should also be kept in mind that any legal concession, admission, or compromises made during these negotiations when made "**without prejudice**" will not hurt the parties if the negotiations fail and litigation results. And it may also be true that successful negotiation, when there has been concession and compromise between the parties, can actually improve the business relationship. **Representatives may conduct negotiation**

Relationship may be enhanced

MEDIATION

Mediation also has a long history in resolving disputes. Its use in labour relations has been mandated by statutes for most of the last century, and its use in family disputes is commonplace. Mediation has always played a role in commercial relations but has become much more vital in recent years. The main difference between negotiation and mediation is that mediation involves a neutral third party, hopefully properly trained, who assists the parties to come to an agreement. The **mediator** does not make decisions but facilitates the discussion, making sure that each side has the opportunity to put his side forward, eliciting information, finding areas of possible compromise, identifying potential problems and solutions, and encouraging settlement. **Neutral third party facilitates communication**

Mediator does not make decision

The mediation process can be very informal or it can be carefully structured with rules of procedure and a set timeframe. Often only a few meetings are necessary, with the main objective of the mediator being to find some common ground between the parties. The mediator will meet with both parties together and separately, using a variety of techniques to find some area of agreement and developing compromises between the parties, which can be used to encourage a settlement. It is this degree of flexibility and creativity that makes the process effective in the hands of a skilled mediator. Mediation has been so successful **Mediator finds common ground**

REDUCING RISK 2.4

There are a variety of circumstances in which mediation might be preferable to and more productive than other means of dispute resolution. One example would be when the benefits of a continuing relationship outweigh the benefits of securing a damage award. In the construction industry, for example, it may appear that a contractor is about to fail to complete the building on time or on budget, leading to a dispute with the owner. Rather than expending time, energy, and expense on litigation, with the likelihood of further delay of the project, it may be more reasonable to call in a mediator who has knowledge of the construction industry. This mediator could help the parties arrive at an understanding of the problems each has faced, such as unexpected illness, increased costs, or the unavailability of materials. This could lead to a solution acceptable to both sides, resulting in the completion of the building and the maintenance of the relationship. In fact, in the construction sector, it is reported that millions of dollars are saved annually in jurisdictions where the first recourse in the event of problems is to mediate rather than to litigate.

because the persuasiveness, skills, and neutrality of a trained third party are introduced, while control of the problem is retained by each party. While the parties are not bound by any solutions suggested by the mediator, once an agreement is reached it can be enforced just like any other contract.

Successful mediators require considerable specialized training. There are organizations that provide membership and certification, and that set recognized professional standards. The disputing parties will normally choose a mediator who is a member in good standing with such an organization. They may, in fact, choose a mediator from a list provided by the organization.[54]

Mediation may be required

In several situations, mediation has been mandated by statute—perhaps the highest-profile of these is in collective bargaining. In many jurisdictions, mediation is also compulsory in family disputes and in the litigation process itself.[55]

Disadvantages of Mediation

Mediation may be inappropriate

Mediation depends on cooperation and good will between the disputing parties. When there has been some wrongdoing involved, or blame is to be attached, it is unlikely that proper disclosure will be made, and crucial information may be withheld. Mediators have little power to compel parties to produce evidence and documentation when they are unwilling to do so.

Successful mediation requires balance of power and willingness to act in good faith

Also, when one of the parties is weaker, mediation may just exacerbate that weakness. This can be a serious problem in family disputes, when the weakness of one of the parties—or his desire to accommodate—leads to an unbalanced result. Also, when one of the parties is suspected of acting in bad faith, mediation is simply inappropriate, because trust is such an important component of the mediation process.

---

54. One example of such an organization is the ADR Institute of Canada, www.adrcanada.ca/.

55. Ontario has introduced a Mandatory Mediation pilot project, which requires that a mediation session take place after a statement of defence has been filed. See *supra* note 36. In several provinces, including Alberta and British Columbia, parties involved in small claims litigation may be required to attempt mediation before a trial date will be fixed. See *Mediation Rules of the Provincial Court—Civil Division*, Alta. Reg. 271/1997 and *Small Claims Rules*, B.C. Reg. 261/93 Rule 7.2.

Mediation does work well when highly confidential or sensitive information that should not be disclosed to the public is involved, a speedy resolution is vital, good ongoing relations must be maintained, there is some trust involved, or both parties are desirous of reaching a settlement.

ARBITRATION

The third major category of alternative dispute resolution involves surrendering the decision making to a third party. In most cases, arbitration is voluntary, but in some situations, such as labour relations, the parties are required by statute to agree to some arbitration mechanism as part of the collective agreement process.[56] In some instances, arbitration is agreed upon before any dispute has arisen by including, in the original contract, a requirement to arbitrate. Often, however, the parties agree to arbitrate after a dispute arises. Arbitration can be very effective when external disputes arise with creditors, suppliers, or customers, and even internally with employees and shareholders or between departments. Arbitration is commonly used in resolving disputes arising from international trade agreements.[57]

Arbitration involves third-party decision maker

Typically, the **arbitrator** is chosen from a pool of trained and certified professionals, often with expertise in the subject matter of the dispute. Organizations of professional arbitrators have been established, and the members offer their services like any other professionals.[58] These organizations not only provide training and certification, but also set professional and ethical standards requiring that their members be properly trained, avoid conflicts of interest, be free of bias, and keep in strict confidence all information they obtain. In more formal instances, retired judges are hired to hold what is essentially a private trial, rendering a decision much like a court but without the attendant publicity or delay.

Arbitrators are chosen by parties

Arbitrators may be experts in the field

Parties can stipulate in their contract the requirement for arbitration, how the arbitrator is to be chosen and, if they want, that provincial arbitration legislation apply to the process. The specific process to be followed may be left to the arbitrator or, alternatively, the procedure may be set out in the agreement,[59] but such procedures, whether determined by the parties or by the arbitrator, must be fair.

Procedure must be fair

Usually, before an arbitration hearing takes place, there is a requirement that information relating to the matter be disclosed by both sides. At the hearing itself, lawyers or other representatives of the parties usually examine witnesses, present documents, make arguments and summarize their cases. Formal rules of evidence need not be adhered to, nor is the arbitrator required to follow precedent in reaching the decision. When the process is mandated by statute, as in labour disputes, the requirements are much more stringent and more closely resemble an actual court hearing. An arbitrator's decision is binding on the parties and is generally not appealable, but it is important to remember that the courts still have the right to supervise and review the decision-making process as discussed above under the heading "Dealing with Regulatory Bodies."

Decision cannot be appealed but process may be reviewed by court

---

[56.] See, for example, s. 48 of Ontario's *Labour Relations Act, 1995,* S.O. 1995, c. 1, Sch. A.

[57.] See the discussion regarding International Commercial Arbitration, at www.bcicac.com/bcicac_ica.php.

[58.] One such organization is the ADR Institute of Canada, *supra* note 53.

[59.] The ADR Institute of Canada has published National Arbitration Rules, which the parties can agree to use to resolve their contractual disputes, www.adrcanada.ca/rules/arbitration.cfm.

Third party makes a decision that is binding

The unique feature of arbitration is that a third party makes the decision. To be effective, it is vital that the parties be required to honour that decision. Most jurisdictions provide that the decisions reached by arbitrators are binding and enforceable.[60] As a result, arbitration is usually an effective process.

Arbitration is, however, still essentially adversarial in nature. In this sense, it is like litigation, with the attendant danger that bitterness and hard feelings may be aggravated. Arbitration is more costly than other forms of ADR, because it is more formal and involves more people, but it is still much less expensive than the litigation process.

Ideally, arbitration should be voluntary, but clauses requiring arbitration are finding their way into standard form contracts at an alarming rate. These contracts often cover consumer transactions, with the consumer unaware that he has surrendered the right to a court hearing until the dispute arises. Because the decision is binding and non-appealable, the disgruntled party may challenge the validity of the arbitration clause in court, compounding an already complex resolution procedure.

Arbitration is private

Arbitration may look much like litigation, but it is still private and still usually within the control of the parties. When expertise is important, an arbitrator with that expertise can be chosen. Arbitration is faster, less costly, and more private than litigation, but it also has disadvantages. Arbitration is still more costly and likely more time consuming than other forms of ADR. Also, there may be little certainty or predictability, as precedents are usually not binding and animosity between the parties may actually increase as a result of this adversarial process.

It should be noted that these ADR mechanisms are not mutually exclusive. Sometimes the tools of mediation and arbitration will be brought together when the outsider starts out as a mediator and, if it grows clear that the parties cannot reach a settlement even with the mediator's help, she becomes an arbitrator, making a decision that is binding on both parties. Of course, such a change of roles must be agreed upon by the parties.

Mediator may become an arbitrator

Finally, mediation and arbitration are becoming more common in resolving online disputes.[61] There are many advantages to using ADR in the context of e-commerce. Many internet transactions involve relatively small amounts of money, so litigation is not practical. Using ADR for online disputes overcomes geographical issues, reduces costs, and enables a quick resolution of disputes. Confidentiality is often important to online businesses, which do not want publicity about problems with their sites or security systems.

Online dispute resolution (ODR) programs have been developed to help resolve disputes between parties.[62] Such programs will continue to improve and become more cost effective. Over time, this may enable businesses to impose mandatory ODR systems that would be effective and acceptable to consumers.[63]

---

60. See, for example, *Arbitration Act*, 1991, S.O. 1991, c. 17, ss. 37, 50.

61. See Derek Hill, "ADR Picking up in Internet and E-commerce Law" *Law Times* (1 August 2008), www.lawtimesnews.com/200808014192/Headline-News/ADR-picking-up-in-internet-and-e-commerce-law.

62. Glenn Kauth, "ODR in Canada Getting a Boost" *Law Times* (8 December 2008), www.lawtimesnews.com/200812084400/Headline-News/ODR-in-Canada-getting-a-boost.

63. See Gary Oakes, "Your Virtual Day in Court: How Online Dispute Resolution Is Transforming the Practice of ADR" *Lawyers Weekly* (16 January 2009), www.lawyersweekly.ca/index .php?section=article&articleid=737. This article indicates that ODR is "the next step to traditional ADR" and that "it's not just for commercial transactions." It can be used for small claims litigation, divorce actions, and even "in the context of world peace or interstate conflict"!

REDUCING RISK 2.5

ADR services are now being offered online. Such services can be very helpful in attempting to mediate between corporations and their customers, when information, services, or products do not meet expectations, or when customers have not fulfilled their obligations. In addition, such intermediaries may serve to set standards, monitor compliance, and warn potential customers when problems exist. As there is little regulation controlling ADR generally, it is likely that there will be even less in the electronic environment. Businesspeople should ensure that the services are being offered by qualified professionals and be aware that they may have little recourse if things go wrong.

SUMMARY

The courts

- Procedural rules govern structure and function, which may vary with jurisdiction
- Open to the public, with some exceptions
- Both criminal and civil functions at trial and appellate levels
- All but lower-level provincial court judges are appointed by federal government

Provincial courts

- Handle less serious criminal offences, civil matters under a set amount, custody and maintenance in family divisions, youth offenders
- Provinces have recently created new specialized courts to deal with societal changes and problems

Superior courts

- Handle serious criminal offences, civil matters with unlimited monetary jurisdiction, divorce

Appellate courts

- Deal with appeals of law from trial courts, usually have three judges, do not rehear the facts, usually hold final hearing for most criminal and civil matters

Federal courts

- Tax Court hears cases involving federal tax matters
- Federal Court hears disputes within federal jurisdiction and appeals from some administrative tribunals
- Federal Court of Appeal hears appeals from Federal Court, Tax Court, and some administrative tribunals

Supreme Court of Canada

- Highest-level appeal court
- Deals primarily with Constitutional and *Charter* matters, as well as cases of national importance

Process of civil litigation

- Limitation periods
  - Set by statute

- Pre-trial
  - Plaintiff files writ of summons (if required) and statement of claim
  - Defendant responds with appearance (if required) and statement of defence
  - Discovery of documents and questioning of parties by opposing counsel
  - Payment into court or offer of settlement to encourage reasonable demands and offers
  - Purpose—to bring information to light and encourage settlement
- Trial
  - Examination of witnesses and presentation of evidence
  - Judgment
  - Jury decides questions of fact
  - Judge decides questions of law
  - Loser usually pays some legal costs
- Enforcement
  - Examination in aid of execution
  - Seizure of property
  - Garnishment
- Remedies
  - Damages—general, special, punitive
  - Accounting, injunction, specific performance, declaration

Alternative dispute resolution (ADR)

- Recent trend to avoid costs and delays associated with litigation
- Advantages
  - Control, timeliness, productivity, cost, privacy, good will, flexibility
- Disadvantages
  - Unpredictable, no precedents set, cannot deal with complex legal problems
  - Must be voluntary, must have a balance of power between the parties
  - Parties must cooperate to ensure agreement and resolution
- Methods
  - Negotiation—direct discussion between parties
  - Mediation—neutral third party facilitates discussion
  - Arbitration—neutral expert makes a binding decision

QUESTIONS

1. Describe the court hierarchy in Canada, including provincial and federal courts.

2. Distinguish between questions of law and questions of fact, and explain why this distinction is significant.

3. Who appoints provincial superior court judges? Provincial court judges?

4. How would the expiration of a limitation period affect the rights of parties to litigate a matter in dispute?

5. What are the pleadings used to commence an action in the superior trial court in your jurisdiction?

6. How does the discovery process take place, and what is its significance in civil litigation?

7. Explain how an offer to settle can affect the judgment award made by the court to the plaintiff.

8. Describe the recent initiatives taken in your jurisdiction to "speed up" the litigation process.

9. Explain the trial process.

10. Compare party–party costs with solicitor–client costs. To whom are these costs generally awarded?

11. Distinguish among the various remedies available to a successful plaintiff in a civil action.

12. Explain the role of the examination in aid of execution in enforcing those remedies (from Question 11), and indicate what methods are available to enforce a judgment against a debtor who is trying to avoid payment.

13. Explain the value of an injunction as a pre-judgment remedy. Discuss other pre-judgment remedies available to aid in the collection of debt.

14. List and describe the principal advantages of alternative dispute resolution.

15. Distinguish between negotiation, mediation, and arbitration, and discuss the advantages and disadvantages of each of them.

Chapter 3

The Law of Torts

1. Describe the role of tort law
2. Explain vicarious liability indicating when it may be imposed
3. Distinguish the torts of assault, battery, and trespass to land, listing the relevant defences
4. Describe three torts that deal with wrongful interference with goods (chattels)
5. Contrast the torts of false imprisonment and malicious prosecution
6. Differentiate private from public nuisance
7. Compare defamation with the tort of injurious falsehood
8. Describe the following torts:
   - Inducing breach of contract
   - Interference with economic relations
   - Conspiracy to injure
   - Intimidation
   - Deceit (fraudulent misrepresentation)
   - Passing off
   - Misuse of confidential information
   - Invasion of privacy
9. Identify torts frequently committed in the online environment
10. Identify remedies awarded to redress torts

THE SCOPE OF TORT LAW

tort
a wrongful act done to the person or property of another

The role of the law of **torts** is to *compensate* victims for harm suffered from the activities of others. In theory *punishment* is left to the criminal law, if the conduct in question happens also to amount to a crime.[1] For example, when a person

---

1. In some cases the courts award "punitive damages"; see the discussion later in this chapter under the heading "Remedies."

punches a neighbour in the nose, the neighbour may sue him in tort for compensation and the state may also charge him with the criminal offence of assault causing bodily harm.

While there is no entirely satisfactory definition of "tort," it is not difficult to compile a list of separate "torts." As a general proposition, tort law identifies those circumstances that create a right to compensation.

The basic issue for society when dealing with such causes of harm as automobile accidents, industrial accidents, or pollution of the environment is to determine who should bear the loss—the victim, the person whose act caused the harm, the group that benefits most directly from a common activity, such as all motor vehicle owners, or an even larger group, such as taxpayers generally. Tort law is one instrument for apportioning loss, along with other instruments such as insurance and government compensation schemes.[2]

DEVELOPMENT OF THE TORT CONCEPT

In the early stages of development, societies usually had simple rules for imposing liability for injurious conduct: anyone who caused direct injury to another had to pay compensation. No inquiry was made into the reasons for the injury or whether the conduct of the injurer was justified. This type of liability is called **strict liability**. Gradually, the idea developed that a person should not be responsible for harm caused to another if he acted without *fault*. The courts also began to consider the way in which the harm had arisen. At first, only direct injuries were recognized by the courts—running down another person or striking a blow. Gradually the courts began to recognize indirect or consequential injuries. For example, suppose *A* carelessly dropped a log in the road and did not bother to remove it although it was near sunset. After dark, *B*'s horse tripped over the log and was seriously injured. In early law, *B* would have been without a remedy. Later, however, the courts recognized that *A*'s act was as much responsible for the injury to *B*'s horse as if *A* had struck the horse by throwing the log at it. They allowed *B* to recover damages.[3]

Therefore, early tort law evolved in two ways: the law took into account the *fault* of the defendant and it also took into account *causation*—whether the defendant's conduct could be considered the cause of the harm. Both these developments present difficult problems, which we will examine more closely in this chapter and in the next chapter on negligence.

strict liability
liability that is imposed regardless of fault

THE BASIS FOR LIABILITY

Fault

Fault, in the context of tort law, refers to blameworthy or culpable conduct—conduct that in the eyes of the law is unjustifiable because it intentionally or carelessly disregards the interests of others. One justification for basing liability upon fault

---

2. For a fuller discussion of the purposes of tort law, see especially J. Fleming, *The Law of Torts*, 9th ed. (Sydney: Law Book Company, 1998). See also A.M. Linden, *Canadian Tort Law*, 6th ed. (Toronto: Butterworths, 1997).

3. This example was discussed by Fortesque, J. in *Reynolds* v. *Clarke* (1726), 93 E.R. 747, and has been cited many times since by both the courts and leading writers as a classic statement of the law.

is a belief in its deterrent effect: people will be more inclined to be careful if they must pay for the consequences of their carelessness. There is little hard evidence to support this theory, although it is reasonable to suppose that large, highly publicized awards of damages have had an effect upon the standards and practices of manufacturers, surgeons, and similar persons affected by those awards. But the modern reality is that many of the activities where tort liability arises—driving a car, operating a factory or store, practising medicine—are covered by insurance. Carelessness is more likely to be deterred by the likelihood of criminal penalties (for example, for dangerous driving) and of increased insurance premiums than by the possibility of being sued in tort.

A compensation system based on fault also has its defects. Accident victims who cannot establish fault on the part of some other person go uncompensated, and the costs and delays of litigation deter many other claims. At the same time, when fault is established there is a tendency for the victim to be over-compensated, especially where the defendant is a large corporation and its conduct is considered particularly blameworthy.[4]

Strict Liability

Not all tort liability is based upon fault. As already noted, early tort law took a narrow approach, imposing the burden of compensation upon the person who caused the injury regardless of whether he was at fault. That offends modern ideas of fairness. However, strict liability persists in some areas of modern tort law. For example, a person who collects potentially dangerous substances or materials on his land, from which they subsequently escape, is liable for any resulting damage even if he were blameless.[5]

ILLUSTRATION 3.1

A manufacturer stored acid in a large container on his property. The container was accidentally punctured by a visitor's truck. The acid leaked out and damaged a neighbouring farmer's crops. The manufacturer is liable to compensate the farmer. The risk of that type of damage is a burden that the manufacturer must bear as the price for storing dangerous chemicals on his land. (The truck driver may also be liable for the damage if he is found to be at fault.)

Some activities are inherently dangerous regardless of the amount of care taken—for example, transporting high explosives. A strong argument may be made that a person carrying on an inherently dangerous activity should be strictly liable for damage, regardless of fault. In other words, a person who undertakes a dangerous activity should charge for his services according to the degree of risk, and should carry adequate insurance to compensate for possible

---

[4.] This is especially so in the United States, where jury trials and awards of punitive damages are more common. That has been the main focus for the recent calls there for "tort law reform."

[5.] *Rylands* v. *Fletcher* (1868), L.R. 3 H.L. 330. In Canada, the *Rylands* v. *Fletcher* rule requires a non-natural use of the land and damage caused by escape. See John *Campbell Law Corporation* v. *Owners, Strata Plan 1350*, 2001 BCSC 1342.

harm done to others. Most often strict liability is imposed by legislation, although some United States courts have done it. In the absence of legislation, Canadian courts still apply the principles of negligence. However, they have raised the standard of care as the danger increases. As a result, in many cases involving hazardous activities the defendant finds that the standard of care is so high that it is virtually impossible for him to show that he has satisfied it. The effect is much the same as if he were strictly liable.

Social Policy

Whether liability should be based on fault, on strict liability, or on some other principles is an important question of policy. Policy objectives change as our social standards change. These standards force the law to adapt in many ways, ranging from direct legislative intervention to more subtle influences on judge and jury in determining liability and the amounts of damages awarded.

The most radical proposals would eliminate lawsuits for all personal injuries and compensate victims through a government scheme. A step in that direction has been taken in Canada with the virtual elimination of fault as the basis for automobile accident claims through a system of compulsory **"no-fault" insurance**. Another example of an alternative to the tort approach is found in the scheme governing **workers' compensation** in Canada. Under this scheme, industrial accidents are seen as the inevitable price of doing business. Employers must contribute to a fund that is used to compensate workers injured in industrial accidents, even when the employer is blameless and the injury is the result of the employee's own carelessness.

But between comprehensive "no-fault" schemes on the one hand and strict liability on the other, there are many circumstances where liability based on fault is still considered to be the fairest principle. In most areas of tort law, liability is imposed on a fault basis.[6]

"no-fault" insurance
a system of compulsory insurance that eliminates fault as a basis for claim

workers' compensation
a scheme in which employers contribute to a fund used to compensate workers injured in industrial accidents regardless of how the accident was caused

Vicarious Liability

One area in which the law has responded to the pressure of social needs relates to torts committed by employees in the course of their employment. In some cases an employer may be personally at fault for an act committed by an employee: for example, he may instruct an employee to perform a dangerous task for which he knows the employee is not trained. In such a case the employer personally is at fault, and it may be that there is no fault on the part of the employee.[7]

But should an employer be liable when the employee alone is at fault? Over the years the courts developed a basis for holding the employer liable for harm caused by the acts of an employee when those acts arose in the course of employment. Now, the employer may be found liable even when he has given strict instructions to take proper care or not to do the particular act that causes

---

[6.] See, for example, *Fiala* v. *Cechmanek* (2001), 201 D.L.R. (4th) 680, where the defendant suffered from a mental illness of which he was unaware. During a manic outburst, he damaged the plaintiff's automobile. The Alberta Court of Appeal held that he was not liable for the damage: there could be no liability without fault.

[7.] See *Edgeworth Construction Ltd.* v. *N.D. Lee & Associates Ltd.* (1993), 107 D.L.R. (4th) 169.

the damage, and he may be held liable for criminal, as well as negligent, acts of an employee.[8]

There are two main justifications for taking this strict approach. First, although an employee is personally liable for the torts he commits while acting for himself or his employer, employees often have limited assets available to pay compensation for the potential harm they can cause—a train driver may injure hundreds of passengers. Second, there is an argument based on fairness: the person who makes the profit from an activity should also be liable for any loss. This is called the principle of **vicarious liability**, by which an employer is liable to compensate persons for harm caused by an employee in the course of employment.[9] (See Figure 3.1.)

vicarious liability
the liability of an employer to compensate for harm caused by an employee

Figure 3.1 Vicarious Liability

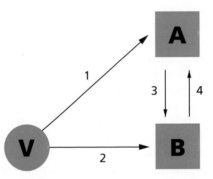

The victim, *V*, is injured by *A* while *A* is acting in the course of his employment. *V* can sue *A* [1]. *V* can also sue the employer, *B* [2], who will normally have a greater ability to pay. (In practice, *V* is likely to sue both *A* and *B*.) If *V* does sue *A*, it is possible that *A* will have a right to be indemnified by *B* [3]. Or, if *B* has to compensate *V*, *B* may be able to sue *A* [4]. These rights [3 and 4] could arise under the contract of employment.

INTENTIONAL TORTS

Intentional physical interference

The following discussion is concerned with torts where the conduct involved was intended or deliberate, as opposed to the following chapter's discussion of negligence, where the conduct is inadvertent. The term *intentional* does not mean that the wrongdoer intended to do harm, only that the conduct itself was wilful as opposed to inadvertent. As with all forms of actionable torts, fault on the part of the wrongdoer must be demonstrated, but when we examine intentional torts as discussed here, that fault is embodied in the wilful act of the wrongdoer.

---

8. *British Columbia Ferry Corp.* v. *Invicta Security Service Corp.* (1998), 167 D.L.R. (4th) 193.

9. For a review of the policy issues underlying the vicarious liability principle, see the decision of the Supreme Court of Canada in *671122 Ontario Ltd.* v. *Sagaz Industries Canada Inc.* (2001), 204 D.L.R. (4th) 542. As that case demonstrates, one difficulty is to determine whether the primary tortfeasor was an employee or an independent contractor. The principle of vicarious liability is not restricted to acts of employees; in some circumstances a person may be held liable for the torts committed by an agent.

Trespass to Person: Assault and Battery

Assault and battery (or **trespass to person**) involve the intentional physical interference with another person. These torts are a concern to businesses whose employees serve the public. Conduct that makes a person think he is about to be struck is an **assault**. If someone fakes a punch, points a gun, or picks up a stone to threaten another person, an assault has been committed. A **battery** takes place when someone intentionally makes unwanted physical contact with another person. Since battery almost invariably involves an assault, the term *assault* is often used to refer to both assault and battery. Assault and battery are actionable, even where there is no injury; "the least touching of another in anger is battery."[10] The purpose of the tort of trespass to the person is to recognize the right of each person to control his body and who touches it. Damages are awarded when this right is violated.

Actual contact—battery

Fear of contact—assault

The test to determine whether an assault has taken place is to look to the victim and ask whether she was fearful or anticipated unwanted physical contact. If the defendant's conduct would cause a reasonable person to feel threatened with imminent harm or even simply unwanted contact, it constitutes an assault. In *Warman v. Grosvenor*,[11] for example, the defendant waged a "campaign of terror" against the plaintiff by posting threatening and intimidating messages on the internet and in personal emails. By virtue of their repetitiveness, their detail regarding the plaintiff's whereabouts, and their level of malevolence, the postings were more than empty threats and insults. Damages of $50 000 were awarded for assault and defamation.

Verbal threats (face-to-face, at a distance, or online) may constitute assault

The anticipated contact might be anything from a physical blow, to unwanted medical treatment, to a kiss. The motive or goodwill of the person attacking is not relevant. The words are taken into consideration as well as the gestures and actions. The action of a person walking toward another can be an assault when accompanied by threatening words, whereas words such as "How nice to see you again" remove the threat.

Intent to harm not required

CASE SUMMARY 3.1

Bouncers Beware! *Tardif v. Wiebe*[12]

There is no dispute that Tardif was drunk when he was refused further service and was asked to leave the hotel on the Friday night in question. He was not usually a fighter but did get obnoxious and rude when he was in an intoxicated state. In the process of leaving the bar with his girlfriend, he got into an altercation with a woman who made some offensive remarks about the two of them. This scuffle resulted in the hotel bouncers, Wiebe and Poburn, being called to intervene and eject Tardif. On the landing above the outside steps of the hotel, Poburn held Tardif while Wiebe struck him twice. As a result of the second blow, Tardif was thrown off the landing and fell down four steps onto the concrete sidewalk below causing serious injuries. Tardif has no recollection of this, but Poburn testified that his head "cracked like an egg."

---

10. *Cole v. Turner* (1704), 6 Mod.149, 87 E.R. 907.

11. [2008] O.J. NO. 4462 (SUP. CT J.).

12. [1996] B.C.J. No. 2254

While Poburn was a professional bouncer, Wiebe was untrained, and both were considerably larger than Tardif, who posed no threat to them. Excessive and unjustified force was clearly used against Tardif.

The bouncers may have had a right to eject Tardif with force if he had been refusing to leave, but that was not the case here. And even if it were, it would not have justified the bouncers using such forceful blows when Tardif was already outside the hotel. The Judge found that Tardif had done nothing to justify the bouncers' actions.

Because of considerable brain and nerve damage and other injuries, Mr. Tardif was unable to return to work. The award against the hotel and bouncers was more than $1 million. Because no malice was involved, there was no award for punitive damages.

SMALL BUSINESS PERSPECTIVE

This, and numerous cases like it, demonstrates the potential liability faced by businesses dealing with the public. Due to vicarious liability, investing in training one's staff will not totally eliminate the risk. The fact that the business has instructed employees not to use force does not operate as a defence. Do these principles in law expose the business to too much liability? Should employers always be liable for their employees' wrongdoing in these situations? Should bouncers face personal liability if they are just "doing their job"? What do you think?

DEFENCES

Consent is a defence

There are several defences that can be raised against an assault or battery claim. Normally, doctors escape liability for their actions when operating on or otherwise treating patients through the principle of consent. Essentially, a person who expressly or implicitly consents to conduct that would otherwise constitute an assault or battery loses the right to sue. This is the reason why injured boxers cannot sue their opponents.

It is important to remember that the level of interference cannot exceed the consent. Excessive violence in a sporting activity will constitute the tort of battery despite the consent. Mike Tyson faced liability after biting his opponent during a boxing match. Excessive violence may also be a crime, as Todd Bertuzzi discovered when he was charged and subsequently convicted of assault causing bodily harm for a vicious hit to the head of Steve Moore in an NHL game in 2004.[13] Also, the consent must be *informed consent;* people must know what they are consenting to.[14] People may refuse or give only limited consent to medical treatment. In *Malette v. Shulman,*[15] the physician administered a blood transfusion, which likely saved the patient's life, and yet the plaintiff successfully sued for battery. The plaintiff had a card in her purse stating that, as a Jehovah's Witness, she refused consent to receive any blood products. If this refusal of consent is made clear to a doctor and

---

[13.] *R. v. Bertuzzi*, [2004] B.C.J. No. 2692, (B.C.P.C.). Note: a civil action has also been commenced by Moore. See: *Moore v. Bertuzzi*, [2008] O.J. No. 347, (Ont. S.C.J.) dealing with an interim application to add a claim against the owners of the Vancouver Canucks.

[14.] See *Halushka v. University of Saskatchewan et al.*, [1965] S.J. No. 208 (C.A.)where medical researchers were unable to establish that the consent was an informed one. The student had agreed to participate in a drug experiment in exchange for $50 but was not fully informed of the risk. His heart stopped when the drug was administered and he had to undergo emergency surgery to restart it. Halushka was paid $50 four days later when he regained consciousness. The battery action succeeded.

[15.] [1990] O.J. No. 450 (C.A.)

the refused treatment is administered anyway, the doctor can be sued for the battery committed.[16] This is true even where the patient would die without the treatment, putting physicians in an unsettling position.[17]

Note that **consent** to conduct that would otherwise constitute a tort, when informed and voluntary, operates as an effective defence to any of the torts discussed in this chapter or the next.

Self-defence can also be raised to counteract an assault and battery accusation. The law entitles people who are being attacked to use necessary force to defend themselves. The test is reasonable force. An attack is not a licence to respond with unrestrained violence. Of course, the experience of the person being attacked will be taken into account in determining what is reasonable. Thus, a boxer is held to a higher standard than an ordinary person not accustomed to such violence. When a bouncer ejects an unruly patron from a bar, the same principle applies. If a patron refuses to leave when asked, he becomes a trespasser, and reasonable force can be used to eject him. But as seen in Case Summary 3.1, use of excessive force may result in liability on the part of the occupier of the premises.

Reasonable force permitted to defend self

Reasonable force permitted to eject trespasser

Trespass to Land

Trespass to land involves going onto another person's property without having either the lawful right or the owner's permission to do so. Such a trespass is an actionable wrong, even when no damage or injury takes place, and even if the intruder does not know she is trespassing. Ignorance of the location of the property line is no excuse. Only if the intruder had no control of where she was would there be a defence. Thus, if she were struck by a car and thrown on the property, there would be no trespass. But if she were running away and went on the property to escape a threat, it is still a trespass and she would be responsible for any damage caused. A mere "bruising of the grass" is trespass; but if only nominal damages are likely, why sue? In some provinces, legislation has been passed enabling occupiers to have trespassers apprehended and fined.[18]

On land without authority

People acting in an official capacity, such as postal workers, meter readers, municipal inspectors, and the police, have the right to come on private property and are not trespassing. In shopping malls and other premises where the public is welcome, visitors have an implied right to be there even when they have not come to shop. Permission is also implied when visitors have been allowed on the property over time without steps being taken to remove them. If such visitors become unruly or dangerous to other patrons, they can be asked to leave. In fact, visitors can be required to leave even though they have done nothing wrong, so long as the reason does not violate human rights legislation (such as refusing entry to

---

[16] When for religious reasons parents refuse treatment needed to save the lives of their children, the courts are often willing to interfere by taking custody of the children away from the parents and ordering treatment. See *B. (R.) v. Children's Aid Society of Metropolitan Toronto*,[1988] O.J. No. 78 (C.A.).

[17] Patients now can indicate what treatment they do and do not consent to by creating an advance directive in the form of a Personal Directive. See Alberta's *Personal Directives Act*, R.S.A. 2000. c. P-6, as an example of legislation validating these directives.

[18] See Alberta's *Petty Trespass Act,* R.S.A. 2000, c. P-11, and *Trespass to Premises Act*, R.S.A. 2000, c. T-7, both of which enable the arrest without warrant of individuals caught trespassing. Fines range from $2000 to $5000 (for subsequent violations).

persons based on their race or religion).[19] If visitors refuse to leave, they become trespassers, and reasonable force can be used to eject them.

REDUCING RISK 3.1

The importance of careful training of employees with respect to how they interact with customers and the public cannot be overemphasized. To protect the business from the possibility of devastating lawsuits, employees must know what they can and cannot do when faced with shoplifting, fraud, and other improper conduct. The courts may be somewhat sympathetic to the plight of businesses when faced with the considerable losses caused by shoplifting, fraud, and other wrongs committed by customers, but people who have done nothing wrong must be protected from assault, intimidation, or improper restraint. The damages awarded are based not only on what the employee has done but also on the plaintiff's status in the community and any injury or humiliation suffered. For example, in the *Osz* case, a 16-year-old struck a city bus with a snowball, splattering the defendant driver with snow. The driver stopped the bus, confronted the teen, hit him twice in the face, breaking the teen's nose, and then kicked him. In addition to suffering a painful and debilitating injury, the plaintiff suffered the embarrassment and indignity of being throttled in the presence of his friends. He was awarded general, special, and punitive damages exceeding $10 000, for which the City of Calgary, as the driver's employer, was vicariously liable. Quite a price to pay for losing one's cool!

Trespass can also occur indirectly. When a person throws some item on another's property, or erects a sign without the occupier's permission, a trespass has taken place. Trespass can also involve a permanent incursion onto the property of another. This is referred to as a **continuing trespass** and can take the form of a building or other structure that encroaches on the property of another. The remedy requested would likely include an injunction. Where multi-storeyed buildings are involved, the costs of correcting the problem can be enormous. Of course, consent (in the form of permission to come onto the property or build the encroaching structure), if there has been full disclosure, will be a complete defence to an action for trespass.

CASE SUMMARY 3.2

Trespassers Present Without Lawful Right: *Costello v. Calgary (City)*[20]

The Costello family owned a property on which a 10-unit motel was situated. They applied for a development permit seeking to build a 40-unit motel on that site, but the application approval was delayed because the city wanted to expropriate the land for a roadway interchange. The subject lands were expropriated in 1972 and leased to a third party. The Costellos opposed the expropriation, and in 1983 the Supreme Court of Canada ruled the expropriation illegal and invalid. The Costellos then commenced an action for trespass against the city.

[19.] See *Russo v. Ontario Jockey Club*, [1987] O.J. No. 1105, where a private racetrack was able to exclude a gambler from the premises simply because she was very successful.

[20.] [1995] A.J. No. 27 (Q.B.), varied [1997] A.J. 888 (C.A.), leave to appeal refused, [1997] S.C.C.A. No. 566.

The trial Court found the city liable and awarded damages. (The subsequent appeal was dismissed, and leave to appeal to the S.C.C. was refused.) The Court held that a trespass occurs if an authority takes possession of land pursuant to an expropriation that is subsequently determined to be invalid. The fact that the city did not intend to commit the tort was not a defence. Neither mistaken belief of fact or lawful authority, nor the absence of fault, operates as a defence in the trespass context.

The trial Judge correctly assessed damages on the basis that the Costellos would have developed a 40-unit motel on the property. Damages were calculated to place the plaintiffs in the position they would have enjoyed had the city not committed the wrong. Damages of $572 265 were awarded to reflect the profits the family would have earned from the proposed 40-unit motel. Additionally, $518 295 in interest plus solicitor and client costs were awarded. The case emphasizes the care that parties must exercise before taking possession of or entering another's property.

DISCUSSION QUESTION

In this case it was clear that neither the good intentions of the parties nor their understanding of the facts or the law amounted to an excuse. Do you think that these factors should be given more consideration in a trespass or other tort action?

Trespassers who cause damage while on private property bear responsibility for any injury or loss caused. This is the case whether injury was foreseeable or not. But what if the trespasser is the one injured? Under common law, the injured trespasser generally has no claim against the occupier. Provincial occupiers' liability legislation generally reiterates this rule, requiring only that the occupier of property not wilfully or recklessly cause harm to a trespasser or someone on the property for a criminal purpose. A greater duty is owed, however, to minors who trespass. If it is foreseeable that minors who trespass may be harmed, a duty may arise to take reasonable steps to ensure reasonable safety.

Occupiers' liability legislation

Trespass to Chattels, Conversion, and Detinue

There are three torts that deal with the wrongful interference with goods. The decision to assert one tort and not another may impact the remedies available. Any direct intentional interference causing damage to the goods of another is a **trespass to chattels**. Generally, the remedy for trespass to chattels is compensatory damages. When vandals smash the windshield of a car or kick the door in, they have committed trespass to chattels and are liable to pay compensation and possibly punitive damages to the victim. They may also face criminal charges.

Trespass to chattels actionable

Conversion involves one person's intentionally appropriating the goods of another person for her own purposes. In addition to being crimes, theft of goods or acquiring possession of goods through deceit are also actionable under the tort of conversion. Conversion takes place when someone sells or otherwise wrongfully disposes of goods belonging to someone else. When goods are damaged or destroyed to the extent that they are no longer of any value to the rightful owner, the wrongdoer should have to pay the market value at the time of the tort.

Conversion actionable

Conversion involves defendant treating plaintiff's goods as his own

In essence, conversion consists of interference with the plaintiff's chattels in such a way that a forced sale is justified. In such circumstances the person converting the goods is forced to purchase them. In exchange for payment, the defendant acquires the property. The courts also have the power to order the return of the goods if that is a more appropriate remedy.

Unfortunately for the unsophisticated buyer, if one purchases an item from someone other than the true owner, one may later be sued by the rightful owner for conversion. The court may require the buyer to return the goods to the rightful owner, or pay damages equal to the market value of the goods when misappropriated. In the end, the buyer may end up paying the price twice—once to the seller who misrepresented ownership, and secondly to the true owner.

Refusal to return goods enables owner to assert detinue

The third tort involving wrongful interference with goods is called **detinue**. Like conversion, it involves the wrongful possession of someone else's goods. But where conversion requires wrongfully taking control of the goods through some intentional act, detinue deals with situations where the person is wrongfully retaining the goods. The defendant may have come into possession of them legally but is now, after a proper request, refusing to return them. As the name of the tort suggests, it is the wrongful detention that gives the plaintiff the ability to sue. For example, if Rick lends Henry his lawnmower and Henry refuses to return it, Rick could bring an action in detinue for compensation. Like conversion, the calculation of damages essentially amounts to a forced sale of the goods, but since detinue is a continuing tort, damages are calculated as at the date of the trial. This distinction proved to be very significant in the *Steiman* case, below.

CASE SUMMARY 3.3

Expensive Selection of Cause of Action: *Steiman v. Steiman*[21]

In this dispute, the defendants were found liable in conversion for taking the plaintiffs' jewellery. Damages were assessed at $186 787 on the basis of the value of the jewellery at the time of trial. The defendants appealed, arguing that the proper date of valuation was 1976, as that was when the loss or taking occurred.

Since the action was framed in the tort of conversion, the plaintiffs were claiming the money value of the goods wrongfully taken. The Court determined that a wrongdoer who destroys a chattel is bound to pay only that amount which will cover the cost of replacing the chattel at the time of the tort (or a reasonable time thereafter) plus loss of use limited to the period of time required to find a replacement.

Had the plaintiffs claimed in detinue instead of conversion, the Court would have been able to order return of the goods or payment of their value at the time of trial. In detinue the plaintiff has a continuing cause of action arising out of the wrongful refusal of the defendant to deliver up the goods. However, in detinue, the plaintiff runs the risk of a falling market and of depreciation in value. In this case, however, the plaintiffs would have been better off to sue in detinue, as the value of the property had appreciated.

---

21. [1982] M.J. No. 21 (C.A.).

SMALL BUSINESS PERSPECTIVE

Examine scenarios where a claim in detinue might arise. For example, if an employer decides to keep the work or project a terminated employee has been working on, might the employee sue in detinue for the return of their intellectual property? What might be done to preclude any such claims by disgruntled employees?

False Imprisonment

False imprisonment, including false arrest, occurs when people are intentionally restrained against their will and the person doing the restraining has no lawful authority to do so. This may be in the form of complete imprisonment, where the person is held in a cell or room, or in the form of an arrest. In either case, the person's liberty to go where he pleases must be totally restrained. Even a person who submits to authority or threat can be considered imprisoned, since in his mind he has been restrained. The second requirement is that the restraint be unlawful. When a security guard arrests someone found shoplifting, there has been no false imprisonment. Generally, a private person has the power to make an arrest, but only when she finds someone in the process of actually committing a crime, such as shoplifting.

A citizen's powers of arrest are set out in section 494 of the *Criminal Code*.[22]

> 494. (1) Any one may arrest without warrant
>
> > (*a*)   a person whom he finds committing an indictable offence; or
> >
> > (*b*)   a person who, on reasonable grounds, he believes
> >
> > > (i) has committed a criminal offence, and
> > >
> > > (ii) is escaping from and freshly pursued by persons who have lawful authority to arrest that person.
>
> (2) Any one who is
>
> > (*a*)   the owner or a person in lawful possession of property, or
> >
> > (*b*)   a person authorized by the owner or by a person in lawful possession of property, may arrest without warrant a person whom he finds committing a criminal offence on or in relation to that property.
>
> (3) Any one other than a peace officer who arrests a person without warrant shall forthwith deliver the person to a peace officer.

A charge of false imprisonment is a significant risk for any business involved in serving the public. This risk is great when, either because of store policy or inexperienced staff, customers are detained whenever they are suspected of wrongdoing. If the customer has not in fact stolen any goods, there is no justification for holding him. A manager will often discourage their employees from apprehending shoplifters, since the potential loss from goods stolen is far outweighed by the danger of losing a false-imprisonment action. Of course, this may encourage more shoplifting. The answer is to carefully select and train security people to deal with these matters and have the other employees only inform the security people of what they observe. Case Summary 3.4 on the next page demonstrates the difficulties a retail store or other business may encounter should its security guards be overzealous.

Restraint without lawful excuse—false imprisonment

Submission to authority can constitute imprisonment

Damage awards for false imprisonment can be significant

[22.] *R.S.C. 1985 c. C-46, s. 494.*

CASE SUMMARY 3.4

Employer Pays for Loss of Temper: *Chopra v. Eaton (T.) Co.*[23]

The plaintiff, Mr. Chopra, went to Eaton's department store seeking a refund. An argument ensued. Mr. Frauenfeld (from security) told Chopra that he would have to leave; Frauenfeld took Chopra's elbow and started to escort him out of the store. Chopra protested but did not create a disturbance. Near the doors, Chopra pushed Frauenfeld away, presumably wishing to go through the doors unassisted. Frauenfeld reacted quickly and violently, putting Chopra into a headlock. Chopra's glasses were knocked off and his lip was cut; he was handcuffed, detained in the security office, and subjected to racial slurs. Chopra asked to leave, asked to call his wife, and asked Frauenfeld to call the police; all of these requests were refused. After Chopra had been detained for four hours or more, the police arrived and charged Chopra with assaulting Frauenfeld and causing a disturbance. Chopra was subsequently acquitted of both charges.

Chopra's complaint to the Alberta Human Rights Commission and his civil action against Eaton's were both successful. The Court awarded damages totalling $38 000 against Frauenfeld and vicariously against Eaton's.

The Court found that once Chopra was told he would have to leave the store, he did not resist. Thus, Chopra never became a trespasser against whom reasonable force could be justified. But Chopra did push Frauenfeld, which constituted an assault, albeit a nominal one, contrary to section 265 of the *Criminal Code*. This offence gave lawful authority to the initial arrest and detention. But the failure to deliver the party arrested to the police forthwith transformed an initially lawful imprisonment into an unlawful one. In addition, the amount of force used by Frauenfeld in restraining Chopra was excessive, constituting an unjustified battery against Chopra. Since the arrest was made while Frauenfeld was acting within the scope of his employment, Eaton's was held vicariously liable for the damages awarded.

SMALL BUSINESS PERSPECTIVE

What instructions should businesses give to their security personnel in light of the tort of false imprisonment? If a cost benefit analysis is conducted, one might conclude that it only makes sense to detain a customer if one has solid proof that a crime has been committed.

Malicious Prosecution

Malicious prosecution available where charges unjustifiably laid

Sometimes the criminal justice system is improperly used. When this happens, the victim may be able to sue for the tort of **malicious prosecution**. The defendant in the tort action must have initiated a criminal or quasi-criminal prosecution in which the accused was subsequently acquitted of the charge or the prosecution was abandoned. In addition, the plaintiff must establish that the prosecution was motivated by malice and that there were no reasonable grounds to proceed with the criminal action in the first place. Successful malicious prosecution actions

---

[23.] (1999), 240 A.R. 201 (Q.B.).

may involve prosecutors who have chosen to ignore important evidence or complainants who have lied or manufactured evidence used to improperly support the charges.

An interesting example of a successful claim for malicious prosecution involved a patron at a restaurant who disputed his obligation to pay for liquor. He had been served the drinks but couldn't consume them before they had to be removed from the table under provincial liquor law.[24] The patron was detained and held for the police. When the police arrived he was arrested, charged under the *Criminal Code* with fraudulently obtaining food, and imprisoned. There was no basis for the criminal charge as this was at worst a civil dispute between the parties. The restaurant owner and police were liable for false arrest, but the restaurant owner was also liable for malicious prosecution. The complaint that led to the charge was initiated at his request. There was no basis for the charge, and it was dismissed for want of prosecution. The fact that threat of criminal charges was used to pressure the patron to pay for the drinks provided was enough to constitute malice. All the elements required for malicious prosecution were thus established.

CASE SUMMARY 3.5

Suppression of Evidence Establishes Malicious Prosecution: *McNeil v. Brewers Retail Inc.*[25]

The employer, Brewers Retail Inc. (BRI) fired McNeil from his job for allegedly stealing $160 from the till. BRI handed over surveillance tapes to the police that incriminated McNeil, but suppressed parts of the tapes that would have exonerated him. Initially McNeil was convicted, but these convictions were quashed on appeal. McNeil commenced a civil action and was awarded over two million dollars in aggravated and punitive damages.

The Court of Appeal upheld the award finding that all four elements of malicious prosecution were established, namely:

1. the proceedings must have been commenced by the defendant;
2. the criminal proceedings must have been terminated in favour of the plaintiff;
3. there must have been an absence of reasonable and probable cause; and
4. there must be malice (or a primary purpose other than that of carrying the law into effect).

SMALL BUSINESS PERSPECTIVE

The jury awarded $100 000 for general damages, $188 000 for aggravated damages $500 000 in punitive damages, $240 000 in pecuniary damages for future loss of income, and $308 000 in special damages for past loss of income and legal expenses. The Court of Appeal found that the award of damages, while generous, was not in error. Do awards such as this deter others from being less than honest with the police?

[24.] *Perry et al. v. Fried et* al. (1972), 32 D.L.R. (3d) 589 (N.S.S.C. Trial Div.). Also see *Bahner v. Marwest Hotel Co.* (1969), 6 D.L.R (3D) 322 (B.C.S.C.); aff'd (1970), 12 D.L.R. (3d) 646 (B.C.C.A.) where the facts were very similar. False imprisonment was established as against both the restaurant and the police.

[25.] [2008] O.J. No. 1990 (C.A.).

Private Nuisance

Private nuisance—use of property interferes with neighbour

The tort of **private nuisance** is committed when an individual or business uses property in such a way that it interferes with a neighbour's use or enjoyment of her property. Such interference is usually ongoing and continuous. When a commercial building, such as a mill, is built near a residential neighbourhood, and the resulting odour and noise interfere with the neighbours' enjoyment of their yards, it is appropriate for them to sue for nuisance. Such an action is possible only where the property is being used in an unusual or unreasonable way and the problem caused is a direct consequence of this unusual activity. A person living in an industrial section of a city cannot complain when a factory begins operating in the neighbourhood and emits noise, smoke, and dust. Nor could the residents of a rural area complain about the normal odours associated with farming. But if the odours create a significant disturbance, far beyond what one would expect from farming operations, liability may follow. For example, in the *Pyke* case the plaintiff's complaint stemmed from odours emanating from the composting phase of the defendant's mushroom farm.[26] The odours were described in graphic terms, including: "nauseating and like rotten flesh," "worse than a pig farm," and "like an outhouse, ammonia, sour, putrid, rotten vegetables." The Court considered the proximity of the neighbours and the fact that the plaintiffs were there first. The degree and intensity of the disturbance exceeded that of a "normal farm practice" and thus damages exceeding $260 000 were awarded.

Private nuisance at a distance

Normally, the properties would need to be in close proximity for private nuisance to apply and for a nuisance action to be brought. However, in an Alberta case a telephone was used to harass people on the other side of the city, interfering with the enjoyment of their property. The Court found this to be a private nuisance, even though the two parties were kilometres apart.[27]

For a private nuisance to be actionable, the consequences must be reasonably foreseeable to the defendant. Reasonable foreseeability will be discussed in the following chapter, but essentially it requires that an ordinary, prudent person, in the same circumstances, would have anticipated the risk. Because nuisance often involves offending substances, it is one of the few common law tools that can be used to enforce environmental protection. In *St. Lawrence Cement Inc. v. Barrette*,[28] the Supreme Court of Canada discussed the common law of environmental nuisance and held that the term *neighbour* must be construed liberally. Residents in the greater Quebec City area who endured dust, smoke, and noise pollution generated by the cement plant during the 1990s were awarded damages despite the fact that St. Lawrence Cement spent more than $8 million to collect the dust emitted by its plant. Liability was nonetheless imposed because neighbours had been exposed to excessive and abnormal annoyances, contrary to art. 976 of the *Civil Code of Quebec*.

---

26. *Pyke v. TRI GRO Enterprises Ltd.* (2001), 55 O.R. (3d) 257 (Ont. C.A.), leave to appeal to S.C.C. refused, [2001] S.C.C.A. No. 493.

27. *Motherwell v. Motherwell* (1976), 1 A.R. 47, 73 D.L.R. (3d) 62 (C.A.).

28. [2008] S.C.J. No. 65.

CASE SUMMARY 3.6

Golf Balls Destroy Enjoyment of Property: *Carley v. Willow Park Golf Course Ltd.*[29]; *Cattell v. Great Plains Leaseholds Ltd.*[30]

The Carleys purchased their home, which was next to the Willow Park Golf Course, about 28 years after the golf course and driving range were constructed. Golf balls from the driving range regularly landed in their yard, making it impossible for them to use their backyard for fear of being hit. Over the years the golf course had taken steps to solve the problem, building several fences and placing nets to stop the balls, but the errant golf balls raining down on their property and those of their neighbours persisted.

They knew of the driving range when they bought their home but were also aware of a 90-foot net and assumed that kept any balls from falling on their property. While some errant golf balls had to be expected living next to a golf course, the Judge at one point characterized this as a "barrage."

The Court found that the driving range constituted a private nuisance. A private nuisance is present when property is used in such a way as to unreasonably interfere with a neighbour's interest in the beneficial use of his or her land. The "bombardment" of golf balls from the driving range constituted such an interference. "No use of property is reasonable which causes substantial discomfort to others or is a source of damage to their property."[31]

The Court ordered damages of $2500, but more importantly a permanent injunction was issued against the golf course ordering it to prevent people using the driving range from hitting balls onto the Carleys' property.

Similarly, in the *Cattell* case, a barrage of misdirected golf balls emanating from the ninth hole of the Emerald Park Golf Course created a nuisance for the plaintiff homeowners. At trial, a permanent injunction was granted, restraining the golf course, its members, their guests, or any other users of the golf course from hitting golf balls on the ninth hole of the course so that they landed anywhere on the plaintiffs' property! This time, the remedies were appealed. The injunction was replaced with an order allowing use of the ninth hole—with conditions.

SMALL BUSINESS PERSPECIVTE

What remedy do you think might be more problematic? A one-time award of damages or an injunction preventing a particular use? Findings of private nuisance have been made in several cases with similar circumstances to these, where injunctions have likewise been granted. From the plaintiff's perspective, obtaining an order to stop the offending conduct may well be the preferred solution, but this could be problematic for the defendant.

[29.] [2002] A.J. No. 1174 (Q.B.).

[30.] [2008] S.J. No. 347 (Sask. C.A.)

[31.] *Carley v. Willow Park Golf Course Ltd.,supran.* 21;para. 27, citing Lewis N. Klar, *Tort Law*, Carswell 2nd edition, at 535.

It should also be noted that private nuisance as discussed here is different from **public nuisance**. Only rarely is an action for public nuisance brought and then usually by the government. A public nuisance takes place when some public property is interfered with. Protesters blocking a road or park, or a mill polluting a river, would be examples. The Supreme Court of Canada found that such a public nuisance had occurred when a forest company in British Columbia allowed a controlled burn to escape.[32] The resulting forest fire caused damage to environmentally sensitive streams and the Attorney General of that province brought an action for public nuisance against the company. The Supreme Court adopted the language of an earlier decision, stating, "any activity which unreasonably interferes with the public's interest in questions of health, safety, morality, comfort or convenience" is capable of constituting a public nuisance.[33] Note that a private individual can bring an action of public nuisance only if able to show that the conduct harmed him or her particularly and more than other members of the general public.

Defamation

Defamation: derogatory, false, and published

Defamation is a published false statement that is to a person's detriment. It is a primary concern for businesses involved in media communications, but all commercial enterprises face some risk over defamation, even if it is only from a carelessly worded letter of reference. For the statement to be an actionable defamation, it must be derogatory, false, and published, and must refer to the plaintiff. If the false statement causes people to avoid or shun someone, it is derogatory. In the *Youssoupoff* case, Lord Justice Scrutton said that a statement was defamatory if it was "a false statement about a man to his discredit."[34] A complimentary statement about a person, even if it is false, is not defamation. Thus, if a manager were to say of an employee that he was the best worker in the plant, it would not be defamation even if false. Once the plaintiff establishes that the derogatory statement was made, he need not prove it was false. This is assumed, and it is up to the defendant to prove it true if he can. If the statement can be shown to be true, it is an absolute defence to a defamation action.[35]

Member of group defamed may not be personally defamed

For a statement to be actionable, it must be clear that it refers to the person suing. Thus, a general negative reference to a group,[36] such as the faculty or student body of a university, will not qualify. It is not possible to defame a dead person; however, it is possible to defame a corporation, which is a person in the eyes of the law, and it is possible to defame a product. (See the discussion of product defamation, trade slander, and injurious falsehood, below.)

---

32. *British Columbia v. Canadian Forest Products Ltd.*, [2004] S.C.J. No. 33.

33. *Ryan v. Victoria (City)*, [1999] 1 S.C.R. 201 (S.C.C.), at para. 52.

34. *Youssoupoff v. Metro-Goldwyn-Mayer Pictures Ltd.* (1934), 50 T.L.R. 581 at 584 (C.A.).

35. *Elliott v. Freisen et al.* (1982), 136 D.L.R. (3d) 281 (Ont. H.C.) aff'd (1984), 6 D.L.R. (4th) 388 (Ont. C.A.); leave to appeal refused (1984), 6 D.L.R. (4th) 388 n (S.C.C.).

36. In *Diffusion Metromedia CMR inc. c. Bou Malhab*, [2008] J.Q. no 10048, the Quebec Court of Appeal dismissed a group defamation action brought against a shock radio host who made negative racist comments against taxi drivers of Arab and Haitian descent. The Court found that because the statements did not target any specific individuals, individual members could not claim their reputation had been damaged by comments aimed at large groups. A group defamed by racist comments may, however, file a complaint under human rights legislation.

Further, the false statement must be published. In this sense, "to publish" means that the statement had to be communicated to a third party. Publication could have occurred in a newspaper, in the broadcast media, on the internet, or simply by word of mouth. It is sufficient publication if just one person other than the plaintiff hears or reads the defamatory statement.

In those situations where legislation does not specifically restrict damages payable, the damages for defamation can be substantial. The courts not only will compensate the victim for actual losses as well as for a damaged reputation, but will go further, awarding damages to rehabilitate the victim's reputation. For this reason, the Supreme Court of Canada upheld a decision to award a Crown prosecutor defamed by a church $1.6 million in damages—far in excess of what would be awarded for general damages in a normal tort action.[37] Justice Cory stated that, unlike non-pecuniary losses in personal injury cases, general damages in defamation are not capped.

Statement must be published

Significant damages available

CASE SUMMARY 3.7

Pricey Condemnation: *WeGo Kayaking Ltd. v. Sewid*[38]

Imagine discovering that a competitor has posted defamatory statements about your businesses on the internet! WeGo Kayaking Ltd. and Northern Lights Expeditions Ltd. brought a defamation action against the defendant Sewid after reading statements posted on villageisland.com. The Plaintiffs offered kayak tours in the vicinity of Vancouver Island and relied heavily on the internet to attract customers. Sewid operated a water taxi service and had provided services for the guides and clients of the plaintiffs in 2003 and 2004. Following his termination, Sewid went into competition with the plaintiffs and posted the following on the web:

Bad Kayak Companies

These are the companies that arenot looked at favourably. They are ones that have done things to try and make First Nations become token Indians who are only needed as items of attraction or convenience. There may be some environmental concerns with their operating practices as well . . .

Fifteen businesses were rated as good kayak companies and the plaintiffs were among the three businesses listed as bad kayak companies. Sewid refused to remove the plaintiffs from the bad list and refused to apologize. He also claimed that the statements on the website were protected by the defence of fair comment. That defence failed because the statements were presented as facts rather than as comments based on true facts; further, the statements were motivated by malice. Evidence that Sewid had published the bad companies list to punish the plaintiffs for not continuing to do business with him, and evidence suggesting he also wanted to remove the competition, supported the finding of malice. WeGo was awarded general damages of $100 000; Northern Lights recovered general damages of $150 000. The Court determined that general damages were not sufficient, and awarded the plaintiffs punitive damages of $2500 and $5000, respectively.

[37.] *Hill v. Church of Scientology of Toronto*, [1995] 2 S.C.R. 1130.

[38.] [2007] B.C.J. No. 56 (B.C.S.C.)

SMALL BUSINESS PERSPECTIVE

This decision suggests that damage awards granted to corporations are getting larger. Earlier case law suggested that a corporation's reputation deserved less protection. *Jameel v. Wall Street Journal Europe SPRL*, [2006] UKHL 44, confirms that all plaintiffs, be they corporations or real persons, are to be treated equally in the assessment of damages.

Innuendo

Mistake no excuse

Statements often contain **innuendo**, which is an implied or hidden meaning. A statement may appear perfectly innocent on the surface, but when combined with other information it may take on a more sinister meaning. It is no excuse to say that the person making the statement thought it was true or did not know of the special facts that created the innuendo. Such a mistake is no defence, and the offending party can be held liable for the defamatory remark. Innuendoes in the form of suggested inferences can be actionable, as the CBC discovered in the *Leenen* case. During a *Fifth Estate* episode, the CBC called into question the plaintiff doctor's honesty and integrity. The program implied that the doctor and research scientist was in a conflict of interest, receiving payoffs from a pharmaceutical company and prescribing "killer drugs." By presenting an unbalanced view of the issue, the audience was lead to draw negative inferences.

Many concerns related to the internet can be examined in the context of topics discussed in this course and applied to this new medium of communication. Because the internet provides direct and inexpensive access to a massive audience, torts that involve the communicating of statements such as deceit, negligent misstatement, and defamation[39] are primary concerns. Contributing to the problem is the absence of an intervener (editor or publisher) to monitor the communication; people can say whatever they want, however they want to say it. The communication may be individual-to-individual (email) or published on a broader scale, such as in chat rooms, through Facebook, or posted on websites generally.

Defamation on the internet—is it libel or slander?

Where the communication is found to be defamatory, the first question to be determined is which rules will apply. Is defamation over the internet libel or slander? As is evident from the *Bahlieda* case,[40] even answering this question is complex. Placing material on the internet, via a website, where it may be accessed by a large audience, has been likened to broadcasting information on television or radio. The Ontario Court of Appeal, however, held that a genuine issue for trial did exist with respect to whether material placed on a website and made available through the internet is "broadcast." That issue is significant because if communication over the web qualifies as broadcasting, provincial legislation concerning

---

[39] See *Hay v. Partridge*, [2004] Nu.J. No. 9 (Ct. J.), where two staff at a correctional facility were sued by their supervisor for defamation, over a newsletter circulated and posted to the internet. Use of the internet was considered an aggravating factor, thus both general and aggravated damages were awarded.

[40] See *Bahlieda v. Santa* (2003), 68 O.R. (3d) 115 (C.A.).

libel rather than slander may apply. One might ask, should the size of the audience make a difference? If the communication is between two individuals, as in an email message, will a defamatory message be considered libel or slander? A definitive answer to these questions is still not available.

Another problem relates to whom an injured party can sue. If the author is known and lives in the same jurisdiction there is little difficulty, but where the author is unknown, uses a false name, or resides in another jurisdiction with different rules, where does one sue? If one doesn't have access to the author, can one sue the service provider (ISP) or website operator for defamation? What happens where an offensive email is intercepted and sent to others? It is now clear that an ISP can be forced to disclose the sources of such material,[41] but even that may not be helpful where they are in a different jurisdiction or without resources. It is likely that these intermediaries will be liable for the defamation only if they encouraged the offending behaviour, or if they knew or ought to have known of it and failed to remove it after notification.[42]

ISP can be forced to disclose source

ISP will be liable only where it fails to remove after notification

---

CASE SUMMARY 3.8

When Will a Court Hear a Case Involving Defamation on the Internet? *Dow Jones v. Gutnick;*[43] *Young v. New Haven Advocate;*[44] *Bangoura v. Washington Post;*[45] *Burke v. NYP Holdings, Inc.*[46]

Two foreign cases illustrate the problems when dealing with defamation over the internet. In the *Dow Jones* case, Gutnick sued in Australia, where he resided, for defamation in an article published by Dow Jones over the internet, originating in New Jersey. The High Court agreed with Gutnick that since the article was read and the damage to his reputation was done in Australia, Australia was the appropriate place to sue. But in *Young v. New Haven Advocate*, a U.S. appeal court decided essentially the opposite. Young, a prison warden residing and working in Virginia, brought an action in that state against the *New Haven Advocate* for publishing a defamatory article over the internet, originating in Connecticut. The Court held that the fact that the defamed person lived and worked in Virginia and his reputation was damaged there was not enough. There also had to be some evidence that the offending party did something to focus on Virginia readers (targeting), and since this wasn't proven, the Court declined to take jurisdiction.

---

41. *Irwin Toy Ltd. v. Doe* (2000), 12 C.P.C. (5th) 103 (Ont. S.C.). But see *BMG Canada Inc. v. John Doe*, [2005] F.C.A. 193, where the plaintiff sought an equitable "bill of discovery" (a form of pre-action discovery) to compel an ISP to assist by providing information, namely the identities of the file sharers downloading music. That request was denied. The court rationalized that there could be no disclosure of a document that did not exist—there was no actual document listing the file sharer's identities and the pseudonyms they used for their IP addresses.

42. See *Society of Composers, Authors and Music Publishers of Canada v. Canadian Association of Internet Providers*, [2004] 2 S.C.R. 427. This case was concerned with copyright law, but the ISPs argued that they should be likened to a postal service and should not be liable for material transmitted by them. The Supreme Court of Canada accepted this position. It appears that ISPs will not be held liable for torts committed over the internet so long as their activities are restricted to the transmission of information.

43. [2002] H.C.A. 56 (H.C.A.).

44. 315 F.3d 256 (4th Cir. 2002).

45. [2005] O.J. No. 3849 (C.A.).

46. [2005] B.C.J. No. 1993 (S.C.).

Courts in Canada appear to be following the *Gutnick* rationale by focusing on the connections with the jurisdiction rather than on whether readers in a jurisdiction were targeted. In the *Bangoura* case, the *Washington Post* published articles online, alleging that Bangoura's colleagues accused him of financial improprieties and harassment during his posting with the U.N. in the Ivory Coast. Bangoura later moved to Ontario and commenced an action there—more than six years after the publication of the articles. Because the connection between Ontario and the plaintiff's claim was minimal at best, the Ontario courts refused to assume jurisdiction

However, in *Burke v. NYP Holdings, Inc.*, the general manager of the Vancouver Canucks was able to pursue a defamation action against the *New York Post* in British Columbia. Burke established a real and substantial connection within British Columbia. Although the *New York Post* published the article on its American website, the material was read in British Columbia and that was where Burke claimed to have suffered damage to his reputation.

The key to a court assuming jurisdiction is evidently the number and strength of the connecting factors between the cause of action and the jurisdiction.

Where several connecting factors exist, Canadian courts thus appear willing to assume jurisdiction. In the *Warman v. Fromm* case,[47] the defendants admitted to posting defamatory articles on different websites hosted by servers in United States and reposted material to other sites by way of email sent to a large distribution list. The Court awarded the plaintiff $20 000 in general damages and $10 000 in aggravated damages. The mode and extent of publication, absence of retraction or apology, and malicious conduct and motive of Fromm impacted the award of damages.

When determining damages, the size of the audience has been regarded as relevant, as in *Ross v. Holley*.[48] Holley emailed statements about an archeologist, accusing her of grave robbing. Ross was awarded general ($75 000) and aggravated damages ($50 000) as Holley urged recipients to republish. Similarly, in *Barrick Gold Corp. v. Lopehandia*,[49] the defendant made hundreds of internet postings accusing Barrick of fraud, tax evasion, money laundering, and genocide. On appeal, Barrick was awarded $75 000 in general damages, $50 000 in punitive damages, and a permanent injunction. The Court considered the internet's unique ability to cause instantaneous and irreparable harm.

Libel and Slander

Slander spoken/ Libel written

Defamation can be either **slander**, which is spoken defamation, or **libel**, which is usually written defamation. The significance of finding a defamatory remark to be libelous rather than slanderous is that libel is easier to prove because there is no requirement to show that special damages have been sustained. Libel is seen to be more deliberate, more premeditated, and also more permanent than slander, thus causing more harm. However, modern means of mass communication give slander a potentially huge audience, so the rationale for distinguishing between

---

47. [2007] O.J. No. 4754 (Ont. S.C.).
48. [2004] O.J. No. 4643 (Sup. Ct. J.).
49. (2004), 71 O.R. (3d) 416 (C.A.).

libel and slander is breaking down. In fact, this distinction has been eliminated altogether in some provinces, while in others, legislation has simply declared that all broadcast defamation will constitute libel whether spoken or written.

While defamation is primarily governed by common law, most provinces have passed statutes modifying those common law provisions in light of the needs of a modern society. Should defamation by the media occur, for example, legislation may reduce the damages plaintiffs can claim where material was published in good faith. If the publisher shows that the damage was done by mistake or misapprehension of the facts, and a full apology or retraction has been made, damages may be restricted to special damages (the actual losses and expenses incurred).[50]

These statutes will need even more modification to take into account the new problems associated with defamation on the internet. It is often difficult to trace the original source of defamation in an internet message because it can be so easily copied and transferred by intermediate parties. Nevertheless, the injury caused by such transmission of defamatory information can be extensive. Another problem is that in a traditional communication environment there is usually a broadcaster or publisher that can be held responsible for the damaging words, but in online communication there is often no intermediary who checks and authorizes material, nor is there any clear way of determining just how far a message has been spread or even who wrote it in the first place.

CASE SUMMARY 3.9

Is Posting a Link Publication? *Crookes v. Wikimedia Foundation Inc.*[51]

The plaintiffs claimed they had been defamed in a "smear campaign." A website known as "p2pnet" published an article examining the implication of defamation actions on those who operate internet forums. The author claimed to be interested in freedom of speech. His article contained hyperlinks to other sites, but the operator of p2pnet did not quote any of the alleged defamatory words from those other websites.

The Court concluded that although individuals who read an article containing a reference to another website may go there, this does not make the publisher of the first website the publisher of the material posted on the second site. Since the publisher of the first site did not reproduce any of the disputed content, nor make any comment on the linked material, he could not be deemed a publisher of the derogatory statements.

The issue in this case is not how accessible the website is, but rather, if anyone followed the hyperlinks posted on the p2pnet site. Without proof that persons other than the plaintiff visited the defendant's website, clicked on the hyperlinks, and read the articles complained of, there cannot be a finding of publication.

Justice Kelleher concluded: "In my view, the mere creation of a hyperlink in a website does not lead to a presumption that persons read the contents of the website and used the hyperlink to access the defamatory words." Accordingly, the action was dismissed.

---

50. See, for example, Alberta's *Defamation Act,* R.S.A. 2000, c. D-7, s. 16, or New Brunswick's *Defamation Act,* S.N.B. c. D-5, s. 17.

51. [2008] B.C.J. No. 2012 (B.C.S.C.)

> *DISCUSSION QUESTIONS*
>
> Might the Court have reached a different conclusion if the author of the article had commented on the material contained on the linked site? Justice Kelleher stated: "It is not my decision that hyperlinking can never make a person liable for the contents of the remote site." When might liability be imposed if mere reference to (or hyperlink to) an article containing defamatory content is insufficient to constitute republication?

DEFENCES

Truth is an absolute defence

Once it has been established that a defamatory statement has been made, several defences are available to the defendant. **Truth**, also called the defence of **justification**, is an absolute defence. But even when a statement is technically true, it can still be derogatory if it contains an innuendo or is capable of being interpreted as referring to another person about whom the statement is false. Note also that substantial truth is sufficient. If the defendant claimed that the plaintiff had stolen $300 000 when in fact he had stolen only $250 000, justification would still be an effective defence.

Absolute privilege

The second defence is called **absolute privilege**. Anything discussed as part of parliamentary debate on the floor of the legislature, Parliament, or in government committees, and statements made or documents used as part of a court procedure cannot give rise to a defamation action, no matter how malicious, scandalous, or derogatory they are.

The rationale for this defence is that there are certain forums where, for the good of society, people should be able to exercise freedom of expression without fear of being sued. For example, even statements made to an investigator in the context of a *Human Rights Act* investigation are privileged.[52] Absolute privilege has also been extended to documents used in the process of a complaint before the College of Physicians and Surgeons in British Columbia.[53]

Qualified privilege, requires duty

The most significant defence for businesspeople is called **qualified privilege**. When a statement is made pursuant to a duty or special interest, there is no action for defamation so long as the statement was made honestly and without malice, and was circulated only to those having a right to know. A manager reporting to a superior about the performance of a worker or members of a professional organization describing the performance of an officer of that organization to other members would be instances protected by qualified privilege. When a manager sends a defamatory email specifically to someone with a shared interest in the matter, such as his superior or the particular group of employees he supervises, that may be protected by qualified privilege, but that privilege would be lost if the defamatory message were sent to a website available to everyone. Since anyone could access the website, the publication would be too broad and privilege could no longer be claimed. Thus, in *Egerton v. Finucan,* a community college professor's claim for wrongful dismissal was complicated by the fact that his supervisor sent a highly critical performance evaluation to all the professors in the institution via email. The Court found that the plaintiff had grounds for a defamation suit

---

[52.] *Ayangma v. NAV Canada* (2001), 197 Nfld. & P.E.I.R. 83 (P.E.I.S.C. (A.D.)), leave to appeal to S.C.C. refused, [2001] S.C.C.A. No. 76.

[53.] *Schut v. Magee,* [2003] B.C.J. No. 1689 (B.C.C.A.).

against his superior.[54] Note that when reporting on matters of public interest, newspapers and other media often claim this defence, but it is normally denied them on the grounds that although they claim that they have a duty to report and that the public has a right to know, there is no legal duty on them to report matters to the public and so no qualified privilege.

A further defence available in the field of defamation is the defence of **fair comment**. When people put their work before the public, as with movies, plays, artwork, books, and the like, they invite public criticism and run the risk that the opinions expressed may not be complimentary. Even when these opinions amount to a vicious attack and may be unreasonable, artists cannot sue for defamation. The defence raised here is fair comment. Public figures are also open to such criticism. To successfully use this defence, the critic or editorial writer must be able to show that what was said was a matter of opinion, drawn from true facts that were before the public, and was not motivated by malice or some ulterior motive. A food critic expressing a negative opinion of a restaurant[55] and a theatre critic attacking a play or movie are examples of fair comment. The same defence should apply where a play, photograph, or musical performance is put on the internet and made available to a wide audience.

Fair Comment

CASE SUMMARY 3.10

Freedom of Expression Clashes with Defamation Law: *WIC Radio Ltd. v. Simpson*[55]

Rafe Mair, a sometimes controversial radio talk-show host, tackled Ms. Simpson on the airwaves. Simpson was a widely known social activist who opposed the introduction of materials dealing with homosexuality into public schools. During a WIC Radio editorial broadcast, Mair disagreed with Simpson's views and compared Simpson to Hitler, the Ku Klux Klan, and skinheads. Simpson commenced an action in defamation against Mair and the station.

Mair argued that the purpose of his words was to convey that Simpson was an intolerant bigot, not that she condoned violence against homosexuals as alleged. The Supreme Court of Canada, like the trial Judge, found Mair's editorial defamatory but allowed the defence of fair comment. The action was thus dismissed.

The Supreme Court considered that the evolution of the common law should be informed and guided by *Charter* values. Whereas the tort of defamation aims at protecting a person's reputation, there is also a need to accommodate the value of freedom of expression.

The fair comment defence is consistent with the values of freedom of expression and freedom of the press. Here there was a public debate about the inclusion of educational material on homosexuality in schools. The subject clearly engaged the public interest.

54. *Egerton v. Finucan*, [1995] O.J. No. 1653 (Gen. Div.).

55. Fair comment was successfully raised in *Sara's Pyrohy Hut v. Brooker*, [1993] A.J. No. 185 (C.A.).

56. [2008] S.C.J. No. 41.

The inflammatory words would most likely be understood as comment, rather than fact. Further, the comment satisfied the objective test regarding whether any person could honestly express that opinion on the proved facts. Having regard to the content of some of Simpson's speeches, the defamatory imputation that while Simpson would not engage in violence herself, she would condone violence by others, is an opinion that could honestly have been expressed. The fair comment defence could have been defeated if the comment was actuated by malice, but Simpson failed to establish malice.

DISCUSSION QUESTIONS

Freedom of opinion, freedom of expression, and freedom of the press all seem to conflict with defamation law. What is the appropriate balance to be struck between encouraging such freedoms and protecting one's good name?

Public interest responsible journalism defence

Canada's media may now be able to utilize a new defence, as the Ontario Court of Appeal recognized the public interest responsible journalism defence in *Cusson v. Quan*[57]. Cusson, an OPP constable, voluntarily went to New York City following the September 11 attack on the World Trade Center to assist with rescue operations. Initially, he was portrayed in the media as a hero, but a newspaper later published three negative articles about him. The Court of Appeal would not allow the public interest responsible journalism defence to be relied upon, since it had not been raised at trial. Nonetheless, it agreed that defamation ought to be subject to this defence, in light of freedom of expression. The Court adopted the rationale of the House of Lords in *Reynolds v. Times Newspapers Ltd.*[58], which identified tenfactors that courts might consider in applying the public interest responsible journalism defence:

1. The seriousness of the allegation. The more serious the charge, the more the public is misinformed and the individual harmed, if the allegation is not true.

2. The nature of the information, and the extent to which the subject-matter is a matter of public concern.

3. The source of the information. Some informants have no direct knowledge of the events. Some have their own axes to grind, or are being paid for their stories.

4. The steps taken to verify the information.

5. The status of the information. The allegation may have already been the subject of an investigation that commands respect.

6. The urgency of the matter. News is often a perishable commodity.

7. Whether comment was sought from the plaintiff. He may have information others do not possess or have not disclosed. An approach to the plaintiff will not always be necessary.

---

[57] [2007] O.J. No. 4348 (C.A.).

[58] [1999] 4 All ER 609, [2001] 2 AC 127 (H.L.); www.bailii.org/uk/cases/UKHL/1999/45.html. [2007] O.J. No. 4348 (C.A.).

8. Whether the article contained the gist of the plaintiff's side of the story.

9. The tone of the article. A newspaper can raise queries or call for an investigation. It need not adopt allegations as statements of fact.

10. The circumstances of the publication, including the timing.

This list is not exhaustive. The weight to be given to these and any other relevant factors will vary from case to case.

Thus the media may avoid liability if they act responsibly when reporting on matters of public interest. What remains to be seen, however, is whether non-traditional journalists, such as bloggers and others posting to websites, will be able to seek the benefit of this defence.

Product Defamation (Injurious Falsehood)

Is the goodwill associated with a product entitled to protection, much like the good reputation of a person or corporation? The tort of **injurious falsehood** addresses such a wrong. This tort takes place when one person attacks the reputation of another's product or business. When a person spreads a false rumour that the wine manufactured by a competitor is adulterated with some other substance, or that his business is about to become bankrupt, she has committed an injurious falsehood. Although this tort is often called **trade slander** or **product defamation**, it must be distinguished from the tort of defamation that involves injury to the personal reputation of the injured party. Injurious falsehood deals with the reputation and value of a person's property. It may reflect negatively on the quality of the product, or it may relate to title. When a person falsely claims that the seller does not own what he is selling or that the product is in violation of patent or copyright, he has uttered an actionable injurious falsehood.

Injurious falsehood actionable

CASE SUMMARY 3.11

Unfounded Accusations Can Be Costly: *Procor Ltd. v. U.S.W.A.*[59]

Procor Ltd., a manufacturer that exports much of its product to the United States, was involved in a serious and difficult labour dispute with its employees. In the air of hostility created by the labour dispute, members of the union accused the company of customs fraud, saying that it was exporting Japanese products into the United States (marked as products made in Canada) without disclosing the fact. This caused an intensive and disruptive investigation into the operations of the company, even stopping production for a time. In addition, there was considerable negative publicity. The investigation exonerated the company, showing the union members to be wrong and the accusations to be unfounded. Procor Ltd. then sued for injurious falsehood the union and the members who had made the accusations. These defendants knew, or should have known, that the statements they were making to customs agents were false, thus instigating the investigation.

In addition to the presence of a false statement made to a party causing damage, it is also necessary to establish malice to succeed in an injurious falsehood action. "Malice"

---

59. [1989] O.J. No. 2156 (H.C.J.).

is usually described as a dishonest or improper motive. While the Judge did not find that they lied outright, he did find that the union officials were "willfully blind to the truth" when they made these false statements to the customs officials. That was enough to establish malice. In addition, their motive was not to act as good citizens but to further their labour dispute and vent their frustrations and hostility toward the company. This was an improper purpose supporting the finding of malice. The Judge also found that the defendants had participated in a conspiracy to accomplish these goals and were, as a result, liable to pay $100 000 general damages and a further $100 000 punitive damages. In a society like ours, we have to be careful about what we say about others. This case is an example of the difficulties that a few misplaced words can cause.

DISCUSSION QUESTIONS

Is this sort of thing just what is to be expected in heated labour disputes? Do you think the prospect of tort action further aggravates hostilities between parties such as these?

Successfully Establishing a Tort Claim

When a plaintiff commences a tort action, he bears the burden of establishing each of the required elements or *ingredients* of that tort. Failure to prove an ingredient should result in the action's being dismissed. See Table 3.1 for a simplified list of ingredients for the torts examined thus far.

Table 3.1 Simplified Ingredients for Torts

Assault	1) Deliberate threat creating fear of imminent harm 2) No consent
Battery	1) Deliberate physical interference (contact) with one's body 2) No consent
Trespass to Land	1) Deliberate interference with property 2) No consent/permission/lawful right to be there
Trespass to Chattels	1) Deliberate interference with goods of another 2) No consent
Conversion	1) Deliberate appropriation of the goods of another 2) In such a way that a forced sale is justified.
Detinue	1) Deliberate possession of another's goods 2) Wrongful refusal to return the goods to the owner
False Imprisonment	1) Deliberate restraint 2 Lack of lawful authority
Malicious Prosecution	1) Initiation of prosecution on criminal or quasi-criminal charges 2) Subsequent acquittal of the plaintiff 3) Prosecution was motivated by malice

Private Nuisance	1) Unusual use of property
	2) Interference caused to neighbour's enjoyment/use of property
	3) Foreseeable consequences
Defamation	1) False statements made
	2) Derogatory to the plaintiff's reputation
	3) Publication or communication to a third party
Injurious Falsehood (trade defamation)	1) False statements made
	2) Derogatory to the reputation of the product or service
	3) Publication or communication to a third party

OTHER TORTS IMPACTING BUSINESS

People involved in business activities can find themselves faced with tortious liability for their conduct or the conduct of their employees and agents. Businesses that deal directly with the public, especially in the service industries, such as restaurants, hotels, and retailers, may find their employees becoming involved in altercations with customers in the course of their work. Vicarious liability for assault and battery, negligence, trespass, and even false imprisonment may follow. When business premises visited by customers or the public are involved, there can be actions for negligence based on occupiers' liability.

Intentional torts more common in some businesses

Negligence will be the primary focus of the following chapter. Those providing consulting services to businesses and private individuals, such as bankers, accountants, auditors, lawyers, financial advisers, engineers, and architects, are only a few of the professionals who find themselves increasingly vulnerable to damage actions for both tort and breach of contract.

In addition to the torts already discussed in this chapter, there are other unique torts that can be important to businesses: inducing breach of contract, interference with economic relations, intimidation, deceit, conspiracy, passing-off, breach of confidence, and invasion of privacy. Most of these are associated with unfair or overly aggressive competition.

Inducing breach of contract actionable

CASE SUMMARY 3.12

Cold and Calculated: *Polar Ice Express Inc. v. Arctic Glacier Inc.*[60]

The trial Judge found that the defendant, Arctic Glacier, ambitious to become the sole supplier of ice to many customers in area, used threats and bribery to get customers to stop doing business with the plaintiff, Polar Ice. Arctic Glacier had a virtual monopoly over ice sales in Alberta to grocery stores, liquor stores, service stations, small confectionary stores, and concrete supply companies. Polar Ice, a fledgling company, adduced

---

60. [2009] A.J. No. 19 (C.A.).

evidence revealing that Arctic Ice threatened to refuse further delivery of ice to Inland Cement, at a critical time, unless Inland Cement stopped buying ice from Polar Ice. A bribe was also offered to Inland Cement's employee to secure an exclusive contract.

Arctic Glacier also made offers to match or undercut Polar's price, but only to the liquor outlets and Sobeys stores that Polar Ice supplied. These direct and deliberate attempts to induce those targeted businesses to breach their contracts with Polar Ice breached the *Competition Act* in addition to being actionable torts. Damages for inducing breach of contract were thus awarded.

To establish the tort of interference with economic relations, the plaintiff had to prove that: (1) the defendant had an intention to injure it; (2) the means employed by the defendant to accomplish this were unlawful; and (3) the plaintiff suffered economic loss or a related injury as a result. All three requirements were met and damages of $50 000 were awarded.

The Court of Appeal upheld the decision and found that the award of solicitor and client costs to the plaintiff was justified. The defendant's employee had lied under oath, which impeded earlier settlement of the action and necessitated a longer trial.

SMALL BUSINESS PERSPECTIVE

Competition is encouraged in Canada but within ethical guidelines. Businesses need to teach their employees that certain lines are not to be crossed to "make a deal."

Inducing Breach of Contract

There are several ways that one can interfere with the operation of another's business. **Inducing breach of contract** usually involves an employer persuading an employee of another business to leave that employment and work for him or her. This practice is more common when that employee has special knowledge about trade secrets or customer lists or has a special relationship with customers, enabling him or her to bring them to the new job. If the employee is contractually committed to stay in that position of employment for a period of time or not to disclose secret information, he will breach that contractual obligation if he submits to the enticement to make the move and make the disclosure. A different employer that persuades someone else's employee to commit such a breach, usually with financial incentives, violates a duty not to intervene in that relationship. As a result, that employer may face the tort action of inducing breach of contract. For the victim to sue for inducing breach of contract, he must be able to establish that there was a contract that was breached and that the person being sued knew about the contract and intentionally induced the breach. The victim likely has the right to sue the employee for breach, but it is often preferable to sue the other employer because it tends to have "deeper pockets" (the funds to make the action worthwhile), and legal action may deter the defendant from luring other employees away and causing the plaintiff such losses again.

Inducing breach of contract can also be committed when one business induces severance of contractual relations with someone else, as when a supplier is persuaded to abandon one customer in favour of another or a customer is persuaded to breach its contract with a competing supplier. Another interesting application of this tort is to sue a director of a corporation for inducing the corporation to breach a contract it had with the plaintiff.

CASE SUMMARY 3.13

The Consequences of Inducing Breach: *Ahmad v. Ontario Hydro*[61]

Dr. Ahmad was an engineer working for Atomic Energy Canada Limited (AECL) as head of the Advanced Engineering Branch. He was working on a project to get the nuclear reactors to work at a higher efficiency, which was of great interest to Ontario Hydro, AECL's primary customer. Each percentage rise in efficiency would reap a reward of $20 million in income. Ahmad was working on a process that would lead to such results but stated in his report that further study was required. Ontario Hydro needed a more positive report to take before the controlling board, so it persuaded Ahmad's employer to transfer him and put someone more "supportive" in charge. Ontario Hydro threatened to withdraw from future joint research projects unless Ahmad was reassigned.

AECL complied, assigning Ahmad to a project where he was no longer in contact with Ontario Hydro. The result was that he could no longer work in his area of expertise and went from managing 24 employees to being in a one-person office with nothing to do. Ontario Hydro produced a press release stating that Ahmad was reassigned due to research delays and inadequate research, accusations that were repeated in *The Globe and Mail*. Ahmad sued Ontario Hydro, and when AECL failed to supply documents he needed for his action, he joined them in the action. As a result he was terminated. In this action Ahmad sought remedies against Ontario Hydro for defamation and inducing breach of contract.

This is a classic example of one company putting extensive pressure on another to breach its employment relationship with a long-term employee. The Court awarded $488 525 in damages against Ontario Hydro for inducing breach of contract and another $40 000 for defamation. The Court even awarded the plaintiff solicitor and client costs. It found that there had been a valid contract between AECL and Ahmad that Ontario Hydro was aware of, and that it had intentionally and wrongfully induced AECL to breach that contract, causing substantial damage to Ahmad. In a separate action, Ahmad was awarded $102 000 against AECL for wrongful dismissal.

SMALL BUSINESS PERSPECTIVE

Knowing that one can sue a third party for wrongfully causing a contract to be breached in effect doubles the potential for the relief following a breach of contract. More importantly, it allows one to pursue the wrongdoer who initiated the damage.

When one business intentionally interferes with the operation of a competitor, problems can develop. When this is done through ordinary competition there is no complaint, but sometimes that competition becomes unfair. Examples of improper interference in business and unfair competition include: one business seeking confidential information from the employees of another; intimidation to discourage someone from opening a business in an area; or one restaurant sending employees to the door of another to redirect customers to the first. Most of these kinds of problems are dealt with by the federal *Competition Act*.[62]

---

61. [1993] O.J. No. 3104 (Gen. D.); [1997] O.J. No. 3047 (C.A.)
62. R.S.C. 1985, c. C-34.

Interference with Economic Relations

Interference with economic relations

Interference with economic relations is also actionable where no breach of contract has taken place, but there must be some other unlawful conduct associated with the complaint, such as bribery or defamation. That unlawful conduct must have been intended to cause harm and, in fact, harm must have resulted. For example in the *Sagaz* case,[63] a company had supplied seat covers to a retailer for over 30 years when that business arrangement was abruptly terminated. A competitor bribed a key employee of the retailer with a 2 percent kickback for every seat cover the competitor supplied. The key employee accepted the bribe and arranged for the change in suppliers. The bribe was sufficient illegal activity to support the claim of illegal interference with the supplier's economic relations.

In *Barber v. Vrozos*,[64] the complaint related to the supply and sale of water at a Rolling Stones concert. The plaintiffs purchased for $100 000 what they thought was the exclusive right to supply and sell water at the concert from the defendant Vrozos, who in turn had acquired these rights through an oral contract with the defendant, Molson, for $120 000. Molson proceeded to breach this contract by negotiating a deal with the defendant, GMIC, giving GMIC "exclusive" rights to onsite food and beverages sales. Vrozos also allowed the sale of water by other vendors in a barbecue area.

The plaintiffs ultimately were awarded damages in excess of $1.3 million—$531 616 for breach of contract and a further $180 000 in tort against Vrozos, and $632 000 against Molson for intentionally interfering with the plaintiffs' economic relations when it breached its exclusive water contract with Vrozos. Note that an additional $50 000 in punitive damages and costs of $481 185 were also awarded.

Intimidation

Intimidation

Even just the threat of violence or some other illegal activity, such as an illegal strike, can constitute the tort of **intimidation** where it forces the businessperson to do something that harms the business. For example, a trade union threatening an illegal strike if a particular employee was not terminated amounted to the tort of intimidation and was actionable in England.[65] Of course, if a union was in a legal strike position, the threat of such a strike would not amount to intimidation since the necessary element of a threat to do an illegal act would be missing. Such intimidation is often associated with the tort of unlawful interference with economic relations. In *Cheticamp Fisheries Co-operative Limited v. Canada*,[66] the Department of Fisheries instituted a fee on the fishers and fish processors at the dock to pay for the weighing and inspection of the catch to ensure that the quotas were being adhered to. This was not supported by statutory authority, and as an illegal fee it was held to be an unlawful interference with economic relations. The fishers also claimed that it amounted to intimidation, but the Judge found that since the unlawful interference had been established it was not necessary to determine

---

[63.] *671122 Ontario Ltd. v. Sagaz Industries Canada Inc.*, [2001] S.C.R. 983.

[64.] [2008] O.J. No. 2616 (Sup. Ct. J.); [2008] O.J. No. 3357 (Sup. Ct. J.) as to punitive damages; [2009] O.J. No. 865 (Sup. Ct. J.) ruling as to costs.

[65.] *Tran v. Financial Debt Recovery Ltd.*, [2000] O.J. No. 4293 (Sup.Ct.J.).

[66.] *Rookes v. Barnard*, [1964] 1 All E.R. 367 (H. of L.).

whether intimidation was present as well. Note that a related tort of **intentional infliction of mental suffering** (or nervous shock) will often also be alleged where such threats and harassing behaviour is involved. Examples include harassing behaviour associated with wrongful dismissal, such as harassing an ill employee for justified absences after she has already been given notice of termination.[67] Another example involves the improper activities of a collection agency, including harassment and threat of physical violence, to encourage repayment of a loan.[68]

Intentional infliction of mental suffering

Deceit (Fraudulent Misrepresentation)

The tort of **deceit** involves the fraudulent and intentional misleading of another person, causing damage. This is where one person lies to another, causing loss.[69] It is an intentional tort and one of the few situations where the court will entertain an application for punitive damages. The case of *Derry v. Peek*[70] established that deceit did not require actual knowledge that what was stated was incorrect. It was enough that the person making the statement did not believe it to be true. This is a common wrong committed in business.

Fraud or deceit actionable

Conspiracy

A **conspiracy to injure** takes place where two or more persons act together using unlawful means to injure the business interests of another. For example, in the *Sagaz* case mentioned above, where the key employee was given kickbacks to change to a new supplier of seat covers, the actions of that employee and the supplier together also constituted a conspiracy. When a group of employees work together to get another employee fired, a conspiracy is involved. In *Meehan v. Tremblett*,[71] the plaintiff worked as a corrections officer. His immediate supervisor and the superintendent got together, creating a false performance evaluation report that led to the plaintiff's forced resignation. This conspiracy to injure involved the wrongful act of creating false and misleading documents and was thus an actionable tort. Not only were the parties to it liable, but due to vicarious liability, the New Brunswick government (as employer) was held liable as well. See also the *Procor* case discussed above (Case Summary 3.11).[72]

Conspiracy

An interesting case where an insurer alleged conspiracy to injure is *Insurance Corp. of British Columbia v. Husseinian*.[73] The plaintiff (ICBC) alleged that the defendants staged motor vehicle accidents to obtain insurance monies for personal injuries and property damage. Most of the motor vehicle accidents involved a stolen car either rear-ending another vehicle or hitting a parked car. The driver

---

[67] [1995] N.S.J. No. 127 (N.S.C.A.); application for leave to S.C.C. dismissed, [1995] S.C.C.A. No. 202.

[68] *Prinzo v. Baycrest Centre for Geriatric Care*, [2002] O.J. No. 2712 (C.A.).

[69] (1889), 14 App. Cas. 337 at 374 (H.L.).

[70] See *Usenik v. Sidorowicz*, [2008] O.J. No. 1049 (S.C.J.), where the plaintiffs purchased a home from the defendants after being assured there were no problems with moisture and flooding. These statements were untrue. The defendants were ordered to redress the water damages suffered.

[71] *Supra* n.40.

[72] [1996] N.B.J. No. 142 (C.A.).

[73] [2008] B.C.J. No. 333 (S.C.).

of the stolen vehicle would flee the scene of the accident on foot without ever being caught. The insurer established that the defendants either knew each other or shared acquaintances. The Court concluded there was conspiracy to injure. Further, this extensive scheme to defraud an insurer of significant monies was the type of reprehensible conduct that warranted an award of punitive damages.

Passing Off

Passing-off actionable

A **passing-off** action is appropriate when a business or product is presented to the public in such a way as to lead the public to believe that the product is being provided by another. When imitation Rolex watches are sold as the real thing, or when a restaurant adopts the golden arches logo, leading the public to believe it is part of the McDonald's chain when it is not, the tort of passing-off has been committed. The court can award damages in these circumstances, but an injunction or an order that the offending product be delivered to the plaintiff for destruction may be a more appropriate remedy.

Misuse of Confidential Information

Misuse of confidential information actionable

A company's trade secrets and other forms of **confidential information**, including customer lists and future plans, are some of the most important assets a business can have, and their improper disclosure to a competitor can do that business great harm. Key employees, agents, and others that do business with that company have a duty not to disclose its confidential information to others or to use it for their own purposes. Persons can be sued where they fail in that duty. As discussed above, an action can also be brought against anyone who induced them to breach that confidence. This duty to maintain confidentiality may be imposed through contract or may arise simply because the information has been provided in confidence. Often it exists because of the fiduciary relationship existing between the parties. A fiduciary duty arises when one party places a considerable amount of trust in another, making himself particularly vulnerable to any wrongful actions of that trusted party. A fiduciary duty may arise, for example, if a client puts his business affairs in an advisor's hands. Fiduciary duty will be one of the topics discussed under the heading of professional liability in Chapter 5.

An example of the misuse of such confidential information is found in *Enterprise Excellence Corporation v. Royal Bank of Canada*.[74] The plaintiffs approached the bank with a promotional idea, including the sponsorship of a radio program and the use of the phrase "Today's Entrepreneur." The bank rejected their proposal and instead went ahead on its own using the phrase "Today's Entrepreneur" constantly over a one-year period while the promotion ran. The Court found that this was a misuse of information that had been given to the bank in confidence and awarded damages of over half a million dollars to the plaintiff. The Judge found that such a breach of confidence took place where (1) the information was of a confidential nature, (2) it was given in confidence, and (3) it was misused by the person to whom it was conveyed. In this case all three requirements had been met.

[74.] [2002] O.J. No. 3086 (Sup.Ct.J.).

CASE SUMMARY 3.14

Cheaters Never Prosper: *Walter Stewart Realty Ltd. v. Traber* [75]

A 200-acre tract of undeveloped land beside a housing development was thought to be unserviceable—at least until the plaintiff, Walter Stewart, discovered a method to service it. He found that the land was available, making it very valuable for residential development. He approached Mr. Traber, a real estate developer, with his plan, disclosing it to him only after receiving a promise that the information would be kept secret and confidential and that he would receive 30 percent of the profits from the venture. The developer then acquired the property and developed it, but refused to give Stewart the funds promised. Stewart sued, claiming that the project amounted to a joint venture and that there had been a breach of confidentiality.

At trial the Judge found that the agreement for a joint venture, while discussed, had never been finalized. Nonetheless, the conduct of the developer amounted to a breach of confidentiality, and Stewart was awarded 15 percent of the profits. On appeal the Court agreed that there had been a breach of confidentiality but also held that the appropriate damages should be based on the original amount of 30 percent of the profits from the development, as originally agreed.

SMALL BUSINESS PERSPECTIVE

The case illustrates that a breach of confidence not only involves conveying that confidential information to someone else but also includes using it inappropriately for one's own purposes.

PRIVACY

Invasion of a person's **privacy** may take the form of a physical intrusion, surveillance, misuse of an image or name, or access to information. Businesses often use information that people would like to keep private. They sometimes use images or likenesses to promote products without permission. Until very recently, there was no tort of invasion of privacy in common law, but several provinces made interfering with a person's privacy a statutory tort.[76] These statutes enabled claimants to sue if, for example, their likeness or voice was used without their consent. In *Heckert v. 5470 Investments Ltd.*[77] a tenant sued her landlord for invasion of privacy by video surveillance and was awarded $3500 in damages. British Columbia's *Privacy Act* was relied upon. In *L.A.M. v. J.E.L.I.*[78] the defendant videotaped the plaintiff and her daughter in the bathroom through a peephole; general and punitive damages were awarded.

Privacy protection initially found only in statutes

---

75. [1995] A.J. No. 636 (C.A.); supplementary reasons [1995] A.J. No. 971 (C.A.).

76. [2008] B.C.J. No. 1854 (S.C.).

77. See *Privacy Act,* R.S.B.C. 1996, c. 373; *The Privacy Act,* R.S.S. 1978, c. P-24; *The Privacy Act,* C.C.S.M. c. P125. *Privacy Act,* R.S.N.L. 1990, c. P-22.

78. [2008] B.C.J. No. 1612 (S.C.).

Pursuant to these *Privacy Acts*, remedies ranging from damages to injunctions and accounting for profits may be awarded. Often, consent of the claimant operates as a defence.

CASE SUMMARY 3.15

Time to Recognize Invasion of Privacy as a Tort: *Somwar v. McDonald's Restaurants of Canada Ltd.*[79]

The plaintiff sued his employer for invasion of privacy after discovering that the employer conducted a credit check on him without his permission.

Can someone whose privacy has been violated by another person pursue a civil remedy in the courts of Ontario? Does our law recognize the tort of invasion of privacy?" The trial judgment begins by asking these two questions.

After reviewing the developing case law and legal commentary on this issue, the trial Judge concluded: "The traditional torts such as nuisance, trespass, and harassment may not provide adequate protection against infringement of an individual's privacy interests. Protection of those privacy interests by providing a common law remedy for their violation would be consistent with *Charter* values and an 'incremental revision' and logical extension of the existing jurisprudence." . . . "Even if the plaintiff's claim for invasion of privacy were classified as 'novel' (which, in any event, is not a proper basis for dismissing it) the foregoing analysis leads me to conclude that the time has come to recognize invasion of privacy as a tort in its own right."

DISCUSSION QUESTIONS

Based on your understanding of *stare decisis*, does this case establish the tort of invasion of privacy across Canada? What level of judicial recognition is required before one can say with certainty that the tort of invasion of privacy exists in its own right?

With judicial recognition of the tort of invasion of privacy increasing, parties may soon be relieved of trying to "fit a square peg into a round hole." Because of the courts' reluctance to recognize invasion of privacy as a tort, parties have tried to characterize the action complained as another kind of tort. For example, where a business uses a person's image, name, or likeness to promote its product without permission, there is an innuendo communicated that the person has endorsed the product. That is a false statement and is actionable as defamation. Obviously, it would be much clearer if parties could simply sue for breach of privacy.

Internet poses new problems   In the last decade, the number of problems arising from abuses with respect to the use of personal and private information, such as the misuse of health and medical records, has increased exponentially, largely as a result of ecommerce. Governments have taken steps to help protect consumers, but still face the challenge of enforcing new regulations in light of the borderless nature of the internet. The encouragement of self-regulation has not been overly successful. This is an area where international treaties may make an important contribution.

Violations of privacy occur when private information is exchanged in a commercial transaction over the internet and then is used again without consent or is sold to another company for another purpose. Legislation has been enacted at both the federal and provincial levels to control the collection, use, and distribu-

---

[79.] [2006] O.J. No. 64 (Sup.Ct.J.).

tion of such personal information. The federal *Privacy Act*[80] gives people the right to access their personal information held by government and government agencies and severely restricts how that information can be disseminated to others. The *Personal Information Protection and Electronic Documents Act (PIPEDA)*[81] regulates the collection and use of personal information at both the federal and provincial level and applies to all organizations including private corporations. It requires them to account for their activities, identify the purposes for which the information is being collected, inform and get the consent of the individuals involved, and limits the use, disclosure, and retention of the information.

The organization concerned must ensure the accuracy of the information, protect it with security safeguards, and be open about policies and practices relating to the management of the information. The *Act* requires that organizations make available to individuals, upon request, the nature of the information and how it is being used. It also outlines how an individual would proceed to have a complaint reviewed and empowers a privacy commissioner to impose fines for violations.

PIPEDA has attached as its central core—and has given statutory standing to— the Code of the Canadian Standards Association (CSA). The CSA code, entitled the "Model Code for the Protection of Personal Information," was approved as a national standard by the Standards Council of Canada and was published in 1996. It sets out ten privacy-protection principles. The European Union enacted legislation to protect privacy in this area some time ago, and the passage of this *Act* provides similar protection here, removing a major barrier that threatened to interfere with international business.

The federal government's *PIPEDA* applies in all provinces except where legislation that provides for equivalent protection has been passed by the province. At the time of writing, Quebec, British Columbia, and Alberta have passed "substantially similar" legislation. It must also be emphasized that while the rights, obligations, and remedies set out in these statutes are important with respect to safeguarding private information, they do not create a general right to sue in tort for a violation of those provisions.

Another problem relating to privacy is the unauthorized interception of communications between individuals. While most sites where important information is transferred have encryption devices, determined hackers can break those codes. If the codes become too sophisticated, then governments that make use of this information in their surveillance activities cannot decode the information and so are reluctant to allow advanced encryption. This creates a serious dilemma.

Another related problem is the widespread use of "cookies" and other related tools associated with internet communication. These are embedded devices that track a user's internet activities and allow others to read private information about their internet browsing. The information may simply be used by the user's internet service provider to improve its service, but it may also be sold to retailers for marketing purposes, or used to incriminate a person who has been downloading and inappropriately using sites.

Businesses are often tempted to extract private information from their employees or even to use surveillance techniques to obtain information about

Collection and use of private information

Requirement of notice and consent

Model Code approved as a national standard for privacy protection

Limits on advanced encryption

Privacy and the internet

---

80. R.S.C. 1985, c. P-21.

81. S.C. 2000, c. 5.

them. Secret surveillance of computer users is a major problem, especially in the work environment, where it seems that employers have the right to read employees' emails and monitor their internet use on their office computers. Telephones and electronic mail are sometimes monitored. Medical information, political or religious affiliations, treatment for alcohol or drug-related problems, even mental conditions, all may be of considerable interest. Surveillance for detecting theft and monitoring other security concerns is also common. This is dangerous territory, as it may violate statutory rights to privacy in place in that jurisdiction. It may also be a violation of human rights legislation, depending on the kind of information being sought and the methods used to obtain it.

As stated at the beginning of this chapter, tort law is continually evolving, with the courts declaring new torts to exist as the need arises. The tort of spoliation, for example, is recognized in the United States and has been recently asserted in Canada. It would provide a remedy where one party has deliberately spoiled or destroyed the evidence needed by the plaintiff to establish a civil case. In *Spasic Estate v. Imperial Tobacco Ltd.*[82] the Ontario Court of Appeal found that in the proper circumstances a trial judge might find that the tort of spoliation did exist; pre-trial dismissal of the action on the grounds that no cause of action was disclosed was therefore inappropriate. The Court stated at para. 22:

Tort of spoliation grants where evidence has been destroyed

> If it is established that the conduct of the respondents resulted in harm to the plaintiff by making it impossible for her to prove her claim, then it will be for the trial judge, in the context of a complete record, to determine whether the plaintiff should have a remedy. This is how the progress of the common law is marked in cases of first impression, where the court has created a new cause of action where none had been recognized before... I can see no reason why the trial judge should be precluded from considering all possible remedies, including a separate tort, on the basis of the record that will be developed.

The evolution of tort law, with new torts being recognized as the need arises, certainly makes tort law interesting from an academic's perspective. From a businessperson's perspective, this constant evolution of law underscores the importance of having an ongoing relationship with a lawyer to keep abreast of changes in the law.

CASE SUMMARY 3.16

Torts in Cyberspace: *Braintech, Inc. v. Kostiuk*[83]

A case heard in British Columbia helps to clarify some of the problems regarding jurisdiction in internet-related disputes. In this case, a Vancouver firm sued a Vancouver investor for defamation over comments he made about the company in a chat room at Silicon Investor. The lawsuit was filed in a Texas court (even though both litigants were in Vancouver, and there was no active presence of the plaintiff in Texas) primarily because the court in that jurisdiction has a reputation for making huge damage awards. The

---

82. [2000] O.J. No. 2690 (C.A.).

83. [1999] B.C.J. No. 622 (C.A.); leave to appeal to S.C.C. refused, [1999] S.C.C.A. No. 236.

defendant did not defend himself, believing that the court had no jurisdiction in the case. The plaintiff was awarded US$300 000 in damages. When the successful plaintiff took the judgment to the British Columbia Court to have it enforced, the defendant argued that the Texas court had no jurisdiction in the matter and was not the appropriate forum to hear the case. He lost at the trial level, but that decision was reversed on appeal.

It was argued that the case should have been heard where there was a "real and substantial connection" to the matter in dispute. Because of the nature of the internet, the only connection with Texas was that a Texas resident could have logged on to an out-of-state internet site and read the alleged libel. But that was true of any location in any country, and to allow any location to have such jurisdiction would have a "crippling effect" on the internet and freedom of expression. The danger is having several different parallel actions going on at the same time. The action should be brought according to American law in a jurisdiction where there was a "real and substantial presence," or according to Canadian law if that was the jurisdiction having a "real and substantial connection" to the case. The Court found that the connection was to British Columbia and not Texas. The Supreme Court of Canada refused leave to appeal. The decision is important because it spells out under what conditions a given jurisdiction can rule on an internet dispute and, by extension, which set of laws ought to apply to cyberspace behaviour.

Note, however, that the use of the internet here was passive. An active use of the internet occurs where the parties use the internet to communicate while engaging in commercial transactions.

DISCUSSION QUESTIONS

In such circumstances, do you think the legal outcome ought to be different? Could several jurisdictions then have a "real and substantial" connection to the case? What impact would that have on the practice of business over the internet?

TORTS ONLINE

The popularity of the internet has given rise to new problems. Because the internet is uncontrolled, people can say whatever they want. All sorts of mischievous, defamatory, and obscene materials appear on the internet every day. Confidential information may easily be leaked, defamation and injurious falsehood may take place, privacy may be invaded, fraud may be perpetrated, and negligent misrepresentations made. What can victims do? The persons making the offending comments are liable for what they say, but litigation may be useless if it is not possible to determine who is responsible. Can the online service provider, the people who operate the internet server, or the operators of the particular website or chat room be sued for allowing their facilities to be used in this way? Arguably, the people who have direct control will have some responsibility, but the larger service providers have been treated more like telephone companies, escaping direct responsibility for the calls unless they have been asked to intervene. Canada's courts and legislators are now addressing these issues.

REMEDIES

punitive or exemplary damages
damages awarded with the intention of punishing a wrongdoer

special damages
damages to compensate for quantifiable injuries

general damages
damages to compensate for injuries that cannot be expressed in monetary terms

restitution
an order to restore property wrongfully taken

injunction
an order restraining a person from doing, or continuing to do, a particular act

mandatory injunction
an order requiring a person to do a particular act

Since the purpose of the law of torts is to compensate an injured party, the usual remedy is an award of a sum of money by way of damages.

Generally, the purpose of damages is to restore the plaintiff, so far as is possible, to the position she would have been in if the tort had not been committed. The object of awarding damages is not to punish the wrongdoer, though **punitive or exemplary damages** may be awarded in rare cases, such as a deliberate libel or malicious false imprisonment.

Tort damages are often classified in two categories: **special damages** and **general damages.** Special damages refer to items that can be more or less accurately quantified—medical bills, the cost of repairing a car, or actual lost wages. General damages include more speculative items, such as future loss of earnings due to disability, and non-pecuniary losses, such as awards for the "pain and suffering" of losing a limb or one's sight. Obviously, it is impossible to put a money value on health and happiness, but the courts must attempt to do so. They have thousands of precedents to guide them.

In some cases, remedies other than damages may be available, although they are rarely granted. Where a defendant has wrongfully converted the plaintiff's property, the court may order its specific **restitution** to the plaintiff, since to restrict the remedy to damages would in effect allow the defendant to compel a sale of the property. Courts may also grant an **injunction**—that is, order the defendant to refrain from committing further acts of a similar nature under threat of imprisonment for contempt of court if he disregards the order. For example, an injunction may restrain the defendant from committing a nuisance or from trespassing on the plaintiff's land. Less frequently, courts grant a **mandatory injunction**, ordering the defendant to take some positive action, such as removing a fence blocking the plaintiff's right-of-way to her property.

INTERNATIONAL ISSUE

Tort Reform

In the United States, tort reform is a hot political topic. Attention focuses on large damage awards and their impact on insurance premiums and availability of services. One of the major concerns is medical malpractice (physician's negligence). Large judgments affect the supply of physicians in high-risk specialties such as obstetrics, and the affordability of medical insurance. Another concern is the use of class actions to pool claims. They often result in huge contingency fees for the lawyers and small compensation for individual plaintiffs.

There are a number of reasons why tort judgments tend to be higher in the United States than in other jurisdictions around the world, including:

- the popularity of juries,
- the common use of punitive damages,
- the absence of a public health-care system, and
- the popularity of class actions and contingency fees.

Among the reform measures being considered are:

- capping the size of damage awards,
- limiting the use of juries,
- adopting the "loser pays" rule, and
- abolishing contingency fees.

As we have noted, some Canadian jurisdictions have undertaken targeted tort reform. Some injuries arising from negligent use of a motor vehicle are now handled by "no fault" schemes.

QUESTIONS TO CONSIDER

1. Should Canada consider capping the size of all damage awards?

2. Do you think tobacco industry litigation would have occurred without class actions and contingency fees?

Sources: R.L. Miller and G.A. Jentz, *Business Law Today: Standard Edition*, 7th ed. (Mason, OH: West Legal Studies in Business, 2006), p. 118; S.D. Sugarman, "United States Tort Reform Wars" (2002) 25(3) *The University of New South Wales Law Journal* 849–53; L. Dobbs, "Tort reform important to U.S. future," *CNN.com*, January 6, 2005, www.cnn.com/2005/US/01/06/tort.reform/index.html (accessed June 27, 2008).

SUMMARY

Intentional torts

- Assault and battery involve deliberate interference with one's person—defences are consent or self-defence (reasonable force)
- Trespass—temporary or permanent intrusion on someone else's property, without lawful right or consent
- Trespass to chattels, conversion, and detinue—involve deliberate interference with another's goods
- False imprisonment—restraint of a person by someone without authority
- Malicious prosecution—pursuing criminal charges in the absence of evidence
- Private nuisance—unusual use of property causing foreseeable disturbance to neighbour
- Defamation—a false, published statement that discredits a person
  - Libel is written defamation; slander is spoken
  - Defences—truth, absolute privilege, qualified privilege, fair comment, and public interest responsible journalism
  - Injurious falsehood (product defamation or trade slander)—false, published statements that damage the goodwill associated with a product or business

Other business torts

- Inducing breach of contract—causing breach of a contract that exists between two other parties
- Interference with economic relations—using unlawful means to disrupt the business of another
- Intimidation—using threats to cause another to act against its interests

- Deceit—deliberately misleading another with false statements
- Conspiracy—acting in concert with others to damage a third party
- Passing-off—misleading the public to think one's goods or services are those of another
- Misuse of confidential information—wrongful use or disclosure of trade secrets and other confidential information
- Invasion of privacy—violation of a person's reasonable expectation of privacy
- Spoliation—destruction of evidence to hide proof of wrongdoing

Online torts

- Problems with jurisdiction and with enforcement

QUESTIONS

1. What is the origin of the word "tort," and what does it mean?

2. What is the principal purpose of tort law?

3. What is meant by "strict liability"? Should liability ever be "strict"?

4. Who should bear the loss resulting from an automobile accident? What are the alternatives?

5. What is the main justification for the principle of vicarious liability?

6. Distinguish between assault and battery.

7. How do doctors avoid liability for the tort of battery when operating on or otherwise treating patients?

8. What limitations are there on the right of self-defence when people are defending themselves against an attack?

9. Describe the situations in which battery may be justified.

10. What are the necessary elements that must be present for a person to be classified as a trespasser?

11. What may the proprietor of a business do when faced with an unruly patron?

12. Distinguish between trespass to chattels, conversion, and detinue.

13. Imprisonment can take the form of confinement, arrest, or submission to authority. Explain.

14. What must be established to sue successfully for false imprisonment?

15. How is malice typically established by a plaintiff who sues in malicious prosecution?

16. Distinguish between libel and slander, and explain the significance of the distinction.

17. Define the terms *innuendo* and *qualified privilege*.

18. Distinguish between defamation, trade slander, and deceit, indicating in what situations each would be used.

19. Explain the nature of the tort of inducing breach of contract and what circumstances would give rise to such an action.

20. How does the tort of interference with economic relations differ from the tort of inducing breach of contract?

21. Differentiate between conspiracy and intimidation.

22. List the remedies that may be appropriate to redress misuse of confidential information.

23. Privacy concerns are becoming more problematic in the technological age. What statutes protect the rights of individuals in this area?

24. How do the courts determine if they have jurisdiction over a tort action where the internet is the means of communicating a defamatory message?

25. What are "punitive damages"? Should they be awarded in tort actions?

26. What is an injunction?

Chapter 4

Negligence

CHAPTER OBJECTIVES

1. Identify the elements of a negligence claim
2. Define when a duty of care arises and explain how the courts determine whether it is owed
3. Describe a breach of the standard of care
4. Identify the test used to determine if a breach has occurred
5. Explain how both physical and legal causation are proven
6. Identify the types of damage or loss that the courts have recognized and deemed compensable
7. Distinguish the defences applicable to the tort of negligence
8. Clarify when product liability may be imposed

NEGLIGENCE

negligence
the careless causing of injury to the person or property of another

By far the most common basis for legal actions in tort, and the one that best illustrates the fault theory of liability, is **negligence**. The concept of negligence is quite simple: anyone who carelessly causes injury to another should compensate the victim for that injury. As it has developed in the courts, negligence has become a complex and sophisticated body of law, covering a wide variety of situations.

CHECKLIST	Elements of a Negligence Action

In establishing the right to recover compensation, a plaintiff must prove three things:
1. The defendant owed the plaintiff a duty of care.
2. The defendant breached that duty.
3. The defendant's conduct caused injury to the plaintiff.

All three of the above requirements must exist for the plaintiff to succeed. The first element requires a *value judgment* by the court—is the activity complained of one that *ought* to create a duty? The second question is a mixed question of policy and fact—did the defendant's conduct fall below the standard of behaviour required in the circumstances? The third question involves difficult philosophical issues as well as fact—what is meant by "cause," and what is "injury"?

Duty of Care

In order to establish liability in negligence a plaintiff must establish a **duty of care** owed to her by the defendant. What is the nature of that duty? Duty focuses on the relationship between the parties.

duty of care
a relationship so close that one must take reasonable steps to avoid causing harm to the other

The principal question is whether the defendant should have foreseen that his actions might do harm to the victim. Another way of putting it, since the defendant cannot be expected to anticipate all the possible consequences of his actions, is to ask, "Would a normally intelligent and alert person—a reasonable person—have foreseen that those actions would likely cause harm?" But the plaintiff must go further: she must establish that the defendant owed a duty of care to *her*. As a general rule, the duty will arise only where the defendant could reasonably have foreseen a risk of harm to the plaintiff or to someone in the plaintiff's position.

CASE SUMMARY 4.1

A courier company contracted with the Province of British Columbia to deliver an envelope to a land registry office in Prince George. Unknown to the courier company, the envelope contained a document relating to land owned by the plaintiff. If delivered on time, the document would have enabled the plaintiff to complete the sale of its land. The courier company was unreasonably slow and delivered the document too late. As a result, the plaintiff was unable to perform the contract of sale, and it suffered a loss of $77 000.

The Supreme Court of Canada held that the courier company was not liable to the plaintiff. It owed no duty of care to the plaintiff since it could not reasonably have foreseen that the delay would cause a loss to some third person outside its relationship with its client, the Province.[1]

Two years earlier, in *City of Kamloops* v. *Nielsen*, the Supreme Court of Canada ruled that, to determine the existence of a duty of care, a court must ask:

> . . . is there a sufficiently close relationship between the parties (the [defendant] and the person who has suffered the damage) so that, in the reasonable contemplation of the [defendant], carelessness on its part might cause damage to that person? If so, are there any considerations which ought to negative or limit (a) the scope of the duty and (b) the class of persons to whom it is owed or (c) the damages to which a breach of it may give rise?[2]

Recently, the Supreme Court of Canada summarized the test for duty of care in one sentence: "Whether such a relationship exists depends on forseeability,

---

[1] *B.D.C. Ltd.* v. *Hofstrand Farms Ltd.* (1986), 26 D.L.R. (4th) 1. For a recent example see *Esser v. Luoma* (2004), 242 D.L.R. (4th) 112.

[2] [1984] 2 S.C.R. 2 at 10 (per Wilson, J.). This test was cited with approval by LaForest, J. in *Hercules Managements Ltd.* v. *Ernst & Young* (1997), 146 D.L.R. (4th) 577 (S.C.C.), in a judgment that provides a comprehensive review of the Canadian law on the duty of care. That case is examined further in Chapter 5.

moderated by policy concerns."[3] Policy concerns consider the effect that recognizing a duty of care will have on other legal obligations, the legal system, and society more generally.[4] Concerns include such things as the proliferation of lawsuits or the ability to insure against a huge new potential legal risk.

The courts have sometimes held that a duty of care is owed to persons other than the individual who is directly injured. For example, a negligent driver was held to be liable to a parent who suffered severe nervous shock when she saw her own child, who was standing nearby, run down and killed.[5] In that case the court considered that the type of injury suffered by the parent was foreseeable.

In recent years more and more duties have been imposed by statute, especially upon the operators of businesses. In addition to statutory penalties, breach of these duties may give rise to liability in tort to persons who are injured as a result. The courts have also shown increasing willingness to hold public bodies liable for the negligent performance of their statutory duties. Municipalities have been held liable to homeowners for issuing building permits for defective designs or for not carrying out proper inspections of construction works.[6] A public body may be liable even where the statute imposes no duty but merely confers a discretionary power on it—for example, to maintain a highway—if it is negligent in the exercise of that power.[7]

CASE SUMMARY 4.2

"Neighbours" Are Owed a Duty of Care: *Donoghue v. Stevenson*[8]

The reasonable foreseeability test was developed in *Donoghue v. Stevenson*, one of the most significant cases of the 20th century. Mrs. Donoghue went with a friend into a café, where the friend ordered a bottle of ginger beer for her. After consuming some of it, Donoghue discovered part of a decomposed snail at the bottom of her bottle. She became very ill as a result of drinking the contaminated beverage. In the process of suing, she discovered that she had some serious problems. She could not successfully sue the café that had supplied the ginger beer for breach of contract; she had no contract with the establishment, as her friend had made the purchase. Similarly, she could not successfully sue the café for negligence, since it had done nothing wrong, the ginger beer having been bottled in an opaque container and served to her in the bottle. Her only recourse was to sue the manufacturer for negligence in producing the product, but

---

[3] *Mustapha v. Culligan of Canada Ltd.*, 2008 SCC 27 at para. 4, relying on the seminal case of *Anns v. Merton London Borough Council*, [1978] A.C. 728 (H.L.).

[4] *Cooper v. Hobart*, [2001] 3 S.C.R. 537.

[5] *Hinz v. Berry*, [1970] 1 All E.R. 1074. Contrast with *Schlink v. Blackburn* (1993), 18 C.C.L.T. (2d) 173, where the plaintiff was at home, asleep in bed, when his wife was injured in a motor accident; his nervous shock occurred some time later when he was told of the accident.

[6] *City of Kamloops v. Neilsen, supra*, n. 11; *Rothfield v. Manolakos* (1989), 63 D.L.R. (4th) 449.

[7] See, for example, *Bisoukis v. City of Brampton* (1999), 180 D.L.R. (4th) 577 (failure to sand a stretch of road where black ice was known to form). The courts will normally not interfere with policy decisions taken by the appropriate body, but once a policy decision has been taken (for example, to guard against rock falls onto a highway), the body will be liable if it is negligent in carrying out that policy: *Just v. British Columbia* (1989), 64 D.L.R. (4th) 689; contrast with *Gobin v. British Columbia*, (2002) 214 D.L.R. (4th) 328.

[8] [1932] A.C. 562 (H.L.).

the bottler claimed it owed her no duty to be careful. The Court had to determine whether a duty to be careful was owed by the manufacturer to the consumer of its product. In the process of finding that such a duty was owed, the House of Lords developed the reasonable foreseeability test. Lord Atkin, one of the Judges in the case, made the following classic statement when discussing how to determine to whom we owe a duty:

> The rule that you are to love your neighbour becomes in law, you must not injure your neighbour; and the lawyer's question "Who is my neighbour?" receives a restricted reply. You must take reasonable care to avoid acts or omissions which you can reasonably foresee would be likely to injure your neighbour. Who, then, in law, is my neighbour? The answer seems to be—persons who are so closely and directly affected by my act that I ought reasonably to have them in contemplation as being so affected when I am directing my mind to the acts or omissions which are called in question.[9]

SMALL BUSINESS PERSPECTIVE

Risk management involves asking whether one's actions put others at risk. If injury is foreseeable, then a duty to take care may be owed. Liability could follow unless reasonable precautions are taken to avoid causing harm.

Standard of Care

The **standard of care** refers to the level of care that a person must take in the circumstances. The law places a general duty on every person to take *reasonable* care to avoid causing foreseeable injury to other persons and their property. What constitutes a reasonable standard of care? It is often said that the standard demanded is that of the ordinary reasonable person, or "the person on the Yonge Street subway."[10] However, the standard of care necessarily varies according to the activity in question: the standard expected of a brain surgeon is that of a competent brain surgeon rather than of the person in the subway.

In addition, the court must balance competing interests. On the one hand the court considers the degree of likelihood that harm will result from the activity in question and the potential severity of the harm. On the other hand it considers the social utility of the activity and the feasibility of eliminating the risk. It may be permissible not to take every possible precaution where the risk of serious damage or injury is small, but where there is danger of a major catastrophe, it would be unreasonable not to take every known precaution.

Legislation not only imposes duties but also sets out the appropriate standard of care for particular activities. For example, safety standards for the food industry are prescribed by statute, and those standards are frequently a good indication of where a court will set the negligence threshold. But it must be remembered that the tort of negligence is based on fault, and the fact that a person may be guilty of a breach of a statutory standard does not of itself make him civilly liable to a person injured as a result of the breach—at least if he can show that the offence occurred without fault on his part.[11]

standard of care
the level of care that a person must take in the circumstances

---

9. *Ibid.* at 580.

10. Linden, *Canadian Tort Law, supra,* n. 2, at 126–7.

11. *R. v. Saskatchewan Wheat Pool,* [1983] 1 S.C.R. 205.

Causation

For an action in negligence to succeed, it is necessary for the plaintiff to show not only that a duty of care was owed to her and that duty has been breached, but also that she has been injured as a result of the breach; that is to say, the breach of duty is the cause of the injury. **Causation** is a complex subject about which whole volumes have been written. An extreme view of the theory of causation can link one act to every other act in the world.

causation
injury resulting from the breach of the standard of care

ILLUSTRATION 4.1

PQR Inc. were having some renovations done to part of their factory building by *STU* (Contractors) Ltd. One of the *STU* workmen negligently sliced through a cable, causing an electric motor to burn out. The motor was an essential part of the factory's cooling system; without it, the factory could continue in operation for only a few hours. The factory manager, *X*, immediately decided to drive to the nearby town to obtain a replacement motor. On the way, his car was struck by a vehicle carelessly driven by *Y*, and *X* suffered slight injuries and concussion. By the time *PQR* were able to get the motor back to the factory, the cooling system had overheated and it had been necessary to close down operations. As a result, four hours of production were lost. Worse, *X*'s injury caused him to miss a meeting with an important client, as a result of which *PQR* lost the opportunity of a lucrative contract.

In Illustration 4.1 it could be argued that the negligence of *STU*'s worker "caused" (1) the shutdown at the factory, (2) the injury to *X*, and (3) the loss of the contract. But for his slicing through the cable, none of those consequences would have followed. The same might be argued with respect to *Y*'s careless driving. Yet it would seem unreasonable to hold *STU* liable for items (2) and (3), or to hold Y liable for items (1) and (3). Clearly, the "but for" approach to causation does not always provide a satisfactory solution.

For the most part the courts have avoided philosophical discussion and have adopted a common-sense approach. No matter how blameworthy a person's conduct may be, he will not be held liable for damage that he did not cause. In a famous case, a passenger in a small boat accidentally fell overboard into ice-cold water and died. The boat's operator was under a duty to try to rescue him. He was negligent in the attempt at rescue, but was held not liable because, even if he had used proper rescue procedures, the passenger would have been dead before he could have been pulled from the water.[12]

remote
unrelated or far removed from the conduct

Again, a person will not be held liable for consequences of his acts that are considered to be too **remote** or unrelated. Generally speaking, the closer in time the occurrence of an injury is to a person's careless conduct, the less chance there is of some significant intervening act happening, and the more likely he is to be found the "cause" of the injury.

---

12. *Matthews* v. *MacLaren*, [1969] 2 O.R. 137, affirmed in *Horsley* v. *MacLaren*, [1972] S.C.R. 441.

CASE SUMMARY 4.3

B and his wife were involved in an automobile accident. *B* received relatively slight injuries but his wife was severely injured. Two years later, *B* was in another accident and some time after that he was diagnosed as suffering from severe depression. In the action arising out of the first accident, *B* claimed damages in respect of the depression.

The claim was rejected. The court held that, if *B*'s depression had resulted from the stress of seeing his wife suffer, day after day, the damage might have been foreseeable. However, the length of time between the first accident and the onset of the depression (more than two years later) cast doubt on the causal relationship. The depression might have been the result of the second accident.[13]

As both Case Summary 4.3 and Illustration 4.1 demonstrate, an injury may be the result of two or more negligent acts by different defendants. In such a case, which of them should be held liable? At one time the courts attempted to determine which of the acts was the "proximate cause" of injury. That sometimes produced an unfair result, and the modern tendency is to hold both defendants liable.[14]

CASE SUMMARY 4.4

An innkeeper allowed a customer to drink too much and then turned him out to walk home along a country road, where he was hit by a careless motorist. Both the innkeeper and the motorist were held to have contributed to the accident.[15]

Remoteness of Damage

Foreseeability is a major element, as we have seen, both in establishing whether or not a duty of care exists and in determining what is the appropriate standard of care. It reappears again when the question of the *extent* of liability for negligence is considered.

Until the 1960s the position seemed to be that, once some sort of damage was reasonably foreseeable as a consequence of a negligent act, the actor was liable for *all* damage resulting directly from that act, however unlikely that damage was.[16]

---

13. *Beecham v. Hughes* (1988), 52 D.L.R. (4th) 625.

14. For an example, see *Economy Foods & Hardware Ltd.* v. *Klassen* (2001), 196 D.L.R. (4th) 413, where a fire was caused by the negligence of one defendant but spread, causing additional damage, due to the failure of the second defendant to install an adequate system of sprinklers.

15. *Menow v. Honsberger and Jordan House Ltd.*, [1974] S.C.R. 239. See also *Murphy v. Little Memphis Cabaret Inc.* (1998), 167 D.L.R. (4th) 190; *Renaissance Leisure Group Inc.* v. *Frazer* (2004), 242 D.L.R. (4th) 229. By contrast, the Supreme Court of Canada held that a restaurant serving alcohol to a party of people, knowing that they had arrived by car, owed a duty to the driver and passengers, but since some members of the party were not drinking, it was entitled to assume that a non-drinker would be driving; consequently, it was not responsible for the accident: *Mayfield Investments Ltd.* v. *Stewart* (1995), 121 D.L.R. (4th) 222. It is still unclear whether "social hosts" (for example, at a private party), will be held liable in the same way as "commercial hosts": see *Childs v. Desormeaux* (2004), 239 D.L.R. (4th) 61.

16. *Re Polemis*, [1921] 3 K.B. 560.

CASE SUMMARY 4.5

Employees of the defendants, who were charterers of a ship called *Wagon Mound*, negligently allowed a large quantity of oil to escape from the ship into Sydney Harbour, Australia. Some of the oil washed up against the plaintiff's dock. Workers on the dock were carrying on welding operations. A spark from a welder ignited some cotton waste floating on the surface of the water and this, in turn, ignited the oil. A severe fire resulted, causing considerable damage to the dock.

The Australian trial judge held the defendants liable. They had been negligent in allowing the oil to escape, and it was foreseeable that some damage to the plaintiff's dock might result from the leakage, though the judge found that damage by fire was not foreseeable. Nevertheless, the actual damage was a direct result of the defendants' breach of their duty to the plaintiff.

The defendants appealed and the Privy Council allowed the appeal, holding that liability existed only in respect of the sort of damage that was reasonably foreseeable.[17]

The *Wagon Mound (No. 1)* decision (Case Summary 4.5) restricted liability to damage that was reasonably foreseeable. A follow-up case known as *Wagon Mound (No. 2)* defined "reasonably foreseeable" as a real risk: "one which would occur to the mind of a reasonable man in the position of the defendant . . . which he would not brush aside as far fetched."[18] A court undertakes an objective assessment of what a *reasonable* defendant would foresee as likely injury to the *average* defendant. The damage is considered from the perspective of the "normal" victim—a person of "ordinary fortitude." It is not based on the actual circumstances of the particular plaintiff.

CASE SUMMARY 4.6

A consumer saw a dead fly in a bottle of water as he replaced a canister in his home. The observation was so upsetting that he developed serious mental disorders including anxiety and phobias. The trial judge found that the mental injuries were caused by the incident and awarded damages of approximately $340 000. The judgment was overturned by the Court of Appeal and leave to the Supreme Court of Canada was granted. The Supreme Court did not interfere with the trial judge's finding that the mental illness was caused by the incident but found that mental illness was not a reasonably foreseeable type of damage in the circumstances. The average person would not suffer a mental disorder as a result of seeing a fly in a water bottle. This was an extreme reaction by a plaintiff with particular vulnerabilities. The same reaction would not be expected in a person of ordinary fortitude. The plaintiff could not recover because the damage was too remote.[19]

[17.] *Overseas Tankship (U.K.) Ltd. v. Morts Dock & Engineering Co. (The Wagon Mound No. 1)*, [1961] A.C. 388.

[18.] *Overseas Tankship (U.K.) Ltd. v. Miller Steamship Co. Pty. Ltd. (The Wagon Mound No. 2)*, [1967] A.C. 617 at p. 643; *Hughes v. Lord Advocate*, [1963] A.C. 837.

[19.] *Mustapha, supra*, n. 12.

However, there is some element of subjectivity in the valuation of the damage. If the type of damage is considered reasonably foreseeable, the court will compensate the victim for his *actual* damage. When a teenager negligently started his father's snowmobile, which escaped from his control, crossed a schoolyard, and collided with a gas pipe just outside the school causing gas to escape into the school and explode, he was held liable for all the resulting damage. The damage was considered to be of a general type that might have been foreseen even if the actual extent of the damage was unusually high.[20]

Economic Loss

As we noted in the previous chapter, the purpose of tort law is to compensate for loss suffered as a consequence of the wrongful act of another. As we shall see, the remedy given in cases of negligence is a sum of money by way of **damages**. A plaintiff injured in an automobile collision may be compensated not only for her physical injuries and for the cost of repairing her car, but also for *economic loss*, such as wages lost due to an enforced absence from work and the cost of renting a replacement car.

damages
a sum of money awarded as compensation

There are two types of cases. In the first type, economic loss is caused without there being any physical damage at all. A classic example is the leading case of *Hedley Byrne* v. *Heller and Partners*,[21] in which the House of Lords established that financial loss suffered as a result of a negligent misstatement may be recovered. This subject is discussed further in Chapter 5. In the second type of case there is physical damage, but not to the plaintiff or her property.

CASE SUMMARY 4.7

B negligently operated a tugboat and it collided with a railway bridge owned by *C*. The bridge was closed for several weeks for repairs. As a result, the railway company, which was the principal user of the bridge, suffered a loss of profit because it had to reroute traffic.

The Supreme Court of Canada held that the railway company could recover its loss.[22]

The decision turned in part on the close relationship that existed between the owner of the bridge and the railway company and, while it established that there *may* be recovery for pure economic loss in some situations, it left open the question of when the courts will hold that a duty is owed to a plaintiff or when the particular damage is not too remote. The answer turns on the particular circumstances of the case. For example, where a supplier sold a quantity of polyethylene resin to a corporation, knowing the resin to be defective and also

---

[20] *Hoffer v. School Division of Assiniboine South*, [1973] W.W.R. 765 (S.C.C.). The father and the gas company that installed the pipe were also held liable.

[21] [1964] A.C. 465.

[22] *Canadian National Railway Co. v. Norsk Pacific Steamship Co.* (1992), 91 D.L.R. (4th) 289.

knowing that the purchaser was part of a group of wholly owned subsidiaries that operated in an interdependent manner, the supplier was held liable to the entire group.[23]

A somewhat different issue was raised in Case Summary 4.8:

CASE SUMMARY 4.8

A land developer contracted with the defendant construction company to build an apartment building, which was later sold to the plaintiffs. About 10 years later, a section of cladding fell from the ninth floor. On examination, defects in the construction were found and the plaintiffs had the entire cladding replaced. They successfully sued the defendants for the cost of the repairs.

Although no damage had been suffered, apart from the cladding on the ninth floor, the Supreme Court of Canada held that it was foreseeable that without the repairs there was a strong likelihood of physical harm to persons or to property. It was right that the defendants should be liable for the cost of replacing the rest of the cladding. In reaching that conclusion, the court recognized the strong underlying policy justification of providing an incentive to prevent accidents before they happen.[24]

Burden of Proof

Like plaintiffs in most court proceedings, a plaintiff in a tort action must prove all the elements of her case. In certain kinds of cases, however, the plaintiff does not know why or how the accident happened. For example, a pedestrian knocked down by a car, or a consumer poisoned by a dangerous substance in a jar of food, may have no way of knowing exactly how the defendant driver's or manufacturer's conduct caused her injury. The car might suddenly have swerved out of control because of some hidden mechanical defect, or the poisonous substance might have been deliberately inserted into the jar after it had left the manufacturer.

The law takes these difficulties of proof into account. A plaintiff may initially meet his burden of proof using circumstantial evidence. If the plaintiff establishes that the behaviour of the defendant is the most likely cause of the injury, the burden of proof then shifts to the defendant to show that he was not at fault. Once the burden has been shifted to him, he will be found liable unless he produces evidence to satisfy the court that, on balance, he was not at fault. Historically, this principle was known as ***res ipsa loquitur***, or, translated, "the facts speak for themselves." It emerged in a 19th-century English case[25] in which the plaintiff, standing in a street, was struck by a barrel of flour falling from the upper window of the

res ipsa loquitur
the facts speak for themselves

[23.] *Plas-Tex Canada Ltd. v. Dow Chemical of Canada Ltd.* (2004), 245 D.L.R. (4th) 650. The supplier was also liable for breach of contract.

[24.] *Winnipeg Condominium Corp. No. 36 v. Bird Construction Co.*, [1995] 1 S.C.R. 85.

[25.] *Byrne v. Boadle* (1863), 159 E.R. 294.

defendant's warehouse. Not unreasonably, the court concluded that, unless the defendant could prove otherwise, the most likely cause was the negligent conduct of the defendant or one of his employees.

In 1998, the Supreme Court of Canada dispensed with use of the Latin phrase, concluding that the principle was really just an application of the circumstantial evidence rules.[26]

The Plaintiff's Own Conduct

Early in the development of the principles of negligence the courts recognized that, even if the defendant had been negligent, the plaintiff might be largely responsible for her own injury. The courts at one time took a rather narrow and mechanical approach to the question. If the defendant could establish that the plaintiff contributed in any way to her own loss, the plaintiff would fail even if the defendant was mainly at fault. The harshness of the **contributory negligence** rule was changed by legislation pioneered in Canada.[27] These statutes required courts to apportion damages according to the respective degree of responsibility of the parties. The statutes do not set out in detail the basis for making the apportionment, but leave it to be decided by judges and juries according to their opinion of what is fair in the circumstances.

contributory negligence
negligence of an injured party that contributes to her own loss or injury

---

CASE SUMMARY 4.9

The plaintiff, a passenger in a truck, was injured when the driver failed to negotiate a sharp curve on a rural access road. The plaintiff had been aware that the driver had been drinking when he accepted the lift. The trial judge held the plaintiff 15 percent to blame, the driver 50 percent, for driving too fast and while impaired, and the municipality 35 percent, for not having erected a sign warning of the dangerous bend.[28]

By applying an appropriate standard of care to the plaintiff as well as to the defendant, the courts have also taken account of changing social standards. For example, it is now common to find that a person injured in a motor vehicle accident has contributed to some extent to her own injuries by failure to wear a seat belt.[29]

Another problem arises when the victim is not to blame for the accident itself but her own *subsequent* conduct contributes to the *extent* of her original injuries— for example, where a plaintiff refuses to undergo safe and simple surgery or

---

[26.] In *Fontaine* v. *Loewen Estate* (1998), 1 S.C.R. 424, the Supreme Court of Canada held that the *res ipsa loquitur* principle was an unnecessarily confusing approach to the circumstantial evidence rule. There was no presumption of negligence simply because a vehicle left the road in a single-vehicle accident.

[27.] Ontario passed the first statute in the field: Negligence Act, S.O. 1924, c. 32.

[28.] The Supreme Court of Canada upheld the trial judge's determination: *Housen* v. *Nikolaisen* (2002), 211 D.L.R. (4th) 577.

[29.] A driver of a vehicle may be held negligent for failure to ensure that a child passenger is wearing a seat belt: *Galaske* v. *O'Donnell* (1994), 112 D.L.R. (4th) 109 (S.C.C.); see also *Heller* v. *Martens* (2002), 213 D.L.R. (4th) 124.

refuses to accept blood transfusions,[30] and thus aggravates her condition. In some cases, the courts have decided that part of the damages were due to the plaintiff's unreasonable conduct and were therefore not recoverable.[31] This result may be justified on the ground that the plaintiff's own conduct has contributed to the seriousness of the injury. Alternatively, it may be regarded as an application of the principle that a plaintiff is expected to act reasonably to minimize, or **mitigate**, any damage suffered.

It is important to note that the statutory defence of contributory negligence may be raised only in actions based in tort law.[32] A farmer whose crops were destroyed sued the manufacturer and supplier of a pesticide. He successfully claimed that the instructions for use did not contain an adequate warning of the risks involved; the alleged negligence of the farmer himself was held to be no defence since the action was based on breach of contract.[33]

PRODUCT LIABILITY

One of the most important areas of tort law, for many businesses, is the liability of manufacturers for injury or loss caused by defects in their products. Consider the four cases below. Who should bear the loss in each one?

CASE SUMMARY 4.10

X runs a small refreshment booth at a beach and buys his supplies from *Y* Bottling Co. Ltd. He sells a dark-green bottle of ginger ale to *A*, who gives it to her friend, *B*. *B* drinks half the contents and becomes violently ill. The balance is found to contain a decomposed snail. *B* is hospitalized and is unable to return to work for several weeks.

CASE SUMMARY 4.11

P buys a *Q* Company sports car from Dealer *R*. On being driven away from the showroom, the car loses a defective front wheel and collides with a parked vehicle, injuring the occupant, *S*.

[30.] *Hobbs* v. *Robertson* (2004) 243 D.L.R. (4th) 700.

[31.] See *Janiak* v. *Ippolito* (1985), 16 D.L.R. (4th) 1 (S.C.C.).

[32.] It also seems that the defence is not available in strict liability torts, such as conversion; see *Boma Manufacturing Ltd.* v. *Canadian Imperial Bank of Commerce* (1996), 140 D.L.R. (4th) 463 (S.C.C.). However, where the breach of duty is identical in both contract and tort, some courts have allowed the defence of contributory negligence to be raised against both claims: see *Crown West Steel Fabricators* v. *Capri Insurance Services Ltd.* (2002), 214 D.L.R. (4th) 577.

[33.] *Caners* v. *Eli Lilley Canada Inc.* (1996), 134 D.L.R. (4th) 730 (Man. C.A.). This aspect of contractual liability is discussed in Chapter 8.

CASE SUMMARY 4.12

M buys from the *N* Ski Shop a set of thermal underwear manufactured by *O* Company. The underwear contains a toxic acid and when it comes in contact with perspiration causes *M* to have a severe skin burn.

CASE SUMMARY 4.13

J buys a bottle of cough medicine, manufactured by the *K* company, from her local drugstore. To try to get rid of her cold she drinks two stiff whiskies, takes a dose of the medicine, and goes to bed. During the night she has a heart attack. The cough medicine is extremely dangerous if taken with alcohol, but there was no warning to that effect on the bottle or package.

The retailer in each of our examples may be liable to the buyer for breach of an implied *contractual* undertaking that a product is not defective. But in Case Summary 4.10, *X* sold the soft drink to *A* rather than to *B*, the injured party: there was no contract with *B*. Similarly, in Case Summary 4.11, the injured person, *S*, has no contractual relationship with Dealer *R*. In these circumstances, contractual remedies are not available. If the injured parties are going to be compensated, it must be by imposing liability in tort law or by providing a special statutory remedy. (See Figure 4.1.)

It was not until 1932 that the British courts recognized the duty of manufacturers to the ultimate consumers of their products as an obligation in tort law. The House of Lords did so in the famous case of *Donoghue* v. *Stevenson*,[34] in which the facts were similar to those in Case Summary 4.10. Case Summary 4.11 is drawn in part from the United States case *MacPherson* v. *Buick Motor Co.*,[35] decided by the New York Court of Appeals in 1916, a decision that may have influenced the later House of Lords decision.

In the years since *Donoghue* v. *Stevenson*, its principle has been applied by the courts in a wide variety of circumstances to protect consumers and other members of the public. The complexity and sophistication of modern manufactured products makes it increasingly difficult for consumers and distributors to detect dangers in those products, and places manufacturers in a position of growing responsibility for the safety of consumers. In Case Summary 4.6, dealing with the fly in the water bottle, the Supreme Court of Canada declared that it is well established that a manufacturer of consumable goods owes a duty of care to the ultimate consumer.[36] This duty also extends to other businesses in the chain of distribution.[37]

[34.] [1932] A.C. 562.

[35.] 111 N.E. 1050 (1916).

[36.] *Mustapha*, *supra*, note 12 at para. 6.

[37.] New Brunswick has made this duty abundantly clear by codifying it in the Consumer Product Warranty and Liability Act, S.N.B. 1978, c. C-18.1.

Figure 4.1 Product Liability

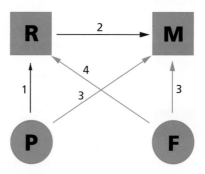

Manufacturer *M* sells a product to retailer *R*, which sells it to purchaser *P*. The product is defective and injures *P* and her friend, *F*. *P* can sue *R* in contract [1], and *R* can sue *M* for its loss, also in contract [2]. *P* and *F* can sue *M* in tort [3]. *F* might also be able to sue *R* in tort, if *R* should have discovered the defect.

To hold that manufacturers owe a duty of care to consumers and others who might be injured is only a partial solution to the problem. Normally, an injured party will have no way of proving that the manufacturer was negligent. However, if the product is defective, then it may be reasonable to assume that there has been negligence in some stage of its design, production, or inspection, unless there is evidence of some other reason for the defect. The circumstantial evidence principle will be applied. The manufacturer will be liable unless it can show that the cause of the defect was not something for which it should be held responsible, or at least that it had taken all reasonable precautions to prevent defective goods from reaching the distribution system.[38]

In Case Summary 4.12, based on the leading case of *Grant* v. *Australian Knitting Mills*,[39] the manufacturing company was placed in the following dilemma: if the inspection process permitted the underwear to pass through undetected, the system was inadequate and the company was therefore negligent. If the inspection process was virtually foolproof, as the manufacturer claimed, then one of its employees must have been personally at fault, making the manufacturer vicariously liable. As a result, manufacturers are liable for injuries resulting directly from all product defects of which, given the present state of technology, they can reasonably be expected to be aware.[40] Manufacturers who choose to reduce costs by omitting necessary safety features, or by using a system of sampling inspection rather than inspecting every item, become responsible for harm that results. In the long run, the savings in production cost may be outweighed by increased insurance premiums for product liability.

[38.] United States courts have gone further. They tend to favour a principle of strict liability, under which the manufacturer impliedly warrants its products to be free of defects regardless of negligence. However, the end result is probably not very different.

[39.] [1936] A.C. 85.

[40.] The situation may be different where the defective item is merely a component that is incorporated into the product of another manufacturer. In that case, the second manufacturer has the opportunity, and duty, to test the component for defects: see *Viridian Inc.* v. *Dresser Canada Inc.* (2002), 216 D.L.R. (4th) 122.

Case Summary 4.13 takes us a stage further. Even though a product is not defective in any way, there may be dangers if the product is not properly used. Courts have ruled that manufacturers owe a duty to consumers to give proper warning of such dangers.[41]

The **duty to warn** is a continuing one, owed to consumers of the product. If, after a product has been placed on the market, the manufacturer becomes aware of potential dangers in its use, it must issue appropriate warnings to the public.[42] Sometimes, however, the duty may be met by issuing the warning to a "learned intermediary." In *Hollis* v. *Dow Corning Corp.*[43] the Supreme Court of Canada considered that the warning of the dangers of silicone breast implants should have been given to the physicians who would perform the implant operation. Had this been done, a direct warning to the public might not have been necessary.[44]

A plaintiff whose claim is based on a failure to warn must also satisfy the court that, had a proper warning been given, she would not have used the product or would not have used it in the way she did; that is, the failure to warn must have been a cause of the injury.[45]

> **duty to warn**
> to make users aware of the risks associated with the use of the product

---

CONTEMPORARY ISSUE

Tobacco Litigation

Astronomical awards of damages in the United States against tobacco manufacturers have received a lot of publicity. Individual smokers who have become ill as a result of smoking have received large sums in compensation. In July 2000, in Florida, for example, a court awarded US $145 billion in punitive damages in a class action on behalf of 700 000 smokers and former smokers. Two years later a Los Angeles court awarded US $28 billion in punitive damages to a single plaintiff (though this was reduced on appeal to a mere US $28 million). State governments have also launched proceedings to recover the extra health-care costs that they have incurred in treating tobacco-related illnesses. In 1998, a settlement was reached under which the major tobacco companies agreed to pay a group of states a total of US $246 billion over a 25-year period.

---

41. *Lambert* v. *Lastoplex Chemical Co. Ltd.*, [1972] S.C.R. 569 (inflammable lacquer); *Buchan* v. *Ortho Pharmaceutical (Canada) Ltd.* (1984), 28 C.C.L.T. 233 (Ont.) (side effects of contraceptive pills); *Plas-Tex Canada Ltd.* v. *Dow Chemical of Canada Ltd.*, supra, n. 30 (defective resin). The duty to warn may be excluded by an express contractual provision; see *Bow Valley Husky (Bermuda) Ltd.* v. *Saint John Shipbuilding Ltd.* (1997), 153 D.L.R. (4th) 385 (S.C.C.). For an interesting analysis of the duty to warn see D.W. Boivin, "Factual Causation in the Law of Manufacturer—Failure to Warn" (1998–99) 30 Ottawa Law Rev. 47.

42. *Nicholson* v. *John Deere Ltd.* (1989), 57 D.L.R. (4th) 639.

43. (1995), 129 D.L.R. (4th) 609.

44. The physician might then be liable if he operated without explaining the risk to the patient.

45. In *Hollis* v. *Dow Corning Corp.*, *supra*, n. 50, the Supreme Court of Canada preferred a subjective approach to causation in product liability cases; would the plaintiff have used the product if she had known of the risk? See also *Arndt* v. *Smith* (1997), 148 D.L.R. (4th) 48 (S.C.C.).

Tobacco litigation in Canada is a more recent development. Claims for compensation have been brought both by individuals[46] and in the form of class actions.[47]

Canadian governments, too, have joined in the action. The federal government brought an action to recover health-care costs in New York State, presumably in the expectation of obtaining much larger damages than a Canadian court was likely to award. The action was dismissed on a technicality, having cost the government about $13 million in legal fees. Meanwhile, British Columbia passed a statute specifically entitling the government to recover health-care costs.[48] The first statute was declared unconstitutional by the B.C. Supreme Court.[49] A replacement statute was promptly enacted[50] and declared constitutional by the Supreme Court of Canada.[51]

Questions to Consider

1. Should individual smokers be compensated for smoking-related illnesses? How can one prove the illness was caused by smoking? Are smokers responsible for their own misfortunes? Should they be held contributorily negligent?

2. What is the basis for the claims to recover health-care costs? Should governments that have permitted the sale of cigarettes, knowing the health risks, and that have collected vast amounts of tax on their sale be entitled to compensation for the costs of providing health care?

3. Is it appropriate for a government to enact a statute for the specific purpose of allowing it to bring a claim? Is that a form of retroactive legislation?

(For an interesting review of these issues relating to tobacco liability, see G. Edinger, "The Tobacco Damages and Health Care Costs Recovery Act" [2001], 35 *Canadian Business Law Journal* 95.)

[46.] See *McIntyre Estate* v. *Ontario* (2003), 218 D.L.R. (4th) 193. That case is notable in that the Ontario Court of Appeal permitted the action to be brought on a contingency-fee basis.

[47.] *Caputo* v. *Imperial Tobacco Limited* (2004), 236 D.L.R. (4th) 348. The action was dismissed for failure to establish an identifiable class.

[48.] Tobacco Damages and Health Care Costs Recovery Act, S.B.C. 1998, c. 45.

[49.] *JTI-Macdonald Corp.* v. *British Columbia* (2000), 184 D.L.R. (4th) 335.

[50.] Tobacco Damages and Health Care Costs Recovery Act, S.B.C. 2000, c. 30. The government of Newfoundland and Labrador has enacted a similar statute: Tobacco Health Care Costs Recovery Act, S.N.L.2001, c. T-4.2.

[51.] *British Columbia* v. *Imperial Tobacco Canada Ltd.*, [2005] 2 S.C.R. 473, 2005 SCC 49.

SUMMARY

Negligence

- Inadvertent conduct falling below an acceptable standard of behaviour
- Plaintiff must establish:
  - A duty of care was owed—using reasonable foreseeability test; in new situations, the court may also refer to policy considerations
  - Breach of duty—by conduct falling below the level expected from a reasonable person
  - Causation—"but for" test establishes physical link; remoteness test used to determine if the injury or damage was unforeseeable; must show that material damage resulted from the conduct
  - Damage—must show that material damage resulted from the conduct
- Defences to negligence
  - If there is contributory negligence, courts may apportion the losses
- Product liability
  - Manufacturers owe a duty of care to consumers of their products, but the plaintiff consumer must establish breach of that duty, causation, and damage

QUESTIONS

1. What must a plaintiff prove in order to succeed in an action based on negligence?

2. In what circumstances may a public authority be held liable for damage resulting from its failure to carry out a statutory duty imposed on it?

3. How do the courts determine the appropriate standard of care to be expected of a defendant?

4. Is the "but for" test an appropriate way of determining causation?

5. What is meant by "economic loss"? What are the two types of economic loss?

6. Should an injured party be able to recover damages despite the fact that her own conduct was negligent and contributed to the injury?

7. When is a manufacturer under a duty to warn?

Chapter 5

Professional Liability

CHAPTER OBJECTIVES

1. Describe the three different ways the law imposes liability on professionals: contract, fiduciary duty, and tort
2. Identify the special duties owed by professionals to their clients and others
3. Explain the role of professional organizations in setting standards for professional conduct

PROFESSIONAL LIABILITY: THE LEGAL DILEMMA

As business becomes more complex, professional services have become one of the fastest growing and most important sectors of the economy; at the same time, the potential for economic harm caused by negligent or fraudulent conduct of professionals has also grown considerably.

We use the term "professionals" here to apply to people who have specialized knowledge and skills that their clients rely on and are prepared to pay for. Usually they belong to some professional body and are licensed by that body to offer their services to the public. Professional opinions, obviously, are not infallible. Their value lies in assisting in clients' decisions and in increasing the likelihood that those decisions will be sound. The purchase of professional services reduces risk. But when a client pays for and relies on professional advice and it turns out to be wrong, the question arises whether the professional is liable for the loss or harm suffered by the client, or even by someone else, who relies on the advice. As we shall discuss, tort is one way to assign liability to a professional. In addition, a professional may be found liable under the contract to supply the advice. Finally, the law may require the professional to honour a fiduciary duty separate from her tort or contractual obligations.

As in other areas of tort law, the courts face a problem in determining when liability for professional incompetence or negligence arises. In theory, there is a persuasive argument to be made in favour of widened liability of professionals. The benefits (or utility) gained by a plaintiff who recovers damages will exceed the losses (or reduced utility) of a professional defendant who has to pay them but who can recoup the loss by increasing fees and by purchasing insurance protection to safeguard against liability. However, if the courts go too far and award damages to compensate everyone who relies on bad advice, the increased costs will likely discourage people from entering the profession and increase the price of advice beyond reach.

In practice, the greater exposure to liability for professional negligence has led to extensive use of liability insurance. Because of uncertainty concerning liability and the risk of heavy damages, insurance premiums have been rising. Professional fees, in turn, increase to cover insurance costs. As fees rise, clients expect more for their money, and when they are disappointed are more likely to sue. The process is something of a vicious circle and striking a fair balance can be a challenge for the courts.[1]

Liability of Professionals

Professional liability may be considered under three headings:

- contractual duty
- fiduciary duty
- duty in tort

In most cases, the professional stands in a contractual relationship with her client. Because of the professional's skill and experience, a special relationship of trust usually also exists between professional and client, giving rise to a fiduciary duty. And a professional, like anyone else, owes a duty of care under tort law to persons who may foreseeably be injured by her negligence.

Contractual Duty

An agreement to provide professional services to a client contains a promise, whether stated expressly or not, to perform those services with due care. A breach of that promise is a breach of the contract, and the client may then sue for damages.

Fiduciary Duty

A professional's duty often extends beyond her contractual duty in an important way. A principle of equity imposes a **fiduciary duty** where a person is in a special relationship of trust, such as often exists in professional–client relations.[2] This fiduciary duty can arise even when the professional donates services free of charge, so that no contract exists.

fiduciary duty
a duty imposed on a person who stands in a special relation of trust to another

The first step to imposing liability for breach of fiduciary duty is establishing that the relationship is one to which the duty applies. According to the judgment of Wilson, J. in the Supreme Court of Canada, in *Frame* v. *Smith*,[3] relationships in which a fiduciary obligation exists possess three general characteristics:

- The fiduciary has scope for the exercise of some discretion or power.
- The fiduciary can unilaterally exercise that power or discretion so as to affect the beneficiary's legal or practical interests.
- The beneficiary is peculiarly vulnerable to or is at the mercy of the fiduciary holding the discretion or power.

[1.] The dilemma is well summarized by Professor Brian Cheffins regarding the potential liability of auditors for incorrect statements in a corporation's financial statements: B.R. Cheffins, "Auditors' Liability in the House of Lords: A Signal Canadian Courts Should Follow" (1991), 18 C.B.L.J. 118 at 125–7; this passage was quoted with approval by LaForest, J. in the Supreme Court of Canada *Hercules Managements Ltd.* v. *Ernst & Young* (1997), 146 D.L.R. (4th) 577 at 593.

[2.] *Nocton* v. *Lord Ashburton*, [1914] A.C. 932 at 943–58; *Hedley, Byrne & Co. Ltd.* v. *Heller & Partners Ltd.*, [1964] A.C. 465 at 486.

[3.] [1987] 2 S.C.R. 99 at 136. See also *Air Canada* v. *M & L Travel Ltd.* (1993), 108 D.L.R. (4th) 592.

The law has long recognized some professional relationships as inherently fiduciary including lawyer/client and doctor/patient. But not every professional relationship is a fiduciary one. For example, the broker and client relationship depends on the particular facts of the case. Five factors applicable to the assessment of a financial advisor/client relationship are: vulnerability, trust, reliance, discretion, and the standards expressed in a professional code of conduct.[4]

CASE SUMMARY 5.1

Mr. and Mrs. Hunt, a retired couple in their 70s, set up an investment account with Mr. Schram of TD Evergreen. Mr. Schram considered Mr. Hunt a person of average investment knowledge. Prior to his retirement, Mr. Hunt was a vice-president and director of a large footwear manufacturer.

The account was "non-discretionary," that is, no trade was to be completed without Mr. Hunt's express authorization. Mr. Schram sold 1349 of the Hunts' 1472 shares in BCE. By the time Mr. Hunt learned of the sale, the BCE stock price had risen and the Hunts sued for the lost profit. The Hunts claimed breach of contract and breach of fiduciary duty. The Court of Appeal found that the unauthorized sale amounted to a breach of contract but disallowed the claim for breach of fiduciary duty. The Court found that the relationship was not a fiduciary one. It lacked the necessary degree of discretion, reliance, and trust; Schram could not exercise unilateral power over the account and all other trades were directed by Mr. Hunt. Although there were some health and age issues, these did not amount to vulnerability in the context of the relationship.[5]

If a fiduciary duty is found to exist, it imposes a wider range of obligations on a professional than is expressly stated in the contract or required under tort law. The professional must act honestly, in good faith, and only in the best interests of the client. The second step to imposing liability involves determining if the professional's behaviour meets the fiduciary duty. For example, a lawyer who entered into a business arrangement with a client of long standing and failed to disclose his own precarious financial situation was held to be in breach of his fiduciary duty to the client.[6] And an accountant may not use information obtained from a client to make an investment without the consent of the client.

Liability for breach of fiduciary duty may arise without any negligence.

Case Summary 5.2 illustrates the principle that a fiduciary should not place herself in a position of **conflict of interest** and has a duty not to profit, or attempt to profit, at the client's expense. A fiduciary obligation requires complete loyalty to the other party to the relationship. Consequently, a professional who acts on behalf of two or more clients who have competing interests (for example, the vendor and the purchaser of a piece of property) may well find it impossible to fulfill her duty to them both. In one recent case, the Ontario Court of Appeal made an order prohibiting a law firm, one of whose lawyers had represented two book stores in an amalgamation five years earlier, from acting for a prospective

conflict of interest
a situation where a duty is owed to a client whose interests conflict with the interests of the professional, another client, or another person to whom a duty is owed

---

4. *Hodgkinson* v. *Simms*, [1994] 3 S.C.R. 377.

5. *Hunt* v. *TD Securities Inc.*, (2003) 229 D.L.R. (4th) 609 (Ont. C.A.).

6. *Korz* v. *St. Pierre* (1987), 61 O.R. (2d) 609; *Strother* v. *3464920 Canada Inc.*, [2007] 2 S.C.R. 177.

> **CASE SUMMARY 5.2**
>
> Hodgkinson, a stockbroker, was inexperienced in tax planning. He wanted an independent professional to advise him in respect to tax planning and tax shelter needs. He retained Simms, an accountant who specialized in these areas. On Simms' advice, Hodgkinson invested in a number of MURBs (multiple unit residential buildings) as tax shelters and lost heavily when the value of the MURBs fell during a decline in the real estate market. The advice was perfectly sound at the time it was given. Unknown to Hodgkinson, Simms was also acting for the developers in structuring the MURBs and did not disclose that fact to Hodgkinson. The Supreme Court of Canada accepted the client's claim that he would not have undertaken the investment had he known of the adviser's conflict of interest. Simms was held to be in breach of his fiduciary duty to Hodgkinson and consequently liable to compensate Hodgkinson for his loss.[7]

purchaser of the amalgamated company.[8] The law firm possessed confidential information that it had acquired in the earlier transaction. The firm was placed in a potentially impossible position: its duty to its previous clients forbade it to disclose the information, which in turn made it difficult to represent the new client effectively.

> **ETHICAL ISSUE**
>
> ## Lessons from Enron
>
> Enron was the seventh-largest public corporation in the United States. The energy giant's collapse into bankruptcy cost investors billions of dollars and was accompanied by revelations of fraud and impropriety on a massive scale.
>
> The Enron affair highlighted the many conflicts of interest that arise when a corporation's external auditors also act as its accountants, business advisers, or management consultants. In theory, a corporation's auditors are appointed by its shareholders: their task is to supervise the financial management of the corporation's affairs by the directors and management and to report any irregularities. In reality, the auditors are usually selected by the management and their appointment is a formality. They consequently owe their position to the very people they are meant to supervise, an obvious conflict of interest.
>
> A second conflict of interest arises when the auditors are themselves members of a firm that has lucrative contracts to supply accounting and management services to the corporation that they are required to audit. If they judge the directors too harshly, they may jeopardize those contracts and lose an important source of income for their firm.
>
> To address these and other governance problems, the United States passed the Sarbanes-Oxley Act of 2002 (SOX), which introduced a number of changes, including:
>
> - prohibiting a company from hiring one accounting firm to provide both auditing and consulting services, and
> - placing auditor selection under the control of directors who do not work at the company.

[7.] *Hodgkinson v. Simms, supra,* n. 4. See also *Martin v. Goldfarb* (1998), 163 D.L.R. (4th) 639 and *Strother* at note 6.

[8.] *Chapters Inc. v. Davies, Ward & Beck LLP.* [2000] O.J. No. 4973.

The application of SOX was not limited to American companies—it applied even to foreign companies trading on an American exchange. As we will discuss in Chapter 17, Canada immediately felt the impact of SOX and has now adopted many of the SOX provisions.

Questions to Consider

1. What other possible solutions would you propose to minimize conflicts of interest?

2. Is it appropriate for American legislation to apply to Canadian corporations?

3. Accountants have always been under a duty to avoid conflicts of interest. Why was this existing duty not sufficient to prevent the auditor/consultant conflict?

Sources: New York State Society of Certified Public Accountants, "The Sarbanes-Oxley Act of 2002," *The Website of the New York Society of CPAs*, www.nysscpa.org/oxleyact2002. htm; L. McCallum and P. Puri, *Canadian Companies' Guide to Sarbanes-Oxley Act*, (Markham: LexisNexis Butterworth, 2004).

Duty in Tort

Until the 1980s the courts appeared to favour the view that a professional's liability to her client should be governed by the duties owed under the contract.[9] They limited a client's right to sue for the tort of negligence to special circumstances where the professional's conduct did not fall within her contractual obligations. Subsequent decisions suggested that a plaintiff might choose to sue either in contract or in tort, and this approach has been confirmed by the Supreme Court of Canada. In a case where a solicitor was negligent in arranging a mortgage that was later found to be void, the Court held that the client was entitled to sue in either contract or tort.[10] The common law duty of care is not confined to relationships that arise apart from contract—it exists independently of the duty owed under the contract.

Of greater importance, usually, is the fact that a duty may be owed in tort to persons other than the client who is paying for the services. Many people may rely on a professional opinion given to a single client, as for example:

- when an auditor expresses an opinion on the fairness and accuracy of the client firm's financial statements

- when engineers or architects recommend design specifications for structures that, if faulty, may present risks to occupiers and others

- when bankers or credit analysts give assessments of creditworthiness for their customers which come to the attention of other lenders

- when accountants provide a corporation with a valuation of the business or its shares, and the valuation is intended for the use of a third party

- when a lawyer prepares a will for a client who intends to leave property to a beneficiary under the will

- when one doctor gives a professional opinion to another doctor concerning the patient of the second doctor

---

9. *Nunes Diamonds* v. *Dominion Electric Co.* (1972), 26 D.L.R. (3d) 699 at 727–8.

10. *Central Trust Co.* v. *Rafuse* (1986), 31 D.L.R. (4th) 481.

Potential **third-party liability** also exists for insurance agents and real estate agents. The contractual duty of a real estate agent is normally owed to the vendor of the property; that of an insurance agent is usually owed to the insurance company with which she arranges insurance.[11] In the course of their work for their principals, however, these agents develop close relations with persons to whom they may refer as "clients"—applicants for insurance and prospective purchasers of houses. While in a strict sense their commissions are paid by their principals, the persons with whom they deal in the course of their work provide them with the opportunity of earning the commissions and frequently rely on their advice.

As we shall see, one of the most difficult questions that the courts have had to answer in recent years is where, precisely, to draw the line in deciding when a professional incurs liability to a non-client for a negligent or inaccurate statement.

third-party liability
liability to some other person who stands outside a contractual relationship

CASE SUMMARY 5.3

A credit union was investigated by the government agency responsible for supervision. The investigation revealed that, over a number of years, the credit union had made various unauthorized and unsecured loans, and its loans department had committed various other irregularities. The credit union brought an action against its former auditors, claiming that they ought to have discovered the irregularities if their audits had been conducted with proper care. The auditors were found to have been negligent and were held liable for losses sustained by the credit union. However, the credit union was held to have been contributorily negligent, in failing to exercise proper supervision over its loan manager, and was held to be 30 percent to blame.[12]

The Choice of Action

Before turning to the tort liability question, one other issue needs to be addressed. As we have seen, sometimes a professional may be liable in tort but not in contract, or may be liable for breach of fiduciary duty without having been negligent. But there will frequently be cases where the professional is liable in both contract and in tort, and perhaps for breach of fiduciary duty as well. Does it matter whether the client sues for breach of contract, breach of fiduciary duty, or for negligence?

The choice may be important. The rules governing the time limits for bringing an action might make it advantageous to sue in tort.[13] On the other hand, in a tort action a client's own contributory negligence may be raised as a defence, though the defendant may still rely upon any term of the contract that excludes

[11.] By contrast, an insurance broker usually acts as agent for the insured: see the discussion in *Adams-Eden Furniture Ltd.* v. *Kansa General Insurance Co.* (1996), 141 D.L.R. (4th) 288.

[12.] *Capital Community Credit Union Ltd.* v. *BDO Dunwoody* [2001] O.J. No. 4249.

[13.] The time limit for a tort action is normally calculated from the moment when the breach is discovered, rather than when it occurs, as is the rule in contract. In *Central Trust Co.* v. *Rafuse, supra,* n. 10, the invalidity of the mortgage was not discovered until some years after it was executed. This difference in time limits is also important in cases of negligence by an architect or builder, where a defect may only be discovered many years after construction has been completed and it would be too late to sue in contract.

Figure 5.1 Contractual and Tort Liability

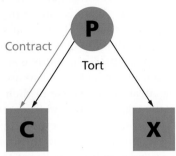

The professional (P) owes both a contractual duty and a duty in tort to client (C). The only duty owed to a third party (X) is a duty in tort. (There may be occasions when a fiduciary duty is owed to C or to X.)

or limits liability.[14] As we saw in Case Summary 5.1, the problem can often be avoided by pleading both, or all three, causes of action in the alternative.[15]

The form of the action may also affect the amount of damages awarded in some cases. The principles for determining the measure of damages are not exactly the same in contract as in tort.[16] In the case of breach of fiduciary duty, a defendant may be under a **duty to account** for any profit derived from the breach in addition to or as an alternative to damages. However, in *Hodgkinson* v. *Simms*,[17] the Supreme Court of Canada held that damages for breach of a fiduciary duty should place the plaintiff in the position he would have been in if the breach had not occurred. In *Martin* v. *Goldfarb*, Finlayson, J.A., delivering the judgment of the Ontario Court of Appeal, expressed the view that, regardless of the doctrinal underpinning, plaintiffs should not be able to recover higher damage awards merely because their claim is characterized as breach of fiduciary duty as opposed to breach of contract or tort.[18]

duty to account
the duty of a person who commits a breach of trust to hand over any profits derived from the breach

LIABILITY FOR INACCURATE STATEMENTS

Misrepresentation

If a person makes an untrue statement, knowing it to be untrue, or at any rate without an honest belief in its truth, and with the intention to mislead some other

---

14. *Central Trust Co.* v. *Rafuse*, *supra*, n. 10; *London Drugs Ltd.* v. *Kuehne & Nagel International Ltd.* (1992), 97 D.L.R. (4th) 261.

15. Where the plaintiff sues in both contract and in tort, it seems that the defence of contributory negligence can be raised against both claims; see *Crown West Steel Fabricators* v. *Capri Insurance Services Ltd.* (2002), 214 D.L.R. (4th) 577: contrast *Caners* v. *Eli Lilly Canada Inc.* (1996), 134 D.L.R. (4th) 730, where the action was brought only in contract.

16. See Chapter 3, under the heading "Remedies."

17. *Supra*, n. 4; see Case Summary 5.1.

18. (1998), 163 D.L.R. (4th) 639 at 652. Clearly, some uncertainty remains: see Waddams, "Fiduciary Duties and Equitable Compensation" (1996), 27 C.B.L.J. 466.

person, the misrepresentation is fraudulent and amounts to the tort of **deceit**. A victim who relies reasonably on the statement and suffers a loss may recover from the person who made it. The tort of deceit may also be committed when a person deliberately conceals or withholds information.

deceit
the making of a false statement with the intention of misleading another person

---

CASE SUMMARY 5.4

A bank allowed a customer to invest in a company that owed a substantial debt to the bank. The bank's employees knew that the company was on the verge of insolvency but did not disclose this fact to the customer. The bank was held guilty of fraud and liable to compensate the customer.[19]

Whereas deceit or **fraudulent misrepresentation** requires at least some guilty knowledge or willful disregard of the falsity of information provided, **negligent misrepresentation** requires only a breach of the duty of care and skill.

One of the most significant developments in the law of torts has been the extension of liability to include negligent acts causing purely economic loss, as distinguished from those causing injury to persons or property.[20] For a long time the courts drew back from holding persons liable for negligent misrepresentation except when there was a contract with the injured party or when they were subject to a fiduciary duty. The courts were especially reluctant to impose liability for negligent misrepresentation, in the absence of a direct contractual or fiduciary relationship, on professionals giving financial advice and information such as accountants, bankers, trust company officers, and stockbrokers, whose statements often reach large numbers of the public. They feared that to extend liability to third persons, for advice given to and intended only for a client, would make the risk so wide as to limit severely the reasonable freedom of professionals to practise their occupations. In a case in 1951, the English Court of Appeal held that an accountant who carelessly audited a misleading financial statement, knowing that it would be shown to a prospective investor, was not liable to the investor for the loss caused by reliance on the audited statement.[21] Lord Justice Denning, who dissented from the majority opinion, considered that such risks were greatly exaggerated: the duty of care need not be owed to every conceivable person, but should be confined to the particular person.

fraudulent misrepresentation
an incorrect statement made knowingly with the intention of causing injury to another

negligent misrepresentation
an incorrect statement made without due care for its accuracy

The *Hedley Byrne* Principle

Twelve years later, Lord Denning's position was accepted by the House of Lords in the famous case of *Hedley Byrne* v. *Heller & Partners*.[22]

The House of Lords found that although Heller neither dealt with nor even knew the identity of Hedley Byrne, Heller should have foreseen that its information would be used by a customer of the other bank. It therefore owed that customer a duty to take reasonable care in expressing an opinion about the financial

---

[19.] *Sugar* v. *Peat Marwick Ltd.* (1988), 55 D.L.R. (4th) 230.

[20.] Negligent misstatements causing physical injury have long been actionable—for example, where an architect's negligent design causes a building to collapse.

[21.] *Candler* v. *Crane, Christmas & Co.*, [1951] 2 K.B. 164.

[22.] *Hedley Byrne* v. *Heller & Partners*, [1964] A.C. 465.

CASE SUMMARY 5.5

Easipower asked Hedley Byrne, an advertising agency, to handle its account in placing ads in magazines and commercials on radio and TV. Since Hedley Byrne would have to extend credit to Easipower in arranging the advertising, it first decided to ask its own bank to obtain credit information on Easipower, and in particular about whether Easipower would be good for a line of credit up to certain limits. The bank manager made inquiries from Heller & Partners (Easipower's bankers) about Easipower's credit-worthiness, without revealing Hedley Byrne's identity. Heller sent the following letter in reply:

Confidential

For your private use and without responsibility on the part of the bank or its officers

Dear Sir:

In reply to your inquiry we advise that Easipower is a respectably constituted company, considered good for its ordinary business obligations. Your figures are larger than we are accustomed to see.

Yours truly,

Heller & Partners.

At no time did Hedley Byrne communicate directly with Heller, but its own bank did inform it of the full contents of the letter, including the disclaimer of responsibility. Hedley Byrne then accepted Easipower as an account and placed extensive advertising for it, running up a large balance. Shortly afterwards Easipower became insolvent and was unable to pay Hedley Byrne more than a small portion of the debt. Hedley Byrne sued Heller for the resulting loss, claiming it was caused by Heller's negligent misrepresentation of Easipower's creditworthiness.

---

disclaimer

an express statement to the effect that the person making it takes no responsibility for a particular action or statement

state of Easipower. On the facts, however, the court held that, because of the **disclaimer** of responsibility, Hedley Byrne could not rely on the information. Nevertheless, the *Hedley Byrne* decision established the principle of liability to third parties for negligent misrepresentation.

The result is that a person who makes such a misstatement may be held liable for losses suffered by a wider group than those with whom she has a direct contractual or fiduciary relationship. The crucial question is, "How wide is that group?"

Limits to the *Hedley Byrne* Principle

If the test of liability for negligent misrepresentation turned entirely on who could foreseeably be harmed, banks, public accountants, and other financial analysts might be faced with an almost unlimited liability. For example, the auditors of a corporation whose financial statements are made public know that the statements will be relied upon by many people who are unknown to them. They could be liable then to anyone who might happen to read the financial statements.[23]

---

23. This fear is largely responsible for the enactment in Ontario of legislation allowing for the creation of limited liability partnerships by accounting and other professional firms.

CASE SUMMARY 5.6

Shareholders in two corporations brought an action against a firm of accountants, alleging that audits of the corporations' financial statements had been negligently prepared, and that in consequence, they had incurred investment losses and losses in the value of their shareholdings. Their claim failed.

The Supreme Court of Canada held that (a) there was no contractual relationship between the auditors of a corporation and its shareholders; (b) the purpose of the auditor's report was to oversee the management and affairs of the corporation, and (c) the auditors owed shareholders no duty of care in respect of their personal investments.[24]

As to the existence of a duty of care, the court applied a two-part test, expressed as follows.[25]

First one has to ask whether, as between the alleged wrongdoer and the person who has suffered damage there is a sufficient relationship of proximity or neighbourhood such that, in the reasonable contemplation of the former, carelessness on his part may be likely to cause damage to the latter—in which case a *prima facie* duty of care arises. Secondly, if the first question is answered affirmatively, it is necessary to consider whether there are any considerations which ought to negative, or to reduce or limit the scope of the duty or the class of person to whom it is owed or the damages to which a breach of it may give rise. . . .[26]

The first branch of the test requires an inquiry into whether there is a sufficiently close relationship between the plaintiff and the defendant that in the reasonable contemplation of the defendant, carelessness on its part may cause damage to the plaintiff. The court held that a *prima facie* duty of care did exist in the *Hercules* case: the possibility that the shareholders would rely on the audited financial statements of the corporation in conducting their affairs, and that they may suffer harm if the reports were negligently prepared, must have been reasonably foreseeable to the auditors.

The second branch of the test raises what is essentially a policy issue. On this issue, LaForest, J. said:

I would agree that deterrence of negligent conduct is an important policy consideration with respect to auditors' liability. Nevertheless, I am of the view that, in the final analysis, it is outweighed by the socially undesirable consequences to which the imposition of indeterminate liability on auditors might lead.[27]

---

[24]. *Hercules Managements Ltd.* v. *Ernst & Young* (1997), 146 D.L.R. (4th) 577.

[25]. The test was first enunciated by Lord Wilberforce in the *House of Lords in Anns* v. *Merton London Borough Council*, [1978] A.C. 728 at 751–2 (H.L.). It was quoted with approval in the *Hercules* case, by LaForest, J., at 586, and has been followed and applied in a number of other important Canadian decisions; for example, *Kamloops (City)* v. *Nielsen* (1983), 10 D.L.R. (4th) 641; *Winnipeg Condominium Corp. No. 36* v. *Bird Construction Co.* (1995), 121 D.L.R. (4th) 193.

[26]. Just as LaForest, J. intended, this test now applies to all negligence cases, not merely those involving negligent misrepresentation: *Mustapha* v. *Culligan of Canada Ltd.*, 2008 SCC 27 and *Hill* v. *Hamilton-Wentworth Regional Police Services Board*, 2007 SCC 41.

[27]. At 593.

Liability, consequently, should be restricted to the use of the information for the same purpose as that for which it was prepared. As a matter of law, the only purpose for which shareholders receive an auditor's report is to provide them with information in order to be able to oversee the management and affairs of the corporation—not for the purpose of guiding their personal investment decisions. Therefore, no duty of care was owed to them in that regard.

It would seem from this test that eligible plaintiffs must not only be "foreseeable" in a general sense, but also more specifically "foreseen" in relation to a contemplated transaction. So when, in an earlier case, an auditor negligently prepared accounts for a corporation, knowing that they were to be shown to a potential purchaser of the corporation, the Supreme Court of Canada held that he was liable for the loss suffered by the purchaser.[28] Securities legislation creates a statutory cause of action for damages arising from misrepresentations contained in financial statements of publicly traded companies, as well as other documents including a prospectus.[29]

Liability for negligent misrepresentation is not restricted to financial information provided by professionals such as accountants and bankers.[30] A municipality has been held liable for loss suffered by purchasers of land who relied on incorrect information given to them by the zoning department regarding permissible use of the land.[31] An engineering firm that was negligent in preparing drawings and specifications for a provincial construction project was held liable for loss suffered by the construction company that had bid successfully for the contract in reliance on the specifications.[32] Although the scope of the *Hedley Byrne* principle has been gradually widened over the years, the courts remain cautious about extending the principle too far. For example, in one recent case the British Columbia Court of Appeal held that a government department, which had negligently certified to a leasing corporation that a piece of contaminated land had been fully cleaned, was not liable to an investor who bought shares in the leasing corporation. There was insufficient proximity between the Crown and the plaintiff to establish a duty of care and, even if a duty of care was owed, it would be negated by the policy consideration of indeterminate liability.[33] In another case the Ontario Court of Appeal refused to extend liability for a defective smoke alarm system to the organization that set the safety standards and approved the product as safe. The parties did not have the necessary close and direct relationship to justify imposing a duty of care. Even if a *prima facie* duty of care did exist, policy considerations would negate the duty, since to do so would effectively create an insurance scheme for dissatisfied purchasers, for which the purchasers had paid nothing.[34]

---

28. *Haig* v. *Bamford* (1976), 72 D.L.R. (2d) 68.

29. Securities Act, R.S.O. 1990, c. S.5, ss. 130–138.14; R.S.B.C. 1996, c. 418, ss. 131–140; R.S.A. 2000, c. S-4, ss. 203–211.095. For a discussion of the statutory liability see *Kerr* v. *Danier Leather Inc.*, 2007 SCC 44.

30. In one recent case a law firm was held liable for a negligent statement regarding the secured status of a loan: *347671 B.C. Ltd.* v. *Heenan Blaikie* [2002] B.C.J. No. 347.

31. *Bell* v. *City of Sarnia* (1987), 37 D.L.R. (4th) 438.

32. *Edgeworth Constructions Ltd.* v. *N.D. Lea & Associates Ltd.* (1993), 107 D.L.R. (4th) 169. Interestingly, the individual engineers employed by the firm, who prepared the drawings, were held not to owe a duty to the contractor.

33. *Border Enterprises Ltd.* v. *Beazer East Inc.* (2002), 216 D.L.R. (4th) 107.

34. *Hughes* v. *Sunbeam Corp. (Canada) Ltd.* (2003) 219 D.L.R. (4th) 467.

A further requirement of the *Hedley Byrne* principle, apart from the existence of a duty, is that the plaintiff's reliance on the misrepresentation must have been reasonable. An interesting issue was raised in *Avco Financial Services Realty Ltd.* v. *Norman*.[35] At trial, the defendant finance company was held liable for a negligent misrepresentation by failing to point out to the plaintiff that he would need to renew a life insurance policy if he wished to renew his mortgage: the plaintiff was held to have been contributorily negligent by not inquiring further into the terms of the mortgage. On appeal, it was argued that the two findings were mutually inconsistent. If the plaintiff's reliance on the misrepresentation was reasonable, then he could not have been negligent himself. Alternatively, if he was negligent, his reliance on the statement would not have been reasonable. The Ontario Court of Appeal rejected both arguments. The two findings could co-exist: it could be reasonable to rely on a statement, but negligent to rely exclusively upon it.[36]

Omissions

The duty to take reasonable care includes the duty not to omit essential steps in providing professional services. It applies to sins of omission as well as sins of commission.

CASE SUMMARY 5.7

Fine's Flowers Ltd. sustained a serious loss from the freezing of flowers and plants in its greenhouse. The freezing conditions were caused by failure of a water pump, which interrupted the supply of water to boilers that heated the greenhouse. Fine's had arranged its insurance with the same agent for many years and its coverage and premium costs were extensive. It relied on the agent to recommend appropriate coverage and paid the necessary premiums without question. An inspector for the insurance company had advised the agent that the insurance policy with Fine's did not cover such matters as the failure of water pumps but the agent did not report this gap in insurance coverage to Fine's.

Since the policy provided no right of recovery from the insurance company, Fine's brought an action against the agent for breach of his duty of care in failing to notify it of the insufficient coverage. The agent defended on the grounds that such a duty of care was so broad and sweeping as almost to make him strictly liable and that it was not part of his duty to know everything about a client's business in order to be in a position to anticipate every conceivable form of loss. The court nevertheless held that on the facts of the case a duty of care did exist, and Fine's succeeded in recovering damages from the agent. The grounds for recovery could equally be classified as negligent omission or breach of a special fiduciary relationship between Fine's Flowers and the insurance agent.[37]

[35.] (2003) 226 D.L.R. (4th) 175.

[36.] See also *M. Tucci Construction Ltd.* v. *Lockwood* [2000], O.J. No. 3192, where an investor was misled by his accountant as to the nature of an agreement, but was held contributorily negligent for making no effort to have the agreement explained to him and for not taking legal advice.

[37.] *Fine Flowers Ltd.* v. *General Accident Assurance Co. et al.* (1974), 49 D.L.R. (3d) 641; affirmed (1977), 81 D.L.R. (3d) 139. See also *Martin* v. *Goldfarb* (1998), 163 D.L.R. (4th) 639.

A surgeon who operates on a patient without the patient's consent commits the tort of battery. In this context, "consent" means informed consent: before operating, the surgeon should explain the procedure and the possible risks to the patient. The modern tendency has been to hold a doctor liable in battery only when it can be said that there has been no genuine informed consent at all. However, the courts have recognized a patient's right to full information about the risks inherent in a treatment and the omission of relevant information normally amounts to negligence.[38] The court also considers a second question: would a reasonable person in the position of the plaintiff have decided against the procedure upon a proper disclosure of the risks?[39] If the court is satisfied that the answer is "yes," then it is also saying that the failure to inform was not only a breach of duty but also caused the harm—and the patient will be awarded damages in compensation. But where the court is satisfied that the patient would still have consented even if the risk had been explained, the physician will not be liable.[40] The question of causation is discussed more fully later in this chapter.

THE STANDARD OF CARE FOR PROFESSIONALS

We noted that the standard of care applied in ordinary negligence actions is that of "the person on the Yonge Street subway." That standard is obviously inappropriate when judging the work of an accountant, a lawyer, or a surgeon. But how should one determine what is an appropriate and acceptable standard?

CASE SUMMARY 5.8

Hodgins wished to add an extension with an indoor swimming pool to his house. Through his contractor, he sought the advice of the local hydro-electric commission on heating the addition. An employee of the commission, Runions, provided an estimate of the cost of heating by electricity. In reliance on the estimate, Hodgins specified electric heating for the extension. The estimate proved to be much below the actual costs. Hodgins sued the hydro-electric commission for negligent misrepresentation, on the authority of *Hedley Byrne*. Runions was found not to have been negligent.[41]

In reaching that conclusion, the Ontario Court of Appeal explicitly rejected a hindsight approach. Mr. Justice Evans observed:

. . . the Court is required to consider the information available in 1967 to one in the position of Runions. The question then arises: Did Runions exercise reasonable skill, competence and diligence in the preparation of the cost estimate or did he not? In the opinion of the expert, Runions calculated the heat loss in the same manner as anyone similarly expert in the art would have done in 1967. In the light of that uncontradicted evidence, it would appear that Runions prepared his estimate according to the skill and knowledge

---

[38.] Alternatively, it may be treated as a breach of fiduciary duty: see *Seney* v. *Crooks* (1998), 166 D.L.R. (4th) 337.

[39.] *Hopp* v. *Lepp* (1980), 112 D.L.R. (3d) 67; *Reibl* v. *Hughes* (1980), 114 D.L.R. (3d) 1. Contrast the "subjective" test applied in product liability cases, in *Hollis* v. *Dow Corning Corp.* (1995), 129 D.L.R. (4th) 609, considered in Chapter 3.

[40.] *Kitchen* v. *McMullen* (1989), 62 D.L.R. (4th) 481.

[41.] *Hodgins* v. *Hydro-Electric Commission of the Township of Nepean* (1975), 60 D.L.R. (3d) 1.

> available to those engaged in that particular field. If Runions met the standard then he was not negligent and no liability can be imputed to the defendant. That the estimate was incorrect is not questioned, but it is not sufficient that the plaintiff establish merely that Runions' estimate was wrong, he must go further and establish that the incorrect estimate resulted from a lack of skill, competence or diligence on the part of Runions.[42]

The approach taken in the *Hodgins* case was to compare the quality of professional work done or advice given with the standards of the profession prevailing at the time. This approach tends to assess the adequacy of professional work without reference to the consequences of relying on it. However, simply complying with normal professional standards is not always an adequate defence. When the case was appealed to the Supreme Court of Canada, Chief Justice Laskin agreed that the action should be dismissed, but added:

> In my opinion, the care or skill that must be shown by the defendant must depend, as it does here, on what is the information or advice sought from him and which he has unqualifiedly represented that he can give. He may assume to act in a matter beyond his then professional knowledge or that of others in the field and, if he does, he cannot then so limit the plaintiff's reliance unless he qualifies his information or advice accordingly or unless the plaintiff knows what are the limitations of the defendant's competence when seeking the information or advice.[43]

Consequently, there seem to be two tests. A professional must exercise the same degree of skill and possess the same level of knowledge as is generally expected of members of that profession: that is to say, she must live up to the standards of the profession.[44] The courts will normally consider two types of evidence in determining what those standards are. Many professions publish a code of conduct for their members, or guidelines to be followed in particular types of work. These can usually be taken as laying down an appropriate standard. Frequently, the courts also hear the testimony of practitioners who state what they consider a proper standard. Sometimes, of course, professional opinion is divided—for example, about the best medical treatment in a particular circumstance. In such a case it will normally be sufficient that the defendant has followed a well-recognized practice, even though some other procedure might arguably have been better.[45]

But established standards alone should not be allowed to become a means for protecting members of a profession from liability.[46] As Chief Justice Laskin pointed out in the *Hodgins* case, sometimes a professional undertakes a task that is

---

42. *Ibid.*, at 4.

43. *Hodgins* v. *Hydro-Electric Commission of the Township of Nepean* (1975), 60 D.L.R. (3d) 1.

44. No allowance appears to be made for experience: a newly qualified professional is held to the same standard as an experienced one. However, within a profession, a higher standard may apply to a specialist than to a general practitioner.

45. *Belknap* v. *Meekes* (1989), 64 D.L.R. (4th) 452; *ter Neuzen* v. *Korn* (1995), 127 D.L.R. (4th) 577.

46. See, for example, the decision of the Supreme Court of Canada in *Roberge* v. *Bolduc*, [1991] 1 S.C.R. 374, in which a notary was held to have been negligent in conducting a title search despite having followed the common practice in the profession.

beyond the usual skills of her profession; she cannot then rely on the normal professional standard. The degree of skill and knowledge must be commensurate with the particular task undertaken.

CAUSATION

In Chapter 4 we defined the elements of negligence, meaning the conditions that must be met before compensation will be awarded to an injured party. The court must find that: the defendant owed a duty to the injured party, the defendant breached that duty, and the breach of duty caused the injury. We have discussed the first two of these conditions in this chapter in relation to the liability of a professional and now turn to the special problems of satisfying the requirement of causation.

The essence of causation, in professional–client relationships, is reliance. Did the client rely and act upon the advice of the professional? Would the client have acted in that way if he had not received that advice?[47]

CASE SUMMARY 5.9

An investment company became interested in acquiring control of an apparently prosperous family business. The company commissioned a report on the proposed acquisition from a well-known firm of investment analysts. The report estimated the family business to be worth more than $4 million and considered it to be a sound investment. Without having read the report, the directors of the investment company decided that they should move quickly—they had heard rumours that there was another prospective purchaser. They purchased all the shares in the family business for $3.5 million. Subsequently, they learned that the major asset of their acquisition was almost worthless and that they had paid several times what the shares were worth.[48]

Despite their negligence, the analysts were not found liable since their conduct was not in any way a cause of the loss.

THE ROLE OF PROFESSIONAL ORGANIZATIONS

Responsibilities and Powers

Most major professions—medicine, nursing, dentistry, accounting, law, engineering, and architecture—are governed by professional organizations established under, and to some extent regulated by, provincial statutes. A typical professional organization has a governing council composed mainly of elected representatives of the profession, but it may also have external lay representatives appointed by

---

[47.] As we have already noted, a surgeon will not be held liable for failure to fully inform a patient of all known risks if it is clear that the patient would have agreed to the procedure in any event.

[48.] Case Summary 5.9 is based in part on the decision in *Toromont Industrial Holdings* v. *Thorne, Gunn, Helliwell & Christenson* (1977), 14 O.R. (2d) 87 (some damages were awarded, however, on other grounds.). See also *Martin* v. *Goldfarb* (1998), 163 D.L.R. (4th) 639.

the government to provide an impartial voice in decision-making and to represent the public interest. Professional bodies have a number of special responsibilities:

- to set educational and entrance standards for candidates wishing to become members
- to examine and accredit educational institutions that prepare candidates for membership
- to set and adjust standards of ethical conduct and professional competence
- to hear complaints about and administer discipline to members who fail to live up to the established standards
- to defend the profession against attacks that it considers unfair, and to look after the general welfare of the profession

The governing statute typically gives members of the organization the exclusive right to use a professional designation to identify themselves and often also gives members the exclusive right to practise their profession.[49] Anyone who identifies himself as a member or attempts to practise when not accredited as a member may be—and usually is—prosecuted for committing an offence under the provincial statute.

Two important consequences flow from these powers. First, the right to discipline gives the organizations great power over individual members—expulsion, or suspension for any extended period, may destroy a member's means of livelihood. Second, exclusivity gives these self-governing professions great power over the quality and cost of their services to the public, and there is consequently a strong public interest in the affairs of the organizations.

CASE SUMMARY 5.10

Schilling had entrusted $600 000 to an accountant, Hofman, to invest for him. Hofman absconded with the money. Hofman was a former member of the Association of Certified General Accountants of British Columbia, and having recently been disciplined for other offences, had been forced to resign from the Association, and had been deprived of the right to describe himself as a "CGA." Schilling sued the Association alleging negligence in not preventing Hofman from continuing to practise—as a result of which Hofman had been able to defraud Schilling.

The British Columbia Court of Appeal held that the Association was not liable. There was no private law duty of care that required the Association to bring a criminal prosecution against a former member or to inform potential clients of his resignation.[50]

The Supreme Court of Canada was faced with a rather similar issue in *Cooper* v. *Hobart*.[51] In that case, an investor who had entrusted funds to a mortgage broker, who dealt with those funds in an unauthorized manner, brought an action claim-

---

[49.] For example, the exclusive right to practise applies to medicine and law, but not to some areas of accounting.

[50.] *Schilling* v. *Certified General Accountants Assn. of British Columbia* (1996), 135 D.L.R. (4th) 669.

[51.] (2001), 206 D.L.R. (4th) 193. The court reached a similar conclusion in *Edwards* v. *Law Society of Upper Canada* (2001), 206 D.L.R. (4th) 211, holding a law society not liable for failure to issue a warning that an investigation was being conducted into the handling of a lawyer's trust account.

ing damages against the Registrar (appointed by a statute regulating the mortgage broking profession). The plaintiff claimed that the Registrar, who had been investigating the broker, should have acted more promptly and suspended his licence earlier. The court held that the Registrar owed no duty of care to individual investors. The regulatory scheme required the Registrar to balance a number of competing interests in order to protect the public as a whole. The decision whether to suspend a broker involved both policy and quasi-judicial elements that were inconsistent with a duty of care to investors. To impose a duty of care in such circumstances would be to create an insurance scheme for investors at the cost of the taxpaying public.[52]

Codes of Conduct

code of conduct
rules of a professional organization setting out the duties and appropriate standards of behaviour to be observed by its members

Many professional bodies require their members to observe a **code of conduct**. As already noted, such codes may be important as evidence of what constitutes an appropriate standard of professional care, and may thus help to determine the extent of the duty owed by members to their clients. Additionally, codes of conduct may impose ethical standards on their members over and above any legal requirements. See the following example of a typical code of conduct.

Uniform Code of Professional Conduct

Canadian Association of Management Consultants

Purpose

The purpose of this Code is to identify those professional obligations that serve to protect the public in general and the client in particular. The Code is also designed to identify clearly the expectations of members with respect to other members and the profession.

Definitions

"Council" is the Council or Board of any provincial or regional institute of Certified Management Consultants affiliated with the Canadian Association of Management Consultants (CAMC). "Member" is any individual registered and in good standing with a provincial or regional Institute of Certified Management Consultants in Canada.

Responsibilities to the Public

Legal: A member shall act in accordance with the applicable legislation and laws.

Representation: A member shall make representation on behalf of provincial, regional, or national Institute members only when authorized.

Public Protection: A member shall be liable for suspension or expulsion from membership where that member has behaved in a manner unbecoming to the profession, as judged by Council.

---

52. The governing statute of the professional organization may provide for immunity in respect of acts done in good faith in the performance of a duty or exercise of a power under the statute; see, for example, Regulated Health Professions Act, 1991, S.O. 1991, c. 18, s. 38, considered in *Rogers* v. *Faught* (2002), 212 D.L.R. (4th) 366.

Responsibilities to the Profession

Knowledge: A member shall keep informed of the applicable Code of Professional Conduct and the profession's Common Body of Knowledge. A member shall strive to keep current with developments in any area of the profession where specific expertise is claimed.

Self-Discipline: A member shall recognize that the self-disciplinary nature of the profession is a privilege and that the member has a responsibility to merit retention of this privilege. Therefore, a member shall report to Council unbecoming professional conduct by another member.

Responsibilities for Others: A member shall ensure that other management consultants carrying out work on the member's behalf are conversant with, and abide by, the applicable Code of Professional Conduct.

Image: A member shall behave in a manner that maintains the good reputation of the profession and its ability to serve the public interest. A member shall avoid activities that adversely affect the quality of that member's professional advice. A member may not carry on business that clearly detracts from the member's professional status.

Responsibilities to Other Members

Review of a Member's Work: A member who has been requested to review critically the work of another member shall inform that member before undertaking the work.

Responsibilities to the Client

Due Care: A member shall act in the best interest of the client, providing professional services with integrity, objectivity, and independence. A member shall not encourage unrealistic client expectations.

Business Development: A member shall not adopt any method of obtaining business that detracts from the professional image of the Institute or its members.

Competence: A member shall accept only those assignments that the member has the knowledge and skill to perform.

Informed Client: A member shall, before accepting an assignment, reach a mutual understanding with the client as to the assignment objectives, scope, workplan, and costs.

Fee Arrangement: A member shall establish fee arrangements with a client in advance of any substantive work and shall inform all relevant parties when such arrangements may impair or may be seen to impair the objectivity or independence of the member. A member shall not enter into fee arrangements that have the potential to compromise the member's integrity or the quality of services rendered.

Conflict: A member shall avoid acting simultaneously for two or more clients in potentially conflicting situations without informing all parties in advance and securing their agreement to the arrangement. A member shall inform a client of any interest which may impair or may be seen to impair professional judgment. A member shall not take advantage of a client relationship by encouraging, unless by way of an advertisement, an employee of that client to consider alternate employment without prior discussion with the client.

Confidentiality: A member shall treat all client information as confidential.

> **Objectivity:** A member shall refrain from serving a client under terms or conditions that impair independence and a member shall reserve the right to withdraw from the assignment if such becomes the case.
>
> Source: Canadian Association of Management Consultants, www.camc.com.

Discipline

One of the most important responsibilities of professional bodies is to maintain and improve standards. That may involve disciplining members of the profession. Most professions inevitably have a minority of members who act in an unprofessional, unethical, or illegal manner. The usual response of governing bodies is to punish serious cases of unethical conduct by expulsion or suspension. (There may also be provision for some form of compensation to the injured client by the governing body itself.) These actions are quite apart from any criminal prosecution of the wrongdoer or from private (civil) liability actions.

The more pervasive and difficult cases are those arising from alleged breaches of professional standards of skill and care. In what may be considered isolated cases of negligence, governing bodies ordinarily leave the matter to the regular courts, where an aggrieved client may bring an action. However, in repeated cases of violations, or where the conduct of the professional is such that her competence to remain in practice is called into question, the governing body will take disciplinary action in the same manner as it would for unethical conduct.

For the conduct of disciplinary proceedings against members, a professional organization usually has a standing discipline committee consisting of experienced members of the profession. In addition, the governing council usually designates one or more other members or a separate committee to act as "prosecutor." Both the prosecutor and the accused member may be represented by lawyers at the disciplinary hearing. Ordinarily, the finding of a discipline committee takes the form of a recommendation to the governing council of the organization, which then acts on the recommendation to expel, suspend, reprimand, or acquit. Disciplinary proceedings of this nature are subject to a general duty to act fairly[53] and are subject to review by the regular courts.

Conflict of Duty Towards Clients and the Courts

A member of a professional body faces a dilemma when required to testify in court proceedings affecting a client or patient. On the one hand, the member is expected to reply to questions under oath when examined and cross-examined in court; on the other hand, the member's testimony may appear to be a breach of confidence in the professional relationship with the client. A member or student member of a professional organization probably has a duty to ask the court for a ruling before divulging any information obtained in a confidential capacity.

A professional who learns that a client may be engaged in or is contemplating possibly illegal activities may experience a further problem of interpreting her

---

[53.] For a discussion of this duty see *Mondesir v. Manitoba Assn. of Optometrists* (1998), 163 D.L.R. (4th) 703. Where the disciplinary body is established by statute, its procedures are also subject to the Charter: see *Costco Wholesale Canada Ltd. v. British Columbia* (1998), 157 D.L.R. (4th) 725.

professional duties to the client. Needless to say, the professional must not assist the client (except to advise on possible illegality), and, in dissociating herself from the client's activities, may have to terminate the relationship. It appears to be generally conceded, however, that a professional would not normally be obliged to reveal confidential knowledge to prosecuting authorities: such information is said to be covered by **privilege**. However, where keeping silent would create a serious threat to public safety, the public interest requires disclosure.[54]

privilege
the right of a professional to refuse to divulge information obtained in confidence from a client

---

INTERNATIONAL ISSUE

International Issue

As discussed earlier, the United States' Sarbanes-Oxley Act of 2002 (SOX) was enacted in response to major corporate scandals including that of Enron. It gave the Securities and Exchange Commission the power to regulate the conduct of attorneys. One measure adopted is known as "up the ladder" reporting.[55] This measure requires very specific conduct from lawyers acting for public corporations. If a lawyer becomes aware of improper activities within the corporation, he or she must report the activity up the chain of command, all the way to the board of directors.

The most controversial part of the reporting requirement is known as "noisy withdrawal." If a corporation refuses to discontinue the improper activity, then the lawyer must withdraw her services AND report the improper activity to the Securities and Exchange Commission.

The American Bar Association raised strong objections to the "noisy withdrawal" proposal. To date the SEC has only implemented the rule in voluntary form. Lawyers may report violations to the SEC.[56]

Questions to Consider

1. Why would the American Bar Association object to "noisy withdrawal"?

2. Is there a public interest argument to counter the position of the Bar Association?

Sources: U.S. Securities and Exchange Commission, "Final Rule: Implementation of Standards of Professional Conduct for Attorneys," 17 CFR Part 205, September 26, 2003, www.sec.gov/rules/final/33-8185.htm; American Bar Association, "Independence of the Legal Profession: Section 307 of the Sarbanes-Oxley Act," December 1, 2004, www.abanet.org/poladv/priorities/sarbanes.html.

MULTI-DISCIPLINARY PARTNERSHIPS

Traditionally, professions have carried on their practice either alone or in partnership with fellow members of the same profession. Many professions forbid their members to incorporate. In the case of some professions—in particular, law—it has, in the past, been unlawful for a lawyer to practise in partnership with a non-lawyer. However, these rules are now changing.

[54.] *Smith* v. *Jones* (1999), 169 D.L.R. (4th) 385 (S.C.C.). The case concerned conversations between a psychiatrist and an alleged serial rapist. See *Canada (Privacy Commissioner)* v. *Blood Tribe Department of Health* 2008 SCC 44 where the Supreme Court prioritized solicitor–client privilege over access rights.

[55.] Title 17, Code of Federal Regulations, Part 205, s. 205.3.

[56.] *Ibid.*, s. 205.3(6)(d)(2).

In the past few years, legislation has been adopted in a number of provinces to permit the creation of "professional corporations"; we discuss these further in Chapter 16. The other major development is the changing attitude towards "multi-disciplinary partnerships" (MDPs). The main focus of the current debate on MDPs is on the combining of accountants and lawyers into a single firm. MDPs of this type are common in Europe, where the major international accounting firms have established their own legal departments. Several provincial law societies have set up working groups to study the implications of allowing their members to participate in MDPs. Advocates of MDPs claim a number of advantages—they benefit clients whose problems cannot readily be compartmentalized into legal and non-legal, and they provide a more efficient "one-stop shop" for business clients who require both accounting and legal services. By working together as a team, the quality of service provided by both professions is improved. There are, however, also concerns. There is a possibility that professional duties and codes of conduct may conflict,[57] and the increased sizes of firms and diversity of services provided may more readily give rise to conflicts of interest.

Although the legal profession has tended to oppose MDPs, it may well be that the fundamental freedom of association, in the Charter, gives a right to establish such partnerships.[58] So far, only Ontario and Quebec allow lawyers to participate in MDPs.[59]

APPENDIX READING

Law and Business Ethics

Business Ethics

corporate social responsibility
a concept that suggests business decision-makers consider ethical issues including the interests of customers, employees, creditors, the public, and other stakeholders, in addition to legal and financial concerns

We have struggled to determine if it can ever be right to break the law. We should also consider whether it is always sufficient merely to abide by the law: are there occasions when a higher standard of behaviour is required? In a commercial context, this raises the issue of business ethics and *corporate social responsibility*. As shown in Figure 5.2, corporate social responsibility can be thought of as having three domains: ethical, legal, and economic. In the wake of recent corporate scandals, businesses are encouraged to live up to a higher ethical standard than is imposed on them by law. One way to promote an ethical climate in a business is to

---

[57.] For example, an accountant may be required to report certain financial information where a lawyer has a duty of confidentiality. These concerns have increased since the "Enron affair."

[58.] In *Black* v. *Law Society of Alberta* [1989] 1 S.C.R. 591, the Supreme Court of Canada struck down a rule that Alberta lawyers could not enter into partnership with lawyers from outside the province. The decision was based on the mobility rights provisions of the Charter, but arguably the right of association would have been equally applicable.

[59.] A 2007 Competition Bureau report supported MDPs for lawyers: "Self Regulated Professions – Balancing Competition and Regulation," December 11, 2007, www.competitionbureau.gc.ca/epic/site/cb-bc.nsf/en/02523e.html. See also, M. Rappaport, "Competition Bureau's Study Draws Tepid Reaction from Legal Community," *The Lawyers Weekly*, January 11, 2008, www.lawyersweekly.ca/index.php?section=article&articleid=599.

introduce a ***code of conduct*** that requires behaviour in line with ethical values such as honesty, trust, loyalty, and responsibility.[60]

code of conduct
a common standard of behaviour that may take the form of a values statement or a prescribed set of rules

Why should a firm commit itself to observing a higher ethical standard than is required by law? The answer may be quite straightforward: a firm behaves ethically because that is how its owners or managers believe it should behave. More often, however, ethical behaviour is a matter of enlightened self-interest. A firm that respects its employees is more likely to have a stable, contented, and productive work force; a firm that operates a liberal "returns" policy is more likely to create consumer loyalty; a firm that shows concern for the environment and the community in which it is located will benefit from an improved public image; and a firm with transparent and independent leadership will benefit from the trust and confidence of the public investor. Finally, as we have noted, the ethical values of society shape the development of the law; proactive legal risk management anticipates where the law may go in the future and prepares for it now. Today's voluntary ethical standard may be tomorrow's mandatory obligation. Most chapters of this book will identify an ethical issue.

Codes of Conduct

Codes of conduct take a variety of forms and may fill gaps that law cannot reach:

(a) *Binding codes*—some activities, particularly of professionals, are regulated by a code of conduct, or a similar set of rules, laid down by a governing body or trade association. Although these rules are not law, their effect is often similar. A member of a profession or trade association who breaches the code of conduct may face disciplinary proceedings and may even be

Figure 5.2 Corporate Social Responsibility: A Three Domain Approach

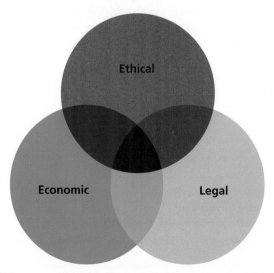

Source: Mark S. Schwartz and Archie B. Carroll, "Corporate Social Responsibility: A Three Domain Approach" (2003), 13(4) *Business Ethics Quarterly* 509.

---

60. Mark S. Schwartz, "A Code of Ethics for Corporate Codes of Ethics" (2002), 41 *Journal of Business Ethics* 27–43; Mark S. Schwartz and Archie B. Carroll, "Corporate Social Responsibility: A Three Domain Approach" (2003), 13(4) *Business Ethics Quarterly* 503–30.

expelled from that body—a very severe sanction, since often it will deprive the offender of the right to work in the profession. These bodies may cross jurisdictional boundaries that the law does not.

(b) *Voluntary codes*—some industries have established voluntary codes of conduct for their activities. Although voluntary, they often have a strong persuasive effect. A voluntary code may even be used as a substitute for government regulation: there is an implicit threat that, if an industry—for example, the advertising industry—does not regulate itself satisfactorily, the government will step in and legislate standards. In other cases, voluntary codes are adopted where there is no effective power to legislate. A well-known example is the United Nations Code of Conduct for Transnational Corporations. Multinational enterprises are urged to observe certain minimum standards—for example, on employment of child labour—even though there are no legal restrictions in countries in which they operate.

(c) *Self-imposed codes*—some firms have adopted and published their own codes of conduct, especially in relation to employment conditions and environmental protection. Codes may be a response to public criticism—for example, to criticism of working conditions in overseas factories of manufacturers of clothing and sporting goods; sometimes they may be used to impress and attract particular groups of consumers. In other cases they simply reflect the philosophy of the owners or managers of the firm. The contents of the code may form part of employment contracts, and employees may be disciplined for violations.

ILLUSTRATION 5.1

Students attending a university are governed by an academic code of conduct that forbids cheating. Cheating is unethical. The code allows the university to expel or suspend a student for cheating. The university does not have to establish that the student broke the law, only that he or she violated the academic code of conduct that forms part of the contractual relationship between the university and the student.

SUMMARY

Professional liability

- Also usually based on negligence
- Professionals may be liable for:
  - False or inaccurate information that causes economic loss
  - Breach of fiduciary duty or of contractual obligations

QUESTIONS

1. What are the arguments in favour of imposing a wide liability on professionals?

2. What is the main effect of increased use of liability insurance?

3. What is the nature of the fiduciary duty owed by a professional? In what way can that duty be wider than a contractual duty?

4. Can a client choose to sue a professional adviser in either contract or tort? What difference might it make?

5. What is the principal basis of a professional's potential liability to persons who are not clients?

6. Why were the courts initially reluctant to impose liability for negligent misstatements?

7. What was the decision reached by the House of Lords in *Hedley Byrne* v. *Heller & Partners*?

8. What is the test now applied in Canada to determine whether a person is liable for a negligent misstatement?

9. Why might it be difficult to establish contributory negligence as a defence in a case involving negligent misrepresentation?

10. How can a person be liable for an omission?

11. What are the objections to a "hindsight" approach in determining the appropriate standard of professional care?

12. What is the essence of causation in most professional–client relationships?

13. What are the main responsibilities imposed or assumed by professional bodies?

14. Should professional bodies be allowed to discipline their members, or should that be left to the courts?

15. What are the potential advantages, and possible disadvantages, of multi-disciplinary partnerships?

Chapter 6

Formation of Contracts: Offer, Acceptance, and Consideration

Along with torts, the second area of private law affecting businesspeople—and by far the most important—is the law of contracts. The world of commerce and most business relationships are based on contracts. In this and the following three chapters, we will discuss how a contract is formed, various factors that affect those contracts, and how they can come to an end. This chapter introduces the first two of the five essential elements necessary for valid contracts. The other three elements will be discussed in the next chapter.

THE CONTRACTUAL RELATIONSHIP

Definition of Contract

Knowledge of contract law is vital to all businesspeople because most commercial transactions are built on contractual relationships. A good starting point would be a practical definition of a contract. We will define a **contract** as a voluntary exchange of promises, creating obligations that, if defaulted on, can be enforced and remedied by the courts.

It is important to understand that when agreeing to the terms of a contract, people are creating and defining their own rules and obligations. This differs

Exchange of promises enforceable in court

from other areas of the law, such as torts, where rules and obligations are imposed on them. A valid contract creates a situation in which parties to the contract can predict, with some certainty, their future relationship because each party knows that the courts will hold them to their agreement.

While the courts will enforce a valid contract after it has been created, what the parties agree to in the first place is generally unrestricted. This approach is referred to as the *freedom of contract*. People can enter into almost any kind of contractual agreement they want to, as long as the contract meets the common law requirements that will be discussed in this and the following chapters. Although the law of contracts is found primarily in the common law, there are a number of specialized areas in which legislation that modifies, restricts, or replaces these common law principles has been enacted, thereby interfering with the freedom to contract. Examples include the sale of goods, consumer protection, employment, partnerships, corporations, and real property, which will be the subjects of later chapters.

Freedom to contract restricted by common law and by legislation

When we study contract law, the focus is usually on the problems that can arise. It may therefore appear that most contractual relationships experience difficulties. In fact, most contracts are honoured or resolved to the mutual satisfaction of the parties. The courts become involved in a small proportion of contractual agreements, when an unresolvable dispute arises.

Elements of a Contract

Not all agreements are contracts. To qualify as a valid contract, an agreement must contain certain elements. They are:

1. **Consensus**. Parties to a contract must have reached a mutual agreement to commit themselves to a certain transaction. They are assumed to have negotiated the agreement from equal bargaining positions. The process by which the agreement is reached usually involves an **offer** and an **acceptance**, although consensus can be implied.

The elements of a valid contract

2. **Consideration**. There must be a commitment by each party to do something or to abstain from doing something. The consideration is the price each is willing to pay to participate in the contract.

3. **Capacity**. Parties to a contract must be legally capable of understanding and entering into the agreement. Limitations in contracting capacity have been placed on infants, insane or intoxicated persons, aliens (persons who are not Canadian citizens), and, in some instances, native people, and corporations.

4. **Legality**. The object and consideration involved in the agreement must be legal and not against public policy.

5. **Intention**. Both parties must be serious when making the agreement, and both must intend that legally enforceable obligations will result from it.

It should be noted that the general rule is that an agreement reached verbally between parties is every bit as binding as a written one. However, legislation (the *Statute of Frauds*) has been passed requiring that certain types of agreements be supported by evidence *in writing* before they will be enforced in the courts. For convenience, this limited requirement of writing will be discussed along with the five elements of a contract.

Sometimes contracts must be evidenced in writing

Important Terms and Definitions

Before addressing the elements of a contract in more detail, it is necessary to outline some basic terminology that is used in the discussion of contractual obligations.

FORMAL AND SIMPLE CONTRACTS

The use of a seal

A formal contract is one that is sealed by the party to be bound. Traditionally, a seal involved making an impression in sealing wax. A modern seal normally consists of a paper wafer affixed to a document, but any mark or impression will do. Simple contracts, sometimes called **parol contracts**, may be verbal or written, but are not under seal.

EXPRESS AND IMPLIED CONTRACTS

Contracts may be implied

An **express contract** is one in which the parties have expressly stated their agreement, either verbally or in writing. An **implied contract** is inferred from the conduct of the parties. When people deposit coins in vending machines, it can be inferred that they intend to create a contractual relationship, and thus an implied contract is in force. Portions of an express contract may also be implied.

VALID, VOID, AND VOIDABLE CONTRACTS

A void contract is no contract

A voidable contract is valid but one party has the right to escape

A **valid contract** is one that is legally binding on both parties. A **void contract** does not qualify as a legally binding contract because an essential element is missing. If the parties to a void contract thought they were bound and followed the agreement, the courts would try to put the parties back to their original positions. A **voidable contract** exists and has legal effect, but one of the parties has the option to end the contract.

The distinction between void and voidable can have important implications for outsiders to the contract who have acquired an interest in the subject matter of the contract. If the original contract is void, the goods must be returned to the seller. If the original contract is voidable, the outsider has acquired good title to the goods and can keep them.

UNENFORCEABLE AND ILLEGAL CONTRACTS

Court won't enforce unenforceable contract

Illegal contract is void

An example of an **unenforceable contract** is one that is required to be in writing under the *Statute of Frauds* and is not. It may be valid in all other respects, but the courts will not force a party to perform such a contract. As well, if an unenforceable contract has been performed, the courts will not help a party to escape the contract.

An **illegal contract** is one that involves the performance of an unlawful act. An illegal contract is void. The parties to such an agreement cannot be required to perform it. If an illegal contract has been performed or partially performed, the court, because of the moral taint, normally will not assist the parties by returning them to their original positions. This would usually be done if the contract was void. For example, if there is an illegal contract, and a deposit has been paid, the court will not order its return. Neither will the court require property to be returned if the contract is illegal, even when one of the parties has been enriched at the other's expense. There is, however, an exception to this general approach:

The courts will help a person who is innocent of any wrongdoing even when the contract is illegal.

BILATERAL AND UNILATERAL CONTRACTS

A **bilateral contract** is one in which both parties make commitments and assume obligations. There is no exchange of promises in a **unilateral contract**. This type of contract comes into effect when one party actually performs what has been requested by the other. For example, a person may offer a reward for the return of a lost item. It is not until the lost item is returned that the offer is accepted and the contract created. Thus, a bilateral contract involves an exchange of promises, whereas a unilateral contract involves a promise followed by an act.[1]

Unilateral contract—performance is acceptance

Consensus

A MEETING OF THE MINDS

The essence of a contract is, at least in theory, the *meeting of the minds* of the contracting parties. The two parties must have a common will in relation to the subject matter of their negotiations, and they must have reached an agreement. They must share an understanding of the bargain struck and be willing to commit themselves to the terms of that contract.

Agreement reached—bargain struck

In practice, however, it is not necessary that both parties fully understand, or even have read, all the terms of the contract. Few people thoroughly read the major contracts they enter into, such as insurance policies, leases, and loan agreements. Of those who do, few fully understand the specific meaning of the documents. The law does not recognize the excuse that one of the contracting parties did not read the contract or that he did not understand it.

Both parties must have had an opportunity to read and understand the contract for it to be valid. The terms of the agreement must be clear and unambiguous. If the terms of the contract are ambiguous, then the court will decide that there has not been consensus between the parties and it will declare the contract void. Case Summary 6.1 provides an example of a court declaring a contract void because of a lack of consensus.

Terms must be clear and unambiguous

CASE SUMMARY 6.1

No Consensus, No Contract! *Sussexinsuranceagency.com Inc. v. Insurance Corp. of British Columbia*[2]

Sussexinsuranceagency.com Inc. (Sussex.com) sued the Insurance Corp. of British Columbia (ICBC) for breach of an oral agreement. It claimed damages for loss of profits of between $26 million and $40 million, as well as punitive damages. Sussex.com claimed that ICBC had promised it an exclusive one-year pilot project to operate a call centre. Sussex.com also claimed that it relied on this promise and incurred significant

---

[1.] See *Speidel v. Paquette* (1979), 20 A.R. 586 (Q.B.), which involved a promise to convey title to a house if the other party moved into the house, looked after it, and paid rent for five years. The Court ruled that a unilateral contract was formed when the other party performed all of the stipulated terms.

[2.] [2005] B.C.S.C. 58.

costs. ICBC denied that a contract had been formed, as there was no intention to be bound and the parties had not agreed to the terms of the contract.

The Court held that the parties did not agree on the essential terms of a contract at their first meeting. There was simply an agreement to continue negotiations. While there was an agreement reached between the parties at their second meeting, the Court ruled that there was not an agreement as to the meaning of "a premium rate finder." In addition, the agreement that ICBC would provide client lists was based on a mistake of fact by ICBC. The Court therefore concluded that there was not a binding contract because of a lack of consensus between the parties.

SMALL BUSINESS PERSPECTIVE

Courts make their decisions based on the evidence presented to them. What types of evidence will a court consider in cases in which the existence of a contract is at issue? In light of this, what can parties involved in contractual negotiations do to ensure that a court will reach the correct decision as to whether there was a meeting of the minds of the parties?

Obviously, mistakes happen, and some very complex rules, which we will discuss later, have been developed to handle them. Nevertheless, contract law is based on the assumption that the culmination of the bargaining process occurs when one party states its position in the form of an offer in the expectation that the other party, through acceptance, will make a similar commitment to be bound by the terms of that offer. It should be stressed that a valid offer and an acceptance are not always obvious and yet, from the conduct of the parties or other factors, it is clear that the parties have a mutual understanding. In such circumstances, the courts are willing to imply the existence of a contract, and no evidence of a specific identifiable offer and acceptance is required.

Offer

Offer—tentative promise

A valid **offer** contains all of the terms to be included in the contract; all that is required of the other party is to give its consent or denial. The offer is a tentative promise on the part of one party to do whatever is set out, providing that the other party consents to do what is requested in return. When a sales person offers to sell a car to a customer for $5000, the offer is a tentative promise by the seller to deliver the car, contingent on the customer's willingness to pay the $5000. The process of making an offer is the communication of a willingness to be bound by the terms and conditions stated in that offer.

This aspect of the offer can be confusing to those involved in commercial activities. People often have documents placed before them and are asked to sign "the contract" (for example, in transactions involving insurance policies or leases). In fact, at that stage, the document is not a contract; it is merely an offer. Only after it is accepted and signed can it be said to be the "contract," and even then it is probably only the written evidence of the contractual relationship between the parties.

Offer—must include all important terms

The offer must contain all significant terms of the proposed contract. The parties, the subject matter of the contract, any price to be paid, as well as any other important terms, should all be stated in the offer. The courts do have the power to imply into contracts the insignificant terms that the parties may not have considered, such as time of delivery, time of payment, and so on. Such terms must be incidental to the agreement, but consistent with the apparent intention of the parties. Courts will often turn to the common practice of the trade or industry for assistance in deciding which terms should be implied. When goods are sold, the *Sale of Goods Act* sets out the terms to be implied if they are not in the contract of sale. Sometimes, as mentioned above, it is even possible for the courts to imply the entire contract from the conduct of the parties, but if it is clear that important terms have been left out, or are to be negotiated later, the courts will rule that there is no contract.

Some terms can be implied

CASE SUMMARY 6.2

An Agreement to Enter into a Contract Is Not Good Enough: *Beacock v. Wetter*[3]

Wetter owned a house. She and Beacock discussed him renting the house for $950 per month and eventually buying it for $200 000. No written contract of purchase and sale was signed by the parties. Beacock moved into the house and paid rent of $950 per month. He made improvements to the house that were worth $23 000. During further discussions, Beacock increased his offer to $215 000. He could not obtain funding, and Wetter would not agree to take back a second mortgage. He filed a builder's lien for the cost of the improvements. Wetter served him with a notice to vacate the house. Beacock sued for specific performance of his agreement with Wetter or, in the alternative, damages for breach of contract. Wetter denied entering into an agreement to sell the house to Beacock.

The Court ruled that there was no consensus, or meeting of the minds, regarding the terms of the alleged agreement. The discussions between Wetter and Beacock resulted in "an agreement or intention to enter into a contract of purchase and sale at some unspecified date in the future." There was no definite offer that contained the specific terms of an agreement that could be accepted. The Court quoted from *Bawitko Investments Ltd. v. Kernels Popcorn Ltd.* (1991), 53 O.A.C. 314, at 327:

> [W]hen the original contract is incomplete because essential provisions intended to govern the contractual relationship have not been settled or agreed upon; or the contract is too general or uncertain to be valid in itself and is dependent on the making of a formal contract; or the understanding or intention of the parties, even if there is no uncertainty as to the terms of their agreement, is that their legal obligations are to be deferred until a formal contract has been approved and executed, the original or preliminary agreement cannot constitute an enforceable contract. In other words, in such circumstances, the "contract to make a contract" is not a contract at all.

The Court also held that there was no option to purchase agreement, as there was no consideration for such an agreement. Finally, the Court denied Beacock's claim for the cost of the improvements, as they had not been requested by Wetter and she did not accept them.

[3.] [2006] B.C.S.C. 951, aff'd [2008] B.C.C.A. 152.

SMALL BUSINESS PERSPECTIVE

Do you think that this is a fair result from Beacock's perspective? What about the expectations that were created? What should he have done to protect himself?

Interim agreement binding

It must be emphasized that the parties can make it clear that, while they intend to put the agreement into a more formal document later, they intend to be bound before the contract is formalized, as long as all of the important terms have been agreed upon. An **interim agreement** (agreement of purchase and sale) in a real estate transaction is an example of such a contract. It is binding even though a more formal document will follow. A letter of intent will also be binding if all significant terms are included in it. If a person does not want to be bound by such a letter, she should clearly state this in the document.[4] A court will consider the common practice of a particular industry when determining whether a particular agreement constitutes a valid contract and at what stage it is considered binding.

Contract not binding until condition satisfied

It should also be noted that **"subject-to" clauses** often raise the same concerns. An offer may include a term making the contract conditional on some future event. A person may offer to purchase a house "subject to" the sale of her house. These types of provisions are not necessarily uncertain or ambiguous, unless the subject-to clause itself is uncertain. If the terms of the offer are clear, and nothing is left to be negotiated or agreed upon, the parties are bound to perform as agreed once the subject-to term has been satisfied.[5]

Note exception for request for goods or services

Some types of contractual relationships, often referred to as **quasi-contracts**, must be viewed as exceptions to the rule that important terms must be clear. These contracts involve requests for goods and services. They will be discussed later in this chapter, with *quantum meruit*, under the heading "Request for Services."

INVITATION TO TREAT

An offer is usually made to an individual or to a group of people, but it is also possible to make an offer to the world at large, such as by posting a notice offering a reward for information, or the return of a lost item. Most newspaper, radio, television, and internet advertisements, however, are just **invitations to treat**. They are simply invitations to potential customers to engage in the process of negotiation. As part of the pre-negotiation process, invitations to treat have no legal effect. The typical process to create a contract is illustrated in Figure 6.1.

---

4. For a case in which an enforceable contract was found, despite an argument that it had been a mere "agreement to agree," see *Knappett Construction Ltd. v. Axor Engineering Construction Group Inc.* (2003), 24 C.L.R. (3d) 120 (B.C.S.C.).

5. See *McIntyre v. Pietrobon*, [1987] B.C.J. No. 1571 (S.C.), in which a sale was made "subject to purchaser obtaining satisfactory personal financing." The Court held that the clause was vague, that there was therefore no contract, and that the deposit paid by the purchasers was to be repaid. This decision was distinguished in *Young v. Fleischeuer*, [2006] B.C.S.C. 1318, in which the condition precedent was "Subject to the Buyer . . . receiving . . . financing satisfactory to the Buyer." The Court held that this condition was not void for uncertainty.

Figure 6.1 Typical Process to Create a Contract

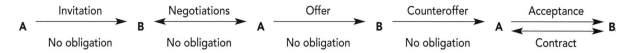

It is sometimes difficult to distinguish between an offer and an invitation to treat. A newspaper advertisement stating, "Automobile tires for sale, two for the price of one" is not an offer. The advertisement is meant to encourage the reader to visit the store and then make an offer to purchase some tires. Catalogues and personal advertisements in the classified section of a newspaper are also invitations to treat. According to the famous English case *Pharmaceutical Society of Great Britain v. Boots Cash Chemists (Southern), Ltd.,*[6] goods displayed on the shelves of self-serve stores are also mere invitations to treat, even though the price of the items may be clearly marked.

Invitation to treat not an offer

Goods displayed on a shelf an invitation only

With the display of such goods being merely an invitation to treat, a customer might be tempted to switch the prices on items displayed for sale in a store. To do so, however, is a crime.[7] The use of scanners and bar codes has made this crime more difficult to commit.

OFFER BY CONDUCT

A customer in a self-serve store takes the goods to be purchased to a cashier and places the goods and money on the counter. A person hails a cab by the gesture of raising a hand and calling, "Taxi!" These are both examples of offers being made by conduct. However, an auctioneer's comment "Do I hear $50?" is merely an invitation to the people in the audience to make an offer. When one of them raises a hand or makes some other acceptable gesture, that is an offer. The auctioneer is free to accept or reject it. A further question "Do I hear $60?" is another invitation for offers. The statement "Sold!" is an acceptance of a person's offer.

Offer may be implied by conduct

COMMUNICATION OF AN OFFER

Before you can accept an offer, it must be communicated to you. You can accept only an offer that has been communicated to you as an individual, to you as a member of a group, or to the world at large. You can't accept an offer made to someone else, no matter how you learn about it. Also, you cannot accept an offer you did not know about. If you return a lost item unaware that a reward has been offered, you have no claim to the reward, because the offer was not communicated to you.

Offer must be communicated

Even where two offers cross in the mail with both parties of the same mind, there is no contract. If one party sent a letter offering to sell, and the other, in

---

6. [1953] 1 All E.R. 482 (C.A.), aff'g [1952] 2 All E.R. 456 (Q.B.).

7. Obtaining goods by false pretences, *Criminal Code*, R.S.C. 1985, c. C-46, ss. 361, 362.

another letter sent at the same time, offered to buy, a particular car for $500, there would not be a contract. Neither letter could be an acceptance, since neither party was aware of the other's offer.

Important terms must be disclosed, especially exemption clauses

It is also important to note that, for a contract to be binding, all important terms must have been disclosed to the offeree. This is especially important with respect to exemption clauses. In contracts with customers, merchants will often include clauses that favour their own position, or limit their liability. There are usually signs disclaiming responsibility for theft or damage to cars or contents posted in parking lots. Tickets to athletic events, or for the use of sporting facilities, will often include terms disclaiming responsibility for injury, damages, or loss of personal property by theft. In cases such as these, an exemption clause will be binding only when it has been reasonably brought to the attention of the customer at the time the contract is made. For example, the sign in the parking lot must be placed in a well-lit location where the driver will see it before, or at the time, the contract is made; this is usually at the cashier's booth or vending machine, as well as at other strategic locations on the lot. When the clause is on the back of a ticket, there must be a reference to it on the front of the ticket for it to be binding. Also, the ticket must be given to the customer at the time the contract is made, not afterwards. Even if these precautions are taken, consumer protection legislation may restrict the effect of an exemption clause.

 REDUCING RISK 6.1

Whether terms are set out in signs or included in written agreements, it is vital that any that are at all unusual be reasonably brought to the attention of the other party, especially if they limit the liability of the first party. It is no longer good enough for the term to appear in small print in a doc-ument, or to put it on a receipt so that it can be seen only after the contract has been created. It is likely that those terms will simply not be considered part of the contract and therefore not binding on the other party.

Fundamental breach may avoid exemption clause

Exemption clauses are also commonly found in written contracts. When people sign contracts, they are generally taken to have read the entire document. Even then, when an exemption clause is unusually restrictive, the court may hold that there was a requirement to specifically bring the clause to the attention of the other contracting party and that the obligation was not met. Even when the clause was brought to the attention of the other party, if the merchant's failure to perform amounts to a fundamental breach, she still may not be able to rely on the exemption clause for protection.

CASE SUMMARY 6.3

An Offer Can't Be Accepted After You Know the Offeror Has Changed His Mind: *Dickinson v. Dodds*[8]

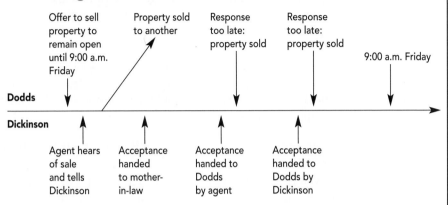

Dickinson v. Dodds, an old case from the latter part of the 19th century, remains one of the best cases to illustrate how offer and acceptance work. Dodds made an offer to sell certain property to Dickinson for £800, stating, "This offer to be left over until Friday, 9:00 a.m." Before the expiration of that deadline, Dickinson learned through his agent that Dodds had been trying to sell, or had sold, the property to someone else.

He quickly went to Dodds's home and left a written acceptance with Dodds's mother-in-law. The next morning, Dickinson and the agent went down to the train station to intercept Dodds as he arrived in town. The agent found him first and handed him a written acceptance. Dodds replied that it was too late and that he had already sold the property. This scenario was repeated a few minutes later when Dickinson intercepted Dodds, with the same response—all before the stated deadline.

This case is important because it illustrates the nature of an offer. The offer is a tentative commitment on the part of the person making it. Until the other party accepts it, there is no obligation on the offeror. Dodds was free to withdraw his offer any time before it was accepted. Even though he had promised to hold the offer open, he was not obligated to do so. He could change his mind and sell the property to someone else, but he had to let the other party know he had changed his mind. In this case, Dodds was extremely lucky, because although he didn't tell Dickinson directly that he had changed his mind, Dickinson found out indirectly. He couldn't accept an offer he knew was no longer available. Had Dickinson not found out about the sale, his acceptance would have been valid and Dodds would have been bound in contract to sell the property to two different purchasers.

SMALL BUSINESS PERSPECTIVE

Do you think that Dodds should have been bound by his promise to hold the offer open? Should a sale to someone else automatically end the offer? Why would a businessperson want to keep her promise, even if she doesn't have to?

---

8. (1876), 2 Ch. D. 463 (C.A.).

THE END OF AN OFFER

Offer ends

For the acceptance of an offer to be effective, the offer must be in force at the time of the acceptance. There are several ways for an offer to come to an end before acceptance.

• when specified

1.   **End of a specified time.** The offer will end at the time stated in the offer. Note that the offeror is still free to revoke the offer before this time expires, unless an option has been purchased. Option agreements will be discussed below.

• after a reasonable time

2.   **Expiration of a reasonable time.** If no time is specified in the offer, it will expire at the end of a reasonable time. What is reasonable depends on the circumstances. Thus, an offer to sell a ship would likely last longer than an offer to sell a load of ripe peaches.

• upon death or insanity of offeror

3.   Death or **insanity** of offeror. The offer will end even if the offeree is unaware of the death or insanity.

• when revoked (revocation must be communicated)

4.   **Revocation** of offer. The offeror may revoke an offer any time before acceptance, but the revocation must be communicated to the offeree to be effective. (When letters are used, the revocation is effective only when received by the offeree.) Until the revocation is communicated to the offeree, the offeree can still accept the offer. The offeror should therefore not contract with another party until she is sure that the message that she has revoked the offer has been received by the offeree. While it is possible for the revocation to be communicated indirectly, as in *Dickinson v. Dodds* discussed above, reliance on such a method would be foolish in the extreme. Dodds was extremely lucky in that case.

• when rejected or counteroffer is made

5.   Rejection and **counteroffer**. During the bargaining process, several different proposals may be put forward, rejected, and then followed by counterproposals. Each counteroffer or rejection ends the offer before it. For example, when a car is offered for sale for $5000 and the customer replies "I'll give you $4500," a counteroffer has been made, and the original offer is thereby ended. If the seller rejects the counteroffer, it is too late for the purchaser to reconsider and accept the original offer, as it no longer exists. Under such circumstances, an attempt to accept the original $5000 offer constitutes a new offer, which the seller is free to accept or reject.

Request for information is not a counteroffer

Note that a simple request for information or clarification, such as an inquiry as to whether the sale of a car includes the stereo, does not constitute a counteroffer or a rejection. It therefore does not end the offer. On the other hand, a counteroffer that is worded like a question will end the offer (such as "Will you take $4500?").

The existence of an offer can be affected by other factors as well. For example, the offer will be ended if the activity contemplated by the contracting parties becomes illegal before acceptance. Also, if the goods forming the subject matter of the contract are destroyed without the parties' being aware of it, the offer is ended.

OFFERS THAT CANNOT BE REVOKED

Often, businesspeople find the uncertainty associated with the offeror's right to revoke any time prior to the point of acceptance very inconvenient, especially when they are arranging their business affairs to take advantage of the offer.

For example, when assembling land, a land developer will get offers from several sellers. He will not accept any of them until he is sure that all of the required properties can be obtained. The right of each of the sellers to revoke is inconsistent with this process. The developer will therefore acquire an option on each property. An option is a subsidiary contract, with separate consideration given to the offeror in exchange for a commitment to keep the offer open for a specific length of time. The developer thereby gains the certainty necessary to accomplish his goal. Such arrangements are quite common; they are found in all areas of finance and business. (Options can also be put under seal; the use of the seal will be discussed below, under "Consideration.")

A similar problem exists when dealing with *tenders,* the normal practice in the construction industry. A purchaser issues a request for bids to get the best possible price on a required product or service. The request for bids is an invitation to treat, and each submitted bid is an offer. The problem is that normally there would be nothing to stop the offeror from withdrawing her offer if she realizes she has made a mistake or, if upon seeing the other bids, she realizes that hers is too low. The Supreme Court of Canada has decided that in some circumstances such tendered bids cannot be revoked.[9] When the original request for tenders made it clear that bids would be considered only when the offeror agreed that the offer could not be withdrawn once submitted, a subsidiary contract exists, and the offer then cannot be revoked. As above, the problem is also avoided when the tendered bid is made under seal.

> Where option exists, offer cannot be revoked

It is likely that the same principle will apply in any situation in which a unilateral contract is involved and performance of the act requested has started. Thus, if an employer promises to give her business to an employee if he stays until she retires, the acceptance is made simply by the employee's staying on. With such an implied subsidiary contract, the employer could not wait until just before her retirement and then revoke the offer.

> Unilateral offer can't be revoked once performance begins

> Subsidiary contracts may be implied

CASE SUMMARY 6.4

The Tendering Process and the Duty to Be Fair: *Martel Building Ltd. v. Canada*[10]

The Department of Public Works issued a call for tenders, pursuant to which it did not have to accept the lowest bid. Martel submitted the lowest bid. However, the Department conducted a financial analysis of the bids and added certain costs to Martel's bid. The tender was then awarded to another bidder.

After reviewing the general principles of the law of tender, the Court stated that a call to tender is an offer to contract and a binding contract may arise when a bid is submitted. The Court held that the parties intended to include an implied term that all bids were to be treated fairly and equally. Pursuant to the call for tenders, the Department did have some discretion in evaluating the bids. It added fit-up costs to all of the bids, using the same approach. This was not a breach of the duty to act fairly. The Department was entitled to add another specific cost to Martel's bid, as this was an express requirement

---

9. *R. v. Ron Engineering & Construction* (Eastern) Ltd., [1981] 1 S.C.R. 111.

10. [2000] 2 S.C.R. 860.

to which all of the bidders had to comply. The Department did breach its duty to treat all bidders fairly and equally, by adding this cost only to Martel's bid. This addition did not, however, cause Martel to lose the tender. Martel's claim for damages was therefore dismissed.

DISCUSSION QUESTIONS

Given the duty to treat all bidders fairly, can a party calling for tenders protect itself simply by including, in the tender documents, a "privilege clause," stating that the lowest or any tender will not necessarily be accepted? Can a privilege clause be used to attach an undisclosed condition to the offer of the party calling for tenders?

STANDARD FORM CONTRACT

Bargaining difficult with standard form contract

The law assumes that the two parties to an agreement are in equal bargaining positions and that both will negotiate the terms of the agreement until a consensus, which represents a fair bargain, is reached. In actual fact, most large businesses do not negotiate with their customers. Rather, they present an offer with fixed terms, which the customer is invited to accept. A passenger purchasing an airline ticket is an example. These are called **standard form contracts** and usually contain one-sided terms favouring the business. Exemption clauses, discussed above, that attempt to limit the liability of the business, are examples of such one-sided terms.

Statutes and attitude of courts mitigate this

In an effort to correct the imbalance in bargaining power, and to alleviate some of the unfairness, *consumer protection legislation* has been enacted in most jurisdictions, controlling the worst abuses. Consumer protection is covered in Chapter 10. Also, when the courts deal with exemption clauses, they interpret them strictly, so that any ambiguity is read in favour of the disadvantaged party. Thus, a business that includes in its contracts terms disclaiming responsibility for "damage" to goods left on the premises would still be held responsible for goods that were stolen. Even when exemption clauses are clear, the courts are showing a willingness to set them aside on the basis of fairness and good faith.[11]

Acceptance

At the heart of contract law are the concepts of consensus and mutual commitment. The manifestation of an intention to commit on the part of the offeror is found in the offer; the offeree's intention to commit is found in the acceptance. The contract is formed, and the parties are bound by it, at the point of acceptance. The key to understanding acceptance is that the commitment must be total. If a condition or qualification is put on the acceptance, it becomes a counteroffer, and is not an acceptance. If a salesperson offers to sell a car and a trailer to a customer for $5000 and $3000, respectively, and the response is "I accept, provided

---

[11.] For a good discussion of the duty of good faith in commercial contracts, see *Transamerica Life Canada Inc. v. ING Canada Inc. (2003)*, 68 O.R. (3d) 457 (C.A.). Unlike American courts, Canadian courts have not recognized a "stand-alone" duty of good faith in the performance or enforcement of commercial contracts. Canadian courts have implied only a duty of good faith that ensures that the parties do not act in a way that defeats the objectives of the agreement that they have entered into.

you include new tires," that response is a counteroffer. Nor is it possible to accept only part of an offer. In this example the purchaser cannot say, "I accept your offer, but I want only the car." For an acceptance to be valid, it must be an all-or-nothing proposition.

Acceptance must be complete and unconditional

A serious problem can arise when customers and suppliers exchange order forms. Sometimes, instead of filling in the supplier's order form, the customer simply sends her own, which may include different terms. This is not an acceptance, but a counteroffer. If the supplier simply sends the product in response, he has accepted and is bound by the new terms. Suppliers often do not realize the difference. Such a mistake is easily made, and care should be taken to watch for such substituted forms.

Even a clear acceptance cannot correct an incomplete offer. When the wording of an offer is unclear, the courts will interpret the agreement to find the most reasonable construction. They will not, however, go so far as to strike a bargain on behalf of the parties. As mentioned, there is no such thing as a contract to enter into a contract.

An incomplete offer cannot be accepted

CASE SUMMARY 6.5

An Incomplete Offer Can't Be Accepted: *Zynik Capital Corp. v. Faris*[12]

A Memorandum of Understanding was signed by Zynik and by Faris, who signed on behalf of a non-existent corporation, Intergulf Developments Ltd. The Memorandum provided that the parties would jointly acquire the Versatile Shipyards property. Zynik alleges that Intergulf repudiated the Memorandum, with the result that the property was purchased by a third party. Zynik claimed damages of $10 million, representing the profits it would have made if it had been able to develop the property.

The Court referred to the paragraph in the *Bawitko* case quoted in Case Summary 6.2. It held that the Memorandum was not a binding contract, as it was missing an essential term. There was no acquisition price for the property provided. Further, there was no evidence that the parties had agreed on an acceptable price. As there was not a binding contract, the action for damages was dismissed.

SMALL BUSINESS PERSPECTIVE

In this case, the offer was incomplete and therefore could not be accepted. No matter how definite the acceptance was, it could not overcome the defect of an incomplete offer. How can parties ensure that the agreements they enter into will be enforceable?

COMMUNICATION OF ACCEPTANCE

Acceptance of an agreement is usually accomplished by communicating it to the offeror. It is possible, however, for an offer to be accepted by conduct. If the offeror has indicated particular conduct to specify acceptance, the offeree must comply with that stipulation for it to be effective. Acceptance may also be implied from conduct as when, for example, a purchaser leaves a deposit on a car she has purchased.

Offer may be accepted by conduct, where specified or implied

---

12. (2007), 30 B.L.R. (4th) 32 (B.C.S.C.).

CASE SUMMARY 6.6

Communication of Acceptance May Be Indirect: *Lanca Contracting Ltd. v. Brant (County) Board of Education*[13]

The president of Lanca was present when the Board of Education passed a resolution to accept Lanca's bid for the construction of a new school. The members of the Board were aware of his presence. Several members of the Board, as well as its architect and controller, spoke at the meeting in terms that implied that Lanca was going to be building the school. Two days later, the Board rescinded its resolution and awarded the contract to someone else. The question facing the Court was whether notice of the acceptance had been given to Lanca sufficient to create a binding contract. The Court decided that it had been, and that the Board was liable for its breach of the contract.

DISCUSSION QUESTIONS

If acceptance can be implied from the conduct of the parties, is the law too subjective? Does it make the law too unpredictable? If acceptance can be implied from the offeror's conduct, it will be the courts that will make the determination as to whether the conduct in a particular case implies acceptance. Does this give the courts too much discretion? Would it be better if the law were that acceptance must be communicated to the offeror to be effective?

Unilateral contract accepted by completion of performance

A **unilateral contract** is accepted by performance of the act specified in the offer.[14] If a prize were offered for the first human-powered flight across the English Channel, acceptance would be by making the flight. Starting the flight would not qualify; only the completion of the cross-Channel flight would constitute effective acceptance of the offer. But what if the offeror tried to revoke his offer when the flight was only partially performed? In theory, an offer can be revoked any time before acceptance. As discussed above, a Canadian court would likely follow the American example, and find a subsidiary contract requiring that once the performance starts the offer cannot be revoked. In any case in which acceptance is by conduct, there is no requirement to communicate the acceptance to the offeror, although there may still be a need to notify the offeror that the required conduct has taken place when this is not self-evident.

Unsolicited offer not accepted by silence

Merchandisers often send unsolicited goods to people along with an invoice stating that if the goods are not returned within a specified time, the customer will have purchased them. But silence, as a general rule, does not constitute acceptance. When goods are supplied in this way, the customer can normally ignore them and just put them away. If the customer uses the goods, he is receiving a benefit and is deemed to have accepted the offer. Consumer protection legislation in many provinces outlaws "negative option practices," reinforcing the common law.

But silence can be acceptance if prior dealings

An important exception to silence not being an acceptance occurs when there is an ongoing business relationship between the parties. It is quite common for a supplier to send materials used by a business on a regular basis, with the understanding that they will continue to be sent unless the supplier is informed

---

13. [1986] O.J. No. 234 (C.A.).

14. See *Speidel*, supra note 1, for an example of a case involving a unilateral contract.

otherwise. A relationship of trust has developed, and the purchaser now has a duty to inform the supplier when he changes his mind. When a person joins a book-of-the-month club, a similar duty is created, and return of the book is likely required to escape obligation. But such clubs sometimes continue to send products when there has not been a request, or even after they have been told to stop. As mentioned above, there is now consumer protection legislation in place in most provinces dealing with negative option practices in an attempt to prevent this kind of abuse.

When acceptance is not by conduct, the general rule is that it is not effective until it has been communicated to the offeror, in the manner stipulated in the offer. The result of this general rule is that the contract is formed when and where the offeror learns of the acceptance. If a supplier of lumber products in Halifax makes an offer to a customer in Winnipeg, and the offeree accepts over the telephone, the contract comes into existence in Halifax, when the offeror hears the acceptance. Where the contract is formed can be an important factor in determining which court has jurisdiction and which jurisdiction's law will apply to the contract.

Acceptance is effective when and where received

THE POSTBOX RULE

Difficulties arise when parties deal with each other over long distances using non-instantaneous forms of communication. Because neither party can be absolutely sure of the other's state of mind at a given time, there can be no certainty of the contract's status. The **postbox rule** was developed to solve this problem. When use of the mail is reasonable, an acceptance is effective when and where it is deposited in the mailbox. This is a clear exception to the general rule discussed above, which states that an acceptance is not effective until the offeror learns of it. Figure 6.2 illustrates how the postbox rule works.

Mailed acceptance effective when and where dropped in postbox

CASE SUMMARY 6.7

Should the Postbox Rule Be Extended? *R. v. Commercial Credit Corp.*[15]

This case dealt with whether a creditor had lost its priority by failing to properly register a security interest as required by Nova Scotia law. If the contract was formed within the province, the creditor would lose any claim to the assets because of the failure to register; if it was formed outside the province, the creditor would have a valid claim. The original offer had been sent by courier by Commercial, from its Nova Scotia office, to the offeree, which was outside of the province. The offer was accepted, and the acceptance was also sent by courier. The Court held that this communication was akin to using the mail and so the postbox rule applied. This meant that the acceptance was effective where sent, which was outside the province. Referring to the offeror, Commercial, the Court said that "They were the ones that chose the method of communication, and having done so on behalf of both parties, the mailbox doctrine was brought into play. Its extension to a courier service was sound in principle and, in my opinion, the contracts were therefore made outside of Nova Scotia when their acceptances were sent back to

---

[15.] (1983), 4 D.L.R. (4th) 314 (N.S.C.A.).

Commercial Credit." This is one of the few cases in which the postbox rule has been extended beyond communication by mail or telegram. The case has not yet been followed in other jurisdictions in Canada.

DISCUSSION QUESTIONS

Is there any justification to extend the postbox rule to other forms of communication? Should it even be in effect today?

Figure 6.2 Postbox Rule

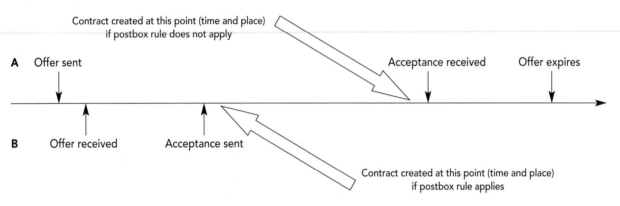

One problem—determining the point of consensus—is solved, but another is created. For a period of time, while the letter of acceptance is still in the mail, the offeror is bound in contract but unaware of that fact. Note that the offeror can avoid this problem by stipulating a different means of communication. When use of the mail is inappropriate, or if another method of acceptance was specified by the offeror, the acceptance will be effective only when received.

Response by mail when an offer is sent by mail is normally reasonable. The problem arises when a means of communication other than mail is used to make the offer, but acceptance is then made by mail. This is illustrated in *Henthorne v. Fraser.*[16] Henthorne was handed an offer in Fraser's office, which was to remain open for 14 days. He took the offer home to think about it and, after several days, posted a letter of acceptance. In the meantime, Fraser sold the property to another party and wrote a letter to Henthorne revoking the offer. The two letters crossed in the mail. The Court decided that even though the offer had been handed to Henthorne, use of the post for acceptance was reasonable. The acceptance was therefore effective when sent. Note that the letter of revocation was not effective until Henthorne received it.

The question must also be asked whether the postbox rule applies to any other form of communication. The postbox rule has been extended to include telegrams. It has not been applied to instantaneous forms of communication, such as telex or fax.

Applies only when response by mail appropriate

Postbox rule extended to telegrams

16. [1892] 2 Ch. 27 (Eng. Ch. D.).

CASE SUMMARY 6.8

Limitation of the Postbox Rule: *Entores Ltd. v. Miles Far East Corp.*[17]

Miles Far East Corp. → Acting through Dutch company

Dutch company ← Offer made by telex

Acceptance by telex → **Entores**

An American company contracted with a British company through a Dutch subsidiary for the purchase of electronic components. The British company wanted to sue the American company in England, but the British courts would have jurisdiction only if the contract came into existence in the United Kingdom. It was argued that since the Dutch company sent the acceptance by telex (similar to a modern fax machine), the postbox rule should apply, meaning that the contract came into existence where the acceptance originated, in Holland. The Court rejected this argument. The Court found that because telex was instantaneous, like the telephone, there was no need to extend the postbox rule exception to that form of communication. Therefore, the general rule applied and the acceptance was effective in the United Kingdom, when and where it was received. The contract thus came into existence in the United Kingdom, and the courts there had jurisdiction.

DISCUSSION QUESTIONS

This case illustrates the operation of the postbox rule and its limitations. There is some question whether there is any justification for the postbox rule in this day of modern high-tech communication. Should the postbox rule be eliminated by legislation, so that it is not possible for a court to apply the rule to any contract, no matter how the acceptance is communicated?

Today, it is becoming much more common to use electronic means of communication, such as electronic mail and fax, rather than the postal service. The question arises whether the postbox rule will be extended to these methods of doing business. Since these new electronic communications are instantaneous, or near-instantaneous, it is not likely that the postbox rule will be extended to them. This conclusion was confirmed, at least with respect to communication by fax, in *Eastern Power Ltd. v. Azienda Comunale Energia and Ambiente,*[18] where it was decided that an acceptance sent by fax was effective only when it was received by the offeror. There is also a U.S. case indicating that an acceptance by email will not be effective until read by the offeree or offeror, which likely indicates the direction our courts will go.[19]

Should postbox rule be extended?

---

[17] [1955] 2 All E.R. 493 (C.A.).

[18] *Corinthian Pharmaceutical Systems Inc. v. Lederle Laboratories*(1984), 24 F. Supp. 605 (S.D. Ind.).

[19] (1999), O.A.C. 54, (1999), 50 B.L.R. (2d) 33, leave to appeal to S.C.C. refused, [1999] S.C.C.A. No. 542.

Law of contracts must adapt to new technology

The applicability of the postbox rule to electronic communications is just one example of how the law of contracts must adapt to the rapid growth of internet transactions. All aspects of contract law will have to be reconsidered, as electronic transactions grow in importance. An advertisement, for example, is usually an invitation to treat, but an advertisement on the internet may be an offer if it can be accepted by clicking on an "I Accept" button.[20]

REDUCING RISK 6.2

People often make the mistake of thinking that, if they make an offer to sell something to several people and then sell it to one of them, their other offers are automatically ended. Normally you must notify the other parties that you have sold the item to revoke the offers. If you fail to do so, you face the risk of one of these parties accepting your offer. You would then be bound to sell the same item to two different people. To avoid the problem of being bound in contract without knowing it, because of the postbox rule, the offeror should be careful to specify the method of acceptance and to clearly state in the offer that it will not be considered accepted until the acceptance is actually received by the offeror. Of course, when a long-term business relationship is involved, this may not be a problem.

It should be noted that there are still significant advantages to using the mail. The use of the mail involves the exchange of a permanent tangible record of the transaction and its terms. Electronic communication, such as email, may be convenient, but it suffers from a lack of permanency or certainty. Such records can be lost through the crash of a system, or simply altered in an undetectable way, making written records and communications through the mail still—and likely to remain—an attractive option as a common aspect of future business transactions.

Postbox rule can also determine what law applies to the contract

As mentioned above, where a contract is formed can also determine which law applies or whether a court has jurisdiction. These things may therefore be determined by the postbox rule. In the *Entores* case, the British court had jurisdiction because the postbox rule did not apply to an acceptance by telex and the contract was thus made in England. In the *Commercial Credit Corp.* case, the transaction was not subject to Nova Scotia law because the postbox rule was held to apply to a couriered acceptance, meaning that the contract was made outside the province.

Postbox rule does not apply to revocation of offer

It must be stressed that the postbox rule is an exception to the requirement that an acceptance must be communicated to be effective. It does not apply to the offer or to a revocation of an offer. In the *Henthorne v. Fraser* case, discussed above, the postbox rule applied only to the letter of acceptance, and not to the letter of revocation, which had to be received before it could have any effect on the transaction.

CONSIDERATION
The Price One Is Willing to Pay

Central to contract law is the *bargaining process*, in which people trade promises for promises, and all parties derive some benefit from the deal. That benefit, essential

---

[20] See, for example, *Electronic Transactions Act*, S.A. 2001, c. E-5.5, which was created to ensure that electronic transactions have the same validity and enforceability as traditional paper-based transactions.

to the existence of a contract, is called consideration, which is defined as the price one commits to pay for the promise of another. Consideration is not restricted to the exchange of money. A bargain may involve the exchange of anything the parties think is of value. For example, when Brown purchases a computer from Ace Computers Ltd. for $2000, there is valid consideration on both sides. The promise to deliver the computer is valid consideration, as is the promise to pay $2000. Note that before the parties actually exchange the computer for the cash, they are bound in contract, because the consideration given is the exchange of commitments or promises, and not the actual money or goods. If one of the parties fails to honour that commitment, the other can successfully sue for breach of contract.

Consideration—not necessarily money

Because it is sometimes difficult to determine the value a person is getting from a deal, it is often better to look at what the parties are giving or paying. For example, if a public-spirited business agrees to pay someone to clean up a public park, the commitment is still binding, even though it might have been made out of a sense of civic responsibility and may result in no actual benefit to the business. Both sides have exchanged promises or commitments. Normally, the promise to make a charitable donation is not enforceable, because it is a one-sided promise, or gift, but when the charity makes a commitment in return—such as a promise to name a building after the donor, or to use the money in a certain way—it has made a commitment, and both parties will be bound.

Promise of charitable donation usually not enforceable

Similarly, a contract is just as binding if the consideration involved is a commitment not to do something, as opposed to a promise to do something. For example, if a business promises to pay its employees $500 to quit smoking, such an arrangement is a valid, binding contract. The consideration on the one side is the promise to pay $500, and the consideration on the other side is the promise to refrain from doing something the party has a legal right to do (that is, smoke). Consideration is a benefit or a detriment flowing between the parties to an agreement as the result of the striking of a bargain (see Figure 6.3).

Consideration can be benefit or detriment

Figure 6.3 Consideration Involves the Exchange of Promises or Commitments

A promises to do X

A ⟶ B

B promises to pay Y ($)

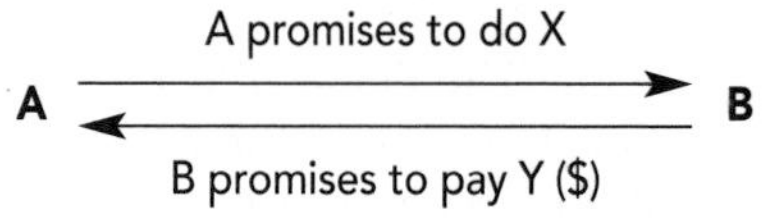

If the agreement is one-sided, and only one of the parties is getting something from the deal, it is called a **gratuitous promise**, or a gift, and the courts will not enforce it. It may well be that such gratuitous promises ought to be honoured from an ethical point of view, but there is no legal obligation to do so. Once the gift has been given, however, the courts will not assist the giver in getting it back. Also, when services are performed gratuitously, there is still an obligation to do a proper job. If through the negligence of the person performing the gratuitous service, damage or injury results, he can be sued in tort. For example, if a skilled carpenter, out of the goodness of her heart, helps her neighbour repair a roof, and because of her negligence the roof leaks and causes damage to furniture and belongings, the neighbour will be successful in suing in tort for compensation.

Courts will not enforce gratuitous promise

CASE SUMMARY 6.9

Promise to Pay Was Gratuitous: *NAV Canada v. Greater Fredericton Airport Authority Inc.*[21]

NAV provided aviation services and equipment to the Authority. The Authority decided to extend one of its runways and requested that NAV relocate its instrument landing system. NAV decided that it made economic sense to replace part of the system rather than move it. The cost of the replacement part was $223 000. NAV asked the Authority to pay for the part. The Authority refused, saying it was not contractually bound to do so. Eventually, the Authority agreed to pay, to ensure that the extended runway became operational. The payment was made "under protest." NAV installed the part, but the Authority refused to pay for it. An arbitrator held that there was nothing in the Agreement between NAV and the Authority that required the Authority to pay for the cost of the part. He held, however, that the subsequent correspondence between the parties resulted in a contract, which required the Authority to pay.

The Court of Appeal held that the Authority was not required to pay for the part because the subsequent correspondence did not create a valid contract. It ruled that the variation of the existing Agreement between the parties was not supported by consideration. Performance of a pre-existing obligation does not qualify as valid consideration. NAV had not promised anything in return for the Authority's promise to pay for a part for which it was not legally obligated to pay.

DISCUSSION QUESTIONS

What step could NAV have taken to ensure that the Authority would be bound by its promise to pay for the part, even if the Court held that there was no consideration given by the Authority for its promise? Should a gratuitous promise to vary an existing contract be enforceable as long as it was not procured under economic duress? If that was the law, would the Court have held the Authority liable to pay for the part?

Adequacy of Consideration

The courts will not bargain for the parties

Consideration need not be fair. The court will not interfere with the bargain struck, even when it is a bad deal for one of the parties. If a person agrees to sell someone a brand new Cadillac for $100, this becomes a valid, binding contract. When businesses deal with each other, the value of a particular deal to the parties is not always apparent, and the wisdom of the courts not reviewing the fairness of the consideration is clear. But when businesses deal with consumers, the courts are much more concerned with fairness. They are therefore sometimes willing to assist consumers who have been taken advantage of by merchants. They have developed such concepts as *unconscionability*, *fraud*, and *mistake*, which give them power to review these transactions. The courts will also examine the fairness of consideration when insanity, drunkenness, or undue influence may have affected the transaction. This power to intervene is now also often found in legislation, such as consumer protection statutes.

Inadequate consideration may indicate fraud, insanity, etc.

[21.] (2008), 229 N.B.R. (2d) 238 (C.A.).

CASE SUMMARY 6.10

Both Sides Must Make Commitments: *Gilbert Steel Ltd. v. University Construction Ltd.*[22]

Gilbert had supplied construction steel to University for a number of its projects. For one particular project, it had a contract for a specified amount of steel to be provided at a set price. But Gilbert's costs for the steel increased, and it requested that University pay a higher price for the steel supplied for that project. University agreed to pay the higher price.

The steel was delivered, but the payments made were never enough to cover the increased price. When Gilbert demanded payment, University refused to pay the amount over the original price, claiming it didn't get anything in return for its promise to pay more. It had agreed to pay more, but Gilbert's position hadn't changed; it still had the same obligation to deliver steel that it had under the original agreement. Such a one-sided agreement was not a binding contract. For a contract to exist, there must be an exchange of promises or commitments between the parties—a one-sided agreement is not enforceable.

The lawyers for Gilbert argued that University received consideration in that Gilbert promised to give University a "good price" on a subsequent project. The Court found that this promise was not specific enough, and that there was no commitment involved. Gilbert also argued that because University did not have to pay for 60 days after the price went up, it was getting free credit, but the Court also rejected that argument. The Court therefore held that there was no bargain struck. Only one side made a commitment, and thus there was no obligation to pay the higher price even though there was a promise to do so. (Note that Gilbert also argued that there was *promissory estoppel* in this case, but this position was rejected by the Court. This aspect of the case will be discussed below.)

DISCUSSION QUESTIONS

What could Gilbert have done to ensure that the promise of University to pay more would be enforced by the Court?

Although the consideration paid does not need to be fair, it must have some legal value. The promise of "love and affection" is not good enough, nor is a promise to stop "bothering" someone's father.[23] Whatever the parties have bargained for must have some material value for the courts to enforce the bargain.

Consideration
• need not be fair but must be specific

---

22. (1976), 12 O.R. (2d) 19 (C.A.).

23. *White v. Bluett* (1853), 23 L.J. Ex. 36 (C.E.).

In addition, the parties must agree to a specific consideration or price. Suppose someone agrees to exchange a car for another's promise to "do some work around the house." Such a promise would not be enforceable because the work to be done is not specified. This was the problem in the *Gilbert Steel* case discussed in Case Summary 6.10, when Gilbert promised to give University a "good price" on a future project. This problem becomes acute whenever a monetary consideration is involved. It is not sufficient to promise to give "some money" as payment for the promise of another. Such a commitment must refer to a specific or calculable amount of money. When the parties agree to pay the "market value" of an item, or when some other objective method or formula for pricing a product at some time in the future is used, the consideration is calculable and is thus sufficiently specific to be binding, thus overcoming the problem. Even then, great care must be taken to make sure the price at that time will be clear.[24]

• **particularly if money is involved**

CASE SUMMARY 6.11

Without Notification, Continued Employment Not Consideration: *Churchill v. Stockgroup Media Inc.*[25]

Churchill was hired by Stockgroup as a sales representative. The employment contract provided that Stockgroup reserved the right "to change compensation and incentive plans at any time . . . " Three years later, Stockgroup provided Churchill with a revised compensation plan that gave it "the right to set targets to be achieved by you and to determine the territory to be covered by you." Churchill agreed to this plan, after some of its terms were changed in response to concerns she raised. Stockgroup assigned Churchill a new sales territory that resulted in her commission decreasing. Stockgroup then became concerned about Churchill's attitude and performance and placed her on probation. Churchill went on disability leave, but did not return to work. She sued, claiming constructive dismissal.

The Court held that Stockgroup was entitled to change the compensation and incentive plans. The change in Churchill's sales territory was, however, constructive dismissal. A fundamental term of the employment contract cannot be changed unless the employer provides the employee with consideration. There was no consideration for the change in the employment contract that entitled Stockgroup to change Churchill's sales territory.

SMALL BUSINESS PERSPECTIVE

Why it is important that employers use detailed employment contracts when hiring new employees?

Gratuitous Promises Are Not Consideration

EXISTING DUTY

Sometimes people enter agreements to do what they are already legally obligated to do. This raises a problem concerning the adequacy of consideration. For

---

24. *Foley v. Classique Coaches* (1934), 2 K.B. 1 (C.A.).

25. 2008 B.C.S.C. 578.

example, Olsen agreed to paint Chang's house for $1500. When the painting was three-quarters finished, Olsen demanded $500 more to finish the job on time. Even if Chang agreed, there would be no binding obligation because Chang got nothing in exchange for the promise to pay more. Olsen was obligated to finish painting the house before the promise to pay the extra $500 was made, and after the promise the obligation remained the same. Olsen's legal position did not change; therefore, there was no consideration. These types of problems often arise in the construction industry, when unforeseen factors may increase the costs significantly, as in the *Gilbert Steel* case discussed in Case Summary 6.10. This is just one more reason for the parties to take great care to predict all costs that are likely to arise and to build into their agreement provisions for resolving conflicts over these unexpected eventualities.

> No consideration where extra pay to do same work

When a duty to act exists, but that duty is owed to a third party, a promise to do the same thing for someone else is enforceable. In the situation above, if Chang's tenant Adams promised to pay Olsen the extra $500 to ensure the job was finished on time, that agreement would be binding. Before Adams's promise to pay the extra $500, Olsen was legally obligated to Chang to finish painting the house. After the promise to Adams, Olsen is now legally obligated to Adams, as well as to Chang, to paint the house. Olsen's legal position has changed because Olsen now runs the risk of having to pay Adams' damages, as well as Chang's, if the contract is breached. There is valid consideration here, and the contract would be binding.

> A new bargain requires new consideration

When a public duty is involved, a demand for further compensation will not be tolerated. A police officer, firefighter, or other public servant can't demand more money to do her job. A firefighter cannot arrive at a blaze and extract a promise from the victim to pay an extra $500 to put out the fire. Such a contract would be against public policy and void. But paying police personnel in their off-duty hours to provide security at a rock concert or celebration is valid, as they are on their own time and not otherwise obligated to help.

PAST CONSIDERATION

There are situations in which there is no consideration even though it appears to be present. One of these is when the consideration was given in the past; that is, the bargain is struck after the price agreed on has been paid. An employer's promise to pay a bonus in recognition of good work already performed by the employee would not be binding: the work has already been done. Although it may appear that both parties have given something (the employer the promised bonus and the employee the good work), such a promise is not enforceable. The key to this problem is in the timing. When the promise to pay the bonus was made, the work had already been performed, so where is the bargain? In fact, the employee is in exactly the same legal position before the promise as afterward. Thus, it is often said, "Past consideration is no consideration."

> Past consideration is no consideration

PAYING LESS TO SATISFY A DEBT

A creditor will often agree to take less in full satisfaction of a debt. Such agreements also raise problems with respect to consideration. A creditor who agrees, after a $5000 debt becomes due, to take $3000 from the debtor as full payment, has received no consideration for the reduction in the debt. In fact, the reduction of the debt is gratuitous. It is quite clear that, under the common law, such a one-sided promise is not binding, and that the debtor can therefore sue for the

> Common law states that agreement to take less to satisfy debt is not binding

remaining $2000. Even if the partial payment is actually made, the creditor can still turn around and sue for the remainder.[26]

But, as a practical business matter, such an arrangement to accept less is often beneficial to the creditor as well as the debtor. The creditor might otherwise have to sue to recover, and then not collect anything. Many jurisdictions have passed legislation providing that when a creditor has agreed to take less in full satisfaction of a debt, and has actually received the lesser sum, the creditor is bound by the agreement and cannot sue for the difference.[27]

Legislation may overrule common law if there is payment of the lesser sum

When the creditor has agreed to take less, but none of the money has yet been paid, the creditor is still free to change her mind and insist on the entire amount being paid. Of course, when the debtor has agreed to pay the lesser amount early, or to do something in addition to the payment, such as pay a higher rate of interest, there is consideration on both sides to support the new arrangement. In cases like these, the creditor is bound by her promise to accept less.

ILLEGAL CONSIDERATION

There are some policy restrictions on what constitutes good consideration. For example, when illegal drugs are sold, the agreement is void because the consideration is illegal. Contracts between businesses to interfere with free competition and unduly restrain trade may also be void due to illegality.

Illegal or impossible consideration is no consideration

In addition, for consideration to be valid it must be possible to perform the consideration promised. An agreement to change lead into gold for a fee would also be void due to the impossibility of performance (at least at this time).

REDUCING RISK 6.3

The old adage that you cannot get something for nothing has been enshrined in the law of contract in the form of the requirement of consideration. In all contracts (with a couple of exceptions, discussed below) there must be a bargain in which both parties make a commitment to each other. The lack of such consideration is often difficult to see, especially in business deals in which pre-existing obligations are being modified. In such circumstances, we have to be especially vigilant in our dealings, to ensure that the deals we make are legally binding and not simply one-sided gratuitous agreements that can be ignored by the other party.

Examples of Valid Consideration

SETTLEMENT OUT OF COURT

Consideration exists in out-of-court settlements

When the parties to a dispute settle the matter outside of court, there is also valid consideration on both sides. When a litigant learns later that he would likely have won, it may look like there is no consideration. In fact, as both parties have given up their right to have the court determine the matter, there is consideration on both sides. As a result, the release signed in such situations is a binding contract.

[26.] *Foakes v. Beer* (1884), 9 App. Cas. 605 (H.L.).

[27.] See, for example, *Law and Equity Act*, R.S.B.C. 1996, c. 253, s. 43.

REQUEST FOR SERVICES

When services are requested from providers, such as lawyers or mechanics, the parties often do not agree on a specific price before the service is performed. When you ask a lawyer for assistance in resolving a contractual dispute, or a mechanic to fix your car, you are often not given a firm price for the service. In these circumstances, the courts will impose an obligation to pay a reasonable price. This is an application of the principle of *quantum meruit*, sometimes called a quasi-contract. *Quantum meruit* means "as much as is deserved." The courts use this principle to impose an obligation to pay a reasonable price when services are requested. The requirement to pay a reasonable price when no specific price has been agreed upon has also been applied to the sale of goods by provincial statutes.[28]

Must pay reasonable amount for services

The courts will also use *quantum meruit* to determine how much should be paid when a person providing the services is not allowed, by a breaching party, to finish the job. For example, when a person has agreed to paint a house and, before the job is finished and payment is due, the other party refuses to allow completion, the court will use the *quantum meruit* principle to require the breaching party to pay a reasonable price for the benefit he has received. The same is not true if the breaching party is the one seeking payment. In the example above, if the painter were the one who refused to finish the job, she could not demand partial payment for what she had done.

Exceptions to the General Rule

PROMISSORY ESTOPPEL

Another exception to the rule that a promise is enforceable only if consideration is present is based on the principle of **promissory estoppel**, sometimes referred to as *equitable estoppel*. The more common or ordinary use of the term *estoppel* involves statements of fact. Promissory estoppel, in contrast, deals with a person making a promise, or a commitment, to do something in the future. As we have discussed, an exchange of such promises or commitments constitutes consideration, and the result is a binding contract. But when the promise is one-sided, or gratuitous, it is normally not enforceable. (Figure 6.4 illustrates how promissory estoppel works.)

Gratuitous promises usually not enforceable

But sometimes the promisee, in anticipation of the promise being performed, incurs expenses or other obligations that otherwise could have been avoided. In the presence of such reliance, unique remedies have been developed to compensate for significant loss. In the United States, when such reliance is placed on a gratuitous promise and injury results, it is possible to sue for compensation. In the United Kingdom and Canada, however, such an unfulfilled promise can be used only as a defence to an action initiated by the person who made the promise.

In London, England, just before World War II, High Trees leased an apartment building from Property Trust under a 99-year lease, with the intention of renting out the individual flats in the building.[29] The two parties agreed to a set yearly rent of £2500. Because of the outbreak of the war, it soon became apparent that High Trees would not be able to rent out all of the flats. Therefore, in 1942, Property Trust agreed to lower the yearly rent to £1250. After the war, it changed its mind, and demanded payment of all of the rent owed under the original lease,

---

28. See, for example, *Sale of Goods Act*, R.S.A. 2000, c. S-2, s. 10.

29. *Central London Property Trust, Ltd. v. High Trees House, Ltd.*, [1947] 1 K.B. 130.

Figure 6.4 Promissory Estoppel

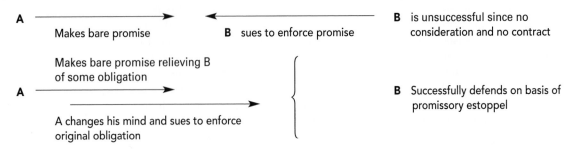

including back rent for the portion that had not been paid since 1942. It argued that the promise to take less rent was one-sided and, as a gratuitous promise, was not binding. The Court agreed that, for the period after the war, High Trees had to again pay the full rent. With respect to the back rent, however, Property Trust was bound by its promise to take the lower amount. The key to understanding this is to realize that High Trees was not suing to enforce the promise; rather, Property Trust was suing for the higher amount in spite of its promise. High Trees was using the plaintiff's promise as a defence to the plaintiff's claim. Thus, in the United Kingdom, the principle of *promissory estoppel* is remedial in nature. In *Combe v. Combe*, Lord Denning made it clear that "it does not create new causes of action where none existed before,"[30] and Lord Asquith, in his concurring judgment, said that promissory estoppel could be used only as "a shield but not as a sword."[31]

> **Promissory estoppel can be used only as a defence**

Canada has followed the English example, limiting the use of promissory estoppel to a defence. That is why, in the case of *Gilbert Steel* (discussed in Case Summary 6.10 above), the argument of promissory estoppel failed. Gilbert Steel argued that because University Construction promised to pay more and Gilbert Steel relied on the promise, it created an "estoppel" and University Construction should be required to pay the higher amount. But Gilbert Steel was not using the promise as a defence; it was suing, claiming payment on the basis of that promise. Since it was using the promise as a sword instead of a shield, it failed. Note that if University Construction had made the higher payments and then sued Gilbert Steel to get them back, promissory estoppel would have been available to Gilbert Steel, as a defence.

> **There must also be reliance placed on the promise**

In fact, in almost every case where promissory estoppel has been successfully used as a defence, there was an existing legal relationship, usually contractual, that was modified by a promise. The promisor was attempting to enforce the original terms of the agreement, ignoring the relied-upon promise to alter the terms. The disappointed promisee was using the promise as a shield, or defence, to the action. To raise this defence successfully, the victim must demonstrate reliance on the promise and suffer an injury as a result of that reliance. That was another reason why the promissory estoppel argument raised in the *Gilbert Steel* case failed. True, it delivered the steel as required, but it was required to do so under the original contract in any case. It did only what it was required to do under the contract; it didn't take on any extra obligation, or incur any extra expense, that could have otherwise been avoided.

---

30. [1951] 1 All E.R. 767 at 769 (C.A.).

31. *Ibid.* at 772.

Do you think we would do better to adopt the American approach and allow an action for compensation whenever someone relies on a gratuitous promise to his detriment?

CASE SUMMARY 6.12

Promissory Estoppel Used by a Government Agency: *Toronto College Street Centre Ltd. v. Toronto (City)*[32]

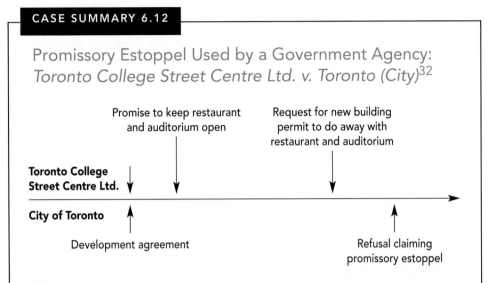

The use of promissory estoppel is not limited to contract. An example of the use of promissory estoppel in a non-contract case involved the owners of a building that was recognized as an important heritage site. The owners had been allowed to develop the building, but they had promised the City to retain a restaurant and auditorium on the seventh floor. When this proved uneconomical, the owners applied for a building permit to change the use of the seventh floor to rental units. The permit was refused, and that decision was challenged by way of judicial review of administrative action, as discussed in Chapter 2. The Court based its decision partly on promissory estoppel. The owners of the building had promised to maintain the seventh floor as a restaurant and auditorium, and the City had refused to grant a permit to do otherwise. The owners were estopped by their promise. Note that the promise of the owners of the property was being used as a defence by the City; it was clear that the City had relied on the promise when allowing them to do other things with the building. The case is interesting in that it involves the enforcement of the doctrine in a non-contract situation and to the benefit of a government entity rather than an individual.

SMALL BUSINESS PERSPECTIVE

In light of this case, businesspeople must be careful in making promises to government agencies while seeking government approval or permission. What should government agencies do to ensure that such promises will be enforced against the promisors?

SEALED DOCUMENTS

The last major exception to the requirement of consideration involves the use of a seal. Seals were originally made by placing melted wax on a document and impressing a signet ring in it, thus lending authenticity or authority to the

Sealed documents do not require consideration

---

32. (1986), 56 O.R. (2d) 522 (C.A.).

document. When the parties went to so much trouble to indicate they were serious, they were bound by their commitment. This practice—which predates modern contract law—has been retained; thus, when a seal is used, it is not necessary to show consideration for the contract to be binding. Today, instead of a wax impression, the seal normally takes the form of a paper wafer, although almost any form of marking on the document that the parties have identified as a seal can be used. A sealed contract is a formal contract, or a deed. The court will not entertain any suggestion that the promise contained in a formal contract is not supported by consideration. Although it is not necessary to look for consideration when a seal is present, the existence of the seal does not eliminate the need for the other elements of a valid contract.

To summarize, consideration (the price one is willing to pay for a promise) is one of the required elements of a contract. There must be some form of valid consideration in the form of a benefit or detriment flowing between the parties for a court to enforce a contract. Only when the document embodying the agreement is sealed, or on those rare occasions when the promise of the promisor is being raised as a defence by the promisee, will the court enforce an agreement without requiring consideration to be established.[33]

APPENDIX READING

Formation of Internet Contracts

Internet contracts are most pervasive in the consumer context. Businesses selling online use standardized terms and conditions just as in the physical world. Two key types of legislation govern the formation of online contracts; e-commerce and consumer protection. The e-commerce legislation has modernized contract formation rules to allow "clicking an icon" to satisfy the acceptance and communication requirements of contract formation.[34]

Consumer protection legislation deals with the problems surrounding long detailed standard terms linked to an order webpage. Most provinces (most notably Alberta, British Columbia and Ontario) regulate Internet consumer agreements. However, these new statutory provisions may in fact alter the traditional rules of offer and acceptance to Internet contracts.

Section 38 of the Ontario Consumer Protection Act, 2002 states that before a consumer enters into an Internet agreement, the supplier shall disclose specific information about, among other things, the total price of the good or service, the terms of payment, and warranties. Subsection 38(2) states: "The supplier shall provide the consumer with an express opportunity to accept or decline the agreement. . . ." This suggests that the Internet consumer is the offeree, and it seems to contradict the general rule discussed in this chapter: that a retailer advertising goods for sale is making only an invitation to consumers to make offers—and typically in retail sales the consumer is the offeror.

[33.] See *Romaine Estate v. Romaine* (2001), 95 B.C.L.R. (3d) 95, (2001), 205 D.L.R. (4th) 320 (C.A.), in which gift documents with wafer seals were enforced as sealed contracts.

[34.] Section 19(1) of the (Ontario) Electronic Commerce Act, 2000 (OECA) states that an offer or acceptance of a contractual offer "may be expressed, . . . (b) by an act that is intended to result in electronic communication, such as, (i) touching or clicking on an appropriate icon . . . on a computer screen. . . ."

Since an Internet consumer is considered the offeree, and after seeing the terms required to be disclosed by the supplier, she will be bound by the terms of the Internet contract at such time as she clicks an "I accept" icon on her computer screen. However, some e-retailers specifically design their websites with multiple acceptances before a "submit" icon is finally clicked. This would appear to satisfy the legislative "agreement to terms" requirement before the entire offer to purchase is submitted. In this context, the contract may not be formed until the retailer communicates acceptance with a confirmation number.

INTERNATIONAL ISSUE

Jurisdiction and Internet Contracts

The ability to contract over the Internet has greatly increased the number of international contracts in which the offeror is in one jurisdiction while the offeree is in another. As we have already described, the laws may be different in each location and jurisdiction is often determined by the place of acceptance. To reduce the likelihood that the rules relating to the formation of electronic contracts might be different in each jurisdiction, the United Nations has undertaken a number of initiatives:

■ The United Nations Convention on the Use of Electronic Communications in International Contracts (2005)

■ The United Nations Commission on International Trade Law (UNCITRAL) Model Law on Electronic Signatures (2001)

■ The UNCITRAL Model Law on Electronic Commerce (1996)

Still, international variation exists. For example, Canadian consumer protection legislation extends protection to Canadian consumers even when they are involved in international contracts governed by a foreign jurisdiction.

Questions to Consider

1. Should Canadian provinces co-ordinate their legislation to avoid international inconsistency?

2. How can a business use its online contractual terms and conditions to ensure that foreign consumers are aware of the law that applies to the contract?

SUMMARY

The contractual relationship

- A contract is an exchange of promises enforceable in court
- There are five elements of a valid contract: consensus (offer and acceptance), consideration, capacity, legality, and intention
- There are many important terms and definitions relevant to the contractual relationship

Consensus

- A contract requires "a meeting of the minds"
- An offer is a tentative promise by the offeror contingent upon an acceptance by the offeree
- All the essential terms of the contract must be contained in the offer; non-essential terms will be implied by the courts
- An invitation to treat, or an invitation to negotiate, is not an offer
- An offer must be communicated to the offeree before it can be accepted
- An offer will end at a specified time, but it may be revoked earlier by notice to the offeree, unless an option agreement has been entered into
- If there is not a specified time limit, an offer will lapse after a reasonable time
- A counteroffer, a rejection of the offer, or the death or insanity of the offeror will also cause an offer to lapse
- A standard form contract is interpreted strictly against the party who drafted it
- An acceptance is an indication of a willingness to be bound; a contract is formed when an offer is accepted
- An acceptance must be complete and unconditional
- An acceptance must be communicated in the manner required by the offer; it is effective when and where received
- Silence may be acceptance if there is an existing business relationship
- The postbox rule says that an acceptance by mail (when reasonable) is effective when and where it is dropped in the mailbox
- The postbox rule has been extended to telegrams, but not to instantaneous forms of communication

Consideration

- Consideration is the price paid for another party's promise and can be anything of value
- Both parties must have experienced some benefit; a gratuitous promise is not enforceable
- Consideration must be specific, but it need not be fair; courts will not review its adequacy
- A promise to do what you are already legally obligated to do is unenforceable
- Past consideration is no consideration
- An agreement to accept less in full satisfaction of a debt is unenforceable in common law, but may now be binding under legislation
- Illegal consideration and impossible consideration are not valid consideration
- An out-of-court settlement is enforceable, as there is valid consideration
- *Quantum meruit* is used when there is a request for services with no agreement as to the amount; a reasonable price must be paid
- Promissory estoppel enables a gratuitous promise to be used as a defence
- When a contract is sealed, consideration is not necessary

QUESTIONS

1. What is meant by "freedom of contract"? Explain the impact of this principle on the development of contract law. What are two types of restrictions on this principle?

2. List and explain the elements that must be present for an agreement to qualify as a valid contract.

3. Explain the difference between a formal contract and a parol contract.

4. Explain the difference between void and voidable. What is a practical result of this difference?

5. Distinguish between unenforceable contracts and illegal contracts.

6. Explain the difference between a bilateral contract and a unilateral contract.

7. What practical concepts does contract law use to determine if "a meeting of the minds" has happened?

8. At what stage in the process of forming a contract are the significant terms of the contract clearly set out?

9. Explain the role of implied terms in a contract. Who has the power to imply terms into a contract? When will the power be used?

10. Is an "agreement to agree" binding? Explain your answer.

11. Distinguish between an offer and an invitation to treat.

12. Can you accept an offer that was made to someone else? Explain your answer.

13. List and explain the various ways an offer can come to an end.

14. What is the effect of the offeror stating in an offer that the offer will remain open for acceptance until a specific date? What can an offeree do to protect herself from the offer being revoked?

15. What risks are faced when a person offers to sell certain goods to A and then sells them to B? How can this problem be avoided?

16. Explain the two types of contracts that result from the tendering process.

17. What do the courts do, when interpreting standard form contracts, to correct the imbalance in bargaining power between the parties?

18. What qualities must an acceptance demonstrate to be effective?

19. When is a contract formed?

20. When will silence be considered an acceptance of an offer?

21. What is the general rule regarding acceptance? What is a practical result of this rule?

22. Explain the effect of the postbox rule on the principles governing acceptance.

23. Discuss the role the postbox rule plays when modern communication methods are used.

24. Define consideration and explain what is meant by the term "the exchange of consideration."

25. Explain under what circumstances a person who fails to properly perform a gratuitous promise can be held legally liable for that failure.

26. Does consideration have to be fair? Explain your answer.

27. What difficulty might be faced by a person who has already agreed to do a specific job and then extracts a promise of more pay from the other party?

28. If a person who is rescued promises to pay the rescuer $1000 but doesn't pay, will the rescued person be successful in suing for breach of contract? Explain your answer.

29. "A creditor is bound by her promise to take less in full satisfaction of the debt." True or false? Explain your answer.

30. Explain why a contract dispute settled out of court is considered binding even though one party would have obtained more if the action had been taken to court.

31. Explain a person's obligation regarding payment when she has requested a service without specifying a particular fee.

32. Describe what is meant by promissory estoppel and the circumstances in which it will arise in contract disputes.

33. How does the presence of a seal affect the requirement that consideration must be present in a contract?

Chapter 7

Formation of Contracts: Capacity, Legality, and Intention

In addition to consensus and consideration (discussed in the previous chapter), contracting parties must have the capacity to contract, the contract must be legal and be performed legally, and both parties must have intended that legal consequences would follow from their agreement. Each of these elements will be discussed in this chapter. Although it is always a good idea to put a contract in writing, the general principle is that a verbal contract is as binding as a written one. There are several situations, however, for which contracts are required by statute to be evidenced in writing. These will also be discussed in this chapter.

CAPACITY

Lawmakers have always recognized that some people are more vulnerable than others and thus require special protection. Over the years, several categories of people have been identified as needing protection. These categories have been protected by having their freedom to enter into contracts limited, or in some cases eliminated completely.

Minors/Infants

The age of majority was 21 at common law, but it has been reduced by statute to 18 or 19, depending on the province. The general principle is that persons under

Age of majority varies with provinces

Minors not bound by their contracts, but adults are

the age of majority, called *infants* or *minors,* are not bound by their agreements, but the adults with whom they contract are bound. The courts try to balance protecting the minor against the objective of not imposing undue hardship on the adult. It is important to distinguish between the actual incapacity of a child who is incapable of understanding what is happening, and the artificial incapacity imposed on a youth who is a functioning member of society.

Test for capacity is objective

Most problems relating to minors and contracts they have entered into arise in situations involving young people who are approaching the age of majority. The test for capacity is objective. When an adult deals with a person who is a minor, it does not matter if the adult was under the impression that the other person was an adult, or even that that person clearly understood the terms of the contract. The only question is whether the other person was under the statutory age of majority at the time the contract was created. As a general rule, whenever a minor enters into a contract with an adult, the adult is bound by the contract, but the minor can choose not to be bound by it.

For example, when a sales representative of a car dealership offers to sell a car for $2500 to a minor who accepts the offer, the dealership will be bound by the contract. If the young person has not yet taken delivery of the car, she has the choice as to whether to go through with the deal or not. If she takes delivery of the car and then chooses not to pay for it, she would have to return the car. She could not, however, be forced to pay or otherwise go through with the contract, even if she wrecks the car or it is stolen.

Legislation supplements common law

In most provinces, these principles are based on English and Canadian case law. British Columbia, however, has a unique *Infants Act.*[1] This legislation states that, in most cases, a contract made by a minor is unenforceable against him. The minor may, however, enforce the contract against an adult party to the contract. The result, then, is the same as in the provinces which rely on the common law. Other provinces may also have legislation dealing with the contractual capacity of minors. For example, the *Minors' Property Act*[2] allows a court to confirm a contract entered into by a minor if it believes it is in the best interests of the child to do so.

Special problems arise when dealing with contracts made online. The law with respect to capacity will be determined by the jurisdiction where the contract is created, which is sometimes not clear. Also, there is no way for online merchants to know the personal characteristics of the parties with whom they are dealing. It is important that such merchants include appropriate restrictions and disclaimers in their online contracts.

NECESSARIES AND BENEFICIAL CONTRACTS OF SERVICE

Except in British Columbia, minors are bound by contracts for the acquisition of necessaries and for contracts of service that benefit the minor. **Necessaries** are things required to function in society, such as food, clothing, lodging, and transportation. What constitutes a necessary will vary with the particular needs of a minor and her status. If the young person is purchasing clothing, but already has a sufficient supply, then that clothing will not be considered a necessary.

[1.] S.A. 2004, c. M-18.1, s. 3.

[2.] *R.S.B.C. 1996, c. 223.*

When a minor is married, or is living on his own, what constitutes a necessary will be broader than would be the case if he were single and dependent on his parents. The courts have held that medical, dental, and legal services, along with toiletries, uniforms, and even a house, will be considered as necessaries in different situations. It is unlikely, however, that they will find that a car qualifies as a necessary, since other alternative forms of transportation are generally available. Even when the subject of the contract is determined to be a necessary, it does not guarantee that the merchant will get paid full price, as the minor is obligated only to pay a reasonable price for such necessaries.[3]

Minors bound by contracts for necessaries

When a minor borrows money to buy necessaries, there is an obligation to repay the debt only if the funds advanced are actually used for necessaries. For this reason, a creditor cannot recover money loaned to a minor to pay for school tuition if it is used instead for gambling. Government student loans are exceptions, because they are supported by legislation requiring repayment regardless of what the money is used for and regardless of the age of the borrower.

Minors must repay money borrowed and used for necessaries

Contracts of employment, apprenticeship, or service are binding if it can be demonstrated that, taken as a whole, the contract is for the benefit of the minor. If it becomes apparent that the minor is being taken advantage of, or the contract is not in the minor's best interests, the minor will not be bound. Today, these kinds of relationships are usually controlled by legislation.[4]

Minors bound by contracts of service that substantially benefit them

Note that in British Columbia's *Infants Act*, all contracts, including contracts for necessaries and beneficial contracts of service, are unenforceable against an infant. Only contracts made specifically enforceable by legislation will be binding on infants.[5] An example of such a contract is a student loan agreement.[6]

Note B.C. exception

ON BECOMING AN ADULT

If a minor agrees to a contract (other than a contract for necessaries or a beneficial contract of service), she is not bound by it. If, however, she ratifies the contract after becoming an adult, she loses the right to avoid the contract. That is, ratifying the contract makes a voidable contract binding. For example, if a minor agrees to pay $5000 for an automobile in a series of instalment payments, she cannot be forced to pay. If, however, the minor, after becoming an adult, makes an instalment payment, or provides a written statement indicating that she intends to be bound, the contract will then be binding. Ratification can be in writing,[7] or it can be implied. Ratification must be complete; a minor cannot affirm the beneficial provisions of the contract and repudiate the rest.

Minor can ratify contract at age of majority

[3.] Some provinces have legislation dealing with the purchase of necessaries by minors. See, for example, the *Sale of Goods Act*, R.S.A. 2000, c. S-2, s. 4, which states that minors need only pay a reasonable price for necessaries, and that necessaries are goods suitable to the "condition in life" of the minor and to the minor's actual requirements.

[4.] See, for example, the *Apprenticeship and Industry Training Act*, R.S.A. 2000, c. A-42.

[5.] See, for example, the *Canada Student Loans Act*, R.S.C. 1985, c. S-23, s. 19, which states that a lender may recover a student loan made to a minor as if the minor "had been of full age at the time the loan was made."

[6.] *Supra* note 1, s. 19.

[7.] In some provinces, ratification must be in writing, and be signed by the minor, to be effective. See, for example, *Statute of Frauds*, R.S.N.S. 1989, c. 442, s. 9.

CASE SUMMARY 7.1

What Amounts to Ratification? *Bayview Credit Union Ltd. v. Daigle*[8]

Daigle was a minor when he borrowed a considerable sum from the Bayview Credit Union. He used his motorcycle as security for the loan. While still a minor, he stopped making payments, and hid the motorcycle. After reaching the age of majority, he disclosed the location of the motorcycle. The Credit Union repossessed and sold the motorcycle, but there was still $4100 owing on the loan. The Credit Union sued Daigle. It claimed that his disclosure of the location of the motorcycle when he was an adult amounted to ratification of the contract, making it enforceable against him.

The Court held that Daigle was not liable. His action was not ratification. He was merely assisting the Credit Union in realizing its security. The Court commented, "Surely the acts of the defendant here, in co-operating as he did to the benefit of the plaintiff, should not place him in a worse position than a person who would refuse co-operation to reduce the plaintiff's loss." The case illustrates the danger of businesspeople dealing with minors as if they were adults. It also shows the implications of a minor ratifying a contract after becoming an adult.

DISCUSSION QUESTIONS

Should a minor lose the protection of the law when, whether out of ignorance or a sense of obligation, he chooses to continue to pay, or acknowledges, a debt after becoming an adult?

Some contracts must be repudiated

There are certain contracts that a minor must repudiate within a reasonable time after becoming an adult to avoid obligations (or, as some cases suggest, a failure to repudiate can be evidence of ratification). These situations tend to involve contracts through which a minor acquires some interest of a permanent and continuous nature. The cases in this area tend to be very old, with little in the way of recent case law.[9] Specific examples of contracts that minors may need to repudiate to avoid being bound by them include those involving land, shares in corporations, partnerships, and marriage settlements.

Description of contractual relationships

Although these principles may seem reasonably straightforward, their application has created a good deal of confusion. To appreciate the reasons for this confusion, it is necessary to understand how the contractual relationship progresses through prescribed stages. At the first stage, when the parties have entered into the contract but the minor has not yet obtained any benefit from it, and has not yet paid, the minor is not bound by the contract. This is an **executory contract**. If the minor has received the goods, but has not yet paid for them, she is not necessarily bound by the contract. This is a **partially executed contract**. When the goods are in the minor's possession, she will be required to return them or pay for them, and upon return is entitled to a refund of any money already paid. If the

---

8. (1983), 3 D.L.R. (4th) 95 (N.B.Q.B.).

9. See, for example, *R. v. Rash* (1923), 53 O.L.R. 245, *Saunders v. Russell,* [1902] B.C.J. No. 65, 9 B.C.R. 321 (S.C.), *Lovell and Christmas v. Beauchamp,* [1894] A.C. 607 (H.L.), and *Edwards v. Carter,* [1893] A.C. 360 (H.L.).

minor has passed the goods on to a third party, or the goods have been destroyed, the merchant will not be entitled to payment, and the merchant also cannot insist that the party to whom the goods have been given return them.

Conflict may arise when the contract has been **executed**. Once minors have obtained the benefit under a contract, can they change their minds and insist on the return of their money? In Canadian law, the conclusion seems to be that minors are bound by the contract unless it can be demonstrated that what was received was of no value at all. That is, a minor can insist that payment be refunded if there is a total failure of consideration and the minor gained nothing from the deal. In general, if the contract is prejudicial to the interests of the minor, it is void.

When contract gives no benefit, minor can escape even executed contract

REDUCING RISK 7.1

Merchants run a great risk when they deal with even mature youths as if they were adults. Contracts cannot be enforced against them and, while security can be taken in goods, even that may not be much protection when the goods used as security are destroyed or otherwise made unavailable, as illustrated by Case Summary 7.1. When dealing with minors, it is advisable not only to take security for the loan, but also to have the parents of the minor co-sign the contract, or to have them give a personal guarantee.

PARENTS' LIABILITY

There is a popular misconception that liability will rest with the parents if a child fails to pay a debt. As a general rule, parents are not responsible for the torts of their children, nor are they responsible for the contractual obligations of their children, in the absence of specific legislation creating such a responsibility. If a minor enters into a contract, she alone is responsible to perform the contract. The adult contracting with the minor cannot turn to the parents if the minor does not perform as required by the contract.

Parents not responsible for minor's contracts

Many jurisdictions have passed legislation making parents liable for the torts, contracts, and even criminal activities of their children.[10] In the absence of such legislation, parents can be held liable for their children's contracts only under specific conditions. Parents can be liable when the minor is acting as an agent having the appropriate authority to bind the parent in contract. Parents will also be bound if they guarantee the minor's obligation at the time the contract is entered into. A guarantee is a written commitment whereby the guarantor agrees to pay the debt if the debtor does not. Since the very purpose of the guarantee is to encourage the merchant to enter the contract, these guarantees have been held to be binding on the parents. Also, because parents are responsible to provide for their minor children, they can be held responsible by the merchant for contracts their children enter into for necessaries.[11]

Parents may be responsible where there is agency or guarantee, or where goods are necessaries

---

[10.] Several provinces have enacted legislation to this effect. See, for example, the *Family Law Act,*R.S.O. 1990, c. F.3, s. 45(2).

[11.] See, for example, the Manitoba *Parental Responsibility Act,* C.C.S.M. c. P8, which makes parents liable if their child "deliberately takes, damages or destroys the property of another person." The parents' liability is limited to $10 000. The parents may avoid liability by showing that they were exercising reasonable supervision and that they made reasonable efforts to prevent or discourage the child from engaging in the kind of activity that resulted in the property loss. For a comment on proposed legislation in Nova Scotia, see "Parental Responsibility: Law Liable to Do Nothing," The *Chronicle Herald* online, 1 June 2009, http://thechronicleherald.ca/Editorials/1125097.html.

INFANTS' LIABILITY FOR TORTS

Minor may be liable in tort

A merchant will occasionally try to get around the protection given to a minor in contract law by suing in tort instead. Sometimes the act that constitutes the breach of contract will also qualify as negligence, or some other tort. It is a basic tenet of tort law that a minor is as liable as an adult for torts committed, although the standard of behaviour expected may differ. But the courts will not allow adults to bring a tort action just to get around the incapacity problem in contract law. If the minor used the subject matter of the contract in a way that would be expected under the contract, then the adult must sue in contract, not tort, despite the protection given to the minor by the law of contracts.

Adults cannot avoid protection given to minors under contract law by suing in tort

On the other hand, if the minor used the subject matter of the contract in a way that was not contemplated in the contract, carelessly causing injury or damage to those goods, the adult would be able to sue for negligence and the minor would not be protected by the defence of infancy. For example, if a minor rents a two-wheel-drive automobile and then damages it while off-roading, the merchant would be able to sue the minor for negligence because the use to which the automobile was put was outside what was anticipated in the contract.

Except when tort arises independent of contract

CASE SUMMARY 7.2

Minor Liable for Tortious Acts Not Contemplated by Contract: *Royal Bank of Canada v. Holoboff*[12]

Holoboff, a minor, entered into an agreement for a savings account with the Bank. He then sold his client card and his personal identification number (PIN) to a third party. The third party proceeded to defraud the Bank by making a "fake" deposit to Holoboff's account and then withdrawing money from the account. Holoboff was convicted of fraud. He was then sued by the Bank.

Holoboff claimed that he should not be found liable because of the common law that allows minors to avoid contracts that are not for necessaries. The Bank argued that the fraudulent use of the debit card by a third party with Holoboff's assistance was not contemplated by the terms of the contract. The Court found that the contract required Holoboff to keep his PIN confidential and to restrict the use of his debit card to his personal use only. Therefore, Holoboff's selling of his card, and revealing of his PIN, were outside the contemplation of the contract. The Court thus allowed the Bank's claim, and found Holoboff liable for the tort of conspiracy to commit fraud.

DISCUSSION QUESTIONS

Is the distinction between liability in tort and in contract artificial? Is it appropriate that an infant may be found liable in tort but not in contract? Should the law be made consistent, so that an infant cannot be found liable for any of her actions?

However, if the minor had an accident while driving the rented automobile on a highway, the adult could not sue in tort, even if the minor was clearly negligent, because that activity would be expected when a car is rented. In short, the adult

---

12. (1998), 221 A.R. 192 (Q.B.).

cannot circumvent the protection afforded to the minor in contract law by suing in tort instead. (This explains why car rental agencies will not rent to minors, but when a minor misrepresents himself as an adult and contracts to rent a vehicle, the agency may be able to get damages from the minor by suing for the tort of fraudulent misrepresentation.) Nor are the parents responsible, since parents are not liable for the torts of their children unless they can be said to have been negligent in their own right, or when there is a statute in place imposing such liability.

Insanity and Drunkenness

The law extends its protection to those incapacitated because of insanity or mental incompetence in a way similar to the protection given to minors. To qualify for this protection, it must be shown that the person could not understand the nature of the act being performed. To take an extreme example, if a man thinks that he is Napoleon and that he is selling his horse when, in fact, he is selling his car, he would be declared to lack the capacity to contract because he does not understand the nature of the transaction. The burden of proving incapacity on the basis of insanity or mental incompetence rests with the person claiming to be incapacitated. That person must lead evidence showing that he did not understand the consequences of his actions.

Insanity or mental incompetence applies if person did not understand

To escape contractual liability on the basis of insanity or mental incompetence, the person (or a representative) must prove not only insanity or mental incompetence, but also that the person he was dealing with knew, or ought to have known, of the incapacity. This is the point illustrated in the case in Case Summary 7.3.

and if other party knew or ought to have known of incapacity

CASE SUMMARY 7.3

Bank Must Know, or Ought to Have Known, of Insanity: *Canadian Imperial Bank of Commerce v. Milhomens*[13]

Milhomens executed a Visa Application Agreement in favour of CIBC and was issued a Visa card. He used the card and, eventually, had an outstanding balance owing of $18 104.29 plus interest at the rate of 18.5 percent. CIBC sued for non-payment of the debt. Milhomens claimed that "he was of unsound mind and incapable of appreciating or understanding the meaning and effect of the Visa Application Agreement when he signed it." The evidence showed that Milhomens had a long psychiatric history. There was no evidence showing that CIBC ever knew, or ought to have known, about his condition.

DISCUSSION QUESTIONS

Should CIBC be awarded judgment for the amount claimed? Is there an obligation on a bank to monitor the spending patterns of its credit card holders to determine if they change and, if they do, the reason for the change? Is there anything else Milhomens could have done with respect to the purchases he made with his Visa card?

---

13. [2004] S.K.Q.B. 168.

Provincial legislation applies to people who are mentally incompetent

A person may be declared mentally incompetent by a court. In such cases, a trustee will be appointed to handle that person's affairs. To understand the precise rights and obligations of a trustee, and the care and use of that person's property, the appropriate provincial legislation should be carefully examined.[14]

Drunkenness treated like insanity

People who lose their ability to reason through intoxication, whether from alcohol or drugs, are treated in the same way as people incapacitated by insanity or mental incompetence. As is the case with insanity, for the contract to be avoided, the person must have been so intoxicated that she didn't know what she was doing, and the other person must have known, or ought to have known, of the incapacity. The person trying to escape a contract on the basis of drunkenness must also be able to show that, on reaching sobriety, the contract was repudiated.

Must repudiate upon becoming sober

For example, an intoxicated person who purchases shares is not permitted, on becoming sober, to wait and see whether the stocks go up or down before repudiating the contract. Hesitation to repudiate makes the contract binding. This requirement of **repudiation** also applies to insane people who regain their sanity. As with minors, the insane, mentally incompetent, or intoxicated person is also required to pay a reasonable price for necessaries.

A person who is of weakened intellect, or otherwise vulnerable, but not insane or mentally incompetent, is still to some extent protected.

LEGALITY

An agreement must be legal and not contrary to public interest to qualify as a binding contract. It is easy to understand that a contract to commit a crime would be void. But contracts involving activities that, while not illegal, are considered immoral or contrary to public interest may also be void. The courts have taken several different approaches when faced with the problem of illegal or immoral contracts.

Contracts Performed Illegally

Difference between contracts formed illegally and contracts performed illegally

When discussing legality, it is necessary to distinguish between illegality as to formation of the contract (the contract itself is illegal) and illegality as to performance (the contract is performed in an illegal way). The Supreme Court of Canada explained this distinction in a case in which a man died when a cocaine-filled condom burst in his stomach.[15] The beneficiaries of his life insurance policy were found to be entitled to the proceeds of the policy. The Court held that the insurance policy was lawful and that the innocent beneficiaries should not be disentitled to the insurance benefits because the insured accidentally died while committing a criminal act. The Court stated: "If the insurance contract purported to cover an illegal activity, the contract would be unlawful and could not be enforced."[16] But, as the case involved a lawful contract that was performed in an

Lawful contracts performed illegally may be enforced

illegal manner, the Court enforced the contract. There was no **public policy** reason to prevent the beneficiaries from receiving the insurance proceeds.

The response of the courts to the illegal performance of a lawful contract will vary. In making their decisions, the courts will consider many factors, such as the

---

14. See, for example, the *Dependent Adults Act*, R.S.A. 2000, c. D-11.

15. R.S.C. 1985, c. I-5. at para. 54

16. *Oldfield v. Transamerica Life Insurance Co. of Canada*, [2002] 1 S.C.R. 742.

intent of the parties, the actions of the parties, and public policy. The case discussed in the previous paragraph shows that in such situations the court may enforce the contract, in appropriate circumstances.

The illegal performance of a lawful contract often involves a breach of legislation that is regulatory in nature. Such legislation may contain provisions declaring that a breach of the legislation will result in the relevant contract being void, or other specified consequences. The courts will apply these statutorily mandated outcomes whenever a contract is performed contrary to the legislation.

Sometimes, however, regulatory legislation does not indicate the result of a violation of the legislation. In such cases, the courts may make a variety of decisions. They may treat the contract as void but not illegal. They will then restore the parties to their original positions, ordering the return of any deposits advanced and property that has been transferred. If the illegal performance can be separated from the rest of the performance of the contract, then they may rule that only that part of the contract is void. If the violation of the legislation is more one of procedure than of substance, the courts may enforce the contract. The current judicial approach is illustrated by Case Summary 7.4.

Several possible results when performance breaches regulatory legislation

---

CASE SUMMARY 7.4

Renovation Contract Void Because of Illegality: *Chung v. Idan*[17]

This case involved what the Court referred to as "renovation hell." The plaintiffs made a claim for payment for extra goods and services relating to a home renovation contract. The defendants denied liability for the amount claimed. The Court dismissed the plaintiffs' claim for several reasons, including their failure to provide required goods and services, their supply of items with deficiencies, their charges for goods and services for which there was no agreement, their charges for goods and services that were within the scope of the initial contract, and because "they supplied goods and services illegally."

With respect to the illegality, one of the plaintiffs did the renovation work without being licensed as required, and without insisting that a required building permit be obtained. The Court referred to older case authorities that held that a building contract contrary to a statutory provision is illegal and unenforceable as a matter of public policy. The Court, however, adopted the approach of more recent authorities stating that a renovation contract may be enforceable notwithstanding a breach of the relevant legislation. The Court stated that

> the recent cases adopt a sophisticated approach to illegality that considers such factors as: (a) the purpose of the statute; (b) the enforcement mechanisms within the statute; (c) whether the statute makes the contract inherently illegal or only illegal if performed without compliance with the provisions of the statute; (d) whether the violation of the statute was only a technical non-compliance because the party intended to comply with the statute and could have done so; and (e) whether the illegality can be severed from the balance of the contract.[18]

[17.] 2006 CanLII 2048 (On. S.C.), aff'd 2007 ON C.A. 544.

[18.] *Ibid.* at para. 53.

The Court held that the plaintiffs made no effort to comply with the licensing and permit requirements. The statutory violations were not just technical, they were "advertent." The Court therefore did not allow the plaintiffs' claim, as it was "tainted by illegality."

DISCUSSION QUESTIONS

Is the modern approach, which may result in enforcement of an illegal renovation contract, appropriate? Does this introduce uncertainty into the law? Would it be better to follow the traditional approach, which makes all illegal renovation contracts unenforceable? Wouldn't this encourage the parties to comply with all relevant laws?

Contracts Formed Illegally

Illegal contracts are illegal when formed

Illegal contracts are void and courts will not assist parties

As discussed above, the Supreme Court has distinguished between illegality as to formation of the contract (the contract itself is illegal) and illegality as to performance (the contract is performed in an illegal way). A reference to an "illegal contract" is to a contract that is illegal at the time it was formed. As the Supreme Court observed, an illegal contract will not be enforced; it is void. Usually, when faced with a void contract, the court will restore the parties to their original position, ordering them to return any deposits advanced and property that had been transferred. But an illegal contract involves unacceptable or immoral conduct. Under such circumstances, while the contract is void, the courts will not assist the parties by restoring them to their original position unless one of them is innocent of any wrongdoing.

An agreement involving immoral conduct is an illegal contract

An illegal contract usually involves the commission of some prohibited conduct, such as the sale of a controlled substance, or the commission of some violent or antisocial act. The conduct may be identified as wrongful and specifically prohibited by the *Criminal Code* or some other statute, or it may simply be inconsistent with the provisions of such a statute. The common law, however, goes even further, and assumes that some types of immoral conduct are unacceptable and against public policy. Even though the immoral conduct is not a crime, or does not result in a violation of a statute, when people make agreements involving such conduct, the agreements are treated like illegal contracts. One example involves an agreement with a prostitute; prostitution is not illegal, but it is considered immoral and against public policy.

CASE SUMMARY 7.5

Contracts with Criminal Rates of Interest—An Exception to the Rule? *Transport North American Express Inc. v. New Solutions Financial Corp.*[19]

The parties entered into a credit agreement that included many payments other than the principal and interest: a monthly monitoring fee, a standby fee, royalty payments, payment of legal and other fees, and a commitment fee. The trial Judge held that the agree-

---

[19.] [2004] 1 S.C.R. 249.

ment contained an interest component greater than the 60 percent allowed by section 347 of the *Criminal Code*. He applied "notional severance" to reduce the effective annual interest rate to 60 percent. The Court of Appeal allowed the appeal and struck out the interest clause, leaving in place the other payments, which amounted to an effective annual rate of 30.8 percent when computed as interest.

The Supreme Court of Canada overturned the Court of Appeal decision. It held that all of the various payments under the agreement were "interest" under section 347. The Court stated, "There is broad consensus that the traditional rule that contracts in violation of statutory enactments are void **ab** initio is not the approach courts should necessarily take in cases of statutory illegality involving section 347 of the Code. Instead, judicial discretion should be employed in cases in which section 347 has been violated in order to provide remedies that are tailored to the contractual context involved."[20]

These remedies range from declaring the contract void if it is very objectionable, to severing the illegal clause if the contract is otherwise unobjectionable. The courts should consider "the specific contractual context" and the illegality involved when determining an appropriate remedy.

The Supreme Court ruled that notional severance was appropriate in this case. It therefore affirmed the decision of the trial Judge. The Court outlined four factors to be considered when deciding whether to declare an illegal contract void, or to partially enforce it, and cited the following:

> In Thomson, at p. 8, Blair J.A. considered the following four factors in deciding between partial enforcement and declaring a contract void ab initio: (i) whether the purpose or the policy of s. 347 would be subverted by severance; (ii) whether the parties entered into the agreement for an illegal purpose or with an evil intention; (iii) the relative bargaining positions of the parties and their conduct in reaching the agreement; and (iv) whether the debtor would be given an unjustified windfall. He did not foreclose the possibility of applying other considerations in other cases, however, and remarked (at p. 12) that whether "a contract tainted by illegality is completely unenforceable depends upon all the circumstances surrounding the contract and the balancing of the considerations discussed above and, in appropriate cases, other considerations."[21]

DISCUSSION QUESTIONS

Does the approach of the Supreme Court lead to uncertainty, as it can result in partial enforcement of an illegal contract? Does it provide the courts with too much discretion, in that they can choose from a variety of remedies when they make their decisions? Would it be better to limit the courts to the simple remedy of severance, rather than to enable them to apply "notional severance," which in effect allows them to rewrite the contract?

---

[20] *Ibid.* para. 4.

[21] *Ibid.* para. 24.

It appears that the approach followed in the *Transport* case applies in all cases, not just those involving section 347 of the *Criminal Code*. The classic approach of declaring every illegal contract void was viewed as harsh and inequitable, as it could result in a windfall to one of the parties. The modern approach means that an illegal contract may be partially enforceable. The courts may sever the illegal provisions of the contract, leaving the balance of the contract enforceable. In the *Transport* case, the Supreme Court said that the severance can even be "notional," meaning that the courts can, in effect, rewrite part of the contract.

New judicial approach to illegal contracts

EXAMPLES

Examples of illegal contracts

The following is a list of some of the types of contracts that have been determined to be illegal. The list includes contracts that are in violation of legislation, as well as contracts that are against public policy.

1. **Contracts to commit a crime.** Agreements involving murder, drug dealing, or even charging a high rate of interest are contrary to the *Criminal Code* and are therefore illegal contracts.

2. **Contracts to commit a tort.** If Mullins offers Nowak $100 to falsely claim that Abercromby did a poor job of repairing his house, that would be defamation. The contract to pay Nowak to defame Abercromby would be illegal.

3. **Contracts involving immoral acts.** As indicated above, prostitution is not illegal in Canada. However, a prostitute could not expect the courts to enforce an agreement made with a client. Prostitution is considered immoral, and the contract would therefore be illegal.

4. **Contracts that are bets and wagers.** Historically, the courts would not enforce contracts related to gambling activities, as they were against public policy. Now this area is covered by statute, and the rules vary from province to province. The statutory provisions are designed primarily to limit and regulate gambling activities. The courts will enforce only contracts for which the activities have statutory approval or are licensed.

Insurance contract is valid when there is an insurable interest

Insurance is like a wager. A person owning property pays for insurance to insure against the destruction of the property. If the property is destroyed, the insurer compensates the owner for the loss. This requirement of loss is called an insurable interest. It must be present for the insurance contract to be valid.

Contracts for the sale of shares have the same difficulty. If the contract merely requires the parties to pay each other the difference if the share price goes up or down, it is void as a wager. To avoid this problem, the contract must provide that the share will actually change hands. Commodities traded in a similar fashion suffer the same problem.

5. **Contracts in restraint of marriage, or in favour of divorce.** Any contract that has as its object the prevention or dissolution of marriage is against public policy. An agreement to pay someone $100 000 in return for a promise never to marry would be an illegal contract.

6. **Contracts that promote litigation.** An agreement in which one person, to satisfy some ulterior motive, pays another to sue a third would be an illegal contract and therefore void, because it promotes litigation. An exception is a lawyer's contingency fee. In such an agreement, the lawyer agrees to proceed with an action without payment, in return for a share of the judgment (often

Contingency fee agreements permissible because they make courts accessible

amounting to 30 percent or 40 percent). This agreement appears to be permissible because it does not promote litigation, and it serves to make the courts more accessible to those who normally could not afford to proceed.[22]

7.   **Contracts that obstruct justice.** If the effect of a contract is to interfere with the judicial process, it is against public policy. An agreement that encourages criminal activity by providing to pay a person a salary whenever he is in jail would involve such an obstruction of justice.

CASE SUMMARY 7.6

An Agreement Made to Avoid Prosecution Is Void: Newell v. Royal Bank of Canada[23]

A woman forged her husband's signature on 40 cheques totalling more than $58 000. He tried to protect her from prosecution by signing a letter prepared by the Bank agreeing to assume "all liability and responsibility" for the forged cheques. The Court found that this was "an agreement to stifle a criminal prosecution which is an illegal contract and unenforceable." Because the contract was illegal, the husband's agreement to accept responsibility for the cheques was void. He was therefore entitled to get his money back. A merchant may find an arrangement such as the husband's letter very appealing. Such an agreement, however, smacks of blackmail and tries to cover up a criminal act. It may even be considered an obstruction of justice. Any such agreement will therefore be an illegal contract and void.

DISCUSSION QUESTIONS

Was the Court's decision appropriate? Should the parties be free to make their own arrangements in these circumstances? Explain your reasoning.

---

8.   **Contracts that injure the state.** An example is a contract to sell secret military information.

9.   **Contracts that injure public service.** Bribing a public official to vote a certain way is an example of an illegal contract.

10.   **Contracts between businesses to fix prices or otherwise reduce competition.** These types of contracts are controlled by the federal *Competition Act*.[24] This statute specifically prohibits agreements that have the "undue" restriction of competition as their primary purpose or objective:

Undue restriction of competition prohibited

> 45.   (1) Everyone who conspires, combines, agrees, or arranges with another person... (c) to prevent or lessen, unduly, competition in the production, manufacture, purchase, barter, sale, storage, rental,

---

[22.] For a case in which a contingency fee agreement that allowed an arbitrator to resolve any disputes was held to not be contrary to public policy, see *Jean Estate v. Wires Jolley LLP*, 2009 ON C.A. 339.

[23.] (1997), 156 N.S.R. (2d) 347 (C.A.).

[24.] R.S.C. 1985, c. C-34.

transportation, or supply of a product, or in the price of insurance upon persons or property, or (d) to otherwise restrain or injure competition unduly, is guilty of an indictable offence and is liable to imprisonment for a term not exceeding five years or to a fine not exceeding ten million dollars or both.

Thus, if two merchants agreed not to sell a particular commodity below a certain price, or not to open up branches that would compete with each other in specified communities, and they were the only ones selling the products in that community, such agreements would likely be illegal contracts and void. Such a conspiracy may also be punishable as a criminal act. This is another example of a contract in restraint of trade. The *Competition Act* prohibits a number of other unacceptable business practices.

Restrictive covenants must be reasonable

11. **Contracts that unduly restrain trade.** When a business is sold, the contract often includes a clause prohibiting the seller from opening another business in competition with the business she is selling. If such a provision is reasonable, and necessary to protect the interests of the parties, it is enforceable. If the provision is unreasonably restrictive, or against public interest, it will be void. An agreement is against the public interest when it interferes with free trade, drives up prices, decreases service, or has any other effect whereby the public may be harmed.

For example, assume Fiona purchases a barbershop from Ahmed for $50 000. A considerable portion of the purchase price may be for the customer relations established by Ahmed. This is called *goodwill*. If Ahmed opens another barbershop next door to the business he sold Fiona, it would destroy the goodwill value of the contract. It would be reasonable for the buyer to include a provision in the contract prohibiting the seller from carrying on a similar business for a specified time (for example, three years) and within a specified geographical area (for example, five kilometres). If the time and distance restrictions agreed to are not excessive, the agreement would be considered a reasonable restraint of trade. The contract would be valid.

CASE SUMMARY 7.7

Helping Business Owned by Daughter-in-Law a Breach of Sale of Goodwill Agreement and Non-Competition Agreement: *Ascent Financial Services Ltd. v. Blythman*[25]

Carolyn and Don Beveridge agreed to combine their financial services business with that of Anna and Art Blythman. Carolyn and Don were told that Anna and Art's son, Brad, and his wife, Marilyn, were not entering the financial services business. Ascent was incorporated; Anna, Art, Carolyn, and Don were its directors and shareholders. Anna and Art sold the goodwill in their business to Ascent. They were to retire over the next five to ten years, with Carolyn and Don taking over the business. Anna and Art signed a non-

---

25. (2006), 276 Sask. R. 23 (Q.B.), aff'd (2002), 302 Sask. R. 118 (C.A.).

competition agreement that required that they not compete with the business nor solicit any suppliers or customers of the business.

The relationship between the couples broke down quickly. Carolyn and Don exercised their right to purchase Anna and Art's shares. Art was upset. He asked clients to pick up their files instead of giving them to Carolyn and Don. He encouraged clients to transfer their business to Lifestyle, a new financial services corporation owned by Marilyn. Art also provided client information to Marilyn. Carolyn and Don sued for breach of the sale of goodwill agreement and the non-competition agreement.

The Court decided that Anna and Art were in breach of both the sale of goodwill agreement and the non-competition agreement, as well as their fiduciary duty, because they did not do what they could have to have the clients stay with the business. The Court assessed damages at $150 000, based on a decrease in the book value of the clients' portfolios transferred from Ascent to Lifestyle.

DISCUSSION QUESTIONS

In cases such as this, who has the burden of proof? What presumption do the courts make in cases involving restrictive covenants? Which party has to rebut this presumption to be successful in litigation regarding the enforceability of restrictive covenants?

When a restriction is excessive and is deemed to be an unreasonable restraint of trade, normally only that provision will be void. It will be severed and the rest of the agreement will be enforced. The effect would be that the purchase price and all other terms of the agreement would be the same, but the seller would have no restrictions at all. He would be free to open a similar business anywhere, at anytime. In the example above, if the provision in the contract for the purchase of the barbershop prohibited Ahmed from opening another shop anywhere in Canada, or imposed an unreasonably long period of time, such as 10 years, the provision would likely be void. Ahmed would then be free to open a new barbershop wherever and whenever he wanted. Great care must therefore be taken to avoid the purchaser's normal inclination to make the restriction on competition as broad as possible. It is best that such a clause go no further than necessary to protect the interests of the purchaser.

Restrictive covenants will be void if too broad

CASE SUMMARY 7.8

When Can Severance Be Used with Restrictive Covenants? *Shafron v. KRG Insurance Brokers (Western) Inc.*[26]

Shafron sold his insurance agency to KRG in 1988. Shafron agreed to be employed by KRG to provide management and insurance brokerage services until 1991. He also agreed to stay out of the insurance brokerage business in the "Metropolitan City of

---

[26.] 2009 SCC 6.

Vancouver" for three years after leaving employment with KRG. In 1991 Shafron agreed to become KRG's president and director and to manage its operations. He also agreed to a restrictive covenant very similar to the one he agreed to in 1988. Intercity purchased KRG's shares in 1991. Shafron's employment contract was subsequently renewed a couple of times. In 2000 Shafron advised Intercity that he would not renew his contract again. Shafron then started working with another insurer; a number of his former customers followed him. KRG sued to enforce the restrictive covenant.

The trial Judge found the restrictive covenant to be unreasonable, unclear, uncertain, and too broad. The Court of Appeal allowed the appeal. It held that the restrictive covenant was reasonable and that to not enforce it would give Shafron a windfall. The Court interpreted "Metropolitan City of Vancouver" to mean Vancouver and the municipalities directly contiguous to it.

The Supreme Court of Canada allowed the appeal. It held that the phrase "Metropolitan City of Vancouver" was uncertain and ambiguous. There was no mutual understanding as to the geographic area the restrictive covenant covered. The Court refused to rewrite the restrictive covenant. The headnote of the case contains the following passage:

> Restrictive covenants generally are restraints of trade and contrary to public policy. Freedom to contract, however, requires an exception for reasonable restrictive covenants. Normally, the reasonableness of a covenant will be determined by its geographic and temporal scope as well as the extent of the activity sought to be prohibited. Reasonableness cannot be determined if a covenant is ambiguous in the sense that what is prohibited is not clear as to activity, time, or geography. An ambiguous restrictive covenant is by definition, *prima facie*, unreasonable and unenforceable. The onus is on the party seeking to enforce the restrictive covenant to show that it is reasonable and a party seeking to enforce an ambiguous covenant will be unable to demonstrate reasonableness. Restrictive covenants in employment contracts are scrutinized more rigorously than restrictive covenants in a sale of a business because there is often an imbalance in power between employees and employers and because a sale of a business often involves a payment for goodwill whereas no similar payment is made to an employee leaving his or her employment. In this case, the restrictive covenant arises in an employment contract and attracts the higher standard of scrutiny.

The Court went on to say that notional severance (reading down a contractual provision to make it legal and enforceable) is not appropriate to apply to an unreasonable restrictive covenant. This approach would encourage employers to draft overly broad restrictive covenants. "Blue-pencil" severance (removing part of the restrictive covenant) may be used when part of the restrictive covenant is severable, trivial, and not part of the main purpose of the restrictive covenant. It is not appropriate with respect to the phrase "Metropolitan City of Vancouver."

SMALL BUSINESS PERSPECTIVE

What should the owner of a small business do to ensure that a restrictive covenant in an employment contract that has been signed by an employee will not be struck down by the courts? Is it a good idea to simply draft the provision as broadly as possible?

An employer will often impose a similar restrictive covenant requiring employees to promise not to compete during, or after, their employment. Although the same test of reasonableness is used, the courts are much more reluctant to find such restrictive covenants valid. It is only when the employee is in a unique position to harm the company (for example, by having special access to customers or secret information) that these provisions will be enforced.

Law applies to employers as well

REDUCING RISK 7.2

There is a great temptation for a purchaser of a business, or an employer, to protect herself from competition. Purchasers of a business and employers are particularly vulnerable to unreasonable competition. They can therefore include terms in their contracts that restrict that competition, but such provisions must not go too far. There is a tendency for the person who is advantaged by such a clause to make it much broader than is necessary to prevent unfair competition. Such clauses, however, must be reasonable in the circumstances and must

not be against the public interest. They must go no further than is necessary to prevent unfair competition. They should have a geographical limit and a time limit to their operation. A clause restricting competition within a 500-kilometre radius, when 50 kilometres would be sufficient, is void. A clause with a five-year restriction, when one year would be enough, is also void. Great care should be exercised in negotiating these non-competition clauses. Legal advice should be obtained to make sure that resulting clause will be enforceable.

The list on pages 204–206 describes some of the types of contracts restricted by statute or held to be against public policy. This list is neither complete nor exhaustive. It may well be that new types of activities made possible by changing technology could also be controlled by statute or be declared as being against public policy in the future. Special care should be directed to activities on the internet. Gambling and pornography account for a large portion of internet use; the validity of the activity depends on the jurisdiction involved, which often is not clear. Several jurisdictions have passed or will soon enact statutes controlling these activities. Great care should be taken, by both businesses and consumers who become involved in such activities, to determine the legality of that involvement.

List of illegal contracts will continue to grow

INTENTION

Not all agreements are contracts. Often, people enter into arrangements or undertakings never intending that legal consequences will flow from them. For example, if a person invited a friend over for dinner and the friend failed to show up for some reason, the delinquent guest would probably be quite surprised if the would-be host were to sue for breach of contract. The law requires that for an agreement to be a binding contract, the parties must have intended that legal obligations and rights would flow from it. Since neither the host nor the guest intended to create a legal obligation, the host's legal action would fail.

Parties must have intended legal consequences from agreements

When determining intention, the courts do not look to the state of mind of the person making the promise. Rather, they look to the reasonable expectations of the promisee. The test is objective. Would a reasonable person have thought that the person making the promise was serious and that the agreement was legally binding? If so, it is not going to help the person making the promise to say, "I was only kidding."

Courts will enforce reasonable expectations

CASE SUMMARY 7.9

When Friends Fall Out Over Money: *Osorio v. Cardona*[27]

Osorio and Cardona went to the horse races together and bought tickets on the "Sweep Six" (betting on six races where they had to predict all six winners). After the third race, they discovered that both their tickets were still eligible to win. They made an agreement that if either of them won, they would split the winnings. Cardona went on to win $735 403 but refused to honour the deal. Because of the odds involved, Osorio was entitled to $147 000. Cardona refused to pay, offering Osorio "$60 000 or nothing." Osorio took the $60 000 and then sued for the remainder. The Court held that the agreement was not a bet or a wager; rather, it was an agreement to pool the winnings, so there was no problem regarding legality. The Court then decided that there was an intention to be bound and thus a valid contract. The fact that they had adjusted the split to reflect the odds indicated that they were serious. Cardona had always acted toward Osorio in a way that led Osorio to believe that he was serious and that he intended the agreement to be in force. Note that because there were threats involved, the agreement to take $60 000 was held to be unconscionable and not binding as a settlement. Osorio was able to collect the other $87 000.

This case illustrates not only the requirement of intention, but also that the test whereby the court seeks to determine the intention of the parties is objective.

DISCUSSION QUESTIONS

When friends enter a contest and agree to divide the prize if they win, and they in fact do win the contest, and then they disagree as to the division of the prize, who will have to convince the court that there was an intention to be bound by the agreement? What is the most convincing evidence to use in this regard? What advice would you therefore give to friends who are entering a contest together?

The following examples illustrate situations in which the issue of intention arises and indicate the courts' probable responses.

Courts will enforce stated intention

1. **Stated intention of the parties.** If the parties clearly state that they do not wish to be legally bound by their agreement, or that their agreement is not to be enforceable in any court, that instruction will be honoured. Such a statement must be embodied in the terms of the contract and be very clear as to the intention not to be bound. Often, in commercial relationships, the parties will make agreements that are convenient, but which they don't want to be legally binding. Sometimes, the parties are in pre-contract negotiations and are not yet ready to be bound. "Letters of intention" are examples of such communications; they clearly do not create legal obligations for the parties.

Courts will presume intention in commercial transactions

2. **Commercial relations.** If the relationship between the contracting parties is primarily commercial in nature, the courts will presume that the parties intended to be legally bound by their agreement. The contract will be binding on them in the absence of any evidence or clear instructions to the contrary.

[27.] (1984), 15 D.L.R. (4th) 619 (B.C.S.C.).

3. **Domestic and social relations.** When an agreement is between members of a family, or friends involved in domestic (non-business) activities, there is a presumption that the parties do not intend legal consequences to flow from their agreement. For example, if members of a family informally agree to make payments to each other, such as a child agreeing to pay room and board, or parents to pay an allowance, the courts would assume that there is no intention to be legally bound and would therefore not enforce the agreement. However, if the parties had gone to the trouble of having a lawyer draw up a formal contract, then the courts would be satisfied that the parties did intend that legal consequences would flow from their agreement and so they would enforce the contract. The presumption of no intention would have been rebutted.

> Courts will presume no intention in domestic and social relations

4. **Social and business relations.** Problems arise when the relationship involved is a mixture of social and commercial relations. Such an example arises when friends jointly enter a contest and then disagree on the distribution of the prize. This problem could become more common in Canada with the increase in the number of lotteries with large prizes. In such cases, the courts must judge each situation on its individual merits. The courts use the reasonable person test to determine whether it is reasonable for the parties trying to enforce the agreement to think that a legally binding contract had been created.

> Reasonable person test applied when social and business relations mix

5. **Exaggerated claims.** Merchants often exaggerate the qualities of their products in advertisements or when they talk to customers. They may, for example, claim that their product is "the biggest" or "the best." To some extent, this enthusiasm is expected, and is not taken seriously by the customers or the courts. The problem is where to draw the line, and the courts again apply the reasonable person test to determine whether, in the circumstances, the customer should have taken the exaggerated claim seriously. Note, however, that even when the exaggeration is obvious, it may still be prohibited by statute, as misleading advertising or an unfair trade practice.

> Reasonable person test also applied when dealing with exaggerated claims

---

CASE SUMMARY 7.10

Are Businesses Permitted to Exaggerate? *Carlill v. Carbolic Smoke Ball Company*[28]

The defendants manufactured a product that they claimed would protect users from influenza. They offered £100 to anyone who used their product as prescribed and still contracted influenza. They stated, in an advertisement, that £1000 had been deposited in the Alliance Bank, Regent Street, and that this showed their sincerity in the matter.

Carlill used the product, got influenza, and claimed the money. The company refused to pay, stating that the advertisement was an advertising puff that merely indicated enthusiasm for the product, and that it was not meant to be taken seriously by the public. The Court held that depositing money to back up the claim had taken it out of the

---

28. [1893] 1 Q.B. 256 (C.A.).

category of an advertising puff. It was determined that a reasonable person would have thought that the advertisement was serious, so there was intention. The offer was held to be valid, and Carlill's use of the product and contracting of the illness were appropriate forms of acceptance. There was therefore a valid contract.

Misleading advertising has become a serious problem and is now controlled by consumer protection legislation, which will be discussed in Chapter 10.

***

DISCUSSION QUESTIONS

Should merchants ever be allowed to make exaggerated claims about their products?

FORM OF THE CONTRACT

We have established that the essential elements of contracts are consensus, consideration, capacity, legality, and intention (as summarized in Table 7.1 at the end of the chapter). Next we will examine the form of the contract.

The Requirement of Writing

Historically, the form of the contract was very important. Promises were enforceable because they were contained in sealed documents, called *deeds*. Today, there is no general rule that a contract must take a certain form, although most jurisdictions have statutory requirements regarding the transfer of land.[29] Contracts may be in writing, they may be under seal, they may simply be verbal, or they may even be implied from the conduct of the parties.

People are often surprised to discover that most verbal agreements have the same legal status as written ones, provided they meet the requirements described in this and the previous chapter.

Verbal contracts binding but writing advised

The importance of a written contract is practical, not theoretical. It is always a good idea to put the terms of an agreement in writing, so that if a dispute arises there is something permanent that establishes the terms to which the parties agreed. In the absence of such a document, it is surprising how differently even well-intentioned people remember the terms of their agreement. If a dispute between the parties does end in litigation, each of the parties will be in a better position to prove her case if she can produce written evidence to support her claim. We can expect changes to what will be required to prove the existence of a valid contract as we move away from a paper-based economy to an electronic one.

WHEN WRITING IS REQUIRED

Statute of Frauds requires writing for enforcement of some contracts

In some limited circumstances, a contract is required by statute to be evidenced in writing to be enforceable. These requirements for writing are found primarily in the *Statute of Frauds*. There are also, however, some other statutes that set out similar requirements.

[29.] See, for example, s. 155 of the *Land Titles Act*, R.S.A. 2000, c. L-4, which requires a Transfer of Land to be signed in front of a witness, who must swear an Affidavit of Attestation of an Instrument.

The first *Statute of Frauds* was enacted in England in the 17th century. It was adopted with some variation by the Canadian provinces. The *Statute* requires that certain types of contracts be evidenced in writing to be enforceable. The *Statute* has been criticized as causing as much abuse as it was intended to prevent. As a result, many important changes have been made by the provinces to the *Statute*. Manitoba[30] and British Columbia have repealed the *Statute* altogether, although British Columbia retains some of its provisions in its *Law and Equity Act.* [31]

Statute of Frauds in force in some provinces

CASE SUMMARY 7.11

Writing Still Needed in Manitoba: *Megill Stephenson Co. v. Woo*[32]

Two parties negotiated by telephone. At the conclusion of their conversation, an agreement was reached regarding the purchase and sale of a parcel of land. However, before any documents were prepared, the vendor changed his mind. The purchaser sued. The Court held that, despite the fact that the *Statute of Frauds* had been repealed in Manitoba, there was the usual expectation of the parties that a contract dealing with the sale of land would not be effective until it was put into writing. The Court honoured that expectation and refused to enforce the agreement.

Note that the Court first had to find that an agreement had been reached. It can be argued that by this decision the vendor was allowed to take advantage of the purchaser for his own profit. It was this type of fraud that led to the adoption of the *Statute of Frauds*.

DISCUSSION QUESTION

Should the requirement of writing therefore be retained for important transactions such as the purchase and sale of land?

The following is a discussion of the types of contracts generally included under the *Statute of Frauds* in Canada. The actual wording varies among provinces.

1. **Contracts not to be performed within one year.** When the terms of the agreement make it impossible to perform the contract within one full year from the time the contract is entered into, there must be evidence in writing for it to be enforceable. For example, if Sasaki Explosives Ltd. agrees in March 2010 to provide a fireworks display at the 1 July celebrations in Halifax in the summer of 2011, that contract must be evidenced by writing to be enforceable. Failure to have evidence in writing will make it no less a contract, but the courts will refuse to enforce it. Some provinces, including British Columbia

When contract cannot be performed within one year

[30.] See *An Act to Repeal the Statute of Frauds*, C.C.S.M. c. F158.

[31.] *R.S.B.C. 1996, c. 253, s. 59.*

[32.] (1989) 59 D.L.R. (4th) 146 (Man. C.A.).

(which has repealed the *Statute of Frauds*) and Ontario,[33] have eliminated the requirement of writing in this area. Note that even when it is impossible for one party to complete performance within the year, written evidence is not required when it is clear in the contract that the other party is expected to perform within that year.

2.   **Land dealings.** Any contract that affects a party's interest in land must be evidenced in writing to be enforceable. It is often difficult to determine what types of contracts affect interest (or ownership) in land and what types do not. Any sale of land (or part of it, such as the creation of a joint tenancy in land) must be evidenced in writing. Any creation of an easement, right of way, or estate (such as a life estate), is also covered by the *Statute of Frauds*. But contracts for services to the land that do not affect the interest in the land itself are not covered. For example, if a carpenter agrees to build a house, such an agreement may affect the value of the land, but not the interest in the land itself. It therefore need not be evidenced in writing to be enforceable. This provision of the *Statute of Frauds* has also been modified in some jurisdictions. For example, in British Columbia[34] and Ontario,[35] a lease for three years or less is exempt from the legislation, but longer leases are treated just like any other interest in land and must be evidenced in writing to be enforceable.

3.   **Guarantees and indemnities.** When creditors are not satisfied with the creditworthiness of a debtor, they may insist that someone else also assume responsibility for the debt. This can be done by using a guarantee or an indemnity. If the third party incurs a secondary liability for the debt, he has given a guarantee. A guarantor promises that, if the debtor fails to pay the debt, he will assume responsibility and pay it. Note that in this type of transaction, the obligation is secondary, or contingent; there is no obligation on the guarantor until the debtor actually fails to pay the debt.

An **indemnity** describes a relationship in which a third party assumes a primary obligation for the repayment of the debt along with the debtor. As a result, both owe the debt, and the creditor can look to either for repayment. When a third party says, "I'll see that you get paid," there is an assumption of a primary obligation, and the promise is an indemnity.

The distinction between a guarantee and an indemnity is important, because in most provinces the *Statute of Frauds* requires that a guarantee be in writing, but not an indemnity. If the court classifies the nature of a third-party agreement as an indemnity, there is no requirement of writing. The distinction can be vital when a person has made only a verbal commitment to pay the outstanding loan to the debtor.[36] In British Columbia, the Law and Equity Act requires that both indemnities and guarantees be evidenced in writing to be enforceable.[37]

When an interest in land is involved

When guarantee is involved

But not an indemnity

[33.] See the *Statute of Frauds*, R.S.O. 1990, c. S.19.

[34.] *Supra* note 39, s. 3.

[35.] *Supra* note 37, s. 59(2)(b).

[36.] For a good discussion of guarantees and indemnities, see *MacNeill v. Fero Waste and Recycling Inc.* (2003), 213 N.S.R. (2d) 254 (C.A.).

[37.] See, for example, s. 6 of the *Sale of Goods Act,supra* note 3, which sets a minimum value of $50.

4.   **Others.** The original *Statute of Frauds* required that whenever the purchase price of goods sold exceeded a specified minimum, there had to be evidence in writing for the sale to be enforceable. This provision has been included in the *Sale of Goods Act* in many jurisdictions in Canada.[38] It is usually sufficient evidence in writing if a receipt or sales slip has been given.

When goods sold over specific value

Parliament and the provincial legislatures have passed many statutes that require certain transactions to be in writing to be valid. Some examples are the *Bills of Exchange Act,* insurance legislation, consumer protection legislation, some of the legislation dealing with employment relations, and the carriage of goods and passengers. For example, while there does not seem to be a provision in the Ontario *Sale of Goods Act*[39] requiring that certain transactions be evidenced in writing, other legislation requires certain types of consumer contracts to be in writing.[40] In many jurisdictions, the *Statute of Frauds* also requires the promises of executors (to be responsible personally for the debts of an estate),[41] and promises made in consideration of marriage,[42] to be evidenced in writing to be enforceable.

WHAT CONSTITUTES EVIDENCE IN WRITING

Note that it is not the whole agreement that must be in writing to satisfy the *Statute of Frauds.* There need be evidence in writing supporting only the essential terms of the agreement. The essential terms are normally an indication of the parties, the subject matter of the contract, and the consideration to be paid. Other terms may become essential, however, depending on the nature of the contract. The evidence in writing can take the form of the actual agreement itself, or simply a receipt, or note, or email. It can even come into existence after the creation of the contract referring to it. The writing can be a single document, or a collection of documents, which taken together provide the required evidence. The document(s) must also be signed, or initialed, but only by the person denying the existence of the contract.

Writing must contain all essential terms

• and may be in more than one document

• and must be signed by party to be charged

• and may arise after agreement

Note that important adaptations have been necessitated because of changing technology. As electronic records and communications become more common, and paper plays less of a role, the traditional requirements of writing and signatures are becoming obsolete. One solution is to give digital records and electronic signatures the status of written documents. Legislation to allow this is now in place in several jurisdictions.[43]

EFFECT OF THE STATUTE OF FRAUDS

It is vital to remember that if a contract is not evidenced in writing this does not make it void under the *Statute of Frauds;* it is merely unenforceable. The contract is

Contract valid when no writing, but unenforceable

---

38. *Supra* note 37, s. 59(6).

39. See the *Consumer Protection Act, 2002,* S.O. 2002, c. 30, Sch. A., which requires future performance agreements, time share agreements, personal development services agreements, direct agreements, and other consumer agreements to be in writing.

40. R.S.O. 1990, c. S.1.

41. See Ontario's *Statute of Frauds, supra* note 39, s. 4.

42. In Alberta, this provision is now subject to the *Matrimonial Property Act,* R.S.A. 2000, c. M-8, s. 37, which deals with pre-nuptial agreements.

43. See, for example, the *Electronic Transactions Act,* S.A. 2001, c. E-5.5.

binding on the parties, but the courts will not assist them in enforcing it. If the parties have already performed, or if there is some other remedy available that does not require the court's involvement, the contract will still be binding. The courts will not assist a person who has performed to get out of the contract. Nor will the court order the return of any money paid (see Figure 7.1). In effect, the party has only done what was required under the contract. Similarly, when there is a lien (a right to seize property), or when there is a right to set off a debt against the obligations created by the contract, the parties themselves may be able to enforce the contract, without the help of the courts. In that sense, such a contract is binding, even though there is no evidence in writing, and it won't be enforced by the courts.

Figure 7.1 Effect of *Statute of Frauds*

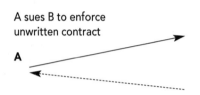

A sues B to enforce unwritten contract

A

B Contract is valid but unenforceable; B can't be forced to perform.

B But if B performs he can't change his mind to get $ back, since contract is valid.

REDUCING RISK 7.3

There are only a few situations in which evidence in writing is required to ensure that a contract is enforceable. However, from a practical business point of view, contractual arrangements should always be put into writing (or, as technology develops, some other permanent form). Even people with the best of intentions will remember things differently as time passes. It is vital, therefore, to have a permanent record that can be referred to later, so that the terms are certain and the good will between the parties is retained. When relations have broken down, there is nothing better than a written document to resolve a dispute that arises over a business transaction that has gone bad. The existence of the document may, by itself, prevent litigation. If it does not, at least there is evidence as to what the parties agreed to that can be used in the lawsuit. So, while in law it may be true that a verbal contract is as binding as a written one, it is poor practice indeed to rely on verbal agreements in business.

PART PERFORMANCE

When part performance consistent with contract, writing not required

The court will waive the requirement of writing if the parties can produce evidence to show that a contract dealing with an interest in land has been partially performed. There are some important limitations to this principle. The part performance must be evidence of the existence of the contract and consistent only with the existence of the contract. The payment of money owed under the contract will therefore not usually be acceptable as proof of part performance, as the payment of money is consistent with any number of different obligations. In British Columbia, however, the payment of a deposit is sufficient part performance with respect to land transactions to make such contracts enforceable.[44] A good example of acceptable part performance when land has been sold is the start of construction. The permission to enter onto the land and start building is consistent with the sale of the land, and so the courts will accept the part performance as sufficient evidence to support the contract.

CASE SUMMARY 7.12

Part Performance Satisfies Statute: *Hill v. Nova Scotia (Attorney General)*[45]

Land was expropriated to build a highway, but the provincial government agreed to allow the owner of the land to move people, livestock, and equipment across the highway. A government department helped the owner by producing fencing and ramps to enable the movement across the highway. This arrangement continued for 27 years. The result was that the owner of the property acquired a right of way (an equitable interest) across the highway.

The Court held that even though the *Statute of Frauds* required evidence in writing, that was not necessary in this case. The 27 years of crossing the highway with the help of the government constituted part performance.

The *Statute of Frauds* was passed originally to prevent fraudulent transactions. The doctrine of part performance provides an exception to the requirement of writing.

DISCUSSION QUESTIONS

Does adoption of the doctrine of part performance therefore increase the likelihood of fraud being committed with respect to transactions involving interests in land?

Table 7.1 summarizes the elements required to make a contract valid and enforceable.

Table 7.1 Summary of Contract Formation

No consensus	Contract void	But must pay for requested services
No consideration	Contract void	But note promissory estoppel, gift, and seal
No capacity	Contract voidable	But infants can enforce contracts with adults
		But infants bound by contracts for necessaries and beneficial contracts of service
	Contract void	But insane persons must show the others knew of insanity
Illegal	Contract void	But depends on statute
No intention	Contract void	Note presumptions
No writing	Valid	But note *Statute of Frauds* exceptions

---

44. *Supra* note 37, s. 59(4).
45. [1997] 1 S.C.R. 69.

SUMMARY

Capacity

- For a contract to be binding, each of the parties must have legal capacity
- In most provinces, contracts with minors are not binding on them, except for contracts for necessaries and beneficial contracts of service
- In British Columbia, all contracts with minors are unenforceable, except those that are specifically made enforceable by legislation, such as government student loans
- The test for the capacity of minors is objective
- Parents are not liable for the torts or contractual obligations of their children unless there is legislation making them liable
- A contract with someone who is insane or drunk will be rendered invalid only when the person was so incapacitated as to not know what he was doing, and the other contracting party knew, or ought to have known, of that incapacity

Legality

- To be binding, a contact must be legal and be performed legally
- If a lawful contract is performed illegally, the courts may rule that the contract is illegal and void, or just void, or they may enforce some, or all, of the contract
- An illegal contract is illegal at the time it is formed. Illegal contracts include contracts that violate legislation and contracts that are against public policy
- The courts may rule that an illegal contract is illegal and void, or just void, or they may enforce some, or all, of the contract
- There are many types of contracts that are illegal because they violate legislation or are against public policy
- One example is contracts that unduly restrain trade, which are usually illegal, but contracts in which one party agrees not to carry on business in competition with another are legal, if they can be shown to be reasonable in terms of the interests of the parties and the public

Intention

- For a contract to be binding, each of the parties must intend to be bound by it
- The courts will enforce the stated intention of the parties
- In family and other social relationships, there is a presumption of no intention. This presumption can be challenged by evidence that shows an intent to be bound
- In commercial relationships, intention is presumed. This can also be rebutted
- In other situations, the courts use the reasonable person test to determine intention

Form of the contract

- Most verbal contracts are valid, if they contain the essential elements of a contract
- Under the *Statute of Frauds,* certain contracts must be evidenced in writing to be enforceable
- The *Statute of Frauds* has been repealed or modified in many jurisdictions
- Most jurisdictions now have legislation requiring certain types of contracts to be in writing
- When part performance is established, verbal agreements dealing with interests in land are also enforceable

QUESTIONS

1. "In determining whether a child has contractual capacity, the court will attempt to determine if she actually understood the transaction." True or false? Explain your answer.

2. Explain the circumstances in which a minor may escape liability for a contract and the circumstances in which a minor is bound by a contract.

3. What is the significance of a minor's contract being designated as a beneficial contract of service?

4. In addition to debts incurred for necessaries, when will a minor be liable for a debt he incurred?

5. What are the three stages of a contractual relationship? Describe the legal situation of a minor in each of these stages.

6. If there is no relevant legislation, when will the parents of a minor be responsible for the minor's contracts? When will they be liable for the torts of the minor?

7. When can an adult sue a minor in tort even though there is a contract between them?

8. What must an insane or drunk person establish to escape liability under a contract?

9. Explain what care businesspeople must exercise when entering into contracts with government corporations or bodies.

10. Explain four other situations where businesspeople must be careful that those they deal with have the capacity to contract.

11. Explain the difference between a contract that is performed illegally and an illegal contract.

12. What decisions can a court make if performance of a contract violates a regulatory statute?

13. What are the two reasons that can cause contracts to be illegal?

14. How has the law regarding the judicial treatment of illegal contracts changed?

15. Give five examples of contracts deemed by the courts to be against public policy, and describe the effect of such a designation.

16. "All contracts that restrain trade are illegal." True or false? Explain your answer.

17. Describe the test the court will use in determining whether the parties had an intention to be bound when they made an agreement.

18. With respect to the element of intention, explain how the courts' treatment of domestic agreements differs from their treatment of commercial transactions.

19. How will a court determine if there was contractual intention when there is a dispute between a brother and his sister over how to operate their business?

20. What is the significance of a written document in contractual relations?

21. Explain why some people have suggested that the *Statute of Frauds* has led to more frauds than it has prevented.

22. Give examples of the types of contracts currently included under the *Statute of Frauds*.

23. What "evidence in writing" is required to satisfy the requirements of the *Statute of Frauds*?

24. "A contract that does not satisfy the *Statute of Frauds* is void." True or false? Explain your answer.

25. Under what circumstances will a contract falling under the jurisdiction of the *Statute of Frauds* be enforceable even though it is not evidenced by writing?

Chapter 8

Factors Affecting the Contractual Relationship

The two previous chapters examined the process of forming contracts. This chapter examines what happens when the parties disagree as to the nature and effect of the contract. The obligations and the extent of the responsibilities of the original parties to an agreement are also discussed, together with how those obligations are affected when an innocent third party, or a stranger to the contract, becomes involved.

MISTAKE

In limited circumstances, the courts will provide a remedy where one or both of the parties have made a mistake with respect to a contract. Where it is clear that because of the mistake, the parties have failed to reach a consensus, the contract is void; there is no complete agreement between them. It must be made clear at the outset that the court will not interfere when the parties have simply made a bad bargain: this is an error in judgment and the person who made it must live with it.

> Misunderstanding that destroys consensus results in void contract

Reviewable mistakes in contract involve a person's mind being at odds with the terms, surrounding circumstances, or other factors relating to the contract. Such a mistake can relate to the terms of the contract, including the identity of the parties. It can relate to an assumption upon which the contract is based, whether as to a matter of fact, some future event, or the law surrounding the contract. And it can also concern an expected result or consequence of the agreement. The mistake can be made by only one of the parties or by both. Where both parties are making a mistake, it can be a *shared mistake*, where both are making the same mistake, or it can be a *misunderstanding*, where each party has a different

> Mistake must go to the very root of the contract

idea as to the meaning of the terms of the contract. This is a complex and difficult area of contract law to understand. It will help to keep in mind that the guiding principle seems to be that the courts will try to do what is necessary to give effect to the reasonable expectations of the parties.

CASE SUMMARY 8.1

Bad Advice Does Not Void Contract Made Based on It: *Works v. Works*[1]

The husband had agreed to transfer his interest in the matrimonial home to the wife in settlement of a claim for spousal support. Later, the husband discovered that he had received incorrect tax advice as to the consequences of this settlement and he tried to avoid signing the formal Minutes of Settlement. He now claimed to have entered a contract based on a mistake. The Court held that a consensus had been reached. The husband knew he was transferring his interest in the home for a release from spousal support. The fact that he had made a "bad deal" because the tax advice given to him was erroneous, did not void the agreement itself.

The issue of tax deductibility was not discussed between counsel, and the wife's counsel had no reason to believe the agreement was based on that assumption. The court concluded that where only one party is mistaken about something significant in a contract, the court will exercise its discretion to set aside the contract only if satisfied that, in light of the circumstances, it would be unfair or unjust to enforce the contract. The issue of a tax saving was never a central issue; thus the deal was deemed fair.

SMALL BUSISNESS PERSPECTIVE

If there are certain assumptions upon which parties are acting, would it be wise to state those assumptions in the contract itself? This decision suggests that would be prudent.

When the mistake relates to the terms of the agreement itself, such as the identity of the parties or the subject matter of the agreement, the courts are more willing to provide a remedy. The courts also will not interfere with contractual obligations unless the demonstrated mistake is significant or material with respect to the agreement. If a person ordering a new car is delivered one that is a slightly different colour than the one he had in mind when he chose it, that will not be enough to allow him to avoid the contract. Finally, where the mistake is caused by the negligence of one of the parties, that party will normally be held responsible for the error.

It should also be noted that if the mistake is one about the facts involved, as opposed to a mistake based on an interpretation of the law or its effect, the court will be more likely to provide a remedy. On the other hand, where one party stands to make a windfall at the expense of the other, the courts likely will review the transaction—whether the mistake is one of law or of fact. For example, when one party receives a payment she is not entitled to because the other has misunderstood his legal obligation, the court will likely order those funds returned on the basis of **unjust enrichment**.

---

[1]. (2002), 206 N.S.R. (2d) 292 (S.C.).

The area of mistake in contract law is evolving; it has not been uncommon over the years for the courts to reverse or modify their position. The discussion below is an attempt to summarize the important aspects of the law in this area. The approach taken concentrates on three different ways that a mistake can be made. It should be remembered that if a contract is found to be *void* it is not a contract at all; if it is *voidable* the contract does exist, but one of the parties has the option of getting out of it. Consequently, when an innocent third party has acquired goods that are the subject of a voidable contract, that party gets to keep the goods; but if the previous contract was void—that is, there never was a contract—the person who sold the goods to the third party never had title to them, and those goods must be returned to the original owner.

Fundamental shared mistake about subject matter—void

Shared Mistake

A **shared mistake** occurs when the two parties are in complete agreement but they have both made the same mistake regarding some aspect of the contract. The courts will review the transaction only where the mistake relates to some fundamental aspect of the subject matter of the contract. The most common example of such a shared mistake resulting in a void contract is where the subject matter of the contract no longer exists at the time the contract is made. Thus, where the parties enter into an agreement for the sale and purchase of the cargo of a ship, without knowing that the ship and cargo were destroyed the night before, the contract is void because of the shared mistake. The courts have also found a contract void because of a shared mistake when, unknown to the parties, the property being sold was already owned by the purchaser. In both these instances, the parties have together made the same significant mistake with respect to a factual aspect of the agreement that has destroyed the basis of the contract. As a result, the contract is void for lack of consensus.

When the shared mistake relates only to the value of what they are dealing with, it normally will not affect the enforceability of the contract. For example, if both vendor and purchaser think that they are dealing with an ordinary violin when, in fact, they are dealing with a rare and valuable Stradivarius, the contract would be binding nevertheless.

RECTIFICATION

If the written document does not reflect the common intention of the parties to the contract, the courts are willing to correct or **rectify** the document. For example, if two parties had agreed to the sale of land for $500 000 and a clerical error made the document read $50 000, the court would add the missing zero and require the parties to perform the corrected agreement. The courts will do this only where it is clear that both understood what they were agreeing to and what was written was different from that understanding.[2]

[2.] See *Pacific Petroleums Ltd. v. Concordia Propane Gas Marketers Ltd.* (1977), 5 A.R. 421 (T.D.), where the contract referred to Canadian gallons instead of American gallons, as agreed. Rectification was ordered.

CASE SUMMARY 8.2

Damages Awarded as Rectification Not Possible: *Sylvan Lake Golf & Tennis Club Ltd. v. Performance Industries Ltd.*[3]

A verbal agreement had been reached between the parties concerning the purchase and operation of a golf course. One of the terms discussed was the future residential development of lands adjacent to the eighteenth hole. The agreement was reduced to writing by a lawyer acting on instructions from the defendant. The plaintiff proved, beyond any reasonable doubt, that he signed the agreement of 21 December 1989 under a unilateral mistake as to the dimensions of the development property and further that the defendant knew he had signed that agreement by mistake.

The preconditions to obtaining the equitable remedy of rectification of the contract were met: (1) The plaintiff established the existence and content of the prior oral agreement. There was a definite project in a definite location to which both parties had given their definite assent. (2) It was found that the defendant had fraudulently misrepresented the written document as accurately reflecting the terms of the prior oral contract. (3) The precise terms of rectification were readily ascertained. All that was required was to change the word *feet* in the phrase "one hundred ten (110) feet in width" to "yards." (4) There was convincing proof of the plaintiff's unilateral mistake and the defendant's knowledge of that mistake. The plaintiff's version of the oral agreement was sufficiently corroborated on significant points by other witnesses and documents.

The court held that the defendant's conduct in attempting to take advantage of the plaintiff's mistake was equivalent to a fraud—or a misrepresentation amounting to fraud—or sharp practice. It would thus be unjust and unconscionable for the court not to offer redress to the plaintiff in the face of that conduct. Rectification itself was no longer a real option as the lands had been developed by the defendant. Accordingly, damages in lieu of rectification were awarded, compensating the plaintiff for the loss of the opportunity to profit from developing residential lots around the 18th hole.

SMALL BUSINESS PERSPECTIVE

The importance of thoroughly reading and comprehending the terms of contract prior to signing it cannot be overstated. The courts are reluctant to rectify contracts where there was a lack of due diligence on the part of the mistaken party. Here, the Court overlooked this lack of care because the defendant's fraud was the greater evil.

Courts will correct an improperly recorded agreement

It is important to remember that the courts are not rewriting the agreement during rectification. They are simply correcting a written document so that it corresponds to the demonstrated intention of the two parties.[4]

Rectification of the contract may be available as a remedy in other situations as well, such as where one person makes a mistake caused by the fraud by the other party.

[3.] [2002] 1 S.C.R. 678.

[4.] For a recent case in which the court rectified minutes of a family settlement, see *Mills v. Mills*, [2004] O.J. No. 3169 (S.C.J.). Both parties had miscalculated what the sale proceeds from their home would be. They believed it would be $65 824, whereas only $22 408 was available for distribution. Nonetheless, the Court found that there was consensus to split the balance equally, so the amounts were rectified but the balance itself was split equally.

The Case of the Million-Dollar Comma: *AMJ Campbell v. Kord Products Inc.*[5]

This case involved AMJ Campbell's selling the assets of a subsidiary to the defendant, Kord. The transaction included the sale of a significant inventory of plant containers with the value determined by calculating the "average sales price" over the prior eight months. This was to be calculated "net of taxes, freight rebates and discounts," but the solicitors for Kord changed that by inserting a comma between the words *freight* and *rebates*. This change, along with some others, was made to the final contract. Before the change only freight rebates would be deducted from the average price, but with the insertion of the comma all of the freight costs as well as any rebates would also be deducted. This resulted in a saving to Kord of more than $759 000 (hence the million-dollar comma).

AMJ Campbell, claiming mistake, asked the Court to rectify the contract by removing the comma. The Court refused, saying that for rectification to take place it had to be clear that both parties had intended the document to read the other way. Here the solicitors for Kord had intentionally inserted the comma and intended that any freight costs be deducted from the purchase price. Only AMJ Campbell had made a mistake by agreeing to the change—and that is not good enough for rectification.

SMALL BUSINESS PERSPECTIVE

This case demonstrates the limited power of the Court to rectify. In light of the restricted situations where rectification can be used, what should a party do before concluding a contract?

Misunderstanding

A different type of mistake occurs when the parties have a misunderstanding about the terms of the agreement itself and neither party is aware of the other's different understanding. When one party to an agreement thinks that the agreement is to do something else, the courts will usually apply the reasonable person test to determine which interpretation of the contract is more reasonable. The court will then adopt the more reasonable position as the correct interpretation of the contract. This point is discussed below in more detail under the heading "Rules of Interpretation." Only if the error is a serious one and the court cannot choose between the two positions because both are equally reasonable will the contract be declared void.

Court will enforce reasonable interpretation

Where equally reasonable and error serious—void

The case of *Raffles v. Wichelhaus*[6] is a good example of such a dilemma. In this case, the contract concerned a cargo being transported on a ship called *The Peerless*. It happened that there were two ships by this name, both leaving the same port but at different times. The seller intended one of these two ships, and the purchaser had in mind the other. The reasonable person test could not resolve this case, and since the disagreement was fundamental there was no consensus between the parties and the contract was void.

---

5. [2003] O.J. No. 329 (Ont. S.C.J.).

6. (1864), 2 H. & C. 906, 159 E.R. 375 (E.D.).

CASE SUMMARY 8.4

Misunderstanding Leads Court to Conclude No Consensus Had Been Reached: *British Columbia (Minister of Transportation and Highways) v. Reon Management Services Inc.*[7]

When the Ministry of Transportation expropriated Reon's land, it offered Reon $75 000 plus interest. Reon countered at $100 000 plus interest calculated under section 46 of the *Expropriation Act*. Section 46(1) provided for regular interest, whereas section 46(4) provided for penalty interest where the expropriating party failed to pay within 90 days of the due date. Reon claimed that its counteroffer had been accepted and that the Ministry had agreed to pay all section 46 interest including any penalty interest.

Counsel for the Ministry had responded to Reon's counteroffer thus: . . . "I am instructed to accept the offer contained therein. I have attached the interest calculation from August 3.1990 to April 7, 2000 on $100,000.00. The total amount payable by month, exclusive of costs, will be $204,324.51...."

Evidently, the Ministry's calculation was based on regular interest, whereas Reon's counteroffer was for a settlement based on regular plus penalty interest.

The Court of Appeal concluded that there was no consensus between the parties. No agreement had been reached as to an essential term, namely the price to be paid. Accordingly the settlement was declared void.

SMALL BUSINESS PERSPECTIVE

It may save parties time (and expense) in the long run to spend a little extra time carefully reviewing every term in a contract before leaving the bargaining table.

One-Sided Mistake

One-sided mistake—"Let the buyer beware"

A one-sided or **unilateral mistake** takes place where only one of the parties to the contract is making a mistake with respect to the contract. This was the situation in *Moss v. Chin* in Case Summary 8.5. As a general rule, there is no recourse for a person who makes such a one-sided mistake. Thus, when the manager of a business buys a computer by name and model thinking it will do a specific job, and it turns out that it does not have the required capacity, a mistake has been made by the purchaser but there will likely be no remedy. This is a one-sided mistake, and if there were no reliance placed on the salesperson and no misrepresentation or misleading information supplied in the documentation and brochures, there will be no remedy. In effect, the purchaser has misled himself, and the principle of *caveat emptor* ("Let the buyer beware") applies. This concept is also discussed in Chapter 10.

---

7. [2001] B.C.J. No. 2500.

CASE SUMMARY 8.5

Unilateral Mistake MAY lead to Rescission of Contract: Moss v. Chin;[8] *Hodder Estate v. Insurance Corporation of Newfoundland Limited*[9]

Mrs. Moss was left unconscious after being struck by a car driven by Mr. Chin. Her representative, the public trustee, started a legal action and negotiated with the driver's insurer, ICBC. ICBC made an offer to settle, but Moss died before it was accepted. The public trustee accepted the offer, on behalf of Moss, without informing ICBC of her death. When ICBC found out what had happened, it applied to have the settlement set aside.

This was a unilateral mistake on the part of ICBC, and normally it would not affect the rights of the other parties. But in this situation, rather than this being a matter of ICBC's misleading itself, the public trustee deliberately set out to make sure ICBC did not discover a mistake. The Court accordingly ordered that the contract be rescinded.

Contrast this decision with the judgment in the *Hodder* case. Marie Hodder died in a motor vehicle accident in January 2001. Four months later, Hodder's widower was diagnosed with terminal cancer. No estimate of life expectancy was given. When counsel for the Hodder family put forward a claim for Marie Hodder's death, he did not disclose that Mr. Hodder had terminal cancer. Several months later, on instructions from the Hodder family, counsel requested a reply to his claim letter. Numerous telephone conversations followed, and Hodder's lawyer was asked why his clients were so anxious to settle the claim. Counsel responded that they just wanted to get it behind them. The insurers thus offered to settle the claim for $35 000, which was accepted. Shortly thereafter, Mr. Hodder died. The insurer submitted that there could be no settlement because Hodder's lawyer failed to disclose this material change in circumstances. But the court concluded there was a binding settlement agreement for $35 000.

There was no duty to disclose the illness or imminent death of Mr. Hodder to the insurers. There was no fundamental change in the nature of the claim prior to the settlement being concluded. There was nothing to indicate that the settlement amount was inequitable or should be set aside for fraud or mutual mistake. Hodder's lawyer had not been untruthful. He had a duty to his client to conduct the litigation according to instructions. While he had a duty to disclose information to the opposing parties as required by law, he had no duty to assist his adversary or volunteer information otherwise.

SMALL BUSINESS PERSPECTIVE

These two cases, when read together, suggest that the courts will be more willing to rescind a contract based on unilateral mistake, where that mistake or error has been contributed to or caused by wrongful behaviour on the part of the other party. Otherwise, the courts are reluctant to set aside an agreement.

It should be noted, however, that when the offeror makes an obvious error in relation to his or her offer, the purchaser will not be allowed to take advantage of this obvious error and snap up the offer. Thus, if the merchant selling the

---

[8.] (1994), 120 D.L.R. (4th) 406 (B.C.S.C.).

[9.] [2002] N.J. No. 47 (Nfld. & L. S.C.).

Snapping up an offer—contract is rescinded

computer misquoted it, agreeing to sell it at $25 instead of the $2500 normal price, the purchaser would not be able to ignore such an obvious error and "snap it up" at the bargain price.[10]

When a one-sided mistake takes place, the person making the mistake usually has a remedy only when he or she has been misled, and then the normal course of action is to claim for misrepresentation with its associated remedies. There are some situations, however, where the one-sided mistake is so fundamental as to destroy consensus between the parties. The lack of consensus may be important to establish even where misrepresentation is involved, since the contract would then be void, providing even broader remedies. For example, if the subject goods are later resold to an innocent third party, the remedy of rescission for misrepresentation would not be available to the mistaken party. However, if a mistake sufficient to destroy consensus takes place, the contract would be void, allowing recovery of the goods involved even from an innocent purchaser.

If mistake goes to identity—void contract

For consensus to be destroyed, the one-sided mistake must be profound. Such a one-sided mistake can occur when there is incorrect identification of one of the parties to a contract. If the person claiming that a mistake has taken place actually thought the deal was with someone else and can demonstrate that identity was an important aspect of the agreement, the court can declare the contract to be void. However, if the error was only about some attribute of the other party, such as her wealth, this will not affect the existence of the contract. The first party has to have thought he was dealing with another person, not just that the person he was dealing with was wealthy.[11]

CASE SUMMARY 8.6

Read the Contract or Live with It: *978011 Ontario Ltd. v. Cornell Engineering Co.*[12]

When is it fair to set aside a contract where only one party suffers a mistake? Apparently, the courts will not exercise their discretion to grant rectification or rescission where the mistaken party is to blame, or as in this case, where the mistaken party contributed to his own mistake.

The shares in Cornell Engineering Co. (Cornell) were owned by Stevens and Bimboga. Bimboga sought to sell his interest and Stevens suggested that Macdonald, whom Stevens had mentored, buy the shares. Negotiations were held and eventually the parties agreed that Macdonald would enter a service agreement and demonstrate to Bimboga that Macdonald was capable of carrying on Cornell's business.

Stevens asked Macdonald to prepare the agreement; Macdonald amended a standard form agreement and presented it to Stevens, asking him to read it. The agreement provided for compensation to be paid to Macdonald in the event of termination of his services. Stevens read only the first page, where salary was laid out, and signed the eleven page contract on Cornell's behalf. Later, when Cornell terminated the service

---

10. See *City of Ottawa Non-Profit Housing Corp. v. Canvar Construction (1991) Inc.* [2000] O.J. No. 1078 (C.A.) for a case involving a tender error. Since the error was evident on the face of the tender, the tenderer was not obligated to perform the construction job at the erroneous tender price.

11. *Cundy v. Lindsay* (1878), 3 App. Cas. 459 (H.L.).

12. (2001), 53 O.R. (3d) 783 (C.A.), leave to appeal to S.C.C. refused, [2001] S.C.C.A. No. 315.

agreement, Macdonald claimed compensation pursuant to the termination clause. Stevens took the position that Macdonald should have brought the alteration to the standard contract, specifically the termination clause, to his attention. The trial Judge held that since termination had not been discussed by the parties during their negotiations, Macdonald had a duty to draw the termination clause to Stevens' attention. The Court thus rectified the contract by striking out the termination clause entirely.

On appeal, however, no such duty was found to exist. Stevens was a sophisticated businessperson. Macdonald had put no pressure on Stevens to sign without reading the contract; in fact, he had asked Stevens to read the contract. The Court thus refused to grant an equitable remedy to correct a mistake that Stevens had allowed, through oversight, to occur.

SMALL BUSINESS PERSPECTIVE

Clearly, the message is "Read before you sign!"

NON EST FACTUM

Where one of the parties is unaware of the nature of the document being signed, the courts will, in rare circumstances, declare the agreement to be void on the basis of *non est factum* ("It is not my act"). If a person were led to believe he was guaranteeing a note and was, in fact, signing a mortgage agreement on his home, he could argue that there was no consensus between the parties and no contract. This might be a valid defence even against an innocent third party who had acquired rights under the agreement. For this defence to succeed and the contract to be void, it must be shown that the mistake about the document went to the very nature of that document rather than merely to its terms. In this example, if the mistake went only to the rates, with the mortgagor thinking he was to pay 10 percent interest when the document actually required 15 percent, he would still be bound, as the mistake only concerned some aspect of the document and not the document itself. Today, negligence, such as failure to read the document before signing, can defeat the defence of *non est factum* and as a result, successful claims of *non est factum* are quite rare.

> If mistake goes to nature of document signed—void
>
> • but not where negligence present

CASE SUMMARY 8.7

Non Est Factum Not Available for Pension Waiver: *Deraps v. Coia*[13]

Mr. Deraps was a labourer who had paid into a pension fund for 20 years when he discovered he had lung cancer. He spoke to his union representative, Mr. Hickey, about a disability pension. Hickey explained to the Derapses that they would receive a higher pension if Mrs. Deraps signed a waiver of spousal benefits. Mrs. Deraps signed the waiver; within a year, Mr. Deraps died. His widow claimed that when she signed the

---

13. (1998), 173 D.L.R. (4th) 717 (Ont. Ct. Gen. Div.); rev'd on other grounds (1999), 179 D.L.R. (4th) 168 (C.A.).

waiver she didn't understand that when her husband died she would be left with nothing. She applied to the Court to have the waiver declared void on the basis of *non est factum*. The trial Court held in her favour, but this ruling was overturned on appeal. The effect of the waiver was clear and it had been explained to her in as simple terms as possible. Also, she read and wrote English and the document she signed was not fundamentally different from what she thought she was signing. In addition, the fact that she did not bother to read the document before signing disqualified her from claiming *non est factum*. In the end the Ontario Court of Appeal did decide in her favour, but on the basis of negligent misrepresentation. The Derapses were dependent on Hickey, who had a duty to supply all material information. His failure to do so was just as misleading as a positive misstatement. Damages were awarded on the basis of what Mrs. Deraps would have received had she not signed the waiver.

DISCUSSION QUESTIONS

This case shows how difficult it now is to succeed in claims for *non est factum*.[14] Fortunately for Mrs. Deraps, she was able to succeed on other grounds. Have we gone too far in limiting the application of *non est factum*? Or do you take the position that individuals should bear more responsibility for their own mistakes?

Rules of Interpretation

Reasonable person test applies when there is a misunderstanding

The test to determine whether a mistake has taken place is objective. The courts are not concerned with what the parties thought they were agreeing to but rather with what the parties should have been aware of and expected when they made the agreement. In such instances, the courts use the reasonable person test. Instead of declaring the contract void because one of the parties has made a mistake about the meaning of a term, the courts will look at the wording to determine what a reasonable person would have understood the term to mean. Only in those rare circumstances in which there is no reasonable interpretation of the agreement, or the positions taken by the two parties are equally reasonable, will the courts declare the contract to be void.[15]

Courts apply literal meaning to specific wording

Ambiguous wording interpreted liberally

Whenever there is a dispute involving the meaning of a specific term, the courts have a choice of applying the literal meaning of the term or adopting a more liberal approach by trying to determine the parties' intent. Usually, the courts will apply the literal meaning of the wording chosen by the parties if there is no ambiguity. If the term is ambiguous, the court will look at what was behind the agreement and apply the most reasonable meaning of the term to the contract.

Determining the literal meaning of the words is not as simple as it might first appear. Even dictionaries often have several different meanings for particular words. Determining the intention of the parties may also be difficult because of the conflicting positions taken by the parties to the dispute. The court will often look at how the terms are normally used in the particular industry involved. The

---

14. For a case where the defence of *non est factum* failed, see *McCoy Brothers Group v. Wilson* (1993), 12 Alta. L.R. (3d) 32. For a case where the defence succeeded, see *Bank of Montreal v. Barath*, [2000] A.J. No. 352.

15. *Raffles v. Wichelhaus*, *supra* note 6; *British Columbia (Minister of Transportation and Highways) v. Reon Management Services Inc.*, *supra* note 7.

court will also look at past dealings between the parties as well as their dealings at the time the contract was formed to determine what they intended by the words they used. The key to the court's approach to such ambiguous terms in an agreement is to choose the most reasonable interpretation. Another rule courts use in these situations is the **parol evidence rule**. Where the terms used in an agreement are clear and unambiguous, the courts will not allow other outside evidence to be introduced to show a different meaning was intended: "What you see is what you get." If you state in your agreement that the contract is for the sale of a "2008 Honda Civic automobile," you cannot later try to introduce evidence that a Honda motorcycle was intended. Of course, if the contract only referred to a "2008 Honda," this term is ambiguous, and evidence then could be introduced to show that a car or a motorbike was intended.

> **Courts will not permit outside evidence to contradict clear wording**

Several exceptions to the parol evidence rule have developed over the years. The courts will override the parol evidence rule when the evidence to be introduced is of a *fraud* or some other problem associated with the formation of the contract, such as *duress or undue influence* (see below). Other exceptions include evidence of a *condition precedent* (a condition that has to be met before the obligations set out in the contract are in force); evidence of a **collateral contract** (a separate contractual obligation that can stand alone, independent of the written one); evidence of a *subsequent agreement* entered into by the parties after the written one; or the *absence of an intention* that all of the contract would be embodied in the written document. When the evidence contradicting the terms of the agreement falls into one of these categories, the court can be persuaded to hear it, despite the parol evidence rule.

> **Exceptions to the parol evidence rule**

> **Courts will imply terms, where appropriate**

CASE SUMMARY 8.8

Judgment Set Aside Due to Incorrect Use of Parol Evidence: *Gainers Inc. v. Pocklington Financial Corporation*[16]

While Peter Pocklington controlled Gainers, a meat-packing company, it had numerous financial dealings and agreements with some of his other companies. Gainers later defaulted on its loans and the government effectively became the owner. Gainers then sued several of its related companies for unpaid debts and for unjust enrichment.

The trial Judge admitted and made repeated use of large amounts of parol evidence about the understanding, intent, and knowledge of Pocklington and his lawyer at various steps in the drama. He found additional agreements created by conduct, and even used the evidence to redefine a number of the terms in the written contracts.

The written contracts were long and detailed, obviously drafted by lawyers. Both sides had legal advice. The Court of Appeal could not find ambiguity or significant lack of clarity in the relevant parts of the written agreements. Yet the trial Judge referred to parol evidence not just to clarify ambiguities, but even to flatly contradict some of the express terms of the contract.

The Court of Appeal outlined its position on use of parol evidence thus: "When the deal is complete in the written contracts, and not subject to an escrow, other evidence

---

[16] [2000] A.J. No. 626 (C.A.).

(parol evidence) is inadmissible to vary or contradict a clear written contract" . . . "Even earlier promises or representations, otherwise having legal effects, may be wiped out by suitable contractual clauses . . . There is such a "whole contract" clause here. Such a clause may also bar side oral contracts". . . . "Similarly, the parties may validly contract, as they did here, that oral modifications of the contract will be ineffective, and that amendments must be written." . . . "The power to imply terms is to be used cautiously, and no implied term can be inconsistent with or contrary to the express terms of the contract" . . . "Nor can the court find a collateral parol contract inconsistent with the express written contract." . . . "Collateral contracts are viewed suspiciously and must be proved strictly, along with clear intent to contract." . . . "The intent of the parties is to be determined from the words which they put in their written contract; their subjective intent is irrelevant . . . . Subjective intent cannot even be used to interpret the written words, if they are clear."

The Court of Appeal thus concluded: "It is apparent that an incorrect use of parol evidence and a misconception of fundamental company law principles underlie almost all of the trial judgment in this suit. The whole approach at trial was misconceived, and the judgment cannot stand."

SMALL BUSINESS PERSPECTIVE

The *Pocklington* judgment illustrates that admission of and reliance upon parol evidence is to be severely restricted. All the more reason to read and fully understand any written contract before signing it!

Statutes may imply terms into contract

The courts are willing to imply terms into an agreement when necessary. It does not occur to most contracting parties to provide terms in their agreement for every possible eventuality, and the courts are willing to supply these missing terms. Where the parties agree to the purchase of a car, for example, they might not specify the time of delivery or when the price is to be paid. The courts will imply what is reasonable in the circumstances, likely that delivery must take place within a reasonable time determined by the nature of the goods, and that the price is to be paid upon delivery. What is reasonable will often be determined by looking at past dealings between the parties or the normal practices and traditions found within that specific industry or trade. Some terms may be implied automatically by statute. The *Sale of Goods Act* has set down, in rule form, the terms that are implied in a contract for the sale of goods when the parties have not addressed them. As well, some consumer protection legislation imposes terms in contracts whether or not the parties have agreed to them. The courts have also been known to impose contract terms on the parties and modify obligations, using the principle of fairness[17] and unconscionability discussed below.

[17.] *Cooper v. Phibbs* (1867), L.R. 2 H.L. 149 (H.L.).

REDUCING RISK 8.1

The interpretation of contracts often leads to confrontation; businesspeople would be wise to review their practices. A deal made on a handshake involves a lot of trust, but this examination of mistake and misrepresentation shows the danger of failing to review contracts carefully. Even the most sincere businessperson can forget just what she has agreed to, or two parties may recall the terms quite differently even when they had the same understanding of the terms of the agreement in the first place. And that does not even consider the instances of wilful blindness and convenient memory loss. Putting an agreement into some permanent form, such as writing, is only the first step. Great care should be taken to ensure that the words used are clear and unambiguous so that there can be no question later of what has been agreed upon. This type of approach will usually contribute to the good will between businesspeople rather than threaten it. Conflict is reduced and confidence increased on the basis of good business practices.

CASE SUMMARY 8.9

Terms Are Sometimes Implied into Contracts: *Dansway International Transport Ltd. v. Lesway and Sons Inc.*[18]

Following the theft of one of its 53-foot trailers, the plaintiff agreed to buy two trailers from the defendant for $100 000. A deposit was paid. No time for payment or delivery was stipulated. The plaintiff contacted the defendant 10 days later, requesting an extension, advising that it was still waiting for insurance proceeds to close the deal. One month later the plaintiff called the defendant to arrange delivery and was told by the defendant that the deal was off.

Since time was not expressed to be of the essence, and since time of payment and delivery were not stipulated, the Court had to determine what would be a reasonable time for payment. One month was found to be reasonable, but the plaintiff was in breach through effluence of time. Nonetheless, where a seller believes the buyer is not taking delivery within a reasonable period of time, the seller must give *notice* requiring the buyer to take delivery, before the contract can be treated as terminated. The defendant failed to give such notice, so the plaintiff's action succeeded. Damages were restricted, however, to loss of profit for one month, that being the time required to buy alternative trailers.

SMALL BUSINESS PERSPECTIVE

This case illustrates that the courts will imply certain terms if the parties fail to do so themselves. Rather than face future clashes with customers, businesses are well advised to anticipate problems and design contracts that deal with contentious issues up front.

MISREPRESENTATION

During pre-contract negotiations, people often say things that are designed to persuade the other party to make the deal but that never become part of the contract. When these statements are false, misleading the other party and inducing it to enter into the contract, an actionable misrepresentation has taken place.

---

18. [2001] O.J. No. 4594 (S.C.J.).

Misrepresentation is a misleading statement that induces a contract

Misrepresentation is a false statement of fact that persuades someone to enter into a contract. The false statement can be made fraudulently, when the person making the statement knew it was false; negligently, when the person should have known the statement was false; or completely innocently, when the misrepresentation is made without fault.

CASE SUMMARY 8.10

Evidence of Fraud Opens Door to Extrinsic Evidence: *Metropolitan Stores of Canada Ltd. v. Nova Construction Co.*[19]

Nova, upon taking over ownership of the Antigonish Mall, tried to evict Metropolitan, resulting in litigation between the two parties. In the process of attempting to reach a settlement, a new lease was negotiated for a 20-year term. The lease contained a non-competition clause, such that no stores in competition with Metropolitan would be allowed to be located in the mall. However, the non-competition clause would not apply if there was any expansion to the existing shopping centre.

When questioned about this exception (or exemption clause) the representative of Nova explained that the only expansion that would take place would be within the present boundaries of the mall and that another clause in the agreement protected Metropolitan from competition within those boundaries. The representative knew that this was false. Seven years later, Nova purchased surrounding property, expanded into that area, and leased property to another department store. It claimed that the exemption clause permitted this.

In the original lease agreement between Metropolitan and Nova, the area of the present mall was specifically covered by the non-competition clause. So when Metropolitan was told that any expansion was going to take place within the present boundaries of the mall, it did not worry about a competing department store moving in. In effect, Metropolitan was tricked into signing a lease that did not protect it the way it thought it would.

The Court found that a fraudulent misrepresentation had taken place, which induced Metropolitan to enter into the contract. Although the parol evidence rule restricts consideration of any outside extrinsic evidence that conflicts with the plain meaning and unambiguous wording of the contract, there are several exceptions. An exception arises if there is evidence of fraud inducing the parties to enter into the contract. Such fraud was found in these circumstances.

This case is unusual because the normal remedies for misrepresentation are rescission or, when fraud is present, rescission and/or damages. In this case, however, Metropolitan asked for rectification of the contract, that is, for the contract to be rewritten to include the terms as it understood it, making the expansion with the inclusion of the rival department store a breach of its lease. The trial Judge thought this was going too far, but the Court of Appeal was willing to rectify the agreement; it added the appropriate words to the lease, and declared Nova in breach of that lease. Rectification, the rewriting of a contract on behalf of one of the parties at the expense of the other, is a drastic remedy, but because of the fraud, it was deemed appropriate.

---

[19]. (1988), 50 D.L.R. (4th) 508 (N.S.C.A.).

SMALL BUSINESS PERSPECTIVE

In the heat of closing a deal, employees or agents may be tempted to hide or misrepresent information so as not to scare the other party away. Insisting that employees and agents deal with third parties honestly is not only ethical—it also makes good business sense, saving money in the long run. The ends do not justify the means, as the above case demonstrates.

Allegation of Fact

The statement that forms the basis of the misrepresentation must be an allegation of fact. Only statements made about the current state of things that prove to be incorrect can be considered misrepresentation. "This car has a new motor" is a statement of fact. "I will have the car inspected next year" is not a statement of fact, but a promise to do something in the future. A promise to do something in the future will qualify as a misrepresentation only when it can be clearly shown that the person making the promise had no intention of honouring that promise at the time it was made. Such promises of future conduct have to be enforced under general contract law, and the buyer should take care to ensure that this commitment is included as a term of the contract. Where the misleading statement being complained of was an expression of opinion rather than fact, it too is not actionable, unless the person making the statement was an expert. When a person declares that the car he is selling is a "good car" or a "good deal" he is entitled to have that opinion, and the statement is not actionable if the car later breaks down. But if a mechanic makes the same statement, and it proves false, it can be actionable as misrepresentation because he is an expert.

misleading.

Misrepresentation must be fact, not opinion or promise

Opinion by expert may be misrepresentation

CASE SUMMARY 8.11

Representation Made by "Expert" Was Relied Upon: *Whighton v. Integrity Inspections Inc.*[20]

The Whightons made an offer to buy a home in Stony Plain, Alberta, and retained the services of an inspector to check the condition of the building. The inspector assured them that the home was in good condition and that the cost of any needed repairs would not exceed $6000. Confident with this information, the purchasers closed the deal and moved in. They then discovered major problems including leaking, corrosion of the sewage pump, water damage, and deterioration of cedar siding and shingles. They sought damages in excess of $100 000. The inspector pointed to an exculpatory clause in the contract, which he claimed limited liability to $10 000.

The Court determined that negligent representations had been made both as to the condition of the building, and beyond that, as to the cost of repairs. This latter representation clearly went beyond the services contracted for. These representations were reasonably relied upon by the purchasers, so in addition to breaching the contract by

made an offer

---

20. [2007] A.J. No. 330 (Q.B.).

failing to adequately inspect the property, the inspector was also liable in tort law. The exculpatory clause did not apply to limit damages for misrepresentation. Further, the Court found the defendant had fundamentally breached the contract by failing to adequately inspect the property, so again the exculpatory clause could not be relied upon to limit damages. The plaintiffs could only produce proof of cost of repairs for approximately $40 000 so damages for that sum were awarded.

SMALL BUSINESS PERSPECTIVE

Clearly if businesspeople give assurances and make representations knowing that the recipient may be swayed by them, extra care must be invested. Those making the statements better be sure the representations are accurate or are made only after due diligence is exercised.

Silence or Non-Disclosure

Silence not misrepresentation, unless there is duty to disclose

For a misrepresentation to take place, there also must be some actual communication of information. Silence or non-disclosure by itself is not usually actionable. There are, however, some special situations where the person contracting is required to disclose certain information. For example, insurance contracts require the parties acquiring insurance to disclose a great deal of personal information that affects the policy. People who apply for life insurance are required to disclose if they have had heart attacks or other medical problems. The sale of new shares involves a similar obligation of disclosure to an investor in a prospectus. If the terms require that the parties disclose all information to each other as a condition of the agreement, the contract can be rescinded if they fail to do so. Professionals also have an obligation to disclose certain information at their disposal that might affect the actions of their clients. These are often referred to as **utmost good faith** contracts. This requirement of good faith is being expanded, and it is now much more common for the courts to find that a misrepresentation has taken place where one party withholds information from the other.

Where a person actively attempts to hide information that would be important to the other contracting party, this also might qualify as misrepresentation. A person anxious to sell a car might be tempted to hide a noisy transmission by using a heavier grade of oil, and such an act might well invite a claim of misrepresentation. It is not necessary that the statement be written or verbal; misrepresentation can occur even if the method of communicating it is a gesture, such as a nod of the head.

Misrepresentation must have misled the victim

Generally, misrepresentation is available as a cause of action only when an actual representation has been made. When individuals mislead themselves, *caveat emptor* applies, and there is no cause for complaint. In *Hoy v. Lozanovski*,[21] the home Mr. Hoy purchased from the Lozanovskis proved to be infested with termites. Hoy sought rescission of contract, alleging misrepresentation, but the Judge determined that since the Lozanovskis did not know of the termites when they sold the house, there was no fraudulent misrepresentation. Also, they had remained silent, so no representation had been made. Finally, since Hoy had had

---

[21.] (1987), 43 R.P.R. 296 (Ont. Dist. Ct.).

the house inspected, he had not relied on any representations from the vendors. In effect, Hoy misled himself about the condition of the building. Accordingly, no remedy against the Lozanovskis was available to Hoy.

False Statement

It is necessary to demonstrate not only that the misleading comment qualifies as an allegation of fact, but also that the statement is incorrect and untrue. Even when a person technically tells the truth but withholds information that would have created an entirely different impression, this can amount to misrepresentation. For example, if a used car salesperson tells a potential purchaser that the transmission of a particular car has just been replaced but fails to say it was replaced with a used transmission, this partial truth can be misrepresentation if it leads the purchaser to believe a new or rebuilt transmission was installed.

Partial disclosure may be misrepresentation

Statement Must Be Inducement

A victim of misrepresentation must show that he or she was induced into entering a contract by a false statement. If the victim knew that the statement was false and entered into the agreement anyway, either because he or she did not believe the statement or believed that the statement did not make any difference, the misrepresentation is not actionable. Similarly, if the person thought the statement was true but would have entered into the contract even if he or she had known it was false, there is no remedy. For there to be an actionable misrepresentation, the false statement must affect the outcome of the agreement, and the victim must have been misled into doing something that she otherwise would not have done. In *Hoy v. Lozanovski,* even if the Court had found that the Lozanovskis had made a misleading statement it likely would not have qualified as an actionable misrepresentation because the purchaser did not rely on it. We know this because Hoy was careful to have the house inspected before it was purchased.

CASE SUMMARY 8.12

False Information Induces Purchase: *Yourside Club Consulting Solution Ltd. v. Exfone Exchange Inc.*[22]

The plaintiff company was in the business of selling long-distance telephone services. The defendant company, through its agent Liang, represented it had a product that would allow customers to place long-distance calls over the internet using an ordinary telephone. This system would be cheaper than using land-line phones. Liang assured the plaintiff orally and in writing that the defendant had a product ready for market and had commitments for $10 million from investors. Based on these representations, the plaintiff invested $200 000 in Exfone in return for 5 percent of the company and 500 000 warrants at $2 each.

In fact, the product was not market ready. It was still in a testing phase.

The plaintiff thus sued seeking its money back. Much of the case rested on the credibility of the parties as to the contents of the oral representations, but the written

---

22. [2006] B.C.J. No. 1231 (S.C.).

business plan clearly suggested that the company had a unique product for which it had patents. The Court found that merely having a prototype that works does not mean the product is market ready. Accordingly, based on this material misrepresentation, the plaintiff company was granted rescission of the contract.

SMALL BUSINESS PERSPECTIVE

Especially when launching a new product or service, businesspeople must temper enthusiasm with caution. Care should be taken not to make unsubstantiated claims in the heat of zealous marketing. If one is reluctant to put representations in writing, that in itself should serve as a warning!

As a Term of the Contract

The law of misrepresentation discussed here applies where the misleading statement induced or persuaded the victim to enter into a contract. Special remedies are needed because the misleading statement usually does not become a term of the agreement itself. If the misleading statement complained of has become a term of the agreement, the normal rules of breach of contract apply, providing much broader remedies that are easier to obtain. If Mills agreed to sell Boothe a used Nissan automobile, which in the contract was described as a 2005 Nissan Murano with a rebuilt transmission, Boothe could sue for breach of contract if the vehicle turned out to be a 2003 Murano and the transmission was used, not rebuilt. But if Mills bought a particular property because the vendor Boothe said that the municipal council had voted to build a new access road nearby, rarely would such a provision be inserted as a term of the agreement. Because the statement is an inducement to buy, not a term of the contract, the victim must rely on the rules of misrepresentation to obtain a remedy. The remedies available will depend on whether the statement was made inadvertently, fraudulently, or negligently.

Breach of contract action may be appropriate if misleading term inserted in contract

Even so, the courts today are more open to the suggestion that such representations have become terms of the contract. Even statements in advertisements now can be taken to be part of the contract. Many provincial consumer protection statutes contain provisions controlling misleading and deceptive trade practices; several specifically state that representations of salespeople are made part of the contract. The topic of consumer protection legislation will be discussed in Chapter 10.

Innocent Misrepresentation

An **innocent misrepresentation** is a false statement, made honestly and without carelessness, by a person who believed it to be true. Where a heavy-duty equipment supplier sells a truck claiming it can haul five tonnes of gravel but its actual capacity is only three tonnes, this is misrepresentation even where the seller believes what he said was true. If the person making the misrepresentation is in no way at fault, the misrepresentation is innocent, and the remedies are limited. The only recourse available to the victim is to ask for the equitable remedy of rescission. As soon as the victim realizes what has happened, he or she can either choose to ignore the misrepresentation and affirm the contract, or refute the contract and seek rescission.

Innocent misrepresentation—remedy is rescission

RESCISSION

Rescission attempts to return both parties to their original positions; the subject matter of the contract must be returned to the original owner, and any monies paid under the contract must also be returned. The courts will also require the party who is returning the subject matter of the contract to return any benefit derived from the property while it was in his or her possession. Similarly, a person can be compensated for any expenses incurred. Damages are not available as a remedy, because both parties are innocent. Although rescission is an important remedy, because it is equitable, it is quite restricted in its application. Rescission is not available in the following situations:

Property returned along with monetary benefit minus expenses

Rescission not available in certain circumstances

1. **Affirmation.** Victims of misrepresentation who have affirmed the contract are bound by the affirmation and cannot later insist on rescission. Thus, where a person uses the proceeds of a contract knowing of the misrepresentation, he has affirmed the contract.

   • if contract affirmed

2. **Impossibility of restoring.** The remedy of rescission is not available if the parties cannot be returned to their original positions because the subject matter of the contract has been destroyed or damaged. Since neither party is at fault with innocent misrepresentation, the court will not impose a burden on either one of them but will simply deny a remedy.

   • if restoration impossible

3. **Third-party involvement.** Rescission will not be granted if it will adversely affect the position of a third party. When the subject matter of the contract has been resold by the purchaser to a third party who has no knowledge of the misrepresentation and otherwise comes to the transaction with "clean hands," the courts will not interfere with that person's possession and title to the goods.

   • if it will affect third party

4. **Failure on the part of the victim.** Where the victim comes without clean hands, rescission will not be available. Where the victim has also misled or cheated, rescission will be denied. Where the victim has caused unreasonable delay, rescission will be denied. These principles apply to all equitable remedies, and these will be discussed in the next chapter.

   • if plaintiff is not blameless—does not have clean hands

Note, as discussed above, that in those few situations where the misrepresentation causes the victim to make a fundamental mistake about the nature of the contract, the agreement may be void due to failure to reach a consensus. When this happens, there is no contract and the victim can recover money or goods supplied despite the effect on third parties or the presence of affirmation.

Fraudulent Misrepresentation

If a misrepresentation of fact is intentional and induces another person to enter into a contract, the victim of the fraud can sue for damages under the tort of deceit in addition to or instead of the contractual remedy of rescission. According to the 1889 decision in *Derry v. Peek*, fraud is established when the false statement was made "(1) knowingly, (2) without belief in its truth, or (3) recklessly, careless whether it be true or false."[23] Essentially, it is fraud if it can be demonstrated that the person who made the false statement did not honestly believe it to be true. The person making the statement cannot avoid responsibility by claiming she did not

Rescission and/or damages for torts for intentional misrepresentation

---

[23.] (1889), 14 App. Cas. 337 (H.L.) at 374.

know for sure that what she said was false, or because she did not bother to find out the truth. Fraud exists even if the victim of the misrepresentation could have found out the truth easily, but relied instead on the statement of the defendant.

CASE SUMMARY 8.13

Disguising Used Goods as New: *Kellogg Brown & Root Inc. v. Aerotech Herman Nelson Inc.*[24]

The plaintiff purchased 282 portable heaters from the defendant, Aerotech. Immediately after delivery, it became apparent that the heaters were not new. The plaintiff made some use of the heaters before deciding to discontinue its attempts to service or use them further. It notified Aerotech that the contract was being rescinded and demanded reimbursement. The Court found an obvious intent to mislead the purchaser. Aerotech tried to disguise the used heaters as new by altering hour meters, repainting, cleaning, re-serializing, and changing the manufacturer's plates on the units. The fact that the plaintiff had tried to repair the heaters to make them useable did not operate as a bar to rescission. Victims of fraud do not, as soon as there is an inkling of a misrepresentation, have to make up their minds whether to rescind or not. The plaintiff was found to have repudiated the contract within a reasonable period of time and the cost of the heaters ($1 359 571) and the cost of shipping ($321 905) *plus* punitive damages ($50 000) were awarded.

SMALL BUSINESS PERSPECTIVE

If one reflects upon all the additional costs incurred—the loss of the sale, the cost of shipping, the punitive damages, and the legal costs—it was hardly a sound business decision to mislead the purchaser just to get a better initial price.

Failure to correct turns innocent misrepresentation into fraud

When a person innocently makes a false statement and later discovers the mistake, he must inform the other person of the misrepresentation without delay. Failure to do so will turn an innocent misrepresentation into a fraud. If during the process of negotiating the terms of a contract, a person makes a statement that was true but later becomes false because of changing circumstances, she must correct the statement upon finding out the truth.

Once it has been established that the false statement was intentional and thus fraudulent, the courts can award rescission or damages:

Rescission

1. **Rescission or avoidance.** The victim of fraudulent misrepresentation retains the right to have the parties to the contract returned to their original positions and to be reimbursed for any out-of-pocket expenses.

Damages

2. **Damages for deceit.** The victim of fraudulent misrepresentation can seek monetary compensation as well as rescission for any loss incurred as a result of the fraud. The damages are awarded for the tort of deceit. Note that to obtain damages there is no obligation to return property, nor is the court attempting to return both parties to their original positions, as with rescission. Rather, the courts require financial compensation to be paid to the victim by the person at

---

24. [2004] M.J. No. 181 (C.A.), leave to appeal to S.C.C. refused, [2004] S.C.C.A. No. 344.

fault. A victim of fraud can seek damages even where rescission is not available. The victim does not lose the right to demand monetary compensation by affirming the contract or where the goods have been resold to a third party. The victim of a fraudulent misrepresentation can also seek punitive damages, that is, damages intended to punish the wrongdoer rather than compensate the victim.

The major problem with fraudulent misrepresentation is the need to establish that the person being sued knowingly misled the victim. This is often difficult to do and is not necessary if only rescission is sought.

Negligent Misrepresentation

An important recent development in tort law is the granting of the remedy of damages for negligent misrepresentation (sometimes called negligent misstatement). Today, if it can be shown that the parties should have known what they said was false, even though they honestly believed it was true, the remedies of damages as well as rescission will be available. Even when the negligent statement becomes a term of the contract or arises out of a contractual relationship, the plaintiff may have a choice about whether to sue in contract or sue in tort for negligence. The Supreme Court of Canada made it clear that such "concurrent liability" may exist, subject to limitations that may be included in the contract.[25] Thus, whether the plaintiff can circumvent the protection provided in an exemption clause by suing in tort instead depends on the wording and breadth of the exemption clause.

As stated by Justices La Forest and McLachlin in *BG Checo International Ltd. v. British Columbia Hydro and Power Authority.*[26]

> In our view, the general rule emerging from this Court's decision in Central Trust Co. v. Rafuse, [1986] 2 S.C.R. 147, is that where a given wrong prima facie supports an action in contract and in tort, the party may sue in either or both, except where the contract indicates that the parties intended to limit or negative the right to sue in tort. This limitation on the general rule of concurrency arises because it is always open to parties to limit or waive the duties which the common law would impose on them for negligence. This principle is of great importance in preserving a sphere of individual liberty and commercial flexibility . . . . So a plaintiff may sue either in contract or in tort, subject to any limit the parties themselves have placed on that right by their contract. The mere fact that the parties have dealt with a matter expressly in their contract does not mean that they intended to exclude the right to sue in tort. It all depends on how they have dealt with it.

Damages for negligence may be available in cases of misrepresentation

---

25. *Central Trust Co. v. Rafuse*, [1986] 2 S.C.R. 147.

26. [1993] S.C.J. No. 1, at para.15.

Damages are available as a remedy where the misrepresentation has become a term of the contract that is breached, where the misrepresentation is fraudulent, and where there is negligence.[27]

Thus, it appears that only when the misrepresentation is truly innocent and without fault is the victim restricted to the remedy of rescission.

DURESS AND UNDUE INFLUENCE

Duress

Duress involves threats of violence or imprisonment—contract voidable

When people are forced or pressured to enter into contracts against their will by threats of violence or imprisonment, the contract can be challenged on the basis of duress. Today, duress includes not only threats of violence and imprisonment but also threats of criminal prosecution and threats to disclose embarrassing or scandalous information.[28]

In Canada, duress also includes threats to a person's goods or property. If O'Rourke threatened to vandalize Tong's store unless Tong agreed to purchase his vegetables from O'Rourke, this would qualify as duress and Tong would have recourse against O'Rourke. To succeed, it is necessary to show that the threat was the main inducement for entering into the agreement.

Economic disadvantage not enough

Even though the threat of loss of employment and other financial losses can amount to economic duress and be actionable,[29] it is important not to mistake the normal predicaments in which we all find ourselves for improper pressure or duress. If a person has no choice except to use a particular taxi because it is the only one on the street, or has to deal with the only airline or telephone company that services a particular area, these accepted conditions of the marketplace do not amount to duress. Likewise, where a person has to pay a high rate of interest because no one else will loan money at a lower rate, it is not duress. Even the threat of suing when the person doing so has a legitimate right to sue is not duress. Rather, it is the legitimate exercise of the rights of that person.

Voidable contracts cannot affect third parties

Note that duress only causes a contract to be voidable, thus a third party's position cannot be jeopardized if the victim of duress seeks a remedy. If someone is forced to sell a gold watch by threat of violence and the watch is then resold to an innocent third party, the watch cannot be retrieved. Because a voidable contract is still a contract, the title has passed on to the third party. Had the watch been stolen from the original owner and then sold to an innocent third party, the original owner would not have given up title to the watch and could, therefore, retrieve it.

[27.] *Beaufort Realties v. Chomedey Aluminum Co.*, [1980] 2 S.C.R. 718.

[28.] See, for example, *Byle v. Byle*, (1990), 65 D.L.R. (4th) 641 (B.C.C.A.), where one son threatened physical harm to a sibling. The parents, fearing that threat, conveyed some land and gave other advantages to the aggressor son. The trial judge declared the transactions void on the basis of duress, but the Court of Appeal reversed this decision, finding the contract to be only voidable. A void contract is no contract and nothing can save it, but a voidable contract could be revived later by affirmation and be binding on the parties.

[29.] For a recent case dealing with economic duress, see *1239745 Ontario Ltd. v. Bank of America Canada*, [2005] O.J. No. 920 (C.A.). The debtors sought to have a restructuring agreement set aside, alleging it was signed under economic duress.

CASE SUMMARY 8.14

Vendor's Threats Fail to Amount to Duress: *Braut v. Stec*[30]

Braut brought an action seeking to enforce an equity sharing agreement allegedly made with Stec. Stec defended the action arguing that Braut, literally, put a gun to Stec's head to force him to sign the agreement.

Braut offered to sell certain properties to Stec, and offered to arrange the financing. Since Stec was impecunious, they falsely reported his income to lenders. and Braut arranged for further financing to be advanced by his friend. After the transfers were complete, Braut presented the equity sharing agreement to Stec, who refused to sign it. Stec consulted with a lawyer, who also advised Stec not to sign. The agreement imposed significant obligations upon Stec and required that he bear all of the risks related to the property.

Duress under gunpoint is a serious allegation and the trial judge stated the amount of proof needed would approach the criminal standard. Such proof was not established. However, the judge had no doubt that Braut threatened Stec, warning he would expose the fact that Stec had lied on the applications for the mortgages (which Braut had completed). Braut also threatened to have his friend demand repayment of the second mortgages.

Braut, a sophisticated businessperson, evidently sought to dupe Stec, an uneducated immigrant. The equity sharing agreement imposed considerable obligations upon Stec but no obligations upon Braut. Stec was to bear all of the risks related to the property. Stec was required to expend considerable work and labour on the properties and to obtain Braut's prior consent before making expenditures on the property. Stec was required to share any income and ultimate gains from sales of the properties, but if losses ensued, Braut was not required to bear any share. Stec was required to give notice to Braut if he intended to sell any property and Braut had an option of first refusal to buy. Braut was to receive half of the profits from the enterprise. The equity sharing agreement was found to be unconscionable.

Reference was made to *Harry v. Kreutziger* (1978), 9 B.C.L.R. 166 (C.A.), where McIntyre J.A. said: "Where a claim is made that a bargain is unconscionable, it must be shown for success that there was inequality in the position of the parties due to the ignorance, need or distress of the weaker, which would leave him in the power of the stronger, coupled with proof of substantial unfairness in the bargain. When this has been shown a presumption of fraud is raised and the stronger must show, in order to preserve his bargain, that it was fair and reasonable." Since inequality existed yet Braut failed to rebut the presumption of fraud, the Court refused to enforce the equity sharing bargain.

SMALL BUSINESS PERSPECTIVE

A presumption of fraud is difficult to dispel. Where the agreement in question is blatantly unfair or one-sided, courts are drawn to conclude that the deal is unconscionable and thus unenforceable.

[30.] *Braut v. Stec*, [2005] B.C.J. No. 2318 (B.C.C.A.), appeal to S.C.C. dismissed without reasons, [2005] S.C.C.A. No. 559.

Undue Influence

The types of pressure brought to bear upon people are often more subtle than those described by duress. When pressure from a dominant, trusted person makes it impossible to bargain freely, it is regarded as **undue influence**, and the resulting contract is also voidable.

In the case of *Allcard v. Skinner*,[31] a woman entered a religious order and gave it all her property. The court determined that there had been undue influence when the gift was given, even though there was clear evidence that there had been no overt attempt on the part of the religious order to influence this woman. The court would have set the gift aside, except that she had affirmed it after leaving the relationship.

Undue influence presumed in certain relationships

CASE SUMMARY 8.15

Undue Influence Presumed: *Rochdale Credit Union Ltd. v. Barney*[32]

Mr. Barney was a friend and client of John Farlow, a solicitor. He reluctantly guaranteed Farlow's $50 000 loan from Rochdale Credit Union. Farlow died, and the credit union demanded payment from Barney. The Ontario Court of Appeal found undue influence on the part of Farlow, in persuading his client to guarantee the loan. Because Farlow represented both the lender and the guarantor, the credit union was also held responsible for that undue influence. Barney thus did not have to pay the debt.

The relationship of solicitor/client leads to a presumption of undue influence. Unless that presumption is overturned with evidence that the contract was freely entered, the contract may be set aside. It is interesting that the credit union was also affected by that presumption.

SMALL BUSINESS PERSPECTIVE

Depending on the line of work one's business is engaged in, a presumption of undue influence may arise particularly when contracts are made with clients. To preserve the enforceability of such contracts, extra precautions need to be taken, including a requirement that the client seek independent legal advice.

The court may find undue influence in the following situations:

Where undue influence must be proven

1. **Presumption based on a special relationship.** In certain categories of relationships the courts will presume the presence of undue influence, and if the presumption is not rebutted the contract will be set aside. Some examples of such relationships are

   - professionals such as doctors or lawyers contracting with their patients or clients and the green para is part of the first nl item as well

   - parents or guardians contracting with infant children in their care

---

[31.] (1887), 36 Ch.D. 145 (C.A.).

[32.] (1984), 14 D.L.R. (4th) 116 (Ont. C.A.); leave to appeal refused (1985), 8 O.A.C. 320 (S.C.C.).

- adult children contracting with mentally impaired parents

- trustees contracting with beneficiaries

- religious advisers contracting with parishioners (as in *Allcard v. Skinner*, discussed above).

Note that in contracts between parents and adult children and between spouses, undue influence is not automatically presumed but may be established upon consideration of special circumstances.

2. **Presumption based on unique circumstances.** If the relationship involved does not fall into one of the protected classes listed above, there still can be a presumption of undue influence on the basis of unique circumstances. The courts then attempt to determine whether one person was in a position to dominate the will of another, in which case the court may still presume undue influence where it is just and reasonable to do so. A husband or a wife signing a guarantee for a spouse's indebtedness might constitute such a situation. If the court makes that presumption, it falls on the party trying to enforce the contract to show that there was no domination or unfair advantage taken of the other party. In *Bank of Montreal v. Duguid*,[33] for example, the issue was whether an automatic presumption of undue influence arises when one spouse guarantees a loan for the other. Although the bank was concerned about the wisdom of the investment, it did not send Mrs. Duguid to get independent legal advice. The Court held that a presumption might arise in a marriage where one partner is unaware of and not involved in financial decisions. In this case, however, the wife was a sophisticated real estate agent who knew what she was doing, and so no such presumption of undue influence evolved. Evidently, for the presumption to arise, there has to be more than just a close relationship; the guarantor has to be vulnerable and the bank has to know of that vulnerability.

> Undue pressure from circumstances

3. **Undue influence determined from facts.** In the absence of a relationship that gives rise to the presumption, it is still possible for a victim to produce actual evidence to satisfy the court that undue influence was, in fact, exerted and that there was coercion. This can be difficult to prove, since the victim must show that a relationship of trust developed and that this trust was abused. When it can be shown that the person trying to enforce the contract took advantage of the fact that he or she was being relied on for advice, the courts may find that there was undue influence.

Even when undue influence is presumed, the contract will be binding if the person trying to enforce the contract can show that the undue influence was overcome and that the victim either affirmed the contract, which was the situation in the *Allcard* case, or did nothing to rescind it after escaping the relationship. The courts may also refuse a remedy if the person trying to escape the contract is not altogether innocent of wrongdoing.

Of course, if the party accused of undue influence can convince the court that in fact there was no such influence, any presumption is rebutted and the contract is binding. It is advisable, therefore, for contracting parties who are concerned about this problem to ensure that the other party secure independent legal

---

[33.] (2000), 185 D.L.R. (4th) 458 (Ont. C.A.).

Independent legal advice
desirable, but contract must
be fair

advice before entering into an agreement. This is especially true for professionals who are contracting with clients for matters outside that professional relationship. When it can be demonstrated that the potential victim followed independent legal advice, it is very likely that the courts will enforce the agreement. It must be stressed that the terms of the agreement must be reasonable in such circumstances. The courts will resist enforcing a contract that conveys great advantage to one of the parties, whether or not independent legal advice has been taken.

Unconscionable Transactions

The concept of **unconscionable transactions** has received a greater acceptance by the courts in recent years. This is an equitable doctrine that permits the court to set aside a contract in which one party has been taken advantage of because of such factors as desperation caused by poverty and intellectual impairment that falls short of incapacity. To escape from such a contract, it must be shown that the bargaining positions of the parties were unequal, that one party dominated and took advantage of the other, and that the consideration involved was grossly unfair.

CASE SUMMARY 8.16

Insurance Settlements Set Aside When Unconscionable: *Woods v. Hubley;*[34] *Gindis v. Brisbourne*[35]

Woods suffered back and neck pain resulting from a car accident caused by the negligent driving of Hubley. A week before her spinal surgery, the insurance adjuster contacted her by telephone offering her a $3500 settlement. "Take it or leave it." She agreed, signed a release, and was paid the $3500. Unfortunately, even after the operation, her condition got worse and she brought an application to the court to have the release set aside. This was done, and she was awarded damages of more than $500 000, but the amount was reduced to $150 000 on appeal.

Woods had been taken advantage of and the original settlement was set aside on the basis of unconscionability. The insurance adjuster had deceived and misled her and "effectively dissuaded her from seeking the services of a lawyer, thereby taking advantage of her ignorance and her need." A transaction can be set aside as unconscionable where the evidence shows that (1) there is an inequality in the bargaining positions of the parties arising out of ignorance, need, or distress of the weaker party; (2) the stronger party has consciously used the position of power to achieve an advantage; and (3) the agreement reached is substantially unfair to the weaker party. The presence of these elements in this case warranted the setting aside of the settlement agreement.

Contrast the *Woods* decision with that in *Gindis v. Brisbourne*, which also involved settlement of a personal injury claim. Brisbourne's insurer offered Gindis $25 000 for a release of his claim and Gindis accepted. Initially, he succeeded in having the settlement set aside and damages were assessed at $249 189. But on appeal, the Court determined that the release was not obtained in an unconscionable manner—especially in light of the

---

[34.] (1995), 130 D.L.R. (4th) 119 (C.A.); leave to appeal refused (1996), 136 D.L.R. (4th) vii (note) (S.C.C.).

[35.] (2000), 72 B.C.L.R. (3d) 19 (C.A.).

fact that the insurer had a duty to the insured to ensure that the settlement was not overly generous or extreme. If a contract is reasonable in light of all the risks and contingencies, it is not unconscionable.

DISCUSSION QUESTIONS

When comparing the above two decisions, one differentiating factor was the deception employed by the insurance agent in the *Woods* case. In light of the dim view the Court took of such behaviour, how should businesses train their employees to conduct themselves? Will one-sided bargains be upheld to favour those who act unethically?

Simple economic advantage does not, in itself, qualify a transaction as unconscionable. If a person having limited assets cannot get a loan from anyone else and must pay 20 percent interest, that alone will not make the contract unconscionable. There must be evidence that the debtor was taken advantage of because of some problem, such as lack of sophistication, age, or desperation, and then it must be shown that the resulting deal was not reasonable. If the 20 percent interest charged was reasonable given the risk, the contract is not unconscionable.

There is some overlap in the principles of unconscionable transactions and undue influence. Although legislation has been passed in most common law provinces prohibiting unconscionable transactions,[36] in most instances the statutory provisions are limited to loan transactions.[37] The recent acceptance of this equitable doctrine makes the defence of unconscionability available even when the contracts in question do not involve the loan of money. Of course, as with other equitable remedies, the court will not grant a remedy based on undue influence or unconscionability where a third party is negatively affected or where the victim also has unclean hands.

Both common law and statute

CASE SUMMARY 8.17

When Is Legal Advice Independent? *Bertolo v. Bank of Montreal*[38]

When Mr. Bertolo borrowed money from the Bank of Montreal to open a restaurant, he needed his mother to mortgage her home as added security. The mother was not fluent in English and didn't really understand what was going on other than that she was helping her son, so the bank sent her to obtain independent legal advice. The bank referred her to the bank's lawyer, who was also Mr. Bertolo's lawyer, and he had his partner advise her of her legal position. There was no actual evidence of just what advice she did

---

[36.] See, for example, the *Unconscionable Transactions Act*, R.S.A. 2000, c. U-2.

[37.] See B.C.'s new *Business Practices and Consumer Protection Act*, S.B.C. 2004, c. 2, particularly Part 2 (Unfair Practices) and Ontario's new *Consumer Protection Act, 2002*, S.O. 2002, c. 30 (in force 30 July 2005), especially Part III (Unfair Practices).

[38.] (1986), 33 D.L.R. (4th) 610 (Ont. C.A.).

receive, but before leaving, the bank's lawyer assured her that she should not worry and that all would be fine. The bank manager later gave her similar assurances.

The Court held that both the lawyer for the bank and his partner were in a conflict of interest position and as a result the advice given was not independent. They should have known better. The manager knew the bank had to provide Bertolo's mother with independent legal advice, and its failure to do so caused the mortgage to be set aside on the basis of being unconscionable. This was a failure on the part of the lawyers as well as the bank manager.

DISCUSSION QUESTIONS

When dealing with vulnerable people, what precautions should thus be taken to ensure that there is no undue influence? If the courts determine that the vulnerable party has been taken advantage of, what is the likely consequence?

REDUCING RISK 8.2

Businesspeople—especially professionals in service industries, such as lawyers, bankers, and accountants—should be careful when dealing with their clients to avoid situations where an accusation of undue influence or unconscionability can arise. Business arrangements outside of those related to the profession should be avoided, and even those related to the profession should be guarded so that conflicts of interest do not arise. When in doubt, the transaction should be avoided. Insisting that the client obtain independent legal advice is another option. If the deal goes well, chances are no one will complain; but if a loss occurs, the client may have grounds to seek compensation from the professional to cover those losses.

PRIVITY OF CONTRACT AND ASSIGNMENT

Privity

When two parties enter into a contract, they create a world of law unto themselves. Contracting is a bargaining process, and only those participating in the bargain can be affected by it (see Figure 8.1). It is a fundamental principle of contract law that the parties to a contract do not have the power to impose benefits or obligations on third parties or outsiders who are not parties to the contract. The contracting parties have created a private agreement, and outsiders to it can neither enforce it nor be bound to perform its terms. This principle is called **privity of contract**.

Contract binds only parties to it

The case of *Donoghue v. Stevenson* referred to in Case Summary 4.2 illustrates the application of the privity principle. In that case,[39] a woman bought her friend a bottle of ginger beer, which contained a decomposed snail. The friend, who consumed the contaminated drink, could not sue the owner of the café for breach of contract because she was not the person who bought it. There was no contract between them. Under normal circumstances, merchants can be sued by the purchaser for breach of contract for selling faulty products, even though they are unaware of the problem. But if there is no contract between the

---

[39.] [1932] A.C. 562 (H.L.).

Figure 8.1

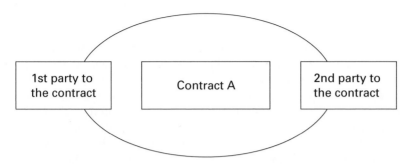

Only the parties to the contract can enforce it, even if outsiders are to benefit from it.

merchant and the individual harmed, the victim can normally sue only the manufacturer in tort.

EXCEPTIONS

There are several exceptions and apparent exceptions to the operation of the privity rule. First, it must be emphasized that while a third party designated to receive a benefit cannot enforce the contract, the original parties still have the right to insist on performance. Thus, if Currah, who operates a landscaping company, contracts with Bermark to mow Kicia's lawn, Kicia cannot enforce the agreement but Bermark certainly can. The court may provide either damages or money compensation calculated on the basis of what it would cost to have somebody else mow the lawn.

Original party to contract can enforce it where benefit to be bestowed on outsider

Where land is involved, the rights of the parties are said to run with the land. If a person leases a suite in a house and the owner sells the house, the new owner must honour the lease, even though the lessee was not a party to the contract of sale.

Where interest in land involved, rights run with the land

When an agent acts on behalf of a principal in contracting with a third party, the actions of that agent are binding on the principal. When a clerk in a store sells a magazine to a customer, the storeowner is bound. This may seem inconsistent with privity, but in fact the contract is between the storeowner and the customer; the clerk is merely acting as a go-between. Agency will be discussed in detail in Chapter 15.

Agents create contract between principal and third party

The concept of the **trust** is a little more complicated. This involves one person's transferring her property to a second person who in turn is obligated to use it to the benefit of a third. This is often done in estate planning, the beneficiaries being the family of the person creating the trust. For this to work, the third-party beneficiary must be able to enforce the contract between the original parties. Since the person creating the trust is often dead and unable to enforce the original contract, it would be an affront to allow the trustee to ignore the obligations set out in the agreement and take the benefits for himself. The Courts of Chancery developed the equitable principle of the trust to overcome this problem, and the beneficiary now can enforce the terms of the original trust agreement even though he is not a party to it.

Trust allows a third party to benefit from the property of another

Beneficiary can enforce trust agreement against trustee

Insurance is handled in a similar fashion, with the beneficiary of an insurance contract having the power to enforce it after the death of the insured. Sometimes, when a contract bestows a benefit on a third party, the courts will infer a trust,

Beneficiary can enforce insurance contract

even though parties did not specifically create one. This is called a **constructive trust** and provides an important method for the third party to obtain the benefit promised.

Novation involves new agreement

Finally, when the parties to a contract agree to substitute someone new for one of the original parties, there is also no problem with privity so long as all three parties agree to the change. This is called a **novation** (see Figure 8.2). If Jones has a contract to provide janitorial services to a college and he sells his business to Brown, there is no problem with Brown taking over that service contract, provided the college agrees. A new contract has been substituted for the old one, and no privity problem arises since all parties have agreed to the change.

In fact, there are signs that the doctrine of privity may be breaking down. The Law Reform Commission of Nova Scotia, for example, recommended reform of the law pertaining to privity, particularly as it relates to third party rights in contract.[40] One of its recommendations is that privity be relaxed by statute, to allow third-party beneficiaries to enforce their rights under contracts.

Contracting parties often protect themselves from contract and tort liability by including exemption clauses in contracts that limit that liability. In the case of *London Drugs Ltd. v. Kuehne & Nagel International Ltd.*,[41] Kuehn & Nagel contracted to store a large and valuable transformer for London Drugs. The contract between them limited a "warehouseman's" liability for damage to only $40. Unfortunately, two employees were careless in their handling of the transformer, causing significant damage, and London Drugs sued. However, instead of suing Kuehne & Nagel for breach of contract, it sued the employees in tort for negligence. By doing this London Drugs thought to avoid the protection of the

Figure 8.2

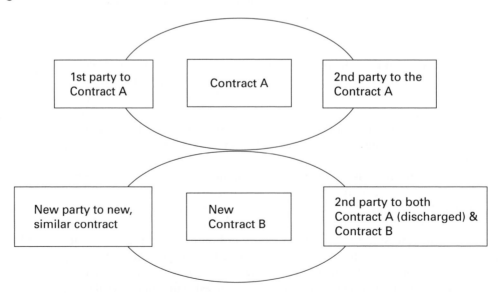

Novation: If the 2nd party agrees to the substitution of the new party, a new contract is formed and Contract A is discharged, replaced by the new Contract B.

---

40. See online: www.lawreform.ns.ca/Downloads/Privity_FIN.pdf.

41. [1992] 3 S.C.R. 299.

exemption clause limiting any claim to $40, the theory being that the employees were not privy to the contract and therefore not protected by it. The Supreme Court, however, found that the protection of the exemption clause extended to the employees, even though they were not party to the contract; the Court created a "principled exception" to the common law doctrine of privity. The rationale underlying this decision is that the employees were third-party beneficiaries under the exemption clause. Obviously, if an employer was exempted from liability for negligence by the exemption clause, employees who would actively be doing the storing of the goods were intended to be included under that exemption as third-party beneficiaries. In essence, the protection from liability given to the warehouseman extended not just to the employer that signed the contract, but to its employees who performed the tasks contemplated by the contract as well. The Court held that in circumstances where the traditional exceptions (such as trust or agency) do not apply, the Court should examine whether the doctrine of privity should be relaxed in the given circumstances. The departure of the Supreme Court from the privity rule in this case indicates a willingness to do so in other circumstances as well.

Employees protected by exemption clauses

CASE SUMMARY 8.18

Exception to Privity Rule Applied: *Tony and Jim's Holdings Ltd. v. Silva*[42]

Norman Silva was the primary shareholder and president of Mamma Mia Pizza (Kingston) Ltd., which operated from a strip mall. The tenancy agreement required that the tenant (Mamma Mia Pizza) pay the premiums for the insurance that was to be purchased by the landlord. The landlord took out insurance on the premises with the Canadian General Insurance Company. Silva caused a fire on the premises when he negligently left a pot of butter on a gas fire while he went next door for a coffee. Considerable damage occurred, and the landlord made a claim to the insurance company. That claim was honoured, but when an insurance company pays out on a claim, it normally takes over the right of the claimant to sue the person who caused the loss. This is called the right of subrogation.

Once the insurance company paid out on the claim, it assumed the right to sue the person who caused the loss, namely Silva. The policy, however, contained a clause whereby the insurance company had given up its right to subrogation: "[A]ll rights of subrogation are hereby waived against any corporation, firm, individual, or other interest with respect to which insurance is provided by this policy." The insurance company took the position that this was a contractual right between its insured and itself and that, under the principle of privity, the clause did not and could not bestow any rights on an outsider (Silva) not party to the contract. Because of privity, it claimed to still have the right to sue Silva despite the non-subrogation clause.

The Court of Appeal had to decide whether the insurance company could override the non-subrogation clause by raising the principle of privity of contract. The Court held that privity did not apply in this situation. In effect, it created an exception to the privity rule, saying that to do otherwise would allow the insurance company to circumvent the provision of the contract. The waiver of the right to subrogate had to be enforced, even to the benefit of the third party (Silva), to give effect to the reasonable expectation of the parties to the insurance contract.

---

42. (1999), 170 D.L.R. (4th) 193 (Ont. C.A.).

A critical case from the Supreme Court of Canada on the doctrine of privity and third-party beneficiaries is *Fraser River Pile & Dredge Ltd. v. Can-Dive Services Ltd.*[43] There the owner of a barge insured it. The policy extended coverage to "charterers" and contained a waiver of subrogation, such that the insurer waived its right to sue charterers. The barge sank while chartered to the respondent and the insurer paid the owner under the policy. But the insurer had the owner waive the "waiver of subrogation clause," and the insurer sued the charterer for the loss of the barge. The issue was whether the charterer could use the "waiver of subrogation" as contained in the insurance policy, as a defence, even though the charterer was not a party to the policy. The Court held in favour of the charterer on the basis of a principled exception to the privity of contract doctrine.

Essentially, where two contracting parties intend to extend the benefit to a third party, who relies on that contractual provision (here the policy stated that coverage was extended to charterers and the waiver of subrogation also applied to charterers) and the activities performed by the third party are the very activities contemplated as coming within the scope of the contract (here the charterer used the barge in stormy weather and it sank), a principled exception to the doctrine of privity applies. The third party will be allowed to raise clauses in the contract, which admittedly it was not a party to, in its defence. The insurer's action against the charterer thus failed.

Another area where the rule of privity of contract may be weakening is in the field of product liability. In *Donoghue v. Stevenson*,[44] the consumer of the ginger beer could not sue the merchant for breach of contract because she was not the one who purchased it. Some provinces have passed legislation allowing the consumer of defective products to sue the seller in contract law, even when the injured person is not the purchaser and not party to the contract. The courts have also extended the right to sue in contract law in product liability cases by finding collateral contracts created by advertising brochures, giving the purchaser a right to seek redress in contract law past the retailer back to the manufacturer.

Assignment

Contracting parties can assign rights

Just as a person buying goods under a contract is then free to resell them, so can a person entitled to receive a benefit under a contract transfer that benefit to a third party (see Figure 8.3). This is called the **assignment** of contractual rights, and the benefit transferred is known as a **chose in action**. While the practice of transferring such rights was originally not permitted because of privity, it is now an essential aspect of doing business. The principle is that a person who has

---

43. [1999] 3 S.C.R. 108.

44. *Supra*, footnote 39.

Figure 8.3

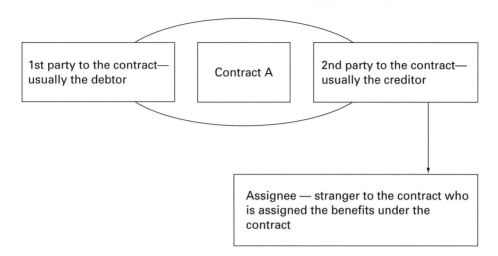

acquired a right or a benefit under a contract has the right to assign that benefit to another. Where Schmidtke does carpentry work for Nehring and is owed money for those services, Schmidtke is free to assign (sell) that claim (or account receivable) to Green. Schmidtke is referred to as the *assignor*, a party to the original contract, and Green as the *assignee*, a stranger to it. It is common for businesses to assign their accounts receivable (money they are owed by their customers) outright to obtain immediate cash or to make a conditional assignment to a creditor to secure a loan.

The ability to make such assignments has become a vital component of our commercial world. There are, however, some important qualifications to keep in mind. First, only a benefit can be assigned, not an obligation. In the example above, if Schmidtke has done poor work or failed to do the job, he is still obligated to Nehring, despite the assignment. Schmidtke cannot say that it is no longer his problem, as he has assigned the contract to Green. Schmidtke has assigned only the benefits, not the obligations.

Only benefits can be assigned

Of course, if Green tried to collect those benefits (the money owed) in face of the defaulted contract, he would fail. While it is true that the assignment of the benefits of the contract between Schmidtke and his client Nehring was valid, Green can be in no better position to collect that benefit than was Schmidtke, and Schmidtke has no claim since he has defaulted; Schmidtke cannot sell something he doesn't have. The principle is that an assignee is "subject to the equities" between the original parties, meaning that the assignee can be in no better position than was the assignor. Schmidtke transferred only what claim he had against Nehring to Green, and that claim was tainted. If the debtor, then, has a good defence against the assignor, he also has a good defence against the assignee.

Assignee in no better position than assignor

CASE SUMMARY 8.19

The Vulnerability of an Assignee: *First City Capital Ltd. v. Petrosar Ltd.*[45]

TDC graphics was to supply specialized computers to Petrosar Limited. For financing purposes, TDC graphics sold the computers to Casselman Financial Underwriters Limited (CFUL), which in turn leased them to Petrosar. An important term of the agreement gave Petrosar the right to terminate the lease at the end of one year and either return the computers or purchase them for "the residual amount left owing." This term was not set out in the lease agreement itself (it was contained in a purchase order and a schedule attached to the lease), but was found by the Court to be an essential part of the lease agreement. When CFUL assigned this lease agreement to First City Capital Ltd. it failed to inform First City of Petrosar's right to terminate at the end of the first year.

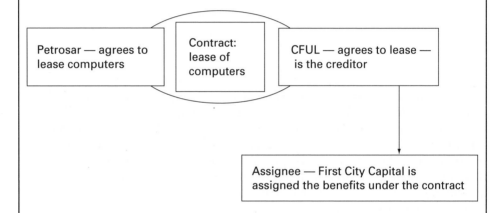

At the end of one year Petrosar opted to purchase the computers, but when a price couldn't be agreed on, Petrosar simply stopped paying and put the computers in storage. First City sued, and the main problem for the Court was to determine whether First City was bound by Petrosar's right to purchase or to terminate. The Court held that, as the assignee, First City could be in no better position than the person who assigned the lease to it. Whether it knew of the provision or not, First City took it "subject to the equities." What First City got was only what CFUL had to give, and that was a lease subject to this right to purchase or terminate. First City's failure to convey the computers to Petrosar for "the residual amount owing" as agreed, entitled Petrosar to stop paying.

SMALL BUSINESS PERSPECTIVE

This case illustrates how an assignee gets only what the assignor has to give. It also shows how careful parties have to be in arranging these kinds of transactions.

---

45. (1987), 42 D.L.R. (4th) 738 (Ont. H.C.)

Although only the benefits can be assigned, that does not mean the original party to the contract always has to be the one to perform. Often, it is understood that the actual work or service involved will be performed by an employee or subcontractor. This is called **vicarious performance** (see Appendix Reading at the end of this chapter). The point is that the original party to the contract remains responsible for the work no matter who does it. But in many cases, the service must be performed by the person so contracting. If a famous artist agreed to paint a portrait, it is likely that the customer would not be satisfied if the actual painting were subcontracted to another.

Because of the restrictions of privity, it was left to the courts of chancery to develop an "equitable" method to enforce assignments. This involved the assignee's bringing an action against the original contracting party through the assignor and is referred to as "joining" the assignor in the action. Joining can be a cumbersome process, and it has since been modified by statute.[46] If the assignment meets certain qualifications, it qualifies as a **statutory assignment** and the assignee can enforce the claim directly without involving the assignor. In the example above, in the past Green would have had to bring an action in Schmidtke's name, to collect funds owing under the contract by Nehring. But today, if the assignment qualifies as a statutory assignment, Green can simply sue Nehring for the money directly.

The qualifications that have to be met to establish a statutory assignment are as follows: First, the assignment must be *absolute*, meaning that it must be both unconditional and complete. The full amount owed must be assigned without any strings attached. Second, the assignment must be *in writing, signed by the assignor*. And third, the original party obligated to pay must be *notified in writing* of the assignment. Only when all these requirements are met will the assignee be able to sue directly; otherwise, he still must join the assignor in any attempt at collection.

Some things cannot be assigned, such as the right to collect support payments or the right to sue another in a tort action. Certain statutes, such as the *Workers' Compensation Act* (in some jurisdictions)[47] prohibit the assignment of benefits provided under the statute. Note, however, that although the right to sue cannot be assigned, there is no such restriction on the assignment of the proceeds from such a lawsuit once awarded.

Sometimes, an assignor may be tempted to assign the same claim to two assignees. This, of course, is fraud, and the victim has the right to seek redress from the assignor. Often, however, that assignor has fled or has no funds. The original debtor against whom the assignment is made is obligated to pay only once, and one of the two assignees will be out of luck. In such circumstances, it is the first assignee to give the debtor notice of the assignment who will collect. The other assignee will be left to seek remedies against the assignor, which may be worthless. It is, therefore, vital in business to take such assignments with care and then to *immediately notify* the debtor. It is only when the debtor makes the mistake of ignoring such notice and paying either the wrong assignee or insisting on paying the original assignor that it may have to pay twice.[48]

The principles discussed so far relate to voluntary assignments. There are some circumstances in which the assignment of rights can take place involuntar-

Contractual obligations can be performed by others

Qualifications for statutory assignment

Some things cannot be assigned

Debtor must pay first assignee who gives notice of assignment

---

[46.] See, for example, Alberta's *Judicature Act*, R.S.A. 2000, c. J-2, s. 20.

[47.] See, for example, Alberta's *Workers' Compensation Act*, R.S.A. 2000, c. W-15, s. 141, which says that benefits may not be assigned without the approval of the Workers' Compensation Board.

[48.] Rights of an assignee and the consequences of notice are also dealt with in provincial legislation. See, for example, the *Personal Property Security Act*, R.S.A. 2000, c. P-7, s. 41.

ily. For example, rights and obligations are automatically transferred to the administrator or executor of the estate when a person dies. This representative steps into the deceased's shoes and is not restricted by the privity of contract rule, unless the terms of the contract require personal performance by the deceased. The second situation of **involuntary assignment** occurs when a party to a contract goes bankrupt. Under bankruptcy legislation, the bankrupt's assets are transferred to a trustee, called the *receiver*, who will then distribute them to pay the creditors as much as possible. Bankruptcy will be discussed in detail in Chapter 14.

Involuntary assignment in cases of death and bankruptcy

REDUCING RISK 8.3

Businesspeople should never ignore a notice of assignment and continue paying the original party. There is no problem so long as the payment is passed on, but you cannot be sure that this will be done. Also, businesspeople often assume that once they have assigned the debt they no longer have anything to do with the transaction. If a product has been sold and the financing arrangements have been assigned to a finance company, the merchant vendor is still responsible with respect to the performance of the product. If it is defective or dangerous, causing injury or loss, it is the vendor that is responsible, not the finance company. One can assign only the benefits, not one's obligations under such a contract.

Negotiable Instruments

Negotiable instruments true exceptions to privity

Another exception to the privity of contract rule recognizes the commercial realities of modern business. As commerce developed it became necessary to devise a method to freely exchange and pass on claims for debt that had been incurred in the process of business. When these claims met certain qualifications, they were defined as **negotiable instruments**, and through them unique rights were bestowed on the parties (we discuss negotiable instruments in Chapter 14 as well). Cheques, promissory notes, and bills of exchange (commonly called drafts) are examples of negotiable instruments. While the use of cheques as a method of payment has significantly decreased as credit and debit cards have gained popularity, cheques are still an important method of transferring funds in business. Promissory notes retain their popularity where credit is involved because of the unique advantages they bestow.

Negotiable instruments give better rights to holder than is the case with assignment

Briefly, a negotiable instrument can be freely passed from one person to another, conveying with it all the rights associated with the original agreement between the parties, and no notice of the transfer is required. This flexibility is completely inconsistent with the doctrine of privity of contract and the law of assignment discussed above. The most significant innovation of negotiable instruments was that better rights or claims than those held by the initial parties could be passed on. As discussed under "Assignment," it is clear that even when it is possible to assign contractual rights, the assignee can be in no better position than was the assignor. Thus, if a defence such as deceit or breach of contract was available against the original party to the contract (the assignor), it was available against the assignee as well. This is not the case with negotiable instruments. When you give a cheque or promissory note to someone (who has deceived or cheated you) once that instrument gets into the hands of an innocent third party who satisfies the qualifications to be a "holder in due course," you can be required to pay despite the existence of the fraud. In other words, if Nehring pays Schmidtke by cheque and then Schmidtke endorses the cheque and delivers it to Carter, Carter is entitled to cash the cheque despite any complaints Nehring might later have with regards to the quality of the work done by Schmidtke.

APPENDIX READING

Vicarious Performance

How It Occurs

A promisor cannot escape his liability to the promisee by appointing a substitute for himself without the consent of the promisee. In other words, he cannot transfer or "assign" his liability by finding someone willing to assume the liability for him.

Nevertheless, in many situations it is normal for a party, without altering the terms of his contract, to arrange for someone else to carry out his duties, though he remains responsible to the promisee for proper performance. Performance of this type is known as **vicarious performance**; typically, an employee of the promisor performs vicariously (that is, on behalf of the promisor). If the work is not done satisfactorily, the promisee may seek a remedy for breach of contract against the promisor, but not against his employee. In turn, the employee can look only to the employer (and not to the promisee) for payment for the work he has done under his employment contract with the employer. The results are consistent with the rule of privity of contract.

> **vicarious performance**
> a third party performs on behalf of the promisor who remains responsible for proper performance

When Is Vicarious Performance Allowed?

When may a promisor employ a third party to perform the work vicariously? He may do so when personal performance by him was not the reason why the promisee entered into the contract. The party entitled to performance generally cannot complain if someone other than the promisor turns up and does the work equally well. However, it would be unacceptable when personal performance is expected, as, for example, when a pianist makes a contract to perform at a concert.

In many contracts, the understanding is that by their very nature they must be performed by a large number of persons who are not parties to the contract: contracts for the construction of buildings, the manufacture of goods, and the transport of people or goods. Moreover, when goods are shipped to a destination that requires the services of more than one carrier, both parties understand that not only employees of the first carrier but also of another carrier will perform: a shipment by rail from Toronto to New York City may be made by Canadian National Railways (CN) and the New York Central. The shipper contracts with CN, whose franchise area includes the point of shipment, and CN arranges for completion of the shipment with the connecting carrier operating beyond the CN area of franchise.

It may not always be clear, as in Illustration 8.1, whether a party is expected to perform personally or whether she may employ someone to perform vicariously.

Sometimes a party arranges for its obligations to be performed vicariously when it should have performed personally, but the other party may have no opportunity to protest until the work is finished. In this situation, the promisor breached a term in the contract (the implied or express promise to perform personally). The promisee may sue for damages to compensate for whatever loss he can show resulted from vicarious, rather than personal, performance.

A Co. Ltd. contracts with a public accountant, B, to have its accounts audited. B sends C, a senior accountant, to carry out the audit program. May A Co. Ltd. object? This is a type of work that can be carried out competently by a qualified accountant and ordinarily would not require B's personal performance unless A Co. Ltd. had expressly bargained for it. Consequently, the vicarious performance by C is permissible, and A Co. Ltd. is not entitled to reject the tender of such performance. (We may, of course, assume that a final review of the audit would always be made by B.)

Tort Liability

Suppose that in performing a contract vicariously, an employee commits a tort: he negligently damages a valuable instrument belonging to the promisee. As we noted in Chapter 3 on torts, the promisee may sue both the employer for vicarious liability and the employee personally. Since the employer ordinarily has a "deeper pocket" than its employee, the promisee almost always sues the employer, but may sue the employee as well, in case the court should find that the employer is not liable because the damage did not occur *in the course of employment.*

Suppose that in Illustration 8.1 above, C does such an inadequate job that he fails to detect a material error in the accounts, and, as a result, A Co. Ltd. suffers a loss. A Co. Ltd. must look to B for damages for breach of contract. In addition, if C's poor work amounted to negligence, he would be personally liable to A Co. Ltd. in tort, and B would also be vicariously liable in tort for C's negligence.

If, while working in the offices of A Co. Ltd., C stole some valuable client records to sell to a competitor of A Co. Ltd., C would, of course, be guilty of a crime as well as of committing a tort. However, the theft would not be considered conduct in the course of employment, and B would not be liable for C's misconduct.

SUMMARY

Mistake

- Must go to the nature of the agreement or the existence of the subject matter, not just to the effect of the agreement when performed

Types	Remedies
• Both parties making a common error	• If serious, there is no contract
• An error in recording the terms	• Can be corrected by rectification
• A misunderstanding between the parties	• Most reasonable interpretation of the contract is enforced
• A one-sided mistake	• *Caveat emptor* applies unless the mistake is so fundamental as to destroy consensus or there is fraud

Misrepresentation

- A false statement that induces a person to enter a contract

Types	Remedies
- Innocent misrepresentation	- Rescission is the only remedy
- Fraudulent misrepresentation	- Damages (and possibly punitive damages) for the tort of deceit and/or rescission
- Negligence	- Damages and/or rescission

Duress, undue influence, or unconscionability

Types	Remedies
- Duress; contract made involuntarily	- Contract is voidable—rescission
- Undue influence	- Contract is voidable—rescission
- Unconscionable contract	- Court may rescind or modify the contract

Privity of contract

- Only the original parties to the contract are bound. Any benefit going to a third party must be enforced by the original party to the agreement
- The trust is a true exception to the privity rule because the beneficiary can enforce it even though he or she is not a party to the original agreement
- Other exceptions include real estate transactions, contracts of insurance, and various principled exceptions as defined by the courts

Assignment

- Only the benefits, not the obligations, in a contract can be sold (assigned) to a third party, and those benefits are to be enforced through the original contracting party, the assignor
- But when an assignment qualifies as a statutory assignment, the assignee can enforce the assigned rights directly, in its own name

Negotiable instruments

- Negotiable instruments may be enforced by third parties without notification to the original drawer (the party who writes and signed the cheque) of the instrument
- Negotiable instruments sometimes convey better rights than existed between the original parties

---

QUESTIONS

1. A mistake may result in a contract being declared void or voidable. What difference does it make if a contract is merely voidable?

2. When will a misunderstanding as to the terms of a contract cause that contract to be void?

3. Distinguish among shared mistakes, misunderstandings, and one-sided mistakes.

4. What approach will the courts usually take when the mistake involves disagreement about the meaning of the contract?

5. What must a party to a contract show to obtain rectification of a document?

6. How will the courts respond to ambiguous wording in a contract?

7. Explain what is meant by *caveat emptor*. What is the significance of this principle in relation to a one-sided mistake?

8. Under what circumstances would a person raise a claim of *non est factum*? What restrictions are there on its availability?

9. Explain the parol evidence rule.

10. What happens when a misrepresentation becomes a term of the contract?

11. Explain how fraudulent, negligent, and innocent misrepresentations differ. Identify the remedies that are available for each type of misrepresentation.

12. Under what circumstances can silence or a statement of opinion become misrepresentation?

13. What factors may affect the availability of the remedy of rescission?

14. Describe the relationship between misrepresentation and mistake.

15. Distinguish among duress, undue influence, and unconscionability and give examples of each.

16. What is meant by privity of contract?

17. Explain what is meant by the term *novation*.

18. Explain the relationship of the privity principle to land transactions, agency, trusts, and assignment. With regard to third-party beneficiaries under a contract, what direction does the law appear to be taking?

19. What qualifications must be realized before there can be a statutory assignment?

20. What limitations are placed on the rights and obligations of the assignee when a contract is assigned?

21. What is meant by "the assignee takes subject to the equities"?

22. Can a "holder in due course" obtain better rights than an assignee? Explain.

Chapter 9

The End of the Contractual Relationship

CHAPTER OBJECTIVES

1. Outline how a contract is discharged by performance
2. Describe when a breach of contract will be sufficient to relieve the opposite party from its obligations
3. Explain how a contract may be discharged by agreement
4. Illustrate the consequences flowing from frustration of contract
5. Detail the remedies available for a breach of contract

Contracts can come to an end or be discharged by performance, breach, agreement between the parties to end or modify, or frustration. This chapter examines each of these and ends with a discussion of remedies for breach of contract.

PERFORMANCE

Contractual obligations are discharged and a contract is ended when both parties have satisfactorily completed their obligations under the contract. Often parties perform their obligations simultaneously. The closing of a sale requires the purchaser to tender the price in exchange for the transfer of title. The purchaser hands over the cash and the seller hands over the goods. With most bilateral contracts, however, one party must complete its side before the other is required to perform. In employment contracts, the employee must perform the work before the employer is obliged to pay wages. If the employee fails to report for a shift, the employer has no obligation to pay the hourly wage. It becomes vitally important, then, to determine whether one party has properly performed its side, thereby obligating the other party to perform in turn. The question that must be asked is: Will anything short of exact performance satisfy the requirement?

In fact, there are two situations where something short of exact performance of the contract will still be considered proper performance. Contracts usually consist of major terms (called **conditions**) and minor terms (called **warranties**)—see the section "Conditions and Warranties" below. When the failure to perform is relatively insignificant, or where failure to perform involves only a warranty or a

Where warranty breached, contract still considered performed

But some contracts must be performed exactly

Contract discharged when contract substantially performed

minor term, that party is regarded as having performed his side of the agreement. The other party will be required to perform, subject to a claim for compensation for whatever loss was caused by the breach of warranty. Thus, if the new car is delivered, but without the ordered fog lights, a minor term or warranty has been breached; but the purchaser will still be required to take delivery and pay for the car minus the cost of the fog lights.

On the other hand, where the breach is significant, as when a condition or major term of the contract is breached, the contract is normally considered discharged and the other party is relieved of performing her obligations under it. Still, when the condition is breached in some minor, inconsequential way, the court will usually treat it like a breach of warranty, requiring the other party to perform subject to a claim for the loss caused by the shortfall. This is called **substantial performance**. For example, if a farmer is required to deliver 2000 kilograms of potatoes and delivers only 1987 kilograms, the contract would be considered substantially performed. The farmer would be discharged from further performance and the purchaser would have to pay for the potatoes that were delivered. Of course, exact performance will be required where only exact performance will do. If a contract with a driller requires a producing well and 25 dry holes are drilled, there has been no substantial performance and there is no obligation to pay.

CASE SUMMARY 9.1

Minor Breach Will Not Discharge Contract: *Sail Labrador Ltd. v. Challenger One (The)*[1]

Sail Labrador Ltd. leased a ship from Navimar Corp. Ltd. with an option to purchase, but only if every payment was properly made. The contract required cash, but the parties agreed to payment through a series of post-dated cheques. One cheque was dishonoured because of a bank error, and despite immediate correction, the owner took the position that the option was no longer available because of this failure.

The Supreme Court of Canada decided that the owners had assumed this kind of risk when they agreed to take post-dated cheques. Since the error was inconsequential and immediately corrected, the contract had been substantially performed and the option was still available. This case illustrates not only the nature of an option but also the doctrine of substantial performance. Here the contract was properly performed except for some minor variation and the owners then had to honour their contractual obligations.

SMALL BUSINESS PERSPECTIVE

Does it strike you as fair that a contract that is substantially performed be enforced despite imperfect performance? If the prospect of incomplete performance is troubling, one might build in penalty provisions for incomplete performance, or bonus provisions for early performance, to encourage the opposite party to perform in a timely and exact manner.

[1.] [1999] 1 S.C.R 265.

Tender

The general rule in common law is that when a person has tendered performance of a contract, it counts as if the contract had been performed. **Tender of performance** means that if a person is ready, willing, and able to perform a contractual obligation and attempts to do so, but the other party refuses to accept it or prevents it, the first party is taken to have completed its obligation and the other party is then required to perform. If it fails to do so then it is in breach, not the party who has tendered performance.

Where goods and services are involved and tender of performance is refused, the tendering party has no further obligation and can sue immediately. If Chan's Renovation Service contracted with Smith to install new gutters on his house, and when Chan shows up to do the job on the specified day he is refused entrance, he has discharged his obligation and can sue. It is no excuse for Smith to claim that the work was not done.

The effect of tendering proper payment of debt is different. It does not extinguish the debt but simply relieves the debtor of the normal obligation to seek out the creditor to make payment. Once proper payment has been tendered and refused, the debtor can just wait for the creditor to collect the debt. Any costs associated with that process will then be borne by the creditor.

Proper payment of a debt requires legal tender. Cheques, even certified cheques, are acceptable only when the parties have agreed to allow cheques to be used to pay debts. This may be an actual agreement between the parties, or it may be implied from accepted business practice.

If there is any question about the acceptable form of payment, it is advisable to present cash and then only the exact amount in proper legal tender. Under the *Currency Act*[2] creditors can refuse to take more than a limited amount in coins, as set out below.

When being paid in coins of this denomination	No more than this need be taken
$2	$40
$1	$25
10, 25, 50 cents	$10
5 cents	$5
1 cent	25 cents

There is no limit on what qualifies as legal tender when paper money is offered, as long as official Canadian bank notes are used. To avoid problems, especially as we move toward a cashless society, the parties should specify the appropriate method of payment in their agreement.

When not specifically addressed in the contract, the tendering of performance must be done at a reasonable time and place.[3] Usually, this means during normal business hours at a person's place of business. Thus, if Aronyk has a contract to deliver five tonnes of ripe grapes to Demers by 10 July, Aronyk would be

Tender of performance ends obligation

Where debt owed and money refused—money still owed, but creditor bears expense

Payment must be in legal tender

Delivery must be as specified or at a reasonable time and place

---

2. R.S.C. 1985, c. C-52.

3. See the *Sale of Goods Act*, R.S.A. 2000, c. S-2,s.29, for example.

expected to make that delivery to Demers's winery rather than to her home or office. The delivery should also take place during the usual working day. Demers would not be obligated to accept delivery at 6:00 p.m. on Saturday, unless such a time was permitted in the contract.

When the parties do specify a time for performance in the contract, the court will have to determine whether it is an important term or not. Where the parties specify (or the court determines) that "time is of the essence," it must be strictly adhered to. Even just a few seconds can make a difference. This was the case in *Smith Bros. & Wilson (B.C.) Ltd. v. British Columbia Hydro and Power Authority,*[4] where a bid was submitted for a job just a few minutes late. Tenders were to be submitted no later than 11:00 a.m. The bid was submitted at 11:01, but could not be considered.

When the contract has been properly performed by both parties, there may still be some continuing obligations. For example, where a product is sold and the purchase price has been paid, title has transferred to the purchaser. Even then, if the product is dangerous or fails to meet the specifications of the agreement, the purchaser can turn back to the seller and seek compensation for the breach. This continuing obligation is imposed, in the case of sales of goods, by legislation. Provincial *Sale of Goods Acts* impose certain implied warranties of fitness and merchantability upon sellers. Breach of these implied warranties can lead to an award of damages.

Some obligations continue after discharge

BREACH

Breach may involve failure to perform or repudiation

Breach of contract involves the failure of the breaching party to properly perform its contractual obligations. Such a breach can take place in two ways: (1) by improper or incomplete performance of the obligations set out in the agreement, and (2) by refusal to perform.

Allegations of improper or incomplete performance are quite common. In the *Olson v. Beaulieu* case,[5] for example, a seamstress performed alterations on a wedding gown so poorly that the bride-to-be was distraught. The hem and bustle were uneven, the sleeves bulged and beads kept falling off. The plaintiff (bride) sued, claiming the cost of the dress and damages for emotional distress. The Court found that the defendant had breached the contract, but limited damages to the cost of having further alterations done in another town, plus travel costs.

CASE SUMMARY 9.2

When Is a Breach Enough to Discharge a Contract? *Baid v. Aliments Rinag Foods Inc.*[6]

It is often difficult to determine just how serious a breach must be to discharge a contract. In the *Baid* case, the father of the groom arranged to have the reception catered. The caterer failed to show and the father hastily arranged to have the reception hall supply food and drinks—at nearly twice the cost. The caterer's truck had broken down and its

---

[4.] (1997), 30 B.C.L.R. (3d) 334 (S.C.).

[5.] [2002] S.J. No. 779 (Prov. Ct.).

[6.] [2003] O.J. No. 2153 (S.C.J.).

cell phone wouldn't work, so the wedding party was not notified. When the caterer finally arrived five hours late, it served food that hadn't been properly warmed. The father sued for breach of contract, claiming the extra costs, plus damages for emotional distress. The caterer counterclaimed, demanding payment of the balance of their unpaid account. Whereas in some situations a five-hour delay in performance would not justify treating the contract as discharged, here the Court determined that the failure to perform was significant. Accordingly, the plaintiff was relieved of paying for the poorly performed task, and the defendant had to pay for the costs that flowed from the breach.

SMALL BUSINESS PERSPECTIVE

Examine the consequences flowing from the above breach. Not only was the defendant caterer unable to get paid, it also had to compensate the plaintiff his costs in hiring a third party to supply the food and drinks. A costly lesson, indeed!

Breach, by refusal to perform, can also lead to discharge of the contract. Refusal to perform will be addressed under the heading "Repudiation," below.

Conditions and Warranties

Conditions are terms essential to the substantial performance of a contract; **warranties** are minor, insignificant terms or terms that are peripheral to the central obligation of the contract. A breach of warranty will not relieve the other party of the obligation to fulfill her side of the agreement. The victim of such a breach of warranty has the right to sue the other party for whatever it costs to overcome the deficiency in performance but still must perform her part of the agreement. However, when a condition or important term is breached, so that the victim of the breach is deprived of the major benefit of the contract, the other party can usually treat his or her obligation as ended and sue for breach of contract. It must be stressed that the breach of condition must be a serious impairment of the performance of the contract. A minor breach of even an important term will not generally allow the victim of the breach to discharge the contract. A common example of this occurs when goods are to be delivered in instalments. A single missed instalment usually will not be enough to discharge the agreement, even though it is the breach of an important term.

> *Breach of warranty—performance required*

Although the breach of a condition normally allows the victim of the breach to treat the contract as discharged, she can elect or choose to treat the contract as still binding. In fact, if the non-breaching party has received some significant benefit under the agreement, she loses the right to discharge and must perform her obligations subject to a claim for compensation for the breach.

> *Breach of condition—party relieved*

It may be tempting for one party to breach a condition of the contract so as to relieve herself of any further obligation to perform. But the breaching party can't choose how the breach will be treated. It takes both parties to end a contract. If Willoughby provided a sculpture of a moose instead of the flying geese agreed to for the foyer of Kubicki's new office building in Regina, this would normally be a breach of a condition, and Kubicki would not have to pay. However, if Kubicki liked the moose sculpture he could keep it, but he would have to pay for it—albeit at a reduced value. Thus, when a breach of condition in a contract has been accepted by the other party, it is treated as a breach of warranty.

What is important to one person might seem unimportant to another. Therefore, terms can be designated as either conditions or warranties in the agreement. Normally, when a person orders a new car, the particular shade of red ordered would be a minor term, and if a car of a slightly different shade were delivered the purchaser would still have to take it. But where the exact shade is important to the purchaser, which might be the case where it is used as a trademark for a business, it can designate the required shade to be a condition and refuse to take the car if a car of any other shade of red is delivered. Similarly, the person supplying goods or services will often designate as a warranty a term that

would normally be a condition in the agreement. The B.C. *Sale of Goods Act* states that in transactions governed by the *Act* the court has the option of treating a term as a condition although it is specified as a warranty in the contract.[7]

Exemption Clauses

Exemption clauses are an attempt by a party to significantly limit or eliminate its liability under an agreement. The courts will generally enforce exemption clauses because the object of contract law is to carry out whatever the parties have freely bargained to do. But they do so reluctantly, especially where the parties are not in an equal bargaining position. If there is any ambiguity in the terms of the exemption clause, the narrow or restrictive meaning will be used.

If a restaurant has a sign above the cloakroom stating that it is "Not responsible for lost or stolen clothing," by bringing this term to the customer's attention, the restaurant would make it part of the contract for care of the goods, or bailment. If clothes left were damaged by fire or water, the proprietor would not be protected, as that kind of loss was not specified on the sign. Similarly, if a briefcase were stolen, the exemption clause would not apply because it was a briefcase and not "clothing" that was stolen.

Exemption clauses are intricate and involved because the people who draft them try to cover all possible eventualities, knowing that the courts will take a restrictive approach in their interpretation. Such clauses usually form a part of the written document, but they could be included in a sign or notice. In any case, the terms cannot be unilaterally imposed and must be brought to the attention of the customer at the time the contract is made. If the clause is on the back of the ticket or receipt, there must be a reference on the front directing the holder to read the back. Where a sign limiting liability is involved, as at a car park or bus depot, it must be in clear view so that a reasonable person would notice it when entering the premises or undertaking a contractual obligation. Even when the exemption clause is part of a written contract, if it is in any way unique or unusual it must be brought to the attention of the other contracting party. If it is buried in other insignificant writing, or so small it cannot be read, it is doubtful that it will have any legal effect.[8]

When goods or services are sold in consumer transactions, these exemption clauses are usually embodied in terms referred to as "limited warranties." The

---

[7.] R.S.B.C. 1996, c. 410, s. 15.

[8.] In *Boutcev v. DHL International Express Ltd.* (2001), 283 A.R. 19 (Q.B.) the defendant was unable to rely on an exclusion (exemption) clause despite the fact that the front of the waybill directed parties' attention to provisions that were printed on the back of the form. The Court found that the exclusion clause was illegible and incomprehensible.

term is misleading and causes confusion, since these are major terms of the contract or conditions, not minor ones. The courts are likely to be much more sympathetic to the plight of a customer in a consumer transaction who has not read the exemption clause than to the more sophisticated parties in a business transaction. It is important to note that under the *Sale of Goods Act* or other consumer protection legislation, the sellers' rights to restrict their obligations in such sales may be extremely limited. Consumer protection and the sale of goods will be discussed in Chapter 10.

Effect of legislation

CASE SUMMARY 9.3

Exemption Clauses Strictly Interpreted: *Meditek Laboratory Services Ltd. v. Purolator Courier Ltd;*[9] *Zhu v. Merrill Lynch HSBC*[10]

A Purolator employee delivered an expensive medical machine meant for Meditek to the wrong address. To make matters worse, the delivery sheets showing where the goods were delivered had been falsified and the goods could not be traced. After a long delay the goods were found, but Meditek had in the meantime obtained a replacement machine. It refused delivery and sued Purolator for damages. Purolator relied on an exemption clause in the contract limiting its liability "whether or not from negligence or gross negligence." But the act of the employee in falsifying the documents had been wilful, not negligent, and the Court found that Purolator was not protected by the clause.

In the *Zhu* case, Zhu used Merrill Lynch's internet trading facility to trade shares from his registered retirement savings account. He cancelled the trade immediately afterwards and shortly thereafter attempted to make the trade a second time. A problem arose because the first cancellation had not been completed, which resulted in a duplicate trade and a short position in Zhu's account. Merrill Lynch then insisted that Zhu buy back the shares—at a higher price. Zhu argued that he relied on the notation on his computer screen that the trade had been cancelled. Merrill Lynch tried to assert a limitation of liability clause, warning that clients had to confirm cancellations, but the Court would not allow that. The disclaimer was deemed unenforceable, for Merrill Lynch could have made it clear that the cancellation was not complete, but it had failed to do so. After all, who would expect one had to telephone to confirm a cancellation, where the entire transaction had been conducted online?

SMALL BUSINESS PERSPECTIVE

In light of the restrictive approach taken by the courts when asked to enforce exemption clauses, a party who wishes to limit its liability should realize that simply inserting an exemption clause may not be enough. Steps should be taken to evidence that the clause was brought to the other party's attention, explained, and assented to.

[9.] (1995), 102 Man.R. (2d) 85 (C.A.), leave to appeal to S.C.C. refused, [1995] S.C.C.A. No. 405.

[10.] [2002] B.C.J. No. 2883 (Prov. Ct.).

Fundamental Breach

Contracting parties often try to limit their liability as much as possible, and sometimes they try to contract out of all obligations and responsibilities. The Supreme Court of Canada, in Hunter Engineering,[11] has made it clear that a properly worded exemption clause can overcome even a **fundamental breach**—particularly where sophisticated businesspeople are involved on both sides. Because of the parties' freedom to contract, the courts may enforce an exemption clause that protects the breaching party even in the face of such a fundamental breach. It must be absolutely clear, however, that the parties understood the exemption clause would cover such a basic failure to perform. In most cases it is unlikely that one party would knowingly exempt the other from such basic obligations, and so the courts usually have no difficulty finding that such an exemption clause, even a carefully worded one, does not apply. The Ontario Court of Appeal has taken the position that it will not enforce exemption clauses where, given a fundamental breach, it would be unconscionable, unfair, or unreasonable to do so.[12]

But in the *Fraser Jewellers* case, where the defendant alarm company was negligent in failing to promptly call the police, thereby allowing the thieves to escape with $50 000 of property, the exemption of liability clause was nonetheless enforced! The Court determined that failing to respond appropriately to the alarm was negligent, but could not be equated to a fundamental breach. More significantly, however, the clause was not unconscionable. The provision was reasonable in the commercial context of this case, the contract was clear and unambiguous, and the clause was evidently drawn to the plaintiff's attention as it was highlighted in bold black letters. Accordingly, company was only liable in the amount of $890.

Exemption clauses usually ineffective in cases of fundamental breach

---

! REDUCING RISK 9.1

In business dealings, people may assume that the courts will enforce all the clauses found in their contracts. This is not necessarily so, especially if terms are oppressive or unconscionable. Furthermore, the courts may even take an expansive role, by implying obligations that may not be stated. The duty to act in good faith toward the other contracting party is such a commonly implied obligation. Whereas lawyers may be familiar with the manner in which courts interpret and enforce contracts, most laypeople are not. Getting legal advice on the enforceability of one's standard form contracts is evidently a good business practice.

---

11. *Hunter Engineering Co. v. Syncrude Canada Ltd.*, [1989] 1 S.C.R. 426; see also *Beaufort Realties v. Chomedey Aluminum Co. Ltd.*, [1980] 2 S.C.R. 718.

12. *Fraser Jewellers (1982) Ltd. v. Dominion Electric Protection Co.* (1997), 148 D.L.R. (4th) 496 (Ont. C.A.).

Franchisor Had a Duty of Good Faith to the Franchisee: *Shelanu Inc. v. Print Three Franchising Corporation*[13]

The franchise agreement in question dealt with the operation of print and copy stores in Toronto. BCD bought one store franchise in 1987 and subsequently, its sole shareholder purchased two further stores through Shelanu Inc. The franchise agreement contained three exclusionary clauses, including one stating that the "written agreement constituted the entire agreement between the parties."

One store was closed in 1991; later a second location was closed. Operations were relocated to the sole remaining store. In 1995, Print Three (the franchisor) and the franchisee orally agreed to cancel the first franchise agreement (made with BCD). Shelanu began reporting its sales as a single franchise, which entitled it to a greater royalty rebate under the franchise agreement than was the case when sales were divided between BCD and Shelanu. Print Three failed to pay the greater royalty rebate, thus Shelanu purported to terminate the franchise agreement and commenced an action against Print Three for damages. Despite the litigation, Shelanu continued to pay royalty remittances—on the basis of one franchise—and continued to use the Print Three name on its store. The issue at trial was whether Print Three had breached its contractual obligations. Shelanu argued that Print Three owed it a duty of good faith, which it breached: (1) by attempting to rescind the agreement; (2) by unilaterally changing the terms of an Air Miles program; (3) by its failures to make royalty payments; and (4) by allowing the establishment of Le Print Express franchise (a new franchise that located in close proximity to Shelanu and competed with it). The trial Judge held that the breach entitled Shelanu to terminate the franchise agreement. Print Three appealed. The Court of Appeal held that the trial Judge was correct in concluding that Print Three had breached a duty of good faith. A duty of good faith may arise out of the nature of the relationship. In *Wallace v. United Grain Growers Ltd.*,[14] the Supreme Court of Canada held that a duty of good faith was found to exist in employment contracts, where there typically is a power imbalance between employer and employee. The situation for franchisees was found to be similar.

A franchisee (such as Shelanu) rarely has bargaining power equal to the franchisor. The franchisee is dependent on the franchisor for information and for training. Courts have thus recognized that a duty of good faith exists at common law in the context of a franchisor–franchisee relationship.

SMALL BUSINESS PERSPECTIVE

Evidently, in light obligations that may be implied or determined by the courts to exist, parties must refrain from acting underhandedly or in bad faith. So when does acting out of self-interest cross the line?

[13.] [2003] O.J. No. 1919, (C.A.).

[14.] [1997] 3 S.C.R. 701.

Repudiation

Repudiation occurs when one of the parties to a contract indicates to the other "an intimation or an intention to abandon and altogether to refuse performance of the contract."[15] Repudiation that takes place after performance is due is just one more way that a contract can be breached; but if this refusal occurs before performance is due, it is called **anticipatory breach** and is treated somewhat differently.

CASE SUMMARY 9.5

Anticipating a Breach: *Driver v. Hrabok (c.o.b. Creative Glass and Mirror)*[16]

Driver entered into an agreement with the defendant, Hrabok, carrying on business as Creative Glass and Mirror, to have a granite countertop installed in her newly renovated kitchen. Driver selected the granite and paid half of the quoted price. When Hrabok arrived to take measurements, he indicated that several cabinets and appliances were not in the right place. He left without completing the measuring, stating he could not go ahead unless several changes were made. The kitchen had been carefully designed and in Driver's view, Hrabok's suggestion to relocate the cabinetry would impede walkways. Further, the changes would cost over $2000.

Believing Hrabok was unable or unwilling to complete the job unless the kitchen was modified, Driver cancelled the job. She hired another contractor who installed a granite counter on the cabinets without difficulty. Driver sought return of her down payment which Hrabok disputed, claiming he suffered a loss as a result of the cancellation of the contract. The Judge stated the issues thus:

- Is Hrabok responsible to refund any or all of the down payment in the amount of $3806.80?
- Is Hrabok entitled to any set off for materials or work he completed on Driver's behalf?

Cases dating back to the turn of the century have determined that if a party states or implies in advance that he will not be able to perform the very thing which is intended by the contract, the other party will be entitled to end the obligation if the threatened non-performance would have the effect of depriving her of substantially the whole benefit under the contract. If a party has acted in such a way as to lead a reasonable person to the conclusion that he does not intend to fulfill his part of the contract, there has been an anticipatory breach.

Accordingly, Driver was entitled to terminate the contract based on anticipatory breach. Hrabok was ordered to repay the down payment and Hrabok's claim for compensation (for his labour and the costs incurred in reserving the granite) was dismissed.

SMALL BUSINESS PERSPECTIVE

Evidently, if through words or actions a party gives the impression that it will not be able to fulfill its primary obligation under the contract, the other party may terminate the contract and go elsewhere.

---

15. Comment of Lord Coleridge, C.J. in *Freeth v. Burr* (1874), L.R. 9 C.P. 208 (Crt. C.P.).

16. [2008] S.J. No. 309 (Prov. Ct.)

In the face of an anticipatory breach, victims have a choice. Victims can choose to immediately treat the contract as breached, refuse to go through with any further performance on their part, and sue. However, the repudiation must relate to an important term of the contract and be a clear refusal to perform, not just a disagreement as to the nature of the contractual obligations. Alternatively, the victim of the repudiation can ignore the breach, demand performance, and continue to perform its side of the agreement. If the repudiating party still fails to perform, the innocent party can then sue for breach of contract, and the party repudiating will be held responsible for damages incurred even after the repudiation.

Victim is discharged and can sue if repudiation occurs before due date—or demand performance and wait

Once made, the choice is binding. This can have serious consequences, for if the victim chooses to insist on performance and then in turn cannot perform, she is then in breach herself, as happened in the *Vanderwal* case discussed in Case Summary 9.6.

Victim is bound by choice

CASE SUMMARY 9.6

Bound by Choice When Faced with Anticipatory Breach: *Vanderwal v. Anderson*[17]

Mrs. Anderson agreed to purchase property from the Vanderwals conditional on the purchaser's selling her house. This condition precedent was subsequently removed. Anderson's obligation to purchase was thus unconditional when she explained to the vendors, through her lawyer, that she didn't understand what she had done and didn't have the money to complete the transaction. She asked that the condition be reinstated and the time extended. The vendors refused, insisting that the contract was binding on her unconditionally. The vendor then sold the property to another purchaser and sued Anderson for breach. The Appeal Court found that the purchaser's claim of insufficient funds and plea for an extension amounted to an anticipatory breach. The vendors had a choice to ignore the breach and insist on performance or treat the contract as discharged. By insisting that the contract was binding unconditionally, they made their choice to reject the repudiation and insist on performance. When they sold the property they abandoned the contract—so they were in breach, and not the purchaser.

SMALL BUSINESS PERSPECTIVE

When the event of anticipatory breach occurs, the innocent party has a right to demand performance or to sue for breach. But if that party demands performance, it had better be prepared to perform its side of the agreement. It would be prudent to seek legal advice before one responds to an apparent breach of contract.

Repudiation can be expressed or implied from the conduct of the parties. Where the goods to be sold are sold to someone else, such repudiation will be implied. Also, repudiation may be implied from the failure to properly perform a term of the agreement. For example, failure to deliver an important instalment

Repudiation may be implied from conduct

---

17. [1999] O.J. No. 2646 (Div. Ct.).

can lead to repudiation being implied. Missing just one delivery will normally not be serious enough, but if non-delivery is serious enough to cast doubt on the proper performance of the rest of the agreement, repudiation may be implied. Thus, if Chan agreed to deliver 10 loads of gravel to Singh's building site and failed to deliver the first two on the specified days, this might well be considered a repudiation of the contract. Singh could then look for another source. See Table 9.1 for a summary of the results of a failure to perform.

Table 9.1 Result of Failure to Perform

Breach of minor term		Other party must perform but can seek damages	
Repudiation	Major refusal	Victim chooses to perform	Contract binding on both
		Victim chooses to discharge	Contract ends but victim can seek damages
Breach of major term	Major failure		Other party can treat contract as discharged and sue for bre--h
	Minor failure	Substantial performance	Other party must perform but can seek damages

DISCHARGE BY AGREEMENT

Contracts can be modified or ended by agreement

Just as the parties to a contract can agree to create contractual obligations, they can also agree to end or modify those obligations. This is referred to as **discharge by agreement**. Whether the intention of the parties is to merely modify the old agreement or to end it and substitute a new one, all the ingredients necessary to form a contract, including consensus and consideration, must be present.

CASE SUMMARY 9.7

Must Be Consideration to Support Change: *Gregorio v. Intrans-Corp.*[18]

Gregorio ordered a truck from Intrans conditional upon financing, which was arranged on 3 July 1984. The only condition was thus removed, creating a binding contract. When the truck was delivered on 2 August, Gregorio was required to sign a one-year limited warranty that excluded all other implied warranties and other liability for consequential damages for failure to perform.

The truck turned out to be a lemon, and when the company couldn't fix it, Gregorio sued to get his money back. It was now 1987. The company claimed to be protected by the limited warranty, but the Court held that this warranty was a modification of the original 12 May agreement. Since Gregorio had received no consideration for the change, he

---

18. (1994), 18 O.R. (3d) 527 (C.A.), additional reasons, [1994] O.J. No. 2834 (C.A.).

was not bound by it. Thus, the statutory protections set out in the *Sale of Goods Act* still applied to the purchase, and Gregorio was entitled to his money back as the truck was defective. (The *Sale of Goods Act* will be discussed in Chapter 10.)

DISCUSSION QUESTIONS

A contract can be modified by agreement, but it is vitally important that all the elements be present. In this case, consideration was missing and Gregorio was not affected by the changes. Would prior legal advice as to the enforceability of the one-year limited warranty have been beneficial to Intrans? How could Intrans have ensured that the limitation would be effective?

If both parties have something left to do under the original contract and the agreement to modify relieves them of their respective obligations, there is valid consideration on both sides to support the change. This is called **bilateral discharge** or mutual release. The problem arises where the discharge or modification is one-sided. Where one party performs its side, yet allows the other out of all or part of its obligations, the discharge, being unilateral, may not be binding because of lack of consideration. The original contract may still be enforceable. When a significant change is introduced that favours only one party, there may also be a problem with consideration. Lack of new consideration was the reason the limited warranty provision, agreed to later, did not bind Gregorio in Case Summary 9.7 discussed above. Of course, the consideration problem can be avoided by putting the agreement under seal. Note, however, that even when the discharge is entirely one-sided, the person being relieved of his obligation may be able to raise the defence of promissory estoppel if sued under the original agreement. In fact, a prime example where the principle of promissory estoppel arises is in the context of such one-sided discharges or modifications of contracts.

Modifications—must have consideration

Where the party benefiting from a modification agrees to do something extra to support the change (or discharge) of the contract, this is called **accord and satisfaction**. The accord refers to the agreement to change (or end) the old contract and the satisfaction is the extra consideration to be supplied by the party benefiting from the change (or discharge). For example, if Groves was renovating her house and paid Grubisich in advance to paint it, there would be a problem with lack of consideration if she simply allowed Grubisich to abandon the contract. But if Grubisich were to agree to do something extra, such as paint Groves' garage instead, there would be a new agreement (an accord) with added consideration (satisfaction), and the new arrangement would be binding.

Accord and satisfaction overcomes consideration problem

Sometimes the old contract is discharged by agreement and a new contract is substituted for it. This is often mistaken for a simple modification of the old contract. Whether a new agreement has been created or the old one modified will be determined by looking at the intention of the parties and what has been changed. The more important the provision changed, the more likely it is that a new agreement has been substituted for the old one. The difference can be important since it may affect whether various terms from the old agreement, such as exemption and penalty clauses, are carried over to the new one. If the original agreement was merely modified (and not discharged and substituted) then the clauses found in the original agreement continue to apply.

When the new agreement involves a new party being substituted for one of the original parties to the agreement, it is called a *novation*. Naturally, both parties

Novation involves new party but all must agree to the change

must agree to the substitution of one party for there to be a consensus. One party cannot unilaterally impose substitution of a party. It may be tempting to cancel a deal when a better one comes along, but if there is a binding contract it must be honoured even when the job has not yet been started.

When a debt is assumed by a new debtor, an issue that can arise is whether the original debtor is still liable if the new debtor fails to repay the indebtedness. When one sells one's home and the new purchaser assumes the mortgage, is the original debtor still indebted to the mortgagee? Or has novation occurred, thereby extinguishing the original debtor's obligation to pay? Madame Justice Wilson explains:

> [T]he burden of establishing novation is not easily met. The courts have established a three part test for determining if novation has occurred. It is set out in *Poulson v. Wuffsohn* (1890), 2 B.C.R. 39 as follows:
>
> 1. The new debtor must assume the complete liability;
> 2. The creditor must accept the new debtor as principal debtor and not merely as guarantor; and
> 3. The creditor must accept the new contract in full satisfaction and substitution for the old contract.[19]

Novation cancels the old contract, substituting it with the new

Must have consensus

It must be emphasized that whether the terms of the agreement or the parties to it are being changed, or the contract is being discharged, there must be complete agreement among all the parties before the new agreement becomes binding.

CASE SUMMARY 9.8

Accord and Satisfaction Can Overcome Significant Defects: *Vandekerkhove v. Litchfield*[20]

Mr. Litchfield borrowed $150 000 from Mr. Vandekerkhove. The agreement required payment of interest and a bonus, which, unknown to them, constituted a criminal rate of interest. Litchfield borrowed a further $145 000, and eventually these two loans plus the unpaid interest were consolidated into one loan for $318 250 at 12.5 percent interest secured by a mortgage on Litchfield's house.

Vandekerkhove subsequently tried to enforce the original bonus but couldn't because it was part of an illegal contract. This prompted the debtor, Litchfield, to bring this action to recover $23 250 of the consolidated loan since it represented the unpaid interest portion of that illegal contract. The trial Judge agreed, but on appeal the Court held that since the parties had renegotiated in good faith not being aware of the illegality, the new agreement was binding on them. There was an exchange of consideration on both sides supporting the modification, and the new interest rate was fair and reasonable.

SMALL BUSINESS PERSPECTIVE

This is an example of the principle of accord and satisfaction with consideration on both sides supporting a renegotiated contract. Especially when loans are being consolidated or the creditor is forgiving part of a loan, the debtor best ensure that some new consideration is being given to the creditor. Otherwise the original contract and original debt may still be payable.

---

19. *National Trust Co. v. Mead*, [1990] 2 S.C.R. 410 at pp. 431–432.

20. (1995), 1 B.C.L.R. (3d) 70 (C.A.), leave to appeal to S.C.C. refused, [1995] S.C.C.A. No. 131.

Contractual Terms

Most contracts, by their nature, will end upon proper performance. However, sometimes they involve an ongoing relationship, with no provision to bring that relationship to an end. In these circumstances, the parties can usually terminate the contract simply by giving the other reasonable notice. Often, the contract will provide for its own termination, usually by specifying a particular period of notice that must be given, and that provision will be binding subject to contrary legislation. In employment relationships and residential tenancy arrangements, for example, such termination provisions must comply with the governing statutes.

When the contract itself specifies that some event or requirement must be satisfied before the parties are bound by it, this is properly referred to as a **condition precedent** but is more commonly called a *"subject to" clause*. For example, if Nishiama were to agree to buy Fafara's house, subject to the sale of her own house, the contract is conditional on that event. Thus, if Nishiama fails to sell her house, she is not obligated to go through with any agreement for the purchase of Fafara's house. When such a condition precedent is not satisfied, there is no contractual obligation.

A **condition subsequent** is a term that brings the obligations of the parties to an end upon some event or condition taking place. Whereas conditions precedent determine when the obligations between the parties begin, conditions subsequent determine when they end. For example, if Halford agreed to pay Perron $400 per month for custodial services "until Perron ceases to be a full-time student," this term is a condition subsequent. Halford will be obligated to pay only until Perron finishes school.

Sometimes the contract anticipates some catastrophic event, such as a riot, invasion, earthquake, or flood that will interfere with the performance of the contract. This is referred to as a *force majeure* **clause**. Such terms might set out the consequences—such as which party will bear the risk of loss—alternatively, they may provide for discharge of the contract. When catastrophic events take place and are not anticipated in the contract, they will likely cause the contract to be discharged by frustration, as discussed below.

Of course, when such terms are not included in the contract, the parties can always agree to end, modify, or substitute obligations with a new agreement, as discussed above. Contracts can also end by operation of law, as would be the case when one of the parties dies, becomes insane, or is declared bankrupt.

FRUSTRATION

Sometimes some unexpected event (out of the control of the parties) makes performance of the contract impossible. For example, where a construction firm agrees to repair a bridge but the bridge is destroyed in a storm before the repair work begins, performance has become impossible. In such circumstances, the contract is considered discharged through frustration. **Frustration** occurs when some unforeseen, outside event (out of the control of either party) interferes with the performance of the contract, making the basic object of the agreement unobtainable.

It is easy to understand frustration when performance of the contract is made impossible, such as when a person agrees to paint a house that is destroyed in a fire before the job can be performed. Difficulties arise because the courts have

Contract may provide for its own discharge

Conditions precedent determine when obligations to perform contract begins

Conditions subsequent determine when contractual obligations end

Frustrating event may end contract

expanded the principle to also cover situations where the foundation of the contract is destroyed. Performance may still be technically possible, but the whole nature of the relationship has changed, making performance something essentially different from what the parties anticipated.

In the case of *Krell v. Henry*,[21] the parties agreed to the rental of an apartment from which the tenant could view the coronation parade of Edward VII. A small deposit was paid at the time the contract was entered into, but because of the King's sudden illness, the coronation parade was cancelled before the balance was paid. It was still possible to occupy the flat, but to require the tenant to do so with no coronation parade to watch would be something essentially different from what the parties had in mind when they entered into the contract. Although performance of the contract was possible in a literal sense, it was no longer possible to obtain the purpose or object of the contract itself. Thus, the contract was discharged through frustration.

Even injury, causing an employee to be unable to perform her work, can be a frustrating event, as was determined by the Court in the *Demuynck* case.[22] Having benefits such as long term disability coverage is a safeguard that employees should seek to secure, for damages for wrongful dismissal may be denied if one is terminated following an injury that prevents one from performing the job. (Note, however, that human rights legislation may offer some relief as employers have a duty to accommodate disabilities, to some extent.)

CASE SUMMARY 9.9

Contract Is Frustrated Even Though Performance Still Possible: *KBK No. 138 Ventures Ltd. v. Canada Safeway Ltd.*[23]

Canada Safeway entered an agreement to sell property to KBK. At the time, the property was zoned for high-density development. But when the city rezoned the property to a much lower density, this destroyed KBK's plans for redevelopment. KBK demanded the return of the $150 000 deposit paid, claiming frustration. Safeway argued that the essential nature of the contract was for the purchase of the property and that remained intact, but the Court found frustration and ordered the return of the deposit. In this case the whole substance of the contract had been radically altered by the unanticipated intervention of the city in rezoning the property. The change struck at the root of the contract, fundamentally changing its nature and thus frustrating it.

SMALL BUSINESS PERSPECTIVE

If certain factors are crucial to one's participation in a contract (such as the zoning in the above the case) parties can make performance conditional upon those factors being present. These key terms should be brought to the attention of the lawyer drafting the contract.

---

21. [1903] 2 K.B. 740 (C.A.).

22. *Demuynck v. Agentis Information Services Inc.*, [2003] B.C.J. No. 113 (S.C.).

23. (2000), 185 D.L.R. (4th) 650 (B.C.C.A.).

Care should be taken not to confuse frustration with shared mistake, discussed in the preceding chapter. With shared mistake, there is no contract because the subject matter had been destroyed before the contract was entered into. Frustration deals with situations where the problems arise after the formation of the contract. If a ship that is the subject of a contract is destroyed before the contract is made, the parties are making a mistake assuming the ship to still be functioning. But if the ship is destroyed after the contract is made, the contract is discharged through frustration.

Shared mistake not the same as frustration

Frustration commonly arises in the following circumstances:

Circumstances constituting frustration

1. Performance of a contract becomes impossible because the subject matter of the agreement is destroyed or is otherwise unusable. Contracts may be frustrated when a person who has agreed to supply personal services becomes ill or dies, or when the specific article that formed the object of the contract is destroyed before the agreement can be performed.

In the case of *Taylor v. Caldwell*,[24] there was an agreement between the parties to rent out a music hall. The hall burned down six days before the performance was to take place. The Court held that the contract was discharged through frustration.

2. An event that forms the basis of a contract fails to take place. An example is the cancellation of the coronation parade in *Krell v. Henry* cited earlier.

3. Acts of the government interfere with performance. Government policy can interfere with the performance of a contract in several different ways. A contract with someone in another country may become unlawful or impossible to perform because of a declaration of war; contracts involving the manufacture and production of particular drugs or foodstuffs may become illegal by statute. A contract may anticipate the acquisition of a licence or permit that the government does not grant. Note as well that all levels of government have the power to expropriate the property that may form the basis of a contract. The above is not intended to be a complete list, but most of the frustrating events that do take place fall into one of these three categories.

Circumstances Not Constituting Frustration

Self-induced frustration involves one of the parties causing—or, if it is within his control, failing to prevent—the frustrating event. It may appear to be frustration, but self-induced frustration is simply treated as a breach of contract. For example, if Moser has a contract to build an apartment building for Wu but the city refuses to grant Moser a building permit, we would expect the contract to be frustrated. However, if the building permit is refused because Moser failed to submit the appropriate plans as required by city bylaw, the frustration is self-induced. Moser is responsible for the misfortune and the refusal of the city to grant a permit will not provide an excuse for Moser's failure to perform the contract.

Self-induced frustration is breach

Secondly, where the parties have anticipated the frustrating event or have provided for one of the parties to bear the risk of such an eventuality, these contractual terms (often called *force majeure* clauses) will prevail. The parties will not be able to claim that their agreement has been frustrated. It is only when the event is an unforeseen interference, not caused by either party, that the courts are willing

Must be unanticipated to be frustration

---

24. (1863) 3 B. & S. 826 (Q.B.).

to find frustration. In *Naylor Group v. Ellis-Don Construction*,[25] for example, the doctrine of frustration was found not to apply because the parties had made specific provision for the supervening circumstances. The defendant contractor had inserted a clause in the contract stipulating it could object to awarding the subcontract to Naylor if it had a good reason. When it failed to utilize that option and awarded the contract to Naylor (despite Naylor's obligation to hire employees from a union other than the IBEW) it could no longer claim that Naylor's inability to hire IBEW workers was a frustrating event.

Increased difficulty is not frustration

Increased cost is not frustration

Finally, the contract is not frustrated if the unforeseen outside event only makes the performance of the contract more costly or more difficult. If a farmer agrees to sell 50 boxes of Golden Delicious apples to a buyer and then his crop is destroyed by hail, this is not frustration unless the terms of the contract specifically stated that the apples were to come from his trees. If the source of the apples is not a term of the contract, the farmer can simply obtain them from another farmer and thus fulfill his contractual obligation, albeit at a higher cost.

In the case of *Tsakiroglou Co. v. Noblee & Thorl G.m.b.H.*,[26] delivery of a cargo from a port in the Sudan on the east coast of Africa to Germany became more onerous when the Suez War closed the canal. The seller claimed that the contract was frustrated. The Court, however, found the seller liable for breach, holding that although it was more difficult and costly to ship the cargo around Africa, the essential nature of the contract remained intact and frustration did not apply. Note that the result would likely have been different had the parties specified delivery through the Suez Canal, since using that route was now impossible.

CASE SUMMARY 9.10

Frustrating Event to Be Unforeseen and Outside of Parties' Control: *Dinicola v. Huang & Danczkay Properties*[27]

Huang & Danczkay Properties sold certain condominiums before they were built, in fact, even before they had finalized the purchase of the property. In the sales contracts there was a clause providing that if municipal approval was not obtained, the developers could terminate the agreement and return deposits paid without further liability up to 30 June 1988. Although things looked as if they were going well, negotiations deteriorated, and the permit to build was eventually refused. This action for damages was brought by a number of the purchasers against the developers for breach of contract. The developers argued that the contract was discharged by frustration because of the failure of the municipality to grant the permit to build.

This position was rejected by the Courts for two reasons. The parties anticipated the possibility that the development might not be approved and provided for an escape for the developer, at least until June 30. Frustration must be an outside event that was not anticipated by either party. Here, the developers not only anticipated that this might take place but provided for it in the contract.

---

25. [2001] 2 S.C.R. 943.

26. [1962] A.C. 93 (H.L.).

27. (1998) 29 O.R. (3d) 161 (Ont. C.A.); aff'g (1996), 29 O.R. (3d) 161 (Ont. Ct. G.D.)

Secondly, the developers had caused the situation that led to the refusal of the permit. In the final stages of the negotiations, the developers' representative wrote to the municipal council declaring that they would not negotiate further. As a result, the permit was refused. Because the letter precipitated the refusal, the Court found that this was an example of self-induced frustration.

To find frustration, performance must be impossible or the foundation or purpose of the contract must be fundamentally or radically changed. Lack of profits or funding will not frustrate a contract. Thus in the *Korol v. Saskatchewan Federation of Police Officers* case,[28] the federation's inability to pay wages did not frustrate the contract. Lack of financial ability alone will not establish frustration and so, the employer was held liable for wrongful dismissal when it terminated Korol on that basis.

Effect of Frustration

The major problem associated with frustration is to determine who shall suffer the loss when the contract is discharged. Under common law, the general principle was "Let the loss lie where it falls." In other words, the party who had done work or provided services before the frustrating event would bear the loss and could not seek compensation from the other party. Similarly, money already paid was lost. Note, however, that where payment was due before the frustrating event, that payment still had to be paid. This is illustrated by *Chandler v. Webster,*[29] a case that also involved the rental of a flat for viewing King Edward VII's coronation parade. But in this case the entire rent of just over £141 was due and payable in advance, but only £100 had actually been paid. Because the principle was that the loss should lie where it fell when a contract was frustrated, the tenant could not get his money back. In addition, because the sum not yet paid was owed before the frustrating event, that sum had to be paid as well.

Problems with deposits

This position was considered unsatisfactory and the House of Lords made a significant change in the *Fibrosa* case,[30] which required the return of a deposit paid by a Polish company to a British manufacturer after the outbreak of war frustrated their contract. Because the Polish company had received no benefit under the contract, it was entitled to the return of its deposit. This represents the common law position today but still leads to some unsatisfactory results. The whole deposit or nothing has to be returned, depending on whether any benefit was received.

Where a benefit has been obtained by one party prior to the frustrating event, legislation in most jurisdictions in the form of the *Frustrated Contracts Act*[31] now permits the court to order that party to pay the other for it.

Legislation allows deposits to be split

Where a deposit has been paid, the legislation usually allows the court to take into consideration the costs that have been incurred in preparation to perform the contract, whether or not the other party has received a benefit. The court can now apportion that deposit on the basis of the costs incurred and the benefits

---

28. (2000), 198 Sask. R. 181 (Q.B.).
29. [1904] 1 K.B. 493 (C.A.).
30. *Fibrosa Spolka Akeyjna v. Fairbairn Lawson Combe Barbouk Ltd.*, [1943] A.C. 32 (H.L.).
31. Such legislation exists in all common law provinces with the exception of Nova Scotia.

received (see Table 9.2). In British Columbia and the Yukon, such costs can be apportioned between the parties whether or not a deposit is involved.

Table 9.2 Effect of *Frustrated Contracts Act*

	Impact on Agent's Actual Authority	Impact on Agent's Apparent Authority
Frustrated contract	No deposit paid or payable With deposit	–Contract discharged –Deposit used to pay for benefit received & contract discharged –Deposit split to cover expenses & contract discharged –No benefit received / costs incurred, deposit returned & contract discharged

Other statutes also modify the common law application of the frustration principle. In common law, frustration does not apply to leases, but most jurisdictions have clearly stated that frustration applies to residential leases.[32] British Columbia extends the application of frustration to commercial leases as well.

CASE SUMMARY 9.11

Reimbursement for Expenses Where Contract Frustrated: *Can-Truck Transportation Ltd. v. Fenton's Auto Paint Shop Ltd.*[33]

The plaintiff's truck was sent to the defendant for repairs after an accident. Repairs worth some $28 000 were completed when a fire destroyed both the shop and the truck, thus frustrating the repair contract. The Ontario *Frustrated Contracts Act* provided that when funds were paid (as with a deposit) or were payable before the frustrating event took place, they could be used to reimburse for expenses incurred. The Court found that payment for repairs was payable prior to the fire, thus the plaintiff had to reimburse the company for the expenses it had incurred in repairing the vehicle even though it had been destroyed.

DISCUSSION QUESTIONS

Here the plaintiff ended up with a destroyed truck, but still had to pay for repairs notwithstanding that it received no benefit from those repairs. Is there a better method for dealing with unforeseen events?

[32.] See, for example, Alberta's *Residential Tenancies Act*,R.S.A. 2000 c. R-17.1, s. 40.

[33.] (1993), 101 D.L.R. (4th) 562 (Ont. C.A.).

When goods are being sold, the *Sale of Goods Act* provides that if the goods, through no fault of the parties, perish before the risk passes to the purchaser, the contract is voided. The effect is that the contract is not binding on the purchaser, and any moneys paid have to be returned.

REMEDIES FOR BREACH OF CONTRACT

Several examples of remedies provided to parties involved in contractual disputes have already been discussed. *Rescission* deals with problems with the formation of a contract and focuses on restoring the parties to their original position. *Rectification* interprets and corrects the terms of contracts, whereas *damages* compensate a victim who has been misled or pressured into the contract. The following discussion looks at remedies available where a party has failed to properly perform its obligations under the contract.

Damages in contract law designed to compensate

Damages

The most common remedy for a breach of contract is an order that the breaching party pay damages. Damages are amounts of money assessed by the court and designed to compensate victims for their losses.[34] The object is to put the victim, as near as monetary compensation can, into the position he would have been in had the contract been properly performed. Thus, in contract law, damages look forward, whereas in tort actions, damages look backward and try to put the victim in the position he would have been in had the tort never taken place. For example, in a contract action, if a person bought defective paint from a supplier that blistered when put on the walls, necessitating repainting, the court would not only award the cost of the paint as damage. The court would also take into consideration the amount it would cost for a painter to scrape the blistered paint off and repaint the house. The court would then order the vendor to pay a sum sufficient to put the purchaser in the position he would have been in if the paint had not been defective.

Victim of breach compensated as if contract had been properly performed

---

CASE SUMMARY 9.12

Damages to Look Forward, Not Backward: *Ed Learn Ford Sales Ltd. v. Giovannone*[35]

Giovannone traded his Lincoln car in for a truck at Ed Learn Ford Sales Ltd., receiving a $9200 trade-in allowance. The dealer resold the car before it discovered the car had been stolen before Giovannone acquired it. The dealer paid $6175.50 to the insurance company to cover what had been paid to the legitimate owner on the original loss. The dealer then sued Giovannone for the $9200 trade-in allowance. But the Court awarded the dealer only the $6175.50 paid to the insurance company. The Judge quoted from *Wertheim v. Chicoutimi Pulp Co.*:"[I]t is the general intention of the law that, in giving

---

34. See *Hamilton v. Open Window Bakery Ltd.*, [2004] 1 S.C.R. 303, which confirms that where a party who has breached a contract had a variety of ways of fulfilling its obligations, damages will be based on the least expensive method of performance.

35. (1990), 74 D.L.R. (4th) 761 (Ont. Gen. Div.).

damages for breach of contract, the party complaining should, so far as it can be done by money, be placed in the same position as he would have been in if the contract had been performed."[36]

DISCUSSION QUESTIONS

What steps could the dealer have taken to prevent this situation? Even though the dealer recovered the amount paid to the insurance company, it still had to pursue legal action to recover that sum.

Damages awarded may be special, general, or punitive

When the damages awarded are to cover specific costs and expenses, they are called *special damages*, but when the funds awarded are an estimate of what has been lost or what will be lost, they are called *general damages*. The calculation of damages may be based on the shortfall from what was expected from proper performance, but sometimes damages are designed to cover what has been lost because reliance was placed on the performance of the contract. Only in rare circumstances involving particularly vexatious conduct will courts award punitive damages for breach of contract.[37] Punitive damages are intended to punish the offending party rather than compensate the injured and may result in a considerably higher award.

Limitations on Recoverable Damages

Not all losses can be recovered

Although damages are designed to compensate a person for injuries suffered, not all losses are recoverable. Remoteness and mitigation are two limitations on the recoverability of damages. As well, the parties are free to place terms in the contract itself limiting the damages recoverable or specifying other courses of action in the event of breach.

REMOTENESS

The important case of *Hadley v. Baxendale*[38] involved the shipping of a broken crankshaft from a steam engine to be used as a pattern for the manufacture of a new one. The shipper was asked to send it quickly but failed to do so. Unknown to the shipper, the plaintiff's entire plant was shut down while waiting for the crankshaft. This caused great expense to the plaintiff, who sued the shipper for lost profits. The shipper claimed that he could not be responsible for the unusual loss because he had no knowledge of it. The Court used the reasonable person test to determine the extent of the shipper's responsibility for damages and held that the shipper was responsible only for the usual damages that could be expected if the contract were breached. The shipper was thus not liable for the plaintiff's lost profits.

The principle that has developed from this and other cases is essentially that a breaching party is responsible only for those damages that, at the time the

---

[36.] [1911] A.C. 301 at 307 (P.C.).

[37.] *Whiten v. Pilot Insurance Co.*, [2002] 1 S.C.R. 595, has become a leading authority on punitive damages. In contract cases, punitive damages should not be awarded in the absence of an independent actionable wrong.

[38.] (1854), 156 E.R. 145 (Ex. Ct.).

contract was entered into, seem a likely outcome if the contract were breached. Thus, the breaching party is responsible not only for the normally expected damages that flow from a breach, but also for any unusual damages resulting from special circumstances that were communicated to it at the time of the contract. In short, the breaching party is responsible in contract law for any damages that can be reasonably foreseen at the time the contract is entered into.

One area where the problem of remoteness often arises is in a claim for damages to compensate for lost profits. Applying this principle, the breaching party will be responsible only for the loss of ordinary profits that could have been expected given his knowledge of the business. In *Horne v. Midland Ry*[39] the defendants were one day late in the delivery of a shipment of shoes, causing the merchant to lose an opportunity to sell the shoes at an exceptionally high price. The shipper knew only that the merchant would have to take the shoes back if they were late, not that an exceptional profit would be lost. The defendants were not responsible for the unusually high lost profit since they were not aware of those special circumstances, and such a loss was not reasonably foreseeable.

Must pay reasonably anticipated losses

When a contract is breached, damages are awarded to compensate for economic losses. Courts have only recently shown a willingness to award monetary compensation for mental distress. These situations are generally limited to cases where some non-monetary benefit was the subject matter of the contract, such as a disrupted vacation or cruise.[40]

General damages compensate for
• economic loss
• even mental distress (recently)

MITIGATION

Victims of a breach are sometimes tempted to do nothing when a contract is breached, allowing damages to accumulate on the assumption that they are the responsibility of—and therefore will be paid by—the breaching party. This is bad practice for several reasons. Victims of breach have a duty to **mitigate** the damages, meaning they must do what they can to keep those damages as low as possible. Also, if they fail to mitigate or minimize losses, courts may actually make a deduction from damages equal to the amount attributable to the failure to mitigate.

Victims must mitigate their losses

The failure to mitigate is a common problem in wrongful-dismissal actions. A person who has been wrongfully dismissed has a right to sue but must make a reasonable effort to find other employment. Damages in such actions are based on the difference between how much notice the employee should have been given as opposed to how much he actually received. If the employer can show that the dismissed employee failed to look for another job, the damages will be reduced by the amount he should have earned during that notice period. For example, if the court concludes that the employee could have found a job, had he looked, after three months, he will recover damages equal to three months' pay notwithstanding that the reasonable notice period was nine months long.

Failure to mitigate may result in damages

Note also that the obligation to mitigate means simply that the victim of the breach must take all reasonable steps to minimize losses suffered. That person is not required to take personal risks or to incur unreasonable expense in the process. Reasonable costs associated with mitigation, such as the cost of flying to another city to attend an interview, can be recovered from the breaching party.

Reasonable costs associated with mitigation are recoverable

---

[39]. (1873), L.R. 8 C.P. 131 (C.P.).

[40]. *Jarvis v. Swan Tours Ltd.*, [1973] 1 All E.R. 71 (C.A.). Here, the vacationer was awarded compensation for the loss of the enjoyment he had been promised. Awards in the travel industry are normally limited to the cost of the holiday, or a portion thereof.

Litigation is expensive and a drain on all parties. Once involved in a court action, it becomes unlikely that the parties will be interested in doing business with each other again. Disputes may be better resolved through negotiation—or with the help of third parties, as with mediation. Alternative measures for resolving disputes should be exhausted. Suing and seeking damages should be viewed as a last resort.

CONTRACTUAL LIMITATIONS

Remedies set out in contract

It is possible for a contract to set out the consequences in the event of breach. The consequences may be quite varied. The contract may call for mediation or arbitration to resolve disputes and determine compensation. The contract might state the maximum amount of compensation to be paid by the breaching party. Businesses often post signs indicating that they are not responsible for losses over a specified amount. Failure to make an instalment payment will often trigger an **acceleration clause**, which makes the entire outstanding debt due and payable immediately. Where the contract involves a consumer transaction, the operation of acceleration clauses are often restricted by consumer protection legislation.[41]

Liquidated damages are specified in contract

When the contract specifies the damages to be paid, they are called **liquidated damages**, and the courts will normally enforce such terms once liability has been determined. Where the amount is actually prepaid with the provision that the funds are to be forfeited in the event of a breach, it is called a **deposit**. For example, to secure the purchase of an automobile, the vendor will usually require the buyer to pay a substantial deposit when ordering. If the purchaser fails to go through with the deal when the car arrives, the vendor can retain the deposit.

Deposit is forfeited—down payment is not

It is important to distinguish between deposits and down payments. Deposits are to be forfeited in the event of a breach, whereas a **down payment** is just the first payment and may have to be returned. Of course, from a practical point of view, once a down payment is made, it may be used as a lever to force performance. But if the matter comes to trial, the court will order the return of the down payment, usually setting off the actual damages to be paid against it. Regardless of what the term is called, it is the provision requiring the forfeiture of the prepayment that will cause the court to treat it as a deposit.

The temptation to take a large deposit entails significant risk. To qualify as liquidated damages, a deposit must be an honest attempt by the parties to estimate the damages that would be suffered if the contract were breached. Too large a prepayment becomes an unreasonable penalty rather than liquidated damages and must be returned.

[41.] See, for example, Alberta's *Fair Trading Act*, R.S.A. 2000, c. F-2, s. 71, which requires written notice of a default to be served on a borrower, and the passage of 10 days from such service, before the acceleration clause takes effect.

A $1000 deposit on a new car might be fair in view of the cost of advertising, the time lost, the extra interest payments, and so on. But a $10 000 deposit on a $15 000 car is no longer an attempt to compensate for possible loss or injury, but becomes an attempt to punish the breaching party for failure to go through with the contract. A penalty clause, if excessive, is unconscionable and void. Such a penalty would have to be returned subject to an action to establish the actual loss. Thus, demanding too large a deposit defeats itself. Even when no prepayment is involved, a liquidated damages clause may be challenged if the amount involved is exorbitant and the object is to unreasonably punish rather than to compensate.

Deposit must be reasonable

CASE SUMMARY 9.13

Liquidated Damages Must Be Reasonable: *Meunier v. Cloutier*[42]

When Cloutier returned to Timmins with his wife, he purchased a hotel only a block away from the one he had sold to Meunier four years earlier. In doing so, he violated a non-competition clause prohibiting him from participating in the hotel business in Timmins for five years following the sale to Meunier. The original contract required him to pay $50 000 for such a breach as liquidated damages, and Meunier brought this action to recover that amount.

The Court determined that on its face, the clause was not a penalty; the amount, time, and geographical area were all reasonable from the point of view of when it was made. Nor was the public interest offended. But, following the Supreme Court of Canada precedent in *H.F. Clarke Ltd. v. Thermidaire Corp. Ltd.*,[43] the Court held that when such a lump sum was involved, it had to be satisfied that the amount was "reasonable in the circumstances." Given the minor nature of the breach and absence of evidence that the plaintiff suffered any damage, requiring Cloutier to pay the $50 000 in these circumstances would be unconscionable. Therefore the non-competition clause was a penalty and unenforceable.

DISCUSSION QUESTIONS

While the courts may be willing to enforce predetermined damages, if the amount is unreasonable, the clause will be characterized a penalty clause and be deemed unenforceable. In this case, the non-competition clause was valid; it was the damages portion of that provision that was unacceptable. Should restraint thus be exercised when imposing penalties in the form of liquidated damages? Would legal advice be beneficial in determining an appropriate sum?

Equitable Remedies

The following are examples of remedies that have been developed by the Courts of Chancery to deal with special situations in which the ordinary remedy of

---

42. (1984), 46 O.R. (2d) 188 (H.C.J.).
43. [1976] 1 S.C.R. 319.

damages would not be adequate. Note that these remedies are discretionary and will be granted only when the judge thinks it right and fair to do so.

SPECIFIC PERFORMANCE

Specific performance occurs when the court orders the defaulting party to live up to the terms of the contract. Where a developer signs up agreements to buy several adjacent properties, and one property owner refuses to go through with the deal, it would be appropriate to obtain a court order for specific performance. The developer won't be assisted by an award of damages if its goal is to build a shopping centre on the total parcel; it wants the court to order that property owner to transfer the property at the agreed-upon price. But if the same developer ordered a number of new trucks from a dealer who then refused to deliver them, specific performance would not be appropriate as equivalent vehicles could be obtained elsewhere. The appropriate remedy would be damages, and they would be assessed on the basis of the extra cost of getting the vehicles from another dealer. Only if the trucks were unique and not available from some other source might specific performance be available.

The courts will not order the defaulting party to perform a contract that requires personal service. If the above developer were to contract with a famous performer to sing at a concert celebrating the opening of the shopping mall and the performer then refused to perform, the court would not order specific performance. Similarly, the courts will not award specific performance as a remedy in any situation that would require close supervision to ensure that the contract is properly performed. Nor will specific performance be available where it would hurt a third party.

On the theory that all land is unique, the courts in the past have been willing to award specific performance whenever the parties to the purchase of land breached their contract. The Supreme Court of Canada has indicated, however, that contracts dealing with the purchase of land will now be treated like any other contract, limiting the availability of specific performance to those situations where damages are inappropriate.[44]

Side notes:
Court orders defaulting party to perform its obligations

Courts will not force performance of contracts for personal services

Specific performance only available if damages are inappropriate

---

CASE SUMMARY 9.14

Specific Performance Ordered Despite Presence of Deposit Clauses: *Romfo v. 1216393 Ontario Inc.*[45]

The vendors of several lots appealed an order of specific performance, which demanded that the sales proceed. The prices of these lots had increased substantially, and the vendors made deals with new purchasers to sell the lots at the higher prices. The vendors argued that since the initial contracts contained deposit clauses, stipulating that if a party breached the contract the deposit would be forfeited, the purchasers would have to be content with the return of their respective deposits. In other words, the vendors argued damages were limited by these "liquidated damages" clauses to the deposits paid earlier.

---

44. *Semelhago v. Paramadevan*, [1996] 2 S.C.R. 415 (S.C.C.).

45. [2008] B.C.J. No. 745 (B.C.C.A.).

The Court of Appeal, however, dismissed the appeal. The parties to the contract could not have intended the deposit clauses to apply where the vendors deliberately deceived the purchasers, by holding onto the deposits while they applied for development approval and then breaching the contracts once approval was granted. The deposit clauses were severed and the contracts were enforced. The vendors were required to transfer the lots to the initial purchasers at the initial price.

SMALL BUSINESS PERSPECTIVE

Here the vendors fundamentally breached the contracts for self-serving reasons. In light of the vendors' questionable conduct, the purchasers were not restricted to seeking damages. This case demonstrates that equitable remedies may be granted to parties who come to the courts with "clean hands."

INJUNCTION

Specific performance involves a court order to do something (to perform the contract) whereas an injunction usually involves an order to refrain from some offensive conduct. In the above example involving personal service by a singer, the court would not order the performer to fulfill the contract by singing at the concert; but the aggrieved party may be able to secure an injunction preventing the performer from performing somewhere else on the day she was to sing at the shopping mall's concert. The injunction is not limited to contractual disputes; it may be available in any situation in which wrongful conduct is involved.

In rare circumstances, the courts may issue a mandatory injunction when a person does something to violate a contractual term and thereby creates an ongoing problem. Striking workers involved in an illegal work stoppage are often ordered to stop breaching their contract and return to work. Another example might involve a shopping centre that erects signs exceeding the permitted height limit set out in a restrictive covenant or a municipal bylaw. The courts may order the shopping centre to remove the sign or reduce it to the permitted height. Such mandatory injunctions are not common.

As with specific performance, there are many instances in which the courts will refuse to issue an injunction. The courts are reluctant to order an injunction that would make it impossible for the person defaulting on the contractual agreement to earn a living. A court might well enforce, by injunction, a term requiring an employee not to work for a competitor for three years upon leaving, but would not enforce a term preventing that employee from working for anyone for three years. Similarly, the courts will not issue an injunction when damages provide a sufficient remedy. An injunction is designed not to punish someone for breaching a contract, but to prevent further injury. An injunction will also not be awarded where it will cause harm to a third party.

An injunction is sometimes ordered even before there has been a trial on the issues. If an employee leaves and works for a competitor, it is important to get an injunction right away and sort out the merits of the dispute later. This is called an **interlocutory injunction**, and is issued by the court when some ongoing injury will increase the damage done to the person seeking the interlocutory injunction. When waiting for the trial to determine the matter is unacceptable, granting an interlocutory injunction becomes the preferable alternative.

Courts may order breaching conduct to stop

• **but not where a person can no longer earn a living**

• **but not where damages are more appropriate**

• **but not where it would hurt a third party**

Interlocutory injunction issued before the trial

ACCOUNTING

It is often difficult for the victim of the breach to determine just what kind of injuries he or she has suffered, especially when the offending party has taken advantage of some opportunities or rights belonging to the victim. This can happen when there is a fiduciary relationship between the contracting parties, that is, a relationship in which the person breaching the contract has a duty to act in the best interests of the other party. In these circumstances, the court can order that the defaulting party disclose all financial dealings and records so that the injured party can determine what he or she is entitled to claim. In some circumstances the court will then order the offending party to pay over to the injured party all or a portion of the profits made from the wrongful conduct. So the court, instead of awarding damages on the basis of what has been lost by the victim, awards damages on the basis of what has been wrongfully obtained by the breaching party.

Court may order accounting and require profits to be paid over

QUANTUM MERUIT

In some situations, the contract is breached when only part of the work has been done and before the amount agreed to in the contract is due and payable to the injured party. In these circumstances, the courts have the power to award compensation for the value of work that has been done on the basis of *quantum meruit*. *Quantum meruit* is the principle that allows the supplier of a service to collect a reasonable fee, even when no price had been agreed upon. Note that only the victim of the breach can claim compensation on the basis of *quantum meruit*. The courts are extremely reluctant to grant any compensation for the breaching party's partial performance of the agreement, unless the contractual obligations have been substantially performed. Sometimes partial payment is payable before completion, and in that case, even the breaching party can collect.

Court may order payment for part performance

If a contractor has agreed to build a house with payment due upon completion of the job and refuses to continue after completing half, he will not be successful in claiming compensation for what he has done. He should finish the job. But if he has finished half the project and the owner of the property with whom he has contracted refuses to let him continue, the contractor, being the innocent party, will be able to claim compensation for the work that has been done under the principle of *quantum meruit*. Only where the contract called for partial payments at different stages of completion will the breaching party be able to collect those payments due before the breach.

Some general requirements must be met before the courts will grant an equitable remedy. If there has been **laches**, an undue delay on the part of the person seeking the equitable remedy, the courts can refuse to grant the remedy. The plaintiff will still be able to pursue any common law remedy, such as damages, without penalty for delay—provided the action is brought within the limitation period. The courts can also refuse to award an equitable remedy in any situation in which it would cause undue hardship to the parties or to some other person or would be inappropriate for any other reason. A person seeking equity must come to the court with **clean hands**, meaning the remedy will be denied when the person seeking the equitable remedy is also guilty of some wrongdoing. These requirements apply to all equitable remedies.

Equitable remedies are discretionary

• unavailable if hardship caused

• only available if claimant applies with clean hands

• unavailable if claim unduly delayed

Equitable Remedies Are Not Always Available: *Island Properties Ltd. v. Entertainment Enterprises Ltd.*[46]

Entertainment Enterprises Limited and Denis Galway made arrangements to sell property through one real estate agent and then made similar arrangements with another. Two different purchasers acting through the two different agents accepted the offer to sell. The Court found that both were valid and that the property had been sold to both purchasers. The property was transferred to Pegasus; Island Property, which had accepted first, sued for specific performance.

At trial, the Judge ordered that the property be returned by Pegasus and transferred to Island Properties. But the Appeal Court ordered that the property be returned to Pegasus. Pegasus was a completely innocent third party, and an equitable remedy cannot be given where it will cause harm to such an innocent party. Because the property had been conveyed to the innocent Pegasus, it could not be taken back. Island Properties was limited to a remedy of damages for breach.

SMALL BUSINESS PERSPECTIVE

This case illustrates the limitations placed on equitable remedies. Even when one's action is successful, the preferred remedy may not be available.

Another factor that may affect the right of the victim of a breach of contract to obtain any remedy is the limitations legislation. The limitation periods outlined in these statutes apply to any action brought to court including contract claims, with the result that once the limitation period has expired, none of the remedies discussed in this chapter will be available to the victim of the breach.

Time limits

Finally, it should be noted that when a judgment or an equitable remedy has been awarded and a defendant refuses to comply, the defendant may be held in contempt of court and can be jailed for contempt, although this is extremely unlikely. The remedies to enforce a judgment are available to the victim of a breach of contract as well.

Contempt

[46] (1986), 58 Nfld. & P.E.I.R. 151 (C.A.).

SUMMARY

Discharge of contracts

- Can come to an end through performance, breach, agreement, or frustration

Performance

- When properly tendered but refused, contract may be discharged
- When payment is tendered but refused, the creditor must bear the cost of its collection

Breach

- Breached condition—the victim may treat the contract as discharged and sue
- Breached warranty—contract is still binding but the victim can sue for damages
- Anticipatory breach—victim can treat the contract as discharged immediately or wait for performance (and later sue) but is bound by choice

Agreement

- Contract may provide for its own end; the agreed-upon method for termination is effective in ending the contract
- Condition precedent—obligations to perform arise if the condition is fulfilled
- Condition subsequent—obligations exist and continue until condition is fulfilled
- Liquidated damages—parties may agree in advance as to sum payable in event of breach
- Deposit, if forfeitable, regarded as liquidated damages

Frustration

- Performance impossible or fundamentally changed
- Monies advanced may be apportioned to compensate for expenses or losses incurred
- Self-induced frustration is breach of contract

Remedies

- Damages paid to compensate the victim
- Damages limited to what was reasonably foreseeable
- Damages must be reduced or mitigated by victim
- Deposits or liquidated damages set out in contract must be reasonable, or treated as a penalty provision—courts do not enforce penalty clauses
- Specific performance requires the breaching party to fulfill agreement
- Injunction—a court order to stop conduct that breaches the contract
- Accounting—requires disclosure of information so other party can assess extent of damages
- *Quantum meruit*—an equitable remedy requiring payment of a fair sum, equal to what the goods or services are reasonably worth

QUESTIONS

1. Describe the various ways in which a contractual relationship can come to an end.

2. Under what circumstances would a breaching party who had partially performed the terms of the contract be entitled to receive part payment?

3. Describe the differences between a condition and a warranty. Why is the distinction significant?

4. When might the victim of a breach of a condition lose the right to treat the contract as discharged?

5. What constitutes adequate tender of performance?

6. What recourse is available to one party to a contract when performance is made impossible by the other party's conduct?

7. What options are available to the victim of an anticipatory breach? Explain the advantages, disadvantages, and risks associated with these options.

8. What is an exemption clause? When might an exemption clause be unenforceable?

9. What is meant by fundamental breach? What remedy is available to the victim of a fundamental breach of contract?

10. Assume the defendant claims that the contract was discharged or modified by agreement; the plaintiff challenges this conclusion and seeks to enforce the original contract. What will the defendant need to prove to avoid having the initial contract enforced?

11. Explain what happens when a creditor agrees to take less than is owed to settle a debt.

12. How do conditions precedent differ from conditions subsequent?

13. Define frustration. List three ways in which frustration can take place.

14. What is the significance of a court's determination that a contract was frustrated through the fault of one of the parties?

15. Explain how the *Fibrosa* case and subsequent statute law have modified the previously accepted common law rule on the obligations of the parties in the face of a frustrating event.

16. Distinguish between a deposit and a down payment. What is the significance of this distinction?

17. What must be shown for the court to conclude that money paid ought to be categorized as a deposit?

18. In light of the decision in *Hadley v. Baxendale*, how is the recovery of damages limited?

19. Describe what is meant by mitigation. Explain how the obligation to mitigate damages limits the ability of the victim of a breach to obtain damages.

20. Distinguish between specific performance and injunction. Explain the restrictions on their availability.

Chapter 10

Special Contracts: Sales and Consumer Protection

CHAPTER OBJECTIVES

1. Describe the scope of the *Sale of Goods Act*
2. Explain the relationship between title and risk and outline the rules for determining who has title
3. Examine the rights and obligations of buyers and sellers
4. Describe the remedies of buyers and sellers upon default
5. Explain what consumer protection legislation is and why it exists
6. Review the *Competition Act* and other federal consumer protection legislation
7. Review the areas of consumer protection covered by provincial legislation
8. Identify the main forms of negotiable instruments and explain their basic characteristics

The preceding four chapters were devoted to a general examination of the law of contracts as developed primarily by the courts and embodied in case law. There are, however, several important areas where legislation has been enacted that profoundly affect the contractual relationship. This chapter is devoted to an examination of sale of goods legislation and various consumer protection provisions. The topics covered in this and the following chapter fall primarily within provincial jurisdiction, resulting in various statutes with considerable provincial variation. In the United States this potential conflict of laws between states is largely overcome by each state's adopting the unified commercial code. Consequently, there are only minor state variations. The Uniform Law Conference of Canada has recommended a modernization of sale of goods legislation and the introduction of other uniform legislative initiatives.[1]

[1.] See the Uniform Law Conference of Canada's "Commercial Law Strategy," online: www.ulcc.ca/en/cls/index.cfm?sec=2.

THE SALE OF GOODS

Scope of the *Sale of Goods Act*

Sale of Goods Act implies terms into contract

The *Sale of Goods Act* is essentially a summation and codification by the British Parliament of the case law in place in the nineteenth century. This statute was adopted with only minor variations by every common law province in Canada.

The primary purpose of the *Act* is to imply the terms that the parties to sale of goods transactions often leave out. For example, the parties may fail to specify a date for payment or time of delivery, and the *Act* will imply the missing terms into the contract. Note that the *Act* provides only missing terms, and so the stated intention of the parties will override the provisions of the *Act*. The *Sale of Goods Act* is not restricted to retail and consumer transactions; rather, it applies to all situations where goods are bought and sold. Even significant commercial transactions involving large machinery such as railway locomotives or earth-moving equipment are governed by this *Act*.

All other contract rules must be complied with

It must be emphasized that the normal contract rules apply to sale of goods transactions except where overridden by the *Sale of Goods Act*. Thus, offer and acceptance, as well as consideration, capacity, legality, and intention must be present for the contract to be formed. Also, the rules with respect to mistake, misrepresentation, privity, and breach apply to the contract.

GOODS AND SERVICES

Act applies only to sale of goods

The *Sale of Goods Act* affects only those contracts involving goods. Goods are tangible items, such as watches, televisions, books, and so on. The term "goods" does not include real estate but does include crops still growing on land. Buildings and building materials are subject to the *Sale of Goods Act* until they become attached to the land. They are then treated as part of the real property and are not subject to the *Act*, unless the contract itself provides for the building to be severed from the land before the sale or under the contract of sale. Contracts for intangibles, such as services or the exchange of negotiable instruments, stocks, bonds and other documents representing rights or claims (referred to as *choses in action*), are not covered by the *Act*.

Transactions involving both goods and services can pose a problem. When a lawyer drafts a will, or an artist paints a portrait, the client gets a physical item, the will or portrait, but the main component of the transaction is the service provided. The *Sale of Goods Act* will therefore not apply.[2] Note that if the client were to then resell the portrait, the *Act* would apply. Sometimes, the service and sale of goods components of a transaction can be separated, as when parts are installed to repair an automobile. The *Sale of Goods Act* will apply to the goods portion of that contract.

When only services are involved, the court may still be willing to imply terms, such as the requirement of a certain level of quality, even though the *Sale of Goods Act* does not apply. For example, in *Borek v. Hooper*,[3] Borek commissioned a large

---

[2.] In cases in which both goods and services are provided, the court must determine if the essence of the contract was the materials or the work provided. See *Keillian West Ltd. v. Sportspace Enterprises Ltd.* (1982), 40 A.R. 586 (Q.B.), in which the Court decided that a contract for the printing of 20 000 copies of 44-page programs was a contract for goods, not services, and was, therefore, subject to the *Act*.

[3.] (1994), 114 D.L.R. (4th) 570 (Ont. Div. Ct.).

painting from Hooper, an artist. When the painting showed serious problems of discolouration and surface deterioration, Borek sued for breach of warranty as to quality under the *Sale of Goods Act*. The appeal court held that the *Act* did not cover this transaction, as it did not involve a sale of goods, but of work, labour, and materials. The court did, however, recognize a similar provision implied into the contract by the common law, in that there was a warranty with respect to quality and fitness for purpose. The case was thus sent back to the trial court for a proper assessment of damages.

CASE SUMMARY 10.1

Has There Been a Sale of Contaminated Goods? *Gee v. White Spot Ltd.* and *Pan v. White Spot Ltd.*;[4] *ter Neuzen v. Korn*[5]

In July 1985, Gee suffered botulism poisoning from food obtained at the White Spot restaurant. He sued. The Judge decided that, since the primary purpose of the transaction was to obtain the food (a chattel), the service component being incidental, the *Sale of Goods Act* applied to the purchase. Section 18(b) of the *Act* required the goods to be of merchantable quality, meaning that they had to be fit for their normal purpose; in this case, fit for human consumption. Section 18(a) required that when the skill of the seller is relied on, and it is in the normal course of the business to supply the goods, those goods have to be fit for the purpose for which they are purchased. The Judge found that the goods failed both of these tests and Gee was successful in his action, the contract of purchase having been breached.

In contrast, consider the facts in *ter Neuzen v. Korn*. In this case, the Court ruled that a patient who contracted an HIV infection from an artificial insemination program could not rely on the *Sale of Goods Act*, as the contract was mainly for the sale of services, not goods. The Court also held that there was not a common law warranty of fitness and merchantability applicable to the contract, which involved the provision of a donor's semen.

DISCUSSION QUESTIONS

Based on these precedents, how would the courts characterize cosmetic services, such as botox injections? What if the sample of botox itself was defective or contaminated? Would the *Sale of Goods Act* apply?

TRANSFER OF GOODS

The *Sale of Goods Act* applies only when it can be demonstrated that the parties intended that the actual possession and property of the goods would transfer to the buyer.

When goods are used to secure a loan with no intention that they actually be transferred, the *Sale of Goods Act* will not apply even though a **bill of sale** may have been used to create the credit relationship. However, when the goods used as security actually do change hands, as in a conditional sale, the *Act* will apply.

Goods must be transferred

---

4. (1986), 32 D.L.R. (4th) 238 (B.C.S.C.).

5. [1995] 3 S.C.R. 674.

MONETARY CONSIDERATION

Act does not apply to barter

It is also necessary that the sale involve the actual payment of some money. The *Act* will not apply to traded goods unless some money is also exchanged.

REQUIREMENT OF WRITING

Some provinces require evidence in writing

Despite the trend to move away from the *Statute of Frauds,* some jurisdictions still require in their *Sale of Goods Acts* that sales of goods sold over a specified amount[6] must be evidenced in writing for the contract to be enforceable. Part performance, when some of the goods have been accepted by the buyer, will likewise make the contract enforceable. Giving something in earnest (anything of value) will also make the contract binding. Other provinces, including British Columbia, New Brunswick, Ontario, and Manitoba, have eliminated any writing requirement in sale of goods transactions, although British Columbia, in its *Consumer Protection Act,* still requires that there be a written contract for direct sales of consumer goods.

Title and Risk

Distinction between sale and agreement to sell

Normally risk follows title

When the title (the property interest in the goods) does not transfer immediately upon the sale agreement's being concluded, it is called an **agreement to sell**. The *Sale of Goods Act* also applies to this future transfer of goods. Determining who has title, at any given time, is important because, under the *Sale of Goods Act,* whoever has the title bears the risk of damage or destruction to the goods—unless the parties have agreed otherwise.

Four common methods are sometimes used to override this provision of the *Act.*

1. **C.I.F. contracts (cost, insurance, and freight)**. In this type of contract it doesn't matter when title transfers, because one of the parties has been designated as being responsible for paying the costs involved in the shipping of those goods as well as arranging insurance, in the process assuming the risk if anything goes wrong.

2. **F.O.B. contracts (free on board)**. With F.O.B. contracts, the parties have agreed that the seller will bear the risk until a specified point in the transport process. For example, if the goods are to be delivered F.O.B. the loading dock at the seller's place of business, the buyer assumes the risk at that point.

3. **C.O.D. contracts (cash on delivery)**. This type of contract entitles the seller to maintain the proprietary rights (or title) as well as control over the possession of those goods, until they are delivered to the buyer's premises and paid for. The risk stays with the seller until delivery at the specified location is complete.

4. **Bills of lading**. Bills of lading are also often used by the seller to maintain control over the goods during shipment. A bill of lading is a document given by the transporter (or carrier) of the goods to the shipper as a form of receipt. The seller can maintain control (and the risk) with respect to those goods by naming itself as the party entitled to receive delivery of the goods at their destination.

---

6. The relevant dollar amount is $50 in Alberta, Saskatchewan, Newfoundland and Labrador, Nunavut, and the N.W.T., $40 in Nova Scotia, and $30 in P.E.I. In the Yukon, the amount is $1000!

REDUCING RISK 10.1

There are many opportunities to exercise control over the various legal aspects of business transactions, such as who bears the risk and when title transfers. While there have been many restrictions imposed when consumers are involved, it is still important to understand what options you can exercise to reduce the risk you face in both consumer and commercial transactions.

TRANSFER OF TITLE

Who has title can not only can determine who bears the risk, but it will also affect which remedies are available in the event of a breach. If title is transferred, the seller can sue for the entire price; otherwise, only damages for breach of contract are available. Who has title can also determine who has first claim to the goods in the event of default or bankruptcy. The rules for determining who has title as found in the *Sale of Goods Act* are set out below.[7]

Remedy may depend on who has title

Rules for determining title

Rule 1

When there is an unconditional contract for the sale of specific goods in a deliverable state, the property in the goods passes to the buyer when the contract is made and it is immaterial whether the time of payment or the time of delivery or both are postponed.

Unconditional contract—title transfers immediately

If the goods are identified and nothing more has to be done to them, the buyer gets title at the point of contracting to purchase. Thus, if Cristina decides to buy a used car, sold "as is" by Mills, and Cristina says, "I'll pay you $15 000 for this Toyota and not a dollar more," title would transfer as soon as Cristina's offer was accepted even though she might take delivery and pay at a later date. Were the car vandalized while parked on the street overnight, before the buyer picked it up, the loss would be the buyer's.

Rule 2

When there is a contract for the sale of specific goods and the seller is bound to do something to the goods for the purpose of putting them into a deliverable state, the property does not pass until such thing is done and the buyer has notice thereof.

Seller required to do something to put goods in deliverable state—title transfers when task completed and notice is given

If some repair or work has to be done on the car in the above example, title and risk would pass to the buyer only after the repair was done and the buyer was notified the goods were ready. If the car was vandalized or otherwise damaged before the notice, the loss would be the seller's, as was the case in *Kovacs v. Holtom*.[8]

Notice required if repairs are needed

Rule 3

When there is a contract for the sale of specific goods in a deliverable state, but the seller is bound to weigh, measure, test or do some other act or thing with reference to the goods for the purpose of ascertaining the price, the property does not pass until the act or thing is done and the buyer has notice thereof.

Seller required to ascertain price—title transferred when purchaser notified

---

[7.] These provisions are taken from s. 19 of the *Ontario Sale of Goods Act*, R.S.O. 1990, c. S.1. Every province has a similar act, although the wording of the provisions may vary.

[8.] See *Kovacs v. Holtom*, [1997] A.J. No. 775 (Prov. Ct.), in which the Court applied Rule 2 with respect to a car that was destroyed prior to the completion of its restoration and delivery.

If Schmidt bought a truckload of potatoes from Naslund, title would not pass until they had been weighed to determine the price and Schmidt had been notified.

Rule 4

Goods delivered subject to buyer's approval—title passes when approval by acceptance is signified or a reasonable time has passed

When goods are delivered to the buyer on approval or on "sale or return" or other similar terms, the property in them passes to the buyer

(i) when the buyer signifies approval or acceptance to the seller or does any other act adopting the transaction, or

(ii) if the buyer does not signify approval or acceptance to the seller but retains the goods without giving notice of rejection, then if a time has been fixed for the return of the goods, on the expiration of that time, and, if no time has been fixed, on the expiration of a reasonable time, and what is a reasonable time is a question of fact.

This rule covers situations in which goods are taken by the buyer to test for a trial period before deciding to keep them. To modify our earlier example, if Mills had allowed Cristina to take the car home for two days, to test drive it and have it inspected by a mechanic, title and risk would not transfer to Cristina until the expiration of those two days unless Cristina notified Mills before that time that she was happy with the car. Title would pass earlier if Cristina resold the car or had repairs done on the car.

Rule 5

When goods are not manufactured or identifiable as goods in question, title passes upon unconditional appropriation and assent

(i) When there is a contract for the sale of unascertained or future goods by description and goods of that description and in a deliverable state are unconditionally appropriated to the contract, either by the seller with the assent of the buyer, or by the buyer with the assent of the seller, the property in the goods thereupon passes to the buyer, and such assent may be express or implied and may be given either before or after the appropriation is made.

(ii) When, in pursuance of the contract, the seller delivers the goods to the buyer or to a carrier or other bailee (whether named by the buyer or not), for the purpose of transmission to the buyer and does not reserve the right of disposal, the seller shall be deemed to have unconditionally appropriated the goods to the contract.

The goods covered by Rule 5 are those that have not been manufactured at the time the contract was entered into or that exist but have not yet been separated out and identified as the particular goods to be used in a given transaction. If one purchases a specific model of a car from a dealer, title does not pass until the specific vehicle is selected from the several like it on the lot. Rule 5 would apply because no specific car has yet been appropriated to the contract at the time of the sale. Rule 5 would also apply when a buyer orders a new car that has not yet been manufactured.

Only when the goods have been manufactured or separated out and unconditionally committed to the buyer with the buyer's assent does title pass. While notice to the buyer that the goods are ready may be the most common method of satisfying the assent or approval provision, assent is often implied from the circumstances. Thus, if a person were to leave her car with a dealer for the installation of a new stereo system, she will be taken to have assented to the selection of the stereo when it is installed, since she left her car there for that purpose.

It must always be remembered that the parties can specify a contrary intention in the contract, overriding these rules with respect to title and risk. Great care should be used in examining the terms of the contract to determine whether this has been done.

CASE SUMMARY 10.2

Did Property in the Fire Truck Pass? *In the Matter of the Bankruptcy of Anderson's Engineering Ltd.*[9]

Anderson's contracted with Online to build and deliver a fire truck. Online paid Anderson's two advances toward the total purchase price of fire truck. Anderson's viewed these billings as advances against the full contract price, consistent with Anderson's procedure on other contracts and with industry practice. Anderson's made an assignment into bankruptcy before the work on fire truck was complete, and listed the chassis and pump that were to be part of the fire truck as assets owned at the time of the bankruptcy. Online claimed ownership of the chassis and pump, the cumulative value of which was approximately equal to the amount paid in advances. An application was brought to determine whether Online's claim to a property interest in these assets was defeated on the grounds that property did not pass to it prior to bankruptcy.

DISCUSSION QUESTIONS

Which provisions of the *Sale of Goods Act* are relevant to Online's claim? Are the chassis and pump "specific goods," "unascertained goods," or "future goods by description"? Was that distinction relevant to the Court's decision? Was the fire truck in a "deliverable state"? Would it matter if there was evidence that the parties intended that the chassis and pump were to become Online's property after the advances were paid?

Rights and Obligations of the Parties

The *Sale of Goods Act* implies both conditions and warranties into the contract. The difference is important. An implied warranty is a minor term. A breach of warranty does not discharge the victim from the rest of his contractual obligations. On the other hand, a breach of an implied condition allows the victim to treat the contract as ended. But a breach of a condition does not always bring a contract to an end. The victim of a breach of a condition has the option to ignore it or to treat it as a breach of warranty. By accepting the goods, the victim of a breach may also lose the right to have a contract discharged by a breach of condition.

The buyer of a television set, for example, would be entitled to return the set and demand a refund if it were specified as a condition of the contract that the television had a remote control device and he did not discover until he got it home that his set did not have one. However, if he assembled the TV knowing that there was no remote and watched it over the weekend, he would be deemed to have accepted the goods. He could not return the set, but he could still sue for damages for the reduction in value.[10] It should also be noted that while the parties

Conditions and warranties under Sale of Goods Act

Acceptance causes victims of breach to lose right of discharge

---

9. (2002), 33 C.B.R. (4th) 1, (2002), 26 B.L.R. (3d) 62 (B.C.S.C.).

10. In *Saville v. Sher-Ell Equipment Sales Ltd.* (1980), 25 A.R. 550 (Q.B.), the buyer who used the defective equipment he had purchased, instead of returning it promptly, lost the right to treat the contract as discharged. He was limited to the remedy of damages.

are free to designate a term as a condition or warranty, the court retains the right to make the final determination.

Contracting parties often try to limit their liability as much as possible, and sometimes they try to contract out of all obligations and responsibilities. The Supreme Court of Canada, in Hunter Engineering, has made it clear that a properly worded exemption clause can overcome even a **fundamental breach**—particularly where sophisticated businesspeople are involved on both side.

Manufacturers and retailers often try to override the implied conditions and warranties set out in the *Act*, especially in the areas related to fitness and quality. They do this in "warranties" that include exemption clauses attempting to limit their liability. If such clauses are carefully worded, they can override the provisions of the *Act* unless prohibited by statute. In the *Hunter Engineering* case, discussed in Case Summary 10.3, the exemption clause was effective with respect to Allis Chalmers but not with respect to Hunter Engineering, which had failed to exclude the implied conditions of the statute. Several provinces have enacted legislation prohibiting the seller from excluding or limiting these provisions relating to fitness and quality in consumer sales transactions. Others will allow parties to a sales contract to exclude any implied terms.

Parties may be free to contract out

THE *CAVEAT EMPTOR* PRINCIPLE

caveat emptor
let the buyer beware

Caveat emptor means "let the buyer beware"—that is, the risk is with the buyer. However, it is not a rigid rule but a flexible general principle, subject to the limits put on it by customary business practice.

The *caveat emptor* principle applies where the goods are in existence and are specific items that may be inspected by the buyer, and when the seller has made no misrepresentations about them. In these circumstances it is a sensible rule. The buyer has the opportunity to exercise her judgment by examining the goods, and if she distrusts her own judgment or has doubts, she may bargain for an express term stating that the goods have the particular quality she requires.

Caveat emptor encourages buyers to take care and to determine that the goods are what they want before they contract to buy them. However, there are circumstances in which the principle, if not qualified, would invite abuse by unscrupulous sellers. For example, a buyer sometimes relies upon the knowledge or expert judgment of the seller, or a buyer may place special confidence or trust in the seller. Consequently, various implied terms to protect buyers evolved and are now found in the Sale of Goods Act.

RIGHT TO CONVEY CLEAR TITLE

The *Sale of Goods Act* implies several terms into sales agreements that cover a seller's right to sell goods to a buyer. Section 13(a) of the Ontario *Sale of Goods Act* makes it a condition that the seller has the right to sell the goods, or will have the right at the time title is to be transferred. Thus, Mills breaches a condition of the contract if he cannot deliver good title at delivery. Cristina would then be free from any further obligation under the contract.

Seller must convey good title
• and quiet possession

Section 13(b) requires that the seller provide **quiet possession** of the goods as a warranty of the contract. This means that the goods must be delivered in such a condition that they can be used and enjoyed by the buyer in the way they were intended, free from any interference. If the car sold to Cristina was subsequently seized by one of Mills' creditors, this would constitute a breach of the covenant of quiet possession.

Section 13(c) of the *Act* specifies that it shall be an implied warranty of the contract that the goods shall be free from any charge or encumbrance that has not been disclosed to the buyer. Such a **lien** gives the lien holder (a secured creditor) the right to retake the goods if not paid. The presence of such a lien without telling the buyer would be a breach of warranty under section 13(c) of the *Act*. The buyer would be well advised to conduct a title search at the appropriate registry office before buying. But even if a search is not done, section 13(c) gives the buyer the right to claim against the seller for any losses if a lien is in fact present— assuming he can still locate the seller!

• and goods free from charge or encumbrance

GOODS MUST MATCH DESCRIPTION

Goods sold on the internet, by catalogue, by mail order, or through other forms of distance shopping, usually with a picture and accompanying text, are being sold by description. Section 14 of the Ontario *Sale of Goods Act* provides that when goods are sold by description there will be an implied condition that the goods delivered must match that description. If Afsari ordered an iPod pictured as "60 GB with video" on the internet and what was delivered was a 30 GB iPod, there has been a breach of the implied condition that the goods match the description, as there was when an odometer in a used car had been tampered with.[11]

Goods must match description

In fact, today the sale of any manufactured good is a sale by description, one item being indistinguishable from another of the same model. When we buy, we are relying on the manufacturer's description, whether that description is found on the box, a specification sheet, a brochure, a catalogue or the internet. All goods delivered must match that description.[12]

Most sales of manufactured goods are by description

Goods bought must match the description or picture provided

GOODS MUST BE OF MERCHANTABLE QUALITY AND FIT FOR PURPOSE

The *Sale of Goods Act* applies to both small and large transactions, whether they are consumer or commercial in nature. But the parties can contract out of its provisions if they wish. Even the principle of fundamental breach can be overcome by a very carefully and specifically worded exemption clause.

The *Sale of Goods Act* requires, as a condition, that when goods are sold by description they must be of **merchantable quality** (section 15 of the Ontario *Act*). This means that the goods must be free of any defect that would have persuaded the buyer not to purchase them at the agreed-upon price if the buyer had known of the defect at the outset.[13] If a sample has been inspected, the defect must not have been readily apparent upon examination. Because of the broader approach taken

Goods must be of merchantable quality

---

11. (2000), 194 Sask. R. 249 (Q.B.).

12. See *Coast Hotels Limited v. Royal Doulton Canada Ltd.* (2000), 76 B.C.L.R. (3d) 341 (S.C.), in which the substitution of the word "Capital" for "Royal Doulton" on tableware resulted in the goods provided not corresponding with the description.

13. See *Eggen Seed Farms Ltd. v. Alberta Wheat Pool* (1997), 205 A.R. 77 (Q.B.), in which the Court held that the sale of contaminated fertilizer was a breach of the implied condition of merchantable quality. Because the buyer had accepted the goods, it was only entitled to damages for breach of warranty. In *Satara Farms Inc. v. Parrish & Heimbecker, Ltd.* (2006), 280 Sask. R. 44, four farmers were successful in a claim relating to defective ostrich feed as the manufacturer and distributor were liable for breach of the implied conditions of fitness for purpose and merchantable quality.

today as to what constitutes goods sold by description, this provision has become much more important, covering virtually all sales of mass-produced goods.

CASE SUMMARY 10.3

Suppliers of Defective Gears Fail to Protect Themselves: *Hunter Engineering Co. v. Syncrude Canada Ltd.*[14]

As part of its tar sands extraction project, Syncrude operated a large conveyor belt to carry sand over long distances. Syncrude ordered a number of gearboxes for this system from two different companies. Both companies, Hunter Engineering and Allis Chalmers, obtained the gears from the same manufacturer. All of the gears were made according to the same design and specifications. After several gears failed, it was determined that all would have to be repaired. Syncrude sued both companies. Both companies claimed that they were protected by clauses in their contracts limiting their responsibility to a specific period of time that had expired. Although the *Sale of Goods Act* applied, requiring the goods to be fit for their intended purpose, the Court had to determine whether the exemption clauses contained in the contracts overrode the operation of the *Act*.

The Hunter Engineering contract did have a clause limiting its liability, but it failed to include a clause exempting the operation of the *Sale of Goods Act* provisions which, still being in force, imposed liability on it. The Allis Chalmers contract specifically excluded all statutory warranties or conditions, and so there was no liability. It was also argued that if the breach were fundamental, this exemption clause could not stand. But the Supreme Court of Canada held that even in the face of such a fundamental breach, it was still possible for the parties to exempt themselves from liability, as Allis Chalmers had effectively done in this case. (Fundamental breach is discussed in more detail in Chapter 9.)

SMALL BUSINESS PERSPECTIVE

Is knowledge of case law important when deciding how to word exemption clauses? Is it worth the expense to have contracts prepared, or at least reviewed, by one's lawyer?

Goods must be suitable for purpose of purchase when sales person relied upon

Sometimes a buyer with a particular need will rely on a seller's recommendation as to what product to use. In these circumstances, there is an implied condition that the goods will be reasonably fit for that purpose. The requirement of fitness applies not only when the goods are being used for some unique purpose, but also when they are being used normally. (This is the section applied in the *Hunter Engineering* case discussed in Case Summary 10.3.)

---

14. [1989] 1 S.C.R. 426.

This protection does not apply when the goods are purchased by trade name in such a way that it is clear that the skill of the seller is not being relied on,[15] or when it is not in the normal course of the seller's business to supply the goods.

If Florio were to buy a particular kind of paint from McGregor's paint company after asking if it were suitable for concrete and later found that the paint peeled, Florio would be able to sue McGregor for compensation because of the breach of the implied condition that the goods would be reasonably suitable for their intended purpose. However, if he bought it by trade name, disregarding any recommendations from the sales staff, he would have only himself to blame.[16]

In British Columbia this protection has been extended to leased goods and a provision has been added that the goods be "durable for a reasonable period of time."[17] While these provisions do not relieve the buyer of the obligation to be cautious, they do provide for a certain minimum level of protection and quality.

In British Columbia, goods leased or sold must be durable

The provisions related to fitness and quality apply in most sale of goods situations.[18] The principle of *caveat emptor* also applies to these situations. The end result is that while the buyer is required to be careful when buying goods, she still has the right to expect a certain level of quality and protection when such care has been shown. Courts have found sellers liable for breach of the implied condition that the goods will be reasonably fit for their purpose in cases involving the sale of a sandwich that contained a piece of wood,[19] a truck that was plagued by constant breakdowns,[20] and a laptop computer that frequently broke down.[21]

Many argue that people don't take enough responsibility for themselves. Have we shifted too much of this responsibility to merchants and manufacturers? Or is it appropriate to force vendors to stand behind their products?

Other examples in which the warranties of fitness or merchantable quality were breached include a vendor of herbicides held liable when the herbicide failed to be effective,[22] a contractor found liable when the sauna heaters it installed were not reasonably fit for the known purpose,[23] a manufacturer of a forklift tractor held liable because the equipment sold never functioned properly,[24] and a farm dealership found liable because a tractor had mechanical problems.[25]

---

15. Baldry v. Marshall, [1925] 1 K.B. 260 (C.A.).

16. For a case in which the Court held that a paint manufacturer breached the implied condition that the paint supplied to the buyer was reasonably fit for its intended purpose, see *McCready Products Ltd. v. Sherwin-Williams Co. of Canada Ltd.* (1985), 61 A.R. 234 (C.A.), aff'g on this point (1984), 53 A.R. 304 (Q.B.).

17. *Sale of Goods Act,* R.S.B.C. 1996 c. 410, s. 18(c).

18. For a good discussion of the implied conditions of fitness and quality, see *Gill v. Kittler* (1983), 44 A.R. 321 (Q.B.).

19. *Coote v. Hudson's Bay Company* (1977), 6 A.R. 59 (Dist. Ct.).

20. *Rosseway v. Canadian Kenworth Ltd.* (1978), 11 A.R. 91 (Dist. Ct.).

21. *Gadd v. London Drugs Ltd.* (1991), 123 A.R. 335 (Prov. Ct.).

22. *Caners v. Eli Lilly Canada Inc.* (1996), 110 Man. R. (2d) 95 (C.A.).

23. *Young Men's Christian Association of Hamilton-Burlington v. 331783 Ontario Ltd.,* [2001] O.J. No. 4152 (Sup. Ct. J.), aff'd [2003] O.J. No. 2201 (C.A.).

24. *Champs Food System Ltd. v. de Koning Manufacturing,* [2004] M.J. No. 174 (C.A.).

25. 2006 AB P.C. 127, [2006] A.W.L.D. 2311.

Goods must match sample and be free of hidden defects

GOODS MUST MATCH SAMPLE

The *Sale of Goods Act* uses a similar approach for the purchase of goods after examining a sample. There is an implied condition that the bulk of the goods must match the sample provided and be free of any hidden defects. For example, if the load of bricks Tsang bought from Cashin after first inspecting a sample brick looked fine, but in fact had not been baked properly and disintegrated after being used in Tsang's building, the bricks would be of unmerchantable quality, a breach of an implied condition of the contract.

Where price omitted— reasonable price

Time, payment and place for delivery implied terms

OTHER IMPLIED TERMS

There are several other terms that are implied by the *Sale of Goods Act* unless otherwise specified by the parties. Where no price is stated, a reasonable price must be paid for goods. Delivery must take place within a reasonable time, and payment is due upon delivery. The time of payment will be treated as a warranty, unless the parties state time is of the essence. Whether the time of delivery will be treated as a condition or a warranty will be implied from the conduct of the parties. When bulk goods, such as grains, lumber and ore are involved, if significantly too little or too much is delivered the buyer is free to either reject the goods or keep them and pay for them at the contracted rate. The provisions affecting delivery, place, time, and quantity of the goods are usually made conditions by the parties.

CHECKLIST	Implied Terms in a Contract for the Sale of Goods

Subject to certain exceptions and qualifications, the *Sale of Goods Act* implies the following contractual terms:

- an implied condition that the seller has (or will have) a right to sell the goods
- an implied warranty that the buyer will have and enjoy quiet possession of the goods
- an implied warranty that the goods will be free from any undisclosed charge or encumbrance
- an implied condition that the goods will correspond with the description under which they are sold
- an implied condition that the goods will be reasonably fit for the purpose for which they are required if that purpose was made known to the seller
- an implied condition that the goods will be of merchantable quality
- in the case of a sale by sample, an implied condition that the bulk will correspond with the sample

EXEMPTION CLAUSES

The *Sale of Goods Act* contains the following provision:

Where any right, duty or liability would arise under a contract of sale by implication of law, it may be negatived or varied by express agreement or by the course of dealing between the parties, or by usage, if the usage is such as to bind both parties to the contract.[26]

As a result, a seller may insist that a contract of sale contains an express term relieving it from the liability normally imposed by the implied terms. A prospective buyer may, of course, refuse to enter into a contract containing such an exemption clause. In some provinces, if she agrees to the clause, she loses the protection given to a buyer by the *Act*.[27]

The courts have restricted the circumstances in which a seller may excuse himself from liability under the *Act*. Clear and direct language must be used to contract out of the statutory protections.

CASE SUMMARY 10.4

Syncrude ordered 32 gearboxes from Hunter, a manufacturer, to drive its conveyor belts in the Alberta tar sands project. Syncrude provided specifications of what the gearboxes were required to do, and Hunter designed them to meet those specifications.

The contract contained an express term guaranteeing the gearboxes for two years. When the period had expired, the gearboxes developed faults that were found to be due to faulty design. Syncrude could not succeed in an action on the express term because the two-year period had elapsed, but the Supreme Court of Canada held that the implied term of fitness under the *Act* could still be relied on. The existence of an express warranty was not inconsistent with the statutory warranties.[28]

If the words used in an exemption clause do not precisely describe the type of liability disclaimed, the courts will normally find that the implied liability is still part of the contract. If a seller includes an express term that "all warranties implied by statute are hereby excluded," the seller will avoid liability under all those implied terms that are *warranties* but not under those that are *conditions*.[29] Moreover, if the seller expressly promised that the goods would be of a certain quality or type, an exemption clause that refers only to implied terms will not free him from obligations under this express term.

CASE SUMMARY 10.5

Allan agreed to purchase a car from Lambeth Motors Ltd. In the contract the car was described as "a new, 190-horsepower, six-cylinder sedan." There was also a clause, inserted by the seller, that "all conditions, warranties, and liabilities implied by statute,

---

[26.] Ont., s. 53: see also Alta., s. 54; B.C., s. 69; Nfld., s. 56.

[27.] In British Columbia, New Brunswick, and Saskatchewan the warranties cannot be contracted out of in the case of retail sales.

[28.] *Hunter Engineering Co.* v. *Syncrude Canada Ltd.* (1989), 57 D.L.R. (4th) 321. See also *Fording Coal Ltd.* v. *Harnischfeger Corp. of Canada* (1991), 6 B.L.R. (2d) 157.

[29.] *Gregorio* v. *Intrans-Corp.* (1994), 115 D.L.R. (4th) 200 (Ont. C.A.).

common law, or otherwise are hereby excluded." After taking delivery, Allan discovered that the car was not new and had only four cylinders, and he sued for damages.

The exempting clause referred only to implied terms. The undertaking that the car was new and had six cylinders was an express term in the contract of sale. The seller had therefore failed to exempt itself from liability.[30]

The courts have also held that a seller cannot so completely exempt himself from liability that he may default on his bargain entirely. They will not give effect to an exemption clause that gives a seller immunity from action if he delivers goods that are totally different from those contracted for by the buyer or if he delivers goods to which he does not have good title.[31] In effect, the courts have held that a contract for the sale of goods would be deprived of all meaning if a seller's obligation were merely to deliver the goods "if he felt like it."

ETHICAL ISSUE

Exemption Clauses

Exemption clauses are an important tool used by businesses to limit their exposure to liability. As the forgoing discussion indicates, the *Sale of Goods Act* recognizes and preserves the role of an exemption clause. This position prioritizes the value of freedom to contract over the protective policy reflected in the implied terms. The Supreme Court seemed willing to accept the possibility that a properly worded exemption clause could protect a business even in cases of fundamental breach.

However, it may not be possible to contract out of the implied terms in the consumer context. In a complete reversal of the *Sale of Goods Act*, the *Ontario Consumer Protection Act* voids any "term or acknowledgement, whether part of the consumer agreement or not, that purports to negate or vary any implied condition or warranty under the *Sale of Goods Act* . . . " (s. 9(3)). This places the retailer in a precarious situation. Few retailers manufacture their own goods; the chain of distribution usually involves a manufacturer and a wholesaler. The retailer is bound by the implied terms of the *Sale of Goods Act* when dealing with consumers, but unable to rely on them when pursing the manufacturer or wholesaler of the goods.

Questions to Consider

1. Does this represent a fair result in today's marketplace?
2. Which legislation should be changed?

---

30. *Andrews Bros. Ltd.*v. *Singer & Co. Ltd.*, [1934] 1 K.B. 17.

31. *Pinnock Brothers* v. *Lewis and Peat Ltd.*, [1923] 1 K.B. 690; *Karsales (Harrow) Ltd.*v. *Wallis*, [1956] 2 All E.R. 866; *Canadian-Dominion Leasing Corp. Ltd.* v. *Suburban Superdrug Ltd.* (1966), 56 D.L.R. (2d) 43.

SALES MADE ONLINE

Many sale of goods transactions are now conducted online, and parties to such transactions are still required to comply with the terms of the *Sales of Goods Act* in place in the jurisdiction that covers the transaction. These *Sales of Goods Acts* vary, and in many jurisdictions it is still possible for the parties to agree to override even the requirements with respect to fitness and quality. Where sellers can, it is normal practice for them to include terms (interestingly, often called "warranties") that override or otherwise limit these provisions. Consumers should be extremely careful to look for such provisions and understand their effect. Some sellers may fail to make those exemptions clear to the buyer by burying them at the end of the site or in pages that most buyers skim or neglect to read at all. Generally, online retailers are required to take reasonable measures to draw such terms to the attention of the other party, and if they fail to do so, these terms do not bind the buyer. But if retailers do direct buyers to these terms and the buyer fails to read them, the buyer will typically be bound.[32]

CASE SUMMARY 10.6

Performance Required Within a Reasonable Time: *Dansway International Transport Ltd. v. Lesway and Sons Ltd.*[33]

Dansway bought two trailers from Lesway, paying a $2000 deposit on the $100 000 purchase price on 16 July 1998. Nothing had been said as to the time of delivery or whether the time for delivery and payment were important. Dansway claimed to have said that payment had to wait for an insurance settlement, but Lesway said it had thought that the deal was to go through within one week. Lesway claimed to have sent notification of termination on 29 July 1998, but Dansway denied receiving it and continued arranging financing. On 27 August Dansway tried to complete the deal, but Lesway told it of the termination and returned its deposit.

Dansway sued. The Judge determined that since neither party had either stated that time was important or specified a time for performance, there was an implied term that performance had to be within a reasonable time. What constituted a reasonable time depended on the circumstances. In this case, a reasonable time would be one month. In any event, the party wishing to terminate the contract had to serve notice on the other that performance was required or that the contract would be considered at an end. Since this wasn't done, the seller was in breach of the contract. Damages were awarded accordingly.

SMALL BUSINESS PERSPECTIVE

If performance of a contract doesn't proceed as expected, parties may grow dissatisfied and attempt to cancel the deal. Can such situations be avoided? If a party feels a need to terminate a contract, what should that party do first?

[32.] See *Kanitz v. Rogers Cable Inc.* (2002), 58 O.R. (3d) 299 (Sup. Ct. J.), in which the Court held that adequate notice of changes to an online agreement was given and that the customers were therefore bound by the amended terms of the online agreement. This result is consistent with general contract law and non-internet cases.

[33.] [2001] O.J. No. 4594 (Sup. Ct. J.).

Remedies on Default

SELLER'S REMEDIES

When the buyer defaults, the seller has an unpaid **seller's lien** against the goods. This gives the seller the right to retain the goods until appropriate payment has been made, even though title may have transferred.

Similarly, if the goods are en route to the buyer, and the buyer defaults, the seller has the right to intercept the goods and retake possession from the transporter, as long as the goods have not yet reached the buyer. This is referred to as the seller's right of **stoppage in transit**. Reference to the specific provincial legislation is necessary to ascertain when this right arises. The *Bankruptcy and Insolvency Act*[34] also allows a seller of goods to recover those goods even after they are delivered to the buyer if, within 30 days of delivery, the buyer has become bankrupt or a receiver has been appointed and, of course, provided the buyer, receiver or trustee still has them. This gives the seller priority over the bankrupt's other creditors.

When the seller exercises this power to retake the goods sold and, after appropriate notice, remains unpaid, the goods can be sold to recover the loss. Such notice of resale is not required when perishable goods are involved.

In the event of a breach of contract, the seller retains all of the normal remedies that were discussed in the previous chapter. He has the right to sue for the price of the goods when title has passed to the buyer. In such a case, if the buyer refuses to accept delivery of the goods, she is rejecting her own goods and may still be required to pay the purchase price. If the time specified for payment passes, the seller can sue for the purchase price even if title has not yet passed to the buyer. Buyers would be wise to refuse delivery only when the seller has breached a condition of the contract. Otherwise, by refusing delivery, the buyer takes the risk of not getting the goods but still being required to pay full price for them. But the seller must be careful and do nothing inconsistent with his continued willingness to perform. If he tries to sell the goods to someone else, for example, he will no longer be able to sue for the whole price, just for what he has lost on the sale.

The seller may be able to claim for damages for breach of contract even in situations in which it is not possible to claim the purchase price of the goods. These losses will normally include the costs involved in restocking and resale. When the goods are resold at a lower price, that loss will be included as well. The seller also has an obligation to mitigate losses, which usually requires the seller to take steps to resell the goods immediately. When a deposit is involved, the seller can keep the deposit. This is not the case when the prepayment is a down payment only. In fact, it may well not be worth the effort to sue for damages if it is not possible to sue for the actual price of the goods.

BUYER'S REMEDIES

The remedies available to the buyer if the seller defaults are those provided by general contract law. Where misrepresentation is involved, the buyer may be able to rescind the contract or seek damages when there has been fraud or negligence. When a condition of the contract is breached, the buyer may refuse to perform or

Right of stoppage in transit

Seller protected in case of bankruptcy

Seller can sue for price in cases of default or refusal of delivery once title has passed

---

[34.] R.S.C. 1985, c. B-3, s. 81.1.

demand return of any money paid. If only a warranty is breached, the buyer must go through with the deal, subject to a right for damages. The damages will usually be based on the difference between what the buyer had agreed to pay for the goods and the cost of obtaining the goods from another source. But when there are additional losses suffered because of the delay in obtaining the goods or the defect involved, the buyer will be able to claim them as well.

Buyer's remedies those of contract law

If title has passed, the buyer may lose his right to discharge the contract in the event of a breach of condition. The damages usually are determined by what it costs to bring the goods up to the specifications in the original contract or by their reduction in value because of the breach.[35] When defective goods have caused physical injury or damage to other property, those damages are also recoverable, provided they were reasonably within the contemplation of the parties at the time the contract was entered into.[36] Thus, people who suffer food poisoning because of poor-quality food at a restaurant can seek compensation for their injuries under the *Sale of Goods Act* provisions, and those damages can be substantial. When unique goods are involved, the buyer may also be able to claim a remedy of specific performance and force the seller to go through with the sale rather than pay damages in compensation.

Extent of damages depends on circumstances

Finally, it should be mentioned that every Canadian jurisdiction (federal, provincial, and territorial) has now enacted an international sale of goods act.[37,38] A great deal of trading today is done in the international arena, and these statutes are intended to bring the same kind of structure and certainty to import and export dealings as the *Sale of Goods Act* provides domestically.

Additionally, the federal government is a signatory to the U.N. *Convention on the International Sales of Goods (CISG)*, which governs trade between Canada and the United States as well as 60 other signatory states. Oddly, many North American legal practitioners are wary of resorting to the *CISG* (adopted by the United States in 1988 and in Canada in 1992), so there is little case law interpreting it. Apparently, legal practitioners prefer the "devil they know" and opt to insert choice of law provisions into contracts to avoid having "uncertain" law applied to their contracts.

 REDUCING RISK 10.2

Businesspeople should always be aware of the operation of the *Sale of Goods Act*, especially the provisions related to fitness and quality. Even in large commercial transactions, it is important to specify the nature and limits of the obligations of the parties to avoid unwanted terms from being implied into the contract. As seen in the *Hunter*

Engineering case (Case Summary 10.3), the failure of one supplier to exclude the operation of the *Sale of Goods Act* made that supplier responsible for substantial damages. Whether buyer or seller, it is important to keep the *Sale of Goods Act* in mind whenever goods are being transferred for money.

[35.] See *A.C. Neilsen Co. of Canada v. Kiosk Design Inc.*, [2003] O.J. No. 4647 (Sup. Ct. J.) for a case in which only nominal damages were awarded after a seller acted promptly to address concerns.

[36.] *Hadley v. Baxendale* (1854), 156 E.R. 145 (Ex. Ct.).

[37.] In Alberta, for example, the *International Conventions Implementation Act*, S.A. 1990, c. 1–6.8., now cited as R.S.A. 2000, c. I-6.

[38.] All of the following have enacted legislation based on the Uniform Law Conference of Canada's *International Sale of Goods Act*: British Columbia (1990, 1992), Alberta (1990), Saskatchewan (1991), Manitoba (1989), Ontario (1988), Quebec (similar act, 1991), New Brunswick (1989), P.E.I. (1988), Nova Scotia (1988), Newfoundland (1989), Yukon (1992), N.W.T. (1988), Nunavut (2006), and Canada (1991).

CONSUMER PROTECTION

Freedom of contract has been significantly affected by legislation in the context of consumer transactions. **Consumer transactions** involve goods or services purchased by individuals for personal use and not for resale or for business purposes.

Consumer transaction involves purchases for personal consumption rather than business use

Consumer protection legislation imposes standards and responsibilities on manufacturers and suppliers of goods and services. It controls the use and disclosure of information and advertising. It controls the safety and quality of the goods sold. This legislation also controls unethical or otherwise unacceptable business practices. The rest of this chapter will examine this area and consider the regulatory bodies created to enforce the legislation. There are both federal and provincial statutes involved, with considerable variety among provincial jurisdictions. Depending on the jurisdiction, the legislation may be contained in one statute or several.[39] Although there has been some limited form of consumer protection in our law for centuries, modern statutes have significantly expanded and modified the law in this area. Until recently, the common contractual themes of *caveat emptor* and freedom of contract dominated consumer transactions. But because of the vulnerability of consumers to abuse and their weakened bargaining position given modern business practices, limits have been placed on those principles.

Statutes prevent abuse

CASE SUMMARY 10.7

Parked Truck Goes Up in Flames: *Prebushewski v. Dodge City Auto (1984) Ltd.*[40]

Fourteen months after the Plaintiff purchased a new truck, it was destroyed by fire. An investigation determined that a defect in the daytime running light module had caused it to short-circuit, leading to the fire. Both Dodge City and Chrysler refused to assist the Plaintiff, even though she had purchased an extended warranty. They simply referred her to her insurer. The insurance settlement did not cover the amount still owing on the Plaintiff's bank loan, so she commenced an action under the *Consumer Protection Act* (*CPA*).

The trial Judge had no difficulty in finding that the module was not durable for a reasonable period, in breach of section 48 of the CPA:

> Where a consumer product is sold by a retail seller, the following warranties are deemed to be given...
>
> (g) that the product and all its components are to be durable for a reasonable period.

---

39. Ontario and British Columbia have each consolidated a collection of consumer protection laws into a single statute. Ontario's *Consumer Protection Act*, 2002, S.O. 2002, c. 30, Sch. A, was proclaimed in force on 30 July 2005. British Columbia's *Business Practices and Consumer Protection Act*, S.B.C. 2004, c. 2, is notable for creating the Business Practices and Consumer Protection Authority. This not-for-profit organization operates at arm's length from the government and has been responsible for overseeing business practices and consumer protection in British Columbia since July 2004. See http://www.bpcpa.ca/.

40. [2005] 1 S.C.R. 649.

Pursuant to the legislation, the manufacturer is also bound by these statutory warranties. The CPA remedies for a substantial breach enable the purchaser to reject the product and recover the price, which the Judge awarded (less $5000 for usage). The Judge also awarded bank interest charges, $560 for property destroyed by the fire and $25 000 in exemplary damages.

The Supreme Court of Canada affirmed the award since Chrysler willfully violated the *CPA*. Chrysler knew about the defective module, but had "made a business decision to neither advise its customers of the problem nor to recall the vehicles to replace the modules.... Chrysler was not prepared to spend $250 million even though it knew what the defective module might do."

SMALL BUSINESS PERSPECTIVE

The Supreme Court held that, since Chrysler's conduct was voluntary, intentional, and deliberate, an award of exemplary damages was justified. The *Consumer Protection Act* purposely sets a low threshold for exemplary damages so that protection for consumers is enhanced. Do you think this is appropriate? Without such a legislative provision, might manufacturers be tempted to maintain secrecy despite risks to consumers?

Federal Legislation

Although the most dramatic developments in consumer protection legislation have taken place provincially in recent years, there are some significant and effective federal statutes as well. Industry Canada was established under the *Department of Industry Act*.[41] Industry Canada, through its various offices, such as Consumer Affairs, the Competition Bureau, and the Office of the Superintendent of Bankruptcy, regulates the various areas of concern. The mission of Industry Canada is to foster a growing, competitive, knowledge-based Canadian economy. Its mandate includes three strategic objectives—a fair, efficient, and competitive marketplace; an innovative economy; and competitive industry and sustainable communities. Product safety is now overseen by Health Canada, which was established under the *Department of Health Act*.[42] Information about these and other consumer-oriented agencies can be found in the *Canadian Consumer Handbook*, discussed below.

Federal department enforces statutes, educates, and protects consumers

THE COMPETITION

The mission of the Competition Bureau "is to protect and promote competitive markets and enable informed consumer choice in Canada."[43] The Competition Bureau is an independent law enforcement agency that administers and enforces the *Competition Act*.[44] This legislation can be characterized as a criminal statute that has as its objective the maintenance and encouragement of competition in

---

[41] S.C. 1995, c. 1.

[42] S.C. 1996, c. 8.

[43] See the website for the Competition Bureau, at: www.competitionbureau.gc.ca/eic/site/cb-bc.nsf/eng/home.

[44] R.S.C. 1985, c. C-34.

Canada so that Canadians can benefit from product choice, competitive prices, and quality services. Hearings pursuant to the *Competition Act* are conducted before the Competition Tribunal, which functions much like a court, prosecuting violations and imposing fines and imprisonment for up to five years on those who are found guilty of violations.

Competition Act controls abuses in free market

Mergers controlled

One purpose of the *Competition Act* is to control mergers. Mergers are no longer treated as inherently bad; the Competition Tribunal just reviews them to determine whether they will have the effect of substantially limiting or lessening competition. The Tribunal must weigh different factors. It will tolerate some lessening of competition if it is justified by the efficiency gained. A **horizontal merger** takes place when one competitor buys another. A vertical merger involves the merger of a supplier and retailer. The danger of this is that the supplier may squeeze out the competition by favouring its own retailer, as explained below. A **conglomerate merger** involves companies not in direct competition. The Tribunal will look to determine if the overall effect is to unduly limit competition.

The "efficiency defence"[45] has recently been successfully raised, for example, in the merger of Superior Propane Inc. and ICG Propane Inc.[46] Acknowledging that the merger would lessen competition, the Tribunal nonetheless approved it because of increased efficiencies of cost savings, improved customer service, and improved position in the overall energy market. These efficiencies were quantified at $29.2 million, while the anti-competitive economic effects were calculated to be $6 million. The decision surprised many. Even mergers that will lead to price increases may pass the merger-review provisions of the *Competition Act* if the efficiencies gained exceed the anti-competitive effects.

Abusive trade practices prohibited

The *Competition Act* criminalizes some anti-competitive practices, including conspiracy to unduly lessen competition (for example, price fixing among suppliers); bid rigging (for example, a group of bidders agreeing in advance who will bid lowest); discriminatory and predatory pricing (for example, using loss leaders to drive competitors out of business); price maintenance and refusal to supply; and certain misleading advertising and deceptive marketing practices (including deceptive notices of winning a prize, pyramid selling, and double ticketing). Criminal prosecutions must be proven beyond a reasonable doubt. Upon conviction, penalties include fines, imprisonment, and injunctions ordering the offender to cease-and-desist its anti-competitive behavior.

Undue restriction of competition prohibited

Some practices are subject to civil, as opposed to criminal, sanctions, including refusal to deal (for example, substantially affecting a business by refusing to supply product on the usual terms); consignment selling; tied selling, exclusive dealing, and market restriction (for example, inducing a buyer to purchase a second product as a condition of supplying a particular product, requiring a customer to deal only or mostly in certain products, or requiring a customer to sell specific products in a defined market); delivered pricing (for example, bait-and-switch selling, selling above the advertised price, or advertising a "bargain price" which is actually the original price); abuse of dominant position; and merger review.

In June 2002, the *Competition Act* was amended to create a new right of "private access." This enabled private persons or businesses to seek a legal remedy against another's anti-competitive conduct. This was a substantial change. Previously, the Commissioner of Competition had an "enforcement monopoly" over civil

---

[45.] *Ibid.* s. 96.

[46.] *Canada (Commissioner of Competition) v. Superior Propane Inc.*, 2003 FCA 53, [2003] 3 F.C. 529.

provisions of the *Competition Act*. Now, competitors can apply for remedies if confronted with a refusal to deal. Suppliers may thus be required to supply product to would-be distributors and customers. Cease-and-desist type orders can also be obtained to counter exclusive dealing, tied selling, and market restriction when such practices have resulted, or are likely to result, in a lessening of competition.

It is conceivable that this extension of remedies to those most affected by the anti-competitive practices may lead to greater enforcement of the *Competition Act*. The Competition Bureau may thus focus on business practices that affect the public generally. For example, on 6 March 2009, the Competition Bureau announced that Moores Clothing for Men had agreed to amend its advertising regarding a two-for-one suit sale.[47] The advertising did not disclose that the sale applied only to select designer suits, contrary to the misleading representations provisions of the *Competition Act*. Moores agreed to "prominently disclose" that the sale applied only to select designer suits.

On 26 March 2009, the Competition Bureau announced that The Brick Warehouse LP had agreed to cancel all advertising related to a national mail-in rebate promotion.[48] The Brick advertised an $80 mail-in rebate, implying that consumers would receive a cash rebate. Consumers were instead sent a Brick gift certificate. This too was contrary to the misleading representations provisions of the *Competition Act*. The Brick agreed to provide consumers who made a purchase under the promotion with an $80 rebate cheque, rather than a Brick gift certificate.[49]

Misleading representations stopped

The primary purpose of the *Competition Act* is to ensure the proper operation of the free-market system. To accomplish that purpose, provisions are included that prohibit any attempt to unduly restrain competition.[50] The key here is "unduly." As a result, it is clear that not all agreements restricting competition will be illegal or in violation of the *Act*. Cynically, one might state that "Not all attempts to lessen competition are prohibited—just those that are successful!" Thus, if two merchants agree not to sell specific goods in the other's area and they are the only source of those goods, this would likely violate the *Act* as an agreement that unduly restricts competition. On the other hand, if competition is not lessened because customers still have alternative sources, then a violation of the *Act* may not have occurred.

47. "Moores Clarifies Advertising to Resolve Competition Bureau Concerns," 6 March 2009, www.competitionbureau.gc.ca/eic/site/cb-bc.nsf/eng/03016.html.

48. "Furniture Chain Cancels Rebate Promotion to Resolve Competition Bureau Concerns," 29 March 2009, www.competitionbureau.gc.ca/eic/site/cb-bc.nsf/eng/03032.html.

49. The Competition Bureau set up a special research group to investigate consumer rebates. See "Competition Watchdog to Warn About Misleading Rebate Offers: Report" CBC News, 8 December 2008, www.cbc.ca/canada/manitoba/story/2008/12/08/competition-bureau.html. The Bureau has issued a Draft Information Bulletin on Consumer Rebate Promotions, www.competitionbureau.gc.ca/eic/site/cb-bc.nsf/eng/03033.html. The Bureau is seeking comments from the public on this Draft Information Bulletin, www.competitionbureau.gc.ca/eic/site/cb-bc.nsf/eng/03037.html.

50. See s. 45(1) of the *Competition Act, supra* note 38.

CASE SUMMARY 10.8

Conspiracy to Fix Prices Not a Violation: *R. v. Clarke Transport Canada Inc.*[51]

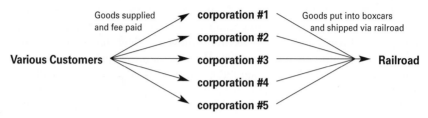

The five corporations agree to fix price charged to customers

Five corporations were involved in providing services to forward freight by pool car. They paid a set price per boxcar and charged their customers a fee based on the weight of the commodities they wanted shipped. Representatives of these five corporations attempted to keep prices high by agreeing not to compete amongst themselves or to undercut each other's prices. This apparently was a clear case of price maintenance or price fixing. The Court, however, found the corporations not guilty of charges laid under the *Competition Act*, because customers could still choose to use another mode of transportation. The Crown thus failed to show that the conspiracy *unduly* limited competition.

DISCUSSION QUESTIONS

Does this interpretation make it too difficult to prosecute those engaged in price maintenance practices? Would the result of this case be different under the amendments to the *Competition Act* discussed below?

Effect of recent amendments unclear

On 12 March 2009, the *Budget Implementation Act, 2009*[52] received Royal Assent. It contained amendments to the *Competition Act*. These amendments address topics such as price fixing, bid rigging, agreements between competitors, misleading advertising, and mergers and acquisitions. Fines were increased to as much as $25 million and jail sentences were increased to as long as 14 years. The conspiracy section of the legislation was toughened so that it is now an indictable office to conspire with a competitor to fix prices, allocate sales, territories, customers, or markets and fix production and supply. It is now assumed that an agreement among competitors automatically impacts competition. That means that existing agreements may be caught by the legislative changes. On the other hand, criminal provisions relating to price discrimination, promotional allowance, and predatory pricing provisions were repealed.

At the time of the initial writing of this chapter, regulations to implement the amendments to the *Act* had not yet been published. The Competition Bureau had just published its draft merger review process guidelines.[53] These were open for

---

51. (1995), 130 D.L.R. (4th) 500 (Ont. Gen. Div.).

52. S.C. 2009, c. 2.

53. "Draft Merger Review Process Guidelines Issued for Comment," www.competitionbureau.gc.ca/eic/site/cb-bc.nsf/eng/03029.html.

public comment for 60 days. Furthermore, the amendments did not undergo the usual parliamentary scrutiny. It is therefore difficult to predict what the results of the amendments will be. On 23 March 2009, Suncor Energy Inc. and Petro-Canada announced a merger that would create a corporation worth \$43 billion.[54] This merger will provide the first test of how effective the amendments will be in protecting competition in Canada.

OTHER FEDERAL LEGISLATION

The Competition Bureau also enforces and administers several other federal statutes that have a consumer protection aspect to them. The *Consumer Packaging and Labelling Act,*[55] the *Precious Metals Marking Act,*[56] and the *Textile Labelling Act*[57] are criminal statutes intended to force proper disclosure of information to help consumers make comparisons among products.

There are several statutes, both federal and provincial, designed to protect the consumer from dangerous products. The federal *Food and Drugs Act*[58] is intended primarily to control the sale of food, drugs, and cosmetics unfit for consumption or use. The legislation also prohibits misleading or deceptive claims associated with the sale, labelling, and advertising of these products. Several categories of drugs are created. Unsafe drugs, such as thalidomide, are prohibited from sale in Canada. Under the *Controlled Drugs and Substances Act,*[59] certain *dangerous drugs* that are useful are allowed to be sold under controlled conditions. The *Act* makes it an offence to traffic in certain *controlled drugs,* such as amphetamines and steroids. Strong and effective enforcement provisions are included.

Food and Drugs Act carries strict penalties

Another federal act, the *Hazardous Products Act,*[60] similarly controls the manufacture, import, and sale of products that are inherently dangerous. Some particularly dangerous products, such as inflammable clothing or dangerous toys, are prohibited from sale in Canada, while the sale of other potentially dangerous products is allowed provided that they comply with the enacted regulations. Examples of the latter are such products as cradles, cribs, carpets, kettles, toys, and pacifiers. The *Act* also contains important inspection, analysis, and enforcement provisions. Some hazardous products are covered by their own legislation, such as the *Explosives Act,*[61] the *Pest Control Products Act,*[62] the *Motor Vehicle Safety Act,*[63] and the *Organic Products Regulation.*[64]

Hazardous products controlled

Of course, consumers injured by dangerous products retain their common law right to seek compensation from the seller or manufacturer. This may be done in the form of a contract action (usually under the fitness and quality provision under

---

54. "Suncor, Petro-Canada Announce Merger" CBC News, 23 March 2009, www.cbc.ca/money/story/2009/03/23/suncor-petro-canada-merge.html.

55. R.S.C. 1985, c. C-38.

56. R.S.C. 1985, c. P-19.

57. R.S.C. 1985, c. T-10.

58. *R.S.C. 1985, c. F-27.*

59. S.C. 1996, c. 19.

60. *R.S.C. 1985, c. H-3.*

61. R.S.C. 1985, c. E-17.

62. S.C. 2002, c. 28.

63. S.C. 1993, c.16.

64. S.O.R./2006-338 enacted pursuant to the Canada *Agricultural Products Act*, R.S.C. 1985, c. 20 (4th Supp.), c. 0.4.

the *Sale of Goods Act* or the consumer protection legislation). It can also be done in tort, suing for negligence as illustrated by the *Donoghue v. Stevenson* case. In that case, the plaintiff consumed a ginger beer purchased for her by her friend that was contaminated by a decomposed snail. She sued the manufacturer for negligence. With the advent of consumer protection legislation, the manufacturer would be in a more precarious position today.

REDUCING RISK 10.3

It is important for businesspeople dealing with the public to keep up with statutory changes in the area of consumer protection, including those within federal jurisdiction. The enforcement sections of consumer protection legislation have become stronger, and abusive practices that may have gone unchallenged in the past are now much more likely to result in bad publicity, censure, fines, or even the loss of a business licence.

Provincial Legislation

RESPONSIBILITY FOR GOODS

When products are defective, causing injury or loss, consumers have recourse in either contract or negligence. The problem with suing in negligence is that there must be a failure on the defendant's part to live up to a demonstrated standard of care. This carelessness is often difficult to prove. Another problem is that often only the manufacturer can be sued, since the wholesalers and retailers don't deal with, or even inspect, the prepackaged goods they sell. An action based on contract law is much simpler, since the consumer need only show that the product delivered was defective and caused loss or injury. But, because of the principle of privity, any action for breach of contract is limited to the actual purchaser suing the merchant that sold the defective product. Also, the contracts involved usually include exemption clauses that attempt to significantly limit the responsibilities of the seller. There are several examples of statutes that overcome these problems.

Statutes overcome problems in contract and tort

Effect of exemption clauses limited by statute

The sections of the *Sale of Goods Act* requiring the delivery of good title, that goods correspond to the description and sample, and that the goods supplied be fit and of merchantable quality, have one serious drawback. In commercial transactions, these can be overridden by properly drafted exemption clauses. Many provinces in Canada have therefore enacted legislation removing the right to override these provisions in consumer transactions. Some do this in their *Sale of Goods Acts*, while others provide similar protection in separate statutes. Some jurisdictions require these goods to be "durable", while some have also extended the protection to leased goods.

Manufacturers usually include a "warranty" with their products stating the extent of their responsibility for fitness and quality. These are in fact exemption clauses that attempt to limit the liability of the manufacturer and retailer for the product. With the recent legislative changes, manufacturers and retailers may not be able to rely on such exemption clauses to relieve themselves of the obligation to deliver fit and quality goods to the consumer. Purchasers can now sue for breach of contract and receive significant compensation for their losses when products are unfit, even after the expiration of a stated warranty period. This also may apply to online consumer transactions depending on the legislation in place in the particular jurisdiction.

If Joyce bought a new vehicle for family use from Ace Dealership and the engine seized three days after the expiration of the three-year warranty period, Ace would not be allowed to claim that the stated warranty had expired and refuse to fix it. The three-year warranty is an exemption clause that is void in a consumer transaction. The vehicle must be of merchantable quality. Since most people would expect a transmission in a modern car to last longer than three years, it is likely that Ace would be required to be responsible for its product and make (or pay for) the repairs in these circumstances.

As mentioned, there are several advantages to suing in contract—as is the case when proceeding under the *Sale of Goods Act*—rather than basing a lawsuit upon tort law. The plaintiff does not need to prove that the defendants failed in their duty of care. The damages awarded in breach of contract cases (like in cases based on negligence) can go far beyond a refund of the purchase price. This was the case in *Gee v. White Spot*, discussed above. However, the principle of privity can pose a significant obstacle to suing in contract, since only the parties to an agreement can sue for breach. In the case of *Donoghue v. Stevenson*, Donoghue consumed a contaminated bottle of ginger beer given to her by a friend. She could not sue the seller for breach, not being "privy" to the contract. She had to sue the manufacturer for negligence instead.

Some provinces have extended the requirements of fitness and quality discussed above to anyone the seller could reasonably foresee might use the product. Through their consumer protection statutes, others have eliminated privity as a defence when warranties of fitness are implied. The result in those jurisdictions is that anyone injured or suffering a loss because of a defective product can sue the seller or manufacturer for breach of the implied conditions, whether he is the purchaser or not.

Privity problem overcome by statute

Defective Bottle Cap Causes Injury: *Morse v. Cott Beverages West Ltd.*[65]

Morse sustained a serious eye injury when she used a nutcracker to remove a difficult bottle cap, which exploded in the process. She sued, relying on Saskatchewan's *Consumer Products Warranties Act*, claiming that the manufacturer's poor quality control caused the accident. The corporation's records showed that on the day the subject bottle was manufactured, more than half of the bottles produced required a pressure greater than that recommended. The Judge therefore concluded that the caps were defective because they were too tight. He awarded damages to Morse, including punitive damages because the corporation, given its own test results, had wilfully jeopardized the safety of the public by distributing a dangerous product.

---

65. (2001), 215 Sask. R. 47 (Q.B.).

> Note that the *Act* imposed contractual obligations with respect to fitness and quality, eliminating the need to prove negligence. It also removed the barrier of privity of contract, allowing the consumer to sue the manufacturer in contract.[66]
>
> ---
>
> *DISCUSSION QUESTIONS*
>
> Is it justifiable to facilitate the consumer's ability to sue in this fashion?

Privity problem overcome by the courts

The right to sue for breach is extended by these statutes beyond the original parties to the contract, making the seller liable even when there is no indication of fault on its part. The courts have also shown a willingness to get around the privity problem. In *Murray v. Sperry Rand Corp.*,[67] the manufacturer was found liable to the consumer in contract even though the purchase was made from a retailer. Because false claims were included in the advertising brochures produced by the manufacturer, the Court found that there was a subsidiary, or collateral, contract between the manufacturer and the consumer that allowed the consumer to sue the manufacturer directly in contract. This is consistent with the tendency of the courts to abandon the privity principle.

It should be mentioned, however, that although exemption clauses in warranties will not protect the seller in consumer transactions, they might still be effective in limiting the liability of the manufacturer, depending on the nature of the contract and the legislation in place in the particular jurisdiction.

 REDUCING RISK 10.4

Most salespeople don't understand the merchant's liability beyond the manufacturer's limited warranty included with the product sold. It is important, however, for merchants to understand their potential liability for defective products. As consumers become more aware of their rights and become more aggressive in enforcing them, a merchant's very existence may depend upon whether appropriate steps were taken to eliminate or reduce such potential liability.

Duty to warn when product hazardous

Some useful products, by their very nature, are hazardous. The obligation of the manufacturer and seller of such products is to make them as safe as possible, to warn the potential user of the dangers, and to provide information on their proper use. An injured consumer can successfully sue in contract or negligence when these steps are not followed. Except when the danger is obvious, a warning incorporated into the product label must alert the consumer to the hazards associated with the product. If the warning is inadequate, the manufacturer and seller may be liable for the injuries that result. Even when such dangers are obvious, as with a sharp knife, the practice is growing for manufacturers to include such a

---

[66.] This legislation has been replaced by the Consumer Protection Act, S.S. 1996, c. C-30.1, which likewise augments the buyer's ability to sue the retailer and manufacturer.

[67.] (1979), 23 O.R. (2d) 456 (H.C.).

warning, out of an abundance of caution. Federal legislation dealing with the merchandising of dangerous products was covered earlier in this chapter.

UNACCEPTABLE BUSINESS PRACTICES

False or Exaggerated Claims

Another major thrust of consumer protection legislation is to prohibit or control certain unacceptable business practices such as making misleading or false statements to persuade people to buy a product. Under the common law, these statements normally do not form part of the contract and generally are dismissed as mere advertising puffs, leaving the purchaser with little recourse. Further, contracts of sale often contain clauses stating that there are no representations other than those contained in the written document, making any false or misleading claims by salespeople not actionable unless they are actually included in the contract itself. Today these statements are controlled by statute, with most provinces incorporating them into the contract and making any attempt to override them void. As a result, when a salesperson makes a false or exaggerated claim, or one is included in an advertisement, it becomes a term of the contract and is actionable as a breach if it proves incorrect or is not honoured. If Mrs. Holberg, the purchaser of a used car from Affleck's Fine Car Co., was informed by the salesperson that the car had been driven "only to church on Sundays," that statement would, under these provisions, be incorporated into the contract, even if it were not contained in the written document. If Mrs. Holberg could convince the court that a false statement had been made, she could successfully sue for breach of contract when the statement proved false. The actual statutes used to accomplish this vary considerably from province to province.

Legislation incorporates misleading statements into contract

Typically, this type of statute lists several different kinds of misleading and deceptive statements which are deemed to be unfair practices. For example, taking advantage of a consumer and exerting undue pressure on a consumer are deemed to be unfair practices in Alberta.[68] In addition to the penalties imposed by governments for violations, the consumer is given the right to have the contract rescinded or specifically performed, or to sue for damages. Any attempt to override these provisions, or to declare in a contract that there are no other representations other than what appears on the written document, will be void, leaving the purchaser free to sue. This is true even when the parties involved have been relatively innocent, for negligence or fraud on the seller's part need not be shown. Innocent but misleading statements may still qualify as deceptive practices under the relevant legislation.

Unfair practices identified in statute

The government department involved is typically given considerable powers to investigate complaints and to deal with complaints against offending merchandisers, including the powers to impose fines, to suspend licences and, in some provinces, to pursue a civil action on behalf of the consumer.

Government bodies have been given significant powers

Perhaps the most effective provisions controlling misleading advertising and other deceptive business practices are contained in the federal *Competition Act*, which was discussed above. The common law provisions concerning false and misleading claims in consumer transactions have been considerably strengthened by these statutory provisions.

---

[68] An example of legislation of this type is the *Fair Trading Act*, R.S.A. 2000, c. F-2.

B.C. Act Controls Frauds Against U.S. Residents: *Director of Trade Practices v. Ideal Credit Referral Services Ltd. et al.*[69]

Ideal was a B.C. company directing misleading advertising to customers in the United States. It claimed it would loan even to those with a bad credit rating. The advertising included such phrases as "Good or Bad Credit!", "Bankruptcies O.K.!", and "Guaranteed Results!" To apply, customers had to pay a non-refundable $300 "processing fee." Ideal did a credit check, refused the application and kept the balance of the $300. The Director of Trade Practices applied for a declaration that this was a "deceptive or unconscionable act" and for an injunction. Ideal claimed that the B.C. *Act* did not apply, since its customers were in the United States. The Court of Appeal held that the *Act* prohibited deceptive and misleading practices that took place in British Columbia no matter where the victim was located. The *Act* was meant to control unethical business practices within the province.

DISCUSSION QUESTIONS

Is this an extraterritorial application of provincial law? Should the provisions of the statute be limited to the protection of B.C. residents? Is this too much of an interference in the operation of a free-market system?

Unconscionable transactions or unfair bargains controlled

Note that in *Robson v. Daimler Chrysler Corp.*,[70] the shoe was on the other foot; the customers were in British Columbia and the car manufacturers were in the United States. The B.C. *Trade Practice Act* was found to apply nonetheless. The customers alleged that the supplier engaged in deceptive acts or practices with respect to consumer transactions by failing to disclose that the paint finishes on the vehicles sold in British Columbia were defective. It was not essential that the alleged deceptive practices or acts took place within the province.

Unconscionable Transactions

Consumers sometimes are taken advantage of because of some vulnerability, such as desperation, poverty, lack of sophistication, or intellectual weakness. To prevent unscrupulous merchants from taking advantage of such vulnerable individuals, legislation has been enacted, either in separate acts (e.g., *Unconscionable Transactions Act*) or included in other statutes.

In some provinces, this legislation is restricted to situations involving the borrowing of money. For a transaction to be found unconscionable when money

---

69. (1997), 145 D.L.R. (4th) 20 (B.C.C.A.).
70. (2002), 2 B.C.L.R. (4th) 1 (C.A.).

is loaned, the actual cost of borrowing must be excessive in the circumstances. If the risk justifies the high rate of interest, it is not an unconscionable transaction, even when the consumer is of weak intellect or in desperate straits. When unconscionability is demonstrated, the courts can set the contract aside, modify its terms or order the return of money paid.

CASE SUMMARY 10.11

Aged Homeowner Protected from Unscrupulous Salesperson: *Dominion Home Improvements Ltd. v. Knuude*[71]

A door-to-door salesperson using intense tactics persuaded Knuude, an 80-year-old homeowner, to purchase a number of home improvements that she didn't need. After four hours of extremely high-pressured selling, including a refusal to leave unless the contract was signed, Knuude agreed to have the renovations done. She signed a $300 cheque as a deposit, but stopped payment on it immediately after the salesperson left.

The next day, workers from the company came to do the work. Knuude insisted that they leave. This brought back the salesperson who, by devious means, persuaded Knuude to reinstate the contract. The work was done. Knuude refused to pay. The company sued for the money owed under the contract.

The Judge determined that the contract was not binding on Knuude as it was fraudulent and unconscionable, and did not conform to the requirements set out in the provincial consumer protection legislation. This kind of unscrupulous business practice has led to the increase in consumer protection legislation.

DISCUSSION QUESTIONS

Has such legislation gone too far? Should consumers assume more responsibility for their own mistakes? Are there occasions when protection is necessary?

In several other provinces, the legislation goes further, extending the concept of unconscionability beyond loan transactions to also cover unacceptable business practices. In these provinces, the courts can look at factors such as physical infirmity, illiteracy, inability to understand the language of an agreement, undue influence, a price that grossly exceeds the value of the goods, and the lack of reasonable benefit to the consumer, in establishing unconscionability. Remedies such as rescission, damages, and punitive damages are available. In some provinces, the government agency may assist in, or even initiate, an action on behalf of the consumer. In addition to these legislative provisions, the common law doctrine of unconscionability in contract law, has become much more accepted. It can also be applied in these consumer situations. In Case Summary 10.11, Knuude was able to escape her contractual obligations because she was taken advantage of and unreasonably pressured by the salesperson. The key to unconscionability is that there

Some statutes do not limit unconscionability to loan transactions

Common law developments

---

71. (1986), 20 C.L.R. 192 (Ont. Dist. Ct.).

must be an inequality of bargaining power. According to Lord Denning, this inequality exists when a person "who, without independent advice, enters into a contract upon terms that are very unfair... when his bargaining power is grievously impaired by reason of his own needs or desires, or [ignorance]... coupled with undue influences or pressures brought to bear on him...."[72] This was certainly the situation with Knuude; however, McHugh v. Forbes (1991), 4 O.R. (3d) 374 (C.A.), the terms of the agreement were not unreasonable. Therefore, although there was pressure and desperation, there was no unconscionability.[73]

Gift Cards

Laws governing gift cards becoming more common

Gift cards are increasingly popular in North America; there are now $80 billion of gift card sales annually in North America.[74] Gift cards do not involve credit. The purchaser pays in advance to "load" a card, which can then be used up to the amount that has been loaded onto the card. The key issues involving gift cards relate to expiry dates and fees. A monthly fee could, for example, eventually consume the entire value of the card.

Because of the increasing popularity of gift cards and the corresponding increase in consumer complaints, governments have begun to introduce laws to deal specifically with gift cards. In Alberta, for example, the *Fair Trading Act*[75] contains general provisions that could be used with respect to gift cards. Section 6(4)(a) indicates that it is an unfair practice for suppliers to do or say anything that might reasonably deceive or mislead a consumer. Section 7(3) entitles consumers to recover the amount by which the consumer's payment under the consumer transaction exceeds the value of the goods or services to the consumer.

Nevertheless, the *Gift Card Regulation*[76] came into force on 1 November 2008. It stipulates that gift cards may not have expiry dates, that only certain fees can be charged with respect to gift cards and that certain activities (such as refusing to accept a gift card as partial payment on a purchase) are unfair practices under the *Fair Trading Act*. It is likely that most jurisdictions will introduce similar provisions to protect consumer interests if the use of gift cards continues to grow.

CONTROLLED BUSINESS PRACTICES

Door-to-door sales controlled

Consumer protection legislation also places controls on several specific kinds of business activities. All provinces restrict **door-to-door** sales, also known as **direct sales**. The main method of doing this is by imposing a **cooling-off period**, which allows a purchaser a given period of time to change his mind and to rescind the contract. Some jurisdictions also require the disclosure of certain information and that the contract be in writing, and provide for an extended cooling-off period.

Other activities controlled including referral selling

Other types of potentially abusive business activities prohibited or controlled in various jurisdictions are unsolicited goods and services or credit cards, discounted

---

72. *Lloyd's Bank Ltd. v. Bundy*, [1975] Q.B. 326 (C.A.).

73. For an article explaining unequal bargaining power, unconscionability, and Canadian legislation dealing with unconscionable contracts, see Donald Manderscheid Q.C., "The Right to a Fair Bargain", *LawNow* (May/June 2008).

74. For a good article on the subject of gift cards, the need for legislation to protect consumers, and a review of some of the existing legislation, see Peter Bowal, "Playing Your Cards Right", *LawNow* (March/April 2008).

75. *Supra* note 67.

76. Alta. Reg. 146/2008.

income tax returns, pre-arranged funeral services, inappropriate debt collection activities, prepaid contracting, time-share contracts, and referral selling. **Referral selling** involves a purchaser supplying a seller with a list of friends or acquaintances. When sales are made to any of those people, the purchaser is given a benefit, such as a reduction of the purchase price.

Methods of Control

Controlling these unacceptable activities through legislation is accomplished by several methods. One method involves requiring that the party supplying these goods and services be licensed. This gives the government an effective control mechanism, as licences can be suspended or revoked. Legislation may also impose fines or imprisonment in the event of abusive behaviour. In addition to the powers to investigate, to seize records and to impose penalties for violations, government bodies are often given the power to initiate actions on behalf of victimized consumers, or to help them start their own actions.

Several methods used to control abusive activity

LOAN TRANSACTIONS

In addition to unconscionable transactions legislation, every province has enacted legislation requiring that the true cost of borrowing be disclosed, thus prohibiting excessive rates of interest and costs in loan transactions. The federal *Interest Act*[77] has similar requirements. The *Criminal Code*[78] also prohibits the charging of excessive rates of interest.

True cost of borrowing must be disclosed

CASE SUMMARY 10.12

Proper Disclosure of Interest Rates Required: *Elcano Acceptance Ltd. v. Richmond, Richmond, Stambler & Mills*[79]

Elcano retained the services of the defendant law firm to draft promissory notes on its behalf, for use in its business. These notes stated interest was to be calculated at the rate of 2 percent per month. Section 4 of the *Interest Act* provided that in any contract for which interest is payable, interest must be stated as an annual rate; otherwise, it is not permissible to collect more than 5 percent interest. Because of this oversight, Elcano was not able to collect the interest due and payable from its customers pursuant to its promissory notes. It sued the law firm alleging negligence, and won.

[77.] R.S.C. 1985, c. I-15.

[78.] R.S.C. 1985, c. C-46, s. 347.

[79.] (1991), 3 O.R. (3d) 123 (C.A.).

CASE SUMMARY 10.13

Excessive Interest Costly for All Concerned: *Garland v. Consumers' Gas Co.*[80]

In a stunning class action suit, Garland brought an action on behalf of over 500 000 customers of Consumers' (now Enbridge Gas Distribution Inc.). He demonstrated that the 5 percent late payment penalties charged on unpaid accounts constituted a criminal rate of interest. Garland established that when a late payment penalty was charged, and the actual bill and late payment were paid within 38 days, the actual annual interest rate was over 60 percent, contrary to section 347 of the *Criminal Code*.

The case went to the Supreme Court of Canada—twice! In the first instance, the Court found that the late payment penalties were collected in contravention of the *Criminal Code* and, as a matter of public policy, criminals should not be permitted to keep the proceeds of their crime. The Court thus ordered Consumers' to repay the late payment penalties collected from the representative class in excess of the interest limit stipulated by the *Criminal Code*.

The issue of restitution brought the matter back to the Supreme Court. It decided that, although late payment penalties had been collected since 1981, only those penalties imposed after the class action was commenced (in 1994) had to be repaid. Prior to 1994, reliance on the Ontario Energy Board's orders gave Consumers' juristic reason for the enrichment; but once Garland's action was commenced, Consumers' was put on notice that it was violating the *Criminal Code*. Collecting excessive interest from that point constituted unjust enrichment.

DISCUSSION QUESTIONS

Consider other situations where consumers must pay late payment penalties. Should it be left to consumers to challenge these in court?

Legislative provisions aim to prevent the practice of hiding excessive interest rates in the payment of a bonus or through some other form of subterfuge. Statutes demand that all this information be fully disclosed to the borrower at the outset. They usually prohibit misleading information in advertisements about the cost of borrowing, require the cost of borrowing to be stated in a standard format and require moneylenders to be registered, which makes them subject to suspension by the governing body for misbehaviour or incompetence.

The payday loan industry has come under attack recently, particularly in British Columbia and Manitoba. In response to public pressure, Manitoba amended the *Consumer Protection Act*[81] by adding Part XVIII, dealing with "Payday Loans." Among other things, these provisions require the Public Utilities Board to hold hearings when it is setting the maximum interest rates that may be charged for payday loans. The *Payday Loans Regulation*[82] allows for the licensing of payday lenders. Because of this statutory framework, Manitoba was the first province to receive

---

[80]. [2002] S.C.C.A. No. 53; [2004] 1 S.C.R. 629.

[81]. C.C.S.M. c. C200.

[82]. Man. Reg. 99/2007.

designation under s. 347.1 of the *Criminal Code*, allowing it to regulate the rates that can be charged for payday loans.[83] Other provinces are likely to follow this lead.

Court Refuses to Enforce Payday Loans Where Interest Is Usurious: *Consolidated Financial Corp. v. Forde*[84]

Consolidated's lawyer, who also represented Consolidated's related company, Intercapital, sought to enforce numerous unpaid loan cases, including loans to Forde, Gentile and 78 other debtors. These "payday loans" were challenged by the debtors on the basis that the effective rate of interest was usurious (excessive) and contrary to section 347 of the *Criminal Code*.

The loans were generally for 14 days. The stated interest was 47 percent per annum. Upon default, a $180 fee would be imposed, as "liquidated damages" (a supposed estimate of the damages) but, in essence, it constituted a penalty. Evidence was given that the lender also inflated the principal. A "fee" of some sort may have been subsumed into the principal, disguising the true amount advanced. If Gentile was advanced $500, but the loan stipulated that $620 was to be repaid in 14 days, on the 15th day, $806.95 was owing (once liquidated damages were included), bringing the effective rate of interest ($306.95 for 15 days) to 1500 percent per annum!

The Court decided *not* to assist Consolidated in the collection of *any* of its contractual debts. Instead, it ordered that no further action by Consolidated or Intercapital on this form of loan agreement could proceed, until the higher court (B.C.S.C.) ruled on the enforceability of this type of contract.

SMALL BUSINESS PERSPECTIVE

The B.C. Supreme Court was already considering the enforceability of these payday loans. Until the superior court rules on this issue, all other collection actions by the lenders are stayed. If denied access to the courts to enforce these debts, will payday lenders survive?

The "unconscionability" of the transaction has an impact on the severity of the penalty imposed by the courts. When it is shown that the parties' bargaining positions were relatively equal and that each had independent advice, the reduction in the eventual interest deemed payable may be less. In the *Transport North American Express* case,[85] in which the parties' bargaining positions were relatively equal and each had legal representation, the Supreme Court of Canada refused to enforce the illegal rate of interest agreed upon. Instead, it imposed interest at 60 percent, the highest rate possible to comply with section 347 of the *Criminal Code*. The rationale expressed for the decision was that if the borrower had been

---

[83] See *Order Designating Manitoba for the Purposes of the Criminal Interest Rate Provisions of the Criminal Code*, S.O.R./2008-212.

[84] 2005 BCPC 0209.

[85] *Transport North American Express Inc. v. New Solutions Financial Corp.*, [2004] 1 S.C.R. 249.

relieved of paying a commercially appropriate rate of interest, it would enjoy a windfall. Partial enforcement of the loan was more likely since the parties stood on equal bargaining positions.

But when the borrower is less sophisticated and the transaction smacks of unconscionability, the court may refuse to enforce the indebtedness in its entirety.[86]

DEBT-COLLECTION PROCESSES

Unpaid creditors often turn to debt collection agencies to assist in the collection process. The actual debts owed are usually assigned to these agencies for a fee. The practices used by such agencies are sometimes abusive, so legislation has been enacted to control their activities. Common law remedies for abusive debt collection practices, such as defamation, assault and battery, trespass and even false imprisonment, are usually ineffective. The legislation enacted requires these agencies to be licensed, adding the threat of a suspended or revoked licence in the event of infractions. These statutes set out specific unacceptable collection practices, such as excessive phone calls, calls at unreasonable hours, collect calls, threats of legal action with no foundation, issuing letters of collection that resemble official court documents, making deceptive or misleading statements, communicating with employers, friends or relatives, and putting pressure on innocent relatives to pay the debt.

Abusive debt collection practices controlled

Some provinces require that debt-collection agencies use only previously approved form letters in their demands for payment. In British Columbia, a collector must not communicate with a debtor, a member of the debtor's family or household, a relative, neighbour, friend, or acquaintance of the debtor, or the debtor's employer in a manner or with a frequency as to constitute harassment. Any use of undue, excessive or unreasonable pressure constitutes harassment.[87] The punishment for a party engaged in such activities may range from the loss of its licence to prosecution and a fine. Some provinces give debtors the right to civil action for any damages suffered because of the abusive practices. The threat of criminal prosecution to pressure a debtor to pay is a violation of the *Criminal Code*[88] and can result in prosecution for extortion against the person making the threat.

Credit reporting practices controlled

Legislation to control credit-reporting agencies is also in place. While providing a valuable service to the lender, these businesses sometimes cause great harm to the borrower through carelessness or indifference. The relevant statutes usually require such bodies to be registered, limit the type of information that they can disclose, make it an offence for them to knowingly include false information in a credit file, give the individual the right to inspect the file and to correct or remove erroneous information, and, in some jurisdictions, prohibit an agency from making any report to a lender without the written permission of the borrower.

[86.] See *C.A.P.S. International Inc. v. Kotello* (2002), 164 Man. R. (2d) 202 (Q.B.), or *Direct Advances (Spruce) Ltd. v. Halgren*, 2003 ABPC 136, in which the Courts refused to enforce any part of the contract due to violation of s. 347 of the *Criminal Code*. In each case, the Court refused to sever the illegal interest clause and enforce the principal indebtedness due to the unconscionability of the loans. But in *Milani v. Banks* (1997), 32 O.R. (3d) 557 (C.A.), the Court ordered the debtor to repay the amount she received and interest at the rate normally charged litigants on money due.

[87.] *Business Practices and Consumer Protection Act*, supra note 33, s. 114.

[88.] *Criminal Code*, supra note 79, s. 346.

CONSUMER SERVICE BODIES

In most jurisdictions, government departments have been empowered to implement and enforce these consumer protection statutes. The authority given to such departments usually includes the right to hear and investigate complaints, seize records, search premises, suspend licences, impose fines, or some other corrective action, and initiate civil actions on behalf of the consumer.

Government agencies enforce statutes

In some jurisdictions, these bodies have become clearing houses of consumer information, with a mandate to collect and disseminate that information to the public. Consumer bureaus can collect information on dangerous products, consumer business scams, or unacceptable practices. They may get involved in advertising to educate the consumer.[89]

Government agencies educate and publicize

Representatives of the federal government and of each of the provinces and territories belong to the Consumer Measures Committee (CMC). The aim of the CMC is to provide, through national cooperation, an improved marketplace for Canadian consumers. To create public awareness, the CMC has published an electronic version of the *Canadian Consumer Handbook*.[90] This publication provides advice and information on a wide range of consumer issues. It includes a Canada-wide directory of names, addresses, and telephone numbers for contacts in government, business, and consumer associations.

Private organizations, such as the Better Business Bureau ("BBB"), are also designed to be clearinghouses for such information. It must be remembered, however, that the BBB is supported and sustained by the business community. It thus has a vested interest in serving that community. The theory is that it is in the best interests of the business community to maintain high standards by weeding out disreputable businesses. The BBB and similar organizations serve that function for members of the business community who join them. Specialized bodies have also been set up to deal with disputes in unique industries. In particular, there are several organizations that are available to arbitrate disputes arising from the sale and repair of automobiles in Canada. The Canadian Motor Vehicle Arbitration Plan (CAMVAP) is a prime example.[91]

Private agencies also provide helpful information and services

 REDUCING RISK 10.5

For businesspeople, it is important to understand that the operation of the consumer protection legislation has shifted the balance. The old principle of *caveat emptor* required the consumers of products or services to be careful in their dealings. Now that principle is often downplayed. Instead, responsibility has shifted to the merchant to exercise care. But, even though these consumer protection statutes may *seem* strong, they will be ineffective if they are poorly enforced. Still, merchants must be aware that the nature of their responsibility has changed and has become much more onerous.

---

89. See, for example, services provided by the government of Alberta, at www.servicealberta.gov.ab.ca/ Consumer_Info.cfm, www.servicealberta.gov.ab.ca/548.cfm, and www.servicealberta.gov.ab.ca/ ConsumerTipsheets.cfm

90. Available online at www.ic.gc.ca/eic/site/oca-bc.nsf/eng/h_ca02058.html.

91. Check CAMVAP online at www.camvap.ca/.

SUMMARY

Sale of Goods Act

- Implies certain terms into a contract unless the parties have agreed otherwise
- Applies only when goods are being sold
- Except where there is agreement otherwise, risk follows title, and the *Act* supplies five rules to determine when title is transferred
- Seller must convey good title and quiet possession
- Goods must be free of any lien or charge
- Goods must be fit for communicated purpose and be of merchantable quality
- Goods must match the sample or description
- In the event of a default, where the goods are not yet in the hands of the purchaser, the seller has an unpaid seller's lien and has the right of *stoppage in transit*

Consumer protection

- The federal *Competition Act* controls practices that unduly lessen competition
- The federal *Food and Drug Act* and *Hazardous Products Act* control dangerous products
- Many other federal statutes protect customers
- Various provincial statutes require that goods be of acceptable quality
- A number of other statutes are in place to protect consumers, including consumer protection acts, trade practices acts, and unconscionable transactions acts
- These statutes control unacceptable business practices, such as misrepresentation and other forms of misleading advertising, unconscionable transactions (that is, when a merchant takes advantage of a weak-willed or otherwise unequal customer), and specific activities, such as door-to-door and referral selling
- Moneylenders are required to disclose the true cost of borrowing to their customers
- Abusive debt collection practices are restricted

QUESTIONS

1. Explain the purpose of the *Sale of Goods Act* in relation to the obligations of the parties to a sale of goods transaction.

2. What three conditions must be met before the *Sale of Goods Act* applies to a transaction?

3. What is the distinction between a sale and an agreement to sell? What is the significance of that distinction?

4. When does the risk transfer to the buyer in a sale of goods transaction? Explain the exceptions to this general rule.

5. What is a bill of lading? How can it affect who bears the risk in a sale of goods transaction?

6. Indicate when title transfers in the following situations:

    a. when the contract for sale is unconditional and the goods involved are in a deliverable state at the time the purchase is made

    b. when the subject of the contract involves specific goods to which the seller is obligated to do something, such as repair, clean, or modify to get them into a deliverable state

    c. when the contract for sale involves specific, identified goods, which must be weighed or measured before being given to the buyer

    d. when the goods are delivered to the buyer on approval

    e. when goods purchased by description have not been selected, separated out, or manufactured at the time the sales contract is entered into.

7. The *Sale of Goods Act* imposes terms relating to goods matching samples or descriptions and meeting standards of fitness, quality and title. Explain the nature of these implied terms and their effect on the parties. Indicate which terms are conditions and which are warranties. Explain the significance of the distinction.

8. Explain what merchantable quality means.

9. Explain the effect of an exemption clause included in a contract that is inconsistent with the terms set out in the *Sale of Goods Act*.

10. Explain the rights of the seller when the buyer of goods:

    a. becomes insolvent

    b. defaults on the contract of sale while the goods are still in the hands of the seller

    c. defaults after the goods have been given to a third party to deliver but before they are received by the buyer

    d. where the buyer becomes bankrupt after the goods have been delivered.

11. Explain why a seller of goods might be less likely to sue for damages than for price.

12. Under what circumstances may a buyer refuse delivery of goods?

13. The *Sale of Goods Act* in each province implies certain terms into contracts of sale relating to the fitness and quality of the product. Some Canadian jurisdictions make these provisions mandatory in consumer transactions. Explain the situation in your jurisdiction.

14. Describe the practices controlled by the *Competition Act* and explain how that control is accomplished.

15. How does the concept of privity of contract limit the effectiveness of many consumer protection provisions? How have some jurisdictions overcome this problem?

16. What common law provisions are available to protect consumers from unscrupulous business practices?

17. Describe the methods outlined in federal and provincial consumer protection statutes to control businesses with a tendency to abusive practices. Discuss the effectiveness of these tactics.

18. Identify the legislation in effect in your jurisdiction that offers relief to victims of unconscionable transactions.

19. What statutory provisions have been introduced throughout Canada to control door-to-door selling, referral selling, and other potentially abusive practices?

20. What services are provided to consumers through organizations set up by the federal and provincial governments? Discuss whether these services are adequate.

Chapter 11

Special Contracts: Employment

A contract for employment is one of the most important contracts in which a person will become involved. This chapter is devoted to exploring the legal ramifications of the employment relationship.

WHAT IS EMPLOYMENT?

Employment involves one person doing work for another, but not all such relationships are classed as employment. The work of independent contractors, such as doctors, lawyers, and plumbers, must be distinguished from employment. Such independent contractors work for themselves and act independently, providing a specific service for the person they contract with, whereas an employee is said to be in a master–servant relationship, acting under the direction of the master.

Not all work is employment

Agency is a third type of business relationship, in which one person acts as a go-between in relationships between others. Agency will be discussed in detail in Chapter 15. Each of these relationships imposes different legal rights and obligations on the parties; understanding which body of rights and obligations governs a particular relationship can be of vital importance.

The Control Test

Employee controlled by employer

The traditional method of determining whether an employment relationship exists is to assess the degree of control exercised by the person paying for the service. A person who is told not only what to do but also how to do it is classed as an employee. But if the person doing the work is free to decide how the job should be done, the position is more likely that of an independent contractor. For example, if Fong hires Kirk to paint a house, Kirk could be either an independent contractor or an employee. If Fong tells Kirk which tools to use, when to work, and how to perform the job, then Kirk is probably an employee. If Kirk supplies the tools and determines what time to start work and the best way to perform the job, then he is probably an independent contractor. Whether the person is paid a wage or salary, or is paid by the job, is also taken into consideration in determining if an employment relationship exists. Courts will also look at who owns the tools used and who profits or runs the risk of loss from the work performed.

The employment relationship involves a contract in which the employee agrees generally to serve the employer, who has the right to supervise and direct. On the other hand, an independent contractor agrees to do a particular job, not to enter into a general service relationship. In other words, employees work for their employer, whereas independent contractors work for themselves. In Case Summary 11.1, it was clear to the court that Ms. Samuda was working for the employer and not for herself.

Independent contractor works independently

CASE SUMMARY 11.1

Control Suggests Employment—But It's Not the Only Test: Samuda v. Recipco Corp;[1] *Algoma Taxicab Management Ltd. v. M.N.R.*[2]

Ms. Samuda initially provided consulting services through her company, pursuant to an oral agreement. She then signed an employment contract with Recipco for the position of Senior Vice-President of Legal and Business Affairs. She was eventually dismissed from this position. She therefore brought an action for wrongful termination and breach of an employment contract. The defendants argued that Samuda was a "consultant," that the relationship was governed by the oral agreement, and that Samuda voluntarily terminated the relationship.

The Court referred to a Supreme Court of Canada ruling in which Justice Major listed a number of factors that should be considered in determining whether a person is an employee or an independent contractor:

[T]he central question is whether the person who has been engaged to perform the services is performing them as a person in business on his own account. In making this determination, the level of control the employer has over the worker's activities will always be a factor. However, other factors to consider include whether the worker provides his or her own equipment, whether the worker hires his or her own helpers, the degree of financial risk taken by the worker, the degree of responsibility for investment and management held by the worker, and the worker's opportunity for profit in the performance of his or her tasks.[3]

The Court held that the oral agreement between the parties was superseded by the written agreement, which clearly stated that the status of Samuda was that of an employee. Furthermore, Samuda did not maintain her own office premises but instead used offices at Recipco's premises, Recipco paid for her laptop computer, her expenses

1. [2007] B.C.S.C. 1013 (CanLII), additional reasons at [2008] B.C.S.C. 192 (CanLII).
2. (2006), 60 D.T.C. 2497 (T.C.C.)
3. 671122 Ontario Ltd. v. Sagaz Industries Canada Inc., [2001] 2 S.C.R. 983, at para. 47–48.

were reimbursed by Recipco, she did not hire her own assistants, her activities were subject to the control and direction of Recipco's Board of Directors, and she did not undertake any financial risk. The fact that her salary was paid to her consulting company was immaterial.

Contrast this with the *Algoma* case, in which Brouillard worked as a taxi driver for Algoma. The contract between Algoma and its drivers entitled the drivers to use a vehicle and Algoma's dispatch services. Algoma paid for the vehicle insurance, as well as the maintenance, fuel, oil, and other supplies for the vehicles. The drivers paid a rental fee that varied from 62 percent to 70 percent of their gross receipts. Algoma did not assign drivers to work at particular times, on particular days, or in specific geographical areas. Drivers could request a vehicle for a specific date and time. Drivers were not required to work any minimum period. They did not have to be consistently available during a shift. Drivers could have customers call them directly rather than calling the dispatcher.

The Court indicated that the central question is whether the person is performing the services as a person in business on his own account. The level of control the employer has over the worker's activities will always be a factor, although other factors will also be considered. In this case, the Court concluded that all of Algoma's drivers, including Brouillard, were performing services as independent contractors.

SMALL BUSINESS PERSPECTIVE

The determination as to whether a worker is an employee or an independent contractor is often important with respect to the applicability of government legislation, such as the Canada Pension Plan or the *Employment Insurance Act*, or in determining whether a terminated worker is entitled to severance pay. Courts consider the level of control the worker is subject to, as well as other factors, when classifying the worker. Should the contract between the parties be the sole determinant of the nature of the relationship? Should the courts defer to the agreement between the parties? What about the imbalance of power between those parties?

The Organization Test

Organization test supplements control test

In recent years, the courts have supplemented the control test with the organization test. Even if there is little direct control, when the individual is an integral part of the organization, working only for that corporation and subject to group control, that person is likely an employee.[4]

On the other hand, if that person is free to offer services to others and bears the risks of profit or loss if work is not completed in a timely manner, she may be an independent contractor.

Definition of employment broadened

It is important to note that, at least for the purposes of establishing vicarious liability, a person can be an independent contractor for most purposes but an employee or a servant in some specific instances.[5] This ruling has prompted the courts to find employment relationships in areas that were traditionally considered purely independent. Jones could be a plumber acting as an independent contractor for Smith for most of the job, but while digging a drainage ditch at Smith's direction he could be considered an employee for that purpose. If someone was

---

4. John G. Fleming, *The Law of Torts,* 8th ed. (Sydney: The Law Book Co. Ltd., 1992), p. 372.

5. *Cooperators Insurance Association. v. Kearney,* [1965] S.C.R. 106.

hurt, Smith could be found vicariously liable for Jones's careless conduct in digging that ditch.

Individual statutes may provide a definition of employment for the purposes of that statute, but there is no general legislated definition. When a court is dealing with vicarious liability or wrongful dismissal, it must therefore turn to the principles enunciated in precedents to determine whether an employment relationship exists.

It is also important to note that while a person normally cannot be an independent contractor and an employee at the same time, the same is not true of an agent. **Agents** can be independent contractors or employees. A sales clerk in a store is both an employee and an agent; a person selling insurance is likely an independent contractor but is also functioning as an agent for her client. It's important to keep these categories separate, as the liability of the parties will likely be determined by the relationship between them.

> An employee can be an agent

> An agent can be independent

The legal principles governing the independent contractor are embodied in the general rules of contract law already covered in Chapters 6 through 9. This chapter will examine the law of master and servant, the relevant federal and provincial legislation, the trade union movement, and collective bargaining.

THE LAW OF MASTER AND SERVANT

Over the years, the common law courts developed special rules to deal with the unique problems associated with employment, which was then referred to as a master–servant relationship. Today, employment law is governed primarily by the general provisions of contract law, supplemented by these special rules as well as by a number of statutes that further define the responsibilities and obligations of the parties.

The Employment Contract

The main responsibility of the employer, in addition to payment of wages, is to provide a safe workplace and good working conditions for the employee. Some types of jobs are inherently dangerous, such as construction, and the employer is obligated to minimize the danger, usually by promoting safe work practices; erecting protective fences, barriers, and nets; and requiring the use of proper safety equipment. The employer must hire competent people. If it can be shown that the employer hired a careless or incompetent worker who caused injury to others, the employer may be held accountable. For example, when an inexperienced crane operator caused the crane to topple, injuring other workers, the employer was responsible because of its failure to ensure that only a competent and experienced worker operated the crane.[6] Job-site health and safety requirements, and injuries caused by other workers, are specialized areas covered by occupational health and safety legislation and workers' compensation legislation; both are discussed below.

> Obligations of employer include
> • payment of wages or salary
> • safe working conditions

The contract of employment usually includes a commitment by the employer to pay a specific wage or salary. That agreement will often also set out bonus arrangements, benefit packages, and promises to repay any reasonable expenses incurred.

The employee also has obligations to fulfill. The employee must possess the skills claimed and exercise them in a reasonably competent and careful manner.

[6.] R. v. A. W. Leil Cranes & Equipment (1986) Ltd., [2003] N.S.J. No. 524.

Obligations of employee:
• competent work
• honesty and loyalty
• punctuality
• action in employer's best interests
• fiduciary obligations in some cases

The employee has an obligation to follow any reasonable order pertaining to the employment and must treat the property of the employer carefully. The employee must be honest, loyal, and courteous; an employee who does the work required but acts in an insubordinate or disloyal way can be fired. Similarly, an employee must be punctual and work for the time specified in the contract. If the employee uses the employer's time or facilities without permission, he may be disciplined. With some types of jobs, there may also be an obligation to generally act in the best interests of the employer. This is referred to as a fiduciary obligation and is usually imposed only on senior-level employees. For normal employees, unless the employment contract provides otherwise, their obligations to the employer end when that employment is terminated. But for those senior level employees who have a fiduciary duty, that duty may continue after the employment ends.

An employee who is also a fiduciary is automatically subject to certain obligations toward an employer. These include a duty to act in good faith, make full disclosure, and not take corporate opportunities for one's own benefit. For example, in the *Felker* case,[7] when the employee secretly engaged in negotiations to become the sales agent for a second company and did not advise or offer his employer the opportunity to represent the second company, the Court found just cause for that employee's dismissal. Failure to disclose this activity and to secure prior consent justified the dismissal.

Restrictive covenants must be reasonable

Employment contracts are often not formal or written documents. It is, however, a good idea to put the contract in writing, clearly stating the provisions that are important for the parties. Such provisions may include the rate of pay, the hours of work, and a description of what services are required and for what period. As with other contracts, all the ingredients necessary for a contract to exist must be present. Employers often try to impose new, one-sided employment contracts on their employees after the commencement of employment. These contracts often include terms adverse to the employee, such as restrictive covenants or terms limiting the period of notice to be given upon termination. When imposed after the fact, these provisions are often not binding because of a failure of consideration. The employment contract is illustrated in Figure 11.1.

General contract law applies to employment

When **restrictive covenants** are included in the original contract, committing the employee not to work in a particular geographic area or in a particular industry after leaving the position, they have to specify a reasonable time and area. If they are too broad, the covenants will not be enforced. Further, such covenants must be the most appropriate way of protecting the employer's interests, and not be against the public interest. For example, if an employer invents a special production method, the secrecy of which could be maintained only by

Figure 11.1 The Employment Contract

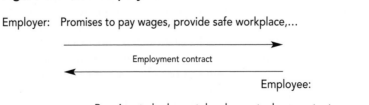

Employer: Promises to pay wages, provide safe workplace,...

Employment contract

Employee:

Promises to be honest, loyal, punctual, competent,...

Breach of these major terms may enable opposite party to treat contract as discharged

---

[7.] *Felker v. Cunningham* (2000), 191 D.L.R. (4th) 734 (Ont. C.A.), leave to appeal to S.C.C. refused, [2000] S.C.C.A. No. 538.

requiring that the employees commit themselves not to work in a similar industry for a reasonable period of time, a restrictive covenant in the contract of employment to that effect would likely be valid. But, in general, there is some reluctance on the part of the courts to enforce restrictive covenants in employment contracts because of the danger of denying the employee the ability to earn a livelihood and because of the normally weaker bargaining position of employees.

CASE SUMMARY 11.2

Injunctions Sought to Enforce Promises Not to Compute: *Herff Jones Canada Inc. v. Todd;*[8] *Lyons v. Multari*[9]

Todd entered into a sales-representative agreement with the respondent whereby he agreed to solicit schools and colleges for the purpose of selling class rings, medals, awards, and yearbooks supplied by the respondent. After six years, Todd severed the relationship and went to work for a competitor, Jostens. By doing so, he breached a promise that he would not compete with his former employer for four years. The respondent sought and obtained an injunction from the trial Judge, preventing Todd from "soliciting or contacting directly or indirectly any of those schools or accounts who were customers" of the respondent as of 20 May 1994, for a period of four years.

Todd appealed, arguing that the trial Judge erred in deciding that the restrictive covenant in the sales representative agreement was valid. Prohibiting an employee from working for a competitor for four years does, at first glance, appear excessive. The Court of Appeal, however, found the trial Judge had applied the correct tests: (1) The covenant was reasonable as between the parties. Its duration, four years, was reasonable in light of the fact that Todd would have been entitled to a split commission for three years after leaving the respondent had he not breached the restrictive covenant. Further, Todd had developed a special relationship with the customers, so the proprietary interest of the respondent would be jeopardized if Todd could approach them on the competitor's behalf. Nor did the covenant cover too large a geographical area. Todd had simply promised not to compete in the area formerly serviced by him on behalf of the respondent. (2) The covenant was also reasonable with regard to public interest.

Contrast the above with the *Lyons* case, in which the plaintiff oral surgeon hired a new associate. They signed a short, handwritten contract containing a non-competition clause. The defendant therein agreed not to compete for three years within a five-mile area. After 17 months, he gave the agreed 6 months' notice and opened his own oral surgery practice, in the same city. The Court of Appeal determined that it was not appropriate to enforce a non-competition clause if a non-solicitation clause would adequately protect the employer's interests. A non-solicitation clause prohibits a departing employee from soliciting clients, patients, or customers of his previous employer. A non-competition clause does more—it attempts to keep the former employee out of the business.

[8.] (1996), 181 A.R. 236 (C.A.).

[9.] (2000), 50 O.R. (3d) 526 (C.A.), leave to appeal to S.C.C. refused, [2000] S.C.C.A. No. 567.

These cases suggest that not only must the non-competition clause be reasonable as between the parties (not overly broad geographically or in terms of time), but the party trying to enforce the same must show that the clause is necessary to protect some proprietary interest. Otherwise, the court might regard the clause as being too restrictive or unnecessary and simply refuse to enforce it.

SMALL BUSINESS PERSPECTIVE

The question again arises, should the parties to such agreements be required to honour them? Remember that the compensation and benefits would have been calculated on what the parties thought their obligations were under the contract of employment. Should the courts be able to disregard what the parties have agreed to, on the basis that they consider the agreement to be too restrictive or unreasonable?

Termination

Contract may stipulate amount of notice to be given

• Otherwise, reasonable notice of termination required of both employer and employee

An employment contract may provide for its own discharge (as when the contract is for a fixed term, say one year, and that term expires), or the parties can mutually agree to bring it to an end. However, most contracts of employment are for an indefinite period of time with no reference to notice requirements. In general, such contracts of employment can be terminated by either party giving reasonable notice, by the employer giving the compensation that should have been earned in that notice period (pay in lieu of notice), or immediately with just cause.

• But note human rights violations

Just as the employee is not bound to the job and can leave after giving reasonable notice, so too is the employer free to terminate the employment relationship for no specific reason as long as sufficient notice is given. Note, however, that the employer's right to terminate even with proper notice is restricted somewhat by provincial and federal human rights legislation and by the *Charter of Rights and Freedoms*, which prohibit such action when it amounts to discrimination on the basis of gender, religion, colour, physical disability, or other protected ground.[10]

REASONABLE NOTICE

What constitutes reasonable notice varies with circumstances
Courts consider
• length of service
• type of job
• age of employee
• qualifications
• availability of similar employment
• bad-faith conduct

The problem for employers is that reasonable notice, especially when long-term employees are involved, can be quite significant. The courts impose notice periods on the basis of such factors as length of service, the type of job, the employee's age, experience, training and qualifications, and the availability of similar employment.[11] In some cases involving long-term senior managers, the required notice period may even exceed two years.

[10.] *Canadian Charter of Rights and Freedoms*, ss. 15 and 28, Part I of the *Constitution Act, 1982*, being Schedule B to the *Canada Act 1982*(U.K.), 1982, c. 11, and, for example, *Human Rights Code*,R.S.O. 1990, c. H.19, s. 5.

[11.] *Honda Canada Inc. v. Keays*, 2008 SCC 39.

CASE SUMMARY 11.3

Bad Faith of Employer May Add Significant Damages: *Honda Canada Inc. v. Keays*[12]

Keays had worked for Honda for 14 years but was persistently absent due to chronic fatigue syndrome. He went on long-term disability for a period, but that was terminated (wrongfully, as later determined by the Court) and he had to return to work. There followed a considerable amount of absenteeism caused by his illness. Honda required him to submit to its doctor, and when he followed his lawyer's advice and refused "pending clarification of the purpose, methodology and the parameters of the assessment," his employment was terminated.

He sued for wrongful dismissal. At trial, the Judge found that Honda had a culture of "lean operation" and production efficiency, which led it to hound Keays because of his absences. It was also clear to the Judge that Honda thought his condition was "bogus." The Judge also determined that the request to see Honda's doctor was not made in good faith but as a pretext to fire him. There was also an internal meeting during which the Honda representatives tried to persuade Keays to reject the advice of his own lawyer. Because of the deceit and insensitive method of termination amounting to bad faith on the part of the employer, the normal notice period was extended by 9 months, from 15 to 24 months. This amounted to an award of $150 000 for wrongful dismissal.

The Judge also found that the harassment and discrimination Keays experienced and the denial of his disability benefits constituted a separate wrong. The Court found that the employer had been guilty of a "protracted corporate conspiracy" and awarded Keays a further $500 000 in punitive damages. This was the largest award of punitive damages in a wrongful dismissal action thus far in Canada.

On appeal, the Court of Appeal upheld the finding of wrongful dismissal and the awarding of the extra damages because of the manner of dismissal. The Court did, however, reduce the punitive damages from $500 000 to $100 000.

The Supreme Court of Canada set aside the damages for the manner of dismissal. It also set aside the punitive damages and reduced the costs awarded to a regular level. The Court indicated that damages for wrongful dismissal do not usually include damages for the actual loss of a job or for pain and distress suffered as a result of being terminated. Damages for the manner of dismissal will only be available if the employer has acted, during the course of the dismissal, in a manner that is (para. 57) "unfair or is in bad faith by being, for example, untruthful, misleading or unduly insensitive." Such damages should be awarded through an award that reflects actual damages, not by extending the notice period.

The Court ruled that the trial Judge had made an error of fact and that Honda's conduct was not deserving of an award of damages for misconduct in dismissal. Punitive damages are awarded for deliberate wrongful acts that are malicious and outrageous. The Court ruled that Honda's behaviour was not deserving of punitive damages.

---

12. *Ibid.*

SMALL BUSINESS PERSPECTIVE

While the sympathy of the lower courts was with the dismissed employee, the Supreme Court took a much more balanced view. As long as an employer's conduct is not untruthful, misleading, or unduly insensitive, the employee will not receive damages for the manner of the dismissal. Aggravated or punitive damages will only be awarded if the employer acts maliciously or outrageously. In a time of recession, does the Supreme Court decision give too much of an advantage to employers who would like to terminate the employment of employees?

Even seasonal employees who are fired at the end of a season and then repeatedly re-hired may be entitled to reasonable notice if not recalled.[13] Short-term or probationary employees may be entitled to extended notice periods if the employee has not been informed of the basis on which his performance will be evaluated, or if he was persuaded to leave another job but is then terminated after a short time. Similarly, if an employer fosters employee loyalty by promising job security, that employer may be required to provide even greater notice of termination to its employees than would otherwise be the case.[14] Trade unions generally include terms in their collective agreements as to when an employee can be terminated and what notice is required. Also, minimum statutory notice periods are set out in employment standards statutes and will be discussed below.

REDUCING RISK 11.1

What the foregoing highlights is that legal advice should be sought if an employer wishes to terminate an employee without cause. In such a situation, adequate notice must be given. If the amount of notice has not been agreed upon by the parties, either in the employment contract or through subsequent mutual agreement, then reasonable notice must be given. If the employer has concerns about the employee's continuing to work during the notice period, pay in lieu of notice (a severance package) can be given instead. A lawyer can advise as to the length of the required notice, and costly litigation may thus be avoided.

JUST CAUSE

Notice not required when there is just cause

When there is just cause, there is no requirement for an employer to give any notice. An employee can be dismissed without notice for things such as serious absenteeism, consistent tardiness, open disobedience, habitual negligence, incompetence, harassing other employees, drinking on the job, or immoral conduct on or off the job that reflects badly on the employer. Even swearing at the employer

---

[13.] See *Levy v. Ken-Wo Country Club* (2001), 194 N.S.R. (2d) 213 (N.S.S.C.), in which the golf course groundskeeper was not recalled after 24 seasons with that employer.

[14.] *Singh v. BC Hydro and Power Authority* (2001), 95 B.C.L.R. (3d) 238 (C.A.), leave to appeal refused, [2002] S.C.C.A. No. 45.

has been determined to be serious misconduct sufficient to justify dismissal. Such conduct may be used to defend a wrongful dismissal action, even if it is discovered after the employee has been dismissed. In the *Dowling* case in Case Summary 11.4 below, it was the employee's dishonesty that justified the dismissal. Such dishonesty need not be tolerated by the employer, regardless the plight of the employee.

When dismissing employees for dishonesty or behaviour such as fraud or theft, great care must be taken to ensure that the accusations are accurate and the evidence firm. The courts have awarded significant damages for wrongful dismissal, augmented by punitive damages, when such charges have not been substantiated.[15]

Also, care should be taken to ensure that when a person is dismissed, the real reason for the termination is not discrimination. The human rights tribunals of the various jurisdictions are very active in prosecuting such violations.

A final word: In rare instances, even dishonesty will not constitute just cause for dismissal when other mitigating factors are present. For example, when a bank clerk was found to have stolen $2500 from her employer and then lied about it, her dismissal was overturned by an arbitrator who substituted a 22-month suspension. This decision was upheld when appealed to a Quebec court.[16] The clerk had an unblemished record of 25 years' employment with the bank. She stole the money because of a pathological addiction to video poker. There was great remorse, along with expert testimony of the family and personal problems she had faced because of the addiction. These factors led the arbitrator, supported later by the court, to decide that dismissal was too harsh in this instance. Proportionality between the offence and the punishment is the key in such decisions.

CASE SUMMARY 11.4

Honesty Is Still the Best Policy: *Dowling v. Ontario (Workplace Safety and Insurance Board)*[17]

Dowling was a manager of an office of the Workplace Safety and Insurance Board. He had worked for that organization for 25 years. He was terminated for cause, with the employer claiming that he had purchased a computer from one of its clients (an account he supervised), receiving a discount in the process and giving an advantage in return. It was also claimed that he had accepted a payment of $1000 on another occasion from the same client. His employer conducted an investigation and, in the process, Dowling made misrepresentations and provided false documents.

At trial, the Judge found that the dishonest conduct was not enough to justify Dowling's termination. On appeal, however, the Court of Appeal found that the receipt of the $1000 payment and the discount with respect to the computers amounted to a conflict of interest. The Court also went on to find that the conduct of Dowling during the investigation in which he lied and presented false documents constituted dishonesty and misconduct sufficient to result in a breakdown of the employment relationship. This

---

[15.] See *Clenndenning v. Lowndes Lambert (B.C.) Ltd.* (1998), 41 C.C.E.L. (2d) 58 (B.C.S.C.), varied (2000), 4 C.C7L. (3d) 238 (B.C.C.A.), in which the trial Court awarded an additional 36 months' salary as damages for the bad faith of the employer. On appeal, this award was reduced as the employer's honest belief that it had cause for dismissal negated bad faith.

[16.] *Banque Laurentienne du Canada c. Lussier*, [2003] J.Q. No. 1468.

[17.] (2005), 246 D.L.R. (4th) 65 (Ont. C.A.).

amounted to cause for termination and was characterized by the Court as giving rise to a fundamental breach of his employment relationship. In the words of Justice Gillese, "It was indispensable to the parties' employment relationship that Mr. Dowling exercise the powers of his position with honesty and impartiality, and exclusively in the interests of the Board and the public. The underpinnings of faith and confidence, necessary to the parties' employment relationship, were destroyed by Mr. Dowling's misconduct. When the various acts of misconduct are considered in the context of Mr. Dowling's position, the degree of trust reposed in him and the public nature of the Board's responsibility, it is clear that summary dismissal was a proportionate response."

DISCUSSION QUESTIONS

What do you think? Should even minor instances of dishonesty associated with the business justify termination? What if that dishonesty is not associated with the business but relates to some private aspect of the employee's life?

DISABLED WORKERS

Illness may constitute frustration of contract

In the past, employees who became seriously ill, even though not "at fault," could be discharged without notice if they could no longer perform their job. The employer did not have to pay for work not done. There was no suggestion of fault here. The employment contract was considered to be frustrated. Even today, when the employee can't work, termination is justified. However, there is a legislated duty to accommodate disabled workers who are still able to work. Human rights commissions are very willing to rule against employers who too quickly fire workers because of illness or disability. The employer must take great care to accommodate such disabled workers and to otherwise comply with the provisions of both the applicable human rights legislation and the workers' compensation legislation, which are designed to protect disabled or injured workers.

Disability is a prohibited ground. In enforcing the prohibition of discrimination against the disabled, the courts have ruled that employers have a legal duty to take reasonable steps to accommodate an employee's individual needs. This legal duty does not apply, however, if the only way to resolve the problem will cause the employer *undue hardship*, that is, hardship that is substantial in nature. To deal with this problem, most businesses offer some form of illness and long-term disability insurance or policy as part of their benefits package.

DISOBEDIENCE AND INCOMPETENCE

Problem when incompetence tolerated

Although an employee is entitled to refuse to work because of dangerous working conditions, failure to perform a reasonable order is also grounds for dismissal without notice. Disobedience justifies dismissal. Incompetence is also just cause for dismissal; however, employers are well advised to let employees know when the level of performance is unacceptable as soon as it becomes apparent, and provide an opportunity for improvement. It may appear to be easier to let the matter go, but the employer may then be faced with the argument that the employer's conduct and acceptance of the employee's performance led that employee to believe that the level of performance was appropriate. This argument will be especially difficult to overcome if bonuses or wage increases were given to the employee in the past despite the poor performance.

LAYOFFS

When an employer simply runs out of work for the employee to do, or runs into financial difficulties, that is not just cause for termination, and reasonable notice is still required. Even when the layoff is only temporary, the employee may be entitled to treat it as termination and demand the appropriate notice and compensation. In the absence of such reasonable notice or just cause, the employee can sue the employer for wrongful dismissal. Provisions in collective agreements often cover layoffs and recalls, and several provinces have included provisions covering temporary layoffs in their employment standards legislation.

For example, Ontario's *Employment Standards Act*[18] stipulates that if an employee has been laid off for a period longer than the defined "temporary layoff" (generally 13 weeks) employment terminates, and the employer must pay the employee termination pay. However, if wages or other payments are made to, or for the benefit of, the employee during the layoff, the length of the temporary layoff can be extended to 35 weeks. (Each province will have different rules in this area.)

Layoff or termination

WRONGFUL LEAVING

Employees are also required to give reasonable notice upon leaving, although what constitutes reasonable notice is usually considerably less. Unless the employee is in a key position, such as senior executive or salesperson, it is usually not worth the effort to sue when an employee leaves without giving proper notice. But key employees may be required to give substantial notice just like employers. When there is a serious breach of the employment contract by the employer, however, the employees are entitled to leave without notice. If the employer gives an unreasonable or dangerous order, if the working conditions are dangerous and the employer refuses to correct them, or if the employer involves the employee in illegal or immoral activities, the employee may be entitled to "quit."

Employees can leave without notice if contract breached by employer first

If former employees are sued, it is usually for breach of fiduciary duty or for disclosing confidential information. Ordinary employees do not have a fiduciary duty and, unless there is a valid restrictive covenant in their employment contract preventing them from doing so, they are free to compete with their former employer as soon as they leave.[19] That competition, however, must start after they leave. Employees cannot gather information, copy customer lists, or solicit customers before termination. If they do, they can be sued. Similarly, if the departing employee takes confidential information and misuses it, that conduct is also actionable.[20] As managers and other executives owe a fiduciary duty to their employer, they may find themselves somewhat restricted in what they can do even after they leave their employment. It is much preferable for the employer to set out such restrictions clearly in the original employment contract.

Employees may be sued for breach of duty

[18.] S.O. 2000, c. 41, s. 56.

[19.] See *Gertz v. Meda Ltd.* (2002), 16 C.C.E.L. (3d) 79 (Ont. Sup. Ct. J.), in which Gertz's wrongful dismissal action succeeded whereas the employer's claims of breach of fiduciary duty and of confidentiality were dismissed. Gertz took certain knowledge about the industry and client needs with him, but the Court held that a mere employee's duty of fidelity to the employer ceases with termination of employment.

[20.] See *CRC-Evans Canada Ltd. v. Pettifer* (1997), 197 A.R. 24 (Q.B.); aff'd (1998), 216 A.R. 192 (C.A.), in which two former key employees set up a competing corporation and used confidential information from the former employer in bidding against that party. They were ordered to pay $305 507.72 in damages for breaching their duty to serve their employer honestly and faithfully, and for breach of their fiduciary duty.

No General Duty Not to Compete with Former Employer: *RBC Dominion Securities Inc. v. Merrill Lynch*[21]

Virtually all of the investment advisers at the Cranbrook RBC branch left without notice. They went to the branch of a competitor, Merrill Lynch. Delamont, the RBC branch manager, orchestrated the move. RBC sued Delamont and the investment advisers, as well as Merrill Lynch and its manager. The trial Judge held that: (1) Delamont and the investment advisers were not fiduciary employees; (2) the investment advisers breached the implied terms of their employment contracts requiring reasonable notice (which was held to be 2.5 weeks) and prohibiting unfair competition with RBC; and (3) Delamont had breached his contractual duty by organizing the departure.

Damages were assessed against the investment advisers and Delamont; Merrill Lynch and its manager were found jointly and severally liable, as the manager had induced the breach of the duty not to compete unfairly. The Court of Appeal overturned the award of damages against the investment advisers and Merrill Lynch and its manager. It also set aside the award against Delamont for breach of a contractual duty of good faith.

The Supreme Court of Canada reinstated the award of the trial Judge except for the damages payable by the investment advisers for losses due to unfair competition based on their actions during the notice period. The Court ruled that damages arising in respect of an employment contract should, as for all contracts, be such as arise naturally, or as may reasonably be supposed to have been in the contemplation of both parties, at the time they made the contract, as the probable result of a breach. The Court decided that an implied term of Delamont's employment contract was the retention of RBC's employees under his supervision. Delamont therefore breached his contractual duty of good faith by organizing the departure of the investment advisers.

The Court also held that an employee who has terminated employment is not prevented from competing with his employer during the notice period. The employer is restricted to damages for the employee's failure to give reasonable notice. The employee could be liable for damages for such things as improper use of confidential information during the notice period. The award of damages by the trial Judge for the investment advisers competing against their former employer was therefore wrong in law. Given the loss of profits award made against Delamont, it was inappropriate to award damages against the investment advisers for loss of profits based on their improper use of confidential information.

DISCUSSION QUESTIONS

In Canada, the required notice periods with respect to termination can be very lengthy compared to those in other countries. Consider the effect of such lengthy notice periods imposed on employers and employees with respect to the flexibility of the labour market and the efficient operation of an employer's business.

[21.] 2008 SCC 54.

CONSTRUCTIVE DISMISSAL

When an employer demotes the employee or otherwise unilaterally changes the nature of the job, this may constitute constructive dismissal, and the employee may be able to sue for wrongful dismissal. Sometimes the employer does this inadvertently; sometimes she does it to humiliate or to make an employee uncomfortable so that the employee will voluntarily leave. From a contractual perspective, one party cannot simply impose a change in the terms of a contract without first securing the consent or agreement of the other party. In essence, the employer is simply refusing to perform the original contract when it demotes an employee.

As with harassment or sexual harassment, even when the problems are caused by other employees, the employer is still responsible. For example, in the *Stamos* case, in which an employee suffered stress-related health issues as a result of another employee and resigned, the Court found that the employer's failure to defuse the hostile work environment constituted constructive dismissal.[22] When there is constructive dismissal, the employee has an obligation to mitigate, possibly to the extent of accepting a new position offered by the employer. The employee is not, of course, obligated to accept such a position when it would cause undue humiliation or otherwise create an impossible working situation, especially if bad relations have been created because of the way the termination took place.

Promoting one employee is fine, but demoting another without cause may prompt a costly lawsuit. An employee may be constructively dismissed even when offered a comparable position. Consider the *Weselan* case, in which an employee was relocated and given a similar position.[23] The new job, however, involved a substantial daily commute at the cost of time and approximately $34 000 per year. This meant that the employee's working conditions and net remuneration would be substantially different, so he was constructively dismissed. The law simply requires reasonable steps to be taken to mitigate damage. One does not have to suffer a substantial loss to mitigate damages.

> **Constructive dismissal—employer breaks contract when nature of job is changed without consent**

CASE SUMMARY 11.6

Employment Contracts Are Binding: *Hilton v. Norampac Inc.;*[24] *Weselan v. Totten Sims Hubicki Associates (1997) Ltd.*[25]

Hilton had worked for Norampac as a mill worker for 15 years when his conditions of employment were unilaterally changed by the employer. He was working as a foreman when the employer demanded that he, along with other foremen, was required to be on call for extensive periods including weekends without any extra pay. He explained that he couldn't do this as it required him to be available on the weekends when his wife worked and he had to look after his young children. He offered to be on call during the

---

22. *Stamos v. Annuity Research & Marketing Service Ltd.* (2002), 18 C.C.E.L. (3d) 117 (Ont. Sup. Ct. J.).

23. *Weselan v. Totten Sims Hubicki Associates (1997) Ltd.* (2001), 16 C.C.E.L. (3d) 184 (Ont. C.A.), varied on issue of costs, [2001] O.J. No. 5145 (Ont. C.A.).

24. (2003), 26 C.C.E.L. (3d) 179, (2003), 176 O.A.C. 309 (O.C.A.).

25. [2003] O.J. No. 1242 (On. S.C.).

week, or to be demoted to a union position, but these offers were rejected and his employment was terminated for cause based on his refusal to obey proper instruction. He sued for wrongful dismissal. The trial Court and the Appeal Court found that this was a material change in his terms of employment, which amounted to constructive dismissal. He was therefore successful in his wrongful dismissal action.

The enforcement of the employment contract does not always favour the employee. Weselan had been working for his employer for more than 10 years, and had been associated with the firm as an independent engineer for much longer than that, when his employment was terminated. The Court found that if the common law prevailed he would have been entitled to 24 months' notice, or $147 400 in lieu of that notice. Unfortunately for Weselan, his original contract of employment contained a provision requiring only 90 days' notice if dismissed without cause. Since this provision was greater than the statutory minimum, it prevailed, and the damage award was limited to only $18 925, representing that 90-day entitlement.

SMALL BUSINESS PERSPECTIVE

Does the ruling against Norampac impose too much restriction on the employer's operation of its business? In light of the law of constructive dismissal, should an employer's employment contracts be very specific as to the duties of the employees, or should they be very broad, outlining the duties of the employees in a general sense?

REMEDIES FOR WRONGFUL DISMISSAL

Compensation based on notice that should have been given

In a wrongful dismissal action, the damages awarded are usually based on what the employee would have received had proper notice been given. If a person is fired and is given only one month's notice when he should have received five months' notice, he will be awarded the difference, including any benefits and pension rights to which he would have been entitled. The employee does, however, have an obligation to mitigate. He must try to find another job.[26] Any damages awarded will be reduced by what is earned from that other employment.[27]

Obligation to mitigate losses

In rare circumstances, the court will also take into account a person's damaged reputation or mental distress, and sometimes will even award punitive damages where appropriate.[28] It is normally the employer, often a corporation, that is sued for wrongful dismissal, but the individual manager implementing the decision may also be sued when defamation or some other actionable wrong has taken place.

Employer must have clear evidence of misconduct

It is evident that great care must be exercised when dismissing an employee for incompetence or misconduct. An employer must have clear evidence of the misconduct or incompetence and, with the latter, must demonstrate that the employee has been given a reasonable opportunity to improve. Failure to substantiate just cause will likely result in a successful action by the employee for wrongful dismissal.

[26.] But see *E.C. & M. Electric Ltd. v. Alberta (Employment Standards Code)* (1994), 7 C.C.E.L. (2d) 235 (Alta. Prov. Ct.). While a duty to mitigate exists under common law, no such duty is imposed on the employee under Alberta's *Employment Standards Code*. Money earned from other employment need not be deducted from the statutory severance pay.

[27.] Efforts to mitigate damages need only be those expected of a reasonable person. See *Bradbury v. Newfoundland (Attorney General)*(2001), 207 Nfld. & P.E.I.R. 181 (Nfld. C.A.).

[28.] See *Honda Canada Inc. v. Keays, supra* note 11.

REDUCING RISK 11.2

Employers are often surprised to learn of the lengthy notice requirements for termination in Canada. Including specified notice entitlements in the contract of employment will go a long way to solving the problem. But if this is done, it is vital not to make the contracted notice period less than the minimum specified in the relevant employment standards legislation. If it is, the contract clause may be void, and the employer may be required to pay a much higher amount based on the common law notice period.

Employers must avoid the temptation to manufacture reasons to justify dismissal without notice or to make an employee so uncomfortable that he will quit. Courts are now willing to find constructive dismissal, and assess higher damages, if there is evidence of false statements, defamation, a poisoned work environment, or damage to the employee's reputation. The sensible way to approach the problem is to negotiate with the employee. Typically, the employee will settle for less when he realizes that he will thereby avoid the significant legal costs of a wrongful dismissal lawsuit.

Damages are the appropriate remedy for wrongful dismissal. It is rare for a court to order that an employee be given back the job. Reinstatement is more common if collective agreements are involved, when the decision is made by an arbitrator rather than a judge. Some statutes, such as the *Canada Labour Code*,[29] provide for reinstatement in non-union situations. Still, in general, reinstatement is rare.

Liability of Employer

Although not directly at fault, an employer can be held liable for torts committed by an employee during the course of employment. Because the employer benefits from the work of the employee, the employer is held responsible for losses caused by the employee. The employer's liability is limited to those activities that take place during the course of employment. This includes not only incidents arising during working hours, but also any conduct that takes place as part of the employment activity. If Pawluk, while delivering a letter to his employer's client on his way home, injures a pedestrian, both Pawluk and his employer would likely be liable. The negligent act occurred during the course of employment, even though it did not happen during working hours. But if Pawluk injures the pedestrian when he goes out to do his personal banking during working hours, the employer would not be liable. In this case, Pawluk is "on a frolic of his own," and the injury did not take place in the course of his employment.

Employer liable for torts committed by employee while on the job

As a general rule, there must be an employment relationship for vicarious liability to apply. This is one reason why the tests discussed above for determining whether an employment relationship exists are so important. Several jurisdictions have legislated vicarious liability in special situations. For example, in Alberta, British Columbia, and some other provinces, the owner of a motor vehicle is vicariously liable for any torts committed by the person driving the vehicle with the

Vicarious liability and motor vehicle

[29.] R.S.C. 1985, c. L-2.

owner's consent. The driver is deemed to be "the agent or employee of the owner of the motor vehicle, employed as the agent or employee of the motor vehicle, and driving the motor vehicle in the course of that person's employment."[30]

This section actually expands the potential liability of an employer that allows its employees to drive its vehicles beyond the normal scope of vicarious liability. Under vicarious liability, the employer escapes liability if the employee negligently hurts the plaintiff while "on a frolic of his own." The statute, on the other hand, deems the driver to be driving in the course of his employment, whether he's driving for a job-related purpose or not. For example, in the *Morad* case, the employer was held liable when an employee borrowed the company vehicle and then deliberately ran over some third party who owed him money![31] Other provinces, such as Ontario, simply make an owner liable for any damage negligently caused by a person driving his car with consent without reference to an employment or agency relationship.[32]

Although the employer has the right to turn to the employee for compensation when it is found vicariously liable, this is usually a hollow remedy, the employee typically being in no financial position to pay such compensation.

Employers often try to separate portions of their operations from the actual business they conduct. Cleaning and office management, as well as sales and product service, may be contracted out. This is done to reduce the number of employees, thereby reducing administrative costs, leaving the organization free to concentrate on what it does best. It may also reduce the risk of the employer being found vicariously liable when injuries take place. Avoiding vicarious liability is more likely when great care has been taken to make sure the people doing those jobs are truly independent. But even then, the courts may still find a sufficiently close relationship to impose vicarious liability on the employer for the wrongful acts committed by these supposedly independent workers. The risk of such liability should be planned for in the operation of the business. Liability insurance is typically advisable.

Legislation

As a consequence of the relatively weak position of individual employees in the employment relationship, employees have tended to band together to exert greater pressure on the employer. Such collective action is now governed by legislation and will be discussed under "Collective Bargaining" later in this chapter.

Provincial legislation applies

A considerable amount of legislation has also been passed that is designed to protect employees, whether unionized or not, by setting minimum standards of safety, remuneration, hours of work, and other benefits. Conditions of employment normally fall under provincial jurisdiction. Most provinces have concentrated their employee welfare legislation into one statute, generally called the *Employment Standards Act*, or *Labour Standards Act*, which sets minimum standards in connection with

- wages
- overtime, work hours, and rest periods

---

30. *Traffic Safety Act*, R.S.A. 2000, c. T-6, s. 187. See also *Motor Vehicle Act*, R.S.B.C. 1996, c. 318, s. 86.

31. *Morad v. Emmanouel* (1993), 9 Alta. L.R. (3d) 378 (Q.B.).

32. *Highway Traffic Act*, R.S.O. 1990, c. H-8, s. 192(2).

- vacation and holiday entitlements
- maternity and parental leave
- termination and severance pay.

Some also provide for bereavement and sick leave.

There are substantial differences in the details. For example, the general minimum wage in Alberta in April 2009 was set at $8.80 per hour, whereas in neighbouring British Columbia it was $8.00 ($6.00 for employees newly entering the workforce). Employment standards legislation varies with each jurisdiction.

There are, however, a number of activities, such as banking, the military, activities on aboriginal reserves, the post office, telephone and broadcast companies, and airlines, railroads, and steamships that fall under federal jurisdiction. The employment relationship in those sectors is governed by the federal *Canada Labour Code*,[33] Part III sets out employment standards. Since it applies across the country, its provisions will be reviewed here to illustrate employment standards.

Federal legislation also may apply

EMPLOYMENT STANDARDS

Notice periods less than the common law standard can be set out in employment contracts, and as long as they are greater than the minimum statutory requirement, they will prevail. This was illustrated in the *Weselan* case (second part of Case Summary 11.6). If a notice period is shorter than the statutory minimum, it will be void and the employer will then have to comply with the longer "reasonable notice" provisions found in common law. The statutory provisions set a minimum standard, thus agreements that waive the protections or remedies available under the legislation may likewise be declared void. When the parties have agreed to a higher standard, or when a higher standard is imposed by common law, that higher standard will normally prevail.[34] But even the minimum statutory provisions do not treat all employees equally. The government may exempt, or modify certain provisions in respect of, certain types of employment. In other words, employers may, for example, be excused from paying minimum wage to managers or students, and overtime may be calculated differently for persons engaged in different lines of work.

Statutes set out minimum standards

---

33. *Supra* note 29.

34. *Ibid.*, s. 168. Note that similar provisions are found in provincial acts.

CASE SUMMARY 11.7

Statutory Notice May Not Suffice: *Machtinger v. HOJ Industries Ltd.*[35]

This case involves two employees who were terminated from their employment with only four weeks' notice, despite the fact that they both had been employed for a number of years. The employees each brought a wrongful dismissal action against the employer, demanding compensation. The issue was whether the four weeks' notice was enough. This notice corresponded with the statutory minimum under the *Employment Standards Act*. The employment contracts required even less notice to be given. If common law applied, each employee would be entitled to more than seven months' notice.

The Supreme Court of Canada held that any contractual term that did not comply with the minimum standards set out in the *Act* was a nullity. The minimal notice provisions found in the contract were therefore void. The Court then observed that, although the notice given satisfied the requirements of the legislation, that was merely a minimum standard. Since common law required more than seven months' notice in such circumstances, that longer notice requirement prevailed. Complying with the statutory minimum was not good enough in this case.

SMALL BUSINESS PERSPECIVE

This case illustrates the confusion and inconsistency involved in enforcing the terms agreed to in the contract, applying the statutory minimums, or requiring the much more lengthy common law notice period to be followed. Because of this complexity, it is important for a small business owner to obtain legal advice with respect to the preparation of employment contracts for employees. Should governments attempt to simplify the law relating to the employment relationship?

TERMINATION

Termination entitlements determined by length of service

As under common law, the *Canada Labour Code* recognizes that no notice is required when the dismissal is for cause; otherwise, notice of termination is necessary.[36] Where the *Code* and common law differ is in the remedies available for wrongful dismissal. When determining adequate notice and severance pay, the *Code* does not consider the nature of the employment, only its length. Employees who have completed three months or more of continuous employment are to receive two weeks' notice of termination (except when the dismissal is for cause). Additionally, employees who have been employed for more than 12 months are entitled to severance pay of two days' wages for each completed year of service, plus five days' wages. The *Code* also provides that when a person has been laid off for a period longer than three months, he may be able to treat this layoff as a termination and claim termination pay and severance pay. (There are exceptions, as when payments are made to the employee during the layoff.)

Layoffs may trigger termination pay

---

35. [1992] 1 S.C.R. 986.

36. *Supra* note 29, ss. 230–237.

Most jurisdictions have passed similar legislation, but the provisions vary substantially; it is thus necessary to review the provisions of the relevant statute to determine the entitlements of a particular employee.

ISSUE ESTOPPEL

Employees who face termination have a real concern. Case law makes it imperative that employees seek legal advice before filing a complaint under employment standards legislation. By simply applying for these minimal legislative benefits, an employee may lose the ability to later sue for damages for wrongful dismissal based on common law. If an employment standards officer determines that the complainant was terminated for cause, not only will the complainant's claim for termination pay under the statute fail, but if the employee later tries to sue for damages for wrongful dismissal, the court may decide that the issue was already settled.[37] This is because the employment standards officer has already decided that the termination was not wrongful. **Issue estoppel** may cause the court to dismiss the wrongful dismissal suit altogether, without even hearing the details. Such were the results in the *Fayant* and *Wong* cases,[38] where the pleadings were struck out after issue estoppel was successfully raised.

Choosing to file complaint may preclude suing later

COMPLAINTS

Employment standards legislation allows employees to file a complaint with a government board; the investigation and determination is then made by civil servants.[39] This process enables the employee to avoid the costs of litigation. Note that time limitations vary between employment standards statutes and may well be as short as a few months. Under the federal legislation, the inspector may dismiss the complaint if it is unfounded, but this determination may be appealed. If the inspector determines that earnings are due to the employee, she may order payment to be made. If the employer is a corporation, the individual directors may be liable personally for up to six months' wages per employee.

HUMAN RIGHTS

An area of employment law that is becoming much more significant is the protection of employee rights. With the passage of the *Charter of Rights and Freedoms*, as well as federal and provincial human rights legislation, employers are required not only to ensure that they do not discriminate in their hiring and employment practices, but that they take active steps to ensure that these basic rights are protected. Although the *Charter* does not apply directly to most employment situations, it does have an important indirect effect, since federal and provincial human rights statutes must be consistent with the provisions of the *Charter*. Indeed, the courts have gone as far as to read into human rights statutes protection for homosexual persons, where no such provision was originally included.[40] Human rights legislation has an impact on employment by prohibiting discrimination on

Federal and provincial human rights legislation prohibit most forms of discrimination in employment

---

[37] *Fayant v. Campbell's Maple Village Ltd.* (1993), 146 A.R. 175 (Q.B.); *Wong v. Shell Canada* (1995), 174 A.R. 287 (C.A.), leave to appeal to S.C.C. refused, [1995] S.C.C.A. No. 551.

[38] *Rasanen v. Rosemount Instruments Ltd.* (1994), 17 O.R. (3d) 267 (C.A.), leave to appeal to S.C.C. refused, [1994] S.C.C.A. No. 152.

[39] *Supra* note 29, ss. 249–251.

[40] *Vriend v. Alberta*, [1998] 1 S.C.R. 493.

the basis of race, national or ethnic origin, colour, religion, gender, sexual orientation, and, in some cases, age, marital status, family status, physical or mental disability, and pardoned criminal convictions.

CASE SUMMARY 11.8

Family Needs Must Be Accommodated: *Health Sciences Assoc. of B.C. v. Campbell River and North Island Transition Society*[41]

Howard was a part-time employee working as a child and youth support counsellor at a women's safe house. She worked between 8:30 a.m. and 3 p.m., giving her time to look after her own son who suffered from ADHD and Tourette's syndrome and who needed special care after school because of these conditions. Her employer decided to change her hours, requiring her to work until 6 p.m. Unfortunately, this interfered with her ability to provide the necessary care of her own son after school. She grieved the decision.

The employer's reason for the change was based on business considerations requiring her to be available so she could spend more time counselling school-aged children. Even after her request and a doctor's letter asking that the decision be reconsidered, the employer refused. The grievance was argued on the basis that the employer's decision amounted to discrimination against Howard on the basis of family status, which was prohibited under the B.C. *Human Rights Code*. The employer argued that the *Code* did not stipulate that employers had an obligation to accommodate an employee's child care needs. The Court held that because this was a change that caused a serious interference with a substantial parental or family duty, a prima facie case of discrimination on the basis of family status had been established. There was a duty to accommodate as long as doing so didn't impose undue hardship on the employer.

DISCUSSION QUESTIONS

Do you think we have taken human rights enforcement too far?

Tribunals hear complaints

Human rights tribunals have been established to hear complaints about violations of human rights legislation. These tribunals have the power to investigate, levy fines, and even order reinstatement of employees if they find that the employees have been terminated in violation of some human rights provision, or forced to quit because of harassment.

The *Canadian Human Rights Act*, for example, prohibits discrimination with regard to any term or condition of employment on the basis of a person's race, religion, and so on. It specifically prohibits the refusal to hire, or the firing of, any person on the basis of one of the prohibited grounds.[42]

For example, to discriminate against a woman because of pregnancy would constitute gender discrimination. Employers cannot, therefore, fire or demote an

---

41. (2004), 240 D.L.R. (4th) 479, 28 B.C.L.R. (4th) 292 (B.C.C.A.).

42. *Canadian Human Rights Act*, R.S.C. 1985, c. H-6, s. 7.

employee because of pregnancy. Also, an employer's refusal to permit an employee to breastfeed in the workplace may constitute discrimination on the basis of gender.[43] Furthermore, employers must refrain from asking women at job interviews whether they are pregnant, or plan to have children, for the legislation also addresses discrimination during pre-employment inquiries.

Job advertisements and application forms must not directly or indirectly express a limitation or preference based on race, colour, gender, or other prohibited ground. The forms used cannot require applicants to furnish information concerning their gender, age, marital status, and so on. Accordingly, unless a bona fide occupational requirement exists that would justify such an inquiry, employers must refrain from requesting photographs or that the applicant's gender, previous name, marital status, date of birth, or religion be provided in the application form.

Harassment is a form of discrimination that occurs when one subjects another person to unwelcome verbal or physical conduct because of his or her colour, gender, age, or other characteristic. Unwanted physical contact, jokes, or insults are harassment when they negatively affect the working environment. Note that interaction between a supervisor and her subordinates, even outside the workplace, can be employment-related harassment. If the supervisor's conduct creates a perception that continued employment is dependent on sexual interaction with that person, then that supervisor has engaged in harassment.[44] Sexual harassment is just one example of harassment. When harassment is committed by an employee, the employer can be held responsible if it has failed to take adequate steps to protect the employee who was harassed. It is, therefore, vital for employers to be proactive and to take positive steps to develop anti-harassment and anti-discrimination policies, clarifying that such conduct will not be tolerated. These policies should also spell out what disciplinary steps might be taken if one employee harasses, or discriminates against, another employee.

Harassment also covered

CASE SUMMARY 11.9

Should the Employer Be Liable? *Robichaud v. Canada (Treasury Board)*[45]

The Supreme Court of Canada had to determine whether the employer was responsible for the sexual harassment committed by an employee. Robichaud worked as a lead hand in a cleaning operation for the Department of National Defence. A supervisor subjected her to unwanted sexual attention. Such behaviour amounts to discrimination on the basis of gender because it differentiates adversely against an employee on the basis of her gender. The Court held that the employer, under the *Canadian Human Rights Act*, was liable for the discriminatory acts of its employees that were committed in the course of their employment, much like vicarious liability in common law. The case indicates the approach taken by courts when faced with sexual harassment.

---

43. *Re Carewest and H.S.A.A. (Degagne)* (2001), 93 L.A.C. (4th) 129 (Alta.).

44. *Simpson v. Consumers' Association of Canada* (2001), 57 O.R. (3d) 351 (C.A.), leave to appeal to S.C.C. refused, [2002] S.C.C.A. No. 83.

45. [1987] 2 S.C.R. 84.

In fact, this precedent has been followed when applying provincial legislation to instances of sexual harassment. In the *Katsiris* case,[46] the corporation owning the restaurant was held liable for the harassment committed by its employee. That case also addressed whether the CEO of the corporation should be personally liable. Since it was not shown that he knew of the sexual harassment, liability was not imposed on him personally.

SMALL BUSINESS PERSPECTIVE

What factors should the court consider in determining whether to hold the employer liable for the wrongful conduct of its employee in these circumstances? What can an employer do to minimize its potential liability (and the liability of the directors, if the employer is a corporation) for the actions of its employees?

Duty to accommodate

This positive obligation on the employer to protect vulnerable employees in the workplace has been taken further. As mentioned above, employers now have an obligation to take steps to accommodate employees with disabilities and special needs. This may extend to changing the physical work environment to accommodate visually impaired people or wheelchair users. It includes allowing workers with chronic illness, such as AIDS, or partial disability, to do lighter work or to work only part-time.[47] Schedules may require adjustment to accommodate different religious holidays, as long as the request does not cause the employer undue hardship.[48]

Employers may find their rules being challenged as discriminatory. Rules requiring employees to be of a certain stature may, for example, discriminate against certain racial groups. Rules requiring uniforms or hard hats to be worn may discriminate against certain religious groups. These rules may, however, be saved if the employer establishes them to be bona fide (genuine) occupational requirements. The hard-hat rule may prevail, even if it violates a religious right to wear a turban, if safety concerns justify its use. But for the requirement to be a bona fide one, it must relate to a necessary part of the job. Also, when a rule adversely affects a particular group, the employer must take reasonable steps to accommodate the disadvantaged group.

CASE SUMMARY 11.10

Effect Duty to Accommodate and Adverse-Effect Discrimination: *Meiorin*[49]

This is a leading case for determining whether a particular occupational requirement is reasonable and justifiable. Meiorin, who worked as a firefighter, failed a running test designed to measure aerobic fitness. She was therefore terminated after three years of

---

[46] *Katsiris v. Isaac* (2001), 204 Sask. R. 52 (Q.B.).

[47] See *Ontario (Human Rights Commission) v. Roosma* (2002), 21 C.C.E.L. (3d) 112 (Ont. Sup. Ct. J.), in which it was held that releasing employees from Friday night shifts to accommodate their religious beliefs would cause undue hardship. Such accommodation was therefore waived.

[48] See the updated Canadian Human Rights Commission Policy on HIV/AIDS, Canadian Human Rights Commission, www.chrc-ccdp.ca/legislation_policies/aids-en.asp.

[49] *British Columbia (Public Service Employee Relations Commission) v. British Columbia Government and Service Employees' Union (B.C.G.S.E.U.)*, [1999] 3 S.C.R. 3.

service. Minimum fitness standards for firefighters had been introduced by the government. The issue before the arbitrator was whether the running test component was discriminatory on the basis of gender. It measured aerobic capacity and women generally have lower aerobic capacity than men. It was argued that this amounted to *adverse-effect discrimination* against Meiorin. This type of discrimination involves a *generally applicable rule* that has a *particular adverse effect* on one group (women) because of a prohibited ground (their gender). In these circumstances, when a rule is shown to have a discriminatory effect, the employer can continue to apply the rule only if it is justifiable as a *bona fide* occupational requirement.

The Supreme Court of Canada stated that the categorization of discrimination as adverse effect or direct effect was no longer appropriate. The Court enunciated a three-part test to evaluate whether an occupational requirement (meeting the fitness standard) is justified. Once the complainant shows that the standard is discriminatory, the employer must prove

1. That there is a rational connection between the test and performance of the job;

2. That the test was adopted under an honest and good-faith belief that the standard was necessary; and

3. That the standard is reasonably necessary to accomplish the employer's legitimate purpose.

The third point implies that the employer may need to show that it cannot accommodate the employee without suffering undue hardship.

The test requires employers to accommodate different members' capabilities before adopting a "standard" or occupational requirement. Before setting the aerobic standard, and setting it so high that most women cannot attain it, it must be shown that such a level of aerobic capacity is necessary to do the job. If it is unnecessary, then the standard cannot be saved as a genuine or bona fide occupational requirement.

No credible evidence was shown to establish that the prescribed aerobic capacity was necessary for either men or women to perform the work of a forest firefighter. The employer also failed to show that it would experience undue hardship if a different standard were used. Accordingly, reinstatement of the claimant was ordered, and she was compensated for her lost benefits and wages. This case underscores the need to be vigilant in setting occupational standards or requirements, for they may be challenged if they have a discriminatory impact on a particular individual or group.

DISCUSSION QUESTIONS

What do you think? Does the Supreme Court's approach result in a lowering of the standards that employers can enforce?

Some jurisdictions have passed **pay equity** statutes requiring equal pay for work of equal value.[50] These provisions usually benefit women, who have traditionally been paid less than men for similar jobs, but they may place considerable hardship on the organization that must bear the extra expense. Most notably, in the *Public Service Alliance of Canada* case, the federal government was required to pay more than $3.3 billion to some 230 000 current and former employees for

Pay equity

[50.] *Canada (Attorney General) v. Public Service Alliance of Canada*, [2000] 1 F.C. 146 (T.D.).

13 years' back pay with interest![51] The Canadian Human Rights Tribunal ruled that the federal government had failed to abide by section 11 of the *Canadian Human Rights Act* by allowing a wage gap between men and women doing clerical work—work of equal value. Note that this must be contrasted to a Newfoundland case where the government refused to honour such a back pay order on the grounds that it was experiencing a financial crisis. This was challenged under the *Charter* and the Supreme Court of Canada held that such a financial crisis was a valid reason justifiable under section 1 to continue the inequity.[52] Discrimination in the workplace has prompted the passage of various **employment equity** acts as

Correction of past imbalance

well.[53] Organizations may be required to take steps to correct employment situations where there has been a tradition of racial or gender imbalance, such as in nursing and engineering. This usually means giving preferential treatment to those job applicants or candidates who belong to underrepresented minority groups. The resulting **reverse discrimination** directed at individuals in the over-represented group is also distasteful to many. Programs that are intended to correct these historical imbalances in the workplace are specifically authorized under section 15(2) of the *Charter of Rights and Freedoms*. They are sometimes referred to using the American terminology "**affirmative action**."

Mandatory retirement at 65 permitted

Mandatory retirement also raises human rights issues. Forced retirement at 65 years is often justified as good social policy, opening up new jobs for youth. But from the point of view of the retiree, it can be a disaster. Although discrimination in employment on the basis of age is usually prohibited, retirement at 65 years is generally exempted in provincial employment standards or human rights statutes. Where "age" is defined as being 18 or older and less than 65, one who faces age discrimination in the form of forced retirement at age 65 may have no remedy. The Supreme Court of Canada has held that where such a mandatory retirement policy is allowed under provincial human rights legislation, it does not violate the provisions of the *Charter of Rights and Freedoms*, being a reasonable exception under section 1.[54] But if an employer tries to impose a retirement policy commencing at a younger age (for example, 60 for firefighters) it can be saved only if the employer establishes the policy as being justifiable in the circumstances of its workplace.[55]

Note that while forced retirement policies may be tolerated in most jurisdictions, there is nothing requiring an employer to have such a policy. Many employers find that keeping older employees on the job after 65 has a positive impact on their business.

As the rules with respect to discrimination in employment change, employers should be particularly vigilant in developing policies that avoid unjust discrimination against same-sex couples, that accommodate disabled workers, and that prevent the various forms of harassment that can take place in the workplace.

[51.] See, for example, *Canadian Human Rights Act, supra* note 42, s.11.

[52.] *Newfoundland (Treasury Board) v. N.A.P.E.*, 2004 S.C.C. 66, 2004 C.L.L.C. 230–035, 244 D.L.R. (4th) 294 (S.C.C.).

[53.] See, for example, *Employment Equity Act*, S.C. 1995, c. 44.

[54.] See "Policy on Discrimination Against Older Persons Because of Age," Ontario Human Rights Commission, http://www.ohrc.on.ca/en/resources/Policies/agepolicyen/pdf.

[55.] *Dickason v. University of Alberta*, [1992] 2 S.C.R. 1103.

WORKERS' COMPENSATION

Common law was often unable to provide an appropriate remedy for an employee injured on the job. This was especially true when the accident resulted from the employee's own carelessness. All provinces and the federal government have enacted workers' compensation legislation that provides a compulsory insurance program covering accidents that take place on the job.[56] The legislation sets rates of compensation to be paid for different types of injuries and establishes a board that hears and adjudicates the claims of injured employees. The system is essentially a no-fault insurance scheme, in which benefits are paid to injured workers, or to their families in the event of death. Careless conduct on the part of the worker will not disqualify an injured employee from receiving compensation. The program is financed by assessments levied by the provincial workers' compensation boards against the employers; the amount levied varies with the risks associated with the industry involved. Some employees, such as casual workers, farmers, and small business employees, are often excluded. British Columbia has, however, extended workers' compensation coverage to almost all workers in the province.

Worker's compensation—compulsory insurance coverage

A significant aspect of workers' compensation legislation in most jurisdictions is that the worker gives up the right to any other compensation. The worker can no longer sue the employer (or the party who caused the injury, if he also contributed to the plan), being limited to the benefits bestowed by the workers' compensation system. When the injury is caused by someone other than the employer or another employee, the plans usually give the injured worker the choice of receiving workers' compensation benefits or pursuing a civil action.

Worker gives up right to any other compensation and cannot sue

Compensation is also limited to injury or disease that arises in the course of the employment. This can sometimes be a problem when it is difficult to establish that a disease, such as emphysema or a heart condition, was caused by the work of the employee. Compensation is typically paid to the employee, but when an employee dies as a result of injuries sustained on the job, payments are then made to her dependants,[57] which may include same-sex partners.[58]

HEALTH AND SAFETY

Related to workers' compensation legislation, in that they work to reduce compensation claims, are statutes controlling health and safety conditions in the workplace. Health and safety requirements are sometimes embodied in general labour statutes, as in the *Canada Labour Code*.[59] Some jurisdictions deal with health and safety in a separate statute, as in Ontario's *Occupational Health and Safety Act*.[60]

Provision of safe workplace

[56.] Further information on workers' compensation in Canada is available through the Association of Workers' Compensation Boards of Canada, www.awcbc.org.

[57.] *Government Employees Compensation Act*, R.S.C. 1985, c. G-5, s. 4.

[58.] For example, see *Workplace Safety and Insurance Act, 1997*, S.O. 1997, c. 16, s. 22.

[59.] R.S.O. 1990, c. O.1.

[60.] *Supra* note 29, Part II.

The main thrust of these statutes and their related regulations[61] is to

1. provide safer working conditions, by requiring fencing of hazardous areas, safety netting, proper shielding of equipment, environmental control, and so on

2. ensure safe employment practices, such as requiring the supply and use of hard hats, goggles, and protective clothing

3. establish programs to educate both the employer and the employee on how to create a safer working environment for all concerned.

Safety boards ensure regulations are adhered to

These objectives are facilitated through the establishment of a board with the power to hear complaints and enforce correction. Officers are empowered to enter the workplace without a warrant. When such officers encounter dangerous conditions (such as lack of fencing or shielding), poor safety practices (such as failure to use hard hats or safety lines), or environmental contamination (caused by hazardous chemicals, fumes, or dust), they can order the problem corrected or, in serious cases, they can shut the job site down. The offending business can be prosecuted for violations, especially when injury or death results. These provisions are effective only if the fines are significant. Ontario, for example, has increased the maximum fines levied and extended liability to make directors of corporations personally responsible for harmful and dangerous practices.

EMPLOYMENT INSURANCE

Employment insurance is federal jurisdiction

The federal government was given jurisdiction over insurance coverage for unemployed workers by an amendment to the *Constitution Act, 1867* in 1940.[62] Under the *Employment Insurance Act,*[63] both employers and employees pay into a government-supplemented fund. Laid-off employees are entitled to receive payments for a specific period of time. This is not a fund from which the employee is entitled to get back what he has contributed. Rather, the payments are insurance premiums, and an employee is entitled to receive only what is set out in the statute and regulations. This amount is based on the number of weeks worked before the claim and the amount of wages received. Workers who voluntarily leave their employment, or are involved in a strike or lockout, are generally not entitled to receive employment insurance benefits. Those who cannot work because others are on strike will receive benefits, provided they otherwise qualify. A severance package from the employer will also limit eligibility, and no benefits will be paid until the severance period is over. Benefits are also paid under the *Employment Insurance Act* to those who are unable to work because of illness, disability, pregnancy, or adoption. Workers may appeal any decisions made, such as entitlement to benefits, to an administrative body set up under the legislation.

Employee must meet qualifications to receive benefits

---

61. These statutes are supplemented by numerous regulations, such as Ontario's *Confined Spaces Regulation*, O. Reg. 632/05, *Training Program Regulation*, O. Reg. 780/94, and *X-ray Safety Regulation*, R.R.O. 1990, Reg. 861.

62. S.C. 1996, c. 23.

63. *Constitution Act, 1940*, 3–4 Geo. VI, c. 36 (U.K.).

REDUCING RISK 11.3

Adhering to the employment standards legislation and dealing with government regulatory bodies can impose considerable hardship on employers, straining their management resources. Health and safety and workers' compensation issues are a fact of life, and enforcement provisions usually put enough pressure on the employer so that there is adherence with the legislative requirements. The same is true with respect to employment insurance and taxation. But human rights standards, including provisions against direct and indirect discrimination and harassment, as well as employment standards, such as minimum wage, hours of work, overtime, holidays, maternity leave, and so on, are usually enforced only when someone makes a complaint. Employees who want to keep their jobs usually do not make such complaints. These complaints therefore usually come after the fact, often after the employee, or a group of employees, has been working in those condi-

tions, sometimes for years. Penalties imposed can be significant.

Ideally, the employer will develop carefully crafted policies and develop training for all, especially those in key decision-making positions, to make sure that the many pitfalls are avoided. When jobs are advertised and potential employees interviewed, great care should be taken to avoid stating qualifications or asking questions that could be construed as discriminatory. Questions relating to a person's place of birth, race, religion, age, language, arrest history, gender, sexual preference, child care arrangements, marital status, or medications being taken should be avoided. Care should also be taken to avoid practices that could be considered discriminatory in promotions, benefits, and bonuses. Clear policies, designed to prevent harassment or discrimination by other employees, should be designed and implemented, with the policy and penalties being made clear to all.

OTHER LEGISLATION

Many other statutes affect the employment relationship. Most jurisdictions have legislation controlling the apprenticeship process and trade schools.[64] Pension benefits are controlled by legislation. Some jurisdictions have legislation controlling the licensing of private employment agencies and restricting the types of payments they can receive from their clients. And legislation such as the *Bankruptcy and Insolvency Act*, the *Wage Earner Protection Program Act*, and the mechanics' or builders' lien acts provide security to the worker in the payment of wages. All jurisdictions have legislation dealing with special categories of employees, such as teachers and public servants.

COLLECTIVE BARGAINING

A significant portion of the legislation affecting employment relates to the collective bargaining process. But because the percentage of unionized workers in Canada has declined over the past few decades, those laws have changed in response to the diminished political strength of the unions. Trade unions today are fighting to hold on to what they have gained and are resisting the further weakening of their position. Since the time of the industrial revolution in the United Kingdom, workers have banded together in an attempt to overcome poor working conditions and low wages. A considerable amount of confrontation and violence flared up between unions and employers, especially when unions first

Consequence of weaker unions

64. See, for example, Alberta's *Apprenticeship and Industry Training Act*, R.S.A. 2000, c. A-42 and Ontario's *Apprenticeship and Certification Act 1998*, S.O. 1998, c. 22.

attempted to organize or unionize the workforce. In North America, earlier governments and courts treated efforts to organize workers as criminal conspiracies, and the activists were severely punished.

Over the years, trade unions gained grudging acceptance, if not respectability, and legislation passed in the first half of the 20th century allowed them to play an increasingly significant role in the economy. The first example of important modern legislation was passed by the United States Congress in 1935 and was known as the *National Labor Relations Act* or the *Wagner Act*.[65]

Legislation designed to reduce conflict

This *Act* reduced conflict by recognizing an employee's right to be a member of a union and eliminating the employer's power to interfere in any way with the organizational process. A trade union successful in persuading more than 50 percent of the employees to join was recognized as the official bargaining agent for all the employees in that workforce. The employer was then required to negotiate with the trade union in good faith. The primary objectives of the *Wagner Act* were to promote labour peace and to give some stability and structure to the field of labour relations in the United States.

Legislation

Canada followed example of American legislation

After a considerable amount of labour strife in Canada, the federal government passed the *Wartime Labour Relations Regulations* by an order-in-council.[66] This order incorporated most of the provisions set out in the *Wagner Act* and, after the war, most Canadian provinces added the provisions of this federal regulation to their provincial statutes. The Canadian legislation, in addition to controlling **recognition disputes** (disputes arising between unions and employers during the organization process), included provisions that reduced conflict in interest disputes and rights disputes. An **interest dispute** is a disagreement between the union and employer about what terms to include in their collective agreement. A **rights dispute** is a disagreement over the meaning or interpretation of a provision included in a collective agreement that is in force. Another type of dispute that can arise is a **jurisdictional dispute**, which is a dispute between two unions over which one should represent a particular group of employees or over which union members ought to do a particular job. For example, should carpenters or steel workers put up metal-stud walls in an office building? The employer is usually caught in the middle in jurisdictional disputes and has little power to affect the situation.

Types of disputes— recognition, interest, rights, jurisdiction

Both federal and provincial legislation covers collective bargaining

The federal collective bargaining legislation is embodied in the *Canada Labour Code*.[67] This legislation covers those industries over which the federal government has jurisdiction, such as railroads, shipping, air transportation, broadcasting, and dock work. Each provincial government has passed collective bargaining legislation covering sectors over which it has jurisdiction. These acts are variously called the *Labour Code, Labour Relations Code, Trade Union Act, Labour Relations Act, Industrial Relations Act*, and *Labour Act*. The statutes cover most labour relations situations arising within the jurisdiction of the provinces as set out in section 92 of the *Constitution Act, 1867*. Some types of activities, such as public services, schools,

---

65. (1935), 49 Stat. 449.

66. 1944, P.C. 1003. (Because of the war emergency, the federal government had the power to pass general legislation for Canada.)

67. *Supra* note 29.

and hospitals, have unique federal or provincial legislation specifically designed to cover labour relations within that industry.[68]

In all jurisdictions, labour relations boards have been established to deal with disputes associated with the collective bargaining process. These boards take the place of courts. It is important to remember that although they quite often look and act like courts, they are not. They are part of the executive branch of government and, as such, they can be used as an instrument of government policy. Labour relations boards have the advantage of expertise in labour matters. Resolution of disputes by such tribunals is usually accomplished more quickly than would be the case in the courts. Administrative tribunals are discussed in more detail in Chapter 2.

Labour tribunals regulate process

Important questions arise with respect to union membership, collective bargaining, and the *Charter of Rights and Freedoms*. Is there a constitutional right to belong to a union, to strike, or even to bargain collectively? Earlier, the Supreme Court of Canada held that there was not. These rights had been created by statute, and the limitations imposed by government were held not to have violated section 2(d) of the *Charter* guaranteeing freedom of association. However, recent case law suggests a different direction by the Court. See the Supreme Court of Canada decision in Case Summary 11.11.

No constitutional right to belong to a union

CASE SUMMARY 11.11

Constitutional Right to Bargain Collectively? *Health Services and Support—Facilities Subsector Bargaining Assn. v. British Columbia*[69]

Several unions and some of their members challenged the constitutional validity of the *Health and Social Services Delivery Improvement Act* (the *Act*), claiming it violated the guarantees of freedom of association (s. 2(d)) and equality (s. 15) set out in the *Charter of Rights and Freedoms*. The *Act* was passed by the B. C. government to deal with problems in the provincial health care system. Costs had increased significantly and it was becoming more difficult for the provincial government to provide health care services. The legislation was designed to resolve both of these issues.

The *Act* came into force three days after it received first reading. There was no meaningful consultation with the affected unions. The legal challenge related to the provisions dealing with changes to transfers and multi-worksite assignment rights, contracting out, job security programs, and layoffs and bumping rights. These provisions gave health care employers greater flexibility in dealing with employees. In some cases, they could do so in ways contrary to existing collective agreements and without consultation or notice. The legislation not only over-ruled existing agreements, it eliminated the need for meaningful collective bargaining on a number of issues. Section 10 of the *Act* said that "Part 2 prevails over collective agreements."

The trial Court and the Court of Appeal both ruled that the *Act* was constitutional. Neither recognized a right to collective bargaining under section 2(d) of the *Charter*, as the Supreme Court had not previously explicitly done so. The Supreme Court, however,

---

68. See, for example, Alberta's *Public Service Employee Relations Act*, R.S.A. 2000, c. P-43.

69. 2007 SCC 27, [2007] 2 S.C.R. 391.

held that section 2(d) protects the capacity of union members "to engage, in association, in collective bargaining on fundamental workplace issues." The Court explained that this protects the right of employees to associate in a process of collective action to achieve workplace goals. The Court was careful to note that this does not guarantee any particular outcomes in labour disputes. If the government substantially interferes with that right, it would be in violation of section 2(d).

The Court based its decision on the historic recognition in Canada of the importance of collective bargaining to freedom of association. Collective bargaining is also an integral component of freedom of association in international law. Canada has ratified international human rights documents that have recognized a right to collective bargaining. Finally, interpreting section 2(d) as including a right to collective bargaining is consistent with, and promotes, other *Charter* rights, freedoms, and values, including dignity, personal autonomy, equality, and democracy.

The Court ruled that the violation of section 2(d) by the *Act* was not reasonable and justifiable under section 1 of the *Charter*. The B. C. government had passed an important piece of labour legislation very quickly and without any meaningful consultation with the unions. The government had not considered achieving its goal by less intrusive measures and the violation of the employees' section 2(d) right of collective bargaining was significant.

DISCUSSION QUESTIONS

Does this decision restrict the power of the government too much? Conversely, does it enhance the power of unions beyond what it should be?

Labour rights have been gained politically and political action must be relied on to retain them. But there is now a constitutional right to bargain collectively. This decision may ensure the continued existence of unions, whose power and influence has dwindled in recent years.

Canadian labour statutes vary considerably from jurisdiction to jurisdiction. Reference herein will generally be made to the federal legislation that has application across the country.

Organization of Employees

CERTIFICATION

Certification of bargaining unit adopted from *Wagner Act*

While in some Canadian jurisdictions it is possible for employers to voluntarily recognize a trade union as the bargaining agent for their employees, the most common method of union recognition in Canada results from the certification process adopted from the *Wagner Act* of 1935. For a union to obtain certification as the bargaining agent for a group of employees, referred to as the bargaining unit, it must apply to the appropriate labour relations board for certification and satisfy the board that a certain percentage of the workforce are members of the union. The particular requirements vary with the jurisdiction.

Majority of workers must be members of union

Under the Canada Labour Code, Division III, if the applicant can show that 50 percent of the workforce has joined the union, it can apply for and receive certification. If the union has less than 50 percent support, but more than 35 percent, a representation vote will be held, and to obtain certification it must receive the support of a majority of those that vote and over 35 percent of the workforce must have participated in that vote. Note that the granting of certification without a vote is unusual. In most provinces, a vote must be taken no matter how much support is included in the initial application. Even in the case of the *Canada Labour Code*, the Canada Industrial Relations Board has the option to order a vote even when the union has over 50 percent support.

BARGAINING AGENT

Once certified, the trade union has exclusive bargaining authority for the employees it represents. A unionized employee loses the right to negotiate personally with the employer, hence the term collective bargaining. The resulting contract between union and employer is binding on all the employees in the designated unit. It is important, therefore, to determine whether the workforce the trade union intends to represent is an appropriate bargaining unit before certification is granted. Labour relations boards discourage bargaining units that are either too small or too large, or that contain groups of employees with conflicting interests. Management employees are, thus, excluded. Also, to obtain certification, the trade union cannot be guilty of any discriminatory practices. A union that has applied for certification and has failed must wait a specified period before trying again.[70]

> Only union has right to bargain for employees

UNFAIR LABOUR PRACTICES

The primary objective of labour legislation is to create an orderly process for the organization and recognition of trade unions, eliminating the conflict that often takes place in such circumstances. Prohibited unfair labour practices include threats or coercion of employees by either the union or management. For example, in the *Convergys* case,[71] the employer implemented a policy prohibiting disclosure of employee contact information to union organizers, and threatened dismissal for violating this policy. Surveillance cameras, positioned near the entry to the workplace, enabled the employer to monitor union organizers' activities. Further, a security guard was posted at the entrance whenever union officials appeared to hand out leaflets. The employer was ordered to stop these unfair labour practices and to schedule paid staff meetings where the union could meet with staff, without employer surveillance.

> Rules of conduct reduce conflict

> Threats, coercion, dismissal—unfair labour practices

The employer cannot threaten dismissal for joining a trade union or require that an employee refrain from joining a trade union as a condition of employment. Once the organization process has begun in most provinces, the employer cannot change conditions or terms of employment to influence the bargaining process. In some jurisdictions, in the face of such an unfair labour practice, if the labour relations board concludes that a vote would not reflect the true feelings of the employees, it can grant certification without a vote. This is rarely done and will take place only when there is clear evidence of intimidation interfering with the reliability of the voting process. What constitutes an unfair labour practice can also vary with the jurisdiction.

> In some provinces, unfair labour practices can result in certification without vote

---

70. Each jurisdiction may specify a different waiting period. In Alberta, for example, the period is 90 days. See *Labour Relations Code*, R.S.A. 2000, c. L-1, s. 57.

71. *Re Convergys Customer Management Canada Inc.*, [2003] B.C. L.R.B.D. No. 62 (B.C.L.R.B.).

Employer retains right of free speech

Requiring that an employer not coerce or intimidate employees does not eliminate the employer's right to state his or her views during the electioneering process that precedes a certification vote. Freedom of expression as set out in the *Charter of Rights and Freedoms* requires that, as long as such statements are merely statements of opinion or fact, and do not amount to threat or coercion, they are permitted. But it is an unfair labour practice for an employer to participate in, or interfere with, the formation or administration of a labour union. Consequently, employers cannot contribute financially or otherwise provide support to a labour union, undermining the independence of the union. Note that many of these unfair labour practices are also crimes under the *Criminal Code* of Canada. For example, when an employer fires, refuses to hire, or threatens an employee with demotion or dismissal because of his union activities, that is a crime punishable with a significant fine and/or imprisonment.[72]

Trade unions, even in the process of organizing the workers, do not have the right to trespass on the employer's property, or to organize during the employees' work time. However, employers will sometimes allow this so that they can at least know what is going on. Once the trade union has successfully completed the certification process, it becomes the certified bargaining agent for all the employees in the bargaining unit. The employer must recognize it as such and bargain with it. The trade union can then serve notice on the employer requiring the commencement of collective bargaining. Employers often wish to join together to bargain collectively with a trade union. In some jurisdictions, such **employers' organizations** can also be certified (or designated to be the "employer" authorized to bargain with the union),[73] creating bargaining agents that are stronger and better able to negotiate with large unions on behalf of their members. These employers' organizations are usually found where there are a number of small employers, such as in the construction industry. In a similar fashion, local trade union organizations are often affiliated with much larger, parent unions, which strengthen the local bargaining units by providing funds to support a prolonged strike and making available research and other expertise to assist in negotiations.

Employer organizations help employers bargain with unions

Unfair labour practices are not limited to the organization process. It remains vitally important to ensure that the union remains independent from employer domination even after certification and to ensure that it can carry on its union activities free from harassment by the employer.

Bargaining

COLLECTIVE AGREEMENTS

Once a union is certified as the bargaining agent for the bargaining unit, it has exclusive authority to bargain on behalf of the employees in the unit. Employees can no longer negotiate "their own deal" with the employer. In a recent Ontario decision,[74] the Arbitration Board found that an employer program, designed to reward good performance by awarding non-cash gifts, violated the collective agreement (compensation above scheduled wage) and breached the requirement that

---

72. *Criminal Code*, R.S.C. 1985, c. C-46, s. 425.

73. *Canada Labour Code, supra* note 29, s. 33.

74. *Re Toronto Hydro and Canadian Union of Public Employees, Local 1* (2002), 103 L.A.C. (4th) 289 (On. L.A.).

the employer recognize the union as the exclusive bargaining agent. By unilaterally implementing this program, the employer was compensating select employees above the wage scales set in the collective agreement. This interfered with the union's exclusive right to negotiate matters of wages, benefits, and other terms of employment.

Any time after a trade union is certified, either party can give notice, requiring bargaining to commence, usually within 10 to 20 days, depending on the jurisdiction.[75] When the union has been certified for some time and a collective agreement is already in place, this notice cannot be given until shortly before the expiration of the old agreement, usually three to four months.[76]

Once this notice has been given, the parties are required to bargain or negotiate with each other, and in most jurisdictions, the bargaining must be "**in good faith**." Whatever the term means, the parties must at least meet with a willingness to explore compromises and to try to find an area of agreement. It does not mean that either party has to agree to the other's terms. Some provinces have adopted the wording used in the federal legislation, requiring the parties to make "every reasonable effort" to reach an agreement.[77]

> Either party can give notice to commence collective bargaining

> Parties must bargain in good faith

CASE SUMMARY 11.12

Employer Must Bargain in Good Faith: *Royal Oak Mines Inc. v. Canada (Labour Relations Board)*[78]

The employer operated a mine in the Northwest Territories. It put forward an offer to contract with its unionized employees. The offer was rejected. A bitter 18-month strike followed in which a number of replacement workers died. Some employees were dismissed, and the employer, when pressured to at least provide for due process in the dismissals, steadfastly refused. After attempts at mediation, an industrial inquiry commission and intervention by the Minister of Labour, there was still no settlement to the strike. The union went to the Canadian Labour Relations Board, complaining that the employer had failed to bargain in good faith. The Board agreed. It ordered the employer to renew the original offer made before the strike. The employer refused and appealed the Board's decision. The Supreme Court of Canada upheld the Labour Relations Board's right to find that the employer had not bargained in good faith and upheld its right to impose the settlement.

DISCUSSION QUESTIONS

While this may constitute interference in the bargaining process to the disadvantage of the employer, the Supreme Court of Canada held that if there is a requisite nexus or connection between the terms imposed and the breach of the duty to bargain in good faith, specific terms can be so imposed. Do you agree with this approach?

---

75. Twenty days under federal legislation, *Canadian Labour Code, supra* note 29, s. 50.

76. Four months under federal legislation, *ibid.,* s. 49.

77. *Ibid.,* s. 50.

78. [1996] 1 S.C.R. 369. See also *Allsco Building Products Ltd. v. United Food and Commercial Workers International Union, Local 1288P* (1998), 207 N.B.R. (2d) 102 (C.A.), which followed this decision.

RATIFICATION

Agreement must be ratified

Once a bargain has been reached, it is presented to the union membership and, when appropriate, to the employer's board, or to an employer's organization, for ratification. If both sides ratify, there is a binding collective agreement. The agreement is a contract but, because of the modifying legislation, it must be viewed as a special form of contract with unique features, such as the method of its enforcement. In most jurisdictions, while bargaining is ongoing, the employer is not permitted to change the terms and conditions of the employment, such as wages, benefits, or hours of work.[79] When it is clear that the parties cannot reach an agreement, it is possible in some jurisdictions for the Labour Relations Board to impose a first contract, although this option is seldom used.[80]

MEDIATION (CONCILIATION)

Mediation, sometimes called conciliation, has been provided for in the various Canadian jurisdictions. When negotiations begin to break down, either party has the right to apply to the appropriate government agency for the appointment of a **conciliator** or *mediator*.[81] This person then meets with the two parties and assists them in their negotiations. The hope is that communications between the two parties will be greatly facilitated by this third-person go-between. The parties are prohibited from taking more drastic forms of action, such as strike or lockout, as long as a conciliator/mediator is involved in the negotiations.

Mediation assists negotiation process

Some provinces provide for a two-tiered process of conciliation with, first, a single officer and, subsequently, a conciliation board consisting of three mediators, but the function is essentially the same. Federally, the Minister must choose among a conciliation officer, a conciliation commissioner, and a conciliation board.[82] It is only after the officer, commissioner, or board has checked out of the dispute and filed a report that the parties are allowed to proceed to strike or lockout. In some jurisdictions, conciliation is a prerequisite to strike or lockout.[83] Although conciliators have no authority to bind the parties, they do have the power to make recommendations that will be embarrassing to an unreasonable party. Note that, in many jurisdictions, conciliation can be imposed on the parties by the Labour Relations Board, even when neither party has requested it.[84] These provisions vary considerably between jurisdictions.

Arbitrators can also play a role in the bargaining process. Arbitration differs from conciliation in that an arbitrator is authorized to make a decision, which is binding on the parties. Under federal legislation, the parties can choose to voluntarily submit any matter respecting renewal, revision, or the entry into a new collective agreement to an arbitrator for a binding decision.[85] Alternatively, legislation may empower labour relations boards to impose a first contract when the parties themselves cannot reach an agreement.[86]

[79.] *Ibid.*, s. 80; *Labour Relations Code*, R.S.B.C. 1996, c. 244, s. 55; *Labour Relations Act, 1995*, S.O. 1995, c. 1, s. 43.

[80.] *Canada Labour Code*, *supra* note 29, 50(b).

[81.] *Canada Labour Code*, *ibid.*, s. 71.

[82.] *Ibid.*, s. 72.

[83.] *Ibid.*, s. 89.

[84.] *Ibid.*, s. 72(2).

[85.] *Ibid.*, s. 79.

[86.] *Ibid.*, s. 80.

Terms of Collective Agreements

The completed collective agreement must satisfy certain requirements, such as having a term of at least one year. If the parties have placed no time limit on the agreement, it will be deemed to be for one year.[87] Federally, when the labour relations board has imposed a collective agreement on the parties, its term will be for two years.[88] Collective agreements may have an automatic renewal clause so that if no notice to bargain is given at the appropriate time, the contract will automatically be renewed, usually for another year. Retroactivity is generally a matter to be negotiated by the parties; if the new collective agreement is to apply retroactively, any changes in terms (such as a new rate of pay) will take effect from the date the old agreement expired. The parties often do not reach an agreement until well after the old collective agreement expires. If the new one then takes effect retroactively, even with this one-year minimum requirement in effect, the new contract will last only a few months. It can be readily seen why every province has taken the approach that any agreement for a period shorter than one year is unworkable.

Contract must be for at least one year

ARBITRATION

All collective agreements must contain provisions for the settlement of disputes arising under the agreement. This is usually accomplished through a **grievance process** that ultimately leads to arbitration. The contract will set out a process involving a series of structured meetings during which the parties can negotiate a settlement. If a settlement is not reached, the matter is submitted to an arbitrator (or panel of arbitrators), who will hold a hearing and make a decision that is binding on both parties. This grievance process is used to resolve disputes not only over the interpretation of the contract provisions, but also as a response to individual employees' complaints of violations of their rights by the employer.

Interpretation of contract disputes to be arbitrated through grievance process

While both arbitration and mediation/conciliation involve the intervention of an outside third party, the distinction is that the parties are not required to follow the recommendations of a mediator/conciliator, but the decision of an arbitrator is binding. Arbitration, therefore, is a substitute for court action. Each party is given an opportunity to put forth its position and present its evidence before the arbitrator makes a decision. Arbitrators are not required to follow the stringent rules of evidence that normally surround judicial proceedings, and their decisions can, in some jurisdictions, be appealed to the Labour Relations Board or to the courts. Some provinces, on the other hand, do not permit appeals, so that the decision of the arbitrator is final. In all jurisdictions, an arbitrator's decision is subject to judicial review when the arbitrator has exceeded the authority given, or when the decision is unreasonable. The collective agreement replaces any individual contract that may have existed previously between the employer and employee, so all disputes between the parties relating to the workplace must be handled by the grievance procedure. This method of dispute resolution is compulsory. It is not permissible for the parties to indulge in strikes or lockouts, or to use the courts, to resolve a dispute over the terms of the contract once a collective agreement is in force.

Decision of arbitrator binding

No strike when contract is in force

---

87. *Ibid.*, s. 80(4).

88. *Ibid.*, s. 67.

CASE SUMMARY 11.13

There Is a Time to Grieve and a Time to Sue: *Goudie v. Ottawa (City)*[89]

A number of unionized animal control officers were transferred from the police force to the City of Ottawa. They were to be covered by a new collective agreement. In the process, their work week increased and other provisions of their employment were changed, to their disadvantage. They claimed that they were promised prior to their transfer that the terms and conditions of their employment would not change as a result of the transfer. In this action they were claiming breach of that contract and negligent or fraudulent misrepresentation.

At the first level of hearing, the dispute was dismissed. The Judge ruled that this was a matter dealing with the collective agreement and that the grievance process should therefore have been used and the matter arbitrated. The case went to the Supreme Court of Canada, which overturned that decision. The Court allowed the animal control officers to bring a civil action on the basis that the dispute arose from a pre-employment contract rather than a labour dispute based on a collective agreement. The Court relied upon a principle developed in an earlier case stating that

> If a dispute between the parties in its "essential character" arises from the interpretation, application, administration or violation of the collective agreement, it must be determined via a grievance procedure by an arbitrator appointed in accordance with the collective agreement, and not by the courts.

DISCUSSION QUESTIONS

In this case, the dispute arose over the terms of a promise or agreement that had been made before these animal control officers became employees of the City of Ottawa. A civil action to determine the matter was thus appropriate. Consider the reasons for restricting a person's right to sue civilly over a collective agreement matter. Do you agree with such restrictions and, if so, was the Court correct in allowing an exception in this case?

OTHER TERMS

Agreement must provide for technological change

In addition to the terms specifically relating to conditions of work, rates of pay, vacations, termination, and the like (which are the main object of the collective bargaining process), there are various other terms that often appear in collective agreements. The federal government and some provinces have passed legislation requiring collective agreements to cover how technological changes in the industry will be handled.[90] Throughout Canada, the parties can agree to terms

---

[89.] [2003] 1 S.C.R. 141, 2003 S.C.C. 14.

[90.] *Canada Labour Code, supra* note 29, ss. 51–55.

that provide for union security. One example is the **union shop** clause, which requires that new employees join the union within a specified period of time. A second arrangement, used particularly in such industries as construction or longshoring, requires that the employee be a member of the union before getting a job. This is a **closed shop** clause. A third option enables employees to retain the right not to join a union, but they must still pay union dues. This arrangement is referred to as the **Rand Formula**, or an **agency shop**. Fourthly, the collective agreement may contain a **check-off provision**, which means that the parties have agreed that the employer will deduct union dues from the payroll. A fifth option, **maintenance of membership**, requires those who are already union members to pay dues and to maintain their membership, though new employees need not join the union.

Union shop and closed shop provisions

Agency shop, check-off, and maintenance of membership provisions

Strikes and Lockouts

Some sort of job action will probably result if the parties cannot agree on what terms to include in the collective agreement. A **lockout** is action taken by the employer to prevent employees from working and earning wages. A **strike** is the withdrawal of services by employees. Although a strike usually consists of refusing to come to work, or intentional slowdowns, other forms of interference with production may also be classified as strikes. For example, postal employees announced just before Christmas 1983 that they would process Christmas cards with 10-cent stamps on them despite the fact that the appropriate rate was 32 cents per letter. This action was taken to draw attention to the fact that certain commercial users of the postal system got a preferential bulk rate not available to the public. The courts declared that the action was a strike. Since a strike would have been illegal under the circumstances, the union reversed its position. Employees can pressure an employer by strictly adhering to the terms of their agreement, or by doing no more than is minimally required. This behaviour is called **work to rule** and will often prompt a lockout. Strikes and lockouts are both **work stoppages**. The lockout is imposed by the employer, while the strike involves the employees' withdrawing their services.

Job action may involve lockout, strike, work to rule

CASE SUMMARY 11.14

There Is No Guaranteed Right to Strike: *Ontario Hospital Assn. v. Ontario Public Service Employees Union*[91]

Health workers in Ontario had been without a contract for over 300 days when they decided to hold a day of protest. On this day, the employees would not work, but would hold rallies and do other things to bring their plight to the public's attention, including picketing at various health-related institutional locations. The employer claimed this was an illegal strike, as health employees in Ontario were prohibited from striking under the *Hospital Labour Disputes Arbitration Act*. The union claimed that this was a political protest rather than a strike, and that its right to strike and to picket was protected under

---

the *Charter of Rights and Freedoms*. The Board held that this was indeed an illegal with-drawal of services amounting to a prohibited strike. While the union's political communi-cations were protected under section 2(b) of the *Charter* (freedom of expression), its right to strike was not. Any restriction on its freedom of expression in connection with the pro-hibition of strike action was also supported as a reasonable exception to its freedom of expression under section 1 of the Charter.

DISCUSSION QUESTIONS

This case illustrates the principle that there is no guaranteed right to strike under the *Charter* and that even the right to freely express opinions can be curtailed when asso-ciated with a violation of a prohibition against striking. Do you think there should be such a right to strike? Should it be included in the *Charter*? Would the result of this case be different in light of the Supreme Court decision discussed in Case Summary 11.11?

Strike or lockout can occur only between contracts in an interest dispute

Since the main objective of modern collective bargaining legislation is to reduce conflict, the right to strike and the right to lock out have been severely lim-ited. It is unlawful for a strike or lockout to occur while an agreement is in force. Strikes and lockouts can take place only after an agreement has expired and before the next one comes into effect.[92] Any strike or lockout associated with the recognition process, or involving jurisdictional disputes between two unions, is also illegal and must be dealt with through the certification process described above. Only when the old collective agreement has expired, and the dispute is part of an interest dispute involving the negotiation of the terms to be included in a new collective agreement, is a strike or lockout legal.

If a collective agreement is in place and a dispute arises as to the terms (a rights dispute), it must be resolved through the grievance and arbitration process described above. Any strike associated with such a dispute is illegal.

Must bargain in good faith first and vote before strike

Even when a dispute concerns what will go into the new agreement (an inter-est dispute), there are still some limitations on strike action. The old contract must have expired and the parties must have attempted to bargain in good faith. A vote authorizing strike action must have been taken, and a specified period of notice must have been given, for example, 72 hours in Alberta, in British Columbia, and under the *Canada Labour Code*.[93] The employer must give the same notice to the employees when a lockout is about to take place. No strike or lock-out can take place until a specified period of time has passed after a mediator/conciliator has made a report to the relevant cabinet minister. Even then, in some areas, a further cooling-off period may be imposed. In some jurisdictions, the employer is prohibited from hiring replacement workers during a strike. This restriction puts considerably greater pressure on the employer to settle the dis-pute and goes some way in reducing the violence associated with such labour–management confrontation. The federal government has amended the *Canada Labour Code* to partially prohibit the use of such replacement workers.[94]

Proper strike notice must be given

[92.] *Canada Labour Code, supra* note 29, ss. 88–89.

[93.] *Supra* note 29, s. 94 (2.1).

[94.] *Labour Relations Code* (Alberta), *supra* note 71, s. 78, *Labour Relations Code* (British Columbia), *supra* note 81, *Canada Labour Code, ibid.*, s. 87.2.

Picketing

Once a strike or lockout is underway, one of the most effective techniques available to trade unions is picketing. As with striking, the use of picketing is severely limited and controlled. Picketing involves strikers standing near, or marching around, a place of business, trying to dissuade people from doing business there. Picketing is permissible only when a lawful strike or lockout is in progress. Employees who picket before proper notice has been given, or somewhere not permitted under the labour legislation, are in violation of the law. A picketer responsible for communicating false information to those who might cross the picket line can be sued for defamation.

When the information communicated does not try to discourage people from crossing the picket line, or dealing with the employer, the action may not qualify as picketing.

Right to picket limited by legislation

CASE SUMMARY 11.15

Leafleting and Picketing Distinguished: *United Food and Commercial Workers, Local 1518 (U.F.C.W.) v. KMart Canada Ltd.*[95]

The UFCW represented employees who were locked out from the KMart department stores in Campbell River and Port Alberni. It decided to escalate the dispute by handing out leaflets to customers in KMart stores in the Vancouver and Victoria areas, explaining the nature of their complaints against the company and encouraging them not to shop at KMart. In British Columbia, the legislation prohibits secondary picketing (picketing at a location other than where the employees work). The issue was whether this leafleting qualified as prohibited secondary picketing. The Supreme Court of Canada held that it did not. The Court determined that "the distribution of leaflets did not interfere with employees at the secondary sites, nor was there any indication that it interfered with the delivery of supplies. The activity was carried out peacefully, and it did not impede public access to the stores. Neither was there any evidence of verbal or physical intimidation." Some customers may have been persuaded not to deal with the stores, but this was a consequence of leafleting rather than picketing.

The court distinguished between picketing and leafleting. It held that leafleting was an expression of free speech and as such was protected by section 2 of the *Charter of Rights and Freedoms*. Because the B.C. *Labour Relations Code's* definition of picketing was overly broad, including leafleting, it was struck down. The prohibition against secondary picketing was also an interference with free speech, but it was justified under section 1 because of its interference in commercial relations. Note that even leafleting is not permitted when the activity involves trespassing on a company's parking lot ordinarily not used by the public.[96]

DISCUSSION QUESTIONS

Consider the delicate balance of power between trade unions and employers that labour relations legislation tries to maintain and whether allowing leafleting or secondary picketing upsets that balance.

[95.] [1999] 2 S.C.R. 1083.

[96.] *RMH Teleservices v. BCGEU* (2003), 223 D.L.R. (4th) 750.

Violence not permitted

Picketing must be peaceful and merely communicate information. Violence will not be tolerated. A tort action for trespass may follow the violation of private property. If violence erupts, the assaulting party may face criminal and civil court actions. When picketing goes beyond the narrow bounds permitted in common law and legislation, the employer can resort to the courts or labour relations boards to get an injunction to limit or prohibit the picketing. Using an excessive number of picketers, as with mass picketing, goes beyond simple information communication and becomes intimidation. The employer can then apply to have the number of picketers restricted.

Strong tradition of union solidarity makes picketing effective

Although picketing limited in this way may seem to be an ineffectual weapon, there is an extremely strong tradition among union members and many others never to cross a picket line. Others simply wish to avoid the unpleasantness of a confrontation. Employers must deal with other businesses that employ union members, and these workers generally will not cross the picket line. It eventually becomes very difficult for an employer to continue in business surrounded by a picket line.

Some provinces permit secondary picketing

Which locations can be legally picketed varies with the jurisdiction. Employees in every jurisdiction can picket the plant or factory where they work. In some jurisdictions, such as New Brunswick,[97] **secondary picketing** is allowed, and striking employees are able to picket not just their own workplace, but also other locations where the employer carries on business. In any case, unrelated businesses cannot legally be picketed, even if they are located on the same premises as the one struck, as might be the case, for example, in a shopping mall. Of course, whether the picketing is directed toward such an unrelated business in a given dispute is a question for the court or board to decide. The more extensive the picketing, the more effective the economic pressure placed on the employer. There is some variation with respect to the specific rules relating to picketing.

No legal obligation to honour picket line

Anyone has the legal right to cross a picket line. Customers are free to continue doing business with an employer involved in a strike or lockout; suppliers are free to continue supplying goods and services to the employer if they can persuade their employees to cross the picket line; and the employer has the right to continue normal business activities. Unfortunately, picketers can lose sight of these basic rights when they think that their picket line is not being effective. As a result, a considerable amount of intimidation, coercion, violence, and injury still takes place, despite all of the precautions that have been introduced into the labour relations system in Canada.

Public Sector and Essential Services

Public-sector employees have limited rights to job action

The discussion thus far relates to people employed in private industry. Many people, however, are employed either as part of the public sector, or in service industries that are considered essential to society, such as hospitals, and police and fire departments. Employees falling into these categories are treated differently than those employed in private industry, and special legislation governs their activities. Although labour issues and disputes in these occupations are virtually the same as those in the private sector, the government and the public regard the position of

---

[97.] *Industrial Relations Act*, R.S.N.B. 1973, c. I-4, s. 104.

public service employees as quite different. Strikes by police, firefighters, hospital workers, schoolteachers, and other public servants are usually considered inappropriate by members of the public.

Every province has special legislation to deal with these groups. Most provinces permit collective bargaining to some extent, but only a few allow public-sector employees to participate in strikes and picketing, the others substituting some form of compulsory arbitration of disputes.[98] Of course, in all labour disputes, including private ones, the government retains the right, either by existing statute, or by the passage of a specific bill, to impose a settlement, or an alternative method of resolving the dispute, such as compulsory arbitration.

REDUCING RISK 11.4

Some employers will feel threatened by the prospect of a union organizing its workforce. Often emotional rather than economic factors come into play, with employers not wanting to give up their right to manage, or to surrender any control to trade unions. This is true especially at the organizational stage and is the main reason the employer's role at that level has been minimized. The certification process, supervised by government, has reduced conflict at that stage. Employers are well advised to exercise care, especially in a newly unionized situation, to avoid unfair labour practices and other situations that poison the atmosphere because of ill-thought-out tactics and strategies.

Union Organization

Trade unions are democratic organizations in which policy is established by vote. Executives and officers are elected. Members can be expelled or disciplined for misbehaviour, such as crossing picket lines after being instructed not to by the union executive. Expulsion can be devastating for a worker, since many collective agreements provide for a union shop in which all employees must be members of the union. Some jurisdictions have passed legislation stipulating that a person who loses her union membership for reasons other than failure to pay dues will be able to retain employment.[99] There are some employees whose religious beliefs prevent them from joining or contributing to such organizations as trade unions, which presents a real dilemma in a union shop situation. Some governments have passed legislation exempting such individuals from joining unions; dues are still deducted but are paid to a registered charity. The other terms of the collective agreement still apply.[100]

Trade unions are subject to human rights legislation. In some jurisdictions, the labour legislation provides that they can be denied certification, or lose their status, as a trade union, if they discriminate.[101] Unions have an obligation to represent all their members fairly.[102] Employees who feel unfairly treated by the union, or who feel that the union is not properly representing them in disputes with employers, can lodge complaints with the Labour Relations Board. The union may find itself required to compensate the wronged employees.

Unions can expel for misbehaviour

---

98. See, for example, *ibid.*, s. 80.

99. *Ibid.*, s. 70(2).

100. *Canada Labour Code, supra* note 29, s. 95(e).

101. *Ibid.*, s. 25(2).

102. *Ibid.*, s. 37.

Trade unions were once considered illegal organizations with no status separate from their membership and therefore no corporate identity. Most provinces have passed legislation giving a recognized trade union the right to sue or be sued on its own behalf, at least for the purposes outlined in the labour legislation.[103]

CASE SUMMARY 11.16

Union Has Duty of Fair Representation: *Dezentje v. Warchow*[104]

The employer usually gave employees extended leaves of absence rather than layoffs. In this case, three employees were laid off by the employer while other employees were given leaves of absence. The three workers went to their union representative for advice about filing a grievance. The union did not help them very much. Eventually, they were told that they had a negligible chance of success. They filed a complaint against the union under a provision that imposed a duty of fair representation on the union.

The Labour Relations Board found that they had a modest chance of success, and that the union had an obligation to represent them and to help them pursue the grievance. In refusing to do so, it had failed its obligation of fair representation. Damages were awarded based on the modest chance of success. One employee was awarded higher damages because the employer had offered to rehire him, and the union had failed to convey the offer to him.

An application for judicial review was made to the Court of Queen's Bench, which overturned the decision. On further appeal to the Court of Appeal the original decision was restored. The Board had dealt with matters within its area of expertise and had done so reasonably. There was evidence that the union representatives had not acted with honesty, or good faith, and that the remedies imposed had been appropriate.

DISCUSSION QUESTIONS

Do you think that giving union members this kind of power puts too many restrictions on the union's ability to effectively maneuver in its relations with the employer?

---

103. See, for example, *Labour Relations Code*(Alberta),*supra*note 71, s. 25.

104. 2002 ABCA 249, [2002] Alta. L.R.B.R. 305, 220 D.L.R. (4th) 566, 25 Alta. L.R. (4th) 249 (Alta. C.A.).

SUMMARY

What is employment?

- Must distinguish employees, independent contractors, and agents
- Control and organization tests used to determine if employment relationship

The law of master and servant

- Employment law governed by contract law, common law, and legislation
- Both employers and employees have obligations to fulfill
- Restrictive covenants will be enforced if not too broad and are reasonable
- Employment contracts can be terminated by the giving of reasonable notice, pay in lieu of notice, or by just cause
- Just cause includes disobedience, dishonesty, incompetence, and absenteeism
- Reasonable accommodation must be provided to disabled workers
- Damages awarded for wrongful dismissal (including constructive dismissal)
- Employer vicariously liable for the acts of the employee during the course of employment
- Employment standards legislation sets minimum standards to protect employees
- Human rights legislation prohibits discrimination and harassment in workplace
- Many other types of legislation affecting the employment relationship now exist

Collective bargaining

- All Canadian jurisdictions now have collective bargaining legislation
- The legislation governs certification of unions to represent a group of employees
- Unions have exclusive authority to bargain on behalf of employees
- Collective agreements must be ratified by union members
- Mediation and arbitration can be used if negotiations break down
- Legislation requires that certain terms be included in collective agreements, including a grievance process
- Strikes and lockouts cannot take place while a collective agreement is in force
- Picketing can only take place during a strike or lockout
- Public-sector and essential service employees not allowed to strike or picket
- Unions are democratic organizations with a duty to represent all members fairly

QUESTIONS

1. Distinguish among an employee, an independent contractor, and an agent.

2. Explain how a court will determine whether a person is an employee rather than an independent contractor.

3. Summarize the employer's obligations to the employee, and the employee's obligations to the employer, under common law.

4. Explain what is meant by a restrictive covenant and what factors determine whether it is enforceable.

5. What is the proper way to terminate an employment contract that is for an indefinite period of time?

6. How is the appropriate notice period to terminate an employment relationship determined?

7. Under what circumstances can an employee be dismissed without notice? When can an employee leave employment without giving notice?

8. What risk does an employer face who ignores an employee's incompetence over a period of time?

9. What is "constructive dismissal"? Be sure to explain it using a contractual perspective.

10. What factors will a court take into consideration when determining compensation in a wrongful dismissal action? Indicate the various types of remedies that may be available to the plaintiff.

11. Explain what is meant by "vicarious liability." Describe the limitations on its application.

12. Describe how the employment standards legislation protects basic workers' rights.

13. Explain how human rights legislation applies to areas of employment.

14. Explain what is meant by a "duty to accommodate" in the field of human rights and how it can affect employers.

15. Explain the object and purpose of workers' compensation legislation and how those objectives are accomplished. If a worker is injured on the job and is not covered by workers' compensation, what course of action need he take to secure a remedy?

16. What is the significance of the *National Labor Relations Act* (*Wagner Act*) in Canada?

17. Compare and contrast recognition disputes, jurisdiction disputes, interest disputes, and rights disputes.

18. Once a collective agreement is in place, what effect will it have on the individual rights of employees? How will it affect the employer?

19. Explain the difference between mediation/conciliation and arbitration. Describe how these tools are used in Canadian labour disputes.

20. Distinguish among a union shop, a closed shop, and an agency shop.

21. Distinguish between a strike and a lockout. What kind of disputes are strikes and lockouts limited to? How are the other types of disputes between union and employer dealt with?

22. Explain what steps must take place before a strike or lockout is legal.

23. Explain what is meant by "picketing," when it can take place, and the limitations that have been placed on picketing in different jurisdictions.

24. What is the legal position of a person who wishes to cross a picket line?

25. How is collective bargaining for public-sector and essential service employees different from that for people employed in private industry?

Chapter 12

Special Contracts: Insurance

1. Define the four types of insurance businesses commonly need

2. Identify when an insurable interest exists

3. Explain the significance of insurance being a contract of utmost good faith

4. Identify the duties imposed on the insured and insurer

INSURANCE

A recurring theme of this text is to encourage risk management and to promote an attitude of risk avoidance. A sound strategy is to learn the law, recognize potential pitfalls, and correct them before any harm takes place. A second aspect of risk management is to reduce the effect of risk by acquiring appropriate personal and business insurance.

Insurance transfers the risk from the insured to the insurer. When property is insured against fire, for example, the risk of loss shifts from the insured to the insurer. The insurer calculates the risk and assesses premiums based on the amount of coverage and the amount of risk involved. As risk increases, so too should the premiums charged. In essence, insurance spreads the loss across a great number of parties in exchange for the payment of a premium.

Insurance transfers risk to the insurer

The industry is tightly regulated by the federal *Insurance Companies Act.*[1] This statute requires all non-provincial insurance corporations to be registered and sets out the amount of reserves that must be retained to cover eventual claims. All provincial jurisdictions have similar insurance legislation. These provincial and federal statutes can be viewed as a type of consumer protection legislation in the field of insurance.

Industry regulated by statutes

The Insurance Industry

Most insurance is purchased through an agent or a broker. Both are agents in the technical sense, but the broker operates an independent business, usually dealing with several different insurance companies in the course of finding the best deal for his client, the insured. Agents and brokers owe significant duties to the people

Insurance can be acquired through agents and brokers

[1.] S.C. 1991, c. 47.

they represent, and so it can be very important whether the person an insured individual is dealing with is acting for the insurance company or for the insured. While **insurance agents** owe important obligations to their principals (the insurance corporations), they also owe a duty of good faith to the customer; thus, agents will be held liable if they fail to provide the insurance coverage asked for, or otherwise fail to properly service the client's needs.

Adjuster values the loss for the insurance company after the insured-against event takes place

Adjusters are employees or representatives of the insurance corporation charged with investigating and settling insurance claims against the corporation after the insured-against event takes place. It is important to remember when dealing with adjusters that they are normally looking after the interests of the insurance corporation rather than those of the person making the claim. Independent adjusters may also be engaged when problems arise with respect to claims.

Insurance companies often re-insure

Often businesses need the assistance of a broker to ensure adequate coverage. In the event of a large risk, a broker may further spread the risk by involving two or three insurance companies, each taking a percentage of the total. The primary company may take 60 percent, the second company 30 percent, and the third company the final 10 percent. Often one company will carry the risk on paper, but turn to the re-insurance market where the risk is divided among a larger number of secondary market companies. Many of these companies operate only behind the scenes so that the policyholder has to deal with only one adjuster in the event of a claim.

Types of Insurance

(A) LIABILITY INSURANCE

The insurance industry is divided between commercial and personal insurance, with the commercial line offering a variety of products. Liability insurance is the type of insurance most closely associated with torts. The main objective of tort law is to determine who should pay when wrongful conduct causes injury and loss, while the function of insurance is to spread that loss. It is important for business-people to maintain appropriate insurance coverage to avoid potentially devastating claims against them or their employees.

Liability insurance covers negligence by self or employees

Only to extent of coverage

Liability insurance is normally designed to cover not only a loss that could be reasonably expected, but legal defence and court costs as well. Should the policy holder purchase an insufficient amount of coverage, she will have to cover any shortfall. It is thus a good idea to follow a broker's advice and insure for an amount that will cover most eventualities. Note that liability insurance will not cover wilful acts, such as assault, theft, arson, or fraud. Nor will it provide coverage where the insured is not the one at fault. There must be negligence or some other basis for liability on the part of the insured for the insurer to pay out on the policy. Liability insurance takes many forms. Professionals, like lawyers and accountants, who exchange their expertise for money, should carry **professional liability insurance**. A contractor should have a **builder's risk policy** in place. Anyone shipping goods should carry insurance that protects the goods while they are in his care. A recent innovation in the industry is **umbrella liability** where several types of liability are bundled together, allowing the insured higher limits of coverage for a more economical premium.

Coverage only when insured is at fault

CASE SUMMARY 12.1

Policy's Terms Determine Coverage: *Omega Inn Ltd. v. Continental Insurance Co.*[2]

There was both fire insurance and business interruption insurance coverage on the Omega Inn when it burned down in 1985. Because the insurance company suspected arson, however, it refused to pay, and with no funds available the insured was not able to rebuild. Finally, after six months of investigation where no evidence of arson was discovered, Continental agreed to pay. The reconstruction took another four months, resulting in a total of 10 months' delay in the reopening of the business. The insurance company claimed that the policy obligated it to pay only for the four-month delay caused by the actual rebuilding. The policy stated that Omega was covered only for the length of time it was actually in the rebuilding process.

At trial the Court held that because the delay had not been caused by the insured, Continental had to pay for the whole 10-month period. But on appeal that decision was reversed.

The policy was clear and required payment only for the time the business would be interrupted while diligent effort was being made to rebuild. That obligation should not be affected by the fact that the insured did not have the funds to rebuild. As stated in the decision, "the impecuniosity of the plaintiff cannot be laid at the door of the insurer because it failed to pay more promptly. Its obligation and the full extent of its obligation, with respect to the business loss interruption coverage under the policy, was to pay for such length of time as would be required with the exercise of due diligence and dispatch to rebuild."[3]

SMALL BUSINESS PERSPECTIVE

Fire insurance and business interruption insurance usually go together, and this case demonstrates how they work. It also highlights the necessity to get back into business as soon as possible, despite any delays attributable to the insurer. The need to read one's policy, to be clear on what is covered and what is not, is likewise critical.

(B) PROPERTY INSURANCE

The predominant form of property insurance covers losses to buildings and their contents due to fire or other named perils. **Comprehensive policies** cover everything except what is specifically excluded. Typical exclusions are acts of war, riots, or illegal activity. Insurance companies often set limits on what the company will pay in the event of a loss or apply a higher deductible. Most insurance contracts require insured parties to maintain certain safety and security standards to protect themselves against the risk of fire and theft.

There are problems with arranging for more or less coverage than is needed. If you take out more insurance than required, you are wasting money since you can collect only on what is actually lost. Carrying too little insurance is also a problem since companies normally include **co-insurance clauses** in most property

---

[2.] (1988), 55 D.L.R. (4th) 766 (B.C.C.A.).

[3.] *Ibid.* at p. 768.

Co-insurance clause may reduce coverage

insurance policies requiring that the insured parties maintain a certain percentage of coverage or bear some of the risk of loss themselves. Thus, in a policy with an 80 percent co-insurance clause, if the policy coverage were for less than that portion of the actual potential loss (say, only $50 000 coverage on property worth $100 000), the insured would have to assume a portion of any covered loss that occurred. The formula is:

The amount of insurance carried, divided by the minimum coverage that should have been in place, times the actual loss.

In this example that would be expressed as

$$\frac{\$50\ 000}{(\$100\ 000 \times 0.8)} \times \$10\ 000 = \$6\ 250$$

Note that the minimum insurance that should have been carried is determined by the co-insurance clause.

REDUCING RISK 12.1

A business that has been categorized as high risk or undesirable because of a claims history, late payments, or generally poor practices may not be able to acquire insurance or may be forced to pay high premiums for limited coverage. Strategies should be developed to avoid such a consequence. Insurance companies and brokers may offer services to help a client identify ways to diminish or eliminate losses.

(C) BUSINESS INTERRUPTION INSURANCE

Business interruption insurance covers lost profits

Often, a business suffering a loss from a fire will have insurance to cover the property damage, but there will be nothing to cover the losses the business suffers during the period it is closed down for repairs. Business interruption insurance is designed to cover that gap, providing coverage not only for lost profits but also any additional expenses incurred to bring the business back into production. Comprehensive property insurance and business interruption insurance together are an attempt to put the insured in the same financial position it would have been in had the fire or other damage not occurred.

(D) LIFE AND HEALTH INSURANCE

Life insurance used in business to cover key personnel

Life insurance provides security for a family or business against the death of the insured. Death is inevitable, and so premiums are calculated on the basis of a prediction of how long a person of a certain age and health can be expected to live. Businesses often take out life insurance against the death of key personnel to cover losses incurred from any disruption that may result from the death or illness of an executive partner or key employee.

CASE SUMMARY 12.2

Consent Given—Insurable Interest Requirement Satisfied: *Chantiam v. Packall Packaging Inc.*[4]

Mr. Chantiam was working as the plant manager for Packall Packaging Inc. when he consented to the company's taking out an insurance policy on his life (called a "keyman" policy). Later he left the company and started another business in competition with it. When he discovered that the insurance policy on his life was still in place, he demanded that it be terminated or transferred to him; when his former employer refused, he brought this action against the company.

Like all forms of insurance there must be an insurable interest to support such a policy. There was no question that an insurable interest for the employer existed in Chantiam's life at the time the policy was taken out, but he argued that conditions had changed, the insurable interest had ended, and it was against the public interest for a business to maintain an insurance policy on the life of a competitor.

The trial Court agreed, ordering the policy to be cancelled. But on appeal the Court held that the appropriate time for determining whether an insurable interest existed or not was at the time the policy was taken out. Once that had been established and it was clear that an insurable interest existed at that time, the company was entitled to continue the policy even where the employment ended and where the subject of the policy became a competitor. Furthermore, the applicable legislation stipulated that where the insured consents in writing to the creation of the policy, as happened here, that satisfies the insurable interest requirement. Since there was an insurable interest at the time the policy was created, there were no grounds to challenge the continuation of the policy.

This case illustrates that with life insurance, the question of insurable interest relates only to when the policy is taken out. Note that Manitoba has changed its legislation, allowing a person to bring an application to the court to have the policy cancelled when that insurable interest is no longer present.[5] But in this case, Ontario (like other provinces) had no similar provision.

SMALL BUSINESS PERSPECTIVE

It is necessary to refer to the applicable provincial legislation for clarity as to when one has an insurable interest in the life of another. Having "something to lose" suggests that an insurable interest may exist. So would a business have an insurable interest in the life of a debtor? Should the size of the debt matter?

There are various forms of life insurance to meet the needs of different individuals. Term insurance provides only a benefit upon death, and the premiums are lower than whole life insurance, which provides coverage in the event of death as well as investment potential and retirement income. These are just two of several variations of life insurance available.

[4.] (1998), 38 O.R. (3d) 401 (C.A.), leave to appeal to S.C.C. refused, [1998] S.C.C.A. No. 358.

[5.] *Insurance Act*, R.S.M. 1987, c. I-40, s. 155(4).

Health and disability insurance provides coverage during the life of the insured and is designed to pay health care expenses and provide an income for a person who is unable to earn a living because of illness or accident. Medical insurance can be arranged individually or as part of group coverage. Health care services in Canada are funded through the government-sponsored medical system, which is often supplemented by plans providing extended coverage.

In most Canadian jurisdictions, disability insurance can be obtained on an individual basis with an insurance corporation, but it is more often acquired by large organizations as part of an employee benefits package.

Health and disability insurance usually part of group coverage

Sometimes, where the husband and wife are both working, there will be overlapping extended benefits coverage such as dental and disability. Usually, there is a deductible amount that must be paid or a limitation on the coverage. When there are two policies, often one can be used to cover the shortfall of the other but not to overpay. Today these policies often include a provision declaring them to be "excess coverage" when another policy is in place, with the result that the first policy will cover up to the deductible or the limit of the coverage and only then will the other kick in and pay the rest. Where both policies declare themselves to be excess coverage, the two insurers will split the cost of the coverage.[6]

Contract governs coverage but where conflict, both share equally

Insurable Interest

For insurance not to be considered a wager, the insured must be able to demonstrate an **insurable interest** in what is insured. That means that when the insured-against event happens, the insured must have suffered a loss for which the insurance payout provides compensation and no more. The contract for insurance is a contract of indemnity. Consequently, except in the case of life insurance, the insured can recover only what he or she has actually lost, up to the limit set out in the policy. When the payout becomes a windfall, the insurance agreement is void as an illegal contract.

The insurable interest, then, is the amount an insured stands to lose if the insured-against event takes place. If Flynn owned a half-interest in a painting worth $150 000, she would have an insurable interest of $75 000. If Flynn carried an insurance policy of $150 000 on the painting and it was stolen, she would be able to collect only $75 000 for herself, even though she had insured it for the higher amount. (Were the painting to be stolen, she would likely collect the entire $150 000 but be required to hold the other $75 000 in trust for the person who owned the other half interest in it.)

Must be insurable interest to avoid illegality

CASE SUMMARY 12.3

Insurance Void Due to Lack of Insurable Interest: *Walton v. General Accident Insurance Co. of Canada*[7]

The Waltons had an insurance policy on their home with the defendant. Because of a dispute with the municipality they stopped making payments on their taxes and mortgage. Even though a final foreclosure order was made they were still living in the house when it

---

6. See *Family Insurance Corp. v. Lombard Canada Ltd.*[2002] 2 S.C.R. 695; [2002] S.C.J. No. 49.

7. (2001), 194 D.L.R. (4th) 570 (Sask. C. A.).

was destroyed by fire. They had continued to pay premiums and so claimed under the insurance policy, but the insurer refused to pay, saying they had no insurable interest in the property. At trial it was held that because the Court still had a right to reconvey the property to them, that was a sufficient insurable interest and the insurance company had to pay. But on appeal that decision was reversed.

The Saskatchewan Court of Appeal found that the Waltons had no right to the property and they were living in it illegally. True, they had a hope that the property would be reconveyed to them, but this was at best a strong expectation. In fact at the time of the destruction of the home they had no legal or equitable right to it and so had no insurable interest.

SMALL BUSINESS PERSPECTIVE

This case dramatically illustrates the nature of insurable interest. Sometimes, following incorporation of a family business, owners fail to distinguish between assets owned individually and assets now owned by the corporate entity. The importance of having the actual owner named as the insured cannot be overstated.

It should be noted that when life insurance is involved, people have an insurable interest in their own life and in the lives of their spouse and other close relatives. A loss, economic, emotional, and otherwise, is assumed if a close relation dies. Depending on the jurisdiction, where the lives of key business personnel are insured, the written consent of that person may be required as was the case in the *Packall* case discussed above (Case Summary 12.2). The value of that insurable interest will be the amount of insurance coverage contracted for.

In the past, it was thought that because a corporation was a separate legal entity, the shareholder had no insurable interest in the assets of the corporation. The Supreme Court of Canada, however, has decided that shareholders may have an insurable interest in those assets even though they don't have a direct legal claim to them. The fact that they would suffer a loss is enough.[8]

Shareholders now have insurance interests in assets of corporation

LIMITATION CLAUSES

Ambiguities Resolved in Favour of the Insured

Insurance contracts take a standard fixed form and often contain limitation clauses favouring the insurer. Where there is ambiguity in the meaning of such clauses the *contra proferentum* rule allows the court to choose an interpretation that favours the insured. Coverage will be broadly construed while exclusions will be narrowly interpreted. Thus courts will apply an interpretation that favours the insured since it was the insurer that chose the language to use.

Ambiguities in contract interpreted in favour of the insured

---

8. *Kosmopoulos v. Constitution Insurance Company of Canada Ltd.,* [1987] 1 S.C.R. 2, at para. 42: "if an insured can demonstrate, in Lawrence J.'s words, 'some relation to, or concern in the subject of the insurance, which relation or concern by the happening of the perils insured against may be so affected as to produce a damage, detriment, or prejudice to the person insuring', that insured should be held to have a sufficient interest."

CASE SUMMARY 12.4

Contra Proferentum Rule Applied: *Heitsman v. Canadian Premier Life Insurance Co.*[9]

The insured's widow sued for death benefits under a policy of accidental death and dismemberment insurance. The insured died after suffering a heart attack while trying to free himself from an overturned tractor-trailer following a motor vehicle accident. Medical experts testified that the heart attack was brought on by the stress, emotional and physical, resulting from the accident. The stress would not have been fatal were it not for the deceased's pre-existing heart problems. The Court determined that both the pre-existing condition and the stress caused by the accident contributed to the death. Neither one was the proximate cause. The insurance policy included an exclusion of liability for loss of life caused by sickness or disease. The Court found the clause ambiguous. It was not clear whether the parties had excluded payment for a death where one of its causes was accidental, the other a pre-existing disease. The *contra proferentum* rule was applied, and the exclusion was narrowly interpreted; thus, judgment was issued to the widow.

DISCUSSION QUESTIONS

This case illustrates that one's insurer may try to avoid payment, relying upon an "exclusion" to justify its actions. Do you think that this rule of interpretation is sufficient to protect the interests of the insured? What if the clause is clear but unfair?

Contract of Utmost Good Faith

Insured has duty to disclose changes in risk

A relationship of *trust* exists between the insured and insurer, creating an *obligation to act in good faith*. An important aspect of that obligation is the duty on the part of the insured to disclose pertinent information, especially where it affects the *risk* assumed by the insurer. After all, it is the insured that knows, has possession of, or has access to the information relevant to that risk. Even after the contract is made, there is often a duty to notify the insurance company when circumstances change, as when an occupied building becomes unoccupied for a length of time.[10]

CASE SUMMARY 12.5

Failure to Notify of Change Voids Policy: *Mueller v. Wawanesa Insurance Co.*[11]

The fire insurance policy in question was taken out by the landlord when the house was rented as a residential family dwelling. The "family" never moved in—instead, the building was occupied by three members of a motorcycle gang. Despite notice from the police that the property was being used as a clubhouse, the landlord did not terminate the

---

9. (2002), 4 B.C.L.R. (4th) 124 (S.C.).

10. See, for example, *528852 Ontario Inc. v. Royal Insurance Co.* (2000), 51 O.R. (3d) 470 (Sup. Ct. J.), where the insured's failure to disclose a change of use, namely that the premises were left unoccupied, was a material non-disclosure that entitled the insurer to deny coverage.

11. [1995] O.J. No. 3807 (Ont. Ct. (Gen.Div.)).

lease. The rent cheques were kept current, so the landlord felt unable to terminate the lease. The property was eventually destroyed by fire and the police suspected arson at the hands of a rival gang.

The insurance company refused to honour the policy, and in this action the Court agreed, finding that the use of the house was not the residential use envisioned under the policy and that there had been a material change in risk. The failure to notify the insurer of the change voided the policy and the insurance company did not have to pay.

SMALL BUSINESS PERSPECTIVE

The case shows how important it is to inform the insurer of any material changes that take place. Could leaving a building vacant, even for a limited period of time, constitute a material change? To be on the safe side, advance notification of changes to risk should be given to the insurer and a written record of the notice should be retained.

When applying for property insurance, the insurer will want to know what the property will be used for, whether it is for a business, whether it will be vacant for extended periods, and what kind of security and safety equipment is in place. For life, disability, or medical insurance, any injury, disease, or other health problems that may affect that person's health must be disclosed.

Insured must disclose relevant information

These factors affect eligibility or the rates charged for insurance, and since the insurer usually has no way of determining this information by itself, it must depend on the honesty of the insured to disclose it. Failure to disclose information material to the loss may be misrepresentation and may result in the loss's being unrecoverable. Even where it is not relevant to the loss, if it is a material misrepresentation it may cause the entire policy to be void. Legislation in some provinces upholds the insurance where the misrepresentation was innocent; but even in those jurisdictions, the policy will be unenforceable if the misrepresentation or failure to disclose was done knowingly. An all too common misrepresentation involves representations as to who owns and who is driving an automobile. The insured may be tempted by potentially lower premiums to misrepresent who the primary driver will be. Such misrepresentations have enabled many insurers to avoid payment following collisions.[12]

CASE SUMMARY 12.6

Perilous Non-Disclosure: *Agresso Corp. v. Temple Insurance Co.*[13]

Since insurance contracts are contracts of utmost good faith, parties must err on the side of caution when completing applications for coverage. The insured software company applied for Information Technology Errors and Omissions insurance from the defendant

---

[12.] See *Demontigny v. Insurance Corp. of British Columbia,*[1989] B.C.J. No. 2475;*Schoff v. Royal Insurance Company of Canada,*[2004] A.J. No. 592 (C.A.).

[13.] [2007] B.C.J. No. 2466 (B.C.C.A.).

insurers for the period of 28 February 2002 to 28 February 2003. Prior to that time, the insured had signed a software license, implementation, and maintenance agreement with the third party, pursuant to which maintenance was to continue until 2005. By 20 January 2003, the insured was aware that the third party was dissatisfied with the insured's progress on solving a major problem with the software. But when the insured applied for a second policy, it did not disclose that there was a potential claim from the third party to the defendant insurers. In April 2003, the third party abandoned the software agreement and retained legal counsel. The insured notified the insurers on 20 January 2004 of a potential claim.

The insurers took the position that the insured had no coverage due to non-disclosure of a potential claim in the application form of 21 February 2003. Questions in the application for insurance required the insured to attach a list and status of all "claims, disputes, suits or allegations of non-performance" made during the past five years against the insured. Further, the insured was asked to advise whether it was aware of any "facts, circumstances or situations that may reasonably give rise to a claim other than advised in the previous question". Negative answers to both of these questions were given.

The Court of Appeal concluded that the insured's failure to disclose a potential claim from the third party constituted a material non-disclosure. There was "ample" evidence that the insured had knowledge of a "dispute" and of "allegations of non-performance." Accordingly, the insurer was able to have the insurance policy set aside.

SMALL BUSINESS PERSPECTIVE

This case underlines the need to be open and forthright with one's insurer. The consequences of keeping silent or failing to disclose information relevant to risk can be disastrous.

Just as the insured has a duty to be honest in its dealings with the insurer, the insurer has a duty to process claims fairly. Where insurers have withheld payments without justification, damages, punitive damages, and solicitor and client costs have been awarded to the aggrieved insured. In the *Fowler* case,[14] for example, the insurer cut off disability payments to the insured even in light of medical evidence supporting the claim. The insurer's actions further exacerbated the insured's condition, by adding to the stress he was already under. Similarly, in the *Whiten*[15] case, the insurer's rejection of proof of loss (without explanation) was regarded as a failure of its duty of good faith. The insured had fled their burning house in their nightclothes, suffering frostbite as they watched their house burn down. After paying their living expenses for only a brief time, the insurer abruptly cut off payments. It raised a weak claim of arson, which was wholly discredited at trial. Punitive damages of $1 million were awarded by the jury, which evidently regarded the insurer's conduct as reprehensible.

Insurer's duty to process claims fairly

Duty to defend

Normally the insurer also has a duty to arrange for legal representation and a defence for the insured. One reason for purchasing liability insurance is to avoid such costs. But this duty does not extend to funding a defence where intentional or criminal acts are involved. In the *Scalera* case,[16] where the insured had a

---

14. *Whiten v. Pilot Insurance Co.*, [2002] 1 S.C.R. 595.

15. *Fowler v. Manufacturers Life Insurance Co.* (2002), 216 Nfld. & P.E.I.R. 132 (Nfld. S.C. (T.D.).

16. Non-Marine Underwriters, *Lloyd's of London v. Scalera*, [2000] 1 S.C.R. 551.

comprehensive general liability policy, the insurer was not required to defend the insured against charges of sexual assault. Also in *Hodgkinson v. Economical Mutual Insurance Company*[17] there was no obligation to provide a defence where the defendant was sued for defamation for making a deliberate verbal attack on the plaintiff on the internet.

Subrogation

The right of **subrogation** gives the insurance corporation, once it has paid out a claim, the right to take over the rights of the insured in relation to whoever caused the injury or loss. The insurer steps into the shoes of the insured and can then sue whoever caused the loss as if it were the insured. Thus, where a neighbour carelessly allows a bonfire to get out of control, causing Mrs. Kostachue's house to burn down, Mrs. Kostachue would normally claim on her insurance and receive compensation. Her insurance corporation would then sue the neighbour for negligence and recoup what it can. In fact, if the neighbour had liability insurance, it would likely be his insurer that would ultimately pay. You should not assume when you are involved in an accident that just because the other person has insurance, you are protected. If it is your fault, that person's insurance company will normally seek to recover its loss from you.

Insurance corporations will also normally have the choice to rebuild, repair, or replace what is damaged so that they can minimize their cost. They also have the right of **salvage**. If stolen goods are recovered, for example, insurers can sell those goods to recover their costs. When personal property has been lost, the insurer usually has to pay only the depreciated value of the goods, not the replacement cost, unless it has agreed otherwise. Most personal household insurance policies today provide for the replacement of destroyed or stolen goods at their full retail value. When a loss does take place, there is a general requirement on the part of the insured to report that loss to the insurance corporation right away so that the insurance corporation can take steps to minimize the damage. There might also be an obligation to report the matter to the police if a crime is involved or if the loss resulted from an automobile accident.

It should also be pointed out that the insured is not permitted to profit from his wilful misconduct. If the insured deliberately causes the loss, he will not be able to collect. Thus, if Fagan burns down his own house, killing his wife in the process, he will not be able to collect on the fire insurance and he will not be able to collect on his wife's life insurance, even where he is named as beneficiary. The **forfeiture rule** (that a criminal should not be permitted to profit from a crime) also extends to those who claim through the criminal's estate. In the above example, if Fagan were also to die in the house fire, his estate would not be able to collect on either policy.

Bonding

While insurance coverage is not generally available for intentionally wrongful acts, such as assault, many businesspeople insist on some protection against losses brought on by their employees or the people they deal with, who may act wrongfully, even wilfully so. Bonding is available in these circumstances, and it takes two forms. Usually, an employer will pay a fee to have an employee bonded against

> **Right of subrogation**

> **Basic rules of contract apply to agency contracts**

> **Depreciated rather than replacement value**

> **Insured can't profit from wilful misconduct**

[17.] *Hodgkinson v. Economical Mutual Insurance Company,* [2003] I.L.R. 1–4168, [2003] O.J. No. 151 (Ont. S.C.J.). *Non-Marine Underwriters, Lloyd's of London v. Scalera,* [2000] 1 S.C.R. 551.

Bonded parties still liable

that employee's own wrongful conduct (**fidelity bond**). If the employee steals from the employer or a customer, the bonding corporation will compensate the employer for that loss. It must be emphasized, however, that this does not relieve the bonded employee of responsibility. The bonding corporation can turn to the employee and collect from that party, which is what distinguishes bonding from normal insurance arrangements.

The second form of bonding, a **surety bond**, occurs when the bonding is designed to provide assurance that a party to a contract will perform its side of the contract. For example, in a large construction project, the corporation doing the foundation may be required to put up a performance bond that it will finish the job at a specified level of quality and by a certain time. If it fails to complete or does not complete on time, the bonding company will be required to pay compensation.

SUMMARY

Insurance

- Designed to spread the risk of loss
- Liability, property, business interruption, life, and health are the primary forms of insurance available
- Insured must have an insurable interest in the subject matter. Recovery limited to the extent of that insurable interest
- *Contra proferentum* rule: policy's ambiguities interpreted in the insured's favour
- Insurance is a contract of utmost good faith
- Insured has a duty to act fairly, fully disclose material facts, and be honest
- Misrepresentation of material facts enables the insurer to have the insurance contract rescinded
- When a claim is paid, the insurance company has salvage rights and is subrogated to the rights of the insured

QUESTIONS

1. Distinguish between business interruption insurance and fire insurance. Why might a businessperson want to have both forms of coverage?

2. What is meant by an insurable interest, and how does it apply to the various types of insurance discussed in the chapter?

3. What remedies does an insurer have if the insured misrepresented material facts when applying for insurance coverage?

4. Explain what is meant by the right of subrogation. How may subrogation affect not only the insured but also the person who has caused the injury or damage? Indicate what other means the insurance corporations have to keep their damages as low as possible.

5. Does a shareholder have an insurable interest in the property of his or her corporation?

6. Is it necessary for an insured to notify the insurer of changes of circumstance that occur after the policy enters into force?

Chapter 13

Special Contracts: Leases

INTRODUCTION

In discussing contracts of Sale in Chapter 10, we saw that ownership and possession of goods do not always go together. In this chapter, we examine leasing, a common type of contract in which ownership and possession are separated. Leasing of personal property is a form of bailment, although from a business point of view, leasing has a very different function from other forms of bailment. A lease of personal property—a chattel lease—is frequently regarded as a form of financing or an alternative to sale. By contrast, most types of bailment involve parting with possession of an item for a relatively short time—for storage, repair, or transportation. Legally, however, they share the same essential features.

LEASING

Leasing is a major growth industry and has become a multi-billion-dollar business in both Canada and the United States. At the consumer level, automobile leasing has become a common alternative to purchasing on credit. In business, it is common to lease capital equipment, such as heavy machinery and aircraft.

The widespread use of leasing in business is a relatively recent development, although the concept of a **lease** is a very ancient one. The essence of a lease is that the owner of an item of property, referred to as the **lessor**, rents the property to the **lessee**—that is, allows the lessee to have possession and use of the property for a stipulated period, in return for the payment of rent. Leasing traditionally has

lease
an arrangement where the owner of property allows another person to have possession and use of the property for a stipulated period in return for the payment of rent

been associated with real estate—leasing, or renting, a house, an apartment, or office space for a business has always been an alternative to purchase.

Although the possibility of renting personal property, or chattels, has long existed and been recognized by the law, such contracts were comparatively rare until recently. A major reason was the risk that an owner ran when he parted with possession of personal property. A person who obtains a lease of land cannot remove it, and if she fails to pay the rent, the owner can repossess it. But chattels are transportable, and there was, until modern systems of registration of property rights were developed, an obvious danger that a lessee might simply disappear with the leased property and stop paying rent for it.

The other factor that led to the great increase in the leasing of personal property was the realization that a lease could be used as a security device. This was first recognized in England more than 100 years ago, in the leading House of Lords decision of *Helby v. Matthews,*[1] which recognized a hiring agreement with an option to purchase at the end of the hiring term as an effective method of selling goods on credit. It opened the way for the popular type of transaction known in Britain as **hire-purchase**. In a typical hire-purchase agreement, the lessee/purchaser agrees to lease an item of property—for a specified number of years, paying a monthly rental—with an option to purchase it at the end of the term, provided the rent has been paid in full, for a nominal amount, such as $1.

This type of transaction is well known in Canada, principally as a means of marketing automobiles. In reality, it is a method of purchasing on credit, and, as such, is an alternative to the conditional sale and to the *chattel mortgage.*[2] However, not all chattel leases are intended as security devices.

TYPES OF CHATTEL LEASE

Two main types of chattel lease exist: *operating leases,* or "true" leases, where the intention is that possession will revert to the owner at the end of the term; and purchase leases, where it is anticipated that the lessee will eventually become the owner. Purchase leases can be further subdivided into *security leases,* where the credit is provided by the lessor/vendor, and *finance leases,* where a third party finances the transaction on credit.

Operating Leases

In an **operating lease**, since there is no intention to transfer ownership, the term tends to be relatively short—substantially less than the expected working life of the property leased. Examples include a car rental for a weekend or a month and the renting of specialized machinery for the duration of a construction contract or of farm machinery for the harvest season.

Purchase Leases

In *Helby v. Matthews,*[3] the House of Lords distinguished between a "true" lease and a hire-purchase agreement according to whether the lessee/purchaser was obliged to pay the full price for the chattel and whether she became the owner on

lessor
the owner of the leased property

lessee
the person who takes possession of the leased property

hire-purchase
an agreement to lease an item of property with an option for the lessee to purchase it at the end of the stipulated term

operating lease
a lease under which there is no intention to transfer ownership

---

[1]. [1895] A.C. 471.

[2]. The 2008 economic crisis has made leasing less popular with the automobile industry.

[3]. *Supra,* n. 1.

completing the payments. That test now appears to be too simplistic. A more modern approach was adopted in Ontario by Henry, J., who considered that in order to determine the true nature of a lease, it is necessary to have regard to the position of the parties, their intention, and the true effect of the transaction.[4] In practice, however, this test has been difficult to apply and has led to contradictory results. The accounting profession has developed a more objective approach to determine whether to classify a lease as an operating lease or a purchase lease. A lease is treated as a **purchase lease**, or "capital lease,"[5] if one of three conditions exists:

- Title passes automatically to the lessee at the end of the lease *or* on the exercise of a "bargain purchase option."
- There is a non-cancellable term for at least 75 percent of the economic life of the asset.
- The present value of the minimum lease payments exceeds 90 percent of the market value of the asset at the time the lease commences.[6]

purchase lease
a lease whereby ownership is intended to change hands at the end of the lease term

The distinction between an operating lease and a purchase lease is important for accounting purposes. If it is a purchase, or "capital," lease, the asset and the accompanying liability must be recorded in the balance sheet of the lessee/purchaser. From a taxation perspective, the distinction determines whether the lease payments are rental payments—and thus deductible by the lessee in determining the profits of the business—or are instalments of the purchase price and not deductible (apart from any interest element). It also determines which party is regarded as the true owner and entitled to claim capital cost allowances in respect of depreciation of the asset. From a legal perspective, all lessor's interest should be registered under Personal Property Security legislation.[7] We will discuss the *Personal Property Security Act* in more detail in Chapter 14.

Security and Finance Leases

In the typical purchase lease arrangement, it is the lessor who effectively provides the credit. The lessee pays what is, in reality, the purchase price by instalments—in the form of "rent." Until the price is paid in full, the lessor has a security interest by virtue of his continued ownership of the leased property—hence the expression **security lease**.

An alternative that is becoming increasingly common is for a third person, such as a financial institution, to provide the credit financing. In this type of transaction, commonly known as a **finance lease**, the supplier of the goods sells them to the financer, who in turn leases them to the lessee. The financer is technically the owner of the goods, even though it probably has never had possession of them and will ultimately pass title to the lessee.

The major auto manufacturing companies commonly establish their own leasing companies to provide consumer financing in this manner.

security lease
a purchase lease in which the lessor provides the credit

finance lease
an arrangement where a third person provides credit financing, becomes the owner of the property, and leases it to the lessee

---

[4.] *Re Speedrack Ltd.* (1980), 1 P.P.S.A.C. 109. In *Adelaide Capital Corp.* v. *Integrated Transportation Finance Inc.* (1994), 111 D.L.R. (4th) 493 (Ont. Gen. Div.), the court attached particular importance to the fact that the lessor was in the business of providing credit financing.

[5.] That is, a lease that acquires a capital asset. Another term commonly used to describe the transaction is "lease-to-own."

[6.] *CICA Handbook*, section 3065. Somewhat different guidelines have been published by the Canada Revenue Agency in Interpretation Bulletin IT-233R.

[7.] *Mitsui & Co. (Canada) Ltd.* v. *Royal Bank of Canada* (1995), 123 D.L.R. (4th) 449; *Adelaide Capital Corp.* v. *Integrated Transportation Finance Inc.*, supra, n. 4.

Figure 13.1 Comparing Purchase Lease and Finance Lease

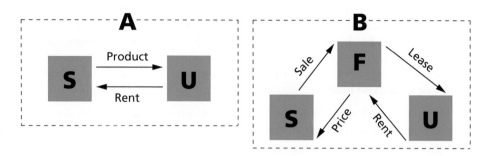

In (A), a conventional purchase lease, the supplier, *S*, leases the property to the user, *U*, who pays rent in return. In (B), a finance lease, the supplier, *S*, sells the property to the financer, *F*, who in turn leases it to the user, *U*. *U* pays rent to *F*.

Sale-and-Leaseback

sale-and-leaseback
a transaction in which the owner of property sells it and immediately leases it back from the new owner

A business with cash-flow problems may enter into a **sale-and-leaseback** transaction to raise working capital. The business sells assets for cash, and leases them back in return for future rental payments. The leaseback may take the form of an operating lease or of a purchase lease. In the latter case, the effect is similar to raising cash by mortgaging the asset.

REASONS FOR CHATTEL LEASING

The reasons for operating leases are obvious. A person is likely to be reluctant to go to the expense of purchasing an item that may be used only for a limited period, even though it may be possible to resell that item when it is no longer needed. Leasing will normally be a more convenient, and frequently less expensive, alternative to outright purchase.

The advantages of purchase leases and finance leases are less obvious. The lessor's perception may be that continued ownership of the asset, until payment has been made in full, provides more security in the case of default or insolvency of the lessee than would a conditional sale or chattel mortgage, though that view is questionable under modern Personal Property Security legislation.[8] The lessee may sometimes find it preferable to lease assets, as a form of *off-balance-sheet* financing; that is, since the asset is not owned by the business, it does not appear on the balance sheet, but neither does the future rental obligation appear as a liability. The net result is to record a lower debt-to-assets ratio than would be the case if the asset had been purchased with borrowed funds. Whether that is, in fact, the case depends upon the proper classification of the lease for accounting purposes.

Initially, the main reason for preferring leasing lies in the way the transaction was treated for tax purposes. Some of these tax advantages have been countered by legislation, but it is nevertheless true that the rapid growth of leasing, and especially of international leasing, owes much to ingenious tax planning.

---

8. See *Re Giffen*, [1998] 1 S.C.R. 91.

COMMON TERMS IN CHATTEL LEASES

What follows are the more important of the terms that are commonly found in chattel leases.

Duration

The lease normally sets out the time period during which it is intended to continue in force. In purchase lease arrangements, this is usually a fixed number of years. Operating leases may not contain a fixed term, but rather provide for termination by one or other party on giving notice. If the term of the lease is shorter than the period for which the lessee is likely to want to use the asset, it is common to include an option for renewal.

Rent

Most leases provide for equal monthly or quarterly payments of rent, usually payable in advance. In a lease-to-own contract, the rent is calculated with reference to the normal selling price of the asset, with an additional "interest" element to take account of the period over which it is payable. Operating lease rentals take more account of the probable depreciation of the asset over the period of the lease and of the cost to the lessor of the asset, with an appropriate profit margin.

Insurance and Other Costs Payable by the Lessee

In short-term operating leases, the lessor normally insures the leased asset and bears the costs of maintenance and repairs. In longer leases, and especially in purchase leases, the lessee is usually required to covenant to keep the asset insured, to maintain it properly, and to pay the costs of maintenance and repairs. Sometimes the lessee is required to provide a "residual guarantee"—that is, a guarantee that the lessor will receive a minimum resale value at the end of the lease or if not, the lessee will be responsible for the difference.

Purchase Option

A purchase lease inevitably contains an option for the lessee to purchase the asset at the end of the term, usually for a relatively nominal amount. In practice, a distinction is often made between fairmarket- value (FMV) leases and lease-to-buy (LTB) leases. In FMV leases, the purchase option corresponds to an estimate of the value of the asset at the end of the lease term; in LTB leases, the price is nominal (for example, $1). This difference is reflected in the rental payments—an FMV lease will have lower monthly payments than an LTB lease. Operating leases sometimes also include a purchase option, at a price to be agreed, with the price reducing over the lease term to offset depreciation.

Early Termination—Minimum Payment

Where the leased asset is new, or relatively new, the decrease in its value due to depreciation will often be greater than the amount of rent payable in the early part of the lease term. Consequently, it is usual for the lessor to insist on a minimum rental payment, to act as a deterrent against default or early termination. In England, hire-purchase agreements at one time contained harsh minimum payment clauses, requiring payment of two-thirds of the full price, or even the entire balance, if the lessee defaulted on even one monthly payment, with no reduction for the value of the asset that reverted to the lessor. Sometimes, such clauses were struck down as disguised penalties, but more effective protection to consumers was later provided by statute. In Canada, by contrast, relatively little statutory protection is provided, and in a number of provinces consumer protection legislation does not apply to leasing transactions.[9]

CHECKLIST	**Terms in a Lease Contract**

A lease contract will normally state

- the duration of the lease
- ■ the rent payable
- ■ the party responsible for maintenance and insurance
- whether there is an option to renew
- ■ whether there is an option for purchase and, if so, the terms of the option
- ■ what is to happen if the lease is terminated before the end of its prescribed term

---

Implied Terms

It is remarkable that there is very little law in Canada relating expressly to chattel leasing. Whereas England has its hire-purchase legislation going back to the 1930s and several U.S. states have legislation adopting article 2A of the *Uniform Commercial Code*, which applies to leases, there is no Canadian legislation specifically dealing with chattel leases. Nor, rather surprisingly, is there much case law. Perhaps this is because the contracts expressly cover most eventualities, there is little room for additional implied terms.

quiet possession
a warranty that there will be no interference with the lessee's possession or use of the asset

Nevertheless, it seems clear that the courts will, by analogy with the law on leases of real property, imply on the part of the lessor a warranty of **quiet possession**—that is, there will be no interference with the lessee's possession or use of the asset so long as the rent is paid and other terms are complied with. It is also likely that implied warranties, such as the warranty of fitness, are equally applicable to purchase lease contracts as they are to sales.[10] It has been held that the lessor impliedly warrants that leased equipment is reasonably fit for the purpose for which it was hired.[11] Some doubt exists as to whether this warranty is limited to defects of which the lessor ought to have been aware. If an analogy is drawn with the corresponding implied term in a contract of sale, a lessor, like a seller, should be liable even if the offending defect in the chattel is something it could not have detected. A number of provinces have resolved these doubts by extending to con-

---

[9.] For example, the cost of credit disclosure provisions apply only in Alberta, British Columbia, Manitoba, and Ontario.

[10.] This has been the case in England; see *Astley Industrial Trust Ltd.* v. *Grimley*, [1963] 1 W.L.R. 584.

[11.] *Griffith S.S. Co.* v. *Western Plywood Co.*, [1953] 3 D.L.R. 29.

sumer leases the implied warranties that apply in the case of sale of goods. For example, in British Columbia the warranties implied under the *Sale of Goods Act* apply equally to retail leases,[12] and in Manitoba and Saskatchewan the implied warranties under the *Consumer Protection Act* are expressly made applicable to consumer leases.[13]

The standard of care required of a lessee who hires equipment is to take such care as a prudent person would exercise in the use of her own property.

CASE SUMMARY 13.1

Roxburgh rented a portable steam engine from Reynolds to power a wood-cutting saw. The engine exploded immediately after it was put into use, killing one worker and injuring another. Reynolds sued Roxburgh for the value of the destroyed engine and boiler. He alleged that Roxburgh had not tested the steam gauge and safety valve before running the machine. The court applied the rule that "the hirer of a chattel is required to use . . . the degree of diligence which prudent men use . . . in keeping their own goods of the same kind." However, the court held that this standard of care did not require the lessee to test the safety gauge and valve. Accordingly, the defendant was not in breach of his duty as a lessee and was not liable to pay for the destroyed steam engine.[14]

The question of who was liable for the injuries to the workers—the lessor or the lessee—was not raised in the case.

RIGHTS OF THE PARTIES
The Lessor

The rights of the parties under a lease contract are, of course, governed by the terms, express and implied, of the contract. The principal remedies available to the lessor are the right to sue for rent that is due and unpaid and the right to retake possession of the leased property at the end of the lease or in the event of earlier default by the lessee. When a lessee contracts to hire a chattel for a given period, she remains liable for the whole rental even if she finds that she has overestimated the time needed to use the equipment. (In the same way, a tenant of a building is liable for rent for the full period of the lease whether she occupies or uses the premises or not.) A lessor may agree to take equipment back ahead of time and to reduce the rental charges; when he does so, he is consenting to a discharge of the original lease contract and to replacing it with a substituted agreement. But it seems that the lessor is entitled *both* to retake possession of the chattel *and* to sue for damages for loss of bargain in respect of the rent that would have been payable if there had been no default, or for any minimum rent stipulated in the contract.[15] Additionally, if the lessee is in breach of her duty to take proper care of the leased property, the lessor will have an action for damages for the loss. Damages should be calculated in accordance with the general principles of contract law.

[12.] R.S.B.C. 1996, c. 410, s. 20. These implied terms cannot be excluded.

[13.] R.S.M. 1987, c. 200, s. 58; S.S. 1996, c. 30.1., s. 48.

[14.] *Reynolds v. Roxburgh* (1886), 10 O.R. 649, per Armour, J., at 655.

[15.] *Keneric Tractor Sales Ltd.* v. *Langille* (1987), 43 D.L.R. (4th) 171 (S.C.C.)

The Lessee

As noted above, the lessor impliedly warrants that the lessee shall have quiet possession and, probably, that the goods are fit for the purpose for which they are hired. Consequently, the lessee is entitled to sue for damages if she is wrongfully dispossessed during the term of the lease, or if she suffers loss because of some defect in the goods.

The law is less clear in the case of finance leases where the supplier sells an article to the financer, who in turn leases it to the actual user, the lessee. The lessee's contract is with the financer, although most of her dealings will have been with the supplier, with whom she has no contract. Where the supplier has made express representations to the lessee to induce her to enter into the contract, a collateral contract may be implied between supplier and lessee—that is, in return for the supplier's warranty that the goods conform to a particular quality or have a particular characteristic, the lessee agrees to enter into the contract with the financer—a contract which is of benefit to the supplier.[16]

The lessee would have the usual contractual remedies against the financer, although in practice finance leases routinely exclude all implied warranties on the part of the lessor.

ETHICAL ISSUE

Consumer Leases

A common complaint about leasing contracts is that the consumer lessee rarely understands the terms of the contract—how much is she really paying, and what happens if she wishes to terminate the lease? According to one recent report,

> People sometimes confuse leasing with renting—when they don't want the car anymore, they think they can just walk away from their monthly payments. . . . In fact, they cannot, without incurring adjustment costs.[17]

During the term of the lease, circumstances may change. The lessee may lose her job and be unable to keep up the payments, or may move and find that the leased article is no longer suited to her needs. It is then that she discovers that she cannot just stop payments and return the article. In the majority of cases the lease terms are quite fair—it is simply that the terms were never properly explained to the lessee. But in some cases, the terms that apply on early termination can be quite harsh.

Some provincial consumer protection legislation (including that of Ontario, British Columbia, Alberta, and Manitoba) specifically addresses the harshness of consumer leasing contracts through the following requirements and limitations:

- a written disclosure statement showing the itemized costs of the lease, including the financed amount, interest rates and calculations, and implicit financing charges

---

16. See *Hallmark Pool Corp.* v. *Storey* (1983), 144 D.L.R. (3d) 56. This is consistent with the principle established in *Shanklin Pier Ltd.* v. *Detel Products Ltd.* "Exceptions to the Privity of Contract Rule."

17. Ken Shaw, "Lease penalties offset costs," *Toronto Star*, July 24, 2004, p. G10.

- caps on termination penalties equal to three months of average payments (British Columbia and Alberta cap this amount if the goods have been returned)
- disclosure and restrictions on form and content of advertising (not in the B.C. statute)

Questions to Consider

1. Does a disclosure requirement provide sufficient protection? Should there be a set of statutory implied terms to protect consumers, as in some provincial Sale of Goods Acts?
2. Does capping the termination penalties unfairly penalize lessors?
3. Why is leasing less popular with the auto industry since the 2008 economic crisis?

SUMMARY

Leases

- There are two main types of chattel leases (or leases of personal property): operating leases and purchase leases.
- Purchase leases can be further subdivided into security leases and finance leases.
- To determine whether to classify a lease as an operating lease or a purchase lease for accounting purposes, one of three conditions must be present.
- Leases are frequently regarded as a form of financing or an alternative to sale.
- To protect their interest in the leased property, a lessor's interest should be registered under provincial personal property security legislation.
- There is an implied condition on the part of the lessor that there will be no interference with the lessee's possession or use of the asset.
- The lessor has the right to sue for unpaid rent and to repossess the property at the end of the leasing period or in the event of default by the lessee.
- The lessee is entitled to sue for damages in the event of wrongful dispossession during the leasing term or if losses occur as a result of a defect in the goods.

QUESTIONS

1. What is the principal difference between an operating lease and a purchase lease?
2. Distinguish between a security lease and a finance lease.
3. What warranties will normally be implied in a chattel lease?
4. What are the main perceived advantages of leasing capital assets as opposed to borrowing in order to purchase them?
5. Why would a business enter into a sale-and-leaseback transaction?
6. If a lessee defaults in paying the rent, is the lessor entitled to retake possession of the leased property as well as to sue for the rent owing?

Chapter 14

Secured Transactions and Priority Interests

1. Outline the process of securing debt, using personal property, guarantees, and other forms of security
2. Review other laws related to creditors
3. Review an introduction to bankruptcy
4. Explain the process of bankruptcy and describe alternatives
5. Distinguish the priorities among creditors in a bankruptcy
6. Describe the bankruptcy offences
7. Explain the situation after discharge from bankruptcy
8. Identify the main forms of negotiable instruments and explain their basic characteristics

A considerable industry has developed around the practices of lending money and granting credit. This chapter will examine the various methods that have been developed to ensure that money owed is paid and the legislation that has been created to control such transactions. Federal bankruptcy and insolvency legislation will also be examined. Other than this federal statute, creditors' rights are generally a matter of provincial jurisdiction. The common principles embodied in the relevant provincial statutes will be the primary area of concentration in this chapter.

METHODS OF SECURING DEBT

Security helps ensure creditor is paid

When a debtor borrows money, or is extended credit, the creditor is at risk that the debtor cannot, or will not, pay the debt. Usually, the creditor requires the debtor to take steps to reduce this risk by ensuring that the creditor will be paid first, before other creditors, even in the event of bankruptcy or insolvency. Several methods have been developed to provide the creditor with this protection. When the creditor is successful in ensuring her **priority** over other creditors, she is said to be a *secured creditor*.

Personal Property

Both real property and personal property have been used as security. *Real property* includes land, buildings attached to the land, and fixtures, that is, items attached to the land or to **fixtures** attached to the land. **Mortgages** are the most common method of using real property as security.

Personal property is also used extensively to secure debt. **Personal property** can be divided into *chattels*, which are tangible, movable things, and *choses in action*, which are intangible rights that are legally enforceable claims. Cheques and promissory notes are examples of choses in action.[1] For a chose in action, the relevant document merely represents an obligation that can be legally enforced. Although a chose in action is often used to secure debt, it is much more common to take real property or chattels as security.

When a pawnbroker lends money, the borrower leaves an item, like a watch or a ring, with the pawnbroker, who holds the item until the loan is repaid. The borrower (debtor) still owns the item. The pawnbroker (creditor) only gains the right to sell the item if the borrower does not repay the loan. This type of transaction is referred to as a **pledge.**

In most situations, however, the debtor needs the use of the goods used as security. When, for example, you borrow money to buy a new car, the assumption is that you will have the use of the car while you are repaying the loan. In such cases, the security of the creditor is the right to take the car and sell it if you fail to repay the loan. In the past, the creditor assumed ownership of the goods used as security, while the debtor had possession of the goods. In the event of default, the creditor would simply take possession of the goods based on this ownership. Under modern legislation, the creditor usually does not actually assume ownership of the goods, but the effect is the same. The creditor has first claim to the goods in the event of a default by the debtor. Note that a default may occur not only when a payment is missed, but also when the debtor fails to meet any obligation (such as maintaining sufficient insurance coverage) that increases the creditor's risk, or that threatens the value of the assets used as security.

> **Real property includes land and anything attached to the land**

> **Personal property can also be used as security**

> **Personal property security involves right to take possession upon default**

CASE SUMMARY 14.1

Is a Fishing Licence "Property"? *Saulnier v. Royal Bank of Canada*[2]

Saulnier held four fishing licences. He and his company signed a General Security Agreement with RBC. Saulnier also signed a guarantee for the debts of his company. The GSA gave RBC a security interest in "all present and after acquired personal property including . . . Intangibles . . . " "Intangibles" was to be interpreted according to its definition in the *Personal Property Security Act (PPSA)*. Saulnier made an assignment in bankruptcy. The Receiver for RBC and the Trustee in Bankruptcy agreed to sell the four licences, but Saulnier refused to sign the necessary documents. He argued that the fishing licences were not "property" available to a Trustee in Bankruptcy or to a creditor

---

[1.] For a case that held that taxi licences were "property" that could be used to secure a loan under the *PPSA*, see *Re Foster* (1992), 8 O.R. (3d) 514 (Ont. Gen. Div.). For a case that held that seismic data was "property", see *Re Gauntlet Energy Corp.* (2003), [2004] 336 A.R. 302 (Q.B.).

[2.] [2008] 3 S.C.R. 166.

under the *PPSA*; they were just a privilege to do what would otherwise be illegal. The trial Judge and the Court of Appeal both ruled that the Trustee in Bankruptcy was entitled to direct Saulnier to sign the required documents.

The Supreme Court of Canada held that fishing licences are indeed "property." They are a "major commercial asset" that gives the holder "a right to engage in an exclusive fishery under the conditions imposed by the licence, and a proprietary right in the fish harvested and the earnings from their sale." The Court referred to the *PPSA* and the *Bankruptcy and Insolvency Act* as "largely commercial instruments which should be interpreted in a way best suited to enable them to accomplish their respective commercial purposes."

This case illustrates the flexibility of the *PPSA* in allowing something unique as a fishing licence to be used as security for the purposes of the legislation.

SMALL BUSINESS PERSPECTIVE

Choses in action are rights to intangible property, such as stocks, bonds, patents, copyrights, and even funds deposited in a bank account. Can a business use such rights as security when obtaining credit? If so, can the rights be taken by the creditor upon default by the business?

THE TRADITIONAL APPROACH

Conditional seller retains title until last payment

Historically, conditional sales agreements, chattel mortgages, and assignments of accounts receivables were the common methods of using personal property as security. A conditional sale involves a two-step process. First, possession of the goods is given to the buyer. The seller, who is also the creditor, retains the title (that is, ownership) as security. Second, after the final payment is made, title to the goods is conveyed to the buyer. It should be noted that the *Sale of Goods Act* applies to conditional sales even though the sale takes place over a protracted period of time.[3]

Chattel mortgage involves transfer of title to goods to secure loan

A chattel mortgage differs from a conditional sale in that the creditor is not the seller of the goods. Typically, the debtor approaches a bank to borrow money. The bank requires the debtor to secure the loan, by transferring the title of some good (such as a car or a boat) to the creditor as "collateral security." Throughout the duration of the loan transaction, chattel mortgages, like conditional sales, involve the creditor's having title to the goods as security, while the debtor has possession of the goods. With a chattel mortgage, when the last payment is made, title of the goods is returned to the debtor. Even though a *bill of sale* is often used to create the security, since no actual sale is contemplated, the *Sale of Goods Act* does not apply to a chattel mortgage transaction.

Accounts receivable can be used as security for a loan

The assignment of book accounts involves using a chose in action as security, rather than goods. Often, a business will have few tangible assets, but will have considerable funds owed to it for goods or services provided to customers. These claims are called **accounts receivable**. If the debtor assigns her accounts receivable, and then defaults, the creditor has the right to intercept the payment of the accounts receivable. The loan is thereby secured.

---

3. See, for example, the *Sale of Goods Act*, R.S.S. 1978, c. S-1, which states, in s. 2(1)(c), that a contract of sale includes an agreement to sell, and then defines, in s. 3(4), an "agreement to sell" as a contract in which the transfer of property to goods is to take place at a future time or is subject to some conditions to be fulfilled in the future.

As previously discussed, **leases** are also a common method of creating a secured relationship between a creditor and a debtor. The most common type of lease is an **operating lease**, in which goods are simply rented to the lessee to use during the lease period, after which the goods are returned to the lessor. Today a **lease to purchase** is being used more frequently. A lease to purchase involves, essentially, a credit purchase. Title to the goods will be transferred to the lessee at the end of the lease period, with the lease simply providing security. In both an operating lease and a lease to purchase, possession of the goods goes to the lessee, while the title to the goods remains with the lessor, providing the lessor with security for the transaction.

> Lease to purchase also provides security to creditor

When the manufacturer or the supplier of goods leases them to the lessee using a lease to purchase, the transaction is much like a conditional sale. The lessee can make claims against the manufacturer or the supplier for the quality and fitness of the goods supplied. But when the goods are sold to a financial institution and then leased to the lessee, the relationship is more like a chattel mortgage, as there is only a financial arrangement between the lessee and the financial institution. The lessee has to deal with the manufacturer or the supplier with respect to problems relating to the goods themselves. This may be difficult because of the lack of a contract with them.

In the past, separate statutes with different provisions governed the various ways of using personal property as security. To further confuse things, when other forms of personal property such as negotiable instruments, shares, or bonds were used as security, there was no legislation at all. Today, personal property security acts are in place in most jurisdictions and govern all situations where personal property is used as security.

> Personal property security acts now in place

THE PERSONAL PROPERTY SECURITY ACT

The *Personal Property Security Act* (*PPSA*) is now used in all jurisdictions in Canada. It creates a unified approach toward the use of personal property as security. (The details of the provincial statutes, however, do vary significantly, so businesspeople must be familiar with the legislation of their province.) As a result, the *PPSA* is more complicated than legislation used previously, but because it uses one set of rules and a common approach to cover both tangible and intangible forms of personal property and the various ways that security can be taken, its application is simpler. A secured transaction is still created by contract in the traditional forms of conditional sales, chattel mortgages, and assignments of accounts receivable, but other forms, such as leases, can also be used, depending on the property used as security. The formal requirements and procedures for all these types of securities are now the same. As well, the *PPSA* allows other, less common, forms of personal property, such as licences, shares, bonds, and even intellectual property (including copyright, patents, and trade-marks), to be used as security and to be treated in a uniform way. The *PPSA* provides for some or all of the assets of a particular debtor to be used as security. It also provides rules to determine the ranking of various claims when several secured creditors have claims against those assets.

> *PPSA* creates common process for using personal property as security

The right to take possession of the goods used as security even when they get into the hands of an innocent purchaser is the essential nature of a secured transaction. Thus, when Lee purchases his car under a conditional sale agreement and then defaults, the creditor must have the right to retake the car even if it has been resold, or if Lee has become bankrupt. In the past, this was accomplished by the creditor's retaining title to the goods and retaking them in the event of default. To protect an innocent third party who might be misled by the debtor having possession of the

Registration protects secured creditors and others

goods, the secured creditor was required to register his secured claim against the goods at the designated government agency. A would-be purchaser, or a potential creditor wanting to use the goods as security, could search the title to the goods and would be forewarned of the prior claim of the secured creditor. Under the *PPSA*, the process is a little more involved but it accomplishes the same purpose.

CASE SUMMARY 14.2

Keep Your *PPSA* Registrations Current! *Royal Bank of Canada v. Wells Fargo*[4]

Meerford Inc. was incorporated in March 2000. It changed its name to Harrison Western Canadian Inc. in December 2000, then to 873052 Alberta Ltd. on 6 July 2004, and finally to Head West Energy Inc. on 8 July 2004. Head West and 876652 Alberta Ltd., a related corporation, entered into two lease agreements with Wells Fargo. Head West alone entered into a third lease with Wells Fargo. Wells Fargo registered its interest in one lease on 23 April 2004 and in the other two on 10 May 2004. Wells Fargo did not amend its registrations to reflect the name change on 8 July 2004 until 18 October 2005. RBC registered a General Security Agreement against Head West on 4 November 2004. Head West became insolvent. The Receiver sold the property. RBC and Wells Fargo both claimed the proceeds of the sale.

The *PPSA* provides that a secured party must amend its registrations within 15 days of having knowledge of the debtor's name change. Wells Fargo said that it first learned of the change of name to Head West on 18 October 2005, when it learned of the appointment of the Receiver.

The trial Judge ruled that Wells Fargo had knowledge (actual and constructive) of the name change prior to RBC's registration on 4 November 2004, as a result of receiving correspondence, credit statements, and credit applications which advised of the name change. The Court of Appeal agreed. RBC therefore had priority to the sale proceeds.

This case illustrates the effect of the perfection of a security under the *PPSA* (and of maintaining perfection). It also demonstrates the unforgiving nature of the *PPSA* and how even minor mistakes can have a dramatic effect on the validity of a claim. Note that the result of this case may not have been the same in other jurisdictions, as the provincial *PPSA*s (and their related case law) are different from one another in many respects. For example, the courts of the various provinces are divided as to whether a misspelled debtor name on a *PPSA* registration invalidates that registration.[5]

DISCUSSION QUESTIONS

Should registration under the *PPSA* have to be perfect to be effective, or should it be possible for an incorrect registration to be valid in certain circumstances? If the latter is the law, what does this mean for someone searching the personal property registry?

[4.] (2008), [2009] 440 Alta. R. 385, (2008), 48 C.B.R. (5th) 15 (C.A.).

[5.] See, for example, *Stevenson v. GMAC Leaseco Ltd.* (2003), 257 N.B.R. (2d) 141 (C.A.), in which the Court held that in cases where the inclusion of a serial number is mandatory, a seriously misleading error in either the name of the debtor, or in the serial number renders the registration invalid. In Ontario, however, if a serial number is correctly stated on a registration form, a misspelled name will not invalidate the registration, as Ontario has a "dual search requirement" requiring debtors to search both the name of the debtor and the serial number of the goods.

Creating a Secured Relationship

The method of creating a secured relationship under the *PPSA* is unique. There are three stages. First, the parties must enter into the contractual agreement. Second, the secured interest must attach to the collateral that has been identified to provide the security. Third, the secured interest must be perfected.

The parties must have entered into a contract that created a secured relationship. While the *PPSA* may deem some relationships to be secured, it does not create security agreements. In a recent case,[6] a lender claimed that it had a perfected security interest in the "capital account" of the borrower, a lawyer in a law firm. The Court ruled that the documents obtained (a loan agreement and a comfort letter from the law firm) did not contain the language required by the *PPSA*. Regardless of the lender's intention, the Court would not accept the lender's claim that a security interest had been taken, in the absence of appropriate documentation.

Contract must be a security agreement

Assuming there is a security agreement in place, **attachment** takes place when the debtor receives some value under the contract. That is, if a person borrowing funds uses his car as collateral security for the loan, that security attaches to the car only when the bank makes the money available to the debtor pursuant to the agreement. Attachment gives the creditor a claim against the security in the event of default by the debtor. This is normally a right to take possession, if so stated in the contract. It is important to remember that the obligations and the remedies of the parties must be set out in the contract. The purpose of the *PPSA* is to give effect to the contractual obligations entered into by the parties.

Security must attach to collateral

It is vital to understand that attachment gives the creditor rights against the debtor only. To protect the creditor's claim if the goods are sold, or if another creditor becomes involved, the secured transaction must not only be attached, it must also be perfected. This **perfection** can be accomplished in one of two ways.

Provisions of contract prevail

Perfection required to prevail against outsiders

The first way perfection occurs is by the registration of the security obligation at the appropriate government agency, as was the case under the old system. This process has been simplified so that the actual contractual documents no longer have to be filed. A single form (a financing statement) is now used to provide notice of the security arrangement. There are some provincial variations but, in general, a financing statement requires the complete name and address of the parties, the type and description (including the serial number) of the security used, and the date and time of registration. When a motor vehicle is used as security, its year, make, model and vehicle identification number must also be set out. There may also be specific requirements when consumer goods are involved.

Perfection through registration

The second, and less common, way of perfecting a secured transaction is for the creditor to obtain physical possession of the collateral used. Whether possession or registration is used depends on the nature of the security. When promissory notes or shares are involved, there is no need for the debtor to keep them, and perfection by possession is appropriate. Note that the original note or certificate must be taken into possession, not a photocopy. When tangible property is involved, such as a car, a truck, or equipment that is required for use by the debtor, registration is the more appropriate process. The purpose of registration is to ensure that others are alerted that the goods have been used as security and that the debtor is not in a position to deal with them. When perfection by possession is involved, this is not necessary, since the goods are not in the possession of the debtor and third parties cannot be misled with respect to them.

Perfection through possession

---

6. *Re Hupfer*, 2003 ABQB 267.

Priority of Secured Creditors

First to perfect usually prevails

If more than one security interest is perfected by registering different financing statements against the same collateral, the priority of those secured parties is generally determined by the date registration takes place. But this is not always the case. For example, sometimes a merchant will secure a loan by granting a security on all of her assets, including after-acquired assets. This can cause a problem if a supplier of goods also claims a security interest in the future acquired goods. The secured creditor selling those goods will have priority with respect to them providing that his security interest is registered within a specified time (for example, 15 days in Nova Scotia). This is called a **purchase money security interest**, or PMSI. A PMSI will prevail over a general security agreement covering all of a merchant's assets, if it is registered within the specified time period.

But PMSIs are an exception

and buyers in the normal course of business are not bound

Similarly, if customers purchase goods from that merchant in the normal course of business, the goods will normally be free of any secured interest of the creditor. If you purchase a car from a dealership, you would get good title even though the assets of the dealership had been used to secure a general loan to operate the business. Since the creditor knows that the inventory will be sold in the normal course of business, an innocent buyer will not be affected by that security.

REDUCING RISK 14.1

For a creditor, it is vitally important that a security interest be properly perfected. Legislation in most jurisdictions has registration requirements that must be carefully followed, including the exact recording of serial numbers and names. Sometimes errors in registration can be corrected, but not if the interests of other parties have been affected. Creditors usually register their security interest first, before advancing their credit. Although perfection takes place when that credit is actually advanced (the point of attachment), it takes place immediately. There are not, therefore, any problems with intervening interests arising, or with subsequent errors that affect the validity of the perfection taking place.

CASE SUMMARY 14.3

When Possession Takes Priority Over Registration: *Royal Bank of Canada v. Steinhubl's Masonry Ltd.*[7]

The Bank took a security interest in all of the undertakings and goods (including equipment) of Pro Masonry Construction Ltd. Pro Masonry then gave Steinhubl's a forklift to secure a debt. Pro Masonry subsequently went out of business, without paying its debts. Both the Bank and Steinhubl's claimed priority over the forklift.

The Court held that the forklift was a "motor vehicle" as defined by the *Personal Property Security Regulations*. As the Bank's financing statement did not describe the forklift by serial number, its security interest did not get the maximum priority available for serial-numbered goods. Steinhubl's had perfected its security interest by taking possession of the forklift. It therefore had priority over the Bank's limited interest.

The Bank's problem was that the *PPSA* required the registration of motor vehicles to include the serial number. At the time it registered its interest pursuant to the general

---

7. (2003), 237 Sask. R. 297 (Q.B.).

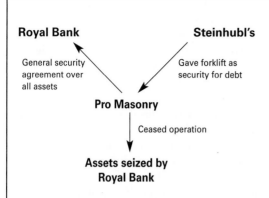

security agreement with Pro Masonry, the Bank did not know the serial number of the forklift.

DISCUSSION QUESTIONS

What else could the Bank have done? The effect is that a creditor in this type of situation gets priority over some, but not all, future acquired property, even though it had done everything it could to secure its position at the time of registration. Is this result consistent with the philosophy behind the *PPSA* and its objectives?

Rights and Remedies Upon Default

In the event of a default by the debtor, the creditor has recourse as set out in the contract and as provided in the *PPSA*. This usually involves taking possession of the goods and selling them to recover the amount owed. In doing so, the creditor not only must comply with the contract, but also must not otherwise violate the law in the process.

Usually, when taking possession of goods, the creditor must hire a bailiff, who can go onto the debtor's property and seize the goods. The relevant legislation usually requires that the bailiff not use force when seizing property. (At least one province, however, allows bailiffs to use reasonable force when entering premises other than the debtor's residence.[8]) If the debtor won't allow a bailiff access to the premises, then the bailiff can apply for a court order. If such an order is not obeyed, then the debtor may be guilty of contempt of court. The police will assist a bailiff only when required to by court order, or when the bailiff has reasonable grounds to believe that an attempt to seize is likely to lead to a serious breach of the peace.

Note that some provinces will not permit the creditor to take possession of the collateral without a court order, when consumer goods are involved and a significant amount of the debt has been paid. With respect to goods (consumer or commercial) that the creditor has taken possession of, the creditor must take "commercially reasonable" care to protect the goods and keep them in good repair. If the goods require repairs to sell them, such "commercially reasonable" expenses will be added to the amount the debtor owes.

> Upon default, creditor can take possession and sell collateral

> Bailiff seizes goods

> Creditor must take reasonable care of goods in possession

---

8. See *Civil Enforcement Act*, R.S.A. 2000, c. C-15, s. 13(2).

Right to redeem

Debtor must be given notice and opportunity to redeem

Before a sale of the goods can take place, interested parties (usually the debtor and other creditors) must be given a chance to redeem the goods by paying any money owing. Notice must be given setting out a description of the goods and the amount owing, that the party receiving the notice has the **right to redeem**, and that failure to do so will result in the sale of the goods. The notice should also declare, when appropriate, that the debtor will be liable for any shortfall between the amount owing plus expenses, and the amount realized from the sale. Sometimes only the missed payments plus expenses need be paid, but there is often an acceleration clause requiring that the entire debt plus expenses be paid to redeem the goods. Some provinces prohibit such acceleration clauses.

Sale—goods taken into possession can be sold to satisfy debt

After possession of the goods has been taken, and the notice period has expired, the goods are usually sold, by private or public sale, to satisfy the debt. Under the *PPSA*, the method chosen must be commercially reasonable.

Debtor may be liable for deficiency

If the proceeds from the sale do not cover the debt, additional costs, and interest, the debtor will usually have to make up the difference. Thus, not only may the debtor lose his collateral, but he may also still owe the creditor a considerable amount of money to pay for the shortfall. In several jurisdictions, this right to sue for a deficiency is lost as soon as the creditor chooses to take possession of the goods. In some provinces, this rule applies only when consumer goods are involved. For example, in British Columbia, if Jones defaulted on a consumer car loan owing $15 000, and only $10 000 was realized from the sale of that car after the creditor took possession of it, the creditor would lose not only the $5000 shortfall on the loan but also any costs and interest incurred.[9]

Creditor must consider alternatives

Because this was a consumer loan in British Columbia, the creditor exhausted her remedies against Jones when she took possession of the car. The creditor must therefore take great care in these circumstances to balance the risks of suing (and possibly getting nothing), against taking possession of the collateral (and getting at least something). The creditor can also lose the right to a deficiency by failing to properly look after the goods, or by failing to get a fair price because of an improvident sale.

! REDUCING RISK 14.2

When a debtor defaults, creditors are often quick to seize property used as security. In some jurisdictions, however, this might prevent the creditor from pursuing other, more effective, remedies. Even in those jurisdictions in which it is possible to sue for a shortfall after the goods have been sold, that right may be lost if the goods are not properly cared for and sold in a commercially reasonable manner. On the other hand, if the debtor defaulted on the original debt, it is likely that any attempt to sue and seize other assets will not result in a significant recovery. Another issue involves the question of whether the debtor can be rehabilitated and kept as a good customer. All of these factors should be carefully considered before deciding to take possession of the collateral. Just because you have the legal right to do something doesn't mean it is always a good idea for you to do it.

[9.] *Personal Property Security Act*, R.S.B.C. 1996, c. 359, s. 67.

Note that, in all jurisdictions, when there is a surplus from the sale, the debtor is entitled to that surplus. In the example above, if the car were sold for $20 000, and costs and interest brought the entire debt up to $17 000, Jones would be entitled to the $3000 surplus from the sale.

Debtor entitled to surplus

In some jurisdictions, instead of taking possession and selling the goods, the creditor can take the goods and simply keep them, in full satisfaction of the debt. This ends any claim the debtor may have to a surplus and any claim the creditor may have to a deficiency. Notice must be given to all interested parties. If someone files an objection, the goods must be sold in the usual way.

Option to retain the collateral

CASE SUMMARY 14.4

If You Elect to Keep the Goods, You Can't Sue: *241301 Alberta Ltd. v. 482176 B.C. Ltd*.[10]

241301 Alberta Ltd. (241) loaned money to one of the defendants, 765918 Alberta Ltd. (765). The loan was to enable 765 to buy equipment and set up a restaurant. The restaurant had only operated for two months when 241 gave notice of its intention to enforce its security on the restaurant's assets. 241 then appointed a receiver for 765, without providing notice. 241 took possession of the assets of the restaurant and operated it for 10 months. It then sold the assets, and sued for the deficiency.

The Court dismissed 241's action. It held that 241 breached the *PPSA* by failing to provide notice of the receivership to 765. The notice it gave of its intention to enforce its security was not sufficient to comply with the legislative requirements. The Court also ruled that, because 241 used the assets to operate the restaurant for 10 months before selling them, there was no deficiency owing. 241 had elected to take the collateral in full satisfaction of the debt. The *PPSA* specifically states that if such an election is made, a deficiency judgment may not be obtained.

SMALL BUSINESS PERSPECTIVE

This case illustrates how important it is to understand and to follow the procedures set out in the *PPSA*. Would 241 have used the assets to operate the restaurant if it knew that doing so would prevent it from obtaining a deficiency judgment? The provisions of the *PPSA* are designed to protect both the rights of the debtor and the rights of the secured creditor. How can creditors (such as merchants who take security interests from their customers) ensure that they are in compliance with the legislation, so that they can realize the benefits of the legislation, rather than suffer its penalties?

The procedures under the *PPSA* may appear very cumbersome, and the legislation itself is very complex, but in actual practice the process outlined by the *PPSA* works quite well. When a person borrows money from a credit union using a car as security, attachment takes place once the contract has been entered into and the moneys have been advanced. Perfection takes place when the credit union files the financing statement with the appropriate registry. A buyer or subsequent creditor interested in the car would search the registry and, finding the

---

[10.] (2003), 341 A.R. 172 (Q.B.).

registered security against the vehicle, would be forewarned to avoid any dealings with the car. If the car is purchased, and a default takes place, the credit union can recover the vehicle even from the innocent third party. This is the essence of the creditor's security. Once there is a default, the credit union has the option of either pursuing its normal breach-of-contract remedies, or taking possession of the vehicle and selling it. If it chooses the latter option, it must follow the proper procedures.

Guarantees

Another method creditors use to ensure the repayment of a debt is the guarantee. When corporations are involved, the use of guarantees is very common as a means of circumventing the limited liability characteristic of incorporation, making the principals of a corporation ultimately responsible for loans and other obligations. In consumer transactions, guarantees are used to make another, more substantial, debtor liable to pay a loan or other debt. Guarantors ensure that the debt will be paid even when the debtor defaults. When Der borrows $5000 from the bank with his mother as a guarantor, and then fails to pay, his mother is responsible to repay the $5000 debt.

Guarantor must pay when debtor defaults

A guarantee involves a secondary, or conditional, obligation that arises only in the event of a default. When a person agrees to be directly responsible for paying the debt of another, the obligation is not secondary, but primary, with the debtors sharing the responsibility. This is referred to as an *indemnity*.

Evidence in writing of guarantee required

The distinction between a guarantee and an indemnity, although subtle, can be important. The *Statute of Frauds* requires that some agreements must be evidenced in writing to be enforceable. In most provinces, only guarantees must be evidenced in writing, but in British Columbia both guarantees and indemnities must be evidenced in writing.[11]

In Alberta, a guarantor must appear before a notary public, acknowledge that he signed the guarantee, and sign a certificate.[12]

Elements of a contract must be present.

Since a guarantee is a separate contract, all of the elements of a contract must be present. Consideration can sometimes be a problem. Because the creditor would not advance funds without the guarantee, the advancement of those funds amounts to consideration supporting the guarantee. When the guarantee is given after default on a loan, the consideration is the creditor's refraining from suing the debtor.

Guarantees often given under seal

When a guarantee is given after the funds are advanced, there can be a serious problem. If Kotsalis borrows money from the Business Bank, and the loans officer fails to obtain a guarantee as required by bank policy, he will face difficulties if he tries to get it later. Since the funds have already been advanced, there is no consideration to support the subsequent guarantee. To avoid any problem with consideration, lending institutions usually require that all guarantees be placed under seal. When a seal is present, consideration is conclusively presumed.

[11.] *Law and Equity Act,* R.S.B.C. 1996, c. 253, s. 59.

[12.] *Guarantees Acknowledgement Act,* R.S.A. 2000, c. G-11.

REDUCING RISK 14.3

People are often persuaded to sign a guarantee thinking that it is just a formality, and that no serious obligations are incurred, since the primary debtor will pay the debt. This is a dangerous assumption to make! Whether in business, or in your personal affairs, you should never sign a guarantee without first carefully weighing the risks. The creditor is insisting on a guarantee because she doesn't have confidence that the debt will be paid by the primary debtor. She wants someone else to also be responsible. You are adding your credit to the transaction, and there is a good chance that you will be required to honour your commitment. Many bankruptcies result from people signing guarantees without realizing the risks they may face.

RIGHTS AND OBLIGATIONS OF THE PARTIES

The creditor has significant duties to protect the interests of the guarantor. At the outset, the creditor should make sure that the guarantor understands the full nature of the guarantee he is signing. Guarantors often escape their obligation by claiming misrepresentation, *non est factum,* or undue influence. When in doubt, the creditor should insist that the guarantor obtain independent legal advice.

Creditor should ensure guarantor understands guarantee

CASE SUMMARY 14.5

Guarantor Released Because of Material Changes: *Toronto-Dominion Bank v. Duffett*[13]

Duffett gave five guarantees to the Bank in support of three mortgages between two companies and various lending institutions who were predecessors in title to the Bank. The mortgagors defaulted and the Bank demanded that Duffett pay the deficiency after the properties were sold.

Duffett gave five guarantees to the Bank in support of three mortgages between two companies and various lending institutions who were predecessors in title to the Bank. The mortgagors defaulted and the Bank demanded that Duffett pay the deficiency after the properties were sold.

   The Court held that Duffett was not liable for the deficiency. Over the years, the Bank had made numerous material alterations to the mortgages, including increasing the interest rates, extending the amortization periods of the mortgages, increasing the monthly payments, and permitting a tax liability to accumulate on the properties. The Court concluded: "The Plaintiff made numerous material alterations to the mortgage contracts between 1988 and 1998 of which the Defendant had no notice or knowledge and to which he did not consent. The guarantees were no longer valid and enforceable against the Defendant and he is discharged from any liability to the Plaintiff."

DISCUSSION QUESTIONS

Why should guarantors be treated with such deference when their involvement persuaded the creditor to loan money to the debtor? Why should the creditor be responsible to protect the interests of the guarantor? And, if it is important for the creditor to protect the position of the guarantor, should we allow this to be changed by a one-sided exemption clause included in the guarantee agreement itself?

---

13. (2004), 234 Nfld. & P.E.I.R. 223 (Nfld. S.C.T.D.).

Creditors must not weaken the position of the guarantor

Significant changes may release guarantor

Creditor should obtain consent of guarantor

The creditor should also avoid any subsequent dealings that may weaken the position of the guarantor. Any substantial change in the nature of the contract between the creditor and debtor without the guarantor's consent will relieve the guarantor of any obligation. If the creditor advances more funds, or even extends the terms of repayment at a higher interest rate, without the consent of the guarantor, the guarantor will usually be discharged from the guarantee. This was the result in the *Duffett* case. Note that a creditor's simply deciding not to sue, and giving the debtor more time to pay, will not be considered a substantial change. Such actions will therefore not discharge the guarantee. In any subsequent dealings with the debtor independent of the guarantor, the creditor should obtain the consent of the guarantor to any material change. The effect will then be that the guarantor will continue to be bound by the original guarantee.[14]

Releasing security may release guarantor

A guarantor is also released from her obligation when other forms of security, such as chattel mortgages, are released. For example, if Kotsalis obtained a loan from the Business Bank, with the Bank taking a guarantee from Bruno and a chattel mortgage against Kotsalis's car as security, such an arrangement would cease to be binding on Bruno if the Bank subsequently allowed Kotsalis to sell the car without Bruno's consent.

Withholding information may release guarantor

The withholding of important information from the guarantor by the creditor may also be enough to discharge the guarantee. The information withheld must be of some substantial and unusual nature, not simply the usual kind of information that would pass between business associates. A creditor is obligated, for example, to advise a guarantor of a priority agreement which reduced the assets available in the event of a default.[15]

Contract can modify rights and obligations

Because the basic rights and obligations of the creditor and the guarantor are determined by contract, they can be modified by contract as well. It is common for creditors to include provisions that attempt to exempt the creditor from the basic obligations discussed above. Like all exemption clauses, exemption clauses in guarantees are interpreted by the courts very carefully. It is becoming common for a guarantee to contain clauses creating a **continuing guarantee**, allowing the creditor to continue to advance funds up to a pre-set limit without affecting the obligation of the guarantor to pay in the event of default. Clauses that allow the creditor to discharge and otherwise deal with security, and to otherwise change the terms of the agreement (including changing terms of repayment and increasing interest rates), are now often included in guarantees. These clauses can be effective if they are carefully worded. They then significantly limit the protection normally enjoyed by a guarantor.

Guarantor assumes rights of creditor upon payment

When a default occurs, the creditor is not required to demand payment from the debtor, or to take steps to seize any other security, before seeking payment from the guarantor, unless that has been agreed to in the contract. A guarantor who pays the debt is *subrogated* to the rights of the creditor, which means, in effect, that the guarantor steps into the creditor's shoes. Any remedy or right available to the creditor after payment is assumed by the guarantor, including the right to seize a chattel used as security for the debt, or to sue the debtor and take advantage of the processes available to assist in collecting the debt.

---

14. For a case in which the Court held that a guarantee was clear in stating that a renewal agreement did not require the explicit approval of the guarantor, see *A.G.F. Trust Co. v. Muhammad* (2005), 73 O.R. (3d) 767 (C.A.), leave to appeal to S.C.C. refused, [2005] S.C.C.A. No. 139.

15 (2004), 47 B.L.R. (3d) 39, (2004), 29 B.C.L.R. (4th) 18 (C.A.).

CASE SUMMARY 14.6

Failure to Register Security Releases Guarantor: *First City Capital Ltd. v. Hall*[16]

First City leased word-processing equipment to Karsha Holdings Ltd., whose principals, Hall and deHaan, signed personal guarantees for the indebtedness. Karsha also owed money to the Royal Bank that was secured against the assets of the corporation. When Karsha defaulted, the Royal Bank, which had perfected its security, was entitled to the word-processing equipment because First City had failed to perfect its security. First City sued Hall on the personal guarantee for payment.

First City had an obligation to the guarantor to ensure that the security was perfected. Its failure to do so relieved Hall of any liability on the guarantee. Note that the Court found that a provision in the contract stating that the guarantee would be enforceable ("notwithstanding that the lease or any other arrangements shall be void or voidable against the lessee... including... by reason... of... failure by any person to file any document or take any other action to make the lease... enforceable") did not apply, since the failure to register did not make those leases void or voidable, just ineffective against third parties.

A similar case in Newfoundland had the opposite result. There, the Bank also failed to perfect its security but the clause in the guarantee stated that the Bank may "abstain from perfecting securities... as the Bank sees fit." The Court held that this term effectively covered the situation, and that the guarantee remained binding despite the Bank's failure to perfect.[17]

DISCUSSION QUESTIONS

These cases illustrate not only the operation of a guarantee, but also the obligations placed on the creditor to preserve and protect the position of the guarantor by doing nothing to weaken it. They also show that carefully worded provisions in the guarantee may change that obligation, and how such provisions are strictly interpreted in favour of the guarantor.

Finally, these cases raise the same question as the *Duffett* case discussed in Case Summary 14.5. Why should the creditor have any obligation to the guarantor? He has guaranteed payment; why shouldn't the creditor be able to choose from whom it seeks payment? And, if the responsibility of the creditor is justified, why should an exemption clause in a one-sided contract change that obligation?

---

16. (1993), 11 O.R. (3d) 792 (C.A.).

17. *Bank of Montreal v. Mercer* (2000), 193 Nfld. & P.E.I.R. 88 (Nfld. S.C.T.D.).

Defences of debtor are available to guarantor

In addition, any defences that are available to the debtor are also available to the guarantor. If breach of contract, fraud, or misrepresentation on the part of the creditor has barred an action against the debtor, it also bars an action against the guarantor. Note, however, that if the reason the guarantee was required was because of the infancy of the debtor, or some other factor known to all parties at the time of the guarantee, the guarantor will normally not be allowed to use that reason as a defence against the creditor.

Other Forms of Security

THE BANK ACT[18]

Anticipated crops can be used as security

As can inventory and goods in process of manufacture

This federal statute predates the passage of the *PPSAs*. It allows banks flexibility in what they can take as security. Under the *Bank Act,* growing crops, inventories, and goods in the process of manufacture can be taken as security by the banks, despite the fact that the nature of the goods changes in the process. For this type of security, it must be possible to sell the collateral during the course of business without affecting the nature of the security. Sections 426 and 427 of the *Bank Act* allow this to happen.

Conflict and confusion between *Bank Act* and *PPSA*

The *Bank Act* is still an important federal statute, but under the provincial *PPSAs,* other lenders now have similar flexibility. There is therefore now more potential conflict between the *Bank Act* and the provincial legislation. Businesspeople must now learn two sets of rules. For example, under the *Bank Act,* security must be registered with the Bank of Canada, creating duplication and confusion. This confusion is compounded because the *Bank Act* enables the banks to continue to use the usual types of secured transactions available to other lenders, such as chattel mortgages, real property mortgages, assignment of debts, guarantees and so on.

BANKRUPTCY

Introduction

As discussed above, debtors will often find themselves in a position where they cannot repay their debts. For that reason, wise creditors take steps at the outset of a relationship to ensure repayment. They may take an asset belonging to the debtor as security, or get someone else, such as a guarantor, to also be responsible for the debt.

Creditors may take security

Unsecured creditors can sue and try to collect

Unpaid unsecured creditors have all of the usual remedies available when someone breaches a legal obligation, including the right to proceed to a civil judgment. A judgment creditor can seize the debtor's assets and sell them to recover the judgment, or she can garnishee wages and other debts. Such action is often ineffective. There may be many creditors with claims outstanding. Secured creditors will have priority with respect to any secured asset that they might claim. The debtor may have limited resources with which to pay. Furthermore, in such a situation, the debtor may choose to declare bankruptcy, or may be forced into bankruptcy.

But debtor may declare bankruptcy

The *Bankruptcy and Insolvency Act*[19] (*BIA*) is a federal statute that is uniformly applicable throughout Canada. It has two purposes. The first is to preserve as

---

[18.] S.C. 1991, c. 46.

[19.] R.S.C. 1985, c. B-3.

many of the debtor's assets as possible for the benefit of the creditors. The second is to rehabilitate the debtor by forgiving the unpaid debt, thus removing an insurmountable burden, and restoring the debtor as a productive member of society.

Purposes of bankruptcy are to protect creditors and to rehabilitate debtor

Bill C-55, which provided a comprehensive insolvency reform, had received Royal Assent on 25 November 2005. When the textbook was written, in November 2006, the Bill (actually S.C. 2005, c. 47) had not yet been proclaimed. Its provisions were therefore not discussed.

Bill C-62 contained amendments to c. 47. It was passed by the House of Commons, but not the Senate. Bill C-12 was then introduced. It was passed by the House of Commons and the Senate. It received Royal Assent in December 2007 (S.C. 2007 c. 36).

Some of the provisions of c. 47 and c. 36 came into force in July 2008. For example, the *Wage Earner Protection Program Act*[20] and its regulations were proclaimed in force as of 7 July 2008; it was subsequently amended by Bill C-10, which came into force on 10 March 2009. (The amendments were retroactive to 27 January 2009.)

Some of insolvency reform now in force

On 8 December 2008, the Canadian Association of Insolvency and Restructuring Professionals, in Bulletin 08-14,[21] indicated that "the remaining insolvency amendments will not come into force in January 2009, as previously anticipated . . . " The Office of the Superintendent of Bankruptcy discussed, on its website, the changes set out in c. 47 and c. 36. It provided a "Summary of Key Provisions of the BIA in Force as of July, 2008."[22] This was last modified on March 17, 2009. This edition of the textbook will discuss only the provisions of c. 47 and c. 36 that were in force in June 2009, as indicated by the updated Summary.

People are often confused by the terms used to describe bankruptcy. **Insolvency** simply means that a person is unable to pay his debts as they become due. **Bankruptcy**, on the other hand, is the process by which a debtor's assets are transferred to a Trustee in Bankruptcy, who then deals with them for the benefit of the creditors. When the debtor makes the transfer voluntarily it is called an **assignment in bankruptcy**. Bankruptcy can be forced on the debtor, by a creditor obtaining a **bankruptcy order** from the court. The *BIA* does not apply to banks, insurance companies, trust companies, loan companies, or railways. Farmers and fishers cannot be forced into bankruptcy, but they can make a voluntary assignment.

Bankruptcy involves transfer of assets to Trustee

The government official responsible for bankruptcy for all of Canada is the Superintendent of Bankruptcy. The Superintendent, in turn, appoints Official Receivers for the bankruptcy districts throughout the country (there must be at least one in each province). A **Trustee in Bankruptcy** is a licensed private professional who, for a fee, assists the debtor in the bankruptcy process—administering the bankrupt's estate for the benefit of the creditors, filing various documents with the Official Receiver, and otherwise shepherding the bankrupt through the process

Superintendent of Bankruptcy responsible

Superintendent appoints Official Receivers

---

20. S.C. 2005, c. 47, s. 1.

21. See Bulletin 08-14, online: www.cairp.ca/english/communications_advo/doc/BUL08-14.doc.

22. See "Summary of Legislative Changes," www.ic.gc.ca/eic/site/bsf-osb.nsf/eng/br01782.html.

from initiation to discharge. A Trustee serves the same purpose when a proposal is involved. A Trustee is called an Administrator when dealing with consumer proposals. The courts become involved when a bankruptcy order is requested and when other types of disputes arise. The superior trial court of each province and territory is designated as a bankruptcy court for the purposes of the *BIA*. Although these are courts of the provinces or territories, they have a national jurisdiction when administering the *BIA* and related legislation, because these are federal statutes.

CASE SUMMARY 14.7

No Act of Bankruptcy, No Bankruptcy! *American Bullion Minerals Ltd. (Re)*[23]

The Court granted the petition of the controlling shareholder of ABML, bcMetals Corporation (bcM), asking for a bankruptcy order for ABML. The minority shareholders of ABML applied for an order annulling the bankruptcy. They claimed that bcM made a number of misrepresentations when it petitioned ABML into bankruptcy, that the sole director of ABML failed to oppose the petition or alert ABML shareholders of it, and that bcM petitioned ABML into bankruptcy to facilitate bcM's acquisition of ABML's interest in mineral claims without compensating ABML's minority shareholders.

The Court found that the petition, the affidavit in support, and the submissions of counsel did not inform the Court of the real relationship between ABML and bcM, fully disclose the circumstances of some of the liabilities of ABML, or provide any information relevant to some of its liabilities. The Court found that bcM was the only creditor of ABML, and that bcM could not prove that there were special circumstances that warranted a bankruptcy order. Also, there was no evidence that ABML had committed an act of bankruptcy. The Court concluded that if the bankruptcy Court had been fully informed, it would not have made the bankruptcy order. The bankruptcy was therefore annulled.

DISCUSSION QUESTIONS

A creditor must prove that the debtor has committed an act of bankruptcy, or the petition will be refused. In such a case, the creditor may be liable for any losses suffered by the debtor. In the *ABML* case, what remedy may the minority shareholders be able to seek?

The Process

Bankruptcy can be forced by creditors

In an involuntary bankruptcy, a creditor petitions the court to force the debtor into bankruptcy. In granting the petition, the court makes a bankruptcy order. This results in a statutory assignment of the debtor's assets to the Trustee in Bankruptcy, ensuring that the assets will be preserved and distributed fairly, so that the creditors will recover as much as possible of what they are owed.

[23.] (2008), 43 C.B.R. (5th) 210 (B.C.S.C.).

To obtain a bankruptcy order, the creditor must specify in the petition that the debtor owes more than $1000 in debt and has committed an act of bankruptcy during the previous six months. Significant acts of bankruptcy include the voluntary assignment of assets to a trustee in bankruptcy, fraudulent transfers of money or assets to keep them out of the hands of the trustee, the giving of a fraudulent preference to one of the creditors, an attempt to leave the jurisdiction without paying debts, and general insolvency. It is usually the failure to pay debts as they become due that is the specified act of bankruptcy. A sworn affidavit must also be filed with the Registrar in Bankruptcy in the district in which the debtor is located, verifying the facts alleged in the petition. If the debtor opposes the petition, as is often the case, a hearing before a Judge will take place. If she is satisfied, the Judge can issue a bankruptcy order, designating a Trustee in Bankruptcy (normally chosen by the creditors) to receive the assets of the bankrupt. When the petition is unopposed, the hearing can be held before the Registrar.

> **If creditor owed more than $1000 and debtor committed an act of bankruptcy**

Petitioning a debtor into bankruptcy is an involved process, normally requiring the assistance of a lawyer. Caution should be exercised before using this approach. Great damage can be done to the business and reputation of the debtor. If the application is refused, the creditor may be liable to pay compensation for the losses incurred by the debtor. See Figure 14.1 for an illustration of the bankruptcy order process.

> **Creditor must be careful when petitioning**

In a **voluntary assignment in bankruptcy**, the debtor must make an "assignment for the general benefit of his creditors," using the prescribed form. The debtor must also prepare a "statement of affairs," summarizing his property and listing all of his creditors, showing the amounts and nature of their claims (whether they are secured, preferred, or unsecured). These documents are filed with the Official Receiver, who then appoints a Trustee in Bankruptcy. The Trustee will receive the debtor's assets and administer the estate. In practice, debtors will first seek out a Trustee in Bankruptcy, who will counsel them, advising of the various alternatives and, if appropriate, assisting them in the preparation of the documents and their filing with the Official Receiver. When larger estates are involved, the debtor will usually also involve the services of a lawyer. The voluntary assignment process is illustrated in Figure 14.2.

> **Bankruptcy can be voluntary by debtor**

It should be noted that not all of the debtor's property is transferred to the Trustee in Bankruptcy. The exempt property is determined by the provincial legislation, so it varies from province to province. It usually includes medical and dental aids, food, clothing, furniture and appliances, and tools and other items used to earn an income, up to a limited value. A vehicle of limited value and a personal residence where the debtor has a limited equity may also be protected. The

> **Exempt property is protected**

Figure 14.1 Bankruptcy Order Process

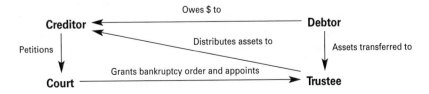

Figure 14.2 Voluntary Assignment

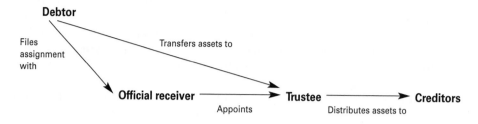

Trustee will not take property of little value, or property that she considers to be worth less than what it will cost to liquidate.

Trustee holds property in trust for creditors

The Trustee in Bankruptcy holds the debtor's property in trust for the creditors. She therefore owes them a duty to preserve the property and to sell it for as much as is reasonably possible. The debtor must cooperate with the Trustee, disclosing all assets, documentation and tax receipts. Often a meeting of the creditors will take place. The debtor must attend, answering the creditors' questions, and otherwise cooperating in the process. The creditors may ask to appoint up to five Inspectors to supervise the Trustee and the process, to ensure their interests are protected. The debtor may also be required to meet with, and answer the questions of, the Official Receiver.

Alternatives to Bankruptcy

Debtor should try to avoid bankruptcy

The debtor should, of course, do all he can to avoid bankruptcy. If he becomes bankrupt, he will lose most of his property. He will also find it difficult in the future to conduct business, or to make personal credit purchases, due to a poor credit rating. A personal bankruptcy will remain on an individual's credit record for about six years. Even after that period of time, it will be obvious to a credit grantor that there must have been serious financial problems, because of the lack of credit transactions during that six-year period. If a corporation becomes bankrupt, it will not be discharged and will therefore not survive.

There are several possible informal solutions

For a debtor who is having financial problems, the first step should be to talk to the creditors involved, to try to make alternative arrangements for paying the debt. Creditors are usually quite responsive to reasonable arrangements for avoiding both commercial and personal bankruptcies. They will often get much less if bankruptcy is forced. There are also many tangible and intangible advantages for creditors to keep their debtor as a functioning customer. Another option, especially when significant credit card debt is involved, is to obtain a consolidation loan from a bank or other lending institution. A consolidation loan enables the debtor to consolidate the various debts he owes. There will then be only one creditor, and a more manageable payment schedule, often at a lower rate of interest. Individual creditors will sometimes agree to take less to pay off the debt. They realize that they will be better off accepting less, rather than risking getting nothing by continuing to demand full payment and thus forcing bankruptcy.

Debtors can make proposal and avoid bankruptcy

If these informal negotiations fail, the *BIA* still provides for an alternative to bankruptcy. Two separate procedures are involved; both allow the debtor to reorganize her affairs and make proposals for partial payment that will satisfy her creditors sufficiently to avoid actual bankruptcy. **Division I proposals** usually involve commercial debtors in the form of corporations or individual debtors with significant claims against them (more than $75 000). The process is started by filing, with the Official Receiver, a proposal, or a notice of intention to file a proposal. The filing should be done with the help of a professional licensed to provide these services (a Trustee in Bankruptcy). Within 10 days of filing a notice of intention, a statement of projected cash flow must also be filed, followed within 30 days by the filing of the proposal itself (although this time limit may be extended). A meeting with the creditors is then held and the proposal is discussed and voted upon. For the proposal to be approved, two-thirds of the unsecured creditors by value and a majority by number, must vote to accept it. (Note that they may be divided into classes of creditors and then vote within that class.) The same approach applies to each class of secured creditors to which the proposal was made. The court also must approve the proposal.

> Division I proposals for corporations and people with debts over $75 000

If the unsecured creditors approve the proposal, all of them are bound by it. If the unsecured creditors (or the court) reject the proposal, the debtor is deemed to have made an assignment in bankruptcy from the day of the meeting of the creditors. Normal bankruptcy procedures will follow. Secured creditors whose class gave its approval are also bound by the proposal. Secured creditors not included in the proposal, or whose class rejected the proposal, can still realize on their security.

> If proposal rejected, debtor into bankruptcy

Division I proposals are very flexible. They may include anything from arranging to reduce the debt, to devising a new payment structure, to helping the creditors wind up the corporation. An important effect of starting this process by filing a proposal, or a notice of intention, is that creditors, including secured creditors who have been included in the proposal process, are prevented from taking action against the debtor or her assets until the vote takes place, at least two months later. In effect, the insolvent debtor is protected from the creditors. If the proposal is accepted, that protection continues.

> Proposals are flexible and they stay proceedings

CASE SUMMARY 14.8

Proposal Abused: *Janodee Investments Ltd. v. Pellegrini*[24]

Pellegrini had two mortgages on his home. When he defaulted on them, the mortgagees/creditors proceeded to judgment and obtained an order to take possession of the house. Before the order could be enforced, Pellegrini served notice of intention to make a proposal under the *BIA*. Normally, such a notice would result in a stay of proceedings, delaying enforcement of the order. However, in this case the Court held that Pellegrini was using the notice as a delaying tactic. He had no serious intention of reordering his affairs. No other secured creditors were involved, and the mortgagees would not be responsive to such a proposal in any event.

This case is instructive in that it shows not only the normal operation of a proposal, but also how such a proposal can be abused. In this case, the Court refused to order the stay, thus preventing such abuse. The difficulty with the operation of such proposals—as well as with the whole bankruptcy process—is that it interferes with the creditors' rights

---

24. (2001), 25 C.B.R. (4th) 47 (Ont. S.C.J.).

to proceed against the debtor and enforce full payment in a timely manner. The justification for this is that, in the long run, the creditors get more and that, after discharge, the bankrupt is able to carry on without overwhelming debt. But, in fact, many creditors get very little or nothing and are barred from further proceedings after discharge.

SMALL BUSINESS PERSPECTIVE

Does the Division 1 proposal process in the *BIA* provide too much protection for insolvent people and businesses, at the expense of legitimate creditors?

Consumer proposals available for people with debts less than $75 000

Consumer debtors with less than $75 000 in claims against them (excluding a mortgage on their home) are similarly protected when they make a consumer proposal under Division II of Part III of the *BIA*. The insolvent debtor must hire an Administrator (a Trustee in Bankruptcy or a person appointed to administer consumer proposals). The Administrator examines the debtor's finances, prepares the consumer proposal and any reports required, provides counselling for the debtor, and files the consumer proposal. This is a simpler process than filing a Division I proposal. No actual meeting is required unless demanded by the creditors. If the creditors reject a consumer proposal, the debtor is not automatically bankrupt. A consumer proposal must contain a commitment by the debtor that the performance of the consumer proposal will be completed within five years. Payments under a consumer proposal are paid to the Administrator, who distributes the funds to the creditors.

Consumer proposals stop all legal actions by unsecured creditors

As long as the debtor complies with the obligations in the consumer proposal, acts honestly and participates in any mandatory counselling required, action cannot be taken against him by unsecured creditors. Even those supplying ongoing services, such as public utilities and landlords, must continue supplying them. But if the debtor defaults on his commitments, the consumer proposal is annulled, and the debtor may face the normal bankruptcy procedures. Court approval of Division II proposals is not required.

Secured debts not affected if not in proposal

For both Division I proposals and consumer proposals, if a proposal is accepted and then properly performed, a certificate is issued and the debtor's obligation is complete with respect to those matters covered by the proposal. There are some matters that cannot be included in a proposal, just as some types of obligations cannot be discharged though bankruptcy. These will be discussed below. If a secured debt was not included in the proposal, then that obligation remains and is not affected by the completed performance of the proposal or the certificate issued.

Orderly payment of debt program available in some provinces

In some provinces, individual debtors may also utilize Part X of the *BIA*, Orderly Payment of Debts (OPD). If the amount the debtor owes is less than $1000, or if the debtor obtains the consent of the creditors, he can apply to the court for a consolidation order. He must provide an affidavit, setting out his relevant financial and personal situation. The application will be approved, unless a creditor objects to it. If there is an objection, there will be a hearing in front of the Clerk of the Court to determine the validity of the objection.

A consolidation order requires the debtor to make the stipulated payments into court, such that all of his debts will be paid in full within three years, unless the creditors consent to a longer period. Such an order acts as a stay with respect to the debts covered by the order, except for secured debts. If the debtor defaults, the creditors can enforce the consolidation order like any other court order, subject to the court's approval. The OPD program is administered by various public and private agencies in the provinces where it is available. In Alberta, for example, Money Mentors (the successor to Credit Counselling Services of Alberta Ltd.) administers the OPD program.[25]

For corporations owing more than $5 million, there is an alternative process available that enables them to restructure their affairs and avoid bankruptcy. This alternative is available under the *Companies' Creditors Arrangement Act (CCAA)*.[26] This is a federal statute providing protection to debtors with some advantages over the *BIA*. The attraction of the *CCAA* is in the protection given to debtors, from their creditors. This may provide more flexibility to the debtor corporation in its restructuring efforts, as it will be protected from its creditors, both secured and unsecured, for a longer period of time. A judge will often combine the flexibility provided under the *CCAA* with the power under section 47 of the *BIA* to appoint an interim receiver to supervise the restructuring process. Many corporations have filed for bankruptcy protection under the *CCAA* in recent years, including Air Canada and Nortel Networks Corp.

Large corporations can ask court for bankruptcy protection

Commercial and consumer proposals under the *BIA*, consolidation orders in the OPD program, and arrangements under the *CCAA* all enable a debtor to avoid the bankruptcy process. Bankruptcy will occur, however, if the creditors reject a proposal, or if the debtor defaults on his obligations under a proposal. Business students should be aware of bankruptcy and its alternatives, from both a consumer and a commercial perspective. Consumer bankruptcies are much more numerous than commercial bankruptcies. Any business dealing with the public must therefore factor this risk into its business considerations. Commercial bankruptcies may be less common than consumer bankruptcies, but they generally involve much more money and have a greater impact on the businesses with which the debtor is dealing. Even very high-profile businesses (General Motors Corp.) are facing bankruptcy or restructuring in these difficult economic times. A businessperson ignores these risks at his peril.

REDUCING RISK 14.4

Bankruptcy is a very serious and drastic step. Both creditors and debtors should do all they can to avoid it. Often negotiation between the parties, perhaps with a mediator, will result in an acceptable alternative. The creditors get more than they would get by forcing bankruptcy, and a valued customer is preserved. If these informal steps fail, and proposals are presented, they should be treated seriously. Bankruptcy should be used only as a last resort.

Priority Among Creditors

Once the Trustee in Bankruptcy has been given the property of a bankrupt debtor (referred to as the bankrupt's "**estate**"), she holds those assets in trust for the benefit of the creditors. The Trustee has the right and responsibility to lease, repair, receive rents or otherwise deal with those assets to preserve their value. The Trustee will eventually sell the assets and distribute the proceeds fairly to the creditors.

Trustee holds property in trust for creditors

---

25. See Money Mentors, online: www.moneymentors.ca/home.html.
26. R.S.C.1985, c. C-36.

Each creditor must file proof of claim

Trustee must evaluate claims of creditors

Suppliers of goods can reclaim goods from bankrupt or Trustee

Secured creditors have prior claim to secured property

Preferred creditors paid before unsecured creditors

Each of the creditors must establish the validity of his claim by filing a **proof of claim** with the Trustee. This document sets out the nature of the debt, how much remains owing, and any claims the debtor might have in return. An important function of the Trustee is to evaluate the claims of the creditors. If they are accepted as valid, they will form part of the body of claims against the estate. Some claims of questionable legitimacy may be rejected by the Trustee. The affected creditors have the right to challenge the Trustee's decision by making application to the bankruptcy court. Mediation is often employed to resolve these and other disputes.

The *BIA* allows a supplier of goods to demand the return of those goods upon learning of the bankruptcy. The supplier must make his written demand for repossession within 30 days of delivery of those goods, and the debtor (or the Trustee) must still have possession of them. Even suppliers of goods that become commingled and lose their identity, such as crops, produce, and fish, have a prior claim. Such suppliers become secured creditors with respect to the value of those goods, provided that the goods were delivered within 15 days preceding the bankruptcy and their claims are filed within 30 days after.

Secured creditors retain their priority position, having a prior claim to at least the value of the property used as security. Most creditors are prevented from taking any further independent action once the assignment or bankruptcy order has been made. (Note that this stay does not apply to criminal prosecutions or matrimonial disputes, which can continue.) A secured creditor, on the other hand, retains a right to take possession of, or otherwise proceed against, the property used as security, without waiting, unless the court orders otherwise. A secured creditor can choose to file a proof of claim for all of what she is owed, giving up any claim for the secured property. She will then be treated as an unsecured creditor for the entire amount. This tactic may be attractive when there is little value in the property, when the property is of such a nature that it would be difficult to sell, or when there are considerable resources in the estate. Otherwise, a secured creditor can, on the basis of a filed proof of claim, take possession of the secured property and sell it. She then becomes an unsecured creditor against the estate for any shortfall. If there is sufficient value in the property, the Trustee may simply pay the secured creditor's claim, retaining that property for the benefit of the other creditors. The Trustee can also serve notice on the secured creditor, requiring her to place a value on the property and deal with it on the basis of that value or, if the Trustee is dissatisfied with the value provided, require the creditor to sell the property.

After the secured creditors have received what they are entitled to, the Trustee distributes the remaining assets, or the proceeds from the sales of those assets, to the other creditors. Preferred creditors are paid first, pursuant to section 136 of the *BIA*. This section indicates that the following are to be paid, in this order: funeral expenses, costs associated with the bankruptcy process, claims for arrears in wages for a limited amount and time period, arrears in maintenance or alimony, municipal taxes, arrears in rent for a limited period, some direct costs incurred by creditors in the execution process, amounts owed for workers' compensation, employment insurance, and income tax that should have been deducted from salaries, and other claims of the Crown. Unsecured creditors, usually suppliers of goods and services, are paid only after all of these obligations have been satisfied. The unsecured creditors will receive a share on a pro rata basis (a share of the remaining estate determined by the percentage of overall claims their particular claim represents).

The federal government has passed legislation that gives it priority over all other creditors, including secured creditors, in certain situations. Examples include section 224 of the *Income Tax Act*[27] and section 317 of the *Excise Tax Act*.[28] These sections essentially create a trust, in situations where there are unremitted source deductions or GST. This gives the government a "super priority." When a Requirement to Pay (the equivalent of a Garnishee Summons) is served by the government on debtors of the tax debtor, any amount that is owed, and which would normally be paid to the tax debtor, becomes the property of the government. It never becomes the property of the tax debtor and is therefore not available to its creditors. The courts have held that this gives the government priority over secured creditors of the tax debtor in the case of a bankruptcy of the tax debtor.[29]

> Government sometimes has priority over secured creditors

Offences

As discussed above, debtors often attempt to keep their property out of the hands of creditors by transferring it to friends or relatives. Debtors also sometimes try to pay one creditor and not others. **Fraudulent transfers** and *preferences* often take place in bankruptcy situations. The Trustee in Bankruptcy can reverse such transactions.

CASE SUMMARY 14.9

Transferring House to Wife Prohibited: *Re Fancy*[30]

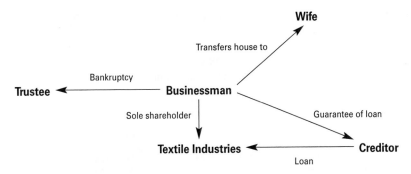

A successful businessman guaranteed the debts of his corporation, Textile Industries, making him personally responsible if it ran into financial difficulties. An action against the corporation resulted in a judgment, causing the corporation to fail and forcing him into bankruptcy. Shortly before his bankruptcy, he transferred his interest in the matrimonial home to his wife. At the time of the transfer, it was clear that the litigation would go to trial and that he was facing substantial losses.

The Court reversed the transfer, determining that the transfer of the house to the wife amounted to a prohibited settlement under the provisions of the *BIA*. A settlement

---

27. R.S.C. 1985, c. 1 (5th Supp.).

28. R.S.C. 1985, c. E-15.

29. See, for example, *Bank of Montreal v. Canada (Attorney General)* (2003), 66 O.R. (3d) 161 (C.A.).

30. (1984), 46 O.R. (2d) 153 (H.C.J.).

can occur when a person transfers property to another to preserve some benefit for himself, which is exactly what was done in this case.

SMALL BUSINESS PERSPECTIVE

Would the result have been the same if the businessman had transferred his interest in the home to his wife before he incorporated his business?

Settlements prohibited

Settlements involve the transfer of assets for nominal or no consideration. A settlement is void if it took place within one year of bankruptcy. This period can be extended to up to five years, if it can be proven that, at the time of the settlement, the bankrupt knew that he was insolvent.

Fraudulent preferences prohibited

A payment made in preference to one creditor over the others is also void. The Trustee can force the return of those funds so that they can be fairly distributed to all of the creditors. This is the situation in the *Speedy Roofing* case discussed in Case Summary 14.10. There is a presumption that a payment was made to create a preference if it was made within three months of the bankruptcy. Such payments can be challenged even if they were made earlier than that, if it can be shown that the debtor was attempting to avoid other creditors.

CASE SUMMARY 14.10

Preferring One Creditor Prohibited: *Re Speedy Roofing Ltd.*[31]

Roofmart supplied materials to Speedy Roofing. As Speedy Roofing was not paying its account, mortgages were given to Roofmart as security for the debt. The mortgages were on the homes of Pompeo and Gaggi, the wives of the principal shareholders of Speedy Roofing. Shortly before the Royal Bank, another creditor, forced it into bankruptcy, Speedy Roofing paid Roofmart $80 000 to discharge the mortgages. The Court

---

[31.] (1987), 62 O.R. (2d) 312 (H.C.J.), aff'd (1990), 74 O.R. (2d) 633 (C.A.).

had to determine whether that payment was a fraudulent preference and therefore prohibited under the *BIA*. Since the payment was made within three months of the bankruptcy, it amounted to a fraudulent preference. The Court ordered Roofmart to repay the
$80 000 it received from Speedy Roofing to the Trustee in Bankruptcy.

SMALL BUSINESS PERSPECTIVE

A debtor cannot choose to pay one creditor over another, or transfer property to a
creditor, to escape a debt. Do you agree with this policy? Should the debtor be able to
choose which creditors will be paid and which will not be paid? If a debtor chooses to
pay money owed to one creditor, should the other creditors be able to complain even if
a legitimate debt has been properly paid?

At the beginning of the bankruptcy process, the debtor is required to file an
affidavit setting out all of his debt, creditors, and assets. He must provide a summary of all of the transactions that have taken place regarding these assets over
the last year (or longer if so ordered). He must disclose any settlements he has
made during the previous five years. A bankrupt also has an obligation to cooperate with the Trustee by disclosing all relevant information and answering any
relevant questions. The bankrupt can also be required to attend before the
Official Receiver, or the court, to answer questions about how he got into financial trouble, as well as questions regarding his debts, creditors, and assets, and
what he has done with them. The bankrupt has many other duties, including
transferring his assets to the Trustee, delivering his credit cards, records, and
documents to the Trustee, and keeping the Trustee advised of his address. The
bankrupt must "generally do all such acts and things in relation to his property
and the distribution of the proceeds among his creditors as may be reasonably
required by the trustee, or may be prescribed by the General Rules, or may be
directed by the court. ..."[32]

> **Bankrupt has many duties, including swearing affidavit about financial information**

In addition to settlements, fraudulent preferences, and a failure to fulfill the
duties of a bankrupt, the *BIA* sets out several other bankruptcy offences for which
a bankrupt may be punished, including refusing to answer questions truthfully,
hiding, falsifying or destroying records, failing to keep proper records, and hiding
or concealing property. If a bankrupt is convicted of a bankruptcy offence, he
may be fined up to $10 000 and/or be imprisoned for up to three years.[33]

Once the assets have been transferred to a Trustee by voluntary assignment,
or through a bankruptcy order, the debtor is a bankrupt. A bankrupt is subject to
several restrictions. If he is involved in any business transaction, or borrows more
than $500, he must disclose his status. He cannot be a director of a corporation.[34]

---

32. *Bankruptcy and Insolvency Act, supra* note 30, s. 158 (o).

33. *Ibid.,* s. 198.

34. See, for example, *Canada Business Corporations Act,* R.S.C. 1985, c. C-44, s. 105.

He may also be restricted from carrying on some professions, such as accounting, depending on the particular rules of the professional body in question.[35]

Once the bankruptcy process is completed and the estate has been distributed, the bankrupt may apply to the court to be discharged. This application is automatic, after nine months, for an individual involved in his first bankruptcy, unless a creditor or the Trustee opposes the discharge. If someone opposes a first-time bankruptcy, or if the bankrupt has been bankrupt before, the matter will be heard by a court. An application for a discharge from bankruptcy may be granted unconditionally, it may be granted subject to certain conditions, or it may be denied.

A lawyer became bankrupt when a business in which he was involved failed. He maintained a very high lifestyle while going through the bankruptcy process. He was looking forward to a reasonable income after his discharge, as well. He had not made any payments to the Trustee. Given these circumstances, the Court ordered that his discharge be conditional on him paying a significant amount to his creditors.[36] A court has the discretion to place such conditions on the discharge of a bankrupt.

On the other hand, the same Court dealt with another lawyer in a different manner. He was 53 years old when he ran into financial difficulties. He did all he could to repay his creditors, including significantly reducing his lifestyle. It was only after his honest efforts failed, through no fault of his own, that he was forced to make an assignment in bankruptcy. In this case, the Court had no hesitation in finding that the bankrupt was entitled to an unconditional discharge and a fresh start, even though his assets were not sufficient to pay back 50 cents on the dollar. In reaching this conclusion, the Court considered the bankrupt's honesty, his struggle for nine years to pay back his creditors, and his need to be free to prepare for his retirement.[37]

> **But discharge may be unconditional, depending on circumstances**

These two cases illustrate the power of the bankruptcy court to place significant conditions on a discharge and the factors that might affect such a decision. Debtors who commit bankruptcy offences will normally not be unconditionally discharged; they may even be imprisoned. The court will also be reluctant to unconditionally discharge bankrupts who have not fulfilled their duties or whose behaviour has not been reasonable. As shown by the *McAfee* case, in such cases the court can grant a conditional discharge, putting conditions or restrictions on the bankrupt. Justice Estey commented on the purpose of the bankruptcy process as follows: "The purpose and object of the *Bankruptcy Act* [now the *BIA*] is to equitably distribute the assets of the debtor and to permit his rehabilitation as a citizen, unfettered by past debts. The discharge, however, is not a matter of right, and the provisions of Sections 142 and 143 [now ss. 172 and 173 of the *BIA*] plainly indicate that in certain cases the debtor should suffer a period of probation."[38]

> **Unconditional discharge not granted if bankruptcy offence committed**

[35.] See, for example, Rule 601.1 of the "Rules of Professional Conduct" of the Institute of Chartered Accountants of Alberta, www.albertacas.ca/Libraries/Rules/Rules_of_Professional_Conduct_2006-newlogo-pol.pdf.

[36.] *McAfee v. Westmore* (1988), 49 D.L.R. (4th) 401 (B.C.C.A.).*Ibid.*, s. 198.

[37.] Re Irwin (1994), 112 D.L.R. (4th) 164 (B.C.C.A.).

[38.] *Industrial Acceptance Corp. v. Lalonde*, [1952] 2 S.C.R. 109, at 120.

REDUCING RISK 14.5

Debtors sometimes use bankruptcy as a convenient way to avoid paying their debts. Some even declare bankruptcy several times. While this is obviously an abuse of the process,, merchants and other creditors must be ever-vigilant to avoid doing business with such people. Use of credit checks can be a great help, even when goods or services are being supplied. On the other hand, debtors who are tempted to abuse the process should realize that, as a rule, committing a bankruptcy offence will likely result in fines and/or imprisonment. Furthermore, the courts will generally not grant an unconditional discharge when faced with abuses such as the debtor failing to cooperate with officials, trying to hide assets, or otherwise abusing the process.

After Discharge

During the bankruptcy process, the bankrupt is required to continue to make regular payments (surplus income payments) to the Trustee to be distributed to the creditors. Any windfall she receives, such as an inheritance or a lottery win, will go to the Trustee for distribution. That all changes upon discharge from bankruptcy (assuming that the discharge is unconditional). When discharged, the debtor is freed from most previous claims by creditors and is in a position to start over. Any assets subsequently obtained by the discharged bankrupt are hers to do with as she wishes. Unpaid creditors cannot claim against them. Pursuant to the *BIA*, some obligations do survive discharge, such as fines, alimony and maintenance payments, and some civil damage awards. Student loans also survive bankruptcy. They are payable for up to seven years after the debtor ceases to be a student.[39]

Effect of absolute discharge is to end most debts

The discussion above focused primarily on the bankruptcy of an individual. The primary difference with a bankruptcy of a corporation is that there will not be a discharge after the bankruptcy unless the corporation has been able to repay all of the money owing. That, of course, is highly unlikely, there being very little likelihood of a bankruptcy in the first place in those circumstances. A Division II consumer proposal under the *BIA* is not available to a corporation, but corporations often try to restructure using Division I commercial proposals. Larger corporations also often restructure using the *CCAA*. If a corporation's proposal is approved, or if it reaches an arrangement with its creditors, and it properly fulfills its obligations, the corporation will be free to carry on its business, avoiding bankruptcy altogether. The obligations of the debtor to supply appropriate information and documents apply to corporations as well. A corporation must provide someone who is familiar with the situation to answer the questions that would otherwise have been put to an individual debtor by the Trustee, the creditors in a creditor meeting, the Official Receiver or the court.

Corporations not discharged after bankruptcy

Corporations may use proposals and arrangements to avoid bankruptcy

A corporation will often face dissolution after the bankruptcy process, although this is usually not worth the trouble. Still, disgruntled shareholders and creditors may have further rights under winding-up acts, or the various business corporations' legislation in place at both the provincial and federal levels. They also may have claims against the directors and other officers of the corporation

Directors of corporations owe creditors a duty of care

Receivers may be appointed by creditors pursuant to security agreement

---

[39]. *Bankruptcy and Insolvency Act, supra* note 30, s. 178. This was changed from 10 years on 7 July 2008, when some of the provisions of the recent amendments to the *BIA* came into force. Also, the period before which an application may be made to request a discharge on the basis of hardship was reduced from 10 years to 5 years.

under those statutes. In this regard, the Supreme Court of Canada recently held that, in certain circumstances, directors owe a duty of care to creditors of the corporation, but that the duty does not give rise to a fiduciary duty. The directors owe a fiduciary duty to the corporation only.[40]

Corporations that go into receivership are usually not involved in bankruptcy at all. When a creditor lends a corporation significant funds, the security agreement usually gives the creditor the right, in the event of default or some other triggering event, to appoint a receiver to take possession of the assets given as security, without the necessity of going through the bankruptcy procedure. Such an assignment of assets to a receiver is not a bankruptcy, but the effect can be every bit as devastating to the business. Some of the rights and responsibilities of receivers are set out in Part XI of the *BIA*. A secured creditor must give the debtor reasonable notice before the appointment of a receiver, or taking possession of the goods used as security. Whether the receiver is appointed by the creditor directly, or it obtains a court order allowing the appointment, failure to give reasonable notice can be devastating to the debtor. This will result in significant liability to the creditor when it is improperly done.[41]

It must be remembered that there are two main purposes of the *BIA* and the other legislation discussed in this section. The first is to ensure that the creditors realize as much of the amount owed as possible. The second is to facilitate the rehabilitation of the debtor. We will continue to see legislative changes as the debate over the proper balance of these two objectives continues.

NEGOTIABLE INSTRUMENTS

Negotiable instruments are often associated with consumer and commercial transactions. They take many different forms, but are primarily *cheques, bills of exchange* (sometimes called drafts) and *promissory notes,* as set out in the federal *Bills of Exchange Act.*[42] The most familiar form of negotiable instruments is the cheque (see Figure 14.3), which is an order made by the drawer to his bank to pay funds to a third party called the *payee;* these funds must be paid as soon as the cheque is presented for payment (on demand).

Negotiable instruments are controlled by federal statute. They include
• cheques

Figure 14.3 Cheque

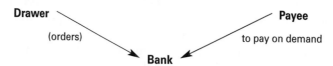

The drawer physically hands the cheque to the payee, who later presents it to the bank.

A bill of exchange or draft (see Figure 14.4) is similar to a cheque, but with two important differences. There are three parties involved, and the *drawer* orders the *drawee* to pay the *payee* a certain sum of money. But with the bill of exchange, the drawee need not be a bank, and the instrument may be made payable at some

---

40. *Peoples Department Stores Inc. (Trustee of) v. Wise,* [2004] 3 S.C.R. 461.

41. See, for example, *Royal Bank of Canada v. W. Got and Associates Electric Ltd.,* [1999] 3 S.C.R. 408.

42. R.S.C. 1985, c. B-4.

future time. (A cheque is defined as a "bill of exchange drawn on a bank, payable on demand.") The cheque is much more common today than the bill of exchange, especially in consumer dealings. Bills of exchange are used in sophisticated financial transactions.

Figure 14.4 Bills of Exchange

• bills of exchange

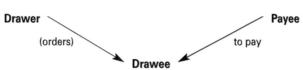

The drawer physically hands the instrument to the payee, who then presents it to the drawee for payment or acceptance.

With these kinds of instruments, the drawer retains the power to countermand even after he has given the cheque or bill of exchange to the payee. To overcome this problem, the payee will often take the instrument directly to the drawee to determine if the latter will honour it. If the drawee "accepts" the instrument, a direct obligation is created on the drawee to pay the payee, ensuring payment. Having a cheque certified has a similar result.

A **promissory note** (see Figure 14.5) involves only two parties. The *maker* promises to pay a certain sum to the *payee* at a specified future date or on demand. Because of their nature, promissory notes are always associated with a creditor–debtor relationship.

• promissory notes

Cheques are used primarily as a convenient means of transferring funds. To a considerable extent, their use has been replaced by tools associated with electronic banking, such as debit cards and credit cards. Cheques are still common,

Figure 14.5 Promissory Note

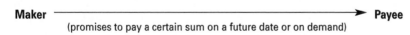

The maker hands the note to the payee, who later presents it to the maker for payment.

however, and students should be familiar with their unique qualities. Often sellers will require payment by certified cheque, which is extremely secure, as payment is in effect guaranteed by the bank. Once the cheque has been transferred to the payee, the bank will no longer honour an order to stop payment. Instead of certifying a cheque, many banks now issue a bank draft in the name of the payee. It will be given by the customer to the payee at the appropriate time. Another common practice when goods are bought on credit is to give the creditor a series of post-dated cheques that are subsequently deposited on the appropriate dates. Negotiable instruments are also regularly used to bolster secured transactions.

CASE SUMMARY 14.11

A Certified Cheque Is Like Cash: *Centrac Inc. v. Canadian Imperial Bank of Commerce*[43]

Officeplus paid for office furniture purchased from Centrac with a $48 000 certified cheque. The CIBC had certified the cheque on the strength of the deposit of another cheque for $76 000. Upon learning that the $76 000 cheque would not be honoured, the CIBC stopped payment on the $48 000 cheque and phoned Centrac to inform it of having done so. The cheque was dishonoured when Centrac presented it for payment. Centrac sued the CIBC. The Court held that after the CIBC had certified the cheque, it was considered equivalent to cash. "Once certification was made, any attempt made by the bank to avoid payment was too late." The CIBC could not hide behind its failure to check the validity of the $76 000 cheque. It had committed to honour the certified cheque, and was required to do so.

REDUCING RISK 14.6

Negotiable instruments can be very dangerous to those who make and endorse them. Great care should be taken in their use. People often think that, if they write a cheque and something goes wrong, they can simply stop payment. This is often not possible, since once that cheque gets into the hands of an innocent third party—even if it is the payee's bank—one will likely have to honour the instrument. The same holds true with respect to the liability of the endorser.

CASE SUMMARY 14.12

Are Money Orders Bills of Exchange? *Bendix Foreign Exchange Corp. v. Integrated Payment Systems Canada Inc.*[44]

Sidhu operated as an agent for IPS, selling money orders. His obligation was to collect the face value of each money order sold, and not to use money orders to pay his debts. He purchased foreign currency from Bendix. He paid for this purchase with money orders. Bendix wired $46 000 to a bank in India. When IPS discovered that the money orders had been stolen by Sidhu, it refused to honour them. Bendix sued to recover the funds. IPS asked for summary judgment, an order dismissing the action.

Bendix argued that the money orders were bills of exchange and that, as it was a holder in due course, it was entitled to payment. The Court disagreed, holding that the money orders were not bills of exchange, as they stated that they were payable only if certain conditions were satisfied. One of these conditions was that the money orders must not have been stolen. Bendix was therefore not entitled to payment and its action was dismissed.

---

[43] (1994), 21 O.R. (3d) 161 (C.A.).

[44] [2004] O.J. No. 4455 (Sup.Ct.).

Bendix appealed, and the Court of Appeal set aside the summary judgment.[45] It said that a judicial definition of a money order would best be decided by a trial court. Accordingly, it ordered that Bendix's action proceed to trial.

SMALL BUSINESS PERSPECTIVE

Money orders are commonly used in consumer transactions. Like certified cheques, they are considered equivalent to cash. What will be the effect if a court rules that money orders are not bills of exchange?

This unique transferability of negotiable instruments also makes their use particularly attractive when used with secured transactions. When a negotiable instrument such as a promissory note or cheque is transferred (negotiated) to some innocent third party, the latter can enforce that instrument despite any difficulties that arise under the original transaction (short of forgery or alteration of the instrument). When a benefit under a contract is assigned, the assignee can be in no better position than the person assigning that right. Thus any defence that the original contracting party has against the person assigning those contractual rights can also be used against the assignee. On the other hand, when a negotiable instrument is signed and passes into the hands of an innocent third party— called a **holder in due course**—the signee almost certainly will be required to honour it.

To qualify as a holder in due course, the person receiving the negotiable instrument (whether it is a cheque or a promissory note) must be innocent in that she must have had no knowledge of the problems with the original transaction. There must also be no indication of alteration or irregularity on the instrument itself. Consideration must have been given for the instrument by someone during the process, and she must have otherwise received the instrument in good faith. For the instrument to be negotiable, it must meet several requirements, including that it be an unconditional promise to pay a specific amount at some future date or on demand.

> Stop payment order may not protect drawer

> Holder in due course can enforce negotiable instrument independent of problems

REDUCING RISK 14.7

People often write cheques, or sign promissory notes, as simply one aspect of the transactions in which they are involved. If they think about a deal going sour at all, they assume that they can either stop payment on the cheque they wrote, or simply not pay the promissory note they signed. But negotiable instruments are much more dangerous than simple contractual obligations. If they are negotiated to a third party (as they are designed to be), and that third party qualifies as a holder in due course, the instruments can be enforced despite any problems with the original transaction. It is wise, therefore, to understand that, when you write a cheque, or sign a promissory note, you could very likely be called on to pay, independent of the transaction for which the cheque or promissory note was given. Even the bank of the payee where the cheque is deposited can be a holder in due course and force you to pay, despite any stop-payment order you may have given.

45. [2005] O.J. No. 2241 (C.A.).

Endorser can be liable for payment

Another important feature of negotiable instruments involves the need for free transferability. As the instruments transfer from holder to holder, others not party to the original instrument will be required to sign or endorse the back of the instrument. There are several different forms of endorsement, but the usual purpose of an endorsement is for the endorser to add its credit to the instrument. This means that if the instrument is not honoured when it is presented for collection, the holder can then turn to the endorser for payment, provided that the holder gave proper notice of dishonour to that endorser immediately after payment was refused.

Promissory notes often part of loan transaction

In most credit transactions, debtors are required to sign *promissory notes* as part of the process. This may seem redundant, given the commitment to pay in the primary contract, but remember that promissory notes provide a great deal of flexibility, making them much more attractive to third parties to whom the creditor may wish to assign the proceeds of the transaction. Merchants supplying goods or services on credit will often assign the debt to a finance company. With the promissory note, the finance company becomes a holder in due course, able to enforce the promissory note independent of any problems that might arise from the original transaction, or with the product sold.

Advantages reduced in consumer transactions

Pursuant to the *Bills of Exchange Act,*[46] any negotiable instrument used to advance credit in a consumer transaction must be marked "Consumer Purchase." This is notice to any third party that the instrument does not convey the usual rights, and that a holder in due course would in fact be subject to the same defences that the drawer would have against the original payee. Thus, most of the advantages of being a holder in due course are lost. This applies only to consumer transactions, however, and when negotiable instruments are used in business transactions, the advantages of being a holder in due course still exist.

SUMMARY

Methods of securing debt—personal property

- Real and personal property may be used as security, giving creditor some assurance that she will be paid even when other creditors are not
- In a conditional sale, the debtor has possession of the goods, while the seller retains title until final payment is made
- In a chattel mortgage, the debtor has possession of the goods but gives title to the creditor until final payment is made
- Assignment of book accounts gives creditor right to intercept payments upon default

Personal Property Security Act

- *PPSA* allows both tangible and intangible forms of personal property to be used as security
- The security must first attach to the collateral, but priority is established through perfection, either by registration or by taking possession of the collateral
- Priority is usually determined by date of registration, but PMSIs and sales in normal course of business are exceptions

---

[46.] R.S.C. 1985, c. B-4, Part V.

- In the event of default, the creditor can take possession of the goods and sell them. Creditor can usually sue for deficiency, but sometimes must make election to take possession or sue
- Debtor has the right to be notified of sale and to redeem the property

Guarantees

- A guarantee is a contingent liability in which someone agrees to be responsible when a debtor fails to pay; an indemnity involves co-responsibility for the debt
- Creditor must protect interests of guarantor, but this protection can be limited by the terms of the guarantee
- If a guarantor is required to pay the creditor, he steps into the shoes of the creditor and can seek repayment from the debtor
- The guarantor usually has the same defences as the debtor

Other forms of security

- *Bank Act* security enables growing crops and goods being manufactured to be used as security

Related laws

- Bulk sales acts protect unsecured creditors from sale of all assets of business
- Fraudulent transfers and preferences are void

Bankruptcy—introduction

- Two main objectives of bankruptcy legislation are to protect creditors and to enable rehabilitation of the bankrupt

The process of bankruptcy

- Bankruptcy can take place voluntarily through assignment, or involuntarily through a bankruptcy order
- Involves the transfer of the debtor's non-exempt assets to a Trustee in Bankruptcy, who sells the assets and distributes the proceeds to the creditors

Alternatives to bankruptcy

- Debtors should try to avoid bankruptcy through informal negotiations
- Division I proposal is used to protect commercial debtors and individuals with significant debts from action by creditors, until the proposal is accepted or rejected
- Division II proposal is used to protect consumers with debts less than $75 000
- The Orderly Payment of Debts program gives individuals protection so they can avoid bankruptcy, if they pay off their debts within three years
- Large corporations can ask courts for protection from creditors under the *Companies' Creditors Arrangements Act*

Priority among creditors in bankruptcy

- Creditors must file proof of claim with Trustee
- Assets go first to secured creditors, then to preferred creditors, and then to unsecured creditors
- Suppliers of goods can reclaim them if make demand within time limits

Bankruptcy offences

- Fraudulent transfers and preferences may be reversed by Trustee
- Bankrupt has many duties; if she fails to fulfill them or commits another bankruptcy offence, she can be fined and/or imprisoned

- Once process is complete, bankrupt can apply for discharge; discharge is automatic for first-time bankrupt unless an objection is made
- Discharge may be granted unconditionally, subject to conditions, or denied

After discharge from bankruptcy

- Absolute discharge relieves responsibility for most prior debts
- A corporation will not survive bankruptcy, but it can make a *BIA* Division II proposal, or a *CCAA* arrangement
- Receivership involves a receiver taking possession of the secured assets

Negotiable instruments

- Negotiable instruments are cheques, bills of exchange, and promissory notes
- They are freely transferable without notice to the maker/drawer
- Holders in due course may be in a better position to enforce the negotiable instrument than the original parties
- An endorser is liable on default by the original drawer/maker only if properly notified of default

---

QUESTIONS

1. Distinguish between the following:

    a. Real property and personal property

    b. Choses in action and chattels

    c. A chattel mortgage and a conditional sale

    d. A chattel mortgage and a mortgage on real estate

2. What kinds of property can be used as collateral under the *PPSA*?

3. What are the advantages of using a personal property security act to govern all transactions involving the use of personal property as security?

4. What significant problem associated with the practice of taking goods as security is alleviated by the registration requirements introduced by legislation? Describe the resulting obligations on all parties.

5. Distinguish among security agreement, attachment, and perfection. Explain the significance of each of them and how each is accomplished.

6. How is the priority of secured parties determined? What are two exceptions to this general approach?

7. What are the rights of a secured party when there is a default by the debtor? What determines the limitations of those rights?

8. What obligations are imposed on a secured creditor who takes possession of goods used as security, after a debtor defaults?

9. Explain the rights of a debtor after she has defaulted and the secured party has taken possession of the collateral.

10. "The debtor is always liable to the creditor for any deficiency after the goods used as security have been sold." True or false? Explain your answer.

11. What is the difference between a guarantee and an indemnity? Why is the distinction important?

12. What duties does the creditor owe the guarantor before and after the guarantee is given?

13. If the debtor defaults, what steps does the creditor have to take before she is entitled to demand payment from the guarantor? If the guarantor pays the creditor, what rights does she have against the debtor?

14. What is the main advantage of the provisions of the *Bank Act* that allow the banks to take security for the loans they grant? Why may these provisions cause confusion?

15. Define the objectives of bankruptcy legislation.

16. Distinguish between bankruptcy and insolvency.

17. Distinguish between an assignment in bankruptcy and a bankruptcy order. Explain the process involved in each case.

18. Explain the role of the Trustee in the bankruptcy process.

19. Discuss the informal options that are available to debtors who are experiencing financial difficulties.

20. Distinguish between Division I and Division II proposals. Explain the advantages of making a proposal.

21. "A consolidation order under the Orderly Payment of Debts program requires the debtor to pay her debts in full." True or false? Explain your answer.

22. What legislation is used by large corporations to obtain bankruptcy protection? What is the main advantage of using this legislation?

23. Who files a proof of claim? What is its purpose? Who evaluates the validity of a filed proof of claim?

24. Describe the order of distribution of the assets, and the proceeds from the sale of assets of the bankrupt. How does a "super priority" affect the order of distribution?

25. How are fraudulent transfers and fraudulent preferences dealt with by the *BIA*?

26. What are the duties of a debtor in the bankruptcy process?

27. Explain what is meant by a bankruptcy offence and the possible consequences of committing one.

28. What restrictions are bankrupts subject to?

29. "An application for discharge by a first-time bankrupt will automatically be granted." True or false? Explain your answer.

30. What factors will a court consider when determining what conditions, if any, to place on a discharge from bankruptcy?

31. What changes for a bankrupt after an absolute discharge?

32. Why is it unlikely that there will not be a discharge after the bankruptcy of a corporation?

33. What can a corporation in financial difficulty do to avoid bankruptcy?

34. When could a creditor who has appointed a receiver to take possession of a debtor's assets face liability for making the appointment?

35. Distinguish among a cheque, a bill of exchange, and a promissory note.

36. Explain how the position of a holder in due course compares to the position of an assignee of contractual rights.

37. Explain the nature of an endorsement and its significance on a negotiable instrument.

Chapter 15

Agency and Partnership

INTRODUCTION

The subject of agency is a vital component in any discussion of business law. The legal consequences that stem from an agency relationship are of utmost concern to businesspeople because at least one of the parties in most commercial transactions is functioning as an agent. Agency law is the basis of the law of partnership, and an understanding of it is essential for coming to terms with corporate law.

Agent represents and acts for principal

An agent's function is to represent and act on behalf of a principal in dealings with third parties. Although by far the most common example of agents representing principals is in the creation of contracts, agents also find themselves involved in other types of legal relationships. Real estate agents do not usually have the authority to enter into contracts on behalf of vendors, but they function as agents nonetheless because they participate in the negotiations and act as go-betweens. Other professionals, such as lawyers and accountants, may make representations or act on behalf of their clients or principals. The term **agency** refers to the service an agent performs on behalf of the principal. This service may be performed as an employee, as an independent agent, or gratuitously. When an agent is acting independently, the business performing the service is often called an agency, such as a travel agency, employment agency, or real estate agency.

Agency refers to service performed by an agent

CASE SUMMARY 15.1

Vicariously Liable for Fraud: *Steinman v. Snarey*[1]

Mr. Snarey was a "well-respected agent" working for the Mutual Life Assurance Company of Canada when he was approached by a customer who wanted to take advantage of one of the investment opportunities offered by the company. Snarey persuaded the customer to part with $16 000 by way of a cheque made out to the agent. The customer was told that his money was going into an "investment vehicle offered to the public by Mutual Life." Actually, the company did not offer this kind of investment plan and never had. This was simply a scheme used by Snarey to cheat a trusting customer out of a considerable amount of money. When the customer discovered the fraud, he turned to the Mutual Life Assurance Company for compensation. In the resulting action, it was determined that Snarey had devised and conducted a fraudulent scheme. Because he was an agent of Mutual Life with the actual authority to enter into this general type of transaction with the company's customer, the company was vicariously liable for his conduct and had to pay compensation to the client.

DISCUSSION QUESTIONS

Evidently, it is critical to retain agents that are well trained, ethical, and trustworthy. Does it place too great a burden on a principal to hold it liable for an agent's fraud that it had nothing to do with? Should such vicarious liability be limited to situations where the agent is an employee as well? Should some degree of wrongdoing, such as negligence on the part of the principal, be required before imposing vicarious liability?

What follows focuses on the law of agency generally, and in most cases no distinction will be made between people functioning as agents as part of an employment contract and those acting independently. Note that where employees also act as agents of the employer, their duties and obligations as agents go far beyond the employment relationship and must be understood as a separate function or set of obligations.

THE AGENCY RELATIONSHIP

The agency relationship can be created by an express or implied contract, by estoppel, by ratification, or gratuitously, the key element being the granting of **authority**.

Formation by Contract

Agency relationship usually created through contract

Usually, an agency relationship is created through a contract, called an **agency agreement**, between the agent and the principal; thus, general contract rules apply. This should not be confused with the contracts agents enter into on behalf of their principals. The agency contract can cover such things as the authority of the agent, the duties to be performed, and the nature of payment to be received (Figure 15.1). It may be imbedded in a contract of employment or the contract

---

1. [1987] O.J. No. 2400 (Dist. Ct.); aff'd [1988] O.J. No. 2917 (H.C.J.).

Figure 15.1 The Agency Agreement

Principal: Grants actual and implied authority

Agency Agreement

Agent: Agrees to act on behalf of principal

may create a more independent relationship between principal and agent. Generally, there are no additional formal requirements for the creation of such a contract. Thus, although it is a wise practice to put the agency agreement in writing, doing so is not necessary except in those jurisdictions where required by the *Statute of Frauds* or other statute. Under the *Bills of Exchange Act,*[2] where the agent is to sign cheques or other negotiable instruments, the granting of the agent's authority must also be in writing. Although there may be other advantages in doing so, it is not necessary that the agency agreement be under seal, unless the agent will be sealing documents on behalf of the principal as part of his or her agency function. An agency agreement in writing and under seal is called a **power of attorney**. Most provinces have powers of attorney acts.[3]

All the elements of a contract, such as consensus, consideration, legality, intention to be bound, and capacity on the part of both parties, must be present for an agency agreement to be binding. The lack of any one of these elements may void the agency contract, but that will not affect the binding nature of any agreement the agent enters into on behalf of the principal. Thus, if Clarke is underage and acts as Drinkwater's agent in the sale of Drinkwater's car to Skoye, the agency contract between Clarke and Drinkwater may be voidable because of the incapacity of Clarke. But the contract between Drinkwater and Skoye for the purchase of the car is still binding. Only when agents are so young, drunk, insane, or otherwise incapacitated that they do not understand what they are doing does the contract between the principal and third party become doubtful on the basis of incapacity or lack of consensus.

> Basic rules of contract apply to agency contracts

The actions of an agent may be binding on the principal even when the agent is acting gratuitously. Only consent is necessary, which explains why, in the above example, the contract for the purchase of the car is binding between Drinkwater and Skoye despite the infancy of the agent, Clarke. Still, most agency relationships are based on contract, either expressly entered into by the parties or implied from their conduct. Often, these are simply employment contracts.

> Consent only essential requirement of agency

AUTHORITY OF AGENTS

Most disputes that arise in agency relate to the extent of the authority of the agent in dealing with third parties. An agent's authority can be derived from the principal in several ways.

---

[2] R.S.C. 1985, c. B-4.

[3] For example, the *Powers of Attorney Act*, R.S.O. 1990, c. P.20.

Actual Authority

The authority specifically given by the principal to the agent and usually set out in the agency agreement is called the agent's **actual authority**. This actual authority may be **expressly** stated by the principal or **implied** from the circumstances, such as from the position the agent has been given. In Case Summary 15.1, the contract entered into by Mr. Snarey was just the kind of contract he was authorized to conclude with his clients. Because of this actual authority, the principal was liable for his fraud. A person who is hired as a purchasing agent has the authority to carry out the customary and traditional responsibilities of purchasing agents as well as the duties necessarily incidental to that function. Of course, if the principal has specifically stated that the agent does not have certain powers, no such authority is implied. Still, even where actual (express or implied) authority is absent, there may be apparent authority.

Any written agency agreement should carefully set out the authority of the agent, eliminating, as far as possible, the need for any implied authority. An agent who exceeds this actual authority may be liable to the principal for any injury caused by his conduct. But no matter how much care is used in drafting an agent's actual authority, the principal may still be bound by the agent's conduct that falls within his apparent authority.

Apparent Authority—Authority Created by Estoppel

When a principal does something by conduct or words to lead a third party to believe that an agent has authority, the principal is bound by the agent's actions, regardless of whether there is or is not actual authority. Even when the principal has specifically prohibited the agent from doing what he did, the principal will be bound because of the agent's **apparent authority**. This is an application of the principle of estoppel. **Estoppel** is an equitable remedy that stops a party from trying to establish a position or deny something that, if allowed, would create an injustice. It would not be fair if a principal could say to a third party, "George has authority to act for me," and then later to be able to deny it and escape liability for George's actions. In these circumstances estoppel applies. If the principal has held out the agent to have authority even if no such authority has been granted, the principal is bound. If a third party has relied on this representation, the principal cannot then claim that the agent had no authority.

CASE SUMMARY 15.2

Apparent Authority of a Sibling: *Willoughby Residential Development Corp. v. Bradley*[4]

The parents of the brother and sister defendants in this action bought property in 1975, which they owned jointly with their daughter, Dawne. When property is owned jointly, the whole property passes to the survivor. After both parents died, the daughter was registered as the sole owner of the property. But her brother had the same first name as the father and claimed that he was the one who had purchased the property in 1975 with his mother. This claim was supported by evidence of contributions he had made toward the

---

[4] [2002] B.C.J. No. 1103 (C.A.).

purchase price. Allegedly, the brother had not raised the issue of ownership earlier as he had been convicted of importing narcotics and did not want his name on the title. Instead he allowed his sister to reside in the house and to become registered as the sole owner of it. But when she tried to sell the house in 1996, he brought an application to stop the sale.

This action was brought by the purchaser who had bought the property in good faith from the sister. By the time of trial the property had increased considerably in value, but the purchaser was granted an order of specific performance forcing sale of the property at the original price. The Court held that as the registered owner, the sister had a right to sell the property. Philip Bradley had allowed his sister to act as the manager of the property and to be the registered owner, and as such she had apparent authority to contract on his behalf as his agent. Even if he was an actual owner of the property, he was bound by the contract entered into by his agent sister.

This case illustrates the nature of apparent authority and the danger of allowing someone to be held out as your representative when they are not. Bradley was estopped from denying that his sister had the authority to act as his agent. It also introduces some important concepts of real property law.

DISCUSSION QUESTIONS

Should liability for an agent's actions be limited to those situations where the agent has been given actual authority? Does the doctrine of apparent authority impose too great a burden on a principal?

The most important example of the application of estoppel is in the field of agency. It is important not to confuse this principle of estoppel with equitable or promissory estoppel as described in Chapter 6. **Equitable estoppel** involves a promise or commitment to do something in the future. Here, we are dealing not with a promise but with a claim or a statement of fact made by the principal.

Although the principal may look to the agent for compensation, so long as that agent has acted within his apparent authority, the principal is still bound in contract with the third party. If Pedersen employed Mohammed as sales manager of his used car dealership, it would be reasonable for customers to assume that Mohammed had the authority of a normal manager to sell cars and to take trade-ins. If after receiving instructions from Pedersen not to accept trades over $2000 without his express approval, Mohammed were to give Kim a $5000 trade-in for a 1995 Mercedes, Pedersen would still be bound by the deal. Pedersen put Mohammed in that position and led Kim to believe that Mohammed had the ordinary authority and power of a sales manager. The agent acted within his apparent authority, and the contract was binding on the principal. If, however, the agent had sold Kim the entire car lot, this would be beyond both his actual and apparent authority and would not be binding on Pedersen.

Agent acting on apparent authority will bind principal

A principal can also be bound by the actions of an agent that would normally be beyond the agent's authority if the principal has sanctioned similar actions in the past. Kim's chauffeur, Green, would not normally be expected to have the authority to purchase automobiles on behalf of his principal. But if he had done so several times in the past and Kim honoured the deals, the dealer, Pederson, would be entitled to assume that the next purchase was authorized as well and Green had apparent authority. Even if Kim specifically told Green not to buy any

Previous acceptance of agent's actions

Actions of principal create apparent authority

more cars, and Green in violation of those instructions purchased another car from Pederson, the contract would be binding on Kim because of apparent authority. The existence of this apparent authority is based on the statements and conduct of the principal, not the agent. When the misleading indication of authority comes from the agent rather than the principal, and the action is otherwise unauthorized, the third party will have no claim against the principal.

Reasonable person test used to determine existence of authority

The **reasonable person test** has a significant role to play in determining the existence of apparent authority. The usual authority associated with the position in which an agent has been placed is based on this test. The reasonable person test is also used to determine whether the third party should have been misled into believing that the agent had authority by the statements and conduct of the principal.

CASE SUMMARY 15.3

When Is It Reasonable to Conclude Authority Exists?
Gooderham v. Bank of Nova Scotia;[5] *LeRuyet v. Stenner*[6]

The first case demonstrates how apparent authority can result in a principal's being bound by the actions of its agent. Mrs. Gooderham and her husband (now deceased) went to the Bank of Nova Scotia for a $55 000 mortgage. The Bank's representative, Braun, provided them with an application for mortgage life insurance supplied by the insurer Canada Life. They properly filled in the form, but the Bank failed to forward it to Canada Life. Had the Bank done so, Canada Life would have denied coverage because of Mr. Gooderham's poor health. The Bank negligently conveyed premium information to the Gooderhams and collected premiums for several months. Mr. Gooderham died and Canada Life denied coverage, claiming the Bank was not its agent and they were not bound by the Bank's actions.

The Court awarded judgment to the Gooderhams, concluding that Braun had apparent authority to represent Canada Life. The Bank had the application forms supplied by Canada Life and supplied them to the Gooderhams. The Bank generally, on behalf of Canada Life, sought out "prospective policy holders," assisted in completing the application for insurance, possessed and supplied rate information, accepted money for premiums, forwarded the money and forms to Canada Life, and was paid for this service by Canada Life. Given these factors it was reasonable for the Gooderhams to assume that the Bank had authority to represent the insurer.

Compare the first case with *LeRuyet v. Stenner*, where the Court found that there was no apparent authority and no agency relationship. LeRuyet approached Stenner seeking assistance with investments. In accordance with Stenner's recommendations, LeRuyet gave Stenner $130 000 to purchase a Great West annuity. Stenner defrauded LeRuyet, showing him false documents and failing to actually purchase the annuity. Stenner was convicted and LeRuyet turned to Great Life to recover his loss, claiming they were vicariously liable for Stenner's fraud. The Court found that although there was a Great Life logo on some of the documents Stenner had been shown, there was no other connection between the two. Stenner did not have Great West business cards, did not work out of

---

5. [2000] O.J. No. 890 (Sup. Ct. J.).

6. [2001] B.C.J. No. 1669 (S.C.).

Great West's premises, nor did he display any connection to Great West. There being no representations made by Great West that would lead a reasonable person to assume that Stenner acted as an agent of Great West, the Court dismissed the claim of apparent authority.

DISCUSSION QUESTIONS

Do you think that Stenner's claim that he was acting for Great Life should have been enough to impose liability on it?

As illustrated by Case Summary 15.3, when a principal puts an agent in a position so that it appears to others that they have authority to make certain commitments, they have that authority, even though it has not actually been given. This is the very nature of apparent authority. It shows how important it is, for public and private institutions alike, to carefully define the authority of those acting for them and then take steps to ensure that their agents act within those boundaries.

To determine whether a principal is bound in contract with a third party by the actions of an agent, a person must first ask, "Was the agent acting within the actual authority given by the principal?" If the answer is yes, then there is a contract, provided all the other elements are present. If the answer is no, then the question to ask is "Did the principal do anything to lead the third party to believe that the agent had the authority to act?" In other words, was the agent acting with apparent authority? If the answer is yes and the third party relied on that apparent authority, there is a contract between the principal and the third party. It is only when the answer to both these questions is no that there is no contract, and the third party must look to the agent for redress.

> Was the action of the agent authorized by principal?

Most people find it difficult to understand the difference between implied and apparent authority, and in most cases the distinction is not important. But to clarify, when a principal has specifically stated that the agent does not have authority, no authority can be implied. In spite of such a declaration, however, there may still be apparent authority because of the principal's comments or conduct in relation to the third party. The principal has then led the third party to believe that the agent has authority; now, because of the principle of estoppel, the principal cannot deny that fact.

Ratification

A principal can still ratify a contract even if the agent has acted beyond both actual and apparent authority. The first time Kim's chauffeur bought a car on Kim's behalf, there would likely have been no apparent authority, since this is not normally a chauffeur's job. If Kim liked the car, however, he could ratify the contract and the deal would be binding on the dealer. The effect of such ratification is to give the agent authority to act on behalf of the principal retroactive to the time of the sale. The result can seem unfair because the principal is not bound when an agent goes beyond the authority given, but if the principal chooses to ratify, the third party is bound and can do nothing to change that.

> If principal ratifies unauthorized contract, it is binding

Third party can set time for ratification

Agent must have been acting for a specific principal

Principal must be capable of entering into contract
• **when it is entered into**

• **when it is ratified**

Ratification can take place inadvertently

In fact, the power of the principal to ratify must meet the following qualifications:

1. The third party has the right to set a reasonable time limit within which the ratification must take place. In the case of a chauffeur buying a car without authority, the dealer cannot simply repudiate the contract but could give the principal a short time to ratify by saying, for example, "You have until noon tomorrow to decide." In the United States, once the third party repudiates, it is too late for the principal to ratify. This may indicate the future direction in Canada, but the courts have not adopted this approach as of yet.

2. The agent must have been acting for the specific principal who is now trying to ratify. A person cannot enter into a contract with a third party while purporting to be an agent and then search for a principal to ratify. The customer would be free to repudiate the purchase, since the would-be agent did not have a particular principal in mind when entering into the contract. There is no one to ratify the agreement.

3. The principal has to be fully capable of entering into the contract at the time the agent was claiming to act on his or her behalf. A principal who did not have the capacity to enter into the original deal because of drunkenness or insanity does not have the power to ratify upon becoming sober or sane. This requirement of capacity can be a problem where pre-incorporation contracts are involved. Often, promoters who are planning incorporation will enter into contracts, such as the purchase of property on behalf of the proposed corporation, assuming that once the corporation is formed it will ratify the agreements. But because there is no corporation at the time the contract is entered into, there can be no ratification, leaving the promoter personally liable for any losses suffered by the third party. Legislation in some jurisdictions has modified this principle to allow a corporation to ratify such pre-incorporation contracts.[7]

4. The parties must still be able to perform the object of the contract at the time of the ratification. For example, if an agent enters into a contract on behalf of a principal to insure a building against fire, the principal cannot ratify the agreement after a fire. There is no building to insure when ratification is attempted, so there can be no contract. Furthermore, the contract the agent enters into must not make any reference to the need for ratification. If the contract includes such terms as "subject to principal's approval" or "subject to ratification," it becomes merely an agreement to enter into an agreement. The contractual requirement of consensus is not satisfied, and there is no contract.

Ratification can work against the principal in other ways. The principal can inadvertently ratify by knowingly accepting some sort of benefit under the agreement. If Kim's chauffeur bought a new Rolls-Royce on Kim's behalf without the actual or apparent authority to do so, Kim would normally not be bound by such a contract. However, if Kim were to use that car in some way, such as driving it to work before returning it to the dealer, Kim would have accepted some benefit under the contract and thus ratified it by his conduct. Kim would be bound to go through with the purchase of the automobile, provided that at the time he received the benefit, Kim knew that the purchase was made on his behalf.

---

7. For example, the Canada *Business Corporations Act*, R.S.C. 1985, c. C-44, s. 14.

CASE SUMMARY 15.4

Delay in Repudiating Unauthorized Act Treated as Ratification: *Community Savings Credit Union v. United Association of Journeymen and Apprentices of the Plumbing and Pipefitting Industry of the United States and Canada, Local 324*[8]

A credit union needed additional supporting security to finance a building project and approached several members for assistance. Mr. Crossett, the business manager of the defendant union local, acted without authority when he pledged, in the form of an indemnity, $80 000 of the local's funds to that purpose. Later he informed the union's governing board that he had made the pledge on the behalf of the local, but they did nothing about it and did not inform the credit union that Crossett's action was not authorized. Still later when the project ran into difficulty, Crossett acting as business manager of the local, informed the credit union that the union had disavowed further financial responsibility for financing the project. Subsequently, when the project failed, the credit union demanded payment from the union under the indemnity agreement. But the union local took the position that the pledge (indemnity agreement) was invalid as it was entered into without authority. The Court of Appeal found that although the business manager acted without actual authority, the failure of the Board to notify the credit union of that fact once they had knowledge of the unauthorized acts was sufficient to constitute ratification. The pledge was thus enforceable against the union.

DISCUSSION QUESTIONS

When should a failure to act be taken as ratification? This case demonstrates that one's silence may be regarded as acquiescence. The union's Board had opportunities to notify the credit union as to its position regarding the indemnity once it learned of the transaction but it chose not to do so. This was sufficient to constitute ratification.

Agency by Necessity

Without authority (apparent or actual) or ratification, the principal cannot be bound. In the past, when communications were less reliable, authority was sometimes implied on the basis of **agency by necessity**. For example, an agent might have to sell deteriorating goods to preserve some value for the principal. If the cargo of a ship might get wet, the shipper may be required to have it sold en route, often without getting authorization from the principal. In these circumstances, authority arises on the basis of necessity. Today, with instantaneous forms of communication, it will be rare indeed for an agency by necessity to arise.

Agency by necessity rarely used today

But where it does, there must be some duty or responsibility placed on the agent to care for those goods. Merely finding another person's property in danger does not, in and of itself, create an agency-by-necessity relationship.

---

8. [2002] B.C.J. No. 654 (C.A.).

EXCEPTION IN FAMILY RELATIONSHIPS

It is common for one spouse to have the actual or even apparent authority to act on behalf of the other when dealing with merchants, especially for the purchase of necessities and other household goods. When the marriage breaks down, those merchants who, because of past dealings, have been led to believe a person has authority to act for a spouse may rely on that apparent authority. In the absence of notice to the contrary, the authority continues, even when the spouse has been specifically prohibited from making such purchases.

In some circumstances, authority can be implied by operation of law against the will of the other party. A wife who is deserted by her husband is presumed to have the authority to bind him to contracts with third parties for the purchase of necessities. But this must be viewed in the light of modern family law legislation. In Ontario, spouses and same-sex partners can be held liable for the purchases of necessities made by the other partner, so long as the purchases were made during cohabitation and the spouse or same-sex partner has not notified the third party that this authority has been withdrawn.[9] In some jurisdictions, this principle has been abolished altogether.[10] For example, in Alberta, a wife's common law right to pledge her husband's credit for necessaries after separation was recently abolished. So too was the common law presumption of implied agency of a wife to render her husband liable for necessaries supplied by a third party.[11]

REDUCING RISK 15.1

A businessperson who deals through an agent runs a risk of that agent's entering into contracts that are not authorized. Whether this is done by mistake or intentionally, the effect on the businessperson can be significant. To avoid the problem, the principal should make the limits of that authority absolutely clear to the agent. Those limitations should be stip-ulated in a written agency agreement. The principal should also, where practical, make the limits of the agent's authority clear to the customers or third parties with whom that agent will deal. Customers should also be notified immediately upon the termination of that agent's authority, otherwise it will continue because of the principle of apparent authority.

THE RIGHTS AND RESPONSIBILITIES OF THE PARTIES

The Agent's Duties

THE CONTRACT

When an agency agreement has been created by contract, the agent has an obligation to act within the actual authority given in that agreement. An agent violating the contract but exercising apparent authority can be sued for breach and will have to compensate the principal for any losses suffered. Failure on the part of the agent to fulfill any other obligation set out in the agreement will also constitute an actionable breach of contract unless the specified act is illegal or against public policy.

---

9. *Family Law Act*, R.S.O. 1990, c. F.-3, s. 45.

10. See Saskatchewan's *Equality of Status of Married Persons Act*, S.S. 1984–85–86, c. E-10.3, s. 5.

11. *Family Law Act*, S.A. 2003 c.F-4.5, ss. 105, 106.

An agent owes a **duty of care** to the principal. The agent must not only have the skills and expertise claimed but also must exercise that skill in a reasonable manner. For example, if Khan hires Gamboa to purchase property on which to build an apartment building, Gamboa must not only stay within the authority given but also must exercise the degree of care and skill one would expect from a person claiming to be qualified to do that type of job. If Gamboa buys a property for Khan and it turns out to be zoned for single-family dwellings, such a mistake would be below the standard of reasonable performance one would expect from someone in this type of business, and Gamboa would be liable to compensate Khan for any loss.

Agent owes duty of reasonable care

Agents often have considerable discretion in carrying out agency responsibilities as long as they act to the benefit of the principal. However, an agent cannot go against the specific instructions received, even if it might be in the principal's best interests to do so. If a stockbroker is instructed to sell shares when they reach a specific price, the broker must do so, even though waiting would bring the principal a better price.

Agent must perform as required by principal

Agents also have a duty to act in the best interests of their principals.

CASE SUMMARY 15.5

Failure to Follow Instructions Can Be Costly: *Volkers et al. v. Midland Doherty Ltd.*[12]

Mr. Volkers, a knowledgeable investor, was assured by the representatives of Midland that he could give instructions to Mr. Hill, or any other trader, and they would be followed. On 28 February, Hill, following instruction from Volkers, purchased on his behalf a substantial number of shares in Breakwater Resources Ltd. Later that day, Volkers phoned and, since Hill had left for the day, gave instructions to Mr. Gurney to purchase additional shares in that company first thing the next morning.

Gurney arrived at 7:00 a.m. but, because of some doubts about the wisdom of the trade, delayed making the purchase until Hill arrived about two hours later. Unfortunately, trading in Breakwater shares had been stopped before Hill's arrival, and when it came back on the market, it had doubled in price. Volkers suffered substantial loss and sued.

It was argued that Gurney had a duty to act in the best interests of his client, and since this was what he was doing, there should be no liability. But the Appeal Court held Gurney had been given specific instructions to purchase the Breakwater shares first thing in the morning, and his duty was to do so, or to tell Volkers that he did not, so that Volkers could make other arrangements. Although the agent was obligated to do what he thought was best for the client, the agent bore an even greater obligation to keep Volkers informed. Volkers was the one to make the decision, not Gurney.

DISCUSSION QUESTIONS

This case illustrates that it is an important aspect of the agent's duty to the principal to follow instructions. Do you think this obligation should apply where it is clear the agent was acting in what he thought was the best interests of the principal?

[12.] [1985] B.C.J. No. 2163 (C.A.); leave to appeal to S.C.C. refused, [1985] S.C.C.A. No. 121.

DELEGATION

Generally, the agent has an obligation to perform the agency agreement personally. An agent is not permitted to delegate responsibility to another party unless there is consent to such delegation, either express or implied by the customs and traditions of the industry. Even then the primary agent has the responsibility to see that the terms of the agency agreement are fulfilled. The authority of an agent is commonly delegated to sub-agents, when that agent is a corporation or large business organization, such as a law firm, bank, real estate agency, or trust company.

Agent cannot delegate responsibility

ACCOUNTING

The agent must turn over any monies earned pursuant to the agency function to the principal. If the agent acquires property, goods, or money on behalf of the principal, there is no entitlement to retain any of it other than the authorized commission. Even when the agent has some claim against the funds, he cannot keep them. If the third party owes money to the agent and pays money to the agent intended for the principal, the agent cannot intercept those funds on his own behalf but must pay over any money collected to the principal. To facilitate this process, the agent also has an obligation to keep accurate records of all agency transactions.

Agent must turn money over to principal

Agent must account for funds

FIDUCIARY DUTY

One may be sympathetic with the position of Mrs. Forbes in Case Summary 15.6 below. She paid over part of her commission to Mr. Halbauer only to preserve the deal. But who was she acting for? If she did not reduce her commission, the property may have been sold by another real estate agent to somebody else, and she would have received nothing. Thus, it is clear that she was acting in her own self-interest above the interest of the principal. This case strongly illustrates the nature of fiduciary duty: a person owing that duty must submerge personal interests in favour of the interests of the principal he or she represents.

CASE SUMMARY 15.6

Conflicting Interests: *Ocean City Realty Ltd. v. A & M Holdings Ltd.*[13]

Mrs. Forbes was a licensed real estate salesperson working for Ocean City Realty Ltd. She was approached by Mr. Halbauer to find a commercial building in downtown Victoria. After some investigation, Forbes approached the owners of a building to determine whether it might be for sale. The owner of the property, A & M Holdings Ltd., entered into an arrangement with her, whereby they agreed to pay a commission of 1.75 percent if she acted as their agent in selling the building. After some negotiations the sale was concluded for $5.2 million, but unknown to the seller, Forbes had agreed to pay back half her commission to the purchaser, Halbauer. When A & M discovered the secret deal between Forbes and Halbauer, they refused to pay any commission.

---

[13] [1987] B.C.J. No. 593 (C.A.).

Forbes had a fiduciary obligation to act in the best interests of her principal, A & M, but she argued that A & M got what it expected and her sacrifice only ensured that the deal went through. That did not hurt A & M but helped it. The Court held, however, that one of the key elements in the duty of a fiduciary is to disclose all pertinent information with respect to the transaction that would be considered important by the principal. In this case, the knowledge that she was paying part of her commission back to Halbauer was important to A & M, and it may have determined whether it would go through with the deal or not. In effect, A & M thought that Halbauer was paying one price, when, in fact, he was paying less for the property. A & M was entitled to this information, and it may have influenced its decision. Therefore, the fiduciary obligation of the agent had been breached, and the agent was entitled to no commission at all.

DISCUSSION QUESTIONS

Is this too harsh an application of fiduciary duty? Should the agent be penalized where the agent was just helping to make the deal go through? On the other hand, is a principal not entitled to have all the relevant information brought to its attention? When an agent profits from a breach of the duty to disclose, the Court's reaction is stern and uncompromising.

Agents owe their principal a positive duty of **full disclosure**. The agent cannot arbitrarily decide what would likely influence the conduct of the principal and what would not. For example, in the *Krasniuk* case,[14] the real estate agent assumed, incorrectly, that she was obligated to forward only written offers to the vendor. She unilaterally turned down the verbal offers for $135 000 and $137 500. Later, when the same purchasers submitted a written offer for $130 000, the vendor, unaware of the earlier offers, accepted it. The agent had breached its fiduciary duty by failing to disclose this information, so no commission was payable. Had the vendors been aware of the earlier offers, they may have accepted them or at least countered the subsequent written offer. Similarly, in the *Skinner* case,[15] the realtors' failure to fully disclose all offers that were made resulted in the Court declining its commission. A listing agent has a duty to ensure that all serious offers communicated to him are presented to the vendor for consideration, whether they are verbal offers or written offers.

> **Agent must disclose information**

Because the principal puts trust in the agent, the principal may be vulnerable; accordingly, the law imposes a fiduciary duty obliging the agent to act only in the best interests of the principal. The relationship is often referred to as an *utmost good faith* relationship, in which the agent has an obligation to

- keep in strict confidence any communications that come through the agency function
- act in the best interests of the principal, even if the agent may lose some personal benefit
- not take advantage of any personal opportunity that may come to his or her knowledge through the agency relationship
- disclose to the principal any personal benefit the agent stands to gain. Only with the informed consent of the principal can the agent retain any benefit.

---

14. *Krasniuk v. Gabbs* [2002] M.J. No. 13 (Q.B.).

15. *D.E.M. Corp. (c.o.b. ReMax Charlottetown Realty) v. Skinner*, [2004] P.E.I.J. No. 90 (S.C. T.D.).

Agent cannot act for both principal and third party without consent of both

If there is a failure to disclose, the principal can seek an accounting and have any funds gained by the agent in such a way paid over to the principal.

An agent cannot act for both a principal and a third party at the same time. It would be very difficult for an agent to extract the best possible price from a third party on behalf of a principal when the third party is also paying the agent. The common practice of agents accepting gifts, such as holidays, tickets to sporting events, and liquor, is an example of the same problem. If the principal discovers the agent accepting payment from the third party, the principal is entitled to an accounting and the receipt of all such funds and will likely have just cause to terminate the relationship. Only where full disclosure has been made at the outset and permission given can the agent profit personally in this way.

In real estate transactions, the agent usually acts for the seller. This can cause problems for purchasers, who often do not realize this and expect the agent to protect their interests as well. In some western provinces, this difficulty is largely overcome by requiring the purchasers to have their own agent acting for them and splitting the commission.

Agent must not profit at principal's expense

Another problem sometimes arises where an agent who is hired to purchase goods or property sells to the principal property actually owned by the agent as if it came from some third party. This is a violation of the agent's fiduciary duty; even if that property fully satisfies the principal's requirements, there must be full disclosure.[16] The reverse is also a breach, where the agent buys for himself what he has been hired to sell to others. An example would be where a real estate agent hired to sell a house recognizes it as a good deal and purchases it for himself, perhaps through a partner or a corporation. The agent then has the advantage of a good price, knowing how low the principal will go, and getting the commission as well. This is not acting in the best interests of the principal, and the agent would be required to pay back both profits and commission to the vendor of the property.

Agent must not compete with principal

It also follows that the agent must not operate his own business in competition with the principal, especially if a service is being offered. Nor can the agent also represent another principal selling a similar product without full disclosure. Finally, the agent must not collect any profits or commissions that are hidden from the principal, but must pay over all the benefit resulting from the performance of the agency agreement. Such a breach of fiduciary duty by an agent who is also an employee will likely constitute just cause for dismissal. Note that with senior employees this duty will probably continue after termination of the employment, but for ordinary employees any duty owed ends when they leave.

> **!** **REDUCING RISK 15.2**
>
> When professionals or independent businesses offer their service to others, a relationship of trust is created that leaves a client vulnerable, so a fiduciary duty is owed. The person providing the service must put the interests of the client ahead of his or her own and follow the instructions given. It is sometimes difficult to keep personal interests and the interests of customers and clients separate, but failure to do so is asking for trouble. It is vitally important that professionals or businesspeople in such a position learn the nature of their fiduciary duty and make sure they honour it.

---

16. *G.L. Black Holdings Ltd. v. Peddle* [1998] A.J. No. 1488 (Q.B.), aff'd [1999] A.J. No. 1083 (C.A.).

The Principal's Duties

THE CONTRACT

The principal's primary obligation to the agent is to honour the terms of the contract by which the agent was hired. If the contract is silent as to payment, an obligation to pay a reasonable amount can be implied on the basis of the amount of effort put forth by the agent, as well as the customs and traditions of the industry. If the agreement provides for payment only on completion, there is no implied obligation to pay for part performance. Thus, if an agent is to receive a commission upon the sale of a house, even if the agent puts considerable effort into promoting a sale, there is generally no entitlement to commission if no sale occurs. Unless there is agreement to the contrary, or a different custom in the industry, the agent is normally entitled to compensation for reasonable expenses, such as phone bills and car expenses.

If the agency agreement is vague about the extent of the agent's authority, the courts will usually favour an interpretation that gives the agent the broadest possible power. Thus, if Jones is hired as a sales manager for a manufacturing business and is given authority to enter into all sales related to the business, a court will likely interpret it to include authority to sell large blocks of product but no authority to sell the plant itself. When the power to borrow money is involved, however, the courts take a much narrower approach. Thus, if Klassen were hired as a purchasing agent with "all the authority necessary" to carry out that function and he found it necessary to borrow money to make the purchases, the courts would not imply an authority to borrow without getting additional approval from the principal. It is necessary for an agent to be given specific authority to borrow money on the principal's behalf in order to proceed.

> Principal must honour terms of contract and pay reasonable amount for services

> Principal must reimburse agent's expenses

> Ambiguous authority will be interpreted broadly
> • except when power to borrow money is in question

Undisclosed Principals

In some transactions principals attempt to conceal their identity from the third parties they are dealing with. These are referred to as an undisclosed principal relationship and might be used, for example, when a well-known company is assembling land for a new project. Agents approach property owners in the area to obtain options on their properties. The options are exercised only if a sufficient number of property owners are willing to sell at a reasonable price. The undisclosed principal approach is used to discourage people from holding out for higher prices once they find out who is really buying the property.

In these circumstances the agent will usually declare that they are acting for a principal whose identity will remain confidential. Sometimes, however, the agent will simply sign in such a way as to be consistent with them being principal or agent or will actually sign as if he or she were the principal contracting party. The rights and obligations of the parties are different in each case. When the agent makes it clear they are acting as agent for an undisclosed principal, the agent has no liability to the third party and only the principal can enforce the agreement. If the would-be agent acts as if he were the principal, only he can be sued by the third party and only he can enforce the contract.

> Where agent makes it clear she is acting as agent for undisclosed principal, the third party cannot sue or be sued by the agent

> Where agent acts as principal, only the agent can sue or be sued by the third party

---

CASE SUMMARY 15.7

No Liability under Contract When Agent Makes It Clear He Is Acting as Agent: *Q.N.S. Paper Co. v. Chartwell Shipping Ltd.;*[17] *Logistec Stevedoring Inc. v. Amican Navigation Inc.*[18]

Chartwell provided stevedoring services for Q.N.S., which operated a chartered ship. Although Chartwell never mentioned specifically who it was acting for, Chartwell made it clear at all times that it was acting as an agent on behalf of others in their dealings with Q.N.S. The deal fell through. Q.N.S. sued Chartwell. The Supreme Court of Canada had to decide whether this was an undisclosed principal situation where the agent could be successfully sued. The Court held that because Chartwell had made it clear at all times that it was functioning as an agent, there was no personal liability for that agent on the contract. Chartwell consistently emphasized that its sole responsibility was as an agent. It identified itself as "Managing Operators for the Charterers" or "acting on behalf of principals" or signed "as agent only." Thus the only option open to Q.N.S. was to sue the principal.

In a subsequent case, *Logistec v. Amican*, Amican also claimed it had acted as agent but in this case didn't make it clear. It signed as an agent on only a few occasions, but this was not done consistently and on several occasions it had acted as if it were the principal party. The Federal Court held that to escape liability the agent acting for an undisclosed principal had to make it clear that it was acting as an agent and this it had failed to do. Thus it could not escape liability, and both principal and agent were liable.

SMALL BUSINESS PERSPECTIVE

In several industries, businesses are engaged as agents. If personal liability is to be avoided, it is necessary to make it clear that one is acting in a representative capacity.

Where agent acts ambiguously as to whether principal or agent, third party can also be sued by either

Where agent acts ambiguously as to whether principal or agent, third party can sue either

Apparent authority does not apply where principal undisclosed

Where the agent acted ambiguously so that it is not clear whether he was acting as agent or the principal party, the third party has a choice. He can choose to sue the agent or when the identity of the principal is determined he can end that action and commence an action against the principal instead. Once the choice is made, however, he is bound by it. For example, when the agent signs a purchase order in a way consistent with being an agent for the purchaser or the actual person purchasing the goods, if the contract is breached the third party/seller can sue either the agent or, upon learning the identity, can sue the principal instead. The injured party cannot sue both; once the choice is made, the third party is bound by it. The converse is also true in that the agent can enforce the contract against the third party unless the principal chooses to take over and enforce the contract himself.

There are some types of transactions done on behalf of an undisclosed principal that are not binding on the parties. The undisclosed principal is liable only when the agent has acted within his actual authority. Apparent authority applies only when the principal has held out the agent to have authority, and since the

---

17. [1989] 2 S.C.R. 683.

18. [2001] F.C.J. No. 1009 (T.D.).

principal is unknown there can be no holding out and no apparent authority. For the same reason an undisclosed principal cannot ratify since the agent must be claiming to be acting on behalf of a specific principal in those dealings with the third party for such a ratification to be valid. Where the agent has made no such claim there can be no ratification of it. Finally an undisclosed principal contract cannot be enforced where the identity of the parties is important to the third party. In a contract involving personal services, for example, the third party would be able to repudiate upon discovering that the deal had been made with an agent rather than with the principal. Similarly, in the case of *Said v. Butt*,[19] a theatre refused to sell a ticket to someone on opening night because he had caused a disturbance in the past. That person arranged for a friend to acquire the ticket on his behalf but was refused admittance even though he had a ticket. He sued for breach, but the Court held that in this situation, the identity of the party was obviously important, and the Court did not enforce the contract.

Undisclosed principal cannot ratify

Third party can repudiate when identity of undisclosed principal important

To further complicate matters, where the contract is made under seal (sealed by the agent) the undisclosed principal cannot be sued. Only parties to a sealed document can have rights or obligations under it.

As can be seen, the responsibilities of the parties in undisclosed principal situations can become very complicated. To avoid the problem of an undisclosed principal, persons acting as agents should be extremely careful to make it clear that they are acting in an agency capacity. This is normally done by writing "per" immediately before the signature of the agent. For example, if Sam Jones were acting for Ace Finance Company, he would be well advised to sign:

Ace Finance Company per
Sam Jones.

The Third Party

When an agent does not have the authority claimed, either actual or apparent, that agent may be sued by the third party for breach of "warranty of authority." This action is founded in contract law and is the most common example of an agent being sued directly by the third party. Also, an agent who intentionally misleads the third party into believing that she has authority when she does not may be sued by the third party for the tort of deceit. Furthermore, agents who inadvertently exceed their authority can be sued for negligence.

Third party can sue agent for unauthorized acts

CASE SUMMARY 15.8

Misrepresentation or Breach of Warranty of Authority: *Alvin's Auto Service Ltd. v. Clew Holdings Ltd.*[20]

The plaintiff was approached by a realtor about making an offer to purchase a building. The plaintiff indeed submitted an offer to purchase and the defendant bank was named as the vendor. A counteroffer was remitted to the plaintiff and again the bank was identified as the vendor.

---

19. [1920] 3 K.B. 497.
20. [1997] S.J. No. 387 (Q.B.).

In fact, the registered owner was Clew Holdings Ltd., (Clew) an insolvent corporation that had defaulted in payment of its mortgage to the defendant bank. Clew had earlier instructed the bank to find a buyer for its commercial premises.

Over two weeks, the bank and plaintiff exchanged offers until they finally agreed on a price. However, before the bank approached Clew about approving the deal, the bank received an offer from a third party for much more money than the bank had originally asked. Clew accepted the third party offer and executed the agreement as vendor.

The plaintiff was forced to purchase another building, which required renovations. Consequently, its business relocation was delayed by a month and a half.

An action for damages for breach of warranty of authority and negligent misrepresentation was commenced. Judgment was granted to the plaintiff. The bank's conduct clearly gave the impression that it was Clew's agent for the purpose of negotiating the sale of the building; it was thus liable for breach of warranty of authority. Further, the bank owed a duty of care to disclose that it did not have the authority to negotiate a binding sale. By conducting itself otherwise, it made a negligent misrepresentation, which the plaintiff reasonably relied upon to its detriment. The plaintiff was entitled to compensation for economic loss suffered in locating and securing an equivalent property for its business expansion.

SMALL BUSINESS PERSPECTIVE

Officers and other employees of corporations often negotiate contracts on behalf of the company. If they do not have actual authority to bind their principal to contracts yet act as though they do, they run the risk of later being sued for breach of warranty of authority, misrepresentation, or both.

Remedies in tort available for fraud or negligence

It is important to distinguish between the tortious liability of the agent based on fraud or negligence and a contract action based on breach of warranty of authority. Where a breach of warranty of authority action is brought, the damages will be limited to those that were reasonably foreseeable at the time the contract was entered into or those that flow naturally from the breach (that is, the damages awarded for breach of contract). If, unknown to the agent, the goods were to be resold at an unusually high profit that was lost because of the breach of warranty of authority, the agent would not be liable for those losses, since they were not reasonably foreseeable. However, if the third party could establish the agent's fraud or negligence, the lost profits might be recovered from the agent because they are the direct consequence of the tortious conduct—and in tort law, damages are awarded to compensate for the loss caused.

Liability for Agent's Tortious Conduct

Vicarious liability limited to employment

As discussed in Chapter 11, an employer is vicariously liable for the acts an employee commits during the course of employment. When an agent is also an employee of the principal, the principal is vicariously liable for any tortious acts committed by the agent in the course of that employment. The difficulty arises when the agent is not an employee but acts independently. In 1938, the Supreme Court of Canada held that the principle of vicarious liability is restricted to those situations in which a master–servant relationship can be demonstrated.[21] This position was reaffirmed in 2001 in the *Sagaz* case[22] when Major J. of the Supreme Court said, "Based on policy considerations, the relationship between an employer and independent contractor does not typically give rise to a claim in vicarious liability."

The courts have been expanding the definition of employment. Fleming points out that "the employment of a servant may be limited to a single occasion, or extend over a long period; it may even be gratuitous."[23] Even if the relationship involves a person who is essentially an independent agent, that agent may be functioning as an employee or servant in a given situation; thus, the courts may impose vicarious liability on the principal by simply asserting that the agent is also an employee. With such a broad definition of employment, judges will have little difficulty imposing vicarious liability on principals when the circumstances warrant. Still it is only in rare cases that a principal will be found vicariously liable for the acts of an independent agent. Of course, the principal can then look to the agent for compensation for any losses incurred.

> • but definition of employment may be broadened

There are some situations in which vicarious liability will apply even if the agent is acting independently. The courts appear willing to hold the principal responsible for theft or fraudulent misrepresentation by an agent, even when no employment exists. In Case Summary 15.1, it made no difference whether Mr. Snarey was an employee or was acting as an independent agent; because fraud was involved, the principal was liable for the agent's wrongful conduct. It does appear, however, that vicarious liability for the acts of independent agents is limited to those situations where the acts complained of are actually committed in the process of the exercise of that agency function. In the *Thiessen* case[24] the B.C. Court of Appeal grappled with the problem of whether vicarious liability ought to be imposed on the principal where the agent was clearly an independent contractor. In that case Mr. Carey Dennis diverted funds to be invested with Mutual Life Insurance and instead put them into his own account. The insurance company had made every effort to ensure that the agent, Carey Dennis, was an independent contractor, even defining him as such in their contract. But the Court found that because he represented only Mutual Life and could sell another company's products only with Mutual Life's permission, and because that company intended that a relationship of trust would be developed between their customers and Dennis, he had apparent authority to represent Mutual in the offending transaction. The act of taking the client's investment funds was the very exercise of that apparent authority and as a result Mutual was vicariously liable for his fraud. Although this was a decision of the B.C. Court of Appeal, it should be noted that an application for appeal to the Supreme Court of Canada was rejected.

> Vicarious liability where independent agent deceitful

---

21. *T.G. Bright and Company v. Kerr*, [1939] S.C.R. 63.

22. *671122 Ontario Ltd. v. Sagaz Industries Canada Inc.*, [2001] 2 S.C.R. 983 at para.3.

23. John G. Fleming, *The Law of Torts*, 8th ed. (Sydney: The Law Book Co. Ltd., 1990) at 371.

24. *Thiessen v. Mutual Life Assurance Co. of Canada*,[2002] B.C.J. No. 2041 (C.A.); leave to appeal dismissed, [2002] S.C.C.A. No. 454.

CASE SUMMARY 15.9

Even Innocent Principals Can Be Liable for an Agent's Negligence: *Betker v. Williams*[25]

The Williamses owned land in Cranbrook, British Columbia, and entered into a listing agreement with a realtor to sell it. The realtor advertised it for sale as a building site and, when asked, indicated that it was suitable for building a residential home.

The property was purchased by the Betkers, and several years later when they decided to build, they discovered a problem. In fact the city bylaws required that such residential building lots either be accessible to city sewers or be more than 2 1/2 acres in size to accommodate a septic filter field. This property satisfied neither requirement and so could not be used as a residential building site. The Betkers sued, and the question in this case was whether the Williamses could be held liable for the negligence of their agent. Also the remedy sought was the rescission of the contract and the return of the purchase price. Linda Williams, in turn, sued the agent in a third-party action.

Although the mistake was entirely that of the agent, the Court found that because of the principle of vicarious liability, the vendors of the property (that is, the Williamses), who had profited from the sale, were responsible. They had to pay significant damages for the negligent misrepresentation of their agent. It is interesting to note that the remedy of rescission was rejected because of the delay in bringing the action. Also, Linda Williams was successful in her third-party action. The Judge ordered the agent to reimburse her for any losses suffered due to their vicarious liability to the Betkers for the agent's wrongful conduct.

SMALL BUSINESS PERSPECTIVE

Many businesses interact with customers through agents. This case illustrates the potential liability principals bear for the wrongful actions of their agents. Even though the principal may be entitled to compensation from the agent, this in itself may be problematic. If the agent is impecunious, securing compensation from the agent may be difficult.

Direct liability if principal is origin of fraud

A principal can also be found directly liable for his own tortious conduct. If the principal has requested the act complained of, has told the agent to make a particular statement that turns out to be defamatory or misleading, or is negligent in allowing the agent to make the particular statements complained of, the principal may be directly liable. In the case of *Junkin v. Bedard*,[26] Junkin owned a motel that was sold to a third party through an agent. Junkin provided false information regarding the profitability of the motel to the agent, knowing that the agent would pass it on to the purchaser, Bedard. The agent did so, and Bedard bought the property. Bedard later discovered the falsification and sued Junkin for fraud. Because the agent had innocently passed the information on to Bedard, Junkin alone had committed the fraud, even though the agent had communicated the information. Here, the principal was directly liable for his own fraud. If

---

25. [1991] B.C.J. No. 3724 (C.A.).

26. [1957] S.C.J. No. 67.

the agent had fabricated the false information, the principal would have been vicariously liable for the agent's fraud.

As is the case with employment law, vicarious liability makes the principal responsible, but it does not relieve the agent of liability for his own tortious conduct. Both can be sued, but the principal can then seek compensation from the agent.

Vicarious liability—both parties liable

Termination of Agency

Since the right of an agent to act for a principal is based on the principal's consent, as soon as the agent is notified of the withdrawal of that consent, that authority ends. When the agent is an employee, the relationship is usually ended with appropriate notice, as discussed in Chapter 11. But even where employment may continue, the authority to act as an agent will end immediately upon notification of the agent to that effect. Sometimes, the agency agreement will set out when the agent's authority will end. If the agency relationship was created for a specific length of time, the authority of the agent automatically terminates at the end of that period. Similarly, if the agency contract created the relationship for the duration of a particular project or event, for example, "for the duration of the 2010 Olympic Games," the authority ends when the project or event ends.

Termination as per agreement

Requirement of notification

REDUCING RISK 15.3

Since most business is done through agents, businesspeople must take care to understand the exposure they have to liability for their agents' conduct. That liability may be based in contract or tort, and both are derived from the duties and authority given. Whether the agent is independent or an employee, care should be taken to carefully define his or her authority and to make sure that the agent stays within those specified parameters. Even then, liability may be incurred when agents do in a careless manner what they are authorized to do. The key here is to minimize exposure, not to eliminate it. In the end, the best practice is to ensure that agents are reliable, trustworthy, and well trained.

When the principal wants to end the agent's authority to act, simple notification is usually sufficient, for there is no requirement that the notice be reasonable, only that it be communicated to the agent. This applies to the termination of authority to enter into new contracts on the principal's behalf, not necessarily to the right to continued payment, which may be based on other contractual considerations. If the activities the agent is engaged to perform become impossible or essentially different from what the parties anticipated, then the contractual doctrine of frustration may apply, terminating the agent's authority. Similarly, an agent's authority to act on behalf of a principal is terminated when the actions the agent is engaged to perform become illegal. If Cantello agreed to act as Jasper's agent to sell products in a pyramid sales scheme, that authority would have been terminated automatically upon passage of the *Criminal Code* provision prohibiting such activities.[27]

Frustration may terminate agency, as will requests to perform illegal tasks

An agent's authority to act on behalf of a principal can be terminated in several other ways, as Table 15.1 shows. The death or insanity of a principal will automatically end the authority of an agent. When the principal is a corporation, its dissolution will have a similar effect. An agent will lose authority when a principal

Death, insanity, or bankruptcy will terminate agency

---

27. *Criminal Code*, R.S.C. 1985, c. C-46, s. 206.

becomes bankrupt, although other people may assume such authority under the direction of the trustee. How third parties are affected by termination of agency varies. Certainly, as far as termination of authority on the basis of agreement is concerned, unless the principal notifies the third party of such termination, the actions of the agent may still be binding on the principal on the basis of apparent authority. Though it is not entirely clear, this may also be the case when the principal becomes insane. However, in the case of bankruptcy or death of the principal, or dissolution of the principal corporation, the agent's actual and apparent authority ceases. Because of the lingering effect of apparent authority, it is vitally important for a principal to take steps to notify current and potential customers, as well as other people and businesses that they may have dealings with, regarding the termination of the agent's authority.

Table 15.1 Other Ways to Terminate an Agent's Authority

	Impact on Agent's Actual Authority	Impact on Agent's Apparent Authority
Death of principal	Ceases	Ceases
Bankruptcy of principal	Ceases[1]	Ceases
Dissolution of principal corporation	Ceases	Ceases
Insanity of principal	Ceases	Unclear—possibly continues[2]
By mutual agreement	Ceases	Continues until the third party is notified of termination[2]

[1.] Other people may assume this authority under the direction of the Trustee.

[2.] Since apparent authority continues, the principal must actively notify third parties that the agent's authority has been terminated. Only then does apparent authority cease.

Specialized Agency Relationships

Many examples of specialized services offered to businesses and the public are essentially agencies in nature, such as those of travel agents, real estate agents, lawyers, accountants, stockbrokers, financial advisers, and insurance representatives. Some of these agents do not enter into contracts on behalf of their clients but negotiate and act on their clients' behalf in other ways. For example, a real estate agent neither offers nor accepts on behalf of a client. In fact, the client is usually the vendor of a property, and the agent's job is to take care of the preliminary matters and bring the purchaser and vendor together so they can enter into a contract directly. Nonetheless, few would dispute that these real estate agents are carrying out essentially an agency function and thus have a fiduciary obligation to their clients. The important thing to remember is that the general provisions set out above also apply to these special agency relationships, although there may be some exceptions. For example, in most of these specialized service professions, the rule that an agent cannot delegate usually does not apply. The very nature of these businesses requires that employees of the firm, not the firm itself, will act on behalf of the client.

General principles apply to specialized agencies as well

Most of these specialized agencies are fulfilling a service function and are governed by special statutes and professional organizations. For example, the real estate industries in each province have legislation in place that creates commissions or boards that govern the industry. The commissions require that anyone acting for another in the sale of property be licensed or be in the employ of a licensed real estate agent. Bodies that license their members often provide training, and discipline them when required. It is beyond the scope of this text to examine these professional bodies in detail; students are encouraged to examine the controlling legislation, as well as to seek information directly from the governing professional bodies. Most of them are concerned about their public image and are happy to cooperate.

Special statutes and professional organizations

Often, agencies perform a service to their customers that involves not only representing those customers but also giving them advice. Because of the specialized expertise provided, customers are particularly vulnerable to abuse should such agencies try to take advantage of them. The governing bodies hear complaints and go a long way toward regulating the industry and preventing such abuses. But abuses still occur, and victims should know that they have recourse based on the fiduciary duty principles set out here as well as remedies in contract and tort discussed before. Such fiduciary duties, in fact, may be imposed on other professional advisers, even when their duties do not extend to being agents.[28]

TYPES OF BUSINESS ORGANIZATION

The law of agency discussed above is of particular importance when discussing different methods of carrying on business. These business organizations almost always conduct their business through representatives or agents.

There are essentially three major types of business organization (see Figure 15.2). The first, the **sole proprietorship**, involves an individual carrying on business alone. Employees may be hired and business may be carried on through the services of an agent, but the business is the sole responsibility of one person, the owner. A second method of carrying on business is called a **partnership**, where ownership and responsibilities, along with both profits and losses, are shared by two or more partners. As was the case with the sole proprietorship, the partnership may also employ others and act through agents. Also each partner acts as an agent for the other partners and has a fiduciary duty to them. The third type of business organization is the incorporated company. Any type of business organization involving more than one person can be called a company; a **corporation**, however, is a legal entity. By statute, it has been given an identity separate from the individual members who make it up. Thus, contracts with a corporation are dealings with the corporation itself as if it were a person in its own right. And because the corporation is a fiction, it must conduct all of its affairs through employees and agents.

Sole proprietorship involves one person

Partners share responsibilities

Corporation is a separate legal entity

---

28. See *Hodgkinson v. Simms*, [1994] 3 S.C.R. 377, where the Supreme Court held that the relationship of broker and client is not necessarily a fiduciary relationship. However, where the elements of trust and confidence and reliance on skill, knowledge, and advice are present, the relationship is fiduciary and the obligations that attach are fiduciary. It thus remains a question of fact as to whether the parties' relationship was such as to give rise to a fiduciary duty on the part of the adviser.

Societies are separate legal entities, but obligations differ

There are other ways for people to work together to carry on a commercial activity. For example, a **non-profit society** can be set up under legislation such as the Nova Scotia *Societies Act*.[29] This also creates a separate legal entity, but the procedure of incorporation and the obligations of those involved are quite different. There are also several ways in which these various types of business organizations can be combined. A **holding corporation** holds shares in other corporations. A **joint venture** involves several different incorporated corporations that band together to accomplish a major project. They may form a separate corporation or a partnership. The discussion in this chapter will be limited to an examination of sole proprietorship and partnership.

Figure 15.2 Types of Business Organization

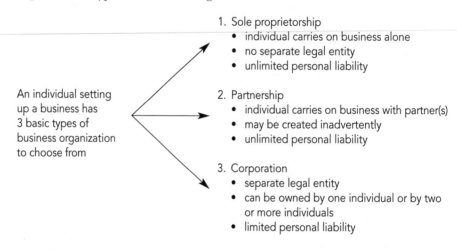

THE SOLE PROPRIETORSHIP

Sole proprietorship carries on business in own right

The sole proprietorship is simply an individual carrying on a business activity on her own. The sole proprietor makes all the decisions associated with the business and is the only one entitled to the benefits derived from the business. A sole proprietor also bears full responsibility for all the costs, losses, and obligations incurred in the business activity. Thus, there is no distinction between the personal assets of the sole proprietor and those of the business. They are all the assets of the proprietor and are available to creditors if things go wrong.

Government Regulations

Must adhere to licensing and governing regulations

The sole proprietor, like all other types of business organizations, must satisfy many federal, provincial, and municipal requirements to carry on business. Usually, the name of the business must be registered if it is different from the sole proprietor's name,[30] and a licence to operate must be obtained from the appropriate level of government. This licensing process is used to control or restrict certain types of businesses, such as door-to-door sales, credit information services, moneylenders, hotels, and cabarets. When the handling of food or dangerous commodities is involved, there are further provincial and federal regulations that must be obeyed. Sole proprietors must also satisfy local zoning bylaws, and if they have employees

---

29. R.S.N.S. 1989, c. 435.

30. See, for example, *Business Names Act*, R.S.O. 1990, c. B. 17, s. 2(2).

they are subject to employment legislation, such as workers' compensation, employment insurance, and income tax regulations. They are also required to remit Goods and Services Tax if the business income is more than $30 000 per year.

As a general rule, sole proprietors are subject to fewer government regulations than partnerships and corporations. Only minimal records need be kept, and sole proprietors are usually not required to disclose information about the business to others. They must keep sufficient records to satisfy government agencies, such as the Canada Revenue Agency. In essence, the sole proprietor has complete control and complete responsibility for the business activity.

Sole proprietor relatively free of outside interference

Liability

Sole proprietors do not have accountability to others and alone are responsible for making important business decisions. They can look only to their own resources to finance the business operation; they cannot sell shares and are restricted to their own credit standing when borrowing money to finance the business. The sole proprietor owns all the assets, receives all the profits of the business, and is responsible for all its debts and liabilities. This **unlimited liability** can be the most significant disadvantage of the sole proprietorship. When liability is incurred for breached contracts or torts, or where there is insurmountable debt, the whole burden falls on the sole proprietor. Under the principle of *vicarious liability*, the sole proprietor is responsible for any tort committed by an employee during the course of employment. Although the sole proprietor's entire personal fortune is at risk, much of this risk can be offset by carrying adequate insurance. Any profit derived from a sole proprietorship is subject to personal income tax, while some tax advantages available to partnerships and corporations are not available to sole proprietors. These factors alone are often enough to encourage the businessperson to incorporate.

Sole proprietor has unlimited liability but can purchase insurance

In most jurisdictions, professional individuals such as doctors, dentists, lawyers, and accountants cannot incorporate their practice, and they derive little advantage from doing so in those jurisdictions where professional incorporations are permitted.[31] They carry on business as sole proprietors or band together in a group as partners. (Note that in some jurisdictions, limited protection can now be obtained as limited liability partners discussed below.) These professionals must join the appropriate professional organization, such as the law society or medical association of the province. Note that it is only the practice of the professional service that cannot be incorporated, and so these professionals obtain many of the advantages of incorporation by establishing companies that supply them with management services and equipment, own the building, and employ the office staff.

Professionals bound by certain rules

PARTNERSHIP

A partnership is the simplest form of business in which people pool their resources and carry on business together with the object of making profit. This relationship is based on contract, and so basic contract law applies, with special provisions to deal with this unique relationship. Unlike a corporation, a partnership is not a separate legal personality from those making it up. However, it is

Partnership—carrying on business together for profit

---

31. See, for example, the *Regulated Accounting Profession Act*, R.S.A. 2000, c. R-12, which, in s. 38, provides that a shareholder or professional corporation is liable as if the business were carried on as a partnership or a sole proprietorship, and that the liability of an accountant is not affected if the practice is carried on by the individual as an employee and on behalf of a professional corporation.

Partnership governed by contract law

possible for the firm to enter into legal relationships so that it is not necessary to contract with each partner individually. This allows the partnership the convenience of functioning as a single business unit. It can own land, contract with others, and sue or be sued in its own name.

Legislation

In 1890, as part of a similar trend in other areas of law in the United Kingdom, the vast body of case law governing partnership was summarized into one statute, the *Partnership Act*.[32] This legislation was adopted in all the common law provinces of Canada, where it has remained in place to the present day, with only a few alterations, such as the creation of limited liability partners. With some minor variations province to province, the law of partnership is basically consistent across Canada. For convenience, this chapter will refer to the Ontario

Partnership Act still used today

legislation, the *Partnerships Act*, and the sections discussed will refer to that statute.[33]

Creation of the Partnership

CASE SUMMARY 15.10

What Are the Damages for Breach of Fiduciary Duty? *Olson v. Gullo*[34]

Mr. Gullo entered into a verbal agreement with Mr. Olson to purchase and develop a 1000-acre (405-hectare) tract of land as an industrial park. They were both to contribute equal funding and their special skills—Gullo in real estate speculation and Olson in marketing and promotion. The pair had difficulty purchasing the designated land from the owners and eventually abandoned the project.

As it turned out, however, Gullo was able to maintain part of the deal by purchasing one 90-acre (36-hectare) parcel for himself, which he then sold at a $2.5-million profit. Olson, who was an employee of Gullo, found out about the deal, quit his job, and sued. It is interesting to note that Gullo died before the trial, but not before trying to have Olson murdered. Gullo's son carried on the defence of this action.

The first problem for the Court was to decide whether a partnership existed between the parties. The Court determined that there was an oral agreement between the parties whereby each was to contribute an equal share of the funds needed to acquire the land; that Gullo was to negotiate the purchases; and that Olson was to find interested investors and prepare promotional material. Thus, as they were carrying on business together with a view to making profits, their relationship was one of partnership. Gullo then had a fiduciary obligation to act in the best interests of his partner. When he secretly purchased the 90-acre parcel for himself, he did so in breach of that obligation.

---

[32] (1890), 53 & 54 Vict., c. 39 (U.K.).

[33] *Partnerships Act*, R.S.O. 1990, c. P. 5. Note that Ontario is the only province for which the name of the partnership legislation is in the plural; all of the other provinces have a "Partnership Act."

[34] [1994] O.J. No. 587 (C.A.); leave to appeal refused, [1994] S.C.C.A. No. 248.

The trial Judge held that because of his breach of fiduciary duty, Gullo should surrender all profit made on the transaction, but the Appeal Court overturned this and determined that despite his bad behaviour, he was entitled to half the profits because the sharing of such profits was the essential nature of a partnership.

SMALL BUSINESS PERSPECTIVE

The case illustrates not only what is necessary for a partnership to exist and the essential nature of that partnership, but also the fiduciary obligation or duty between the partners to act in the best interests of each other. Unless one is prepared to accept the obligation to act in the best interests of others, care should be taken to avoid creation of a partnership.

A partnership is not always created by formal agreement between the partners. The *Partnerships Act* provides that a partnership is created when two or more people carry on business in common with a view toward profits.[35] A profit does not actually have to be made, only that profit is the object of the exercise. It should be noted that the sharing of gross returns from a business activity does not in itself create a partnership. It is the sharing of the net proceeds after expenses have been deducted (the profits) from the enterprise that gives rise to the presumption of a partnership. The splitting of the commission on a sale by two real estate agents does not create a partnership, but when they split what is left after expenses the presumption of a partnership will arise.

Partnership created by agreement or inadvertently

The *Partnerships Act* sets out a number of other circumstances, which, though they involve the sharing of income, by themselves will not establish a partnership.[36]

1. Owning property in common, even when it is rented out for profit.

2. When a debt is repaid by the creditors' taking a share of the debtor's profits. For example, Pallas owes Clegg $10 000, and Clegg agrees to let Pallas pay it back by paying 20 percent of the profits of Pallas's furniture store per month until repaid.

Partnerships Act lists exceptions—refer to MyBusLawLab for specific provincial wording

3. When the payment of an employee is based on a share of sales or profits, such as commission selling or profit-sharing schemes.

4. When the beneficiary of a deceased partner receives the deceased partner's share of the profits.

5. When a loan is made in relation to a business and payment of interest varies with the profit. For example, Pallas loans Clegg $10 000 to start a furniture business, and Clegg pays interest on that $10 000 principal by paying 10 percent of the store's profits per month.

---

[35] *Supra* note 35, s. 2.

[36] *Ibid.*, s. 3.

6. When a business is sold and the payment of the goodwill portion varies with the profitability of the business. For example, Pallas sells Clegg a furniture business for $10 000 for the assets and 50 percent of the first year's profits for goodwill.

When partnership presumed

The question remains: What constitutes carrying on business together with a view to profit? When evidence indicates that there has been one of the following, a partnership will be presumed:

- joint contribution of capital to establish a business
- intention to share expenses, profits, or losses
- joint participation in the management of a business.

Partnership must carry on continuing business

If two people operate a restaurant together by sharing the work and expenses and jointly making decisions, and the business has not been incorporated, the relationship is a partnership. It should be further noted that the *Partnerships Act* requires that the parties carry on a continuing business together. A single joint project, for example a school dance put on by two university students who combine their resources, would probably not be classed as a partnership. (If the students put on several dances, they would be in the "business" of providing this type of entertainment and, thus, would be in legal partnership, whether they looked at it that way or not.) Whether a business relationship is held to be a partnership will always depend on the circumstances.

CASE SUMMARY 15.11

Failure to Establish Partnership Means "No Team": *Blue Line Hockey Acquisition Co., Inc. v. Orca Bay Hockey Limited Partnership*[37]

Gaglardi, Beedie, and Aquilini, three experienced and prominent businesspersons, agreed to work together to acquire an ownership interest in the Vancouver Canucks hockey team. The Canucks were owned by the Orca Bay companies. The purchase was to occur through a tax-efficient entity to be created at a later date. Aquilini subsequently left the group but later asked to rejoin it. This request was rejected by the plaintiffs. The plaintiffs continued to negotiate an agreement to purchase the Canucks, but no agreement was reached.

Aquilini began negotiating the purchase on his own and eventually acquired the team. The plaintiffs sued Aquilini, alleging that a partnership had been formed among the three individuals and that Aquilini misappropriated a business opportunity belonging to the partnership by acquiring the Canucks on his own behalf. A breach of fiduciary duty by Aquilini was also alleged.

The action was dismissed. There was a common understanding among the parties that each member of the group was free to leave at any time. This finding was consistent with the fact that neither Gaglardi nor Beedie objected when Aquilini withdrew from the group. The plaintiffs failed to establish that the parties shared an "intention to carry on

---

[37.] [2008] B.C.J. No. 24 (S.C.); aff'd [2009] B.C.J. No. 136 (C.A.).

business in common with a view to profit." They were careful not to commit to anything except to the payment of their lawyer's fees in equal shares. They refrained from entering into any other obligations to third parties and did not make any actual offer to Orca Bay but simply advanced "expressions of interest." Since the parties could withdraw at any time from the talks without legal consequences, the claim that they intended to carry on business together failed.

As to the breach of fiduciary duty, the Court concluded that there was no expectation that the three men would forward each other's best interests. All were experienced businesspersons who were familiar with partnerships and partnership agreements. No evidence was submitted indicating that they discussed or assumed that each of them would act in the others' best interest. Aquilini was as entitled as the others to pursue the acquisition on his own. Further, since there was no intent to form a partnership, the claim of misappropriation of a business opportunity also failed.

SMALL BUSINESS PERSPECTIVE

The courts are often called upon to determine whether parties intended to "carry on a business" or simply to create an agreement for the regulation of their rights and obligations. Evidently, more than a mere common pursuit to purchase an opportunity must exist to found a partnership.

CREATION BY INADVERTENCE

It is important to realize that the existence of a partnership relationship is a question of fact that a court can imply from the conduct of the parties. A partnership can therefore be created inadvertently. Because of the liability of one partner for the contracts and misdeeds of other partners, the finding of such a relationship can have significant consequences for that person. This must be a consideration whenever someone is involved in any kind of business activity with another. Failure to appreciate this possibility can have disastrous financial consequences when one partner incurs liability to a third party.

Partnership can be created by conduct

The partnership relationship is primarily one of contract, usually created by agreement, but this agreement often does not take a written form. The *Olson v. Gullo* case summarized above is an instance where a court found that a partnership had been created by an oral agreement.

In addition to setting out the responsibilities of partners to third parties, the *Partnerships Act* also sets out the rights and obligations of the partners to each other. But like the *Sale of Goods Act*, the *Partnerships Act* provisions, at least as far as the rights between the partners themselves are concerned, can be modified by the partnership agreement. It is important for the partners to enter into an agreement, preferably in writing, setting out the exact nature of the relationship between them.

But should be created by agreement

> ### CASE SUMMARY 15.12
>
> ## Does Co-owning Property Create a Partnership? *A. E. LePage Ltd. v. Kamex Developments Ltd.*[38]
>
> A number of people owned an apartment building together under the name of one of them, "M. Kalmykow in trust"; that is, in trust with the other owners as well. A corporation, called Kamex Developments Ltd., was created to control the property. The co-owners met monthly to discuss the property and what should be done including the possibility of sale. One of these parties, Mr. March, took it upon himself to list the property for sale under an exclusive listing agreement. He was not authorized to do so by the others. The property was eventually sold by a different agent, and A. E. LePage claimed their commission of $45 000 on the basis that March was in partnership with the rest and therefore bound the partnership to the exclusive listing agreement. Looking at the nature of the agreement, the Court found that although all these people owned the property together, this was not enough to constitute a partnership, and so the others were not liable for the commission.
>
> *SMALL BUSINESS PERSPECTIVE*
>
> When parties own property together with others they run the risk of being identified as "partners." The courts may be called upon to determine whether the intention of the co-owners was to "carry on a business" or simply to create an agreement for the regulation of their rights and obligations as co-owners of a property. The determination that a partnership exists will impact not just the "partners'" rights, but also those who do business with the group.

CREATION BY CONTRACT

Written contract not always conclusive proof of a partnership

As is the case with most business relationships, it is best to create the partnership through contract, preferably in writing, setting out the rights and obligations of the partners. But the terms of that contract are not always conclusive of the relationship. Even where the parties clearly state they are acting in partnership, this may not be enough to create such a partnership. See the *Backman* case set out in Case Summary 15.13 below. On the other hand a court may find that a partnership exists even where the parties clearly state in their agreement that they are not partners.[39]

> ### CASE SUMMARY 15.13
>
> ## Intention to Create Partnership Is Not Enough: *Backman v. Canada*[40]
>
> Some Canadian investors took an assignment of the interests of the American partners in a limited partnership established in Texas to build an apartment building. The project

---

38. [1977] O.J. No. 2273 (C.A.); aff'd [1979] S.C.J. No. 38.

39. *See Foothills Dental Laboratory Ltd. v. Naik (c.o.b. Apple Dental Group)*[1996] A.J. No. 583, (Prov. Ct.). The court determined a partnership existed despite the contract, which stated "It shall be an express term of this agreement that the Association herein provided for shall, under no circumstances, be deemed to create an employer and employee or partnership relationship between Naik and Goldstein respectively."

40. [2001] 1 S.C.R. 367.

failed, and the day after acquiring the interests the new owners resold the apartment building back to the original American owners at a significant loss. Each of the new Canadian partners then claimed that loss to be used against their Canadian taxes as was permitted of a Canadian partnership experiencing losses in another country. But this claim was rejected and the partners' taxes were reassessed on the basis that this was not a valid partnership. The would-be partners appealed first to the Tax Court, then to the Federal Court of Appeal, and finally to the Supreme Court of Canada.

From the documentation it was clear that the parties involved intended to create a partnership but that was not good enough. The partnership had been formed not to make a profit; instead it was formed with the predominant motive of acquiring a tax loss. A further problem was that there was no ongoing business relationship. The object of the transaction was to acquire the apartment building and sell it the next day, not to create or continue an ongoing business. And so no partnership was created.

SMALL BUSINESS PERSPECTIVE

For the partners to obtain the benefit of carrying on business as a partnership they must do more than simply call themselves partners. They must create an ongoing business relationship where they carry on business in common with a view of sharing any profits they make from that ongoing business.

A partnership agreement should deal with all of the matters important to the partnership, such as

- the duties of each partner
- what type of work or talent each is expected to contribute
- the amount of time to be committed to the business
- how the profits are to be shared and how the capital is to be distributed
- any limitations on the powers or authority of each partner
- methods of resolving any disputes between the partners
- the circumstances in which the partnership will be dissolved.

Rights and obligations of partners can be modified by agreement

It must be remembered that the rights of outsiders dealing with the partnership are, without notice, unaffected by any agreement between the partners. Outsiders' rights are determined by the provisions of the *Partnerships Act* and partnership law generally.

It should also be noted that a partnership relationship can arise because of estoppel. If one of the parties represents to a third party, either by words or by conduct, that another person is a partner and that representation is relied on, the existence of a partnership cannot be denied, even if it can be clearly demonstrated that the two were not carrying on a business together. The principle of estoppel applies to partnership just as it does to agency.

Partnership can be imposed by the principle of estoppel

CASE SUMMARY 15.14

Does Holding Someone Out as a Partner Create a Partnership? *Brown Economic Assessments Inc. v. Stevenson*[41]

Cara Brown provided consulting services to Mr. Stevenson and his law firm and submitted a bill for $23 242.59, which was never paid. Since bankruptcy overtook Stevenson in this action, Brown sued the other members of the law firm for what was owed. The other members of the law firm claimed that there was no partnership. The claim was that they were not partners with Stevenson or with each other, and therefore they were not liable for the claimed amount.

When Brown first met with Stevenson, he introduced himself as "senior litigator and partner" in the firm, presenting her with a business card with the name of the firm listed as "Stevenson, Gillis, Hjelte, Tangjerd, Barristers and Solicitors." She also received correspondence from time to time on a letterhead containing that name.

The Court found that although there was no actual partnership, because the defendant lawyers had allowed themselves to be held out as partners and that holding out had been relied on by the plaintiff, they were estopped from denying that they were partners and were liable to pay the amount owing.

SMALL BUSINESS PERSPECTIVE

This case shows how dangerous it is to hold yourself out as a partner or even to allow yourself to be held out as a partner because it is not likely that you will be allowed to deny that fact later.

The Partner as an Agent

Every partner is the agent of the other partners and so has the power to bind them in contract as long as the contract involves the business of the partnership.[42] To properly understand the law of partnership, this discussion must be read in conjunction with the material above on agency. Even where the authority of a partner has been limited and the partner exceeds the power given, that contract will be binding if the third party is unaware of the limitation and the contract relates to the partnership business.[43] Assume Akbari and Carlson operated a shoe store in partnership, and Akbari, while visiting his regular supplier in Toronto, purchased 500 pairs of yellow patent-leather oxfords he was unable to resist for $5000. That contract would be binding on Carlson, even if the partnership agreement specifically set out that neither partner could make any purchase over $1000 without the other's approval. However, if Akbari bought a new boat during his trip to Toronto, this purchase would not be binding on his partner because the purchase could not be said to be made pursuant to the partnership business of selling shoes.

Laws of agency apply to partnership

---

41. [2004] S.J. No. 377 (C.A.).

42. *Partnerships Act, supra* note 35, ss. 6, 7.

43. *Ibid.,* ss. 6, 9.

Vicarious Liability

All partners are also vicariously liable in tort for both careless and intentional conduct of their partners in all business-related activities, including personal injury. Thus, if Agostino and Paradis were partners selling firewood, and Agostino negligently dropped a load of wood on a passing pedestrian, both Agostino and Paradis would be liable to pay compensation for the injury. There are many cases showing vicarious liability for intentional wrongs, such as an Ontario case in which the partners of a lawyer, even though they were completely innocent, were required to make good the loss when that lawyer fraudulently acquired $60 000 from his client by forging a cheque.[44]

Partners liable for each other's acts

Partners can also be held responsible for the breach of trust of their partners, such as the misuse of their clients' money. In such situations, all the partners are responsible for compensating the victim's loss. Note, however, that under the *Partnerships Act* the other partners are liable only if they have notice of the breach of trust.[45]

Partners liable for breach of trust

Since a partnership can employ individuals, the principles set out in Chapter 11 on employment law apply. Partners are vicariously liable for the misdeeds of their employees committed in the course of their employment. They must also adhere to government regulations on workers' compensation, employment insurance, and income tax.

Partners liable for wrongful acts of employees

REDUCING RISK 15.4

For a businessperson, a serious risk associated with the law of partnership is the danger of becoming a partner inadvertently. This can come about by carrying on business together without realizing that a partnership has been created, or by allowing oneself to be held out as a partner by someone else. The danger is the liability imposed by such a partnership both in tort, on the basis of vicarious liability, and in contract, on the basis of each partner being an agent. This unlimited liability means a partner's entire fortune is at risk, and can lead to devastating results. Care should be taken to avoid the risk that an inadvertent partnership can create.

Unlimited Liability

Like that of a sole proprietor, a partner's liability is unlimited, and her personal fortune is at risk to satisfy the claims of an injured party. With partners, however, they are liable not only for their own wrongful acts and those of their employees but also for the conduct of their partners. If the assets of a partnership are not sufficient to satisfy the claims of the creditors, the partners must make up the difference out of their own personal assets. This is typically done in the same proportion that they share the profits. Thus, if a partnership agreement provides that a senior partner gets 40 percent of the profits and each of the three junior partners gets 20 percent of the profits, the senior partner will bear 40 percent of the loss and the junior partners will each bear 20 percent of the loss. But it is pos-

Partners share losses equally or proportionally by agreement

---

44. *Victoria & Grey Trust Company v. Crawford* (1986), 57 O.R. (2d) 484 (H.C.J.).

45. *Partnerships Act, supra* note 35, s. 14.

sible for the partners to agree to a different sharing of losses or profits if so stipulated in their agreement.[46]

Third party can collect from any partner regardless of agreement

Note that such a provision in the partnership agreement will affect only the relations between the partners. An outsider is not affected by any term in the partnership agreement that limits the liability of one of the partners and can collect all of what is owed from any partner. If one partner is particularly well off and the other partners have few personal assets, the injured party will look to the partner with significant assets for compensation once the assets of the partnership have been exhausted. That partner can seek contributions from the other partners on the basis of the partnership agreement if they have anything left to contribute.

In most provinces, partners are only **jointly liable** for the debts and obligations of the partnership, as opposed to jointly and **severally liable**.[47] This means that for someone to seek a remedy against all the partners, they all must be included in the original action, as there is only one cause of action. Thus, if only two of the three partners are sued and it later turns out that they do not have enough assets to satisfy the judgment, it is then too late to sue the third. It must be emphasized, however, that when liability arises because of wrongful conduct (tort) or because of breach of trust, this liability is both joint and several.[48] This means that it is possible for the injured party to sue one partner and still maintain the right to sue the other partners if the claim is not satisfied. In any case, when an action is brought against the partnership in the partnership name, the plaintiff will be able to enforce the judgment against any of the partners. The result of this vicarious liability is that all the partners are personally responsible for the injuries incurred to the extent of their entire personal fortunes. The liability of partners for each other's conduct is one area where there are some provincial differences.

All personal assets at risk

Retiring partner remains responsible

A retiring partner remains liable for any wrongs committed or liability incurred during the partnership period. This liability also continues for acts committed after the dissolution of the partnership or the retirement of the partner, unless the third party has been given notice that the retiring party has left the firm. The remaining partners or a new partner coming in can agree to take over these obligations in the partnership agreement, but the new partner is not automatically liable for them.[49] This is why such care is taken to notify colleagues and customers when the membership of a partnership changes.

CASE SUMMARY 15.15

Was the Loss Incurred in the Normal Course of Business? *McDonic v. Hetherington (Litigation Guardian of)*[50]

In 1985, two elderly sisters, Ms. McDonic and Ms. Cooper, on the advice of Cooper's son-in-law, retained Mr. Watt, a solicitor, to advise them on investments. Watt invested a considerable sum of money for them but failed to properly secure those investments. The result was that McDonic lost more than $230 000 and Cooper lost more than $10 000.

---

46. *Partnerships Act, supra* note 35, s. 24.

47. *Ibid.,* s. 10.

48. *Ibid.,* ss. 12, 13.

49. *Ibid.,* s. 18.

50. [1997] O.J. No. 51 (C.A.); leave to appeal dismissed, [1997] S.C.C.A. No. 119.

Watt was successfully sued on the basis that he failed in his fiduciary duty to these clients. The problem here was for the Court to determine whether his partners were also liable for these losses on the basis of vicarious liability. The partners denied liability, claiming that this was misconduct on the part of Watt outside the scope of the business, as Watt was acting as an investment adviser, not a lawyer, in these transactions. The lower Court agreed. However, the Ontario Court of Appeal decided that the partners were liable for the losses caused by their partner because Watt did what he did as a partner in the normal course of that partnership's business. The money went into a partnership trust account. It was dealt with like all other accounts, and the other partners actually dealt with those funds as well. In addition, he was liable as an agent acting within the apparent authority given by the other partners.

It is true that the transactions were not expressly authorized by the partners, but it is clear that he was acting within his apparent authority and, as such, made the other partners liable for his conduct. His office was part of the firm's offices, he used the firm's letterhead, and in making the investments for the sisters he used the facilities of the law office as well as the firm's accounts in the normal course of the firm's business.

SMALL BUSINESS PERSPECTIVE

This case emphasizes the need to be vigilant in knowing what dealings partners are engaging in. Evidently a great deal of trust is required between partners as well as a thorough understanding of partnership law.

Registration

Most provinces require that a partnership be registered. Some provinces, such as British Columbia[51] and New Brunswick,[52] require registration only when the partnerships involve trading, manufacturing, and mining. Alberta also requires registration of partnerships involving contracting.[53] Ontario prohibits partners from carrying on business or identifying themselves to the public unless the firm name has been registered.[54] Registration may also be required when the partners are in limited partnerships or limited liability partnerships, as discussed below.

Registration usually required

REDUCING RISK 15.5

All partners are liable to the extent of their personal fortune for the wrongful acts and mistakes of their partners. Case Summary 15.15 deals with the misuse of trust money in a law firm, but this is just one of the many examples that could be used where one partner's liability for the acts of another is present. We must use great care in choosing our partners and even then we face great risk of loss. This is one reason that incorporation has become much more popular as a method of doing business.

---

51. *Partnership Act*, R.S.B.C. 1996, c. 348, s. 81.

52. *Partnerships and Business Names Registration Act*, R.S.N.B. 1973, c. P-5, s. 3.

53. *Partnership Act*, R.S.A. 2000, c. P-3, s. 106.

54. *Business Names Act*, S.O. 1990, c. B.17, s. 2.

Failure to register properly can result in the imposition of a fine[55] but typically will prevent the unregistered partnership from maintaining an action[56] and cause joint liability to become joint and several liability.[57] Note that an unregistered partnership can still be sued, and so there are pressing reasons to register and no advantage in not doing so.

Rights and Obligations of the Parties

FIDUCIARY DUTY

Fiduciary duty exists between partners

Each partner has a fiduciary duty to act in the best interests of the other partners. This duty imposes an obligation to account for any profits that have been made or for any partnership funds or property used. A partner who uses partnership property for personal benefit without the consent of the other partners must pay over any profit made and reimburse the partnership for any deterioration of the property. Property brought into a partnership for the purposes of the business becomes the property of the partnership, even though the title documents might not reflect this ownership. The partner with title is said to hold the property in trust for the partnership. This was the situation in *Olson v. Gullo*, discussed in Case Summary 15.10, and why Olson had the right to one-half of the profits from the sale of the property that Gullo had secretly purchased. It also underlines why the Appeal Court found it necessary to reverse the lower Court's decision to award all the profits to Olson. This was inconsistent with the true nature of the partnership where they shared the ownership of the property and thus the rights to the profits.

Partners must account for any profits or use of property

Partners cannot compete with partnership

If a partner operates a similar business without consent, he will be required to pay over any profits made to the partnership, which will then be distributed normally to all the partners. That partner, however, will not be reimbursed for losses. If a partner in a restaurant in Vancouver were to open another in Victoria without consent, any profits made from the Victoria operation would have to be paid over to the partnership and then be distributed equally among them. However, any losses sustained would be borne by that partner alone.

Information must be disclosed

Any information obtained through a person's position as partner must be used to the benefit of the partnership, not for personal use. If Grubisich came across a deal for some mining claims because of his position as a partner in a mining partnership, he would be required to inform his partners about the opportunity. If he bought the claims for himself without his partner's consent, he would have to turn over any profits earned to the partnership but suffer any losses himself. In effect, the information he used was the property of the partnership.

---

55. In Alberta, for example, a fine not exceeding $500 can be imposed on each partner who fails to register. See *Partnership Act, supra* note 55, s. 112.

56. *Ibid.,* s. 113.

57. *Ibid.,* s. 115.

CASE SUMMARY 15.16

Partner Must Account for Income from Other Sources: *McKnight v. Hutchison*[58]

McKnight and the defendant, Hutchison, were partners in a law firm. The partnership agreement stipulated that partners were allowed to conduct business other than the practice of law, provided that notice was given to the other partners and that the business did not compromise the law practice. Hutchison became a director of a corporation that was a client of the partnership and accepted an honorarium as well as company shares that subsequently returned substantial dividends. McKnight contends that Hutchison breached a fiduciary duty to disclose the activities giving rise to these and other subsequently revealed privately retained earnings.

Hutchison advised his partners of his directorship, but he did not disclose that he was retaining the honorarium and dividends privately. The parties had entered a partnership agreement that expressly incorporated provisions of the *Partnership Act*, thus sections 22–33 of the *Act* were binding on the parties:

> 22(1) A partner must act with the utmost fairness and good faith towards the other members of the firm in the business of the firm.

> 31 Partners are bound to render true accounts and full information of all things affecting the partnership to any partner or his or her legal representatives.

> 32(1) A partner must account to the firm for any benefit derived by the partner without the consent of the other partners from any transaction concerning the partnership, or from any use by the partner of the partnership property, name or business connection.

> 33 If a partner, without the consent of the other partners, carries on any business of the same nature as and competing with that of the firm, the partner must account for and pay over to the firm all profits made by him or her in that business.

The Court held that Hutchison owed his partner duties of disclosure, loyalty, utmost good faith, and avoidance of conflict and self-interest. While Hutchison's acceptance of the directorship and his activities of directorship did not place him in a position of conflict with his partner, his entitlement to the shares and stock options, however, should have been disclosed. Hutchison's silence and his failure to account for the payments received was in breach of his duties. The Court determined that Hutchison's partner was thus entitled to an accounting of these benefits.

SMALL BUSINESS PERSPECTIVE

Again, we see just how important fiduciary duty is. It is present when there is a relationship where one party places trust in another and is vulnerable if that trust is not honoured.

---

58. [2002] B.C.J. No. 2211 (S.C.).

PROVISIONS OF THE *PARTNERSHIPS ACT*

The rights and obligations of partners to each other are set out in the *Partnerships Act*, and these provisions apply except where modified by the partnership agreement.[59] Some of the provisions of the *Act* are as follows:[60]

Profits and losses shared equally or modified by agreement

1. The partners will share profits equally between them. Similarly, any losses incurred are shared equally between the partners. This provision is often modified by a partnership agreement, but outside third parties will not be affected by any agreement, as they can recover losses from any partner who has assets. That partner may then look to the other partners for reimbursement.

Partners' expenses reimbursed

2. The partners are entitled to reimbursement for any expenses they incur in the process of the partnership business. They are also entitled to be reimbursed for any money other than capital they have advanced to the partnership, before the other partners can claim a share of the profits. In addition, the partner advancing such funds is entitled to the payment of interest on that money.

Partners participate in management

3. All partners have the right to take part in management. This provision is often modified by partnership agreements, which create different classes of partners, particularly in firms with a large number of partners.

No salaries paid to partners

4. A partner is not an employee and is not entitled to wages or other remuneration for work done, only to a share of the profits. To provide partners with a steady stream of cash flow, the firm may pay partners a monthly draw against the yet-to-be-calculated profits of the partnership.

Unanimous agreement needed for major changes

5. No major changes can be made to the partnership business without the unanimous agreement of all the partners. No new partner can be brought into the partnership, nor can a partner be excluded from the firm without the unanimous consent of all the partners.[61] However, for the ordinary matters of the firm a simple majority vote is sufficient, unless the partnership agreement states otherwise.

Assignment requires consent of other partners

6. Partners do not have the right to assign their partnership status to some other party without the consent of the other partners. The benefits can be assigned, but the assignee will not be a partner and will not have the right to interfere in the management or administration of the partnership business.[62]

Partners must have access to records

7. The business records of the partnership must be kept at the partnership office, and all the partners have the right to inspect them.

As can be seen from this summary, the general principle governing a partnership relationship is that the partners function as a unit and have a considerable responsibility to look after each other's interests.

Advantages of Partnership

Insurance coverage important

Although the problems associated with a partnership may appear overwhelming, many of these difficulties can be overcome by proper insurance coverage. It

---

59. *Partnerships Act, supra* note 35, s. 20.

60. *Ibid.,* s. 24.

61. *Ibid.,* ss. 24, 25.

62. *Ibid.,* s. 31.

should also be noted that a disadvantage to one person may be an advantage to another. For example, the unanimous consent required for important changes in a partnership may appear to interfere with effective management, but it does provide considerable protection to the individual partner. Such an individual partner cannot be outvoted by the majority, as is the case with a minority shareholder in a corporation. Similarly, the right of the individual partner to inspect all records of the business confers advantages not shared by minority shareholders in corporations to the same extent.

Unanimous consent protection

It may be less expensive to set up a partnership than a corporation and less costly to operate a partnership because there are few formal requirements once the business has been established. For example, a corporation must keep certain types of accounting records and file annual reports with the appropriate government agency. A partnership, on the other hand, has only the needs of the partners to satisfy in this regard. But, as with sole proprietorships and corporations, there are other government regulatory bodies that require records, such as the Canada Revenue Agency, the Workers' Compensation Board, and the Employment Insurance Commission.

Partnership less costly to form and operate

REDUCING RISK 15.6

Businesspeople should not be too quick to discard partnership as a valuable method of carrying on business with others. From the individual's point of view, all partners have an equal say, and in all important matters there must be unanimity. This eliminates the "tyranny of the majority" problem usually associated with corporations. The disadvantages, such as unlimited liability, can be overcome, to a large extent, by obtaining appropriate insurance. Before a decision is made to incorporate, consideration should therefore be given to the pros and cons of using a partnership to carry on the business instead.

It should not automatically be assumed that, because of the unlimited liability and unwieldy management structure of partnerships, incorporation is a better way of carrying on business. For a small business operating in a "low-risk" industry, for example, it may be advantageous to start up and then carry on business as a partnership until the business becomes profitable. This would enable the partners to personally take advantage of the business losses for tax purposes.

Dissolution of a Partnership

Usually, a partnership is easy to dissolve, requiring only notice to that effect by one of the partners.[63] Such notice can be implied, as in the case where a partnership was terminated when Mr. Singh, one of two partners driving a shared taxi cab, stopped driving.[64] While it is an advantage to the leaving partner to be able to dissolve the partnership simply by giving notice to the other partners, it can be a considerable disadvantage to the others, requiring the sale of the partnership assets and distribution of the proceeds to the partners. Usually, this is overcome by providing in the partnership agreement a mechanism whereby one partner can leave without causing the remainder of the partnership to dissolve.

Dissolution by notice

[63.] *Ibid.*, s. 32.

[64.] *Singh v. Taggarh*, [2000] M.J. No. 237 (Q.B.).

Dissolution by death, bankruptcy, or insolvency

Subject to the partnership agreement, a partnership is dissolved by the death or insolvency of any partner.[65] This provision varies slightly from province to province.[66] Dissolution can give rise to significant problems in ongoing, long-term partnerships of professional groups. Therefore, professionals will typically set out in partnership agreements that the death or insolvency of one partner will not dissolve the partnership and that, instead, the partner's share will be made available to the heir or creditor of the partner. Insurance coverage is often taken out to cover such a contingency.

British Columbia's partnership legislation is unique because it establishes that, when more than two partners are involved, the partnership will be dissolved only in relation to the partner who has died or become bankrupt. This provision can be modified by agreement, but its unique feature is that the death or bankruptcy of one partner will not bring to an end the whole partnership relationship in the absence of an agreement among the partners.[67]

Partnership established for specified time will end at expiry

Partnership can be dissolved by request to the court

A partnership that has been entered into for a fixed term is dissolved by the expiration of that term.[68] Similarly, a partnership that is entered into for a single venture or undertaking is dissolved by the termination of that venture or undertaking.[69] A partnership is automatically dissolved if the business engaged in by the partnership becomes illegal.[70] In addition, a partner can apply to the court to dissolve the partnership if any of the following factors are present:[71]

1. One of the partners has become mentally incompetent, or otherwise incapable of performing partnership responsibilities.

2. The conduct of one partner is prejudicial to the partnership relationship, or the partner is otherwise in breach of the partnership agreement.

3. It is clear that the partnership business can be carried on only at a loss.

4. It is just and equitable that the partnership be dissolved.

Public notice may prevent liability

The effect of dissolution is to end the partnership relationship, oblige the partners to wind up the business, liquidate the assets to pay off any obligations to creditors, and then distribute any remaining assets and funds to the former partners. Individual partners should take care to give public notice of dissolution.[72] The law may require that such notice be filed with the partnership registration office or registrar of corporations, depending on the jurisdiction. For further protection, such notice should be sent to all regular customers of the business. Failure to do so may render each partner liable for the acts of the other partners even after dissolution. Note that although dissolution takes place, the partners

---

[65]. *Partnerships Act, supra* note 35, s. 33.

[66]. In Alberta, for example, a partnership is dissolved by the death or bankruptcy of a partner, or by an assignment of a partner's property in trust for the benefit of his creditors. See s. 37 of the *Partnership Act, supra* note 51.

[67]. *Partnership Act, supra* note 53, s. 36(1)(b).

[68]. *Partnerships Act, supra* note 35, s. 32(a).

[69]. *Ibid.,* s. 32(b).

[70]. *Ibid.,* s. 34.

[71]. *Ibid.,* s. 35.

[72]. *Ibid.,* s. 37.

still have the authority to act as partners and bind the firm by their actions in doing whatever is necessary to wind up the affairs of the partnership.[73]

Distribution of Assets and Liabilities

Subject to the partnership agreement, when dissolving a partnership the debts must be paid first out of profits and, if they are insufficient, out of the capital the partners originally invested. If there is still not enough money to pay the debts, the creditors can then turn to the partners themselves, who are liable in the proportion in which they were entitled to share profits. On the other hand, once all creditors have been paid and the other obligations of the partnership satisfied, any assets still remaining are applied first to pay back the partners for advances and then to pay back the original capital investment. Any remaining funds are divided among the partners on the established basis for sharing profits.[74]

Debts paid out of profits first, then capital, then personal assets of partners

The dissolution of the partnership and the distribution of assets may be a problem, especially when some of the partners want to continue the business in a new partnership. To avoid this problem, the partners often agree in the partnership agreement to a different process than that described above. It should be noted that if one partner owes a debt to an outside creditor that has nothing to do with the partnership business, that creditor can claim against only the assets of that partner, including his or her share of the partnership assets left after all other claims against the partnership are settled.

Limited Partnerships

Additions to the legislation governing partnership in every province provide for the creation of limited partnerships.[75] This measure gives some of the advantages of incorporation to partnerships. But partners can lose their status as limited partners if they fail to carefully adhere to all the requirements of the governing legislation, with the result that they are then deemed to be general partners with all the consequences inherent in that designation. The main advantage of a limited partnership is that it allows the partners so designated to invest money in a partnership but to avoid the unlimited liability that goes with being a general partner. The only loss a limited partner can incur is the original investment.[76]

Limited partners liable only to the extent of their investment

If Gingras and Gitter were general partners with Leopold, a limited partner, and Gingras were to negligently injure a customer to the extent of $300 000 damages, Leopold would lose only his investment in the firm. Both Gingras and Gitter would be liable for the entire $300 000, but Leopold's liability would be limited to the amount he invested, even if the combined assets of Gingras and Gitter were not enough to cover the loss.

Unfortunately, it is relatively easy for the limited partner to lose that special status, thus becoming a general partner with unlimited liability. In the preceding example, if Leopold had allowed himself to be represented as a partner in the business, taken part in the control of the business, allowed his surname to be used

---

[73] *Ibid.*, s. 38.

[74] See *Partnerships Act, supra* note 35, s. 44, for the rules governing the distribution of assets on final settlement of accounts.

[75] These additions vary from province to province. In Ontario, see the *Limited Partnerships Act*, R.S.O. 1990, c. L.16. In Alberta, see the *Partnership Act, supra* note 55, ss. 49–80. The discussion in the text refers to the Ontario legislation.

[76] *Limited Partnerships Act, Ibid.*, s. 9.

in the name of the business, or contributed services to the partnership, he would have become a general partner and would have been required to pay along with Gingras and Gitter, with no limitation on his liability.

Registration required to become a limited partner

To form a limited partnership, it is necessary to file a declaration at the appropriate government registry. This declaration will set out information such as the term of the agreement, the amount of cash and other property contributed, and the way profits are to be shared.[77] The name used by the limited partnership can contain the name of the general partners, but the surname of a limited partner cannot be included in the firm name unless it is also the surname of one of the general partners. It is not possible to form a partnership with only limited partners; there must be at least one general partner in the firm.

REDUCING RISK 15.7

Limited partnerships may be attractive to people because of favourable tax implications. To obtain these tax benefits, limited liability may have to be sacrificed to a considerable extent through modifications set out in the partnership agreement. Often, these changes are not brought to the attention of prospective investors. Great care should be taken before entering into investment vehicles structured as limited partnerships, to ensure that one understands exactly what one is getting into.

Limited partners cannot take part in control of the business

A limited partner can contribute money and other property to the business, but not services. A limited partner cannot take part in the control of the business, without becoming a general partner. The limited partner is not prohibited from giving the other partners advice as to the management of the business, but since it is often difficult to determine where advice stops and control of the business starts, there is a considerable risk in doing so. When a business starts to fail, there is a great temptation for the limited partner to jump in to preserve the investment, but doing so raises the risk of becoming a general partner and should be avoided.

Limited Liability Partnerships

Historically, professionals have not been allowed to incorporate their businesses and have therefore carried on business using partnerships. This has caused increased concern as the size of professional partnerships has grown and the number and size of liability claims against professionals have increased significantly. Ontario addressed this issue in 1998, by introducing the limited liability partnership (LLP).[78] At the time of writing, all provinces except Newfoundland and Labrador and Prince Edward Island have enacted provisions for limited liability partnerships.

[77.] In Ontario, the specifics of what is to be included in the declaration are prescribed by the *Limited Partnerships Act* General Regulation, R.R.O. 1990, Reg. 713.

[78.] The general provisions regarding LLPs are found in the *Partnerships Act, supra* note 35, ss. 44.1–44.4.

An LLP is formed when two or more persons enter into a written agreement that designates the partnership as an LLP and states that the agreement is governed by the *Partnerships Act*.[79] Only professionals belonging to professional organizations permitted to do so in legislation and requiring their members to carry a minimum amount of professional liability insurance coverage[80] can practise their profession through LLPs. They must include "LLP" or "L.L.P." or "Limited Liability Partnership" (or the French equivalent) in their name[81] and be registered as a limited liability partnership.[82] Initially, lawyers and accountants took steps to form LLPs in most jurisdictions. It is likely that other professions will follow suit. Eligible professions include accountants, chiropractors, dentists, lawyers, optometrists, and physicians.

The main advantage to professionals carrying on business in an LLP is that potential liability is limited. A limited liability partner is not liable for the liability of the partnership arising from the negligent acts or omissions of another partner, or an employee, agent, or representative of the partnership.[83] This does not apply to liability caused by the partner's own negligence, or the negligence of a person under the partner's direct supervision or control.[84] The result of these provisions appears to be that the partnership's assets are at risk with respect to liability caused by negligent acts or omissions of partners, employees, agents, or representatives of the LLP, but the victim of the negligence may not pursue the individual assets of non-negligent partners.

These provisions apply, however, only to negligence. They do not apply to actions for other torts, breaches of contract, or breaches of trust. While one partner may not be liable for another partner's negligence, the innocent partner will not be protected from losing her share in the partnership's assets, and all partners, including "innocent partners," will be liable for the ordinary debts of the partnership. Of course, insurance coverage will be available to satisfy any claims against the negligent partners, who will also be personally responsible for any shortfall.

Note that there are some differences between jurisdictions. While in Ontario a partner will be liable for the negligent acts or omissions of someone he supervises, in Alberta that personal liability will only be imposed where the partner failed to provide adequate supervision.[85] The Saskatchewan legislation states that limited liability partners are liable for any partnership obligation for which they would be liable if the partnership were a corporation of which they were directors.[86]

Keep in mind the distinction between a limited partnership and the more recent limited liability partnership. A limited partner is in effect an investor who does not participate in the partnership business. His liability is limited to losing what he has invested, whereas a limited liability partner is an active professional

Limited liability partners must be professionals authorized by statute, maintain minimum insurance coverage, be registered with LLP in name

LLP has unlimited liability only for own negligent acts and for those they supervise

[79.] *Partnerships Act, supra* note 35, s. 44.1. LLP legislation varies from province to province. The discussion in the text is based primarily on the Ontario legislation.

[80.] *Ibid.,* s. 44.2.

[81.] *Ibid.,* s. 44.3(3).

[82.] *Ibid.,* s. 44.3(1).

[83.] *Ibid.,* s. 10 (2).

[84.] *Ibid.,* s. 10(3).

[85.] *Ibid.,* s. 12(2).

[86.] *Partnership Act,* R.S.S. 1978, c. P-3, ss. 80, 81.

who practises his profession with other partners and who is liable for his own negligent acts and for those committed by others under his supervision.

Refer to Table 15.2 for a comparative summary of the different types of business organizations.

Table 15.2 Comparison of Different Types of Business Organizations

Type of Business Organization	Created by Registration?	Number of Participants?	Separate Legal Entity?	Unlimited Personal Liability?	Vicarious Liability?
Sole proprietorship	No, but registration of business name is usually required	1	No	Yes	Yes, for employees
Partnership	No; can even be created inadvertently	2 or more	No	Yes	Yes, for employees and partners
Limited partnership	Yes	2 or more; must be at least one general partner	No	Only general partner	General partners for employees and other general partners
Limited liability partnership	Yes	2 or more members of eligible profession	No	No, except for own negligence	No except for those supervised

SUMMARY

Agency

- Exists with consent from the principal
- Agents act for a principal in dealings with third parties
- Authority
  - Actual authority is defined in the contract
  - Apparent authority arises from the position of the agent or from the conduct of the principal
    - When the principal has done something to lead the third party to believe that the agent has authority, even when such authority has been specifically withheld
  - Even when the agent has exceeded both the actual and apparent authority, the principal may ratify the agreement
  - When the agent acts beyond all authority he or she can be sued (breach of warranty of authority)
- Agent's duties

- - Involve performing terms of contract, providing an accounting of funds, and fiduciary duty
  - Cannot be delegated
- Principal's duties
  - To honour terms of contract and reimburse agent's expenses
- Undisclosed principal
  - Third party's recourse is against agent if existence of principal is not disclosed
  - Third party has a choice to sue the agent or the undisclosed principal to enforce the contract, once existence of the principal is revealed
  - Undisclosed principal cannot ratify contracts
- Vicarious liability
  - In the absence of an employment relationship, the principal may escape vicarious liability for the acts of the agent, except when fraud is involved
  - Principal may be vicariously liable if misconduct of agent applies to acts within agent's actual or apparent authority
- Fiduciary relationship
  - Exists between the agent and the principal
  - Agent has obligation to act in the best interests of the principal
  - Full disclosure by the agent is required
- Termination
  - The agency relationship is typically terminated by simple notification or as agreed in the agency contract
  - Bankruptcy, death, or insanity of the principal or, when the principal is a corporation, the dissolution of that corporation, will also terminate the agent's authority

Sole proprietors

- An individual, carrying on business independently, without co-owners
- Must nonetheless deal with some government regulation
- Have unlimited liability for their debts and obligations

Partnership

- Involves two or more partners carrying on business together with a view to profits
- Controlled by partnership legislation and by specific agreement of the partners
- Can be created by agreement but often comes into existence by inadvertence when people work together in concert in a business activity
- Partners' duties
  - Each partner is an agent for the partnership, and all partners are liable for the contracts and torts of the other partners and employees. That liability is unlimited, and all the assets of the partners, including personal assets, are at risk to satisfy such debts and obligations
  - Fiduciary duty—partners must act in the best interests of the partnership
  - Unanimous agreement required to effect major changes, offering partners control over firm's direction
- Dissolution
  - Unless the partners have agreed otherwise in their partnership agreement, dissolution occurs:
    - Upon notice to that effect from a partner
    - Upon death or bankruptcy of one of the partners

- Limited and limited liability partnerships
  - Limited partnerships involve general and limited partners
  - Limited partners are liable only to the extent of the investment made in the business, but must be careful to protect that limited liability status
  - Limited liability partnerships now available for professionals who cannot incorporate their businesses
  - Qualifying professions include accountants, lawyers, doctors, dentists and others as identified by legislation

---

QUESTIONS

1. What is the agent's function? Why is it important to understand the law of agency in business?

2. Explain what effect an agent's limited capacity will have on the contractual obligations created between a principal and a third party. What effect would the incapacity of the principal have on this relationship?

3. Distinguish between an agent's actual, implied, and apparent authority. Explain why this distinction can be important from the agent's point of view.

4. Explain the role estoppel plays in agency law.

5. Explain what is meant by "ratification" and describe the limitations on a principal's right to ratify the actions of his or her agent. How can the principle of ratification be as dangerous to the principal as it is to the third party?

6. What effect does it have on the relationship between the principal and the third party when an agent writes on an agreement "subject to ratification"?

7. Agents owe a fiduciary duty to their principals. What are the requirements of that duty?

8. What options are open to a third party who has been dealing with an undisclosed principal if the contract is breached? Does an undisclosed principal have the right to ratify an agent's unauthorized act?

9. Explain how the doctrine of vicarious liability applies in a principal–agent relationship.

10. Distinguish among a sole proprietorship, a partnership, and a corporation.

11. What advantages and disadvantages are associated with carrying on business as a sole proprietorship? As a partnership?

12. Distinguish between sharing profits and sharing revenues.

13. If two people enter into a business together with the object of making money but lose it instead, can the business still be a partnership?

14. Why must a person understand the law of agency to understand the law of partnership?

15. What danger exists when a third party is led to believe that two people are partners when, in fact, they are not? What legal principle is applied in this situation?

16. What is the significance of the existence of a partnership agreement for outsiders dealing with the partnership? What is the advantage of entering into a formal agreement?

17. Explain the different ways in which a person can become responsible for the acts of his or her partner and describe the limitations on this responsibility. Describe the liability of retiring and new partners.

18. Partners have fiduciary obligations to each other. Explain what this means and give examples.

19. What events may bring about the end of a partnership prematurely? Under what circumstances might it be necessary to get a court order to end a partnership?

20. What will the normal effect be on a partnership when a partner dies or becomes insolvent? How is the law of British Columbia significantly different?

21. When a partnership is being dissolved and does not have sufficient assets to pay its debts, how is the responsibility for these debts distributed? How are excess assets distributed?

22. What must a person do to qualify as a limited partner? What happens when a limited partner fails to meet one of these qualifications?

23. What is the main advantage of limited liability partnerships? In light of this, what does the law require to protect those who suffer losses through the actions of a partner or an employee of a limited liability partnership?

Chapter 16

The Nature of a Corporation

CHAPTER OBJECTIVES

1. Define a corporation
2. Discuss what the consequences are that flow from incorporation
3. Outline what is meant by "limited liability"
4. Explain how a corporation formed
5. Identify what the usual provisions are of the "corporate charter"
6. Discuss what is meant by corporate "capital"
7. Discuss the concept of shares
8. Compare the main distinctions between shares and bonds

INTRODUCTION

This is the first of two chapters concerned with corporations. In it we discuss some of the most fundamental issues concerning the nature of the corporation.

THE NATURE OF A CORPORATION

The corporation, or limited company, has become the dominant feature of the modern business world. Not only is it the main instrument of big business, it also rivals sole proprietorship and partnership as a means of carrying on smaller enterprises.

The Corporation as a Legal Person

legal person
an entity recognized at law as having its own legal rights, duties and responsibilities

A corporation is a person in the eyes of the law; that is, it is a **legal person**. A legal person is an entity recognized by law as having rights and duties of its own. A distinction is commonly drawn between legal persons and natural persons. Natural persons—that is, human beings—automatically have rights and obligations. Their rights and obligations may vary according to age, mental capacity, and other factors,[1] but they are all "persons." By contrast, a legal person is entirely a creation of

---

[1]. The contractual capacity of minors and persons of unsound mind was considered in Chapter 7.

the state. A legal person has rights and duties under the law, but it cannot insist on those rights or carry out its duties except through human agents.

Although legal systems create other legal entities, for our purposes the most important one is the **corporation**. The corporation evolved from the need to look after the common interests of a group of natural persons. It is a well-established legal principle, in both common law and civil law countries, that a corporation may be created as a separate and distinct legal person apart from its members.[2]

There are numerous types of corporations: publicly owned corporations created by governments to carry on special activities (for example, the Bank of Canada, the Canadian Broadcasting Corporation, Central Mortgage and Housing Corporation, and Canadian National Railway); municipal corporations to run local government; charitable corporations (for example, the Red Cross, the Heart and Stroke Foundation, the Ford Foundation); educational institutions; and business corporations—the most numerous type of all. For the purposes of this book, we are concerned only with business corporations.[3]

corporation
a legal person formed by incorporation according to a prescribed legal procedure

Characteristics of Corporations and Partnerships

The significance of the separate legal personality of a business corporation can be appreciated when compared with partnership.

LIABILITY

In a partnership each partner is normally liable for the debts of the firm to the limit of his or her personal assets.[4] A corporation is liable for its own debts. If, as is usually the case, a shareholder has paid the full price for his shares, he can lose no more in the event that creditors seize the corporation's assets. It is for this reason—the limited liability of their *shareholders*—that business corporations are referred to as limited companies, although this is really something of a misnomer since the corporation itself is liable to the full extent of its assets.[5]

Limited liability is widely regarded as one of the main advantages of incorporation. However, the benefits of limited liability are sometimes over-estimated since, for a small corporation to obtain credit, its directors or shareholders are often required to give personal guarantees or mortgage their own property as collateral security. In addition, as we shall see in the next two chapters, when shareholders become directors—as they often do in smaller enterprises—they are subject to a wide and increasing range of personal liability to other shareholders, to those doing business with the corporation, and to society as a whole, from which their limited liability as shareholders does not protect them.

limited liability
the liability of shareholders is limited to the amount of their capital contributions

TRANSFER OF OWNERSHIP

A partner cannot release herself unilaterally from her liabilities—to her partners, to the firm, and to its clients—simply by retiring. She must bargain for her release

---

2. See Bonham and Soberman, "The Nature of Corporate Personality," in *Studies in Canadian Company Law*, Ziegel, ed., Vol. 1, Ch. 1 (Toronto: Butterworths, 1967).

3. As we shall see later in this chapter, business corporations can be divided into a number of categories.

4. Exceptions are the limited liability partnership and limited partnership.

5. In British Columbia, Alberta, and Nova Scotia it is possible to form an unlimited company, in which the shareholders are liable for the company's debts. The main attraction of this form has been to create tax planning opportunities for U.S. businesses.

with both her partners and her creditors. She may even be liable for debts contracted after her retirement, unless she has given notice to persons who regularly deal with the firm and has fulfilled the other requirements of the Partnership Act. Since a shareholder has no liability for corporate debts even while he retains his shares, creditors of the corporation have no interest and no say in what he does with his shares. The shareholder may sever all connections with the corporation simply by transferring his shares to another person. However, as we shall see later in this chapter, it is usual in closely held corporations to impose special restrictions on the transfer of shares.

MANAGEMENT

A partnership is unsuitable for a venture involving a large number of investors. Each partner, as an agent of the firm, may enter into contracts on behalf of the firm. By contrast, shareholders have no authority to bind their corporation to contractual obligations—only officers of the corporation may do so.

A partnership usually requires unanimity on major business decisions, a requirement that could stalemate a firm with a large number of partners. In a corporation, management is delegated to an elected board of directors that normally reaches decisions by simple majority votes. Major decisions that are referred back to the shareholders do not require unanimity, but at most a two-thirds or three-quarters majority, depending upon the issue and the requirements of the corporation law statutes in the jurisdiction.

This separation of ownership and management ranks with limited liability as a primary feature of the business corporation. These two features enable an investor to invest a specific sum of money and receive a return on it, without either taking any additional risk beyond the sum invested or having to take an active part in the management of business affairs.

Although at one time the major shareholders in a corporation were usually its managers as well, there has been an increasing separation between those who invest and those who manage.[6] The separation is, however, less pronounced in Canada than in the United States because many large Canadian corporations are still controlled by a single individual or by members of a family, or are wholly owned subsidiaries of foreign parent corporations.[7]

DUTY OF GOOD FAITH

Partners owe each other a duty of good faith or fiduciary duty. It would normally be a breach of duty for a partner to carry on another business independently without the consent of her other partners (especially if it were a competing business), or to enter into contracts with the firm on her own behalf. A shareholder owes no such duty to the corporation:[8] he may carry on any independent business himself and may deal freely with the corporation as if he were a stranger.

[6.] The classic study of this subject is that by Berle and Means, *The Modern Corporation and Private Property* (New York: Macmillan, 1932). It is still well worth reading.

[7.] Randall K. Morck, David A. Stangeland, and Bernard Yeung, "Inherited Wealth, Corporate Control, and Economic Growth: The Canadian Disease?" in *Concentrated Corporate Ownership*, Randall K. Morck, ed. (Chicago: National Bureau of Econcomic Research and University of Chicago Press, 2000).

[8.] See *Blacklaws* v. *470433 Alberta Ltd.* (2000), 187 D.L.R. (4th) 614. Directors owe a duty of good faith to their corporation.

CONTINUITY

We have seen that in the absence of special provisions in the partnership agreement, the death or bankruptcy of a partner dissolves a partnership. Even when provisions are made in advance to continue the partnership and to buy out the share of the deceased or bankrupt partner, the procedure is often cumbersome and expensive. A corporation, by contrast, exists independently of any of its shareholders.[9] A person's shares may be transferred by gift or by sale, by will or by statute transmitting them to the personal representative on death, or by creditors seizing them, yet none of these events affects the existence of the corporation. A corporation continues in existence perpetually unless it is dissolved by order of a court or by a voluntary resolution of its shareholders, or it is struck off the register for failure to comply with statutory regulations.

TAXATION

Unlike a partnership, a corporation is a taxable entity. Income of a corporation is taxed first in the corporation and again in the hands of a shareholder when a dividend is declared. To offset this double taxation, small corporations are taxed at an especially low rate and dividends receive preferential tax treatment.[10]

CHECKLIST	Partnerships and Corporate Ownership Contrasted	
	partnership	corporation
separate legal entity	no	yes
personal liability of owners	yes*	no
duty of good faith	yes	no
agency	yes	no
transferability of ownership	no	yes
participation of owners in management	yes	no
continuity	no	yes
taxable entity	no	yes

*There are exceptions.

Consequences of Separate Corporate Personality

CAPACITY

A corporation is created by law and has the characteristics that the legislators give it. Originally, corporations were formed for specific purposes and could act only for those purposes expressly stated in their constitution. Any act outside the scope of those objects was ***ultra vires***—beyond the powers—of the corporation. Contracts made for an unauthorized purpose were invalid.

ultra vires
beyond the powers

---

9. It survives even the death of all its shareholders: *Re Noel Tedman Holdings Pty. Ltd.*, [1967] Qd. R. 561 (Queensland S. C.).

10. The small business tax rate in Ontario was 16.5% in 2008.

The *ultra vires* doctrine, as it applied to corporations, has now been abolished throughout Canada. Under the federal Canada Business Corporations Act,[11] and most of the provincial statutes under which business corporations are formed, a corporation has the capacity and all the rights, powers, and privileges of a natural person (section 15).

As an artificial person, a corporation can, of course, act only through its human agents—its directors and officers. When a corporation purports to make a contract, it is necessary to determine whether its agent had authority.

SEPARATE EXISTENCE: SALOMON'S CASE

As we noted in the previous section, a corporation is a legal entity distinct from its shareholders. The classic case on the existence of the corporation as a separate entity came before the House of Lords in 1897 in *Salomon v. Salomon & Co. Ltd.*[12] It is probably the most widely quoted decision in the whole of corporate law.

CASE SUMMARY 16.1

Salomon had carried on a successful business as a shoe manufacturer for many years. In 1892, he formed a corporation in which he held almost all the shares (20 001 out of 20 007, the remaining six shares being held by members of his family, in order to meet what was then the statutory requirement of seven shareholders). He then sold his business to the corporation. Soon afterwards, a downturn in the shoe industry, caused by loss of government contracts and a series of strikes, drove the corporation into insolvency, and a trustee was appointed to wind it up. The trustee claimed that the corporation was merely a sham, that Salomon was the true owner of the business and the real debtor—and, as such, he should pay off all debts owed by the corporation. The lower courts supported the trustee's position, but the House of Lords decided in favour of Salomon. The Lords said that either the corporation was a true legal entity or it was not. Since there was no fraud or any intention to deceive, all transactions having been fully disclosed to the parties and the statutory regulations complied with, the corporation was properly created and was solely responsible for its own debts.

The decision in the *Salomon* case was important because it recognized the separate legal personality of the so-called one-man company at the time when it was becoming a common form of doing business.[13] As a leading writer on the subject has said, "Since the *Salomon* case, the complete separation of the company and its members has never been doubted."[14]

For the most part, the principle of separate legal personality has worked well in the commercial world, but there are some circumstances where the shareholders' interests may be recognized. In the 1987 *Kosmopoulos* case, the Supreme

---

[11.] R.S.C. 1985, c. C-44, referred to hereafter as the CBCA.

[12.] [1897] A.C. 22.

[13.] The CBCA, s. 5, now allows a corporation to be formed with only one shareholder, as do the laws of almost all provinces.

[14.] *Gower's Principles of Modern Company Law* (6th ed.), pp. 79–80. London: Sweet & Maxwell, 1997.

Court of Canada held that a shareholder, even one who owns all the shares of a corporation, does not own its assets, but still has an insurable interest in those assets. If they are destroyed, his shares will lose value, and, consequently, he should be entitled to insure against their destruction.[15]

It remains unclear how far the principle in the *Kosmopoulos* case can be taken and whether it is restricted to insurance claims. Certainly, it does not seem to follow that, where an injury is done to a corporation, a shareholder will always have a claim for the consequent reduction in the value of his or her shares. As the Ontario Court of Appeal has since ruled, the fact that the plaintiff was the principal shareholder and directing mind of corporations that were defrauded did not entitle him to personal compensation for the losses suffered by the corporations. To hold otherwise would enable him to jump in front of the queue to the prejudice of other corporate creditors. Where a wrong is done to a corporation, a shareholder has no claim for damages in respect of that wrong.[16]

CASE SUMMARY 16.2

An oil exploration company had formed two subsidiaries, apparently to take advantage of government financing. One subsidiary owned a drilling rig; the other contracted to provide drilling services. The rig was damaged due to the alleged negligence of the defendant. The defendant was *prima facie* liable to the corporation that owned the rig, but not for the economic loss sustained by the service corporation. The two corporations were separate entities, and the loss to the service corporation was too remote.[17]

In other cases, the hardship is suffered not by the owners of the corporation but by the persons who deal with it.

CASE SUMMARY 16.3

K, a Toronto lawyer, had incorporated a real estate company, Rockwell, of which he effectively owned almost all the shares. Rockwell became involved in a contractual dispute with another corporation, Newtonbrook, and eventually brought an action against Newtonbrook for specific performance of the contract. Rockwell lost the action, and Newtonbrook was awarded costs of $4800. When Newtonbrook sought to recover the costs, it found that Rockwell's entire assets consisted of $31.85 in its bank account. Newtonbrook's attempt to recover from K personally failed.[18]

---

15. *Kosmopoulos* v. *Constitution Insurance Co. of Canada* (1987), 34 D.L.R. (4th) 208.

16. *Martin* v. *Goldfarb* (1998), 163 D.L.R. (4th) 639; *Meditrust Healthcare Inc.* v. *Shoppers Drug Mart* (2002), 220 D.L.R. (4th) 611.

17. *Bow Valley Husky (Bermuda) Ltd.* v. *Saint John Shipbuilding Ltd.* (1997), 153 D.L.R. (4th) 385.

18. *Rockwell Developments Ltd.* v. *Newtonbrook Plaza Ltd.* (1972), 27 D.L.R. (3d) 651.

Limitations on the Principle of Separate Corporate Existence

When application of the *Salomon* decision leads to unfair results, should the courts refuse to follow it? Should legislation disregard the principle of separate legal identity?

EXCEPTIONS TO LIMITED LIABILITY

The limited liability of shareholders is not absolute. We have already noted that, in practice, shareholders of small private companies are often required to provide security or personal guarantees for loans made to their corporations. The Canada Business Corporations Act (CBCA) provides a further exception to the principle: where shareholders have received an improper distribution of corporate assets, for example, where a dividend has been paid although the corporation had made no profits, they are liable for the corporation's debts to that extent (section 45).[19] Other statutes, such as the federal Bankruptcy and Insolvency Act,[20] require shareholders who have received property from a corporation before it became insolvent to repay the amounts received in certain circumstances.

It is also important to note that the principle of limited liability does not protect persons who happen to be shareholders of corporations from *personal* liability. For example, a director who drives dangerously and causes an accident while on company business is not absolved from liability in tort, even though the corporation may also be vicariously liable.[21] And directors who make negligent misrepresentations regarding the affairs of their corporation may be personally liable for any resulting loss.[22]

OTHER STATUTORY PROVISIONS

There are numerous examples, especially in taxation and labour law, where statutes require the separate personality of corporations to be disregarded. For example, Canadian-controlled private corporations are taxed at a lower rate on the first $400 000 of their annual income; but it is not possible to multiply this concession by forming several distinct corporations, because **associated corporations** are only entitled to a single concession between them.[23] Again, employers are not allowed to avoid statutory employment standards by transferring their assets to an associated corporation, thereby leaving the employer unable to meet employee claims for unpaid wages, vacation pay, and other benefits.[24] Nevertheless, the courts and legislature have stopped short of imposing any form of group liability. Thus, it is only in exceptional circumstances that a parent company will be held liable for the debts of its subsidiary or vice versa.

associated corporations
corporations that are related either (a) vertically, as where one corporation controls the other (parent–subsidiary), or (b) horizontally, as where both corporations are controlled by the same person (affiliates)

[19.] There are also several provisions that make directors liable for the debts of their corporation.

[20.] R.S.C. 1985, c. B-3.

[21.] See *Berger* v. *Willowdale* (1983), 41 O.R. (2d) 89.

[22.] *NBD Bank of Canada* v. *Dofasco Inc.* (1999) 181 D.L.R. (4th) 37; contrast *Montreal Trust Company of Canada* v. *Scotia McLeod Inc.*, (1995), 26 O.R. (3d) 481.

[23.] Income Tax Act, R.S.C. 1985, c. 1 (5th Supp.), s. 125. Corporations are associated where one corporation controls the other (parent–subsidiary relationship), or where both corporations are controlled by the same person or group of persons (affiliates).

[24.] See, for example, Employment Standards Act, R.S.O. 1990, c. E.14, which defines "employer" to include any associated corporation.

ILLUSTRATION 16.1

Holdco is the parent company of a major marketing group. It has a number of divisions, each operated by a wholly owned subsidiary corporation. Retailco, its retailing subsidiary, recently became bankrupt, owing $100 million. At the same time, Creditco, the corporation that operates its credit financing division, has profits of $20 million. The assets of Creditco are not available to pay the creditors of Retailco.

LIFTING THE CORPORATE VEIL

There have also been cases—although in Canada they have been quite rare—where the courts have been prepared to disregard the separate existence of corporations and "lift the veil" of incorporation to impose liability on those that control it. It seems that, in order to identify an individual within a corporation, three conditions must be met:

- The individual must control the corporation.
- That control must have been exercised to commit a fraud, a wrong, or a breach of duty.
- The misconduct must be the cause of the plaintiff's injury.[25]

Rather than equate a controlling shareholder with the corporation that he controls, Canadian courts have generally preferred to seek other routes to secure a just result. As we saw in the *Kosmopoulos* case,[26] the Supreme Court of Canada refused to lift the veil and to hold that the corporation and the individual who owned all of its shares were one and the same person, but reached the same result by finding that he had an insurable interest in the corporation's property.

INTERNATIONAL ISSUE

Foreign Investment in Canadian Corporations

Foreign investment in Canadian corporations is monitored and controlled by Industry Canada pursuant to the Investment Canada Act.[27] In addition, the Canada Business Corporations Act requires that 25 percent of a Canadian corporation's directors be resident Canadians (as does the Ontario, Alberta, Saskatchewan, and Manitoba legislation). However, there are variations among the provinces in the related legislation. To encourage foreign investment, British Columbia and Nova Scotia have dropped directors' residency requirements.

Another recent strategy to increase foreign investment (particularly by Americans) is the introduction of a new type of corporation: the unlimited liability corporation (ULC). As the name suggests, these corporations do not benefit from the protection of limited liability. On wind-up or dissolution, shareholders in a ULC are personally liable

---

25. *W.D. Latimer Co. Ltd. v. Dijon Investments Ltd.* (1992), 12 O.R. (3d) 415. Courts are more likely to pierce the corporate veil when a shareholder engages in conduct amounting to fraud. See *Gilford Motor Company v. Horne*, [1933] Ch. 935 (C.A.).

26. *Supra*, n. 15.

27. R.S.C. 1985, c. I-21.8.

to the ULC's creditors for any unsatisfied debts.[28] So far, Nova Scotia, Alberta, and British Columbia have introduced ULCs in their provincial incorporation legislation. Ontario did not authorize ULCs when it amended its incorporation legislation in 2007. The attraction of ULCs for investors lies in the different tax treatment they receive in the United States. Although ULCs are taxed like any other corporation in Canada, in the United States they are viewed as "flow through" vehicles and no federal income tax is collected from them. When considering investing in this type of corporation, potential shareholders must weigh the tax benefits against the potential liability involved.

Questions to Consider

1. What impact will provincial variation in the availability of ULCs have on foreign investment decisions?

Sources: Geoff Kirbyson, "Alberta's Unlimited Liability Corporations Will Draw Them In," 27(41) *The Lawyers Weekly*, April 7, 2006, available online at www.lawyersweekly.ca/index.php?section=article&articleid=260; Business Corporations Act, S.B.C. c. 57 s. 51.3; Cassels Brock Lawyers, *Business Law Group e-COMMUNIQUÉ*, Vol. 7 No. 2, June 2007, corporate newsletter,,www.casselsbrock.com/publicationdetail.asp?aid=1349.

METHODS OF INCORPORATION

Early Methods of Incorporation

royal charter
a special licence given by the Crown to form a corporation for the purpose of carrying on a particular activity

The oldest method of incorporation in the common law system—dating back to the 16th century—is by **royal charter** granted by the sovereign. Until the 19th century, all corporations were created by charter. Some of these are still in existence—the best known to Canadians being the Hudson's Bay Company, founded in 1670. A few royal charters are still issued today to universities, learned societies, and charitable institutions, but none to business corporations.

special Acts of Parliament
legislative acts creating a specific corporation

From the end of the 18th century, corporations began to be created by **special Acts of Parliament**, especially for large projects of public interest—railroads, canals, waterworks, and other public utilities. Today, special acts are still used to create such corporations as Bell Canada and Canadian Pacific, and also to create special government corporations such as the Central Mortgage and Housing Corporation, the Canadian Broadcasting Corporation, and Air Canada. Parliament and the provincial legislatures have also passed statutes setting out procedures for the incorporation of particular types of businesses, such as banks and trust and loan companies. Such businesses may be incorporated only under those acts.

Incorporation Statutes

Today, however, almost all business (for profit) corporations are incorporated under general incorporation statutes. Under a statute of this type, any group of

---

28. There is some provincial variation in the extent of shareholder liability. Alberta extends shareholder liability beyond liquidation and windup situations. Liability also applies to former shareholders.

persons that complies with its requirements may form a corporation. In Canada, there is both federal and provincial incorporation legislation. The systems in use vary from one province to another.

INCORPORATION ROOTS: THE MEMORANDUM AND LETTERS PATENT SYSTEMS

In 1862, a system was introduced in England that depended upon Parliament rather than the royal prerogative, and that system was adopted by five provinces. It now remains in force in only one—Nova Scotia. The system requires applicants to register a document that sets out the fundamental terms of their agreement, called a **memorandum of association**. If the memorandum and certain other prescribed documents comply with the statute and the registration fee is paid, the authorized government office issues a **certificate of incorporation** and the corporation comes into existence. We shall call corporations incorporated in this manner "memorandum corporations."

The other five provinces and the federal government employed a different system that survives today only in Quebec and Prince Edward Island. There, the incorporating document is called the **letters patent**, an offspring of the royal charter, but issued under the authority of the Crown's representative in each jurisdiction. Under the letters patent system, a general statute regulates the conditions under which the letters patent may be issued. Although in theory the granting of letters patent is discretionary, in practice, the steps taken by applicants do not differ greatly from those for registering a memorandum under the English system.

THE ARTICLES OF INCORPORATION SYSTEM

In 1970, Ontario passed a substantially different Business Corporations Act, creating a new method of incorporation adapted from a system in use in the United States. In 1975, the federal Parliament adopted the same system in its new statute, although many of the provisions of the federal act were quite different from those of the Ontario version. The CBCA has become the model for the new system: Alberta, Manitoba, New Brunswick, Newfoundland, Ontario, Saskatchewan, and, most recently, British Columbia[29] have followed with acts based on the federal scheme, although with local variations. Under the articles of incorporation system, persons who wish to form a corporation sign and deliver articles of incorporation to a government office and, in turn, are issued with a certificate of incorporation.

As the articles of incorporation system is now the most widely used one in Canada, our discussion will focus on it.

---

memorandum of association
a document setting out the essential terms of an agreement to form a corporation

certificate of incorporation
a certificate that a corporation has come into existence

letters patent a document incorporating a corporation, issued by the appropriate authority, and constituting the "charter" of the corporation

---

29. The memorandum system was in force in British Columbia until 2004, when the new Business Corporations Act, SBC 2002, c. 57, came into effect. The system combines features of both the memorandum and letters patent systems. Unfortunately, the terminology chosen is unnecessarily confusing in the Canadian business and legal context; the new statutes have adopted terms used in various parts of the United States, in particular, the word "articles," which has a different meaning in the memorandum system used in Nova Scotia, as well as in Britain and most Commonwealth countries. Canada Business Corporations Act, R.S.C. 1985, c. C-44; Ontario Business Corporations Act, R.S.O. 1990, c. B-16; Alberta Business Corporations Act, R.S.A. 2000, c. B-9; New Brunswick Corporations Act, S.N.B. 1981, c. B-9.1; Saskatchewan Corporations Act, R.S.S. 1977, c. B-10 and Newfoundland Corporations Act, R.S.N.L. 1990, c. C-36.

The Choice of Jurisdiction

The first decision to be made in forming a corporation is whether to incorporate federally or provincially. The CBCA is especially suitable for large businesses that carry on their activities nationwide; but even a small, local, one-person business may incorporate under it.[30]

The activities of a business incorporated under provincial jurisdiction are not restricted to that province. It may carry on business anywhere inside or outside Canada. However, corporations not incorporated within a province—and this includes federally incorporated corporations as well as those incorporated in other provinces—must comply with certain registration requirements in order to carry on business there.[31] Nevertheless, the act under which it was incorporated governs its *internal* operating rules for holding shareholder meetings, electing directors, declaring dividends, and other matters. The checklist below outlines some of the considerations involved in choosing whether to incorporate under federal or provincial jurisdiction.

CHECKLIST	Federal or Provincial Incorporation	
Considerations	**Federal**	**Provincial**
Type of business activity	Mandatory for federally regulated activities (s. 91) such as banking	
Location of business activity	All across the country	One province
Registered office	In Canada	In the province
Name selections	Pre-screened	Variation (many leave burden on business)
Name use	Throughout Canada	Within province
Prestige value	Increased prestige	
Initial fees	Approx. $200	Approx. $300
Directors' Canadian residency	25%	0%–25%*
Annual filings	Multiple separate	Combined

*Saskatchewan, Ontario, Alberta, Manitoba, and Newfoundland require 25 percent and British Columbia, Nova Scotia, P.E.I., New Brunswick, and Quebec have eliminated the residency requirement.

---

30. Federally incorporated corporations (that is, under the CBCA) make up about one-half of the largest corporations in Canada but less than 10 percent of small corporations.

31. See, for example, the Ontario Extra-Provincial Corporations Act, R.S.O. 1990, c. E. 27. The formalities that must be complied with vary to some extent according to whether the corporation is incorporated federally, elsewhere in Canada, or abroad; for example, only non-Canadian corporations require a licence to do business in Ontario. The Corporations Information Act, R.S.O. 1990, c. C.39, requires registration of certain information—for example, place of registered office, names of directors, and place within the province where notice may be served.

THE CONSTITUTION OF A CORPORATION

Articles of Incorporation

Under the articles of incorporation system, a corporation is formed by filing **articles of incorporation** in the prescribed form and paying the required registration fee.[32] The articles of incorporation are often referred to as the "charter" or "constitution" of the corporation and set out essential information about the corporation. In those provinces that have not adopted the articles of incorporation system, the corresponding "charter" document is the letters patent or the memorandum of association.

articles of incorporation
founding corporate document, often referred to as the charter or constitution of the corporation

---

CHECKLIST   Content of the Articles of Incorporation

- name of the corporation
- place where the registered office is situated
- classes and any maximum number of shares that the corporation is authorized to issue
- if there are two or more classes of shares, the rights and restrictions attached to each class
- any restriction on the transfer of shares
- number of directors
- any restrictions on the business that may be carried on
- other provisions that the incorporators choose to include

Occasionally, matters not usually found in a charter will also be included. This may be done in order to give certain "entrenched" rights to minority shareholders. Normally, the charter can only be altered by a special resolution, requiring the approval of a two-thirds majority of the shareholders,[33] and the filing of the amended charter. In most circumstances, however, the charter is an unsuitable instrument for reflecting special arrangements among the shareholders. Instead, shareholders enter into a separate shareholders' agreement outside the corporate constitution, setting out how they will exercise their powers. This topic will be discussed further in the next chapter.

The Corporate Name

As noted above, the articles must include the name of the proposed corporation. The registration of corporate names is closely regulated. The appropriate government office must approve the name and will refuse to register the corporation if it falls within certain prohibited categories (in particular, those that falsely suggest

---

[32.] The incorporation fee under the CBCA is $250 (reduced to $200 for electronic filing). The corresponding Ontario fee is $360 ($300 for electronic filing).

[33.] The procedures for altering letters patent or a memorandum tend to be more cumbersome than those under the newer articles of incorporation system.

an association with the government or with certain professional bodies, or that are scandalous or obscene), or if it is likely to be confused with the name of some other existing corporation. In order to avoid the inconvenience and delay caused by the rejection of a chosen name, intending incorporators normally first make a "name search" to check that no existing corporation is registered with a similar name and undertake trademark searches. Records of corporations are now computerized,[34] which greatly facilitates such checks. If the name is not important to the incorporators, the problem can be avoided by using a "number name," where the registry simply assigns a number to the new corporation.[35]

By-laws

NATURE OF BY-LAWS

by-laws
the internal working rules of a corporation

Incorporators generally keep the incorporating documents as short as possible to gain flexibility in the operation of the corporation, but detailed operating rules are needed for its day-to-day affairs. Under both the articles of incorporation and letters patent systems, these operating rules are called **by-laws**.[36] By-laws are flexible, requiring confirmation by only a simple majority of shareholders, although corporation acts do specify some matters that must be dealt with by special resolution requiring a two-thirds majority.

It is not strictly necessary to have by-laws at all. However, it is normal and convenient to have them, and they may be amended or new by-laws may be adopted, as and when required, with a minimum of formality. Usually, the directors amend by-laws or adopt new ones, but the new or amended by-laws need confirmation at the next general meeting of shareholders in order to remain valid. By-laws fall into two main categories: general operating rules and specific director authorizations.

GENERAL OPERATING RULES

The first category provides general operating rules for the business of the corporation that are usually passed at the first meeting of the shareholders. The first by-laws are often quite long and elaborate, dealing with such matters as the election of directors, their term of office, the place and required notice for meetings of directors, the quorum necessary (that is, the minimum number who must be present) before a meeting of directors can act on behalf of the corporation, the categories of executive officers, provisions for the allotment of shares and for the declaration of dividends, and procedures for holding the annual general meeting and other meetings of shareholders.

---

34. The NUANS (newly upgraded automated name search) system, operated by Industry Canada, provides a computerized search system for all federally (and some provincially) registered companies and trademarks.

35. CBCA, s. 11(2). A number name may be subsequently changed to a "normal" name without the usual formality that is required to amend the articles: CBCA, s. 173(3).

36. For a memorandum corporation they are called articles of association, which causes confusion. The one really important difference is that, in the memorandum system, articles of association can only be altered by a special resolution of the shareholders, requiring a three-quarters majority.

| CHECKLIST | Provisions Included in Typical By-Laws |

- The qualification of a director shall be the holding of at least one share in the capital stock of the corporation.

- A director shall hold office until the third annual general meeting following his appointment.

- Notice of a meeting of directors shall be given in writing to each director not less than seven days before the meeting.

- Three directors shall constitute a quorum for the transaction of any business, except as otherwise provided in these by-laws.

- Questions arising at any meeting of directors shall, except as herein provided, be decided by a majority of votes: in the event of an equality of votes, the Chair of the meeting shall have a second or casting vote.

- Any contract entered into by the corporation that involves the expenditure or the incurring of a liability in excess of $10 000 must be approved by a majority of all the directors.

- Written notice of not less than 28 days, in the case of an annual general meeting, and 21 days, in the case of other shareholder meetings, shall be given to all shareholders entitled to vote at the meeting.

- A quorum is present at a general meeting of shareholders if not less than 10 shareholders, together holding a majority of the shares entitled to vote at the meeting, are present in person or by proxy.

- Shares in the corporation shall be allotted by resolution of the board of directors, approved by not less than two-thirds of all directors, on such terms, for such consideration, and to such persons as the directors determine.

- The directors may at any time by resolution, approved by not less than two-thirds of all directors, declare a dividend or an interim dividend, and pay the same out of the funds of the corporation available for that purpose.

AUTHORIZATION TO DIRECTORS

Most statutes no longer require a by-law to be passed in order to confer any particular power on the directors (unless the corporation's own constitution does).[37] Certain matters, such as the sale of substantially all of a corporation's property or the amalgamation with another corporation, are required to be approved by special resolution of the shareholders, and although directors now normally have the power to borrow money on the security of the corporation's assets without special authorization, it is common for them to ask the shareholders to confirm a major

---

[37.] See CBCA, s. 16(1).

loan transaction, because creditors may insist upon such confirmation. Shareholder resolutions of this type are still often referred to as "by-laws."

TYPES OF BUSINESS CORPORATIONS

Public and Private Corporations

Initially, legislators believed that limited companies would be used primarily for large undertakings having many shareholders (i.e., be public corporations). Consequently, the regulations focused on protection of the general public through disclosure and publication obligations. By the end of the 19th century, it became evident that incorporation was also a useful and fully effective tool for family businesses. Since these small corporations did not seek investment from the general public, the disclosure and publication requirements were unnecessary.

private company
a corporation with a restricted number of shareholders prohibited from issuing its shares to the general public

In 1908, the British Parliament enacted provisions to permit the formation of **private companies**, which were not permitted to offer shares to the public and in which the right to transfer shares had to be restricted in some manner. Those provisions found their way into Canadian incorporation statutes, but now exist only in Prince Edward Island and Nova Scotia. The CBCA and most other provincial statutes now permit even a single shareholder to form a corporation, and do not maintain a formal distinction between public and private corporations. Instead, a more realistic distinction is made between those corporations that issue their shares to the general public[38] and those that do not. The two types of corporation are commonly referred to, respectively, as "widely held" and "closely held."

WIDELY HELD CORPORATIONS

distributing corporation
a corporation that issues its securities to the public; also referred to as issuing corporations, reporting issuers, and publicly traded corporations

Incorporation statutes, such as the CBCA, apply to both widely and closely held corporations but draw a number of distinctions between them. The CBCA, for example, imposes various obligations upon what it terms a "**distributing corporation**" with respect to such matters as proxy solicitation, the number of directors, and the need for an audit committee. But the most important difference is that distributing corporations are also subject to regulation under the relevant provincial securities acts in those provinces in which their securities are issued or traded. Increasingly, and especially since the Enron affair, securities legislation and the policies of securities regulators and of stock exchanges have come to play an important role in the way in which Canada's larger corporations are structured and conduct their business and affairs.

CLOSELY HELD CORPORATIONS

The main use of the closely held corporation is to incorporate small- and medium-sized business enterprises where the number of participants is small. A closely held corporation is a true limited company with the same legal significance and corporate independence as the widely held corporation. In fact, when a large corporation creates a subsidiary, it usually does so by incorporating a closely held corporation. Many large U.S. and other foreign corporations operate wholly owned subsidiaries in Canada that are closely held. All the shares are held by the parent corporation, except for a few that may be held here by corporate

---

38. The CBCA describes these as "distributing" corporations. Securities legislation refers to these as issuing corporations or reporting issuers.

officers. A number of these subsidiaries rival our own large public corporations in size.

The vast majority of corporations are closely held—over 90 percent in Canada. It is therefore rather surprising that they are largely neglected as a subject of study in business administration. The literature of economics, finance, accounting, and management directs its attention to widely held corporations. Closely held corporations have been permitted the luxury of operating in an atmosphere of relative privacy. In a closely held corporation, the owners are usually the managers as well, thus focusing questions of management and ultimate decision making within a small group. We shall examine the legal implications of this characteristic of closely held corporations in the next chapter.

Corporate Groups

The largest businesses, in Canada and internationally, frequently comprise a group of corporations, one or more of which is widely held, with shares held by the public and listed on one or more stock exchanges, together with a number of subsidiaries that are closely held, in the sense that they are often wholly owned by their parent company. For example, the corporate structure of the Hollinger companies and related entities (formerly controlled by Lord Black) involved over 60 companies—some public, some private—and were subject to a number of different jurisdictions.[39] Groups of this nature can give rise to extremely complex relationships to possible conflicts.

Professional Corporations

Members of many of the leading professions have been prohibited from incorporating their practices, either by the rules of the professional body to which they belong or under the statute governing the profession. They have consequently been restricted to practising as sole proprietors or in partnership with the disadvantage, in the latter case, of being liable for obligations incurred by their co-partners. One response to that problem, which we have already discussed, has been the adoption of legislation permitting the establishment of limited liability partnerships (LLPs).

Most provinces now allow for the incorporation of the **professional corporation (PC)**.[40] Under the legislation, members of listed professions may form a PC, provided it is permitted by the rules of the profession itself and the professional controls the voting shares.[41] The Saskatchewan act provides:

> One or more members of an association may incorporate a corporation pursuant to the Business Corporations Act for the purpose of carrying on, in the name of the corporation, the business of providing professional services that may lawfully be performed by members of the association.[42]

professional corporation (PC)
a special type of business corporation that may be formed by members of a profession

---

[39] See *Catalyst Fund General Partner I Inc. v. Hollinger Inc.* [2004] O.J. No. 4722.

[40] Alberta has allowed the creation of PCs for more than 20 years. The Ontario and Saskatchewan legislation only came into effect in 2001. Manitoba adopted a rather different approach, by amending the relevant statutes governing those professional bodies that are now allowed to incorporate: Professional Corporations (Various Acts Amendment) Act, S.M. 1999, c. 41. Quebec still does not allow professional corporations for dentists, doctors, or engineers.

[41] In Ontario, for example, the Chartered Accountants Act, the Public Accountants Act, and the Law Society Act have been amended to permit the formation of PCs. The legislation is contained in the oddly named Balanced Budgets for Brighter Futures Act, S.O. 2000, c. 42.

[42] Professional Corporations Act, S.S. 2001, c. P-27.1, s. 4(1).

The words "Professional Corporation" or the abbreviation "PC" must appear in the name of the corporation,[43] and all members of the corporation must be members of the profession.[44] Regarding liability, the act provides:

> The liability of a member of an association to a person who receives services from the member is not affected by the fact that the services were provided by the member as an employee of, or on behalf of, a professional corporation.[45]

In effect, a member of a profession who incorporates (either alone or together with other members) remains responsible for her own negligence or misconduct towards clients, although the principle of limited liability does seem to provide protection against the claims of other creditors—for example, lessors of premises or suppliers of equipment. The principal advantage of professional incorporation is not to obtain a degree of limited liability, but rather to enjoy a number of tax advantages that are not available to sole proprietorships and partnerships.[46]

Only members of listed professions may form a PC, but one should remember that not all professions are prohibited from incorporating. For example, engineers and geophysicists are not "listed" and consequently cannot form a PC; however, that is no disadvantage since they are able to establish a "normal" corporation.

ETHICAL ISSUE

Undermining Professional Standards?

Recent legislative changes have introduced the LLP and the professional corporation as alternative vehicles for conducting professional activities, and the concept of multi-disciplinary partnerships is also gaining ground. This has led to fears, in some quarters, that professional standards are being undermined. In particular, it is argued that such developments may lead to the destruction of the professional–client relationship. Would you really want to have your teeth pulled by a corporation?

Others would argue that there are adequate safeguards to ensure that professional standards are maintained, and that there is no valid reason for denying to professionals the benefits of incorporation that are enjoyed by other businesspersons (and by some professions).

Questions to Consider

1. Are the recent changes discarding the traditions of a century, or are they simply keeping up with the times?

2. Is there any reason why professionals, such as accountants, doctors, and lawyers, should not be allowed to incorporate in the "normal" way?

---

[43] *Ibid.*, s. 4(2).

[44] *Ibid.*, ss. 5(2), 6(1). Thus, multi-disciplinary PCs are not (yet) permitted.

[45] *Ibid.*, s. 15.

[46] In particular, the lower rate of income tax on small corporations and greater flexibility in providing for retirement pensions. However, there may also be tax disadvantages, so the decision to form a PC must be considered very carefully.

CORPORATE CAPITAL

Equity and Debt

There are two principal ways in which a corporation can raise funds: by issuing shares (equity) and by borrowing (debt). A third method—financing the corporation's activities out of retained profits—is really akin to the first, since the shareholders are effectively reinvesting part of their profit. Although borrowing increases the funds that are at the disposal of the corporation's management, it is really misleading to speak of "debt capital," since borrowing increases both assets and liabilities. A corporation's true capital is its "equity capital" or "share capital."

Share Capital

Every business corporation must have a share capital.[47] The word "capital" has different meanings in different contexts. In letters patent and memorandum jurisdictions, when a corporation is incorporated, its charter places an upper limit on the number or money value of shares it may issue. This limit is called the **authorized capital**. A corporation need not issue all its authorized share capital. The **issued capital** and **paid-up capital** of a corporation are, as their names indicate, the parts of the authorized capital that have been issued and paid for.

In articles of incorporation jurisdictions, by contrast, a corporation may state the maximum number of shares that can be issued if it so wishes, but does not have to do so. A corporation must, however, still keep a **stated capital account** disclosing the consideration received for each **share** issued. Shares must be fully paid for at the time of issue.[48] Consequently, there is no difference between issued capital and paid-up capital.

There are several ways of becoming a shareholder:

- by being one of the original applicants for incorporation
- by buying shares issued by a corporation subsequent to its incorporation, or
- by acquiring (by purchase or gift) previously issued shares from another shareholder

The first two ways result from contracts between the shareholder and the corporation, and the transactions increase the issued capital as shown in the accounts of the corporation. The third way is the result of a transfer to which the corporation is not a party at all, and does not affect its accounts.

authorized capital
the maximum number (or value) of shares that a corporation is permitted by its charter to issue

issued capital
the shares that have been issued by a corporation

paid-up capital
the shares that have been issued and fully paid for

stated capital account
the amount received by a corporation for the issue of its shares

share
a member's proportionate interest in the capital of a corporation

Par Values

Until the early part of the 20th century, all shares had a nominal or **par value**—a fixed value established in the charter like a bank note or a bond. Shares were issued by the corporation at their par value. However, par value provided little indication of a share's real value; once issued a share rarely had a market price identical with its par value.

A corporation was prohibited from issuing its shares for less than their par value (that is, at a "discount"). If a corporation's shares were selling on the market

par value
a nominal value attached to a share at the time of issue

[47.] Charitable and non-profit corporations need not have a share capital.

[48.] CBCA, s. 25(3). Previously, shares could be issued "partly paid," with the corporation being able to make a subsequent "call" for the remainder of the price.

below their par value and the corporation required additional capital, investors would not purchase a new issue at par. In order to make an issue, the corporation would be compelled to reduce the par value of the shares to a more realistic figure and to reduce its capital accordingly by obtaining an amendment to its charter, causing delay and expense.

no par value share
a share that has no nominal value attached to it

The United States introduced **no par value shares**—that is, shares that represent a specific proportion of the issued capital of the corporation, rather than a fixed sum of money. The advantages of no par value shares, in particular, the fact that they may be issued from time to time at prices that correspond to their current market value, resulted in their adoption by all the jurisdictions in the United States; soon afterwards they were permitted in Canada. The articles of incorporation system has now abolished par value shares entirely.

ILLUSTRATION 16.2

Pliable Plastics Inc. is incorporated under the articles of incorporation system. Its articles contain no restriction on the total number of shares that may be issued, and its shares have no par value. Initially, it issued 50 000 shares at $100 each, giving it a stated capital of $5 000 000. The directors wish to raise a further $3 000 000.

If the current market price of the shares has fallen to $60, they can raise $3 000 000 by issuing 50 000 new shares at that price. On the other hand, if the market price has risen to $120, they will need to issue only 25 000.

---

preferred share
a share carrying preferential rights to receive a dividend and/or to be redeemed on the dissolution of the corporation

Until the introduction of the articles of incorporation system, **preferred shares** were almost always issued with a par value. They paid a preferred dividend expressed as a percentage of the par value and the corporation could redeem them at par value. For example, a share might have a par value of $100 (and be redeemable at that price) and pay a dividend of 8 percent (that is, $8 per share). With the abolition of par values, preferred shares are now stated to have a redemption price ($100), with a preferred dividend expressed simply as a sum of money ($8).

CORPORATE SECURITIES

The Distinction Between Shares and Bonds

bond
a document evidencing a debt owed by a corporation

A corporation may borrow money in a number of ways, but when it borrows substantial sums on a long-term basis it normally does so by issuing **bonds**. The classic distinction between shares and bonds (or "debentures," as they are sometimes called) is that the holder of a share is a member of, and owner of an interest in, the corporation. The holder of a bond is a creditor. In the business world, there is no such clear-cut distinction. In the language of modern business, the true *equity* owner of a corporation, and the person who takes the greatest risk, is the holder of **common shares**. From this end of the scale, we proceed by degrees to the person who is a mortgagee or bondholder, where the holder takes the least risk. In between we may have the holders of preferred shares. Today, most larger corporations have, in addition to an issue of common shares, one or more classes of bonds or debentures and probably also a class of preferred shares.

common share
a share carrying no preferential right

When deciding whether to invest in the shares or the bonds of a corporation, an individual usually does not make a conscious choice between becoming a member (that is, an equity owner) and becoming a creditor. She regards herself in both instances as an investor. Her investment decisions are determined primarily by economic considerations. Bonds provide a fixed and guaranteed return (provided the corporation remains solvent), in the form of regular interest payments and the right to be redeemed in full at their maturity date. Common shares carry no guarantee that their holders will receive anything, either in the form of dividends or on dissolution, but their holders participate in any "growth" of the corporation. Preferred shareholders come somewhere in between. They are entitled to receive dividends and to have their shares redeemed on the dissolution of the corporation, before payments are made to the holders of the common shares, but those rights are often restricted to a fixed dividend and a fixed amount payable on redemption.

The line between shareholder and bondholder is nonetheless a distinct and important one in its legal consequences for a corporation. First of all, since bondholders are creditors, interest paid to them is a debt of the corporation. It must be paid whether or not the corporation has earned profits for the year. Shareholders are not creditors and receive dividends only when the directors declare them. One consequence, especially important for taxation, is that interest payments are normally an expense of doing business and are deducted before taxable income is calculated; dividends, on the other hand, are payable out of after-tax profits. Second, bonds are usually secured by a mortgage or charge on the property of the corporation. If a corporation becomes insolvent, its secured bondholders are entitled to be repaid not only before the shareholders but also before the general creditors. They are secured creditors, and the trustee acting for them can sell the corporation's assets to satisfy the debt owed to them.

Rights of Security Holders

BONDHOLDERS

Bondholders do not normally have a direct voice in the management of the corporation unless it is in breach of the terms of the trust deed or indenture under which the securities were created. Only when a corporation gets into financial difficulty or is in breach of the trust deed may the trustee step in and take part in management on behalf of the bondholders. It is true, however, that bondholders do exert an indirect form of control over management in the restrictive clauses commonly written into bond indentures, which may place a ceiling on the further long-term borrowing of the corporation, on the amount of dividends it may pay, and even, in smaller corporations, on the salaries it pays to its officers.

COMMON SHAREHOLDERS

By contrast, common shareholders have, in theory at least, a strong voice in the management of the corporation. As we shall see in the next chapter, it is they who elect the board of directors and who must approve major changes in the corporation's activities. Otherwise, however, their rights are limited. They have no entitlement to a dividend and can receive one only after bondholders and preferred shareholders have been paid. And, on the liquidation of the corporation, their entitlement is to share what is left after the claims of creditors and preferred shareholders have been satisfied.

PREFERRED SHAREHOLDERS

Preferred shareholders are in an intermediate category. Usually, they are entitled to be paid a fixed dividend before any dividend is paid to the common shareholders, and they are entitled to be paid the fixed redemption price of their shares on liquidation of the corporation before any surplus is distributed to the common shareholders. Frequently, they have no right to vote unless the payment of dividends to them is in arrears. In this respect they are more like creditors than investors. However, payment of preferred dividends is not a contractual commitment of a corporation as is bond interest; a preferred shareholder must enforce her rights as an individual and is not dependent upon a trustee taking action, as a bondholder normally is.

CLASS RIGHTS

Where a corporation issues more than one class of shares—for example, common shares and preferred shares—the precise rights of each class must be set out in its constitution.[49] The various combinations of rights and privileges that may attach to a class of shares are extensive and may relate not only to dividend rights and rights of redemption, but also to voting rights, rights to appoint directors, and sometimes to the right to convert a security of one class into a security of another class.

cumulative right
the right of the holder of a preferred share to be paid arrears from previous years before any dividend is paid on the common shares

participating right
the right of a holder of a preferred share to participate in surplus profits or assets of the corporation in addition to the amount of the preferred dividend or redemption price

Problems of interpretation arise in the drafting of rights for various classes of shareholders. Two questions with respect to preferred shareholders' rights to dividends are particularly important. The first is whether the rights are **cumulative**: if the full preferred dividend is not paid in one year, do the arrears accumulate so that they must be paid in a subsequent year or on winding up the corporation, before the common shareholders are entitled to anything? The second is whether on winding up, their rights are **participating**: if after the preferred shareholders have been fully paid, do they still participate in any remaining surplus along with the common shareholders? This uncertainty makes it all the more important to draft class rights with the greatest care.

CHECKLIST	**Priority of Payment on Liquidation of a Corporation**

On liquidation of a corporation its assets must be distributed in the following sequence. (Note that bondholders are creditors—and usually they are secured creditors.)

(1) secured creditors

(2) unsecured creditors

(3) preferred shareholders

(4) common shareholders

The Transfer of Corporate Securities

NEGOTIABILITY

We have seen that share and bond certificates are a type of personal property subject to different rules of transfer and ownership from those that apply to sales of

---

[49.] See CBCA, s. 6(1)(c).

goods. We noted further that these choses in action may in some circumstances be treated as negotiable instruments. Thus, bond certificates in bearer form may be considered as a type of negotiable instrument at common law. Articles of incorporation statutes expressly treat share certificates as a type of negotiable instrument.[50]

In theory, if bonds and shares are to serve the purposes of a capital market, they should be readily transferable (that is, "liquid"). When bonds and shares are treated as negotiable instruments, an innocent holder for value may often acquire a better title than his predecessor had, as, for example, when he purchases bonds or share certificates that have been stolen. However, two unfortunate results have also flowed from this development: first, there has been an increased temptation to indulge in theft as it is easy to sell stolen certificates; second, it has become easier to pass off forged (and therefore worthless) certificates on purchasers. The innocent holder of a forged negotiable instrument, as we have seen, obtains no title.

RESTRICTIONS ON SHARE TRANSFER

In a widely held corporation, shares are almost always freely transferable; if they are not, the shares will not be accepted for listing on a stock exchange. In contrast, closely held corporations almost invariably restrict the transfer of shares; otherwise, it would be difficult for them to remain closely held.

Restrictions on share transfer are required to be set out in the corporation's constitution,[51] and can take almost any form. Such restrictions must also be noted on the share certificate; otherwise, they are not binding on a purchaser who has no notice of the restriction.[52] In practice, the most common restriction is to require the consent of the board of directors to any transfer, but there are other varieties, such as giving the right of first refusal to existing shareholders or directors before a shareholder can sell to an outsider, or giving a major shareholder the right of veto. Requiring the consent of directors gives them the discretion to approve or reject a proposed member of the corporation, much as partners determine whether they will admit a new partner.

SUMMARY

The process of incorporation

- A corporation is a fiction or a myth that has a separate status as a legal person from its shareholders
- Methods of incorporation in Canada are registration, memorandum of association, letters patent, and articles of incorporation

---

[50.] Unless there are restrictions on transfer noted on the certificate: CBCA, s. 48(3).

[51.] See, for example, CBCA, s. 6(1)(d).

[52.] CBCA, s. 49(8). See *Bank Leu AG* v. *Gaming Lottery Corp.* (2003), 231 D.L.R. (4th) 251.

Separate legal entity

- The corporation is a separate legal entity
- Shareholders own the shares of the corporation; the corporation owns the assets it buys
- Sometimes the courts "lift the corporate veil" and find directors or officers liable
- Shareholders are not liable for the debts of a corporation; they have limited liability so can lose only what they have invested
- Corporations have capacity of natural person, except for special statute corporations, whose capacity may be limited

Corporate Capital

- Funding may be derived from the selling of shares (which may be common shares or preferred shares with special rights and restrictions), or through borrowing (which can involve the sale of bonds or debentures, secured or unsecured)
- Shareholders are participants in the corporation, while lenders are creditors
- Broadly held corporations (many shareholders) have more stringent government controls and greater reporting requirements than closely held corporations (few shareholders)

QUESTIONS

1. What is meant by a "legal person"?

2. What is meant by "limited liability"? Whose liability is limited?

3. What are the main differences between partnerships and corporations?

4. What were the principal arguments made by the creditors in the Salomon case in attempting to make Salomon personally liable?

5. In what ways may two or more corporations be said to be "associated"?

6. What is meant by "lifting the corporate veil"?

7. How does the articles of incorporation system of forming a corporation differ from (a) the letters patent system and (b) the memorandum and articles system?

8. What information must be set out in articles of incorporation?

9. Why must care be taken in selecting a corporate name? What is a "number name"?

10. What is the main function of a corporation's by-laws?

11. What are the principal characteristics of closely held corporations?

12. What are the main advantages of forming a professional corporation?

13. What is the function of a corporation's stated capital account?

14. In what way are par values for shares likely to be misleading?

15. What special rights are normally carried by preferred shares?

16. What are the usual rights of bondholders?

17. What factors influence an investor's choice between shares and bonds?

18. In what sequence should a corporation's assets be distributed on liquidation of the corporation?

19. In what circumstances are restrictions on the transfer of shares binding on purchasers of the shares?

Chapter 17

Corporate Governance:
The Internal Affairs of Corporations

INTRODUCTION

This chapter addresses corporate governance. It discusses the internal affairs and the business of a corporation.

WHAT IS CORPORATE GOVERNANCE?

Corporate governance
the rules governing the organization and management of the business and affairs of a corporation in order to meet its internal objectives and external responsibilities

Corporate governance refers to the organization and management of the business and affairs of a corporation in order to meet its internal objectives and external responsibilities. Where do we find the rules of corporate governance? The incorporating documents—the articles of incorporation and the by-laws—create the management structure within the corporation and this is one set of corporate governance standards. Also, as noted earlier, each incorporating jurisdiction—Canada and each province—has corporation legislation that must be followed. It is in this legislation that we find the legal rules of corporate governance.

The Canada Business Corporations Act (CBCA)[1] and the corresponding provincial statutes draw a broad distinction between two aspects of a corporation's activities. Section 102 states that "the directors shall manage, or supervise the management of, the *business and affairs* of a corporation" (italics added). The difference between these two terms is explained in section 2(1), where "affairs" are defined as "the relationships among a corporation . . . and the shareholders, directors and officers . . . but *does not include the business carried on* [by the corporation] . . ." (italics added). The distinction, which is helpful in understanding the complex activities of corporations, is between

   (a) the *affairs*: the internal arrangements among those responsible for running a corporation—the directors and officers—and its main beneficiaries—the shareholders—which we discuss in this chapter; and
   (b) the *business*: the external relations between a corporation and those who deal with it as a business enterprise—its customers, suppliers, and employees—as well as relations with government regulators and society as a whole.

There is at least one group for which the distinction is blurred: the shareholders in a publicly traded corporation. An invitation to the public to invest in a corporation is directed towards those who may not yet be part of its internal relations, but if the members of the public accept an offer to buy shares, they will subsequently become involved in its "affairs." These potential public shareholders are protected through special provincial securities regulations imposed on only those companies issuing shares to the public. In this chapter we will review the basic legal rules of corporate governance and the liability arising from their breach. The rules discussed in this chapter apply to both *privately* and *publicly held* corporations and are codified in federal and provincial legislation. Breach of the rules may give rise to civil, regulatory, or even criminal liability or a combination of all three.

CORPORATE GOVERNANCE OF PUBLICLY TRADED CORPORATIONS

Recent public corporate scandals such as those involving Enron and WorldCom led securities regulators to tighten the rules of corporate governance for **publicly traded corporations** (this chapter will also use the CBCA term, *distributing corporation*). First, the United States passed the Sarbanes-Oxley Act of 2002 (SOX), and next, the Securities and Exchange Commission introduced new rules, policies, and recommendations for the internal operations of public companies.[2] Canadian

publicly traded corporations corporations that issue shares to the public, also known as public corporations, widely held corporations, reporting issuers, and issuing corporations

---

[1] R.S.C. 1985, c. C 44. The Act was substantially amended by Bill S-11, S.C. 2001, c. 14. Unless otherwise stated, statutory references in this chapter are to that Act, as amended. Corresponding provincial legislation: Business Corporations Act, S.B.C. 2002, c. 57; Business Corporations Act, R.S.A. 2000, c. B-9; Business Corporations Act, R.S.S. 1978, c. B-10; Corporations Act, C.C.S.M. c. C225; Business Corporations Act (OBCA) R.S.O. 1990, c. B-16; Companies Act, R.S.N.S. 1989, c. 81; Companies Act, R.S.N.B. 1973, c. C-13; Companies Act, R.S.P.E.I. 1988, c. C-14; Corporations Act, R.S.N.L. 1990, c. C-36. Most provincial legislation is similar to the federal legislation. Relevant major departures will be noted.

[2] 15 U.S.C. s. 7201 et. seq.

securities regulators adopted some of the SOX standards.[3] This means publicly traded companies are required to meet the standards in both the CBCA (or the relevant provincial incorporating legislation) *and* the provincial securities legislation. These rules increase the protection available to the public stakeholders— public shareholders, creditors, employees, and lenders. The general themes of the legislation are independence of decision makers, transparency, disclosure, accountability, and organizational checks and balances.[4] Some of the recommendations include:

- A majority of directors should be independent.
- The CEO should not also hold the position of chair of the board.
- The corporation should establish separate, independent committees of the board to regulate executive compensation and nomination of board members.
- The corporation should adopt and publish a "code of ethics."
- The board should perform regular self-assessments.

Many privately held corporations choose to comply with the higher standard of corporate governance in order to meet their ethical responsibilities and in preparation for a **public offering** in the future. Where relevant, this chapter will identify the heightened requirements for public companies.

public offering
selling shares to the public, which must be done in compliance with provincial securities regulations

THE STRUCTURE OF THE MODERN BUSINESS CORPORATION

Business corporations differ greatly from one another in their size and composition. Modern legislation tries to take these differences into account. However, there are certain elements that are essential to all corporations.

The three basic groups common to all corporations are the shareholders, the **board of directors**, (generally referred to as "the board") and the **officers**. In small private corporations, such as family companies, it often happens that most or even all of the shareholders are also directors and officers. Even if the distinction between shareholders and directors may sometimes become blurred in practice— for example, when they get together to discuss business, they may not specify whether the meeting constitutes a directors' meeting or a shareholders' meeting— the distinction remains important legally.

In a large corporation, by contrast, the board of directors may have as many as 15 or 20 members who are elected by shareholders. Generally, in such cases the board will appoint or hire a *chief executive officer* (CEO, also often called the president or managing director) or a smaller committee of directors (the *management committee or executive committee*) to direct the affairs and business of the corporation

board of directors
the governing body of a corporation, responsible for the management of its business and affairs

officers
high-ranking members of a corporation's management team as defined in the by-laws or appointed by the directors, such as the president, vice-president, controller, chief executive officer, chief financial officer, general counsel, and general manager

---

3. National Policy Instrument 58-201. Although securities regulation is a matter of provincial jurisdiction and each province has its own legislation and Securities Commission, the 13 provincial and territorial regulators cooperate on most regulation through the Canadian Securities Administrators (CSA). The result is nationally consistent instruments, guidelines, and policies that are adopted under the same numbering system.

4. Richard DeGeorge, Chapter 9, "Corporate Governance, Accounting Disclosure and Insider Trading," in *Business Ethics*, 6th ed. (Upper Saddle River, NJ: Prentice Hall, 2006).

and to supervise its other officers and employees. CEO's are most often full-time employees of the company who, together with other officers, manage the corporation. It is this team, not the board, that are known collectively as "the management." The management refers only the important policy matters to the full board of directors. In turn, the board of directors usually calls no more than the required annual meeting of shareholders, at which it reports to them on the state of the corporation's affairs and holds elections to determine the board of directors for the coming year.

Public or distributing corporations are required to have an **audit committee**, whose members include at least three directors. Originally, the audit committee's task was only to review the financial statements of the corporation before they were submitted to the full board for approval.[5] Recent provincial securities regulations expand the responsibilities of the committee and require *all* audit committee members to be independent directors; the auditor must be retained by and report to the audit committee rather than the board or corporate management.[6] A **compensation committee**, responsible for setting director and officer compensation, and a **nominating committee**, responsible for finding new directors, are also recommended but not mandatory.[7] Figure 17.1 illustrates the general structure of a corporation.

audit committee
a group of directors responsible for overseeing the corporate audit and the preparation of financial statements. The committee has wider responsibilities in a distributing corporation.

compensation committee
committee responsible for setting director and officer pay

nominating committee
committee responsible for proposing and recruiting new directors

Figure 17.1 Corporate Structure

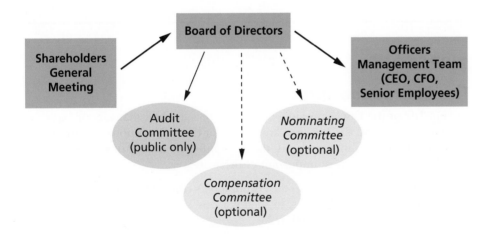

Power originates with the general meeting of shareholders. The shareholders elect a board of directors to manage the corporation. The directors, in turn, appoint or hire a chief executive officer, who is the highest-ranking employee in charge of the day-to-day running of the corporation.

---

5. CBCA, s. 171. Any other corporation (that is not public or distributing) may have an audit committee.

6. National Instrument No. 52-110, s. 2.3, 3.1. This instrument also creates an expanded definition of "independent" that means free of "any direct or indirect material relationship." Previously, only the majority of the directors on this committee had to be independent.

7. National Policy No. 58-201; Multilateral Instrument 58-101.

INTERNATIONAL ISSUE

Sarbanes-Oxley Act of 2002

The U.S. Sarbanes-Oxley Act of 2002 (SOX) set new standards for the internal organization of publicly traded companies. These standards go beyond the Canadian regulations and include mandatory codes of ethics and compensation committees, expanded disclosure requirements, and CEO and CFO compensation clawbacks. Compliance does not come cheaply: American businesses are complaining about the high cost of implementing SOX standards.

SOX has also had a large influence on the corporate governance of Canadian businesses. Its reach extends beyond American geographic borders and applies to many Canadian corporations. Canadian corporations trading on an American stock exchange must comply with SOX, as must Canadian subsidiaries of U.S. parent corporations. If Canadian corporations want to find investors internationally, they must be aware of the corporate governance rules in foreign jurisdictions.

Question to Consider

1. Should public corporate governance rules be those of the incorporating jurisdiction or those of the jurisdiction where the shares are sold? Or both?

Sources: L. McCallum and P. Puri, *Canadian Companies' Guide to the Sarbanes Oxley Act* (Toronto: Butterworths, 2004); Kevin Drawback, "Reform Backlash Gathers Momentum: Restriction on Class-action Suits Part of a Trend," *National Post*, February 21, 2005.

DIRECTORS

The Role of the Directors

Section 102 of the CBCA provides that the directors shall manage, or *supervise* the management of, the business and affairs of the corporation. In addition to the general power of management, the Act confers a number of specific powers on the directors. The most important of these are:

(a) to issue shares—subject to the corporation's constitution, the directors may issue shares at such times, to such persons, and for such consideration as they may determine (section 25).

(b) to declare dividends—the directors determine whether, or to what extent, profits should be distributed to the shareholders or retained in the corporation.

(c) to adopt by-laws governing the day-to-day affairs of the corporation—the directors may adopt new by-laws or amend existing ones. Although they must be submitted for approval at the next meeting of shareholders, the by-laws remain effective until then (section 103).

(d) to call meetings of shareholders (section 133). The directors must call an annual general meeting each year, but they may call additional meetings whenever they wish.

(e) to delegate responsibilities (except those outlined in (a) to (d)) and appoint officers (sections 115 and 121). Officers do not have to be directors.

> ## CHECKLIST   Powers of Directors
>
> In relation to the internal affairs of the corporation, the most important powers given to the directors are:
>
> - to issue shares
> - to declare dividends
> - to adopt by-laws
> - to call meetings of shareholders
> - to delegate responsibilities and appoint officers

A corporation is required to have one or more directors.[8] A distributing corporation must have a minimum of three directors, at least two of whom must be *independent*; that is, they must not be officers or employees of the corporation (section 102(2)). Provincial securities regulations define "independent" more broadly as "no direct or indirect material relationship with the corporation."

Where a corporation has more than one director, decisions of the board of directors are normally taken by majority vote, unless the corporate constitution requires a higher special majority or unanimity. Usually, the by-laws make provision for the holding of meetings of the board, the election of a chairperson, rules on voting, quorums, and like matters.

Shareholders play little or no part in management. They have certain rights, the most important being to vote at meetings, but generally, once the shareholders have elected a board of directors, they have no further power to participate in management. If they do not like the way the directors are running the corporation's business and affairs, they cannot interfere. Legally, their main course of action is to dismiss the directors and elect new ones in their place.[9] It is consequently of vital importance that the shareholders select competent and trustworthy individuals as their directors.

> ## CASE SUMMARY 17.1
>
> The majority shareholder of a corporation wanted the corporation to sell its main asset. At his request the directors called a general meeting of shareholders, which passed a resolution (over the opposition of some of the minority shareholders) instructing the board of directors to go ahead with the sale.
>
> The board refused to do so, believing that the sale was not in the best interests of the corporation. The majority shareholder sought a declaration that the board was bound to carry out the instructions of the general meeting of shareholders.

---

8. Even a corporation with only a single shareholder must have one or more directors, though there is no reason why the shareholder should not also be the sole director. The articles of incorporation are required to state the number (or the minimum and maximum number) of directors that the corporation is to have (section 6(1)(e)).

9. If dissatisfied shareholders hold a sufficient proportion of the shares, they need not wait until the next meeting called by the directors; they may requisition a meeting (s. 143) to elect a new board. As will be discussed under the section called Protections of Minority Shareholders, in some situations there may be court remedies available.

> The court refused to grant the declaration, ruling that it is the directors who manage the business of a corporation and, until such time as they are replaced, they must act as they think best for the corporation and are not bound to follow instructions from the shareholders.[10]

One very important effect of this rule is that the shareholders cannot compel the directors to declare a dividend, unless there is an express requirement in the corporation's constitution that a dividend be paid in particular circumstances.

Appointment and Removal of Directors

A director of a corporation must be a minimum of 18 years of age, be of sound mind, and not have declared bankruptcy (section 105). In addition, at least 25 per-cent of the directors of a corporation must be resident Canadians.[11] Unless required by the articles of incorporation, a director need not hold shares in the corporation.

A corporation's first directors are appointed at the time of incorporation and hold office until the first meeting of shareholders, which must be held not less than 18 months after the corporation comes into existence (section 133). Subsequently, directors are elected, re-elected, or replaced on a regular basis. Normally this occurs at the annual general meeting of the corporation, but elections may be held at any time at a special meeting called for that purpose. Casual vacancies on the board—for example, where a director dies or becomes seriously ill—may normally be filled by the remaining directors.

Directors are elected by ordinary resolution of the shareholders (section 106(3)); that is, a simple majority vote is sufficient.[12] The effect of this rule is that a single shareholder or a group of shareholders, holding anything more than 50 percent of the total votes, is able to elect the entire board of directors. (Conversely, complete equality between two competing groups can lead to deadlock—as sometimes happens when two equal partners incorporate their business.) An exception to the general rule may be made by providing, in the articles of incorporation, that directors be elected by a system of **cumulative voting**—a form of proportional representation designed to ensure that any substantial minority of shareholders will be represented on the board. Such systems, however, are quite rare in Canadian corporations.[13]

A director's term of office may not exceed three years, and even during that term a special meeting may be called to vote on the removal of a director

cumulative voting
a method of electing directors by a form of proportional representation

---

[10.] *Automatic Self-Cleansing Filter Syndicate Co. Ltd. v. Cuninghame*, [1906] 2 Ch. 34 (U.K.C.A.).

[11.] S. 105(3), as amended. Prior to November 2001, the CBCA required a majority of directors to be resident Canadians. Some provinces still require a majority of directors to be resident Canadians, while others have no residence or citizenship requirement. If there are fewer than four directors, at least one director must be a resident.

[12.] The Alberta and Saskatchewan statutes allow for directors to be appointed by a class of shareholders, or by creditors or employees, if the articles so provide: Business Corporations Act, R.S.A. c. B-9, s. 106(9); R.S.S. c. B-10, s. 101(8).

[13.] Except in New Brunswick, where cumulative voting is mandatory: Business Corporations Act, R.S.N.B. c. 9.1, s. 65.

(section 109). Except where cumulative voting is provided for, an ordinary resolution (simple majority) is sufficient for the removal of any director, and the articles may not prescribe a greater majority (section 6(4)).

OFFICERS

As noted, officers are responsible for the day-to-day "hands on" management of the corporation. Officers derive their power from the directors. The CBCA defines an officer as "someone appointed by the directors" with functions similar to "a president, vice-president, secretary, treasurer etc . . ." (section 2(1)). It is for the directors to define and designate responsibilities of each officer (section 121) and this is usually done in the by-laws. The only statutory requirement is that the officer be of "full capacity." Officers may be removed by the directors. In most corporations, officers exercise tremendous power and, as will be discussed in the next section, they are subject to the same duties as directors. The responsibilities of officers of distributing corporations are attracting more attention from provincial regulators, which now require CEO's and CFO's to cerhtify contents of a corporation's audited financial statements.

CHECKLIST	Corporate Governance Legislative Overview		
	Private Corporations	**Public Corporations**	
	CBCA	CBCA	Securities Regulation
Minimum directors	1 s. 102(2)	3 s. 102(2)	3
Independent directors	Not required	2	Majority Recommended NP 58-201 s. 3.1
Financial statements	Unaudited s. 163 (1)	Audited s. 161	Audited by Public Accountant and certified by CEO/CFO
Annual general meeting of shareholders	Required	Required	Required
Audit committee	Optional	Required s. 171	Required All members must be financially literate, independent directors NI 52-110 s. 3.1
Compensation committee	Not Required	Not Required	Optional Disclose alternate method if used NP 58-201 s. 3.10
Nominating committee	Not Required	Not Required	Optional NP- 58-201 s. 3.15
Disclosure of corporate governance practices	Not Required	Not Required	Required NI 58-101 F1
Code of ethics	Not Required	Not Required	Recommended NP 58-201 s. 3.8

ETHICAL ISSUE

Who Is "Independent"?

When Bill Gates was appointed to Berkshire Hathaway Inc.'s Board of Directors in 2004, he was designated by the board as an independent director. His only pre-existing relationship with the corporation was as a shareholder. Still, critics complained about the designation, citing his long friendship with chairman Warren Buffet.[14]

What does independent mean? The commonly understood meaning of the word is that an independent party is free of any conflicting interests or ties. The CBCA definition designates only employees and officers of the corporation as being non-independent. The provincial securities regulation definition excludes anyone with a "direct or indirect material relationship with the corporation" and it leaves the determination of what a "material relationship" is up to the directors themselves to decide with some minor direction.

The regulation suggests that a material relationship is one that could "reasonably interfere with the exercise of independent judgment." It goes on to suggest that examples include employees, officers, and their immediate family members. But what about friends, distant relatives, or competitors?

Questions to Consider

1. Should a director be free of any potential conflict of interest to be considered independent?
2. Is it appropriate to let the board of directors determine its own members' independence?
3. How can a nominating committee or a code of ethics help with this issue?

Sources: National Instrument 52-110 s. 1.4; Belle Kaura, "The Corporate Governance Conundrum: Re-inventing the Board of Directors and Board Committees," in P. Puri and J. Larson (Eds.), *Corporate Governance and Securities Regulation in the 21st Century* (Toronto: Butterworths, 2004).

DUTIES OF DIRECTORS AND OFFICERS

Section 122 of the CBCA describes the statutory duties of directors and officers:

(1) Every director and officer of a corporation in exercising their powers and discharging their duties shall

    (a) act honestly and in good faith with a view to the best interests of the corporation; and

    (b) exercise the care, diligence and skill that a reasonably prudent person would exercise in comparable circumstances.

(2) Every director and officer of a corporation shall comply with this Act, the regulations, articles, by-laws and any unanimous shareholder agreement.

To fully understand these responsibilities we must consider *what* duties are owed and also *to whom* the duties are owed.

[14.] David Pauly, "Just How "Independent" Is Berkshire's Board?" *National Post*, January 26, 2005.

What Duties Are Owed?

SECTION 122(1)(A): FIDUCIARY DUTIES

The CBCA requires that directors and officers "act *honestly* and in *good faith* with a view to the *best interests* of the corporation" (section 122(1)) (italics added). This is the language associated with fiduciary duty, a duty with which we are already familiar. It imposes a high standard of conduct on directors and officers involving loyalty, integrity, and trust.[15] This duty addresses the motives, considerations, and factors that influence decision-making separately from the decisions themselves. We will discuss particular examples of common conflicts of interest in the section called Specific Conduct. All of the examples involve, in one way or another, situations where there is a conflict, at least potentially, between a director's personal interest and that of the corporation. However, it is important to understand that Section 122 (1) (a) imposes a general duty on directors and officers to avoid any *conflict of interest* with their corporation.

SECTION 122 (1) (B): DUTY OF CARE, DILIGENCE AND SKILL

Section 122 (1) (b) of the CBCA requires directors and officers to exercise the care, diligence, and skill that a *reasonably prudent person* would exercise in *comparable circumstances*. A director or officer owes a duty not to be negligent in carrying out his or her duties. This is an objective standard; no greater diligence is required of a director than is required of the average person. We have not yet developed standards for a professional class of directors.[16] By contrast, a director who is also *employed* by a corporation, for example, as its chief executive officer, its treasurer, or its chief engineer, will normally owe a professional duty of care, but that duty is owed in respect of the employment, not as a director.

Directors are not expected to give continuous attention to the affairs of the corporation and, unless there are suspicious circumstances, they are entitled to rely on information received from the officers of the corporation.[17] However, they may not willfully close their eyes to mistakes and misconduct. If they acquiesce in such matters, they may be liable in damages to the corporation for any losses that result.

To Whom Are Directors' and Officers' Duties Owed?

TO THE CORPORATION

Although the Act does not expressly say so, it is implicit, especially in the words "with a view to the best interests of the corporation," that the duties of directors and officers are owed, at least primarily, to the corporation. The interests of "the corporation" are normally taken to mean the interests of the corporate legal entity, *present and future*. Directors and officers may—and should—consider the long-term interests of the corporation and not merely the present interests or wishes of the shareholders. But do directors and officers owe duties to anyone other than the corporation? How should they balance competing interests?

---

15. It may also extend to senior employees. See MacMillan-Bloedel Ltd. v. Binstead (1983), 22 B.L.R. 255.

16. The members of the audit committee of a distributing corporation are required to be "financially literate." That is not a statutory requirement but a rule adopted by Canadian securities regulatory authorities under Multilateral Instrument 52-110. Financial literacy means that the individual "has the ability to read and understand a set of financial statements."

17. *Dovey v. Corey*, [1901] A.C. 477.

TO THE SHAREHOLDERS AND OTHER STAKEHOLDERS

Although directors are elected and can be removed by a majority of the shareholders, it would be wrong to conclude that their first duty is to those shareholders who have elected them—as was demonstrated in Case Summary 17.1. The duty of a director is owed to the corporation *as a whole*.

However, this does not answer the question whether, in addition to the duties owed to the corporation as a whole, any duty is owed to *individual* shareholders or other stakeholders. Modern corporate governance theory recognizes that the conduct of a corporation's business affects not only shareholders but many other sectors of the public as well. If a large corporation is badly managed, the well-being of many people and even the national interest may be seriously affected. Creditors of a bankrupt corporation go unpaid. Employees may lose their jobs, as may other members of the community where the corporation carries on business. A corporation that produces defective products may injure consumers, and one that does not take effective measures to prevent pollution may cause severe damage to the environment. Consequently, the public in general has a "stake" in good corporate management.

The traditional English and Canadian answer to the question is *no:* directors' and officers' duties are owed to the corporation only, and it is the corporation that may seek a remedy if the duties are breached.[18]

THE *PEOPLE* VS. *WISE* DISTINCTION

Recently, the Supreme Court of Canada considered the duties in section 122 and drew a clear distinction between the fiduciary duty and the duty of skill and care.[19]

CASE SUMMARY 17.2

Wise Stores Inc. (Wise) bought Peoples Department Stores Inc. (Peoples). The three sons of the Wise founder (Wise brothers) were the majority shareholders, officers, and directors of Wise. After the purchase they also became the sole directors of Peoples. The integration of the two operations did not go smoothly, especially in the area of inventory control and bookkeeping. The Wise brothers reviewed the inventory problems and accepted the recommendation of the Vice-President of Administration and Finance. They implemented a joint inventory procurement policy which divided purchasing responsibilities between the two operations. Peoples would make purchases from North America and Wise would make all other international purchases. Within a year of implementation the inventory system was in total chaos; suppliers went unpaid. Eventually both Wise and Peoples declared bankruptcy and Peoples' bankruptcy trustee sued the Wise brothers personally, claiming they breached the duties owed to Peoples' creditors.

[18.] *Percival v. Wright*, [1902] 2 Ch. 421. The conduct described in this case is now forbidden by statute but the general principle remains. Only if the directors offer to act on behalf of other shareholders, thereby creating an agency relationship, or if they stand in some other fiduciary relationship, will they be under a duty to them: *Allen v. Hyatt* (1914), 17 D.L.R. 7; *Malcolm v. Transtec Holdings Ltd.* [2001] B.C.J. No. 413. Under securities legislation, directors are required to disclose to the shareholders information relating to takeover offers.

[19.] *Peoples Department Stores Inc. v. Wise* (2004), 244 D.L.R. (4th) 564, at p. 582. In Alberta, a director who is appointed by a particular class of shareholders (or by creditors of employees) may give special (but not exclusive) consideration to the interests of that class: R.S.A. c. B-9, s. 122(4). There may be special circumstances in which directors owe a fiduciary duty to others—for example, to clients of the firm; see *Air Canada v. M & L Travel Ltd.* (1993), 108 D.L.R. (4th) 592.

> The Supreme Court of Canada held that there was no fiduciary duty owing to the creditors or other stakeholders, stating "At all times directors and officers owe their fiduciary obligation to the corporation. The interests of the corporation are not to be confused with the interests of the creditors or those of any other stakeholders."[20] However, the Court held that the duty of skill and care was not limited to the corporation: "the identity of the beneficiary of the duty of care is much more open-ended, and it appears obvious that it must include creditors."[21]
>
> On the facts, the Court held that the Wise brothers met the required objective standard of skill and care by acting prudently and on a reasonably informed basis. The creditors were denied a remedy.

TO THE PUBLIC

In *Peoples* v. *Wise*, the Supreme Court extended the duty of skill and care to other stakeholders including shareholders, creditors, and employees. In refusing to extend the fiduciary duty the same way, the Court noted the broad protection afforded to these groups under other statutory provisions. Some of that legislation will be discussed later in this chapter where we examine other aspects of the external relations of corporations. As we shall see, corporate directors must manage their corporations in conformity with the law, and they may incur personal liability if they fail to do so.

In *Peoples*, the Court also noted that it may be in the best interests of the corporation to consider the interests of others.[22] A corporation that promotes good labour relations by considering the welfare of its employees, enjoys good customer and community relations, and is perceived as socially responsible and responsive to environmental concerns is likely to prosper better in the longer term than one that does not. A corporation's management rightly devotes considerable attention to its public image and relations. It may even be argued that directors owe a duty to the corporation to do so.[23]

The situation is different in Ontario. In August 2007, possibly in response to the *Peoples* decision, the Ontario Business Corporations Act was amended to make it clear that both the fiduciary duty and the duty of skill and care are owed *only* to the corporation.[24]

Defences to Breach of Duty

Directors and officers are personally liable for a breach of duty. If the corporation goes bankrupt, disgruntled shareholders, employees, and creditors often accuse officers and directors of breach of duty or "mismanagement." How can directors and officers protect themselves? What defences are available? What risk-management strategies should be in place? Both legislation and the common law provide some guidance.

---

[20] *Ibid.*, at para. 43–44.

[21] *Ibid.*, at para. 57.

[22] *Ibid.*, at para. 42.

[23] *Re Olympia & York Enterprises Ltd. and Hiram Walker Resources Ltd.* (1986), 59 O.R. (2d) 254 at 271 (On. Div. Ct.).

[24] Section 134 (1).

The CBCA includes the following defences and risk-management strategies:[25]

due diligence defence
establishing that an acceptable standard of care and skill was exercised by a director or officer

(a) Reasonable diligence, also known as the **due diligence defence:** By establishing that the required degree of care was taken, directors and officers can defend themselves against claims of breach of the articles, by-laws, and the act (section 123(4)).

(b) Good faith reliance: Good faith reliance on audited financial statements or expert reports is a defence to breach of fiduciary duty or duty of skill and care (section 123 (5)). Therefore, obtaining expert reports prior to key decisions is a good risk-management strategy.

(c) Corporate indemnity: An agreement with the corporation to reimburse a director or officer for any costs associated with liability for breach of duty is enforceable provided that the director acted honestly, reasonably, and in good faith (section 124). Naturally, the effectiveness of this risk-management strategy depends on the financial health of the corporation.

(d) Directors' and officers' liability insurance: A corporation may purchase directors' liability insurance on behalf of its board (section 124(6)). These policies have many exclusions, including bad faith and fraud, and are very expensive.

The key common law defence available to directors and officers is known as the **business judgment rule**. Under this rule, courts will grant business experts the benefit of the doubt and not easily criticize a business decision. Judges recognize that they are not business experts and even sound decisions may ultimately be unsuccessful. Therefore, courts focus on the process used to arrive at the decision; as long as directors and officers exercise an appropriate degree of prudence and diligence while making the decision, the court will hold that the duty of skill and care is met. As was noted in *Peoples*, establishing and *following* good corporate governance rules can protect directors and officers from allegations that they have breached their duty of care.[26]

business judgment rule
courts will defer to the business decisions of directors and officers provided they are arrived at using an appropriate degree of prudence and diligence

The business judgment rule has its limits. It will not protect a director from liability for a failure to comply with specific legal obligations such as mandatory disclosure under securities legislation.[27]

Strict Liability

Directors may also be subject to strict liability, where no breach of duty need be established. The CBCA and corresponding provincial statutes make directors liable to their corporation when they vote at meetings of the board on specified matters that cause financial losses to the corporation, such as the improper redemption of shares or the payment of a dividend in circumstances that leave the corporation unable to meet its liabilities (section 118(2)). In addition, if the corporation becomes insolvent, the directors are personally liable to all employees

---

[25.] There is some provincial variation: Ontario's reasonable diligence and good faith defence extends to interim financial reports and reports or advice of an officer or employee (section 135(4)).

[26.] *Peoples, supra* note 19, at para 64.

[27.] *Kerr* v. *Danier Leather Inc.*, 2007 SCC 44 at para 55.

of the corporation for unpaid debts for services performed while they were directors, up to the amount of six months' wages (section 119).[28] Directors may also become liable for failure to comply with other statutes. For example, if the corporation is insolvent, the federal government may collect from the directors the income tax that the corporation was required to withhold from the wages and salaries of employees.[29] Even the volunteer directors of a non-profit corporation have been held liable under this provision.[30]

Specific Conduct Involving Conflicts of Interest

CONTRACTS WITH THE CORPORATION

Perhaps the most important fiduciary obligation is the duty to disclose any interest that the director may have in contracts made with the corporation. This duty arises where a director negotiates the sale of her own property to the corporation, or the purchase of property from the corporation. It may arise indirectly, for example, a director may be a shareholder in another corporation that is selling to or buying from her corporation. The problem occurs frequently among related corporations, where a director of one corporation is a shareholder and perhaps a director of a second corporation.

ILLUSTRATION 17.1

Brown holds a large number of shares in each of World Electric and Universal Shipbuilding, and is a director of each of these corporations. Universal Shipbuilding requires expensive turbo-generator sets for two large ships under construction. World Electric is one of several manufacturers of turbo-generators.

Brown is faced with an obvious conflict of interest: can she encourage or even support a contract between the two corporations? On one side, it is in Brown's interest to see Universal Shipbuilding obtain the equipment at the lowest possible price. On the other side, it is in her interest to see World Electric get the contract and obtain the highest possible price.

Under section 120 of the CBCA, a director who has an interest in a contract must disclose this fact at a meeting of the board of directors that considers the contract and must not vote on the matter. If, after learning of the interest, the remaining independent members of the board still wish to go through with

---

[28.] Section 119 uses the word "debts," though it limits the amount to 6 months' wages. It is, however, not necessary to establish that the debt claimed is for "wages," provided it was incurred for services performed. The section 123(4) defence of reasonable diligence applies to both section 118 and section 119. In *Proulx* v. *Sahelian Goldfields Inc.* (2001), 204 D.L.R. (4th) 670, the Ontario Court of Appeal (considering s. 131 of the Ontario act) held that vacation pay owing constituted a debt, whether or not it should be regarded as "wages," and was within the section.

[29.] Income Tax Act, R.S.C. 1985, c. 1 (5th Supp.), s. 227.1.

[30.] *MNR.* v. *Corsano* (1999), 172 D.L.R. (4th) 708.

the contract, they may enter into a binding contract. If the remaining independent directors are not enough to form a quorum, the contract should be ratified at a general meeting of the shareholders. Failure by a director to disclose an interest gives that director's corporation the right to rescind the contract upon learning of the interest.

One type of contract in which a director clearly has a personal interest is the contract providing for their own remuneration, so it is perhaps surprising that the CBCA simply provides that the directors may fix the remuneration of the directors, officers, and employees of the corporation (section 125). There is an obvious risk that the directors will be excessively generous to each other or to their CEO.[31] Securities regulations require distributing corporations to disclose executive compensation and to develop independent methods of establishing executive compensation, and the creation of compensation committees is recommended.

INTERCEPTION OF CORPORATE OPPORTUNITY

A different situation arises when it is a director's duty to acquire a particular item of property for the corporation or to give the corporation the chance of first refusal, and instead she acquires the property for herself. In that case, she has *intercepted* an opportunity belonging to the corporation and has committed a breach of duty. If a director has received a mandate to act as agent for the corporation to purchase a specific piece of property or a particular type of property, she is under the same duty as that placed upon any agent to acquire property for her principal. If she buys the property for herself, she has breached her duty. The property is deemed to be held in trust for the corporation, as is any profit made.

CORPORATE INFORMATION

A rather different situation arises when a director receives information about a profitable venture or an opportunity to buy property at an advantageous price. She may be under no duty to acquire the property for the corporation, but if the information is received in her capacity as a director of the corporation, then it is her duty to give the corporation first chance of acquiring an interest in the

---

CASE SUMMARY 17.3

R was a director of a large corporation that was in the process of expanding its chain of retail grocery stores. A major part of his duties was to travel around the country looking for suitable independent stores for the corporation to purchase. *R* entered into an arrangement with a friend to buy those stores that seemed especially good bargains and to resell them to the corporation, concealing the fact of his ownership. When this was later discovered, the corporation brought proceedings against him.

The court held that *R* was under a duty to acquire the stores for the corporation, and therefore was held to have done so as its agent.[32]

[31.] See *UPM-Kymmene Corp.* v. *UPM-Kymmene Miramichi Inc.* (2002), 214 D.L.R. (4th) 496, where the board approved a "compensation agreement" for the chairman that included a "signing bonus" of 25 million shares. The court held that there had been inadequate disclosure and set aside the agreement.

[32.] *Canada Safeway Ltd.* v. *Thompson*, [1951] 3 D.L.R. 295. Note that in reselling the stores to the corporation, the director was also in breach of his duty to disclose his interest. The corporation could have chosen instead to rescind the contracts. See also *Slate Ventures Inc.* v. *Hurley* (1998), 37 B.L.R. (2d) 138.

CASE SUMMARY 17.4

C was a director of a corporation involved in exploration and natural resource development. *C* was approached by a prospector, who asked if the corporation would be interested in acquiring certain claims. He reported this at a meeting of the board of directors. A majority of the board considered that the corporation was already over-committed financially and decided against taking up the offer.

When the prospector approached *C* again, *C* decided to take up the claims for himself. He later left the corporation, after a disagreement. The corporation learned of his acquisition of the claims and brought proceedings against him.

The court held that, once the corporation had rejected the opportunity, it no longer belonged to the corporation and *C* was free to take advantage of it.[33]

venture or property. If the corporation decides not to acquire the property, the director is probably free to do so. But she makes a dangerous decision if she assumes that the corporation would not want the property anyway, and then acquires it in her own name without consulting the corporation. In practice, it is sometimes difficult for a court to decide whether in the circumstances the information came to the director personally or in her role as a director of the corporation. But once the court decides that the opportunity belonged to the corporation, the result is quite clear: purchasing on her own behalf is a breach of duty.

COMPETING WITH THE CORPORATION

Another aspect of the conflict of interest principle is the rule that a director may not carry on a business competing with that of her corporation, except with the permission of the corporation.

The corporation is entitled to claim all the profit made by the director and to obtain an injunction prohibiting the director from any future competition.

CASE SUMMARY 17.5

O'Malley was a director of Canaero, a corporation specializing in aerial surveying. He had been engaged on a project for the corporation in Guyana, during which he learned a lot about the terrain and made some useful contacts. He subsequently resigned from Canaero, formed his own corporation, and successfully tendered for a surveying contract with the government of Guyana.

O'Malley was held to be in breach of his duty to Canaero and accountable to them for his profit on the contract.[34]

RELATED PARTY TRANSACTIONS

As noted in the previous chapter, large businesses often operate through a group of related corporations. Those corporations deal with each other on a regular basis. Frequently, they share some of the same directors. The potential for conflicts of

---

33. *Peso Silver Mines Ltd.* v. *Cropper* (1966), 56 D.L.R. (2d) 117 (S.C.C.). In contrast, where a majority of the directors (and shareholders) of a corporation purported to pass a resolution rejecting a contractual opportunity offered to the corporation and then took it for themselves, that was held to be a breach of their duties. The resolution was not adopted in good faith: *Cook* v. *Deeks*, [1916] A.C. 554.

34. *Canadian Aero Service Ltd.* v. *O'Malley* (1973), 40 D.L.R. (3d) 371 (S.C.C.).

interest is obvious. Almost inevitably, some inter-group contracts or arrangements will be more beneficial to one party than to the other. The situation becomes especially perilous where the two or more corporations concerned do not have the same shareholders or creditors.

The likelihood of impropriety (or at least of perceptions of impropriety) is further increased where the corporate group is effectively controlled by a single individual or family—a situation that is quite common in Canada.

CASE SUMMARY 17.6

Hollinger Inc., a corporation in which 12 percent of its voting shares were held by the public and the remainder were owned by Lord Black and his associates, made a loan of $1.1 million to Ravelston Corp., all of whose shares were owned or controlled by Lord Black. Minority shareholders in Hollinger alleged that the loan had not been properly approved.[35] In related proceedings it was alleged that improper payments totalling $32 million were made from one Hollinger corporation to another corporation and its directors. The court appointed an inspector to investigate.[36]

Insider Trading

Insider trading is one type of conduct for which English and Canadian courts were reluctant to impose liability, so the legislatures intervened to create a duty. Insider trading attracts all three types of liability: civil liability, regulatory liability, and criminal liability.

insider trading
the use of confidential information relating to a corporation in dealing in its securities

Insider trading occurs when a director or officer of a corporation, or some other person (for example, a shareholder or employee of the corporation), buys

---

ILLUSTRATION 17.2

(a) The directors of a small family company are approached by a large public corporation that offers to buy all the shares of the family company at a price considerably above that at which the shares had previously been valued. The next day, one of the directors is approached by her uncle, who is a shareholder and who offers to sell some of his shares to her. Without disclosing the proposed takeover, she buys the shares at a price well below that of the offer.

(b) The directors of a mining corporation receive a confidential report from their surveyor that very valuable mineral deposits have just been discovered. One of

the directors immediately instructs her broker to buy as many of the corporation's shares as possible on the stock exchange, before the good news is released and forces up the price.

(c) The directors of a corporation learn that their major customer has just declared bankruptcy, owing the corporation a large sum of money. Default on the account by their customer is likely to result in the corporation showing a substantial loss in the forthcoming half-yearly accounts. One of the directors promptly sells her shares just before the news becomes public and the shares drop in value.

---

35. *Catalyst Fund General Partner I Inc. v. Hollinger Inc.* [2004] O.J. No. 4722 aff'd. [2006] O.J. No. 944 (On. C.A.).

36. *Ibid.*, O.J. No. 3886. In criminal proceedings initiated by the American Securities and Exchange Commission, Lord Black was convicted of fraud and obstruction of justice arising from redirection of sale proceeds from Hollinger corporations to directors through artificial non-competition agreements.

or sells the corporation's shares or other securities, making use of confidential inside information in order to make a profit or avoid a loss.

In each of the hypothetical cases in Illustration 17.2, a director has made use of information that came to her in her capacity as a director for her own benefit.

Originally, at common law, courts did not see this conduct as harmful to the corporation and so it did not consider it a breach of the fiduciary duty owed to the corporation. The legislatures stepped in to fill the void. Securities legislation imposes strict disclosure requirements whenever a director or other insider trades in the securities of her own corporation, and has made insider trading a criminal offence, punishable by fines or imprisonment or both. Under the Ontario Securities Act, for example, fines of up to $5 million and prison terms of up to 5 years may be imposed.[37] A recent amendment to the Criminal Code

---

CHECKLIST	**Directors' Liability**

A director faces the following types of personal liability for breach of her duties:

Type of Personal Liability	**Available Remedy**
(a) Civil liability	
(i) to the corporation	
• breach of fiduciary duty, s. 122(1)(a)	• damages for losses arising from breach
• specific conduct involving conflicts of interest, s. 120	• accounting of amounts paid for improper dividends or share redemption
• breach of duty of skill, diligence, and care, s. 122(1)(b)	• rescission of contract involving conflict of interest
	• constructive trust of property
	• accounting of profits
	• injunction to restrain breach of duty
(ii) to others	
• breach of duty of skill, diligence, and care, s. 122(1)(b)	• damages for losses arising from the liability
• liability for unpaid wages	
• liability for unpaid taxes	
• liability for insider trading	
(b) Regulatory and criminal liability	
• insider trading	• fines and imprisonment (Criminal Code)
	• fines and imprisonment (Securities Act)

[37.] Securities Act, R.S.O. 1990, c. S. 5, s. 122. An offender may also be required to pay back three times the amount of any profit made. In *R. v. Harper* (2003), 232 D.L.R. (4th) 738, a fine of almost $4 million was imposed, though it was reduced to $2 million on appeal.

has increased the potential penalty to 10 years' imprisonment.[38] Despite the heavy penalties, however, the number of prosecutions for insider trading seems to be increasing, both in Canada and in the United States.

The above provisions apply principally to corporations whose securities are publicly traded as a way of promoting public confidence in the markets. However, section 131 of the CBCA provides that, even in the case of a private corporation, an insider who purchases or sells a security of the corporation with knowledge of specific, confidential, price-sensitive information is liable

(a) to compensate the seller or purchaser (as the case may be) for any loss suffered as a result of the transaction, and

(b) to account to the corporation for any benefit or advantage obtained.

For the purposes of the legislation, "insider" includes a director or officer, an employee, any shareholder who holds more than a prescribed percentage of the corporation's securities, and a "tippee"—that is, a person who knowingly receives confidential information from an insider.

SHAREHOLDERS

The Role of Shareholders

PUBLICLY TRADED CORPORATIONS

In large, publicly traded corporations, shareholdings may be widely distributed with no single shareholder or group holding more than 5 percent of the voting stock. Less frequently, one entity may control a majority of shares. Both situations make changing management difficult. Management may respond to calls for change with a piece of practical advice to investors: "If you don't like the management, sell!" In other words, "Do not get into costly corporate struggles. Cut your losses by getting out and reinvesting in a corporation more to your liking." All that may be changing with the recent attempts to strengthen corporate governance and the role of independent directors. However, the new rules do not directly expand the shareholders' power or influence over the affairs of the corporation.

Private Corporations

In private corporations, shareholders' problems are radically different. The usual problem is a serious disagreement among the principal shareholders, who are frequently also directors and senior employees of the corporation. In the absence of careful contractual arrangements providing safeguards, a minority shareholder may find himself "locked in" and "frozen out" at the same time.

The minority shareholder is "locked in" in the sense that he probably cannot sell his shares except at a fraction of what he believes they should be worth. There are two reasons for this. First, in most private corporations the transfer of

---

[38] Criminal Code, R.S.C. 1985, c. C-46, s. 382.1, as amended by S.C. 2004, c. 3. In Canada, few inside traders are given jail time. Most receive fines and are banned from the securities industry and public boards.

shares is restricted, usually requiring the consent of the board of directors. They may be unwilling to agree to the transfer of his shares except to someone of their own choosing. Second, even if the minority shareholder is free to sell the shares, he will have great difficulty in finding a buyer who would consider acquiring a minority position in a private corporation.

The minority shareholder may be "frozen out" in the following manner. First, the majority directors may fire him from his job with the corporation, or, at the very least, refuse to renew his employment contract when it expires. Second, they may remove him from the board of directors or elect someone else in his place at the next election. Third, they may increase salaries to themselves, so that the corporation itself earns no apparent profit. Even if a profit is shown, it may be retained by the corporation, since dividends are payable only at the discretion of the board of directors. Therefore, a minority shareholder may find himself deprived of his salary-earning position, his directorship, and his prospect of any dividends on his investment. Worse, he is often left without a marketable security.

In these circumstances the majority shareholders may not have broken any law, and no remedy existed at common law. However, a number of statutory provisions empower the courts to give relief to minority shareholders. We will discuss these, as well as strategies to avoid the problem, under "The Protection of Minority Shareholders" later in this chapter.

Rights Attached to Shares

Shareholder rights come from two principal sources—the rights attached to their shares by the articles of the corporation and the rights conferred on them by the relevant corporate legislation.

The corporate constitution sets out the rights attached to each class of shares. For example, the CBCA requires that the articles state the classes of shares that may be issued and, if there are to be two or more classes of shares, the rights, privileges, restrictions, and conditions attaching to each class (section 6(1)(c) and section 24(4)). If there is only one class of shares, the rights of the shareholders include the rights

- to vote at any meeting of shareholders

- to receive any dividend that is declared

- to receive the remaining property of the corporation (after payment of its debts) on dissolution (section 24(3))

Additional rights may be attached to shares, and, if there are different classes of shares, rights may be granted to some shares and not others; but the three basic rights must exist and be exercisable by one or other class of shares.

Meetings and Voting

NOTICE AND ATTENDANCE AT MEETINGS

If shareholders wish to voice their objections about the management, they need a forum to do so. The forum provided under all statutes is the **general meeting of shareholders**. The corporation may hold other meetings of shareholders in

general meeting of shareholders
a formal meeting of shareholders at which they are able to vote on matters concerning the corporation

annual general meeting
the general meeting of shareholders that is required by law to be held each year to transact certain specified business

the course of the year, but it is required by statute to hold at least one **annual general meeting**.[39] Shareholders are entitled to advance notice of all general meetings and are entitled to receive copies of the financial statements before the annual general meeting. They may attend the meetings, question the directors, and make criticisms of the management of the corporation.[40]

THE RIGHT TO REQUISITION MEETINGS

What if shareholders want to call a meeting and the board of directors refuses to do so? All the provinces provide in their statutes that the shareholders themselves may call a meeting. However, these provisions require a relatively large proportion of the shareholders to petition for the meeting, a requirement that is virtually impossible to meet in large corporations where even a large number of shareholders may hold only a small percentage of the total shares.[41] The right

special meeting
any general meeting of shareholders other than the annual general meeting

to requisition a **special meeting** is therefore of limited use in large corporations, but is especially valuable in the smaller, private companies.

THE RIGHT TO VOTE

The right to attend meetings and to criticize must ultimately be backed by some form of power in the hands of the shareholders. This power is found in the right to vote. The collective power of the shareholders is exercised through the passing (or defeating) of resolutions—an **ordinary resolution**, which is adopted by a simple majority of votes cast, and a **special resolution**, which requires a two-thirds majority.[42] The CBCA sets out a number of matters that must be approved by either an ordinary or a special resolution, the most important being

ordinary resolution
a resolution adopted by the general meeting and passed by a simple majority

special resolution
a resolution of the general meeting required to be passed by a special (usually two-thirds) majority

(a) the approval of alterations to the articles of incorporation—special resolution (section 173)
(b) the approval of certain other fundamental changes, such as amalgamation with another corporation (section 183) or the sale of all, or substantially all, of the corporation's property—special resolution (section 189)
(c) the approval of any amendments made by the directors to the by-laws—ordinary resolution (section 103)
(d) the election of the auditor—ordinary resolution (section 162)
(e) the election or removal of directors—ordinary resolution (sections 106, 109)

---

[39] CBCA, s. 133. The Act requires that an annual meeting be held not more than 15 months after the previous annual meeting and no more than 6 months after the end of the corporation's financial year; thus it is possible for a calendar year to pass without a meeting.

[40] The CBCA (ss. 132(4),(5)) now makes provision for shareholder meetings to be held by electronic means. A corporation's by-laws may provide for voting by means of telephonic or electronic communications facilities.

[41] CBCA, s. 143, requires a requisition to be made by 5 percent of shareholders, and this is the requirement in most provinces. Prince Edward Island specifies the impossibly high figure of 25 percent.

[42] S. 2. In Nova Scotia, a special resolution requires a three-quarters majority.

Excepting the items described in (a) and (b), the most important matter voted upon by the shareholders is the election of directors, since, as we have seen, it is the directors who control the management of the corporation's affairs.

CLASS VOTING RIGHTS

Not all shareholders necessarily have the right to vote. A corporation's shares may be divided into different classes, with different voting rights. Common shares almost invariably carry the right to vote; preferred shares often carry a right to vote only in specified circumstances, such as when preferred dividends are in arrears. The founders of a corporation may create several classes of shares and weigh the voting heavily in favour of a small group of shares held by themselves. For example, they could give Class "A" shares 100 votes per share and Class "B," issued to a broader group of shareholders, only one vote per share. It would be virtually impossible for a publicly traded corporation to have such a share structure today. Securities commissions, stock exchanges, and underwriters would probably refuse such an issue, and without their concurrence a public offering is impossible. Virtually all common stock offered on the public market today carries one vote per share. By contrast, in private corporations there is no restriction upon the different rights that may be attached to various classes of shares, provided at least one class has voting rights. Within a particular class, however, all shares must enjoy the same rights (section 24).

Class rights, which may relate not only to voting but also to other matters such as rights to priority in payment of dividends or to receive the surplus on liquidation of the corporation, must be set out in the articles of incorporation. Consequently, they may only be varied by special resolution of the shareholders. In addition, to alter the rights of a particular class requires approval by the votes of two-thirds of that class and of any other class that may be adversely affected (section 176).

class rights
special rights attached to a particular class of shares

PROXIES

In most publicly traded corporations, only a small proportion of shareholders actually attend general meetings. All corporation statutes permit a shareholder to nominate a **proxy** to attend a general meeting and to cast that shareholder's votes at the meeting as instructed. This is done by signing a form, naming the proxy, and sending it to the corporation before the meeting. Most jurisdictions now go further and require all corporations, except the smallest private ones, to send a **proxy form**, the contents of which are prescribed in detail, to all shareholders at the same time as notice of a meeting is given.

In the event of a proxy fight between two groups of shareholders—usually the board of directors and a dissenting group—each group solicits all the shareholders by mail in order to persuade them to give their proxy forms to the group making the solicitation. The dissenting group may go to the corporation's head office to obtain lists of all the shareholders from the share register in order to make their solicitations. Here the board of directors has a great advantage. As a matter of practice, they include proxy forms, offering one of themselves as the proposed proxy, with the mailed notice of the annual general meeting.[43]

proxy
a person appointed to attend a general meeting of shareholders and to cast the votes of the shareholder appointing him or her

proxy form
a form required to be circulated to shareholders before a general meeting, inviting them to appoint a proxy if they so wish

---

[43.] This advantage is only partly offset by disclosure requirements and by compelling management to provide shareholders with a means to nominate a different proxy.

Financial Rights

Shareholders expect to receive a return on their investment in one or both of two forms—earnings distributed regularly in the form of dividends and growth that can be realized by selling the shares or on dissolution of the corporation. Holders of common shares may be satisfied with smaller dividends if there is capital appreciation in the corporation's assets or if a significant part of the profits is retained within the business and has the effect of increasing the value of the shares. Preferred shares often do not participate in growth, and their holders are primarily concerned with receiving dividends.

DIVIDENDS

dividend
a distribution to shareholders of a share of the profits of the corporation

A fundamental right attached to shares is the right to receive any **dividend** that is declared by the corporation. The declaration of dividends is entirely within the discretion of the board of directors. Shareholders normally have no right to be paid a dividend, even when the corporation makes large profits.

There can be no discrimination, however, in the payment of dividends among shareholders of the same class. Each shareholder is entitled to such dividends as are declared in proportion to the number of shares of that class held. In addition, directors are bound to pay dividends in the order of preference assigned to the classes of shareholders. They may not pay the common shareholders a dividend without first paying the whole of any preferred dividends owing to preference shareholders.

DISTRIBUTION OF SURPLUS

On the dissolution of a corporation, provided it has assets remaining after paying off all its creditors, shareholders are entitled to a proportionate share of the remaining net assets. The distribution of these net assets among the various classes of shareholders must also be made in accordance with the respective priorities of each class.

PRE-EMPTIVE RIGHTS

One of the more important powers given to the board of directors is the power to issue shares. The issue of new shares involves two possible risks for existing shareholders. First, the issue of shares to some other person will necessarily reduce the proportion of the total number of shares that a shareholder holds. Second, there is the risk of "stock watering"; if new shares are issued for a price that is less than the value of the existing shares, the value of the existing shares will be diluted.

ILLUSTRATION 17.3

A owns 34 of the total of 100 shares issued by *XYZ* Inc. The assets of *XYZ* Inc. are worth approximately $1 million. The directors wish to raise additional capital and resolve to issue 20 new shares to *T*, at a price of $5000 per share. As a result, *A* will now own only 28.3 percent of the total shares and can no longer block the adoption of a special resolution. A's shares, previously worth $10 000 each, will be worth only $9167.

---

pre-emptive right
a right to have the first opportunity to purchase a proportionate part of any new shares to be issued

American courts have held that a shareholder has a **pre-emptive right** to retain his proportionate holdings in a corporation, but this right is subject to various qualifications. When a corporation proposes to issue more shares, it must normally offer each shareholder a proportion of the new issue equal to the proportion he holds of the existing shares. A shareholder who has 3 percent of the issued shares of a corporation is entitled to purchase 3 percent of any further issue. A right of pre-emption preserves the balance of power in the corporation. It also ensures that, if the new shares are issued at a price that is less than the value of the existing shares, the existing shareholders are not prejudiced, at any rate, if they exercise their right of pre-emption. Any reduction in the value

---

CASE SUMMARY 17.7

Bonisteel was a director of Collis Leather Co. and the owner of 458 of a total of 1208 issued shares. He entered into an agreement with another shareholder to buy that shareholder's 150 shares. The purchase would have given him control of the corporation. Collis, the general manager and the person most responsible for the corporation's success, threatened to leave if Bonisteel took control. In order to forestall Bonisteel, the directors resolved to issue 292 new shares, and each director was asked how many shares he wished to subscribe for. Most of the new shares were taken up by directors other than Bonisteel, with the result that he would be left with less than 50 percent of the total shares. Bonisteel brought an action to restrain the directors from making the allotment.

The court held that such an allotment would be invalid. The corporation was not in need of additional funds, and it was improper to issue new shares for the purpose of altering the balance of control.[44]

CASE SUMMARY 17.8

Afton was a "junior" mining company, incorporated in British Columbia. As was common in the industry, it was looking for a "major" company to help finance a large drilling program. Teck, a large resource corporation, became interested in Afton and made an offer to buy a controlling block of its shares. The directors of Afton, led by its chief engineer, Millar, rejected the offer and preferred to enter into an arrangement with Canex, the subsidiary of another Canadian corporation, even though Canex was not prepared to match the Teck offer. Following the rejection, Teck started buying Afton shares on the stock exchange, and soon announced that it had acquired more than 50 percent of the issued shares. The Afton directors then entered into a long-term contract with Canex, which involved issuing a large block of new shares to Canex. This arrangement reduced the Teck holding to less than 50 percent.

The share issue was challenged by Teck but upheld by the court. The Afton directors had entered into the arrangement with Canex and had issued the new shares, because they genuinely believed that the interests of Afton would be better served as a "partner" of Canex than as a subsidiary of Teck.[45]

---

of their existing shares will be exactly balanced by the gain they receive in buying the new shares at an undervalue.

Canadian courts have never recognized a general principle of pre-emption. In limited circumstances, however, they have recognized rights somewhat similar to pre-emptive rights. Directors have the right to issue authorized share cap-

---

44. *Bonisteel v. Collis Leather Co. Ltd.* (1919), 45 O.R. 195.

45. *Teck Corp. v. Millar* (1973), 33 D.L.R. (3d) 288.

ital of the corporation at their discretion, but they must issue shares only for the purpose of raising capital or for purposes that are in the best interest of the corporation. If they have a bona fide intention of raising capital, they may distribute the shares to whomever they wish upon payment of a fair price. But if directors issue shares not for the benefit of the corporation but to affect voting control, the issue may be declared void. For example, if directors were to issue shares to themselves for the purpose of out-voting shareholders who, up to that point, had a majority of the issued shares, the extra share issue could be set aside by the court.

While not required to do so, most corporations give shareholders a pre-emptive right. When it proposes to issue further shares, it may first issue subscription rights or share rights to all existing shareholders, giving each shareholder one right for each share held. The shareholder then has an option to purchase a new share at a specified price for a specified number of subscription rights. For example, a shareholder owning 50 shares may receive 50 rights entitling him to buy 10 shares (one share for every five rights) at a specified price per share. Subscription rights are normally made transferable, and if the market value of the existing shares significantly exceeds the specified price for the new shares, the rights themselves will have a market value; they may be sold to anyone who wishes to purchase them and exercise the option.

The Right to Information

Disclosure is one of the fundamental principles of modern corporate governance. Disclosure of relevant information enables investors to evaluate the effectiveness of management, and publicity may be an effective deterrent to high-handed behaviour or misconduct in management.

THE FINANCIAL STATEMENTS

financial statements
annual accounts that are required to be presented to the shareholders at the annual general meeting

Annual **financial statements** must be presented to the shareholders prior to the annual general meeting. All corporation acts require that basic information be part of the financial statements, though the detailed requirements vary. Generally, the basic items required are:

- the income statement, showing the results of operations for the financial year
- the balance sheet, showing the corporation's assets as of the financial year-end (including details of changes in share capital during the year)
- a statement of changes in financial position, analyzing changes in working capital
- a statement of retained earnings showing changes during the year, including the declaration of dividends
- a statement of contributed surplus

The annual financial statements should be in comparative form, showing corresponding data for the preceding financial year. In addition, some statutes require that shareholders be sent comparative interim quarterly financial statements. New securities regulations require CEOs and CFOs of distributing companies to certify that the statements fairly reflect the financial condition of the corporation.[46]

[46.] Multilateral Instrument 52-109; full compliance for year ending December 31, 2005.

DOCUMENTS OF RECORD

A corporation must maintain certain documents of record at its head office, which may be inspected by any shareholder during usual business hours. These **documents of record** include:

- minutes of shareholders' meetings
- a register of all transfers of shares, including the date and other particulars of each transfer
- a copy of the corporation's charter, a copy of all by-laws (or articles) and special resolutions, and a register of shareholders
- a register of the directors

documents of record
documents that a corporation is required to keep and make available to shareholders

These documents may often be useful to a minority group of shareholders attempting to collect evidence to support a claim of misconduct or ineffectiveness on the part of the directors. Access to the share register permits a dissentient group to obtain the names and addresses of all other shareholders so that they may communicate with them, explain their complaints, and attempt to enlist their support.

Another document of record is the collection of minutes from directors' meetings. Unlike the other documents of record, however, directors alone, not the shareholders, have a right of access to it.[47]

THE AUDITOR

To assist in the analysis and evaluation of the financial statements, and to ensure their accuracy so far as possible, the acts provide for the appointment of an independent auditor by the shareholders. Private companies may dispense with this requirement, but only if the shareholders unanimously agree to do so. The auditor must be an independent person who is not employed by the corporation.[48] In order to confirm the accuracy of the financial statements, the auditor examines all the records and books of accounts of the corporation. The auditor provides an opinion on whether the statements fairly present the financial position of the corporation in accordance with generally accepted accounting principles.[49] Both the auditor's report and the financial statements must be sent to all shareholders before the corporation's annual general meeting; the period usually specified is at least 21 days before the meeting. These items are included in the corporation's **annual report** to shareholders.

annual report
the report on the business and affairs of the corporation, which the directors are required to present at the annual general meeting

Only the auditor and the directors have the right to examine the books of account; shareholders as such do not have access to them. If a shareholder suspects that something is wrong, he may communicate his information to the auditor, but the auditor has no duty to undertake a special examination at the request of a shareholder; the auditor's duty is owed to the corporation itself rather than the shareholders.[50] As a last resort, a shareholder may apply to a court for the appointment of an inspector.

---

[47] Ss. 20, 21. An exception is made in the case of minutes that record the disclosure of a director's interest in a contract with the corporation: s. 120 (6.1), introduced in 2001.

[48] Although the shareholders appoint the auditor, they do so as an organ of the corporation (the general meeting), and the auditor's contract is with the corporation, not with the shareholders: see *Roman Corp.* v. *Peat Marwick Thorne* (1992), 8 B.L.R. (2d) 43. The auditor's duty is owed to the corporation, not to the shareholders who appointed her: see *Hercules Managements Ltd.* v. *Ernst & Young* (1997), 146 D.L.R. (4th) 577 (S.C.C.).

[49] See section 5400, *CICA Handbook* (Canadian Institute of Chartered Accountants), for a complete statement of the form and content of the auditor's report.

[50] *Hercules, supra*, n. 48.

In a distributing corporation, the audit must be completed by an auditor registered with the Canadian Public Accountability Board. The audit committee, made up of independent directors, supervises the auditor and must create a process to receive anonymous complaints and reports of irregularities in the financial affairs of the corporation, often referred to as whistleblower protection.[51]

APPOINTMENT OF INSPECTOR

Case 17.6 provides an example of the typical situation where an inspector is appointed. All the jurisdictions, with the exception of Prince Edward Island, have statutory provisions enabling shareholders to apply to the courts to appoint an **inspector** to investigate the affairs of the corporation and to audit its books. The statutes give inspectors sweeping powers of inquiry, and the remedy can be a very effective one. In some jurisdictions there are a number of obstacles that undermine this effectiveness; in particular, a substantial proportion of shareholders may be required to join in the application, and the applicant may be required to give security to cover the costs of an investigation, which may be very high. However, the CBCA and most of the provincial acts based on it now permit a single shareholder to apply, and they expressly state that the applicant is not required to give security for costs (section 229). A concerned shareholder may choose either of two options: he may request the Director—a government official appointed to supervise the affairs of corporations—to apply to the court to order an investigation, or he may apply directly to the court himself. In either event, it is necessary to make out a *prima facie* case—that is, produce sufficient evidence of the probability of serious mismanagement to warrant further investigation.

inspector
a person appointed by the court to investigate the affairs of a corporation

Duties of Shareholders

We have seen that directors of corporations are under strict duties of good faith. They must use their own best judgment as to what is in the best interests of the corporation and are not bound to follow the instructions of the shareholders. However, when there is a controlling shareholder (or group of shareholders)—with the power to call a general meeting, dismiss directors, and appoint new ones in their place—it is usually the controlling shareholder who determines corporate policy, and the directors often merely act as a "rubber stamp." That being the case, one must ask whether shareholders—and especially controlling shareholders—owe any duty to their corporation.

Unlike some U.S. courts, Canadian courts have consistently held that a majority shareholder owes no positive duty to act for either the welfare of the corporation itself or the welfare of his fellow shareholders.[52] His obligation ends when he has paid the full purchase price for his shares. He has no obligation to attend meetings or to return proxy forms, and he is free to exercise his vote in whatever way he pleases and for whatever purposes he desires. His share is an item of property that he is free to use as he pleases, even if that is against the interests of the corporation or of his fellow shareholders. This freedom may be complicated if the

---

[51.] National Instrument 52-108 and 52-110.

[52.] See *Brant Investments Ltd. v. Keeprite Inc.* (1991), 3 O.R. (3d) 289.

shareholder is himself a director of the corporation. A director owes a duty to act honestly and in good faith with a view to the best interests of the corporation (section 122), but when he votes as a shareholder he is entitled to consider his own personal interests.[53]

THE PROTECTION OF MINORITY SHAREHOLDERS

Majority Rule

At the very least, a shareholder's freedom to use his vote as he chooses means that the courts will not substitute their judgment for his when his actions are based upon business considerations. As a consequence, a controlling group of shareholders, through its ability to determine the composition of the board of directors, to approve their actions or decline to do anything about their misdeeds, and even (if they have a two-thirds majority) to amend the corporation's constitution, could ensure that the affairs of the corporation were managed entirely for their own benefit and to the detriment of the minority. As we saw when we considered the dilemma of the "frozen-out" shareholder, these things can happen without any law being broken.

Under traditional principles of corporation law, the aggrieved minority shareholders in the above illustrations received little or no help from the courts. However, special statutory remedies have greatly improved the situation of the minority. In examining the more important of these, we shall concentrate upon the remedies provided in the CBCA, bearing in mind that almost all the provinces have adopted essentially similar rules.

The Appraisal Remedy

In some situations, where the majority shareholders make fundamental changes to the corporation, section 190 offers a procedure whereby a dissenting shareholder need not go along with the change. He may elect instead to have his shares bought out by the corporation. If a price cannot be agreed, the court will fix a fair price. However, this **appraisal remedy** is limited to specific actions by the majority, the most important of which are:

appraisal remedy
the right to have one's shares bought by the corporation at a fair price

- changing any restriction on the issue, transfer, or ownership of shares
- changing any restriction on the business that the corporation may carry on
- amalgamating or merging with another corporation
- selling, leasing, or exchanging substantially all the assets of the corporation
- "going private" or "squeezing out" transactions

The remedy is of most use in private corporations, where no ready public market exists for minority shareholdings, since a dissenter in a public corporation would normally just sell his shares on the stock exchange. However, the procedure is a complicated one, and the dissenter must comply with every step

---

53. *North-West Transportation v. Beatty* (1887), 12 App. Cas. 589.

prescribed by the Act in order to take advantage of it. If, instead, the shareholder can show that his interests have been "unfairly disregarded," he is more likely to resort to the "oppression remedy" discussed below.

ILLUSTRATION 17.4

A, B, C, and D are the equal shareholders and directors of a corporation, Traviata Trattoria Ltd. The articles of incorporation restrict the business of the corporation to the operation of one or more restaurants. Contrary to D's wishes, A, B, and C decide to sell the restaurant to a property developer and to invest the proceeds in a casino business. They use their votes to pass two special resolutions: (1) approving the sale of the restaurant (substantially the only asset of the corporation) and (2) amending the articles to remove the restriction on the business that may be carried on by the corporation.

In this example, no wrong has been done to the corporation, and the majority has acted within its rights. Nevertheless, D may justifiably feel aggrieved since the whole basis upon which he became a shareholder in the corporation has been changed.

ILLUSTRATION 17.5

Sixty percent of the shares of Figaro Ltd. are held by Almaviva Inc., a large public corporation, and 40 percent by its original founder, Susanna. Following a disagreement over company policy, Almaviva used its majority voting power to appoint three of its own directors to be directors of Figaro. The new directors subsequently sell an important piece of Figaro's property to Bartolo Ltd., a corporation wholly owned by Almaviva. The sale is at a gross undervalue.

Here, the directors of Figaro have probably been in breach either of their duty of care and skill or their duty to act in good faith and in the interests of their corporation. The corporation, Figaro, has been injured, since the value of its assets has been reduced, but the loss falls entirely on its minority shareholder, Susanna, since the majority shareholder, Almaviva, gains more as shareholder of the purchaser, Bartolo (100 percent of the undervalue), than it loses as shareholder of the vendor, Figaro (60 percent of the undervalue). Consequently, Almaviva, as controlling shareholder of Figaro, will not complain about any breach of duty by its directors.

ILLUSTRATION 17.6

The shares in Jenufa Ltd. are held in equal proportions by A, her husband B, and his two sons by a previous marriage, C and D, all of whom had until recently been directors. After an acrimonious divorce, B, C, and D use their majority voting power to remove A from the board. Subsequently, instead of distributing the profits as dividends, they decide to reinvest them in a fund to provide for the long-term capital needs of the corporation. They also refuse to consent to A transferring her shares to any third party.

In this example, A is locked in and frozen out. But the corporation has not been injured, and, unless it can be shown that B, C, and D acted in bad faith, there may have been nothing improper in their actions.

The Derivative Action

When a corporation has suffered an injury, as in Illustration 17.5 or, for example, where directors have made a secret profit for themselves by exploiting a "corporate opportunity," the corporation may sue the wrongdoer to recover its losses.

Ordinarily, an action on behalf of the corporation must be started by its directors—it is part of the management function. However, if the directors are the wrongdoers, they are hardly likely to commence an action against themselves. The common law recognized the right of a minority shareholder to start an action on behalf of the corporation, frequently called a **derivative action**—but it was procedurally difficult.

The modern statutory derivative action (section 239) overcomes most of the procedural barriers. It permits a shareholder to obtain leave from the court to bring an action in the name and on behalf of the corporation. To do so he need only establish that the directors refuse to bring the action themselves, that he is acting in good faith, and that it appears to be in the interests of the corporation or its shareholders that the action be commenced. If he establishes these things, then the court may make an order to commence the action. The acts prohibit the court from requiring the shareholder to give security for costs. At any time, a court may order the corporation to pay to the complainant costs, including legal fees and disbursements (sections 242(4) and 240(d)). The court may also direct "that any amount adjudged payable by a defendant in the action shall be paid, in whole or in part, directly to former and present shareholders of the corporation . . . instead of to the corporation . . ." (section 240(c)). In Illustration 17.5, Susanna could receive direct compensation for her loss, rather than being compensated only indirectly through an increase in the assets of the corporation.

Although the statutory derivative action has substantially improved the position of minority shareholders, the remedy has been somewhat overshadowed by the oppression remedy, discussed below.

derivative action
proceedings brought by one or more shareholders in the name of the corporation in respect of a wrong done to the corporation

Winding Up

Minority partners have better protection than most minority shareholders. They are entitled to an accounting of profits and to receive their share of them regularly. In the event of a total breakdown in relations, they can normally insist on a dissolution and sale of the assets and receipt of a proportionate part of the proceeds. Since the other partners cannot continue to use the partnership assets for their sole benefit, they must either face dissolution or come to a reasonable settlement. Not so in a private corporation. In the absence of a separate agreement among the shareholders, a minority shareholder has none of the rights of a partner.

Corporation statutes have, however, followed partnership law in one important respect. They give the courts discretion to make an order **winding up** a corporation where it is "just and equitable" to do so.[54] But because of the drastic nature of the remedy, the courts have been reluctant to use it if the corporation is flourishing or is fairly large. Typically, the remedy is available where the corporation is a small family business or an "incorporated partnership," where there is deadlock, where relations between the participants have broken down, or where a "partner" has been frozen out. In these cases, the remedy has proven quite effective, since the mere threat of its use has often been sufficient to persuade the majority to reach a compromise.

winding up
the dissolution (or liquidation) of a corporation

---

[54] CBCA, s. 214(1)(b)(ii). The "just and equitable winding up" rule has been a feature of English and Canadian company law statutes since around the end of the 19th century.

CASE SUMMARY 17.9

G Corp. was a joint venture corporation with two shareholders—*J*, who owned 52 percent of the shares, and *P*, who owned the remaining 48 percent. The relationship between *J* and *P* broke down, largely as a result of different expectations that they had with respect to the objectives and operation of the venture. *P* applied for an order directing the winding-up of the corporation and its sale as a going concern. *J* responded by offering to purchase *P*'s shares, but *P* rejected the offer, and instead made a counter-offer. No agreement was reached.

The court found that the circumstances justified winding up the corporation, since the parties had lost confidence in each other, but since each party would prefer to continue the business alone, it ordered a "buy/sell shotgun" solution.[55]

Oppression Remedy

oppression remedy
a statutory procedure allowing individual shareholders to seek a personal remedy if they have been unfairly treated

Beginning in the 1970s, an alternative remedy—usually called the **oppression remedy**—was introduced and widely adopted in Canada. It is by far the broadest and most flexible remedy available to shareholders. In fact, it is available to more than just shareholders; section 238 of the CBCA describes a "complainant" as any person the court approves. Courts will approve persons with a legitimate interest. It is not necessary to establish wrongdoing; complainants need only show that they been treated *unfairly or oppressively*. Courts are empowered to make any order they consider just and appropriate to remedy the situation.

The oppression remedy is typically sought where a minority shareholder is frozen out, as in Illustration 17.6,[56] but it has also been applied in cases of deadlock or breakdown in the relations between shareholders or directors;[57] in a few cases, the oppression remedy has been used where a wrong has been done to the corporation and a minority shareholder has suffered in consequence, even though a derivative action would seem to be more appropriate in such circumstances. It is possible that Susanna, in Illustration 17.5, might seek an oppression remedy rather than bring a derivative action.[58]

To justify the making of an order under section 241, a complainant[59] must show that the action complained of has been "oppressive or unfairly prejudicial or . . . unfairly disregards the interests" of the complainant. However, the courts have emphasized that the conduct need not be wrongful or in bad faith, though this will be a factor to take into account.[60] It is particularly well suited to deal with the breakdown of family companies, where both or all sides allege wrongdoing by the others.

---

55. *Patheon Inc.* v. *Global Pharm Inc.* [2000] O.J. No. 2532 .

56. *Re Ferguson and Imax Systems Corp.* (1983), 150 D.L.R. (3d) 718; *Daniels* v. *Fielder* (1989), 52 D.L.R. (4th) 424.

57. *Eiserman* v. *Ara Farms* (1989), 52 D.L.R. (4th) 498; *Tilley* v. *Hailes* (1992), 7 O.R. (3d) 257.

58. See, for example: *Journet* v. *Superchef Food Industries Ltd.* (1984), 29 B.L.R. 206. However, it seems that the plaintiff must still show that he has been affected in a way different from that of other shareholders: *NPV Management Ltd.* v. *Anthony* (2003), 231 D.L.R. (4th) 681; *Pasnak* v. *Chura* [2004] B.C.J. No. 790. For discussion of this issue, see MacIntosh, "The Oppression Remedy: Personal or Derivative?" (1991), 70 Can. Bar Rev. 29.

59. In some circumstances a creditor has been held to be a proper "complainant" for the purposes of the section: *Piller Sausages & Delicatessen Ltd.* v. *Cobb International Corp.* [2003] O.J. No. 2647; *Dylex Ltd.* v. *Anderson* (2003), 63 O.R. (3d) 659.

60. *Brant Investments Ltd.* v. *Keeprite Inc.*, supra, n. 41; *Westfair Food Ltd.* v. *Watt* (1991), 79 D.L.R. (4th) 48 (leave to appeal refused).

CASE SUMMARY 17.10

Elaine brought an application against her brother, Abraham, and nephew, Matthew, each of whom owned or controlled one-third of the shares of the furniture company built up by their deceased parents (or grandparents). It was the ninth piece of litigation involving those parties commenced during a period of two years. The judgment delivered by Herold J. of the Ontario Superior Court of Justice paints a graphic picture of the dispute:

> Each time one reads a judgment involving an oppression remedy claim or hears a case with respect to the same, one wonders if one hasn't considered the worst possible corporate scenario—this case is no different. There is a great deal of animosity amongst the various protagonists and there is a great deal of disagreement with respect to both the facts and the inferences and legal conclusions to be drawn therefrom. . . . A portion of the complaint by Elaine . . . involves the lack of what were referred to as the "corporate niceties", such mundane things as annual meetings of shareholders and directors, minutes of same, formal resolutions and the like. The reality is that there were no such corporate niceties. . . .

Among Elaine's allegations of oppressive conduct were the following:

- She never received any dividends (in fact, no dividends were ever paid to anyone).

- Abraham took $210 000 from the corporation without authority. (Abraham responded that maybe he did but Elaine took money too.)

- Abraham and Matthew increased six-fold the rent paid by the corporation to another corporation owned by themselves.

- There were numerous instances of improper loans and payments for personal expenses (by all three parties).

- Abraham and Matthew were financing the litigation, to the tune of $65 000, out of corporate funds—in effect using Elaine's money to sue herself.

The judge found that there had been an irreconcilable breakdown in relations. The parties had not spoken to each other for two years. Not only could the parties not agree on the time of day, "I don't believe they could even agree on what day it was." In the event, it was unnecessary to decide who had been oppressed and how. It was sufficient that there had been a breakdown, which triggered the statute. The only real question was, "What are the appropriate terms of disentanglement?" Since Abraham's whole life was wrapped up in the business, and it was Matthew's main livelihood, whereas Elaine had nothing to do with its operation, the respondents were ordered to buy out Elaine's shares at a fair value to be determined by an independent auditor.[61]

Section 241(3) allows the court to make any order it thinks fit. By far the most common remedy granted has been to require the majority to buy out the minority interest at a fair price, but a wide range of other orders may be made.[62] Judges may customize a solution that suits the particular needs of the corporation. Because of its great flexibility and the absence of technical obstacles, the oppression remedy is quickly becoming the most widely used shareholder remedy in Canada.

[61.] *Viner* v. *Poplaw* (2003), 38 B.L.R. (3d) 134. For another example of a protracted family dispute under the oppression procedure, see *Waxman* v. *Waxman* [2004] O.J. No. 1765 (leave to appeal refused).

[62.] In some cases the court has allowed the minority petitioner to buy out the majority oppressor: see *Tilley* v. *Hailes*, supra, n. 57.

CASE SUMMARY 17.11

In proceedings related to the improper loan described in Case Summary 17.6, Catalyst, a Hollinger non-voting minority shareholder, sought an oppression remedy removing 8 of the 10 Hollinger directors. Lord Conrad Black resigned prior to the hearing. The trial judge ordered the removal of every Hollinger director who was also associated with Ravelston except Peter White. Although Mr. White's conduct was found to be oppressive, he was allowed to remain on the board "at the pleasure" of the remaining independent Hollinger directors. The trial judge felt that Mr. White's continued service as an officer and director of Hollinger was in the best interests of the corporation "at least on a transitional basis." Approximately six months later, at the request of the independent Hollinger directors, the judge ordered Mr. White's permanent removal. Mr. White appealed both orders, arguing that the trial judge had stripped the shareholders of their right to select directors and changed the nature of his director's duties when the independent directors were given the power to remove him.

The Ontario Court of Appeal upheld both of the orders declaring that section 241 gives the court the power to "directly interfere with the corporate governance of a corporation and the rights and obligations of directors, officers and shareholders."[63]

SHAREHOLDER AGREEMENTS

Advantages

Although the oppression remedy has greatly increased the protection given to the minority shareholder, it still depends on the court exercising its discretion in their favour. A shareholder is still in a less secure position than is a partner.

This uncertainty is a factor to be considered if a small group of equal partners propose to transform their business into a corporation. It may make good business sense to incorporate because of the nature of the business, its growth, and its tax position. Yet each of the partners, if aware of the dangers of being a minority shareholder at odds with the others, might well hesitate to give up the protection of partnership law.

Fortunately, it is possible to approximate the protection available to partners with two agreements. One agreement is a long-term employment agreement between the corporation and the shareholder. The second is an agreement among the shareholders that is outside the constitution of the corporation. This process is not simple because, as we have seen, directors owe their primary duty to the corporation. They must not compromise their duty to act in the best interests of the corporation. Subject to an important exception to be discussed below, any agreement among shareholders must be restricted to their role as shareholders and must not infringe on their role as directors.[64] This danger can be avoided in a well-drafted **shareholder agreement**. Each

shareholder agreement
an agreement between two or more shareholders that is distinct from the corporation's charter and by-laws

---

[63]. *Catalyst Fund General Partner 1 Inc.* v. *Hollinger Inc.* (2006), 79 O.R. (3d) 288 (On. C.A.) at para. 50. In *BCE Inc.* v. *1976 Debenture Holders*, 2008 *SCC* 69, the Supreme Court denied an oppression remedy to debenture holders objecting to the leveraged buyout of BCE, saying no single set of stakeholders' interests has priority over others

[64]. *Motherwell* v. *Schoof*, [1949] 4 D.L.R. 812.

agreement must be tailored to the needs of the individual business, but it may be useful to examine briefly the chief elements normally included in a shareholder agreement.

RIGHT TO PARTICIPATE IN MANAGEMENT

The shareholders promise to elect each other to the board of directors at each annual meeting and not to nominate or vote for any other person. They may also promise not to vote for any major change in the corporation's capital structure or in the nature of its business except by unanimous agreement.

RIGHT TO A FAIR PRICE FOR A SHARE INTEREST

The shareholders may agree to a regular method of valuation of their shares. They may agree not to sell their shares to an outsider without giving the right of first refusal proportionately to the remaining shareholders. If one of them commits a major breach of the shareholder agreement and remains unwilling to remedy it, he can be required to sell his interest to the others at the appraised value. In addition, if any shareholder is wrongfully expelled or dismissed by the others, he may require them to buy out his interest at the appraised value. This provision may also state that in the event of a dispute about appraisal, a named person, usually the auditor, will arbitrate and assess the value of the interest.

Unanimous Shareholder Agreements

The CBCA and most provincial statutes formally recognize **unanimous shareholder agreements** and permit them to govern relationships among shareholders in a private corporation in much the same manner as in a partnership. The CBCA states that "an agreement among all the shareholders . . . that restricts in whole or in part the powers of the directors to manage the business and affairs of the corporation is valid" (section 146(2)), and that the shareholders who are given the power to manage "have all the rights, powers, duties and liabilities of a director . . . and the directors are thereby relieved of their rights, powers, duties and liabilities to the same extent" (section 146(5)).

> **unanimous shareholder agreement**
> a shareholder agreement to which all shareholders are parties

The Act also states that "a purchaser or transferee of shares subject to an unanimous shareholder agreement is deemed to be a party to the agreement" (section 146(3)). Thus, on the sale of a share interest in a private corporation that is subject to such an agreement, the transferee not only receives an assignment of rights as a shareholder, but is also bound to carry out the duties of the transferor. A unanimous shareholder agreement must be "noted conspicuously" on the face of a share certificate in order to bind subsequent transferees (section 49(8)).

These provisions modify the common law rule that no agreement may fetter the discretion of directors. However, only *unanimous* agreements have special status under the acts. The CBCA makes frequent reference to unanimous shareholder agreements and treats them almost as if they were part of the corporate constitution, rather like by-laws. In doing so, it has provided the opportunity to develop a new, flexible device for business planning in private corporations.

APPENDIX READING

Contractual Liability

Generally speaking, a corporation is liable for the contracts made by its agents in the ordinary course of business under the rules of agency. Agents of a corporation acting within their actual or apparent authority[65] bind the corporation to contracts made with third parties.

The by-laws and other internal corporate documents will describe agency powers and the proper process for contract ratification. Still, the courts have held contracts to be enforceable even when the proper rules were not followed. In the absence of notice of an irregularity or of suspicious circumstances, everything that appears normal may be relied upon by an outsider and the contract will bind the corporation.[66] This principle is known as the **indoor management rule**,[67] and is really just an application of the apparent authority principle in agency law. An innocent third party may rely upon the regularity of a corporate act, just as he may rely upon the apparent authority of an agent, if it is reasonable for him to do so in the circumstances.

Certain corporate documents must be filed in a government office and are available to the public for examination. At one time, the public was deemed to have notice of the contents of those documents whether they had read them or not. If the documents prohibited either the corporation or one of its officers from carrying out certain acts, a third party could not rely upon what otherwise might be the officer's apparent authority to perform those acts. That rule often led to substantial injustice and has now been abolished by statute. For example, section 17 of the Canada Business Corporations Act (CBCA) provides:

> No person is affected by or is deemed to have notice or knowledge of the content of a document concerning a corporation by reason only that the document has been filed by the Director or is available for inspection at an office of the corporation.

indoor management rule
the principle that a person dealing with a corporation is entitled to assume that its internal procedural rules have been complied with unless it is apparent that such is not the case

---

ILLUSTRATION 17.7

W, the chief executive officer of A Ltd., negotiates a contract to buy equipment from B Inc. for $1 million. The by-laws of A Ltd. provide that any contract involving expenditure of more than $50 000 must be approved by the board of its Japanese parent company. That approval had not been obtained. Consequently, W was acting outside the scope of her actual authority. Can B Inc. enforce the contract?

The answer is "yes" unless B Inc. knew of the restriction in the by-laws and that the approval of the parent board had not been obtained.

---

[65] Where a director or officer acts within the scope of her usual, or apparent, authority, even though she has no actual authority to do so, the corporation will be bound unless the third party knew (or ought to have known) of the lack of authority.

[66] *Royal British Bank* v. *Turquand* (1856), 119 E.R. 886.

[67] This rule receives statutory recognition in the Canada Business Corporations Act (CBCA), R.S.C. 1985, c. C-44, s. 18. Subsequent references in this chapter are to the CBCA unless otherwise stated.

A contracting third party who actually has read or knows the contents of a restriction will be bound by it, but in saying this we are merely restating the common law rule of agency—a third party who knows of an express restriction between the principal and agent cannot claim to rely upon an apparent authority that ignores the restriction. For large or important contracts, one should not take the indoor management rule for granted. Third parties usually hire corporate lawyers to review the corporation's documents of record and ensure that all necessary authorizations have been obtained.

SUMMARY

Corporate directors, officers, and shareholders

- Directors are elected by shareholders to manage the corporation
- Directors owe fiduciary duty and duty to be careful to the corporation
- Directors and officers may be personally liable for decisions they make
- Directors, officers, and the corporation itself may incur criminal liability
- Officers run the affairs of the corporation and owe it a fiduciary duty and a duty of care
- Shareholders owe very few duties to the corporation or other shareholders unless they have sufficient shares to be classed as insiders
- Shareholders have rights and remedies
- Shareholders do not have a right to sue the directors when they act carelessly or wrongfully in carrying out their duties, as the duty of the directors is owed to the corporation, not to the shareholder
- Shareholders can bring a derivative action against the directors on behalf of the corporation, they can commence an oppression action or apply for an appraisal remedy, or they can apply to the courts to wind up a corporation
- Shareholders do not have a right to demand dividends

QUESTIONS

1. What is the distinction between the "business" and the "affairs" of a corporation?
2. Where are the rules of corporate governance found?
3. What are the principal powers given to the board of directors of a corporation incorporated under the CBCA?
4. How are directors appointed? How may they be removed?
5. To whom are directors' and officers' duties owed?
6. What defences are available to a director accused of breach of duty?
7. When a director enters into a contract with his or her own corporation, what precautions should be taken to ensure the validity of the contract?
8. What is meant by "intercepting a corporate opportunity"?
9. In what circumstances might a director have a conflict of interest?
10. What is "insider trading"?
11. Who is an "insider"?

12. What is meant when one says that a minority shareholder is (a) "locked in" and (b) "frozen out"?

13. What are the principal rights attached to shares in a corporation?

14. What is the difference between an ordinary resolution and a special resolution?

15. What are "class rights"?

16. What is a "proxy"? How are proxies appointed?

17. Do shareholders have any right to receive a dividend if the corporation is profitable?

18. What are "pre-emptive rights" in relation to a corporation's shares?

19. Are there any restrictions on the directors' powers to issue new shares?

20. What information must be provided in a corporation's annual financial statement?

21. What is the role of a corporation's auditor? To whom is the auditor's duty owed?

22. What are a corporation's "documents of record"?

23. Do shareholders owe any duty to their corporation?

24. What is the "appraisal remedy"?

25. What is meant by a "derivative action"?

26. What are the principal differences between the "just and equitable" winding-up procedure and the oppression remedy?

27. What matters are commonly dealt with in shareholder agreements?

28. What are the main effects of a unanimous shareholder agreement?

Glossary

A

ab initio from the beginning; an agreement is void *ab initio* if it has at no time been legally valid **203**

absolute privilege exemption from liability for defamatory statements made in some settings (such as legislatures and courts), without reference to the speaker's motives or the truth or falsity of the statement **100**

acceleration clause a contractual term that comes into effect when there is a failure to make an instalment payment and which requires that the entire debt plus expenses be paid **284**

acceptance agreement by one party to the terms of the offer made by another **161**

accord agreement by both parties on some change in the contract **273**

accord and satisfaction agreement to end a contract, with extra consideration to be supplied by the party benefiting from the discharge **273**

accounting court-ordered determination of the injuries suffered; agent must pay over money or property collected on behalf of principal; court order that any profits made from wrongdoing be paid over to victim **63**

accounts receivable funds owed to a business for goods or services provided to customers **398**

actual authority authority given to agent expressly or by implication **436**

adjusters employees or representatives of the insurance corporation charged with investigating and settling insurance claims against the corporation after the insured-against event takes place **376**

administrative law the rules and regulations governing the function and powers of executive branch **47**

administrative tribunals government decision makers (committees, commissions, tribunals, or individuals) who act with quasi-judicial powers **54**

affidavit a written statement made by a witness out of court, but under oath **61**

affirmative action programs intended to correct racial, gender, or other imbalances in the workplace **354**

agency the service an agent performs on behalf of a principal **433**

agency agreement an agreement creating an agency relationship between principal and agent **434**

agency by necessity consent to act as an agent, which is implied when there is an urgent reason **441**

agency shop *see* **Rand formula** **367**

agent person representing and acting on behalf of a principal in dealings with third parties **333**

agreement to sell an agreement that title will be transferred at some time in the future **296**

annual general meeting a meeting where shareholders elect directors and vote on other important resolutions

the general meeting of shareholders that is required by law to be held each year to transact certain specified business **524**

annual report the report on the business and affairs of the corporation, which the directors are required to present at the annual general meeting **529**

anticipatory breach repudiation of contract before performance is due **270**

apparent authority authority as suggested to third party by conduct of principal; may exist even when there is no actual authority **436**

appeal a formal process whereby a higher court will reexamine a decision made by a lower court **5**

appearance document filed by the defendant indicating that the action will be disputed **59**

applications interim applications and questions that are brought before a judge (before the actual trial) for a ruling **59**

appraisal remedy the right to have one's shares bought by the corporation at a fair price **531**

arbitration submission of parties in a dispute to having an arbitrator make a binding decision on their claims **68**

arbitrator a panel or other third party that has been given the authority to make a binding decision on a dispute between parties **73**

articles of association internal regulations setting out the procedures for governing a corporation in a registration jurisdiction **492**

articles of incorporation a method of incorporating based on a U.S. approach and used in some jurisdictions in Canada **491**

assault a verbal or physical threat; an action that makes a person fear physical interference **83**

assignment the transfer of rights under a contract to another party **252**

assignment in bankruptcy the voluntary transfer of a debtor's assets to a Trustee in Bankruptcy so that they can be administered for the benefit of the creditors **411**

associated corporations corporations that are related either (a) vertically, as where one corporation controls the other (parent–subsidiary), or (b) horizontally, as where both corporations are controlled by the same person (affiliates) **486**

attachment under the *PPSA*, the situation in which value has been given pursuant to the contract, giving the creditor a claim against the assets used as security if there is a default by the debtor **401**

audit committee a group of directors responsible for overseeing the corporate audit and the preparation of financial statements. The committee has wider responsibilities in a distributing corporation **507**

auditor party responsible for ensuring that financial statements for an organization are properly done **105**

authority the right or power to act or to make a decision **434**

authorized capital the maximum number (or value) of shares that a corporation is permitted by its charter to issue **497**

B

bailee person acquiring possession of personal property in a bailment **298**

bailment temporary possession by one person of chattels owned by another **387**

bankrupt a person who has made an assignment in bankruptcy or been forced into bankruptcy through a court order obtained by a creditor, and who has not been discharged from bankruptcy **103**

bankruptcy process by which an insolvent person voluntarily or involuntarily transfers assets to a trustee for distribution to creditors **411**

bankruptcy order a statutory assignment of a debtor's assets to a Trustee in Bankruptcy **411**

bargaining agent a body certified to act on behalf of a group of employees or employers **358**

bargaining unit group of employees who have been certified **360**

battery unwelcome physical contact; non-consensual physical interference with one's body **83**

bias prejudice against or partiality towards one party, for example, based on a decision maker's personal interest in the decision **73**

bilateral contract a contract in which there is an exchange of promises: both parties assume an obligation **163**

bilateral discharge agreement by both sides to terminate the contract or to disregard a term of the contract **273**

bill the form in which legislation is introduced into Parliament or legislature **18**

bill of exchange a negotiable instrument by which the drawer directs the drawee to pay out money to the payee; drawee need not be a bank, and the instrument may be made payable in the future **424**

bill of lading a receipt for goods in the care of the shipper, accompanied by an undertaking to move the goods or deliver identical goods to a designated place **296**

bill of sale a written agreement which conveys title from seller to buyer **295**

board of directors the governing body of a corporation, responsible for the management of its business and affairs **506**

bond a share interest in the indebtedness of a corporation; often used synonymously with debenture, though a bond is normally secured against specific assets, while a debenture is likely not **498**

book accounts accounts receivable that can be used as security for a loan **398**

breach of contract failure to live up to conditions of a contract **105**

breach of trust misuse of property held in trust for another by a trustee **142**

broadly held corporations corporations that are publicly traded on the stock market; also called distributing corporations in some jurisdictions **502**

brokers agents retained by the insured to ascertain their insurance needs and secure the necessary coverage **375**

builder's risk policy insurance against liability and other forms of loss taking place during the construction process **376**

business interruption insurance a form of insurance that compensates the insured for continuing expenses incurred while the business is not earning income **378**

business judgment rule courts will defer to the business decisions of directors and officers provided they are arrived at using an appropriate degree of prudence and diligence **516**

"but for" test a test for causation used in negligence actions to determine whether the injury would have occurred had it not been for the act of the defendant **135**

by-laws the internal working rules of a corporation **492**

C

Canadian Charter of Rights and Freedoms a document entrenched in the Canadian Constitution in 1982 listing and guaranteeing fundamental rights and freedoms **21**

canon or church law legal system of the Catholic Church, from which common law drew principles relating to families and estates **8**

capacity the freedom to enter into a contract, which is sometimes limited by law, as is the case, for example, with minors, the insane, the intoxicated, aliens, bankrupts, and Indians **161**

causation determining whether the act actually caused the injury **124**

caveat emptor "let the buyer beware"; principle that purchaser must examine, judge, and test for herself **226**

certificate of incorporation a certificate that a corporation has come into existence **489**

certified cheque means of transferring funds by cheque where payment is, in effect, guaranteed by the bank **263**

chattel mortgage a loan for which a creditor provides credit to the debtor, securing the loan by taking title of a good such as a car **398**

chattels tangible, movable personal property that can be measured and weighed; also known as goods **397**

check-off provision provision in collective agreement whereby employees agree to have employer deduct union dues from payroll **367**

cheque a negotiable instrument consisting of a bill of exchange drawn on a bank, payable on demand **425**

chose in action the thing or benefit that is transferred in an assignment; intangible personal property, such as a claim or the right to sue **252**

C.I.F. contracts (cost, insurance, and freight) sales contracts in which one of the parties has been designated as being responsible for paying the costs involved in the shipping of those goods as well as arranging insurance **296**

circumstantial evidence facts or evidence that lead one to infer the existence of other facts **128**

civil law legal system the legal system used in most of Europe based on a central code, which is a list of rules stated as broad principles of law that judges apply to the cases that come before them **3**

civil liability responsibility arising from a breach of a private law enforced through a lawsuit initiated by the victim **43**

civil litigation the process of one party's suing another in a private action, conducted in a trial court **47**

class rights special rights attached to a particular class of shares **525**

clean hands absence of wrongdoing on the part of a person seeking an equitable remedy **288**

closed shop workplace where only workers who are already members of the union can be hired **367**

closely held corporations corporations in which there are relatively few shareholders; referred to as "non-distributing corporations" in some jurisdictions **482**

C.O.D. contracts (cash on delivery) sales contracts in which the seller maintains the proprietary rights or title as well as control over the possession of those goods until they are delivered to the buyer's premises and paid for **296**

code of conduct a formal statement that sets out the values and standards of business practices of an organization **152**

co-insurance clauses requirements that the insured bear some risk **377**

collateral goods or property used to secure a debt **401**

collateral contract a separate contractual obligation that can stand alone, independent of the written contract **231**

common law courts the three historical English courts (Court of Common Pleas, the Court of King's Bench, and the Exchequer Court), where in theory law was discovered in the customs and traditions of the people **8**

common law legal system the legal system developed in England based on judges applying the customs and traditions of the people and then following each other's decisions **5**

common shares shares to which no preferential rights or privileges attach

a share carrying no preferential right **498**

compensation committee committee responsible for setting director and officer pay **507**

conciliator a neutral third party who facilitates discussion between parties to a dispute to encourage and assist their coming to an agreement; also known as a mediator **364**

conditional sale sale in which the seller provides credit to the purchaser, holding title until the goods are paid for **295**

conditions major terms of a contract **261**

condition precedent condition under which the obligations of a contract will begin; also called "subject to" clause **275**

condition subsequent condition under which the obligations of a contract will end **275**

Confederation the process that united the British colonies in North America as the Dominion of Canada in 1867 **11**

confidential information private information, the disclosure of which would be injurious to a business; a type of intellectual property **110**

conflict of interest a situation where a duty is owed to a client whose interests conflict with the interests of the professional, another client, or another person to whom a duty is owed **138**

conflict of laws rules used to resolve questions as to which jurisdiction's laws are to be applied to a particular issue; includes paramountcy, a principle that if there is overlapping jurisdiction, federal law prevails and provincial law goes into abeyance; also, the area of law dealing with disputes with parties in other jurisdictions **293**

conglomerate merger a merger of companies not in direct competition **312**

consensus factor in validity of a contract: both parties must objectively know and agree to its terms **161**

consent permission or assent to conduct that would otherwise constitute a tort such as assault and battery; can be expressed or implied; an informed consent constitutes a defence to torts such as assault and battery **85**

consideration the price one is willing to pay for the promise set out in the offer **161**

conspiracy to injure coordinated action of two or more persons using illegal methods to harm the business or other interests of another **109**

constructive dismissal unilaterally demoting or changing the duties of an employee, contrary to what was agreed to in the employment contract; conduct that essentially terminates a pre-existing contractual relationship, which could be treated as dismissal **343**

constructive trust a trust inferred by the courts to benefit a third party to a contract **250**

consumer transactions purchases by individuals of goods or services for personal use and not for resale or for business purposes **310**

contingency fee a fee paid to a lawyer that is based on a percentage of the sum recovered by the client **67**

continuing guarantee a provision in a guarantee allowing the creditor to advance further funds without affecting the obligation of the guarantor to pay in the event of default **408**

continuing trespass permanent incursion onto the property of another **86**

contract a voluntary exchange of promises creating obligations that, if defaulted on, can be enforced and remedied in the courts **160**

contra proferentum rule rule interpreting ambiguities in an insurance policy in favour of the insured **381**

contributory negligence a failure to take reasonable care, which contributes to the injury complained of

negligence of an injured party that contributes to her own loss or injury **129**

control test test of whether an employment relationship exists based on whether the person being paid for work is told how, when, and where to do it **330**

conversion intentional appropriation of the goods of another person **87**

cooling-off period a statutorily defined period during which purchasers in door-to-door sales may change their minds and rescind a contract **322**

copyright control over the use and reproduction of the expression of creative work; type of intellectual property **399**

corporate governance the rules governing the organization and management of the business and affairs of a corporation in order to meet its internal objectives and external responsibilities **504**

corporate social responsibility a concept that suggests business decision-makers consider ethical issues including the interests of customers, employees, creditors, the public, and other stakeholders in addition to legal and financial concerns **156**

corporation a business organization that is a separate legal entity from its shareholders **455**

a legal person formed by incorporation according to a prescribed legal procedure **455**

counterclaim a statement of claim by the defendant alleging that the plaintiff is responsible for the losses suffered and claiming back against the plaintiff for those losses **59**

counteroffer a new offer, proposal of which rejects and terminates the offer available until then **170**

Court of Chancery court developed as a supplement to the common law

courts; sometimes referred to as the Court of Equity **9**

crimes wrongs that affect society as a whole and are punishable by the state **87**

criminal liability responsibility arising from commission of an offence against the government or society as a whole **43**

cumulative right the right of the holder of a preferred share to be paid arrears from previous years before any dividend is paid on the common shares **500**

D

damages monetary compensation to victim **63**

a money award to compensate an injured party for the loss caused by the other party's breach

debenture an acknowledgment of debts by a corporation normally involving more than one creditor; often used interchangeably with bond, but whereas a bond is typically secured against a specific asset, a debenture may be unsecured or secured by a floating charge against inventory **498**

deceit the fraudulent and intentional misleading of another person, causing injury

the making of a false statement with the intention of misleading another person **109**

declaration official statement by the court on the law applicable to a particular case, as an outcome of a trial **63**

defamation a false statement published to a person's detriment **94**

delegation entrusting someone else to act in one's place; an agent normally cannot turn his responsibilities over to someone else **444**

deposit money prepaid with the provision that the funds are to be forfeited in the event of a breach **284**

detinue wrongful retention of goods legally obtained but subsequently not returned in response to a proper request **88**

derivative action a lawsuit where certain shareholders are given the right to launch a civil action against the directors on behalf of an injured company; sometimes called representative action

proceedings brought by one or more shareholders in the name of the corporation in respect of a wrong done to the corporation **533**

directors' circular indoor management rule the principle that a person dealing with a corporation is entitled to assume that its internal procedural rules have been complied with unless it is apparent that such is not the case **538**

direct sales sales made to consumers at their dwellings or places of business; also known as door-to-door sales **322**

disbursements out-of-pocket costs incurred by the lawyer on the client's behalf **67**

discharge by agreement agreement by parties that a contract is ended **272**

disclaimer an express statement to the effect that the person making it takes no responsibility for a particular action or statement **144**

discovery pre-trial disclosure of information, consisting of discovery of documents (records) and examination for discovery **59**

discovery of documents (records) pre-trial inspection of any document that is held by the other party and may be used as evidence **60**

dissent and appraisal right of minority shareholders who are adversely affected by major changes to indicate their opposition and force the company to buy back their shares at a fair price **531**

distinguishing the facts the process judges use to decide which case is the binding precedent; involves comparing the facts relevant to the issues being determined **7**

distress seizure by landlord of any property left by tenant and holding of it until the rent is paid or sale of it to pay rent owing **242**

distributing corporation a corporation that issues its securities to the public; also referred to as issuing corporations, reporting issuers, and publicly traded corporations **494**

dividends payments to shareholders out of company profits **526**

a distribution to shareholders of a share of the profits of the corporation **526**

Division I proposals an alternative to bankruptcy, created by the *Bankruptcy and Insolvency Act*, whereby the debtor secures some time to reorganize his or her affairs and make a proposal for partial payment that will satisfy its creditors; if the creditors reject the proposal, the insolvent debtor is deemed to have made an assignment in bankruptcy from the day of the meeting of the creditors, and the normal bankruptcy procedures follow **415**

documents of record documents that a corporation is required to keep and make available to shareholders **529**

door-to-door sales same as direct sales **322**

down payment an initial payment that must be returned to the purchaser in the event of a breach **284**

drawee person or institution ordered to pay out the amount indicated on the negotiable instrument **424**

drawer person creating the negotiable instrument **424**

due diligence doing everything reasonable to avoid a problem leading to legal liability **224**

due diligence defence establishing that an acceptable standard of care and skill was exercised by a director or officer **516**

duress force or pressure to enter into a contract **242**

duty in a negligence action an obligation to live up to a reasonable standard **4**

duty of care an obligation to take steps to avoid foreseeable harm; an essential element for establishing liability in the tort of negligence

a relationship so close that one must take reasonable steps to avoid causing harm to the other **443**

duty to account the duty of a person who commits a breach of trust to hand over any profits derived from the breach **142**

duty to warn to make users aware of the risks associated with the use of the product **133**

E

easement the right of a person other than the owner to use a portion of private property **214**

electronic commerce retail selling using the Internet **189**

employee a person working for another who is told what to do and how to do it **4**

employers' organizations bargaining agents representing groups of employers **362**

employment equity correction of employment situations where there has been a tradition of racial or gender imbalance **354**

endorser person who signs the back of a cheque usually assuming the obligation to pay it if the drawee or maker defaults **428**

enduring power of attorney the power to act as the donor's trustee or representative following the donor's lack of capacity **435**

equality rights basic rights, enumerated in the *Canadian Charter of Rights and Freedoms*, including the right not to be discriminated against on the basis of grounds such as gender, age, religion, race, or colour, and the guarantee of equal benefit of and protection by the law **23**

equitable estoppel the principle that when a gratuitous promise to do something in the future causes a person to incur an expense, the promisor

may be held liable for those expenses if he fails to live up to the promise; also known as promissory estoppel **437**

equity legal principles developed in Courts of Chancery to relieve the harshness of the common law; and value left in an asset after subtracting what the owner owes **497**

error of fact a decision maker's making an incorrect conclusion with respect to the facts in the matter in dispute **337**

errors and omissions insurance insurance to protect holder should the holder cause injury by negligence **383**

estate all the property the owner has power to dispose of, less any related debt; also an interest in land **417**

estoppel an equitable remedy that stops a party from trying to establish a position or deny something that, if allowed, would create an injustice **436**

ethics a system of moral principles governing the appropriate conduct for an individual or a group **41**

evidence in writing any document that provides information or proof **213**

examination for discovery a pre-trial meeting in which lawyers from opposing sides question the plaintiff and defendant in a civil suit under oath— their responses can be entered as evidence; a method of making all relevant information known to both sides before trial **60**

examination in aid of execution (examination in aid of enforcement) court-ordered review of judgment debtor's finances to arrange for payment of the judgment **65**

executed contract a fully performed contract; a contract at the stage when both parties have performed or fulfilled their obligations **196**

executive branch part of government comprised of the Queen acting through the prime minister, cabinet, deputy ministers and government departments and officials; also known as the Crown **359**

executory contract a contract yet to be performed; a contract at the stage when an agreement has been made but before performance is due **196**

exemplary damages damages in excess of plaintiff's actual losses, intended to punish the wrongdoer for outrageous or extreme behaviour; also known as punitive damages **63**

exemption clause an attempt to limit liability under an agreement (also exclusion or exculpatory clause) **168**

express contract contract in which the parties have expressly stated their agreement, either verbally or in writing **162**

F

fair comment defence available when defamatory statements are made about public figures or work put before the public **101**

fair hearing a hearing conducted in accordance with the rules of procedural fairness; person affected negatively by a decision has a right to receive proper and timely notice of all the matters affecting the case and be given a chance to put forward her side **70**

false imprisonment holding people against their will and without lawful authority **89**

fidelity bond employer's insurance against an employee's wrongful conduct **386**

fiduciary duty a duty to act in the best interests of another; such duty may arise between directors and officers and the corporation they serve, between business associates including senior employees and their employer, between agents and their principals, and between partners **137**

finance lease an arrangement where a third person provides credit financing, becomes the owner of the property, and leases it to the lessee **389**

financial statements annual accounts that are required to be presented to the shareholders at the annual general meeting **528**

fixed fee a predetermined fee paid to a lawyer for completing a specific task **67**

fixture a thing attached to land or to a building or to another fixture attached to the land **397**

force majeure clause contract term anticipating some catastrophic event usually exempting liability when such an event interferes with performance of the contract **275**

foreclosure court process ending the mortgagor's right to redeem **480**

forfeiture requirement by the landlord that the tenant who breached the lease vacate the property **284**

forfeiture rule principle that a criminal should not be permitted to profit from a crime **385**

formal contract an agreement under seal **162**

franchising arrangements based on contracts of service and the supply of products between larger and smaller units of one organization **269**

fraud the tort of intentionally or recklessly misleading another person, or making statements without belief in their truth **86**

fraudulent misrepresentation misleading (false) words said knowingly, without belief in their truth, or recklessly, causing injury

an incorrect statement made knowingly with the intention of causing injury to another **143**

fraudulent preference a debtor's payment of money to one creditor to give that creditor preference over the other creditors **420**

fraudulent transfer a debtor's transfer of property in an attempt to keep it out of the hands of creditors; not a valid sale at a fair price to an innocent third party **419**

F.O.B. contracts (free on board) sales contracts in which the parties have agreed that the seller will bear the risk until a specified point in the transport process **296**

frustration interference with a contract by some outside, unforeseen event that makes performance impossible or essentially different in nature **275**

full disclosure obligation to reveal all details of a transaction **445**

fundamental breach breach of a fundamental aspect of the contract that is not covered by an exclusion clause; a breach that goes to the very root of the contract **268**

fundamental freedoms basic rights, enumerated in the *Canadian Charter of Rights and Freedoms*, including freedom of conscience and religion, of thought and belief, of opinion and expression, and of assembly and association **23**

G

garnishment court orders that monies owed to the judgment debtor by third parties be paid into court and applied towards judgment debts; a portion of the defendant's wages may be so directed to payment of the judgment **66**

general damages compensation for future pecuniary losses and incalculable losses such as pain and suffering **116**

general meeting of shareholders a formal meeting of shareholders at which they are able to vote on matters concerning the corporation **523**

good faith the decision maker must act with honesty and integrity **4**

goodwill a business's reputation and ongoing relations with customers and product identification **103**

goods tangible, movable personal property that can be measured and weighed; also known as chattels **397**

gratuitous promise a one-sided agreement that the courts will not enforce **179**

grievance process procedure for settling disputes arising under a collective agreement **365**

guarantee a written commitment whereby a guarantor agrees to pay a debt if the debtor does not **197**

guarantor person assuming obligation to pay if the debtor does not **406**

H

hire-purchase an agreement to lease an item of property with an option for the lessee to purchase it at the end of the stipulated term **388**

holder in due course an innocent third party entitled to collect on a negotiable instrument despite any claims of the original parties **256**

holding corporation a corporation that owns shares in other corporations **456**

horizontal merger a merger in which one competitor buys out another **312**

I

illegal consideration a promise to commit an unlawful act or to do something against public policy, which is not valid consideration and will not be enforced by a court **184**

illegal contract one that is void because it involves the performance of an unlawful act **162**

implied authority the authority of the agent as implied from surrounding circumstances, such as the position or title given (by the principal) to the agent **436**

implied contract an agreement inferred from the conduct of the parties **162**

in camera hearings part of trial proceedings closed to the public **48**

in good faith characteristic of bargaining that makes every reasonable effort to reach an agreement **363**

indemnity a primary obligation of a third party to pay a debt along with the debtor **214**

independent contractor a person working for himself who contracts to provide specific services to another **331**

inducing breach of contract encouraging someone to break her contract with another **106**

infant a person under the age of majority **194**

injunction court order to stop offending conduct **63**

injurious falsehood defamation with respect to another's product or business; also known as product defamation or trade slander **103**

innocent misrepresentation a false statement made honestly and without carelessness by a person who believed it to be true **238**

innuendo an implied statement that is detrimental to another **96**

insanity when a person cannot understand the nature or consequences of his acts **199**

insider trading the use of confidential information relating to a corporation in dealing in its securities **520**

insolvency inability of a person to pay her debts as they become due **411**

inspector a person appointed by the court to investigate the affairs of a corporation **530**

insurable interest a real and substantial interest in specific property or in someone's life **380**

insurance agents person acting on behalf of insurer to handle policies **376**

intellectual property personal property in the form of ideas and creative work **13**

intention desire or aim; parties must objectively intend an agreement to be legally binding; must intend to assume the obligations of the agreement **161, 209**

intentional infliction of mental suffering a tort constituted by harassment or prank causing nervous shock **109**

interest dispute disagreement about the terms to be included in a new collective agreement **358**

interference with economic relations a tort consisting of unlawful competitive practices such as inducing breach of contract **108**

interim agreement binding contract that will subsequently be put into a more formal document **166**

interlocutory injunction court order issued before a trial to stop an ongoing injury **287**

intimidation a threat to perform an illegal act, used to force a party to act against its own interest **108**

intra vires within one's jurisdiction or scope of power **15**

invitation to treat invitation to engage in the bargaining process **166**

involuntary assignment assignment of rights that takes place involuntarily, as in the cases of death and bankruptcy **256**

issued capital the shares that have been issued by a corporation **497**

issue estoppel principle preventing an issue from being litigated again on grounds that it has already been determined in an earlier trial or hearing **349**

J

joint liability liability under which all parties must be sued together; partners may face joint liability for debts of the firm **468**

joint tenancy shared property ownership with right of survivorship **214**

joint venture the collaboration of several businesses to accomplish a major project **456**

judicial branch part of government comprised of courts and officers of the court **10**

judicial review power held by the courts to review decisions made by administrative decision makers **372**

judgment creditor person to whom court awards damages or costs **63**

judgment debtor person ordered by court to pay damages or costs **63**

jurisdiction legal authority and scope of power; the Constitution Act (1867) delegated responsibility for matters to federal or provincial governments, thus giving them distinct jurisdiction to create laws in those areas **4**

jurisdictional dispute a disagreement over who has authority; in the labour context, a dispute between two unions over which one should represent a group of employees, or over which union members ought to do a particular job **358**

just cause valid reason to dismiss an employee without notice

justification the truth of a statement, applied as a defence to a defamation action **338**

L

laches undue delay; neglect, or omission to assert a right or claim **288**

law the body of rules that can be enforced by the courts or by other government agencies **1**

law of equity the system of law developed by the Court of Chancery **9**

law merchant laws developed by the merchant guilds and source of common law relating to negotiable instruments such as cheques and promissory notes **8**

law society self-governing body whose mandate involves regulating the legal profession, in the public interest; law societies set, and enforce, ethical and professional standards for lawyers **457**

lease a secured arrangement whereby possession of the goods goes to the lessee, while the title to the goods remains with the lessor **387**

lease to purchase a lease in which title to the goods is transferred to the lessee at the end of the lease period **399**

legal advice the giving of an opinion by a lawyer regarding the substance or procedure of the law **67**

legal liability responsibility for the consequences of breaking the law **43**

legal person an entity recognized at law as having its own legal rights, duties, and responsibilities **480**

legal representation a lawyer who has the authority to represent a person in court proceedings or in other legal matters **325**

legal rights basic rights, enumerated in the *Canadian Charter of Rights and Freedoms*, such as the right to life, liberty, and security of the person; and security against unreasonable search and seizure, or arbitrary imprisonment or detention **23**

legality one of the elements of a valid contract; the object and consideration of the contract must be legal and not against public policy **161**

legislation laws passed by Parliament or provincial legislatures; also referred to as statutes **18**

legislative branch part of government comprised of Parliament and legislatures **10**

letters patent a method of incorporating used in some jurisdictions in Canada whereby the government grants recognition to the company as a separate legal entity **489**

liability the situation of being potentially or actually subject to some obligation **5**

liability insurance insurance covering loss caused by the negligence of oneself or one's employees **376**

libel the written or more permanent form of a defamatory statement **98**

licence a non-exclusive right to use property; revocable permission to use another's land **14**

lien a claim registered against property, such as a mortgage; charge giving the creditor the right to retain what is in his possession until his demands for payment are satisfied **301**

life estate an interest in land ending at death **214**

limitation periods rules requiring that legal action be undertaken within a specified time from when the offending conduct occurs **55**

limited liability liability is restricted to capital contributed; shareholders are shielded from liability for the corporation's debts **481**

the liability of shareholders is limited to the amount of their capital contributions

limited partnership a partnership with general and limited partners; limited partners are liable only to the extent of their investment **473**

liquidated damages a remedy requiring party responsible for a breach to pay an amount specified in the contract **284**

lockout an action in which the employer prevents employees from working **367**

M

maintenance of membership requirement in collective agreement that union members pay dues and maintain their membership, though new employees need not join the union **367**

malicious prosecution a tort action based on criminal or quasi-criminal prosecution motivated by ill will towards the accused and lacking reasonable evidential grounds for proceeding **90**

mandatory injunction an order requiring a person to do a particular act

mandatory retirement forced retirement from employment generally at 65 years **116**

mediation a discussion, between the parties to a dispute, that is facilitated by a mediator in an effort to encourage and assist them in coming to an agreement **71**

mediator a neutral third party who facilitates discussion between parties to a dispute to encourage and assist their coming to an agreement; also known as a conciliator **71**

memorandum of association constitution of a corporation in a registration jurisdiction **489**

merchantable quality freedom of goods from defects that, if known, would impact the price **201**

minor a person under the age of majority **194**

misrepresentation a false statement of fact that persuades someone to enter into a contract or take some other action **234**

mistake an error about some aspect of a contract that destroys consensus **221**

mitigate lessen a loss, for example, by victims of a breach, who have a duty to take all reasonable steps to minimize losses suffered **283**

duty to act reasonably and quickly to minimize the extent of damage suffered

mortgage means of securing loans; title of property is held by the moneylender as security in some jurisdictions; in other jurisdictions, a mortgage is simply a charge against title **397**

N

necessaries the essential goods or services required to function in society, such as food, clothing, and shelter **194**

negligence an unintentional careless act that results in injury to another

the careless causing of injury to the person or property of another **120**

negligent misrepresentation an incorrect statement made without due care for its accuracy **143**

negligent statements failure to live up to a duty not to communicate misleading words causing economic loss **241**

negotiable instruments substitutes for money that bestow unique benefits; vehicles for conveniently transferring funds or advancing credit **256**

negotiation direct communication between the parties to a dispute in an effort to resolve the problems without third-party intervention; transferring negotiable instruments to third parties **70**

nominating committee committee responsible for proposing and recruiting new directors **507**

non est factum "it is not my act"— grounds for court to declare a contract void because a party is unaware of the nature of the contract **229**

non-disclosure silence constitutes misrepresentation only when there is a duty to disclose **236**

non-profit society separate legal entity with different rules for incorporation than corporations **456**

no par value share a share that has no nominal value attached to it **498**

novation creation of a new contract through the substitution of a third party for one of the original parties to a contract, by the consent of all **273**

O

offer a tentative promise to do something if another party consents to do what the first party requests **164**

offer to settle a formal offer by either party to modify or compromise its claim to settle the matter before trial, refusal of which offer may affect costs **60**

officers high-ranking members of a corporation's management team as defined in the by-laws or appointed by the directors, such as the president, vice-president, controller, chief executive officer, chief financial officer, general counsel, and general manager **506**

operating lease a lease in which the goods are returned to the lessor at the end of the lease period **388**

oppression action action against the directors who have allegedly offended the rights of creditors or minority shareholders **539**

oppression remedy a statutory procedure allowing individual shareholders to seek a personal remedy if they have been unfairly treated **534**

option agreement a subsidiary contract creating an obligation to hold an offer open for acceptance until the expiration of a specified time **170**

ordinary resolution a resolution adopted by the general meeting and passed by a simple majority **524**

organization test test of whether or not a service-provider is an employee and part of employer's organization **332**

P

paid-up capital the shares that have been issued and fully paid for **497**

par value a share with a stated value at issuance (most shares are now no-parvalue)

a nominal value attached to a share at the time of issue **497**

paramountcy principle that when a matter is addressed by both valid federal and provincial legislation and there is a conflict, the federal legislation takes precedence **16**

parliamentary supremacy principle that the primary law-making body is Parliament or the provincial legislatures in their respective jurisdictions, and that statutes take priority over the common law **1**

parol contract a simple contract that may be verbal or written but is not under seal **162**

parol evidence rule principle that courts will not permit outside evidence to contradict clear wording of a contract **231**

partially executed contract a contract at the stage when one party has performed and the other has not **196**

participating right the right of a holder of a preferred share to participate in surplus profits or assets of the corporation in addition to the amount of the preferred dividend or redemption price **500**

partnership ownership and responsibilities of a business shared by two or more people, with a view towards profit **455**

party and party costs court costs determined by a tariff establishing what opposing parties in a civil action ought to pay **63**

passing-off the tort of misleading the public about the identity of a business or product **110**

past consideration something completed before an agreement is made; it is not valid consideration **183**

patent government-granted monopoly prohibiting anyone but the inventor from profiting from the invention; gives inventors the right to profit from their inventions **13**

pay equity principle or statute requiring equal pay for work of equal value **353**

pay in lieu of notice an amount paid to a dismissed employee rather than notice to terminate **336**

payee the person designated on the instrument to receive the money to be paid out **424**

perfection protection of a secured creditor's claim, either by registering the secured obligation or by taking possession of the collateral **401**

performance completion by both parties of the terms of a contract **261**

permanent injunction court order prohibiting offending conduct **98**

personal guarantee a guarantee of payment for another's obligation **197**

personal property tangible, movable goods (chattels) and intangible claims (choses in action); also known as personalty **481, 486**

picketing job action during a legal strike when employees circulate at the periphery of the jobsite to persuade others not to do business with struck employer **369**

pleadings the documents used to initiate a civil action, including the statement of claim, the statement of defence and counterclaim, and any clarification associated with them **59**

pledge an item that a creditor (such as a pawnbroker) takes possession of as security and holds until repayment **397**

postbox rule principle that mailed acceptance is effective when and where it is dropped into a mailbox **175**

power of attorney an agency agreement in writing and under seal **435**

precedent an earlier court decision; in a common law system, judges are required to follow a decision made in a higher court in the same jurisdiction **5**

pre-emptive right a right to have the first opportunity to purchase a proportionate part of any new shares to be issued **526**

preferred creditors creditors who, by legislation, must be paid before other unsecured creditors **66**

preferred shareholders holder of preferred shares who may have a right to vote arising if dividends are not paid **500**

preferred shares shares giving the shareholder preference over other classes of shares; that preference often pertains to payment of dividends

a share carrying preferential rights to receive a dividend and/ or to be redeemed on the dissolution of the corporation **498**

prima facie case a judicial finding that circumstantial evidence establishes a case "on the face of it" **530**

principles of fundamental justice principles set by tradition and convention that protect the right to a fair hearing by an impartial decision maker acting

in good faith to implement a valid law **30**

priority when there are two or more creditors, the one entitled to be paid first has priority; for example, a registered lien usually has first claim (over other interests) to goods used as security **396**

privacy the right to be let alone, to protect private personal information, and to be free of physical intrusion, surveillance, and misuse of an image or name **111**

private company a corporation with a restricted number of shareholders prohibited from issuing its shares to the general public **494**

private law the rules that govern our personal, social, and business relations, which are enforced by one person's suing another in a private or civil action **2**

private nuisance the use of property in such a way that it interferes with a neighbour's enjoyment of his or hers **92**

privilege the right of a professional to refuse to divulge information obtained in confidence from a client **155**

privity of contract principle that contract terms apply only to the actual parties to the contract **248**

probate courts specialized courts dealing with wills and estates; also known as surrogate courts **50**

procedural fairness rules of natural justice that a hearing must follow **30**

procedural law law determining how the substantive laws will be enforced, for example, the rules governing arrest and criminal investigation, pre-trial and court processes in both criminal and civil cases **2**

product defamation defamation with respect to another's product; also known as injurious falsehood or trade slander **103**

product liability manufacturers owe a duty when users are injured by their products **130**

professional corporation (PC) a special type of business corporation that may be formed by members of a profession **495**

professional liability liability owed by persons failing to live up to the standard expected of a reasonable member of a group with special expertise **136**

professional liability insurance specialty insurance for lawyers, doctors, and other professionals designed to cover risks occurring in their practices **376**

prohibition an order not to proceed with a hearing or other administrative process **17**

promissory estoppel principle that when a gratuitous promise to do something in the future causes a person to incur an expense, the promisor may be held liable for those expenses if she fails to live up to the promise; also known as equitable estoppel **185**

promissory note a promise to pay the amount stated on the instrument **425**

promoter a person who participates in the initial setting up of a corporation or who assists the corporation in making a public share offering **440**

proof of claim document filed with the Trustee in Bankruptcy establishing validity of a creditor's claim **418**

prospectus public document disclosing relevant information about a corporation **146**

proxy shareholders' designation of another person to vote on their behalf at an annual general meeting

a person appointed to attend a general meeting of shareholders and to cast the votes of the shareholder appointing him or her **525**

proxy form a form required to be circulated to shareholders before a general meeting, inviting them to appoint a proxy if they so wish **525**

public interest responsible journalism defence a defence to defamation, excusing incorrect statements on matters of public interest, where conclusions were reached following responsible investigation **102**

public law the public good; law concerning the government and individuals' relationship with it, including criminal law and the regulations created by government agencies **2**

public nuisance unreasonable interference with public property **94**

public offering selling shares to the public, which must be done in compliance with provincial securities regulations **506**

publicly traded corporations corporations that issue shares to the public, also known as public corporations, widely held corporations, reporting issuers, and issuing corporations **505**

public policy the public good; some acts, although not illegal, will not be enforced by the courts because they are socially distasteful (against public policy) **200**

punitive damages damages in excess of plaintiff's actual losses, intended to punish the wrongdoer for outrageous or extreme behaviour; also known as exemplary damages **116**

punitive or exemplary damages damages awarded with the intention of punishing a wrongdoer **116**

purchase lease a lease whereby ownership is intended to change hands at the end of the lease term **389**

purchase money security interest (PMSI) a security interest on specific goods that has priority over a general security agreement provided it is registered within a specified time **402**

Q

qualified privilege exemption from liability for defamatory statements made pursuant to a duty or special interest, so long as the statement was made honestly and without malice, and was circulated only to those having a right to know **100**

quantum meruit "as much as is deserved"; reasonable price paid for requested services; sometimes called a quasi-contract **185**

quasi-contract contractual relationship involving a request for goods and services where there is no agreement on price before the service is performed; courts impose obligation to pay a reasonable price; also known as *quantum meruit* **166**

quiet possession a condition that the seller, or anyone claiming through the seller, will not interfere with the buyer's use and enjoyment of the property

a warranty that there will be no interference with the lessee's possession or use of the asset **392**

R

Rand formula option in collective agreement enabling employees to retain the right not to join the union, though they are still required to pay union dues; also known as agency shop **367**

ratification majority agrees with terms of collective bargain; principal confirms a contract entered into by his or her agent **364**

real property land, buildings attached to the land, and items called fixtures, that is, items which are attached to the land or to a building or to another fixture attached to the land **397**

reasonable foreseeability test test of whether a duty of care is owed, based on what a person should have anticipated would be the consequences of his or her action **122**

reasonable notice length of notice to be given an employee to terminate an employment contract of indefinite term; determined with reference to length of service and nature of employee's position amongst other factors **336**

reasonable person test in a negligence action, the judicial standard of socially acceptable behaviour; standard to determine the existence of apparent authority of an agent **438**

receivership proceeding in which a receiver is appointed for an insolvent corporation, partnership, or individual to take possession of its assets for ultimate sale and distribution to creditors **424**

recognition dispute dispute arising between a union and employer while union is being organized **358**

rectification correction, by the court, of the wording of a mistake in the contract **224**

referral selling a type of sales practice in which the purchaser supplies a seller with a list of friends or acquaintances and receives a benefit when sales are made to those people **323**

registration a legislated requirement for incorporating a company in some jurisdictions in Canada **401**

regulators government agencies including ministries, departments, boards, commissions, agencies, tribunals, and individual bureaucrats at the federal, provincial, and municipal levels **505**

regulatory or **quasi-criminal liability** responsibility arising from breaches of less serious rules of public law often enforced through specialized regulatory tribunals set up by the government for specific purposes **43**

remoteness test determining whether the damages were too far removed from the original negligent act; a breaching party is only responsible for reasonably expected losses **135**

repudiation an indication by one party to the other that there will be a failure to honour the contract (expression can be expressed or implied) **200**

res ipsa loquitur principle of establishing negligence based on facts that "speak for themselves"; this no longer applies in Canadian tort law **128**

the facts speak for themselves

rescission returning of the parties to the position they were in before the contract **239**

restitution an order to restore property wrongfully taken; repayment or recovery of a loss **116**

restrictive covenant in property law, a condition imposed by the seller as to what the purchaser can use the land for; in employment law, a commitment not to work in a certain geographical area for a designated period of time **334**

retainer a deposit paid by a client to a lawyer before the lawyer commences work on behalf of the client **67**

reverse discrimination prejudice or bias exercised against a person or class for purpose of correcting a pattern of discrimination against another person or class **354**

revocation withdrawal of an offer before acceptance (must be communicated to the offeree) **170**

right of salvage an insurer's right after paying the insured to sell damaged or recovered goods to recover losses **385**

right of way type of easement that allows the crossing of another's land **116**

right to redeem after a creditor has taken possession of collateral, the right of the debtor to reclaim it on payment of any money owing **404**

rights dispute disagreement about the meaning of a term in a collective agreement **358**

risk potential loss due to destruction or damage to goods, injury, or other eventuality **15**

Roman civil law law of the Roman Empire, from which the common law drew its concepts of property and possessions **8**

royal assent the final approval of the representative of the British Crown, by which a bill becomes law in Canada **18**

royal charter a special licence given by the Crown to form a corporation for the purpose of carrying on a particular activity **488**

rule of law unwritten convention inherited from Britain that recognizes that although Parliament is supreme and can create any law considered appropriate, citizens are protected from the arbitrary actions of the government **11**

rules of evidence rules governing the kind of evidence that will be accepted by the courts **62**

S

sale a transaction in which the seller transfers possession and property to a buyer, for valuable consideration **65**

sale-and-leaseback a transaction in which the owner of property sells it and immediately leases it back from the new owner **390**

salvage that portion of goods or property which has been saved or remains after a casualty such as fire or other loss **385**

satisfaction a substitute in consideration accepted by both parties **405**

secondary picketing picketing by striking employees not just of their own workplace but also of other locations where the employer carries on business **370**

secured creditor a creditor who has claim on property of the debtor, giving priority over other creditors **65**

secured transaction collateral right to debt giving the creditor the right to take back the goods or intercept the debt owing used as security in the event of a default **396**

securities commission provincial agency that serves as watchdog on stock market **525**

security lease a purchase lease in which the lessor provides the credit **389**

seizure court authorizes property of the defendant to be seized and sold to satisfy the judgment **65**

self-defence the right to respond to an assault with as much force as is reasonable in the circumstances **85**

self-induced frustration frustration arising when one of the parties to a contract causes or fails to prevent a frustrating event; treated as a breach of contract **277**

seller's lien seller who holds the goods has a lien against defaulting purchaser **308**

sentencing circles meetings to suggest sentences in cases involving Aboriginal offenders and victims **52**

separate legal entity a corporation exists separately from the people who created it **381**

service contract an agreement to perform a beneficial service **250**

settlement transfer of assets where nominal or no consideration is involved **420**

several liability liability under which each partner can be sued separately **468**

severance owner's removal of chattel he or she has affixed; separation or division of joint ownership; action by one of the co-owners that is inconsistent with joint tenancy **106**

share the means of acquiring funds from a large number of sources to run a corporation; an interest in a corporation held by an investor

a member's proportionate interest in the capital of a corporation **497**

shared mistake the same mistake made by both parties to a contract **223**

shareholder agreement protects the rights of shareholders in relations with the corporation

an agreement between two or more shareholders that is distinct from the corporation's charter and by-laws **536**

simple contract written or verbal contract not under seal, also called a parol contract **162**

slander spoken defamation **98**

sole proprietorship an individual carrying on business alone **455**

solicitor and client costs costs based on what a lawyer ought to actually charge his client **63**

special Acts of Parliament legislative acts creating a specific corporation **488**

special damages monetary compensation awarded by court to cover actual expenses and calculable pre-trial losses

damages to compensate for quantifiable injuries **63**

special meeting any general meeting of shareholders other than the annual general meeting **524**

special resolution a resolution of the general meeting required to be passed by a special (usually two-thirds) majority **524**

specific performance order by a court to a breaching party that it live up to the terms of an agreement **63**

standard form contract contract with fixed terms prepared by a business **172**

standard of care the level of care that a person must take in the circumstances **123**

stare decisis a principle by which judges are required to follow the decision made in a similar case in a higher court **5**

stated capital account the amount received by a corporation for the issue of its shares **497**

statement of claim the document setting out the nature of complaint and facts alleged forming the basis of the action **59**

statement of defence response by the defendant to a statement of claim **59**

statutes law in the form of legislation passed by Parliament **10**

statutory assignment an assignment that meets certain qualifications and under which the assignee can enforce a claim directly without involving the assignor **255**

stoppage in transit seller's right to stop the shipment during transit in event of default **308**

strict liability liability even in the absence of fault **79**

strike withdrawal of services by employees **367**

"subject to" clause term making a contract conditional on future events **166**

subrogation the right of insurer upon payment to take over the rights of the insured in relation to whoever caused the injury **385**

substantial performance performance of a contract in all but a minor aspect of it **262**

substantive law law establishing both the rights an individual has in society and also the limits on her conduct **2**

surety bond insurance arranged in case a party to a contract fails to perform **386**

surrogate courts specialized courts dealing with wills and estates; also known as probate courts **50**

T

tender of performance an unsuccessful (because it is rejected or prevented by the other party) attempt by one of the parties to a contract to perform its obligations under the contract **263**

third-party liability liability to some other person who stands outside a contractual relationship **141**

tort an action that causes harm or injury to another person **78**

trade secret confidential information that gives a business competitive advantage **106**

trade slander defamation with respect to another's product or business; also known as injurious falsehood or product defamation **103**

trade-mark any term, symbol, design, or combination of these that identifies a business service or product and distinguishes it from a competitor **399**

trespasser one who intentionally and without consent or privilege enters another's property **118**

trespass to chattels direct intentional interference causing damage to the goods of another **87**

trespass to person intentional physical interference with another person; also known as assault and battery **83**

trust provision in equity whereby one person transfers property to a second person obligated to use it to the benefit of a third **249**

Trustee in Bankruptcy the licensed professional appointed to administer the estate of a bankrupt for the benefit of the creditors **411**

truth accuracy of a statement, applied as a defence to a defamation action; also known as the defence of justification **100**

U

ultra vires beyond the jurisdiction, power, or authority of a decision maker **483**

umbrella liability a package of several kinds of insurance **376**

unanimous shareholder agreement a shareholder agreement to which all shareholders are parties **537**

unconscionable transaction equitable principle allowing courts to set aside a contract in which a party in a superior bargaining position took advantage of the other party, and the consideration was grossly unfair **246**

undisclosed principal a principal whose identity is concealed from the third parties with whom the agent is dealing; the rights and obligations of the parties depend on whether the agent makes it clear that he is representing an undisclosed principal rather than operating on his own behalf **447**

undue influence pressure from a dominant, trusted person that makes it impossible for a party to bargain the terms of a contract freely **244**

unenforceable contract an otherwise binding contract that the courts will not enforce, such as a contract that does not satisfy the *Statute of Frauds* **162**

unilateral contract a contract formed when one party performs what has been requested by the other party; there is a promise followed by an act, but not an exchange of promises **163**

unilateral mistake a mistake made by only one of the parties about the terms of a contract **226**

union shop workplace where new employees must join the union **367**

unjust enrichment a windfall that one party to a contract stands to make at the expense of the other **222**

unlimited liability the liability of the business owner or partners for all debts incurred by the business to the extent of their personal resources **457**

utmost good faith another term for fiduciary duty **236**

V

valid contract an agreement legally binding on both parties **162**

vertical merger a merger of a supplier and a retailer **312**

vicarious liability liability of an employer for injuries caused by employees while carrying out their employment duties **82**

vicarious performance performance by another qualified person of the obligations under a contract **155**

void contract an agreement that is not legally binding because an essential ingredient is missing **162**

voidable contract an agreement that has legal effect but that one of the parties has the option to end **162**

voluntary assignment in bankruptcy an assignment of assets to a Trustee in Bankruptcy for the benefit of creditors, made voluntarily by a debtor **413**

W

warranties minor terms of a contract **261**

without prejudice words that, when used during negotiation, are a declaration that concessions, compromises, and admissions made by a party cannot be used against that party in subsequent litigation **71**

workers' compensation a scheme in which employers contribute to a fund used to compensate workers injured in industrial accidents regardless of how the accident was caused **81**

work to rule job action in which employees perform no more than is minimally required, so as to pressure an employer **367**

work stoppages strikes (initiated by employees) and lockouts (initiated by employers) **367**

writ of summons the written judicial order by which legal actions are commenced in some jurisdictions **59**

wrongful dismissal dismissal without reasonable cause or notice **100**

Index

A

ab initio, 203
Aboriginal persons
 Aboriginal and treaty rights, 34
 sentencing circles, 52–53
absolute discharge, 423
absolute privilege, 100
abusive trade practices, 312
acceleration clause, 284
acceptance, 172–173
 communication of, 173–178
 effective acceptance, 170
 implied acceptance, 174
 and incomplete offers, 173
 indirect communication of, 174
 postbox rule, 175–178, 176f
Access to Justice Network, 18
accord and satisfaction, 273–274
accounting, 63, 288, 444
accounts receivable, 398
acquisitions, 314
actual authority, 436
adequacy of consideration, 180–182
adjourn Parliament, 12
adjusters, 376
ADR. *See* alternative dispute resolution
ADR Institute of Canada, 72
adverse-effect discrimination, 352
affirmation, 239
affirmative action, 354
affirmative-action programs, 32
age of majority, 193–194
agency
 see also agents; principal
 accounting, 444
 agency agreement, 434–435, 435f, 442–443, 447
 agency by necessity, 441–442
 agency relationship, 434–435
 authority, 434–442
 defined, 433
 described, 330
 formation by contract, 434–435
 fraud, vicarious liability for, 434
 introduction, 433
 liability for agent's tortious conduct, 450–453
 power of attorney, 435
 ratification, 439–441
 reasonable person test, 438
 rights and responsibilities of parties, 442
 specialized agency relationships, 454–455
 termination of agency, 453–454
 third parties, 439, 449
 undisclosed principals, 447–449
 vicarious liability, 450–453
agency agreement, 434–435, 435f, 442, 447
agency by necessity, 441–442
agency shop, 367
agents
 see also agency
 actions binding on principal, 435
 authority, 435–442
 best interests of principals, 443
 competing with principal, 446
 conflict of interest, 444

delegation of responsibility, 444
discretion, 443
duties of, 442–446
duty of care, 443
fiduciary duty, 444–446
full disclosure, 445
function of, 433
independent contractors or employees, 333
insurance agents, 376
liability, 450
obligations under contract, 442–443
partner as agent, 464
and privity of contract, 249
real estate agents, 446
third parties, acting for, 446
tortious conduct, 450–453
training of, 434
undisclosed principals, 447–449
utmost good faith, 445
vicarious liability, 434
agreement to sell, 296
Alberta
 see also Law Society of Alberta
 examination in aid of enforcement, 65
 examinations for discovery, 60
 limitation periods, 55
 limited liability partnership (LLP), 475
 minimum wage, 347
 Money Mentors, 417
 party and party costs, 63
 small claims courts, 50
allegation of fact, 235–236
alternative dispute resolution, 68–75
 advantages of, 68–69
 arbitration, 68, 73–74
 disadvantages of, 70
 vs. litigation, 68–70, 69t
 mechanisms, 70–75
 mediation, 68, 71–72
 negotiation, 68, 70–71
 online dispute resolution (ODR) programs, 74
alternatives to court action, 68
ambiguous authority, 447
American Bar Association, 155
annual general meeting (AGM), 524
annual report, 529
anti-competitive practices, 312
anticipated contact, 83
anticipatory breach, 270–272
apparent authority, 436–439, 442
appearance, 59
appellate courts, 53–54
appraisal remedy, 531
arbitrary detention, 31
arbitration, 68, 73–75, 365–366
arbitrator, 73
articles of incorporation, 489, 490
assault, 83–85
assignee, 253, 254
assignment, 252–256
assignment in bankruptcy, 411
assignments of accounts receivables, 398
assignor, 253
associated corporations, 486
Association of Certified General Accountants of British Columbia, 151
attachment, 401

authority
 actual authority, 436
 agency relationship, 434, 435–442
 ambiguous authority, 447
 apparent authority, 436–439, 442, 448–449
 breach of warranty of authority, 449
 expressly stated authority, 436
 implied authority, 436, 439
 ratification, 439–441
 termination of authority, 453
authorized capital, 497

B

bad advice, and contracts, 222
bailiff, 403
Bank Act, 410
Bankruptcy and Insolvency Act (1985) (BIA), 410
bankruptcy
 absolute discharge, 423
 act of bankruptcy, 412
 after discharge, 423–424
 alternatives, 414–417
 assignment in bankruptcy, 411
 bankruptcy order, 412, 413f
 Bill C-12, 411
 Bill C-62, 411
 Companies' Creditors Arrangement Act (CCAA), 417
 conditional discharge, 422
 consolidation order, 416
 consumer proposals, 416
 corporations, 423
 defined, 411
 discharge, 422
 Division I proposals, 415
 Division II proposals, 416
 estate, 417
 failure to fulfill duties of bankrupt, 421
 fraudulent transfer and preferences, 419–420
 government, priority of, 419
 insolvency reform, 411
 introduction, 410–412
 involuntary bankruptcy, 412
 offences, 419–423
 Orderly Payment of Debts (OPD), 416
 preference of one creditor, 420
 preferred creditors, 418
 priority among creditors, 417–419
 process, 412–414
 proof of claim, 418
 purposes of, 411
 restrictions on bankrupts, 421
 secured creditors, 418
 seller's protection, 308
 settlements, 420
 unsecured creditors, 415, 418
 voluntary assignment in bankruptcy, 413–414, 414f
bankruptcy courts, 50
bankruptcy order, 412, 413, 413f
bargaining, 362–364
bargaining agent, 361
bargaining process, 178
beneficial contracts of service, 194–195
bets, 204
Better Business Bureau (BBB), 327

BIA. *See* Bankruptcy and Insolvency Act (1985) (BIA)
bid rigging, 312, 314
bilateral contracts, 162–163
bilateral discharge, 273
bill, 18, 19f
bills of exchange, 410, 424, 425f
bills of lading, 296
bonding, 386
bonds, 498
borrowing funds, 320–321
bouncers, 83–84
breach of contract, 264–272
 allegations of improper or incomplete performance, 264
 anticipatory breach, 270–272
 conditions and warranties, 265–266
 damages, 281–285
 described, 264
 as discharge, 265
 equitable remedies, 285–289
 exemption clauses, 266–267
 fundamental breach, 268–269
 inducing breach of contract, 106–107
 limitations on recoverable damages, 282–285
 minor breach, 262
 remedies, 281–289
 repudiation, 270–272
 Sale of Goods Acts, 308
 when contract still binding, 265–266
breach of warranty of authority, 449
bribery of public official, 205
British Columbia
 see also Law Society of British Columbia
 examinations for discovery, 60
 guarantees, 406
 indemnity, 406
 limitation periods, 55
 minimum wage, 347
 small claims courts, 50
brokers, 376
builder's risk policy, 376
burden of proof, 49, 61, 128–134
business ethics, law and, 156
business interruption insurance, 378
business judgment rule, 516
business organization
 comparison of types of, 476t
 corporations, *See* Corporations
 partnership, 455, 457–476
 sole proprietorship, 455, 456–457
 types of, 455, 456f
business relations, 211
business torts
 conspiracy to injure, 109–110
 deceit, 109
 inducing breach of contract, 106–107
 relations, 108
 intimidation, 108–109
 misuse of confidential information, 110–111
 passing off, 110
buyer's remedies, 308–309
by-laws, 492

C

CAMR. *See* Canada's Access to
  Medicines Regime (2004)
  (CAMR)
Canadian Association of
  Management
  Consultants, 152–154
Canada
  agreements to share powers, 17
  Confederation, 11–12
  conflicting powers, 15–16
  Constitution, and division of
    powers, 12–13
  delegation of powers, 17
  federal government. *See*
    federal government
  Government of Canada. *See*
    federal government
  investment in corporations
    in, 487–488
  law in Canada, 11–20
  legislation, 18–20
  outline of court system, 51*f*
  paramountcy, 16
  power to prorogue
    Parliament, 12
  provincial governments. *See*
    provincial governments
Canadian Bill of Rights, 20–21
Canada Business Corporations Act
  (CBCA), 487–490, 494, 495,
  504–506, 508, 511–513, 516,
  523, 534, 537
Canadian Consumer Handbook, 327
Canadian Legal Information
  Institute, 18
Canadian Motor Vehicle
  Arbitration Plan (CAMVAP),
  327
Canadian National Railways
  (CN), 257
Canadian Public Accountability
  Board (CPAB), 529–530
canon law, 8
capacity, 193–200
  defined, 161
  drunkenness, 199–200
  insanity, 199–200
  minors and infants, 193–199
catastrophic event, 275
causation, 79, 124, 125
  professional, 150
caveat emptor, 266, 273, 300, 303,
  327
certificate of incorporation, 489
certification, 360–361
certified cheques, 410, 426
Charlottetown Accord, 36
Charter of Rights and Freedoms, 21–35
  cost of *Charter* challenges, 35
  democratic rights, 27–28
  effect of inclusion in
    Constitution, 21
  equality rights, 23, 32–34
  fundamental freedoms, 23,
    25–27
  interests of the public, 22
  language rights, 34–35
  legal rights, 23, 30–31
  limitations, 21–24
  mobility rights, 29–30
  non-application of, 25
  provisions, 24–35
  reasonable limits, 21–24
  Section 52 of *Constitution Act,
    1982*, 21
chattel lease, 388
  implied terms, 392
  reasons for, 390
  terms, 391–392
chattel mortgage, 388, 398
chattels, trespass to, 87
chattels, 96–98, 293–327, 396–397

check-off provision, 367
cheques, 424
chief executive officer
  (CEO), 506, 511
chief financial officer (CFO), 508,
  511
children. *See* minors
choses in action, 252, 397
church law, 8
C.I.F. contracts (cost, insurance,
  and freight), 296
circuit court, 52
citizen's powers of arrest, 89
civil actions, 48
Civil Code, 3
civil law. *See* private (civil) law
civil law legal system, 3–4
civil liability, 43
civil litigation, 55–85
  vs. alternative dispute
    resolution, 68–70, 69*t*
  contracts that promote
    litigation, 204
  costs, 62–63
  discovery, 60
  enforcement, 63–66
  judgment, 62–64
  judicial remedies before
    judgment, 66–67
  jurisdiction of court, 56–57
  limitation periods, 55–57
  offer to settle, 60
  pre-trial procedures, 59–61
  process, 56*f*
  remedies, 63–64
  statement of claim, 59
  statement of defence, 59
  trial, 61–62
class rights, 525
clean hands, 288
clerical error, 223
closed shop, 367
C.O.D. contracts (cash on
  delivery), 296
code of conduct, 149, 152, 156
  binding, 157
  forms of, 157–158
  self-imposed, 158
  voluntary, 157–158
collateral contract, 231
collective agreements, 362–363,
  365–366
collective bargaining, 354–372
  agency shop, 367
  arbitration, 365–366
  bargaining, 362–365
  bargaining agent, 361
  certification, 360–361
  check-off provision, 367
  closed shop, 367
  collective agreements,
    362–363, 365–366
  and constitutional rights, 359
  employers' organizations, 362
  essential services, 370
  federal legislation, 358
  as freedom of expression, 27
  in good faith, 363
  grievance process, 365–366
  interest dispute, 358
  job action, 367–368
  jurisdictional dispute, 358
  labour relations boards, 359
  leafleting, 369
  legislation, 358–360
  lockouts, 367–368
  maintenance of membership,
    367
  mediation (conciliation),
    364–365
  organization of employees,
    360–362
  picketing, 369–370

  public sector, 370–371
  Rand Formula, 367
  ratification, 364
  recognition disputes, 358
  rights dispute, 358
  secondary picketing, 370
  strikes, 367–368
  terms of collective
    agreements, 365–366
  unfair labour practices,
    361–362
  union organization,
    371–372
  union shop, 367
  work stoppages, 367
  work to rule, 367
commercial relations, 210
common law
  common law courts, 8
  distinguishing the facts, 7
  legal system, 5–7
  stare decisis, 5–7
common law courts, 8
common shares, 498
communication
  of acceptance, 173–178
  electronic communications,
    and postbox rule, 178
  of offer, 167–169
Companies' Creditors Arrangement Act
  (CCAA), 417
compensation committee, 507
compensation, 79, 80, 81
competition
  agents and, 446
  contracts that reduce, 205
  restrictive covenants, 206,
    208, 334–335
Competition Act, 311–315
Competition Bureau, 311–312,
  315
Competition Tribunal, 312
competitive approach, 71
compilations, 18
complaints
  employees, 349
  of human rights violations, 38
comprehensive policies, 377
compulsory mediation, 72
conciliation, 364–365
condition precedent, 275
condition subsequent, 275
conditional sales agreements, 398
conditions, 261, 265–266, 298–299
Confederation, 11–12
confidentiality
  misuse of confidential
    information, 110–111
  online businesses, 74
conflict of interest, 138, 444
conglomerate merger, 312
consensus, 161, 163–164, 199
consent, 85
consideration
  adequacy of consideration,
    180–182
  described, 161, 178–180, 179*f*
  examples of valid
    consideration, 184–185
  exceptions to general rule,
    185–187
  existing duty, 182–184
  gratuitous promise,
    179–180, 182–184
  illegal consideration, 184
  past consideration, 183
  payment of less to satisfy a
    debt, 183–184
  promissory estoppel,
    185–187, 186*f*
  quantum meruit, 185
  request for services, 185
  sealed documents, 187–188

  settlement out of court, 184
  specific consideration or
    price, 182
  to support change in terms,
    272
consolidation order, 416
conspiracy to injure, 109
conspiracy to unduly lessen
  competition, 312
Constitution of Canada
  agreements to share powers,
    17–18
  *Charter of Rights and Freedoms.
    See Charter of Rights and
    Freedoms*
  collective bargaining and, 359
  conflicting powers, 15
  delegation of powers, 17
  division of powers, 12–15
  intra vires, 15
  paramountcy, 16
  Section 52 of *Constitution Act,
    1982*, 21
  significance of 1982 changes,
    36
  ultra vires, 15
  validity of legislation, 14
constructive dismissal, 343–344
constructive trust, 250
Consumer Measures Committee
  (CMC), 327
consumer proposals, 416
consumer protection, 188
consumer protection legislation,
  310–327
  anti-competitive practices, 312
  borrowing funds, 320–321
  Competition Act, 311–315
  consumer service bodies, 327
  consumer transactions, 310
  controlled business practices,
    322–323
  cooling-off period, 322
  dangerous products,
    protection from, 315–316
  debt-collection processes, 326
  direct sales, 322
  door-to-door sales, 322
  federal legislation, 311–316
  gift cards, 322
  limited warranties, 267
  loan transactions, 324–325
  payday loans, 324–325
  provincial legislation,
    316–327
  referral selling, 322–323
  responsibility for goods,
    316–319
  role of, 310
  standard form contracts, 172
  unacceptable business
    practices, 319–322
  unconscionable transactions,
    320–322, 325–326
  undue restriction of
    competition, 311–312
  unsolicited goods, 174
consumer transactions, 310
contingency fee agreement, 67
continuing guarantee, 408
continuing trespass, 86
contra preferentum, 381, 382
contract formation
  see also contract formation
  acceptance, 172–178
  capacity, 161, 193–200
  consensus, 161, 163–164
  consideration, 161, 178–188
  contracts formed illegally,
    202–209
  the contractual relationship,
    160–171
  counteroffer, 170

form of contract, 212–217
intention, 161, 209–211
legality, 161, 200–209
offer, 164–171
summary of, 217*t*
typical process, 167*f*
contracts
acceleration clause, 284
acceptance, 174–178
agency agreement, 434–440,
435*f*, 442–443, 447
assignment, 252–256
and bad advice, 222
bargaining process, 178
beneficial contracts of service,
194–195
bilateral contracts, 162–163
breach of contract. *See* breach
of contract
capacity, 161, 193–200
C.I.F. contracts (cost,
insurance, and freight), 296
collateral contract, 231
condition precedent, 275
condition subsequent, 275
conditions, 261, 265–266,
299–300
consensus, 161, 163–164
consideration, 161, 178–188
contra preferentum, 381, 382
with criminal rates of interest,
202–203
defined, 160–161
discharge by agreement,
272–275
duress, 242–243
duty of good faith, 172
elements of a contract, 161
employment contract,
333–348
end of contractual
relationship. *See* end of
contract
evidence in writing, what
constitutes, 215
executed, 197
executory contracts, 196
exemption clauses, 168,
250–251, 266–267
express contracts, 162
F.O.B. contracts (free on
board), 296
force majeure clause, 275, 277
form of contract, 212
formal contracts, 162
formation of. *See* contract
formation
formed illegally, 202–209
freedom of contract, 161
frustration, 275–280
illegal contracts, 162
illegal performance, 200–202
implied contracts, 162
implied terms, 232–233
inducement, 237–238
intention, 161, 166, 209–212
internet, 188–189
invitations to treat, 166–167
lease, 392
legality, 161, 200–209
limitation clauses, 381–382
major terms, 261
minor terms, 261
misrepresentation, 233–242
mistake, 211–233
negotiable instruments, 256
not performed within one
year, 213–214
novation, 250, 273–274
offer, 164–171
oral contracts, 161
parol contracts, 162

parol evidence rule, 232–233
part performance, 216–217
partially executed contract,
196
performance. *See* performance
postbox rule, 176*f*
privity of contract, 248–252
quasi-contracts, 166
ratification. *See* ratification
simple contracts, 162
standard form contracts, 172
subject-to clauses, 166
suing in contract, 317
tendering process, 171
terms and definitions, 162–163
unconditional contracts, 297
unconscionable transactions,
246–248
undue influence, 244–246, 247
unenforceable contracts, 162
unilateral contracts, 163, 171,
174
utmost good faith, 236,
382–384
valid contract, 162
void contracts, 162
voidable contracts, 162
warranties, 261–262,
265–266
writing, requirement of, 161,
212–216
contractual duty, 137
contractual relationship, 160–171
control test, 330–332
controlled business practices,
322–323
*Convention on the International Sales
of Goods* (CISG), 309
conversion, 67–68
cookies, 113
cooling-off period, 322
corporate governance, 504
annual report, 529
documents of record, 529
inspector, 530
publicly traded
corporations, 505–506
corporate groups, 495
corporate securities, 498
negotiability of, 500
share transfers, 501
corporate social responsibility,
156, 157*f*
corporations, 480
articles of incorporation, 489,
490–491
as legal entity, 484, 485
associated, 486
auditors, 529
bondholders, 499
by-laws, 492
class rights, 500
class voting rights, 525
closely held, 494–495
common shareholders, 499
continuity, 483
contractual liability, 538
corporate veil, 487
defined, 455
directors' authorization, 493
distributing, 505, 509, 530
duty of good faith, 482
equity and debt, 497
groups of, 495
holding corporation, 456
incorporation methods, 488
incorporation
statutes, 488–489
jurisdiction, 490
liability, 481
limited liability, 486
liquidation of assets, 499

management, 482
name of, 491–492
operating rules, 492
ownership transfer, 481–482
preferred shareholders, 500
private, 494
professional, 495, 496
public, 494, 505–506
receivership, 424
share capital, 497, 498
shareholders, 497
structure, 506–507, 507*f*
taxation, 483
types of, 480
ultra vires, 483, 484
widely held, 494
winding up, 533
cost of borrowing, 323–324
costs
of litigation, 62–63
party and party costs, 63
solicitor and client costs, 63
true cost of borrowing,
323–324
counterclaim, 59
counteroffer, 170
Court of Chancery, 9
Court of Equity, 9
courts
burden of proof, 49
circuit court, 52
civil litigation process, 55–84
civil *vs.* criminal actions, 48
common law courts, 8
with criminal jurisdiction, 50
domestic violence courts, 52
drug treatment courts, 52
of equity, 9
federal courts, 54
generally, 48
jurisdiction, 56–59
open to public, 48
outline of Canada's court
system, 51*f*
probate courts, 50
provincial courts of appeal,
53–54
provincial trial courts, 50–53
recent developments, 51–52
sentencing circles, 52–53
small claims courts, 50
Supreme Court. *See* Supreme
Court
surrogate courts, 50
unified family courts, 52
courts of appeal, 53–54
credit-reporting agencies, 326
creditors
see also security for debt
acceptable forms of payment,
263
acceptance of less in
satisfaction of debt, 183–184
bankruptcy order, 411,
412–413, 413*f*
care of goods in possession, 403
debt-collection processes, 326
forcing bankruptcy, 414
guarantees, 406–410
methods of securing debt,
396–410
novation, 273–274
possession of collateral, 403
preference of on creditor, 420
preferred creditors, 65, 418
priority, 410–411, 417–419
secured creditors, 65–66,
410, 418
unsecured creditors, 410, 418
crimes
contracts to commit a crime,
204

unauthorized interception of
communications, 113–114
criminal actions, 48–49
Criminal Code
citizen's powers of arrest, 89
threat of criminal
prosecution, 326
criminal jurisdiction, 50
criminal liability, 43
criminal rates of interest, 202–203
cumulative right, 500
cumulative voting, 510

D

damages, 127
and bad faith of employer,
337
breach of contract, 281–285
breach of fiduciary duty,
458–459
cap for non-pecuniary
damages, 95
contractual limitations,
284–285
deceit, 240
defined, 63
economic losses, 283
exemplary damages, 63
general damages, 63, 116, 282
limitations on recoverable
damages, 282–283
liquidated damages, 284, 285
for misrepresentation, 242
mitigation, 283
negligent misrepresentation,
241
punitive (exemplary), 116
punitive damages, 63, 282, 344
and remoteness, 282–281
special damages, 63, 116, 282
dangerous products, 315–316
debt
see also debtors; loan
transactions
acceleration clause, 284
acceptable forms of payment,
263
consumer protection
legislation, 321
methods of securing debt,
396–410
payment of less to satisfy
debt, 183–184
promissory notes, 401
security for debt. *See* security
for debt
tender of performance, 263
debt-collection processes, 326
debtors
see also debt
bankruptcy. *See* bankruptcy
default by debtor, 403
liability for deficiency, 404
payment of less to satisfy a
debt, 183–184
threat of criminal
prosecution, 326
deceit, 109–110, 240
deceptive marketing practices, 312
declaration, 63
defamation, 94–103
defective products, 316–319
defences
absolute privilege, 100
guarantors, 410
unconscionability, 247
defendant, 55
delegation of powers
agents, 444
government, 17
democratic rights, 27–28
demotion without cause, 343

deposits, 279, 284, 286
derivative action, 533
direct sales, 322
directors,
    appointment of, 510
    board of, 506
    breach of duty, 515, 516
    conflict of interest, 517–518
    corporate information, 518, 519
    duties of, 512
    duty of care, 513
    duty to corporation, 513
    duty to public, 515
    duty to shareholders, 514
    fiduciary duty, 513
    independent, 509
    insider trading, 520–521
    liability, 521
    opportunity interception, 518
    powers of, 509, 510
    qualifications, 510
    related party transactions, 519–520
    removal of, 510
    role of, 508
    share issues, 526, 527
    strict liability, 516–517
disability insurance, 380
disabled workers, 340
discharge by agreement, 272–275
    accord and satisfaction, 273–274
    bilateral discharge, 273
    condition precedent, 275
    condition subsequent, 275
    force majeure clause, 275
    mutual release, 273
disclaimer, 144
disclosure
    during contractual negotiations, 168
    cost of borrowing, 323–324
    full disclosure, 445
    of important terms, 168
    non-disclosure, and misrepresentation, 236
discovery
    discovery of documents, 60
    examination for discovery, 60
discovery of documents, 60
discrimination
    adverse-effect discrimination, 352
    affirmative action, 354
    duty to accommodate, 39–40
    employer's rules, challenges to, 352
    employment equity, 354
    equality rights, 32–33
    harassment as, 351
    human rights legislation, 36–44
    mandatory retirement, 354
    reverse discrimination, 354
    sexual orientation, 38
    in the workplace, 354
discriminatory pricing, 312
dishonesty, 339
dismissal from employment. See termination of employment
disobedience, 340
dispute resolution
    alternative dispute resolution, 68–75
    alternatives court action, 68
    civil litigation process, 55–66
    courts. See courts
dissolution of partnership, 471–473
distinguishing the facts, 7

distributing company, 494
distributing corporation, 494, 505–506, 509
dividends, 526
Division I proposals, 415
Division II proposals, 416
divorce, contracts and, 204
documents
    discovery of, 60
    sealed documents, 187–188
domestic relations, 211
domestic violence courts, 52
door-to-door sales, 322
double ticketing, 312
down payment, 284
drug treatment courts, 52
drunkenness, 199–200
due diligence defence, 516
duress, 242–243
duty of care, 121–122, 132, 513
    see also standard of care
    agents, 443
    omissions and, 147–148
    prima facie, 145
duty of fair representation, 372
duty of good faith, 172, 482
duty to accommodate, 39–40, 352
duty to account, 142
duty to act, 182–183
duty to assist citizens, 30–31
duty to be fair, 171
duty to warn, 133

E

e-commerce (electronic commerce)
    jurisdiction, 189
e-commerce legislation,
    see also Internet
economic advantage, 247
efficiency defence, 312
electronic commerce. See e-commerce (electronic commerce)
electronic communications, and postbox rule, 178
electronic transactions. See Internet
employees
    disabled workers, 340
    dishonesty, 339
    fiduciary duty, 334, 341
    obligations, 334
    seasonal employees, 337
    termination of employment. See termination of employment
    unfair labour practices, 361–362
    unionization. See collective bargaining
    wrongful leaving, 341–342
employers
    bad faith, and damages, 337
    liability of, 345–346
    obligations, 333
    unfair labour practices, 361–365
    vicarious liability, 345–346
employers' organizations, 362
employment
    see also employment law
    conditions of employment, 346
    control test, 330–333
    described, 330–333
    expanded definition, 451
    vs. independent contractors, 330
    organization test, 332–333
employment contract, 333–345, 334f

binding nature of, 343
    employee's obligations, 334
    employer's obligations, 333
    non-competition clauses, 335–336
    restrictive covenants, 207, 208, 334–335
    termination, 336–345
employment equity, 354
Employment Insurance, 356–357
employment law
    collective bargaining. See collective bargaining
    constructive dismissal, 343–344
    demotion without cause, 343
    disabled workers, 340
    disobedience and incompetence, 340
    employment contract, 333–345
    human rights legislation, 349–354
    just cause, 338–340
    law of master and servant, 333
    layoffs, 340–341
    legislation, 346–357
    liability of employer, 345–346
    reasonable notice, 336–338
    remedies for wrongful dismissal, 344–345
    termination of employment, 336–345
    termination without cause, 336–338
    wrongful leaving, 341–342
employment legislation, 346–357
    affirmative action, 354
    complaints, 349
    employment equity, 354
    Employment Insurance, 356–357
    employment standards, 347–348
    health and safety conditions, 355–356
    human rights, 349–354
    issue estoppel, 349
    mandatory retirement, 354
    other legislation, 357
    pay equity, 353–354
    termination of employment, 348–349
    workers' compensation, 355
employment standards, 347–348
enabling statute, 10
end of contract
    accord and satisfaction, 273–274
    bilateral discharge, 273
    breach of contracts. See breach of contract
    contractual terms, 275
    discharge by agreement, 272–275
    frustration, 275–280
    mutual release, 273
    performance, 261–264
enforcement
    examination in aid of execution, 65
    garnishment, 66
    of judgment, 63–66, 65f
    seizure of property, 65–66
equality rights, 23, 32–33
equitable estoppel, 185–187, 186f, 437
equitable remedies
    accounting, 63, 288
    clean hands, 288

injunction, 63, 66, 287
    interlocutory injunction, 287
    laches, effect of, 288
    quantum meruit, 166, 185, 288–289
    specific performance, 63, 64, 286–287
    when unavailable, 288–289
equity
    courts of equity, 9
    described, 9
    law of equity, 9
essential services, 370
estate, 417
estoppel
    apparent authority, 436–439
    defined, 436
    equitable estoppel, 437
    issue estoppel, 349
    ordinary use of, 185
    promissory estoppel, 185–187, 186f
ethics,
    business, 156
    law and, 41–42
evidence
    burden of proof, 49, 61
    evidence in writing, what constitutes, 215
    extrinsic evidence, 234
    parol evidence rule, 231–232
    rules of evidence, 62
    suppression of evidence, 91
exaggerated claims, 211, 212
examination for discovery, 60
examination in aid of execution, 65
excessive interest rates, 321, 324, 325
executed, 197
executory contracts, 196
exemplary damages, 63
exemplary damages. See damages, punitive (exemplary)
exemption clauses, 168, 250–251, 266–267, 316, 318
    Sale of Goods Act, 304
existing duty, 182–183
express contracts, 162
expressly stated authority, 436
extrinsic evidence, 234

F

fact, allegation of, 235–236
fair comment, 101
fair-market-value (FMV) leases, 391
false claims, 319
false imprisonment, 89–90
false statements, 237
    see also misrepresentation
family needs, accommodation of, 350
family relationships, and apparent authority, 442
fault, 79–80
Federal Court, 54
Federal Court of Appeal, 54
federal courts, 54
federal government
    see also government; Parliament
    agreements to share powers, 17–18
    compilation of statutes, 18
    conflicting powers, 15–16
    consumer protection legislation, 311–312
    delegation of powers, 17
    division of powers, 12–15
    paramountcy, 16
    transfer-payment schemes, 18

fees
 contingency fee agreement, 67
 disbursements, 67
 fix fees, 67
 hourly rates, 67
 lawyers' fee, 67–68
 lawyers' fee, 67–68
 retainer, 67
fidelity bond, 386
fiduciary duty, 136, 137–138, 513
 agents, 444–446
 breach of, 458–459
 conflict of interest, 444
 employees, 341, 374
 partnership, 459, 468
 specialized agency
  relationships, 454–455
 utmost good faith, 445
financial statements, 528
fit for purpose, 301–302
fixtures, 397
F.O.B. contracts (free on board), 296
force majeure clause, 275, 277
forfeiture laws, 14
forfeiture rule, 385
form of contract, 212–213
formal contracts, 162
formation of contracts. *See* contract
 formation
franchise agreements, and duty of
 good faith, 269
fraud
 of employee, 339
 extrinsic evidence, 234
 failure to correct innocent
  misrepresentation, 240
 insurance for, 375
 vicarious liability, 434
fraudulent misrepresentation,
 109–117
fraudulent transfer and
 preferences, 419–420
free transferability, 428
freedom of assembly and
 association, 25
freedom of conscience and
 religion, 25
freedom of contract, 161
freedom of expression, 25, 26
frustration, 275–280
 circumstances constituting
  frustration, 277
 circumstances not
  constituting frustration,
  277–279
 described, 275
 effect of, 279–281, 280*t*
 self-induced frustration, 277
 unforeseen and outside of
  parties' control, 278
full disclosure, 445
fundamental breach, 268–269,
 300
fundamental freedoms, 23, 25–27
future transfer of goods, 296

G

garnishment, 66
garnishment before judgment, 66
Gates, Bill, 512
general damages, 63, 282
general meeting of
 shareholders, 523
gift cards, 322
good faith, 382–384
goods. *See* personal property; *Sale
 of Goods Acts*
goodwill, 206
government
 see also federal government;
  provincial governments
 contracts that injure the state,
  205

functions, 10
 priority, 413
government agencies, 2, 18
Government of Canada. *See* federal
 government
Governor General, 18
gratuitous promise, 179–180,
 182–184
grievance process, 365, 366
guarantees, 406–410
 vs. indemnities, 214
 personal guarantees, 481
 writing, requirement of,
  213–215

H

harassment, 38, 337, 343, 351
hard-hat rule, 352
hazardous products, 315–316,
 318–319
health and safety conditions,
 355–356
health insurance, 378–380
Hedley Byrne Principle, 143–144, 148
 limits to, 144–147
hire-purchase, 388
holder in due course, 427–428,
 410
holding corporation, 456
horizontal mergers, 312
hourly rates, 67
House of Lords, 59, 63, 127, 131
human rights legislation, 36–40
 complaints of human rights
  violations, 38
 employment equity, 354
 and employment law, 38–39,
  349–354
 harassment, 38–39
 human rights tribunals,
  350–351
 mandatory retirement, 354
 pay equity, 353–354
 sexual orientation, 37
 unions and, 371
human rights tribunals, 350–351

I

illegal consideration, 184
illegal contracts, 162
illness, 340
immoral acts, 204
implied authority, 436, 439
implied contracts, 162
implied repudiation, 271–272
implied terms, 232–233
implied warranties, 299–300
impossibility of restoration, 239
in good faith, 363
incompetence, 340
incomplete offer, 173
inconsistent interpretations, 6
indemnities
 vs. guarantees, 214
 writing, requirement of,
  213–215
indemnity, 406
independent contractors, 330
Indians. *See* Aboriginal persons
indoor management rule, 538
inducement, 237–238
inducing breach of contract,
 106–107
Industry Canada, 487
infants. *See* minors
infants. *See* minors (infants)
information technology. *See*
 Internet
informed consent, 84–85
injunction, 63, 66, 116, 287
 mandatory, 116
injurious falsehood, 103–104
injury to the state, 205

innocent misrepresentation,
 238–239
innuendo, 96
insanity, 170, 199–200
insider trading, 520
insolvency
 defined, 410
 reform, 411
inspector, 530
insurable interest, 379, 380–381
insurance
 adjusters, 376
 applications for coverage,
  383–384
 bonding, 386
 brokers, 376
 builder's risk policy, 376
 business interruption
  insurance, 378
 co-insurance clauses,
  377–378
 comprehensive policies, 377
 contra preferentum, 381, 382
 contract of utmost good faith,
  382–384
 described, 375
 disability insurance, 380
 Employment Insurance,
  356–357
 excess coverage, 380
 failure to notify of change,
  382
 forfeiture rule, 385
 insurable interest, 379,
  380–381
 insurance agents, 376
 insurance industry, 375–376
 insurer's duty, extent of, 385
 liability insurance, 376–377
 life and health insurance,
  378–380
 limitation clauses, 381–382
 policy terms, and coverage,
  377
 and privity of contract,
  249–250
 professional liability
  insurance, 376
 property insurance, 377–378
 regulation of industry, 375
 salvage, 385
 subrogation, 385
 third-party beneficiaries,
  252
 types of, 376–380
 typical exclusions, 377
 umbrella liability, 376
insurance agents, 375
intention, 161, 166, 209–212
intentional torts, 82–103
 assault, 83–85
 battery, 83–85
 conversion, 87–88
 defamation, 94–103
 detinue, 88
 false imprisonment, 89–90
 libel, 98–99
 malicious prosecution, 90–91
 private nuisance, 92–94
 product defamation, 103–104
 slander, 98–99
 successfully establishing a tort
  claim, 104
 table of, 104–105*t*
 trespass to chattels, 87
 trespass to land, 85–87
 trespass to persons, 83–85
interest dispute, 358
interest rates, excessive. *See* excessive interest rates
interests of the public, 22
interference with economic relations, 108

interim agreement, 166
interlocutory injunction, 287
international trade
 disputes, 73
internet
 consensus, 161
 cookies, 113
 damages, determination of, 96
 defamation, 94–98
 jurisdictional issues, 57, 97
 Sale of Goods Acts, 304–307
interpretation
 rules of interpretation,
  230–233
 strict interpretation of
  exemption clauses, 267
intimidation, 108–109
intoxication, 199–200
intra vires, 15
invasion of privacy, 111–114
Investment Canada Act (1985), 487
invitations to treat, 166–167
involuntary assignment, 256
irrevocable offers, 170–171
issued capital, 497
issue estoppel, 349

J

job action, 367–368
joint venture, 456
jointly liable, 466
judges, 50
judgment, 62–64, 65*f*
judgment creditor, 63
judgment debtor, 63
judicial remedies before judgment,
 66–67
jurisdiction, 56–59
 Internet contracts and, 189
 Internet issues, 57, 96
 postbox rule, 178
jurisdictional dispute, 358
just cause, 338–340
justice
 law and, 42
justification, 100

L

labour law. *See* collective bargaining
labour relations boards, 359
labour unions. *See* unions
laches, 288
land. *See* real property
language rights, 34–35
law
 in Canada, 11–20
 behaviour and, 43–44
 business ethics and, 156
 canon law, 8
 categories of law, 2
 church law, 8
 civil law, 5–6
 common law, 5–7, 8
 defined, 1–2
 ethics and, 41–42
 equity, 9
 justice and, 42
 map of, 3*f*
 morals and, 41–42
 origins of law, 3–7
 private law, 2–3
 procedural law, 2
 public law, 2
 Roman civil law, 8
 sources of law, 8–9, 10*t*
 statute law, 10–11
 substantive law, 2
law merchant, 8
law of equity, 9
law of master and servant, 333
 see also employment law
Law Society of Alberta
 lawyers' fees, 67

Law Society of British Columbia
see also British Columbia
contingency fee agreement, 67
lawyers' fees, 67
Law Society of Upper Canada
lawyers' fees, 67
lawyers
contingency fee agreement, 67
fees and billing, 67–68
fixed fees, 67
hourly rates, 67
layoffs, 340–341
leafleting, 369
lease to purchase, 399
leases
consumer, 394–395
contracts, 392
defined, 398
duration, 391
finance, 389, 390f
FMV, 391
lease to purchase, 399
LTB, 391
minimum payment, 391–392
operating, 388
operating lease, 399
purchase option, 391
purchase, 388–389, 390f, 391
rent, 391
secured transactions, 401
security, 389
lease-to-buy (LTB) leases, 391
leasing, 387–388
legal liability, 43
legal person, 480
legal positivism, 1
legal realists, 1
legal rights, 23, 30–31
legal system
see also law
civil law legal system, 3–4
common law legal system, 5–6
outline of court system, 51f
legality, 200–209
avoidance of prosecution, 205
bets and wagers, 204
competition, reducing, 205
contracts formed illegally, 202–209
contracts performed illegally, 200–201
contracts to commit a crime, 204
contracts to commit a tort, 204
defined, 161
examples of illegal contracts, 204–209
immoral acts, 204
injury to public service, 205
injury to the state, 205
litigation, promotion of, 204
obstruction of justice, 205
price fixing, 205
restraint of marriage or in favour of divorce, 204
restraint of trade, 206–207
restrictive covenants, 207, 207–208
legislation
see also regulations; statutes
collective bargaining, 358–360
consumer protection employment legislation, 346–357
gift cards, 322
human rights legislation, 36–41

introduction of legislation, 18–19
partnership, 457–458
personal property as security for debt, 399–400
lessee, 387
costs paid by, 391
rights, 394
lessor, 388
rights, 393
letter of intent, 166
letters patent, 489
liability
of agents, 450–451
agent's tortious conduct, 450–451
basis for, 79–82
civil, 43
corporation, 481, 486
criminal, 43
directors, 521
jointly liable, 466
legal, 43
negligent misrepresentation and, 146
of employer, 345–346
of retiring partner, 466
parents' liability, 197
partnership, 465–466
principal's tortious conduct, 452–453
product, 130–133, 132f
regulatory (quasi-criminal), 43
severally liable, 466
social standards and, 81
sole proprietorship, 456–457
strict, 79, 516–517
third-party, 141
tort, 258
unlimited liability, 457, 465–466
vicarious, 82, 82f
vicarious liability. See vicarious liability
liability insurance, 376–377
libel, 98–99
lien
described, 301
free from lien, 301
seller's lien, 308
Lieutenant-Governor, 18
life insurance, 378–380
limitation clauses, 381–382
limitation periods, 55–57
limitations on rights and freedoms, 21–24
limited liability partnership (LLP), 474–476, 495, 496
limited liability, 481
limited partnerships, 474–475
limited warranties, 266–267
liquidated damages, 284, 285
litigation. See civil litigation
litigation,
tobacco, 133–134
loan transactions, 320–321, 323–325
see also debt
lockouts, 367–368
lost profits, 283
LLP. See limited liability partnership (LLP)

M

maintenance of membership, 367
malicious prosecution, 90–91
managers. See directors
mandatory mediation, 72–73
mandatory retirement, 354
Manitoba
writing, requirement of, 213
MDPs. See multi-disciplinary partnerships (MDPs)
mediation, 68, 72–75

mediator, 71
Meech Lake Accord, 36
memorandum of association, 489
mental health concerns, 52
merchantable quality, 301–303
mergers, 312, 314
minors
age of majority, 193–194
on becoming an adult, 195–197
beneficial contracts of service, 194–195
capacity, 193–199
executed contracts, 197
executory contracts, 196
necessaries, 194–195
parents' liability, 197
partially executed contract, 196
ratification, 195, 196
repudiation, 196
tort liability, 198–199
misleading advertising, 312, 314
misleading claims, 319
misrepresentation, 142–143, 233–242
actual representation, 236
allegation of fact, 235–236
defined, 233
false statement, 237
fraudulent, 143
fraudulent misrepresentation, 239–241
inducement, 237–238
innocent misrepresentation, 238–239
negligent, 143
negligent misrepresentation, 241–242
reliance on, 235
rescission, 239
silence or non-disclosure, 236
as term of contract, 238
mistake, 221–233
bad advice, 222
facts vs. law, 222
implied terms, 232–233
misunderstanding, 225–226
non est factum, 229–230
one-sided mistake, 226–230
parol evidence rule, 231–232
rectification, 223–225
reviewable mistakes, 221
rules of interpretation, 230–233
shared mistake, 223–225
terms of agreement, 222
unilateral mistake, 226–230
misunderstanding, 225–226
misuse of confidential information, 110
mitigate, 130
mitigation, 283
mobility rights, 29
money orders, 410
morality,
law and, 41–42
mortgages, 397
multi-disciplinary partnerships (MDPs), 155–156
mutual release, 273

N

Napoleonic Code, 3
National Arbitration Rules, 73
National Instrument 80–82
natural law theorists, 1
necessaries, 194–195
necessities of life, 66
negligence, 120
contributory, 129–130
insurance and, 120–130
innocent principals, 452

and limited liability partnership (LLP), 475
negligent statements, 241–242
negligent misrepresentation, 241–242
negotiable instruments, 256
negotiation, 68, 70
neighbours, and duty of care, 122–123
New Brunswick
garnishment before judgment, 66
secondary picketing, 370
Newfoundland and Labrador, small claims courts, 50
no-fault insurance, 81
noisy withdrawal, 155
nominating committee, 507
non-competition clauses, 335–336
non-disclosure, 236
non est factum, 229–230
non-profit society, 456
notice
reasonable notice, 336–338, 348
statutory notice, 348
termination of authority, 453
notional severance, 208
Nova Scotia
garnishment before judgment, 66
non-profit society, 456
small claims courts, 50
novation, 250, 273–274
nuisance
private nuisance, 92–94
public nuisance, 94
nuisance(s). See public nuisances; private nuisances
Nunavut Court of Justice, 52

O

obstruction of justice, 205
occupational requirements, 352
off-balance-sheet financing, 390
offences, bankruptcy, 419–423
offer, 164–171
communication of, 167–169
by conduct, 167
counteroffer, 170
defined, 164
disclosure of important terms, 168
end of an offer, 170, 178
incomplete offer, 173
insanity of offeror, 170
intention to be bound, 166
interim agreement, 166
invitations to treat, 166–167
irrevocable offers, 170–171
nature of an offer, 169
revocation, 170
valid offer, 164–165
offer to settle, 60
official capacity, 85
officers, 506, 511
breach of duty, 515, 516
duties of, 512
duty of care, 513
duty to corporation, 513
fiduciary duty, 513
insider trading, 520
one-sided agreement, 179
one-sided mistake, 226–230
online contracts. See Internet
online dispute resolution (ODR) programs, 74
Ontario
see also Law Society of Upper Canada
limitation periods, 55
limited liability partnership

(LLP), 475
Mandatory Mediation pilot project, 72
small claims courts, 50
Ontario Business Corporations Act, 515
Ontario Consumer Protection Act (2002), 188
Ontario Court of Appeal, 138, 142
oppression remedy, 534
operating lease, 399
oppressive terms, 268
oral contracts, 161
Orderly Payment of Debts (OPD), 416
ordinary resolution, 524
organization of employees, 360–362
organization test, 332–333
origins of law, 3–7
out-of-court settlements, 184

P

paid-up capital, 497
par values (of shares), 497, 498
paramountcy, 16
parents' liability, 197
Parliament
  see also federal government
  prorogue (adjourn), 12
  supremacy of, 23
parol contracts, 162
parol evidence rule, 231–232
part performance, 216–217
partially executed contract, 196
participating rights, 500
partnership, 457–476
  advantages of, 470–471
  breach of fiduciary duty, 458–459
  creation by contract, 462–464
  creation by inadvertence, 461
  creation of partnership, 458–464
  defined, 455
  dissolution of partnership, 471–472
  distribution of assets and liabilities, 473
  fiduciary duty, 468–470
  holding out as partner, 464
  income from other sources, 469
  intention to create partnership, 462–463
  jointly liable, 466
  legislation, 458
  limited liability partnership (LLP), 474–475
  limited partnerships, 473–474
  multi-disciplinary, 496
  partner as agent, 464
  provisions of *Partnerships Act*, 470
  registration, 467–468
  retiring partner, liability of, 466
  rights and obligations of parties, 468
  severally liable, 466
  unlimited liability, 465–466
  vicarious liability, 465
party and party costs, 63
past consideration, 183
pay equity, 353–354
payday loans, 324–325
payment of debt. *See* debt
pension benefits, 357
perfection, 401–402
performance, 261–264
  contractual terms, 275

illegal performance, 200–202
impossibility of, 275
part performance, 216–217
result of failure to perform, 272*t*
specific performance, 63, 64, 286–287
substantial performance, 262
tender of performance, 263–264
time for performance, 264
vicarious performance, 255
person, trespass to, 83–84
personal property,
  choses in action, 397
  Personal Property Security Act (PPSA), 399–406
  as security for debt, 397–406
Personal Property Security Act (PPSA), 399–406
picketing, 369–370
plaintiff
  burden of proof, 61
pleadings, 59
pledge, 397
postbox rule, 175–178, 176*f*
power of attorney, 435
pre-emptive right, 526
pre-trial procedures, 59–61
precedent, 7
predatory pricing, 312
preferred creditors, 65, 418
preferred shares, 498
price fixing, 205, 312, 314
price maintenance, 312
principal
  see also agency
  authority, delegation of, 435–442
  delay in ratification, 441
  duties, 447
  liability for agent's tortious conduct, 450–453
  ratification of contract, 439–441
  tortious conduct of, 452–453
  undisclosed principals, 447–449
priority
  among creditors, 417–419
  defined, 396
  government, 419
  and *Personal Property Security Act* (PPSA), 399–406
  preferred creditors, 418
  secured creditors, 411, 418
  unsecured creditors, 410, 418
privacy
  cookies, 113
  invasion of privacy, as tort, 112*t*
  private information, use of, 112
  protection, 111
  surveillance of employees, 114
  unauthorized interception of communications, 112
private company, 494
private law, 2
private nuisance, 92–94
privilege, 155
  absolute privilege, 100–101
  qualified privilege, 100
privity of contract, 248–252
Privy Council, 126
probate courts, 50
Probate Court. *See* Surrogate (Probate) Court
procedural fairness
  entitlement to, 30

procedural law, 2
product defamation, 103
product liability, 252
professional corporations (PC), 156, 495, 496
professional liability insurance, 376
professional organizations,
  codes of conduct, 152
  conflict of duty, 154–155
  discipline, 151, 154
  exclusivity, 151
  powers, 150–152
  responsibilities, 150–152
professionals
  incorporation of practice, 457
  limited liability partnership (LLP), 474–476
promissory estoppel, 185–187, 186*f*
promissory note, 425, 425*f*, 410
proof of claim, 418
property
  co-ownership, and partnership, 462
  damage by trespassers, 87
  real property. *See* real property
  seizure, 65–66
property insurance, 377–378
prorogue Parliament, 12
protection of rights and freedoms
  Canadian Bill of Rights, 20–21
  Charter of Rights and Freedoms, 21–35
  human rights legislation, 36–41
  limitations on rights and freedoms, 21–24
provincial courts of appeal, 53–54
provincial governments
  see also government
  agreements to share powers, 17–18
  compilation of statutes, 18
  conditions of employment, 346
  conflicting powers, 15–16
  consumer protection legislation, 316–317
  delegation of powers, 17
  division of powers, 12–15
  forfeiture laws, 14
  regulatory offences, 49
provincial trial courts, 50–53
public interest responsible journalism defence, 102–103
public law, 2
public nuisance, 94
public offering, 506
public policy, 200
public sector, and labour issues, 370
publicly traded corporations, 505–506
published false statements, 94–96
punishment, 78
punitive damages, 63, 282, 344
purchase money security interest (PMSI), 402
pyramid selling, 311, 312

Q

qualified privilege, 100
quantum meruit, 166, 185, 288–289
quasi-contracts, 166
quasi-criminal liability. *See* liability, regulatory (quasi-criminal);

regulatory (quasi-criminal) liability
Quebec
  Charlottetown Accord, 36
  Civil Code, 3–5
  and constitutional changes, 36
  Meech Lake Accord, 36
quiet possession, 300, 392

R

Rand Formula, 269
ratification, 195, 196, 364, 439–441
real property
  dealings with land, and writing, requirement of, 214
  part performance, 216
  and privity of contract, 231
reasonable notice, 336–338, 345, 348
reasonable person test, 211, 438
receivership, 424
recognition disputes, 358
rectification, 223–225
referral selling, 322–323
refusal to supply, 312
registration of partnership, 467
regulations
  see also legislation; statutes
  as law, 9
  sole proprietorship, 456
regulatory (quasi-criminal) liability, 43
regulatory offences, 49
remedies
  accounting, 83, 288
  breach of contract, 281–289
  buyer's remedies, 308–309
  damages. *See* damages
  declaration, 63
  equitable remedies, 285–289
  garnishment before judgment, 66
  injunction, 63, 66, 287
  interlocutory injunction, 287
  judicial remedies before judgment, 66–85
  quantum meruit, 166, 185, 288–289
  rescission, 239
  Sale of Goods Acts, 308
  seller's remedies, 308
  specific performance, 63, 64, 286–287
  types of, 63–64
  wrongful dismissal, 344–345
remote, 124
remoteness, 282–283
remoteness of damage, 125–126
repudiation
  as anticipatory breach, 270–272
  expressed or implied, 271–272
  insanity, 200
  intoxicated persons, 200
  by minor, 196
request for services, 185
res ipsa loquitor, 128
rescission, 239, 240
restitution, 116
restraint of marriage, 204
restraint of trade, 206–209
restrictive covenants, 207, 208–209, 334–335
retainer, 67
retiring partner, liability of, 466
reverse discrimination, 354
revocation, 170
right to convey clear title, 300–301

right to die, 31–32
right to life, liberty, and security of
the person, 30
right to redeem, 404
right to strike, 367
rights and freedoms. *See* protection
of rights and freedoms
rights dispute, 358
risk
Sale of Goods Acts, and title,
295–298
risk reduction
agent, authority of, 442
alternative dispute resolution,
284
bankruptcy, 417, 422–423
competition, protection from,
209
consideration, 184
consumer protection
legislation, 316, 327
debtor's default, 404–405
defective products, potential
liability for, 318–319
disclosure during contractual
negotiations, 168
discovery stage, 60
employees' interactions with
customers, 86
employment standards, 357
enforcement of judgments,
66–67
evidence in writing, 216
fiduciary duty, 446
guarantees, 406–407
human rights legislation,
understanding of, 41
insurance strategies, 378
Internet transactions, and
jurisdiction, 59
large deposits, 284
limited partnerships, 474
litigation, decreasing
popularity of, 62
mediation, 72–73
minors, contracting with, 197
mistake, 233
negotiable instruments, 410,
426–427
notice of assignment, 256
offer, ending of, 178
online ADR services, 74
oppressive or unconscionable
terms, 268
partnerships, value of, 467
perfection of security interest,
402
reasonable notice
requirements, 345
Sale of Goods Acts, 309
termination of employee
without cause, 338
title transfers, and risk, 296
unconscionability, 248
undue influence, 248
unionization of employees,
370–371
Roman civil law, 8
royal assent, 18
royal charter, 488
rules of evidence, 62
rules of interpretation, 230–233
rules of natural justice
see also procedural fairness

S

Sales of Goods Act
exemption clauses, 304–305
implied terms, 304
Sale of Goods Acts
agreement to sell, 295

bills of lading, 295
breach of contract, 308
buyer's remedies, 308–309
C.I.F. contracts (cost,
insurance, and freight), 295
C.O.D. contracts (cash on
delivery), 295
exemption clauses, 316, 318
fit for purpose, 301–303
F.O.B. contracts (free on
board), 295
fundamental breach, 299
future transfer of goods, 295
goods and services, 293–294
goods must match
description, 299–300
implied conditions, 298–299
implied terms, 293
implied warranties, 298–299
Internet transactions,
304–305
merchantable quality,
301–302
monetary consideration, 295
other implied terms, 304
quiet possession, 300
remedies on default, 308
right to convey clear title,
300–301
rights and obligations of
parties, 298–307
sample, 304
scope of, 293–295
seller's remedies, 308
suing in contract, 317
title and risk, 295–298
transfer of goods, 294
transfer of title, 296–298
writing, requirement of, 295
sale-and-leaseback, 390
Salomon case, 484
salvage, 385
sample, 304
Sarbanes-Oxley Act (US, 2002)
(SOX), 140, 155, 505–506,
508
Saskatchewan
small claims courts, 50
sealed documents, 187–188
search, unreasonable, 31
secondary picketing, 370
Section 52 of *Constitution Act, 1982*,
35
secured creditors, 65–66, 411,
418
Securities and Exchange
Commission (SEC), 155
security for debt, 396–410
see also creditors
attachment, 401
Bank Act, 410
guarantees, 406–410
other forms of security, 410
perfection, 401–402
personal property, 397–406
Personal Property Security Act
(PPSA), 399–406
purchase money security
interest (PMSI), 402
right to redeem, 404
traditional approach, 398
seizure
execution process, 65–66
necessities of life, exemption
for, 66
of property, 65–66
unreasonable search and
seizure, 31
self-defence, 85
self-induced frustration, 277
seller's lien, 308

seller's remedies, 308
sentencing circles, 52–53
settlement offer, 60
settlement out of court, 184
settlements, 420
severally liable, 466
sexual harassment, 39, 343, 351
sexual orientation, 38
share, 497
shared capital amount, 497
shared mistake, 223–225
shareholder agreements, 536
shareholders,
agreements, 536
appraisal remedy, 531
class voting rights, 525
derivative action, 532–533
dividends, 526
duties, 530
majority rule, 531
meetings, 523, 524
minority, 522–523, 531, 534
oppression remedy, 534,
535, 536
proxies, 525
right to vote, 525
rights, 525
role in private corporations,
522–523
role in publicly traded corporations, 522
silence, 236
simple contracts, 162
slander, 98–99
small claims courts, 50
social relations, 211
sole proprietorship, 456–457
defined, 455
government regulations,
456–457
liability, 457
vicarious liability, 457
solicitor and client costs, 63
sources of law, 8–9, 10*t*
SOX. *See* Sarbanes-Oxley Act
(U.S., 2002) (SOX)
special Acts of Parliament, 488
special damages, 63, 282
special meeting, 524
special relationship, and undue
influence, 244–245
special resolution, 524
specialized agency relationships,
454
specific performance, 63, 64,
286–287
standard form contracts, 172
standard of care, 80, 123
see also duty of care
professional, 148–149
stare decisis, 5–7
stated intention, 210
statement of claim, 59
statement of defence, 59
Statute of Frauds, 212–216, 216*f*,
246
statutes. *See* law, statute; statute law
(statutes)
see also legislation; regulations
bill, 18, 19*f*
compilation of statutes, 18
enabling statute, 10
intra vires, 15
as law, 10–11
royal assent, 18
ultra vires, 15
statutory assignment, 255
statutory notice, 348
stoppage in transit, 308
strikes, 367–368
subject-to clauses, 166, 275

subrogation, 120, 385
substantial performance, 262
substantive law, 2
Sunday shopping, 25–26
sunset clause, 24
Superintendent of Bankruptcy,
411
Supreme Court
appeal to, 54
described, 54
significance of having, 5–6
Supreme Court of Canada, 126
conflict of interest, 138
damages, 128
duty in tort, 140
duty of care, 121–122
duty of directors, 514
fiduciary duty, 137
lapse of offer, 106
product liability, 132, 133
professional organizations,
152
professional standard of
care, 149
res ipsa loquitor, 128
surety bond, 386
surrogate courts, 50

T

tangible personal property. *See* personal property
Tax Court of Canada, 54
tender of performance, 263–264
tendering process, 171
termination of agency, 453–454
454*t*
termination of contract. *See* end of
contract
termination of corporation, 502
termination of employment,
336–345
constructive dismissal,
343–344
demotion without cause,
343
disabled workers, 340
disobedience and
incompetence, 340
employment legislation,
348–349
issue estoppel, 349
just cause, 338–340
layoffs, 340–341
punitive damages, 344
reasonable notice, 336–338,
345
remedies for wrongful
dismissal, 344–345
termination without cause,
336–338
wrongful leaving, 341–342
termination of partnership,
471–472
theft by employee, 339
third parties
and agents, 446, 449–450
involvement of, and
rescission, 239
third-party beneficiaries, 252
threats, 242–243
title
right to convey clear title,
300
and risk, 296–299
transfers, 297–299
torts, 78
agent's tortious conduct,
450–453
conspiracy to injure, 109
contracts to commit a tort,
204

in cyberspace, 115
deceit, 109
fraudulent misrepresentation, 109
inducing breach of contract, 106–107
intentional torts, 82–103
interference with economic relations, 108
intimidation, 108–109
minors, liability of, 198–199
misuse of confidential information, 110–111
other business torts, 105–111
negligence. *See* negligence
parents' liability, 197
passing off, 110
principal's tortious conduct, 452–453
privacy, 111–114
successfully establishing a tort claim, 104
tort law
development of, 79
duty in, 137, 140–141
insurance and, 120–130
product liability, 130–133, 132*f*
reform of, 116
remedies, 116
scope of, 78–79
tort liability, 258
trade slander, 103
trade unions. *See* unions
transfer of title, 297–299
transfer-payment schemes, 18

trespass to chattels, 87
trespass to land, 85–87
trespass to person, 83–85
trial, 61–62
trial periods, 298
true cost of borrowing, 323–324
trust, 382, 175
Trustee in Bankruptcy, 411, 414
trusts
constructive trust, 250
and privity of contract, 249
truth, 100

U

ULC. *See* unlimited liability corporation (ULC)
ultra vires, 15
umbrella liability, 376
unacceptable business practices, 319–322
unanimous shareholder agreement), 537
unauthorized interception of communications, 113
UNCITRAL. *See* United Nations Commission on International Trade Law (UNCITRAL)
unconditional contracts, 297
unconscionable terms, 268
unconscionable transactions, 246–248, 320–322, 325–326
undisclosed principals, 447–449
undue influence, 244–246, 247
undue restriction of competition, 311–312
unenforceable contracts, 162
unfair labour practices, 361–362
unified family courts, 52

unilateral contracts, 163, 171, 174
unilateral mistake, 226–230
union shop, 367
unions
see also collective bargaining
bargaining agent, 361
duty of fair representation, 372
human rights legislation, 371
organization, 371–372
United Nations Commission on International Trade Law (UNCITRAL) Model Law on Electronic Commerce (1996), 189
United Nations Commision on International Trade Law (UNCITRAL) Model Law on Electronic Signatures (2001), 189
United Nations Convention on the Use of Electronic Communications in International Contracts (2005), 189
unjust enrichment, 222
unlimited liability, 457–458, 465–466
unlimited liability corporation (ULC), 487
unreasonable search and seizure, 31
unsecured creditors, 410, 415, 418
unsolicited goods, 174
utmost good faith, 382–384, 236

V

valid contract, 162

vicarious liability
agency, 434, 450–453
employers, 105, 345–346
for fraud of agent, 434
partnership, 464
sole proprietorship, 456
vicarious performance, 255, 257
application of, 257
void contracts, 162
voidable contracts, 162
voluntary assignment in bankruptcy, 413–414, 414*f*
voting rights, 27–29

W

wagers, 204
Wagon Mound (No. 1), 126
Wagon Mound (No. 2), 126
warranties, 261–262, 265–266, 299–300, 317
winding up, 533
without prejudice, 71
work stoppages, 367
work to rule, 367
workers' compensation, 81, 355
writ of summons, 59
writing, requirement of, 161, 212–216, 296, 406
wrongful dismissal, 344–345
see also termination of employment
wrongful leaving, 341–342

Y

youth justice courts, 50
Yukon, small claims courts, 50